THE PLANTS OF THE
PACIFIC CREST TRAIL

Photo credits appear on page 466.

Endpaper maps by Vincent James
Map on page 19 by Jeffrey Kane

Species nomenclature follows current taxonomy as presented on the
Jepson Herbarium eFlora website (ucjeps.berkeley.edu/eflora/). Com-
mon names, often missing from the eFlora, are mainly drawn from the
CalFlora website (calflora.org).

The information in this book is true and complete to the best of our
knowledge. The authors and publisher disclaim any liability in con-
nection with the use of this information. In particular, eating wild
plants or using them medicinally is inherently risky. Plants can be
easily mistaken and individuals vary in their physiological reactions
to plants that are touched or consumed. This book is primarily a guide
to identification and is explicitly NOT a foraging guide.

Published in association with the Pacific Crest Trail Association in
2023 by Timber Press, Inc., a subsidiary of Workman Publishing Co.,
a subsidiary of Hachette Book Group, Inc.

1290 Avenue of the Americas
New York, NY 10104

timberpress.com

The publisher is not responsible for websites (or their content) that are
not owned by the publisher. The Hachette Speakers Bureau provides
a wide range of authors for speaking events. To find out more, go to
hachettespeakersbureau.com or email HachetteSpeakers@hbgusa.com.

The Hachette Speakers Bureau provides a wide range of authors for
speaking events. To find out more, go to hachettespeakersbureau.com
or email HachetteSpeakers@hbgusa.com.

Printed in China on responsibly sourced paper

Cover design by Johnny Bertram
Series design by Vincent James

ISBN 978-1-60469-995-1

Catalog records for this book are available from the Library of
Congress and the British Library.

Cover: PCT through brittlebush; San Bernardino Mountains, near
Cabazon
Right: Joshua trees in the Tehachapi foothills
Back cover: Stephen Ingram (fifth); Steve Mason (bottom)

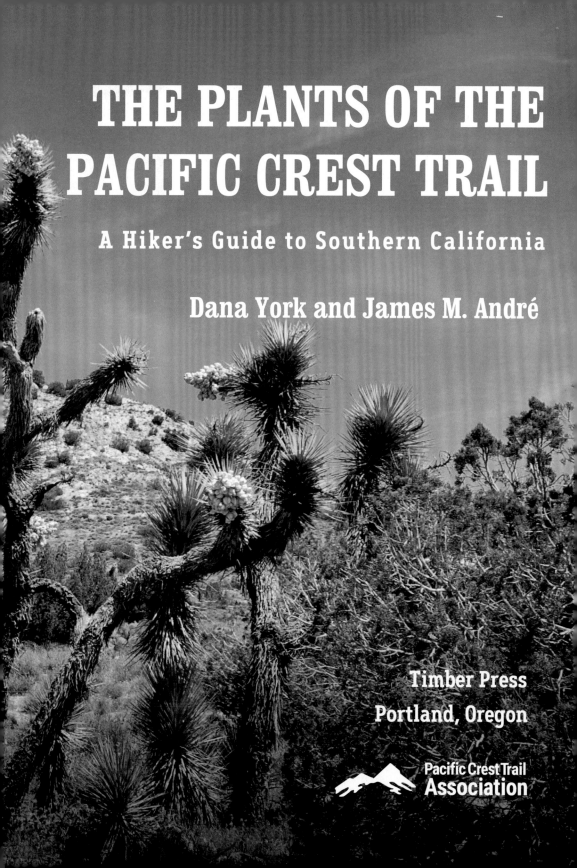

THE PLANTS OF THE PACIFIC CREST TRAIL

A Hiker's Guide to Southern California

Dana York and James M. André

Timber Press
Portland, Oregon

Pacific Crest Trail
Association

CONTENTS

PREFACE

What better way to experience California's unique plant diversity than to hike the state from end to end along the Pacific Crest Trail (PCT)? We have, and we hope you will too—with the help of this book, which covers the first 11 of California's 24 PCT sections, heading from south to north and ending at Tuolumne Meadows (see front endpaper map). We have hiked, extensively explored, and researched plant collections from every California ecoregion (see back endpaper map), covering all 1692 miles of the PCT, from Mexico to Oregon.

According to the 2022 Consortium of California Herbaria (ucjeps.berkeley.edu/consortium), the earliest scientific plant collection on the California PCT was of Lemmon's draba (*Draba lemmonii*), collected by Mark Kerr on 16 September 1941 near upper Woods Creek in Fresno County; John Muir Trail is specifically noted on the specimen label. Likely collections were made even earlier along the trail, but either the collector left the trail name off the specimen label or the trail was not yet formally named. In total, over 5000 vascular plant collections have been made from or near the trail in California. Using those collections as a baseline, we undertook three years of extensive fieldwork, beginning in 2019, to develop this guidebook.

The PCT is a very popular trail for hikers around the world, gaining prominence with Cheryl Strayed's 2012 book and subsequent 2014 movie, starring Reese Witherspoon, *Wild*. But despite all its fame and use, we found surprisingly little information about the trail's vegetation; and as we explored the trail, we were amazed by how many previously unknown populations of rare plants we found, often in plain sight. Having a way to identify plants along the California portion of the trail was lacking—until now.

This guide to Pacific Crest Trail Sections 1–11 covers more than a third of the 3000-plus native plants that occur along the California PCT. Plants were included if they have local significance (rare or endemic to a region), have showy flowers or fruits, are common along the trail, and/or would be of interest to hikers. Some rare plants and grasses and grass-like species were not included because they're either hard to find or hard to identify, and (especially for rare plants) impacts from hikers could negatively impact them.

This guidebook is your treasure map to discovery. Have fun, be safe, and take time to smell the flowers!

INTRODUCTION

A t over 2650 miles, the Pacific Crest National Scenic Trail, as it is officially known, traverses some of the most outstanding natural landscapes in the western United States, spanning three states and crossing numerous national parks and monuments, national forests, wilderness areas, state and county parks, and tribal lands. The trail climbs as high as 13,153 ft. elevation (at Forester Pass) and drops as low as 180 ft. (at the Bridge of the Gods on the Columbia River). Although it may be tempting to have help negotiating the trail's rugged terrain, the PCT is intended for hiking and equestrian travel only. Motor vehicles and bicycles are prohibited.

The concept of a crest trail started over 100 years ago when the US Forest Service designated the Oregon Skyline Trail, from Crater Lake to Mt. Hood; the trail was later extended to traverse the entire state. An effort to create a trail traversing Washington began in 1928 with the designation of the Cascade Crest Trail. The US Forest Service eventually designed PCT markers and in 1937 started marking the trail from Canada to the California border.

The idea for California's portion of the PCT began with Clinton Clarke, a prosperous oilman and avid scout leader. In 1932, he founded the Pacific Crest Trail System Conference, which included Ansel Adams as a member. He also made a proposal to the US Forest Service and National Park Service to form a continuous wilderness trail across the US from Canada to Mexico, eventually recommending linking the existing trails in Oregon and Washington with California's Tahoe–Yosemite and John Muir trails.

In 1968, the PCT was named a national scenic trail, along with the Appalachian Trail. Over the following 20 years, land management agencies, the Pacific Crest Trail Association, and other groups and volunteers completed nearly 1000 miles of trail; the entire PCT was finished in 1993.

Today, the overall management of the PCT is the responsibility of the US Forest Service. Trail maintenance and permits for hikers going less than 500 miles are generally at the discretion of the agency/organization that manages the land being traversed. Thru-hikers, or anyone going more than 500 miles, are required to obtain a long-distance permit. Check the PCT Associations permit website for more information (pcta.org/discover-the-trail/permits). Although the trail has been complete for nearly

30 years, there are still over 200 miles of private land traversed and places where you are routed on roads, highway shoulders, and vehicle bridges.

The Washington portion of the PCT is around 506 miles long, with an additional 7 miles to hike from the Canadian border to Highway 3 in British Columbia's Manning Provincial Park. Washington's southern end begins at the Bridge of the Gods on the Columbia River. The main ecoregions (geographical areas with ecological similarity) traversed are the Cascades and North Cascades. Because ecoregions are based on relationships of climate, precipitation, geology, soils, hydrology, and wildlife, the plants are generally similar within them. The North Cascades ecoregion (275 trail miles) is the most rugged and pristine along the PCT. Unlike the volcanic Cascades ecoregion to the south, its geology is mostly metamorphic and sedimentary rocks. Much of the area was under glaciers until 10,000 years ago. Elevations above 4000 ft., which happens a majority of the time along this section of the PCT, are associated with subalpine and alpine vegetation. Because of the harsh, long winters, upper elevations are less species-rich than Washington's coniferous forests below the subalpine zone.

The Cascades ecoregion (850 trail miles), spanning from Washington to California, is discontinuous along the PCT. From northern California into southern Oregon, the Cascades ecoregion is interrupted by the Klamath Mountains. The Cascades ecoregion is home to active and dormant volcanoes and has a predominantly volcanic geology. The vegetation of California's portion of the Cascades and the Klamath Mountains is strongly associated with the species in the Cascades of Oregon and Washington. Mainly due to its relatively young surficial geology, the Cascades' plant biodiversity is lower than California's Klamath Mountains and Sierra Nevada.

The Oregon portion of the PCT (456 trail miles) falls mostly in the Cascades ecoregion. Volcanoes (both active and dormant) along or near the trail include (south to north) Mt. McLoughlin, Mt. Mazama (Crater Lake), the Three Sisters, Mt. Washington, Three Fingered Jack, Mt. Jefferson, and Mt. Hood. Moist, temperate conditions support extensive Douglas-fir (*Pseudotsuga menziesii*) forests with a mix of many other conifers, especially as you head north or gain elevation.

California (at 1691.7 trail miles, to be precise) accounts for nearly 64% of the PCT's length. California's high biodiversity is well known, especially when it comes to vegetation. Over 6600 native plants occur in the state. Its plant diversity is a result of surficial geology, physiography, climate (mostly temperature and precipitation), biotic influences (critters, other plants, and humans), and fire. California's ecoregions traversed by the PCT (south to north) are Southern California/Northern Baja Coast (30 trail miles), Southern California Mountains (445 discontinuous trail miles), Sonoran Basin and Range (35 discontinuous trail miles), Mojave Basin and Range (33 discontinuous trail miles), Sierra Nevada (756 trail miles), Cascades (153 trail miles), and Klamath Mountains (242 trail miles). Almost half the PCT miles in California are in the Sierra Nevada ecoregion. Although the Sierra Nevada has more plants than any other California ecoregion, the PCT stays mainly in the upper elevations, missing much of that diversity. With that said, the flora of the Sierra Nevada is still spectacular and well documented in such places as Yosemite, Sequoia, and Kings Canyon National Parks.

USING THIS GUIDE

This guide was developed to help hikers or equestrians identify native plants along the southern half of the California portion of the Pacific Crest Trail (CA PCT). We aimed to include as many plants as possible, particularly those that are easily visible from the trail itself. Our general intent was that special tools or equipment would not be needed for identification. With that said, a phone camera can make identification much easier. Photos can be reviewed at your leisure and magnified if necessary. At times a hand lens would be beneficial, especially if fruits, nutlets, or seeds are helpful for identification.

Please practice good conservation techniques by staying on the trail and not picking flowers or collecting plants. Although we point out various cultural, medicinal, or historical uses for some species that you may be interested in trying yourself, always obtain proper permission from the land manager or owner before collecting any plants or plant parts. Also, do not consume any plant part unless you're completely sure of a plant's identity. Color is never a good sole indicator of edibility; red fruits are notorious for being either tasty or poisonous, for example. If in doubt leave them be—it's not worth taking a chance along the trail, far away from medical facilities. The most poisonous plants have notes to that effect in the descriptions.

PCT Sections. We have divided the CA PCT into 24 sections (again, see front endpaper map), numbered and listed in entries from south to north; these divisions were based on likely access points and defined ecoregions as natural borders to those sections, as much as practicable. This volume covers Sections 1–11. We tried to select sections that have vehicle access (or close to it) at each end to accommodate section users. Section locations for plants covered by this book are from personal observations, historic records, and professional judgment as to the likelihood it would occur along the PCT within a particular section. We fully expect that some plants will be found by our readers in sections where previously unknown and not indicated.

Organization. Plants are presented in the following main categories: Conifers, Trees and Shrubs, Wildflowers, and Ferns, Horsetails, and Grasses. Further groupings based on characters such as leaf arrangement, color, etc., are alphabetically arranged, first by the family scientific name then the full species name. **Conifers** groupings are based on leaf type and number of needles per

cluster. **Trees and Shrubs** groupings are based on leaf type and arrangement. **Wildflowers** (Flowering Herbs) are grouped by color. They are further grouped by type of flower or number of petals/sepals. Flowers with 5 petals or petal-like sepals are further divided by having symmetric/irregular flowers with free or fused (into an obvious tube) petals. **Ferns, Horsetails, and Grasses** are split into two sections (ferns and horsetails; grasses, sedges, and rushes).

Scientific Name. Species nomenclature follows current taxonomy as presented on the Jepson Herbarium eFlora website (ucjeps.berkeley.edu/eflora/). Variety and subspecies are included for plants where we felt it necessary to differentiate at a level below species. We often include the origin and/or etymology of scientific names. For more information, Wikipedia maintains an ongoing list at "plant genera named for people," with links to publications where those names first appeared.

Common Name. Many sources were used for common names, with the main source being the CalFlora website (calflora.org). If more than one common name is often associated with a plant, we sometimes include alternative (aka = "also known as") common names.

Abundance. You can use abundance information to help with plant identification. For example, if you keep seeing a species along the trail that you initially identified as a rare plant, then you probably misidentified it. **Common** plants are those found in great numbers along many miles of the PCT, in various habitats, and generally in many PCT sections. **Locally common** plants can have a large range with gaps of few to no plants in between. They're not common along long portions of the PCT, but where they do occur, they tend to have large populations. **Occasional** plants are those encountered infrequently along the PCT. They could also be considered as uncommon. **Rare** plants are those with 1 to few populations on or near the CA PCT; many are restricted to one PCT section. For more details, see the California Native Plant Society (CNPS) Rare Plant Inventory at rareplants.cnps.org.

Height. Given in inches or feet, and represents typical heights of mature plants under normal conditions. If the height is off for a plant that you are looking at, try to find other individuals to see if there's a range that makes more sense.

Flowering. The range indicated is the most likely time the plant blooms. With that said, atypical climatic conditions or other factors can result in plants blooming outside their normal time of year.

Flower Color. Flower color can vary, so you may have to check other colors for the plant you're trying to identify. Detecting the difference between colors can be challenging, or flowers can change color as they mature. We recommend that if you don't find your plant under a certain color, such as orange, you should try something similar like red. Using color and basic flower characters to identify plants is not perfect, but it is a system that doesn't require learning tons of jargon. With a little practice, you will be efficiently figuring out flowering plants along the trail.

Habitat-Community. Where a plant grows is just as important as your address or phone number. A plant's habitat is its natural home. It includes the living and nonliving conditions of a plant's surrounding environment. The next chapter gives a detailed discussion of the habitats and communities used in this guidebook.

Elevation. The CA PCT mostly stays several thousand feet above sea level throughout the state. Since most plants have a clear upper elevation limit (due to things like snow, ice, etc.), you will notice that most entries don't indicate a lower limit. The elevation given for a plant represents the most likely place to find it growing, but outlier populations at extreme low or high elevations are always possible.

Ecoregions. The ecoregions used in this guidebook are designated by the US Environmental Protection Agency. Their California map is too detailed and large to reproduce well in a book but can be accessed and downloaded at epa. gov/eco-research/level-iii-and-iv-ecoregions-state. Again, a simplified ecoregions map appears inside the back cover of this book.

Descriptions. Each begins with the plant type (such as tree, shrub, annual, or perennial) and generally stem and branch characters. Next, character and size information is presented for the leaves, flowers, and fruits. Entries often include explanations of a plant's name or information about its uses.

Photographs. We took almost all the photos; any exceptions are listed in the photo credits. Most wildflowers have only a single photograph, and we acknowledge these may or may not show all important characteristics needed to identify the plant, especially if it's not in bloom. Knowing that having a single photograph can make identification difficult, we recommend you look at all the information given for a plant in order to make a determination.

CALIFORNIA PCT FIRE ECOLOGY

– By Jeffrey M. Kane

Given recent and ongoing patterns of increased wildfire activity in California, it is likely that most PCT hikers will be impacted by fire in some way. Since 2000, over 350 fires have occurred along the PCT. Smoke from nearby wildfires may pose serious health risks. Hikers may need to evacuate areas due to wildfires. Sections of the trail will be closed because wildfire is actively burning or because recent fires have damaged the trail or pose other risks. These circumstances will inevitably pose challenges to planning and may affect the experience, but fires also provide opportunities to learn about its ecological role and the history of past practices that have led to these concerning wildfire trends.

The following table presents wildfire information for ecoregions that occur along the CA PCT. Fire information refers to large fires (≥500 acres) that occurred between 2000 and 2020. Burned area includes areas that have reburned during this time period.

Ecoregion	No. of Fires	Burned Area (acres)	Burned Area (%)
Cascades	15	94,301	2.7
Klamath Mountains	41	455,045	5.6
Mojave Basin and Range	28	70,139	0.4
Sierra Nevada	21	949,167	7.4
Sonoran Basin and Range	32	44,478	0.6
Southern California/ Northern Baja Coast	208	951,680	24.3

For most ecosystems along the PCT, fire is an ecological and cultural process that is integral to numerous plant and animal species. A hike along the trail serves as tour that highlights the diverse roles of fire within and among many ecosystems in California. However, the ability of a hiker to observe the influence of fire on the landscape requires understanding the fundamental concepts of fire science and ecology.

Fire is a chemical reaction that, in the presence of sufficient heat and oxygen, combusts live and dead vegetation, commonly referred to as fuel. Fire behavior, or the pattern of movement and intensity of fire across a given area over time, is influenced by the interaction of weather, topography, and fuels. Depending on the fuels present and the patterns of fire behavior, there are generally three types of fire that can occur alone or in combination: surface fires, crown fires, and ground fires. Fires that burn through litter, grasses, or small woody fuels are surface fires and typically burn at relatively low intensities (amount of energy released during a fire) and low to moderate rates of spread (speed of the fire). Crown fires carry through the canopies of plants (shrubs and trees) and are typically much more intense and rapidly moving than surface fire. Ground fires predominantly burn by smoldering in the organic soil layers of duff or peat.

Fires can ignite by lightning, typically by striking a tree or ground that combusts by smoldering, which ignites the dead and dry litter or grasses that allows the fire to spread. Generally, lightning strike density in California increases from west to east as well as from lower to higher elevations, with the highest lightning density observed in the high Sierra. Fires are also intentionally ignited by humans. Across California, numerous Indigenous peoples utilized fire to manage the landscape for a diverse array of benefits for most of the previous 11,000 years, a practice that was villainized and violently disrupted in the 19th century and afterward but that persists in many regions today. In many regions, most modern ignitions are the result of unintentional human ignitions that result from a number of activities.

In the early 20th century, many foresters perceived wildfire as damaging to forests in the western US due to the loss of merchantable timber. These perceptions were largely generated because nascent federal foresters were trained in regions and countries where forests did not regularly experience fire–a perspective that was strongly reaffirmed following the 1910 fires, referred to as the "Big Blowup," which burned over 3 million acres (an area approximately the size of Connecticut) in the northern Rocky Mountains. Soon after, federal forest policy decisions focused on a zero-tolerance philosophy of fire, in which all fires are to be prevented and extinguished–perhaps best exemplified by the 10 a.m. policy from 1935 that mandated all wildfires were to be suppressed by 10 a.m. the morning of or following wildfire ignition.

The perception that fire was a damaging agent to be eliminated was not uniformly shared. Indigenous peoples in many regions resisted these policies by continuing their burning practices, which had helped sustain their communities for many millennia but were now deemed as illegal. Other groups, primarily ranchers

and private foresters who likely learned about burning through interactions with Indigenous peoples, actively advocated for the beneficial role of "light burning" fires. Unfortunately, these voices ultimately lost out to fire suppression practices that aimed to "protect" forests from fire.

It is also important to point out that direct fire suppression was not the sole means of change contributing to the fire-related issues of today. The removal of fire from the landscape was indirectly facilitated decades earlier through the intentional genocide and removal of Indigenous peoples from their ancestral lands. Intensive grazing practices of the past also contributed to the removal of fire. Many grasslands were effectively denuded by sheep and cattle that would have limited fire spread throughout much of California, conditions that would have also favored conifer and other tree establishment. Furthermore, the fire suppression policies coincided with intensive and extensive logging that cut most of the old legacy forests that were once much more prevalent in California. Following logging, areas were subsequently planted or allowed to naturally regenerate, eventually becoming the dense, young forests that make up a large portion of the forest conditions today. The consequence of these past actions and policies all contributed to the circumstances of fire we are now dealing with. Denser, more contiguous young forests that established across many landscapes due to fire exclusion can yield more damaging and destructive fires when they burn.

Beginning around 1960, western US researchers began to realize the limitations of excluding fire from ecosystems. These perspectives highlighted the need to reintroduce fire to many of California's landscapes. Soon after, many managers began to use prescribed or controlled burning to manage historically fire-prone ecosystems. In the 1970s, the National Park Service and Forest Service incorporated a policy of allowing lightning-ignited wildfires in wilderness areas in the Sierra Nevada of California and other regions in the western US to burn under desired conditions to reduce fuels, improve forest conditions, and promote other resource benefits.

Despite the increasingly aggressive (and more costly) efforts to suppress fires in California throughout much of the 20th century, the recognition of fire's ecological importance, and the increased use of prescribed and managed wildfires for resource benefit, the frequency of large wildfires increased in the mid-1900s. This increase in fire activity over the past few decades is largely attributable to increasing temperatures and greater aridity, a direct impact of climate change—a pattern that was most pronounced in 2020 and 2021, when nearly 7 million acres burned in California. Changes in fire severity (amount of living vegetation killed by fire) across California have been more varied. In the Sierra Nevada, there has been demonstrated increases in fire severity over the past four decades. However, in the Klamath Mountains, increased fire activity has not coincided with increases in fire severity, but the size of high severity patches has increased. While the fire activity in California has increased, it remains below pre-EuroAmerican settlement levels (one estimate is that an average 4.5 million acres burned annually in California), and a substantial fire deficit persists.

Prior to fire exclusion, California ecosystems burned in relatively consistent patterns of seasonality, intensity, severity, size, patchiness, and frequency, or what is commonly referred to as a fire regime. Similar to the way that climate represents the culminating patterns of day-to-day weather fluctuations in an area, fire regimes reflect the cumulative pattern of individual fires over time for a given area. Fire regimes vary over time and space within and among plant community types but still can be classified broadly into three broad categories based on frequency (number of fires that occur over time) and severity (proportion of living biomass killed by fire): 1) low severity (high frequency), 2) mixed severity (moderate frequency), and 3) high severity. All three fire regime types are found along the PCT in California. Fire severity is often inversely related to fire frequency so that high frequency fire regimes typically have low severity fires and low frequency fire regimes have high severity fires. Yet, there are some ecosystems where low intensity fire can result in high severity.

California contains a diverse array of plant communities, each of which can be characterized by one of the three general fire regime types just described. In the desert regions of southern California, plants communities such as creosote bush scrubs, mixed woody scrubs, and Joshua tree woodlands are typically fuel-limited, meaning that low levels of precipitation result in relatively low productivity that limits the spread of fire. These conditions result in very low frequency fires (>500 years) with burns resulting in predominantly high severity. Other plant communities in arid regions, containing species such as pinyon or juniper, are also fuel-limited, burning at high severity every 50–100 years. Foothill and montane chaparrals will also burn at high severity, with fires occurring historically, on average, every 30–60 years. High-elevation plant communities, such as subalpine coniferous forests and alpine, also are characterized as low frequency–high severity fire regimes that historically burned every century or so. However, fire in these communities is limited due to higher fuel moisture content because of the higher precipitation levels and cooler temperatures in these environs. Plant adaptations to fire in these fuel-limited plant communities tend to be uncommon. Most plant species persist through unburned

refugia or by recolonizing areas from the unburned edges. The exception to this is chaparral plant communities that have a number of plant adaptations that facilitate fire or promote recovery following fire. Many chaparral shrub species have the ability to resprout following fire, while others prolifically regenerate from seed stored in the soil. The germination of these seeds are often stimulated by the presence of heat and smoke. The architecture of the shrubs and retention of dead branches also facilitate the spread of high severity fires, which provides growing space for seedlings. Many species also experience enhanced flowering following fire including many fire ephemerals or followers (short-lived plant species that establish in the first few post-fire years).

Lower-elevation plant communities, such as California prairies, oak woodlands, and lower montane conifer forests, often tend to have high frequency–low severity fire regimes. Fires in these ecosystems tend to result in low severity, burning every 15 years or less. Many of the tree species in these ecosystems tend to have relatively thick bark (e.g., ponderosa pine, California black oak) and self-pruning branches. The leaves and needles of these species are also highly flammable due to their creation of dry porous litter beds that promote rapidly moving low intensity fires that are helpful to limit fire damage to the bole and reduce potential competitors, among other benefits. Evidence of frequent fire in these forest types is determined based on fire scars at the base of trees. In the prolonged absence of fire, these ecosystems are most impacted because they typically result in substantial increases in shade-tolerant competitors; these lead to dense stand conditions with higher amounts of fuel and greater continuity, which can result in higher intensity fires that can kill otherwise fire-resistant trees.

Upper montane conifer forests tend to have low or mixed severity fire regimes. Fires in these forests historically burned every 10–40 years. Fire severity in these forest types is usually a mixture of low, moderate and high severity patches, with most burning at low and moderate severity. Many conifers in these forests have adaptations similar to those present in low severity fire regimes. However, some forests contain species that require higher severity fires such as knobcone pine. These species have serotinous cones that open with fire. The adult trees have thin bark and die after the fire, but the seeds from serotinous cones prolifically establish on the exposed mineral soil the year following fire. The upper montane zone also contains lodgepole pine forests. Fire's role in these forests is interesting because although they are not technically serotinous (all cones open within a year), seedlings commonly establish after fire similar to serotinous species. This is likely because most fires occur in the late summer or early fall when the current cone crop contains mature seeds and is still closed. Thus, once fire comes through, the seeds stored in the cone can establish after the fire, though presumably at lower densities than truly serotinous species.

The role of fire in the many ecosystems present along the PCT is quite evident and in most cases ecologically and culturally beneficial. However, the unfortunate legacy of past management practices and the ongoing challenges related to climate change can result in undesired impacts from wildfires. Still, a hike along the PCT would not be representative without the clear evidence of fire on the landscape.

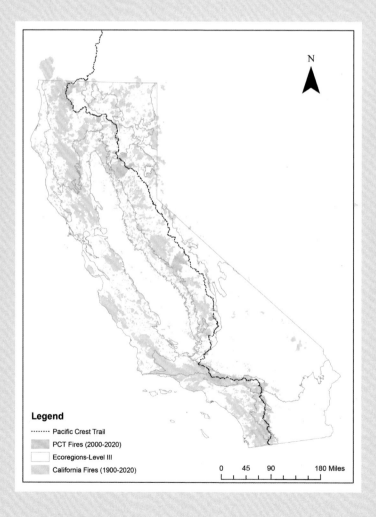

N

Legend

······ Pacific Crest Trail
    PCT Fires (2000-2020)
    Ecoregions-Level III
    California Fires (1900-2020)

0   45   90   180 Miles

PLANT COMMUNITIES AND HABITATS

Y ou may notice vegetation occurring in repeating patterns as you traverse California's various landscapes on the PCT. For 100 years or more, ecologists have mapped and classified these patterns using methods that included species composition, structure, and/or environmental conditions. As practicable, the plant communities are presented here in order of increasing elevation.

WETLAND-RIPARIAN COMMUNITIES

PCT SECTIONS: All

ELEVATION: Below 10,500 ft.

Found from desert arroyos to subalpine zones throughout California. Habitats include bogs, fens, lakeshores and lakebeds, marshes, wet meadows, ponds, riparian forests and scrubs, seasonally wet depressions, seeps, shallow lakes, springs, and streambanks. Meadows, streams, lakeshores, and other wet places above tree line are included in Alpine Communities.

Basically, when you go to fill your water bottle below the alpine zone, you're in a wetland-riparian community. It also includes areas of near-surface water. These are important places not only for us, but for wildlife. Indigenous peoples have used fire over the past 10,000 years in California to keep meadows open and accessible for themselves and game species. While keeping tree species such as lodgepole pine (*Pinus contorta* subsp. *murrayana*) from encroaching, burning also removed old, decadent vegetation from meadows and riparian habitats, allowing for species such as rushes (*Juncus* spp.), grasses, and sedges (*Carex* spp.) to thrive with lots of new growth. With new, nutritious foliage to munch on, plus plenty of available drinking water, grazing animals such as elk and deer would gather and thrive in burned wetlands. Yosemite and other national parks have brought fire back to their shrinking meadows to open them up again or at least to slow the encroachment of woody vegetation. Using controlled burning, or allowing natural fires to burn through meadows and riparian habitats, is gaining popularity with land managers throughout California.

CREOSOTE BUSH SCRUBS

PCT SECTIONS:
1–4 & 7
ELEVATION:
Below 4500 ft.

Structurally dominated by creosote bush (*Larrea tridentata*, pictured above), this ubiquitous desert scrub community is limited to the most arid low-elevation stretches of the CA PCT that bisect the Sonoran and Mojave Basin and Range ecoregions. Habitats include gravelly slopes and alluvial fans to sandy well-drained basins. It intergrades with Sonoran and Mojave Mixed Woody Scrubs and Joshua Tree Woodlands at higher elevations, and with Saltbush Scrubs where soils have higher salinity.

White bursage (*Ambrosia dumosa*) is often codominant with creosote bush, and the two species together represent the most common species in California's Sonoran and Mojave deserts. Creosote bush clonal rings are known to live up to 11,000 years, and undisturbed ancient stands represent the oldest of California's old growth vegetation! While a few widely spaced shrub species dominate this plant community, it's worth noting that annual plants comprise 50–70% of its species composition. Urbanization, off-road vehicles, and the recent sprawl of solar and wind development threaten this plant community, especially along the PCT in Kern County.

SONORAN MIXED WOODY SCRUBS

Found along the CA PCT on the desert flanks of the eastern Peninsular Ranges (San Felipe Valley region and lower Snow Creek drainage of the San Jacinto Mountains) and the southeastern San Bernardino Mountains. It is generally a transitional vegetation between the Creosote Bush Scrubs at lower elevations and the Pinyon-Juniper Woodlands and Montane Chaparrals above. Habitats include alluvial fans, rolling hills, and steep, rocky slopes with shallow soils. Plants are generally of Sonoran and southern Mojave Desert affiliation, with no clear dominant species. The various assemblages are highly diverse, containing a mix of both deciduous and evergreen woody shrubs and succulent species, including desert agave (*Agave deserti* var. *deserti*), California barrel cactus (*Ferocactus cylindraceus*), and Mojave yucca (*Yucca schidigera*). Species composition is influenced by summer precipitation; numerous shrubs and summer annuals are able to initiate growth and late-season flowering when activated by a warm-season precipitation event.

PCT SECTIONS:
1–4
ELEVATION:
Below 4500 ft.

MOJAVE MIXED WOODY SCRUBS

PCT SECTIONS:
3–8
ELEVATION:
Below 5000 ft.

This diverse scrub community is common throughout the Mojave Desert at mid-elevations. Along the CA PCT, it is intercepted only along Mojave Desert–influenced stretches of the Transverse Ranges and southern Sierra Nevada, where it is a transitional vegetation between Creosote Bush and Saltbush Scrubs below and Pinyon-Juniper Woodlands above. It may also intermingle with Joshua Tree Woodlands and Black Bush Scrubs. Often occurs on moderate slopes or on dynamic alluvial fans; soils are shallow, well drained, and gravelly to somewhat rocky, usually derived from granitic materials. These complex scrubs may contain 15–20 codominant shrubs and as many as 45 shrub species per acre! White bursage (*Ambrosia dumosa*), black bush (*Coleogyne ramosissima*), narrowleaf goldenbush (*Ericameria linearfolia*, pictured above), creosote bush (*Larrea tridentata*), Joshua tree (*Yucca brevifolia*), and Mojave yucca (*Y. schidigera*) are often key constituents, but none are dominant.

SALTBUSH SCRUBS

A low-diversity scrub type found intermittently in the valleys and drainages traversed by the CA PCT in the southern trail segments. Habitats include dry basins, sandy benches along watercourses, mudflats, and disturbed areas. Soils are fine-textured, poorly drained, and of high alkalinity or salinity. Because soils with high salt content are toxic to most species, total shrub cover is usually low, and few herbaceous plants occupy the open ground between shrubs. Saltbush Scrubs are typically dominated by one or more shrub species in the Chenopodiaceae, or by other salt-tolerant species. These "xero-halophytes" are well adapted to tolerating dry, saline soils; some absorb salts and store them in their tissues and in doing so may balance the pH of soils. Native species such as four-wing saltbush (*Atriplex canescens*, pictured above) and various goosefoots (*Chenopodium*) have been used in the rehabilitation of over-irrigated agricultural soils or soils contaminated by road salt or depleted by groundwater pumping.

PCT SECTIONS:
1–7
ELEVATION:
Below 4000 ft.

SAGEBRUSH SCRUBS

PCT SECTIONS:
All
ELEVATION:
Below 10,000 ft.

Found in all the CA PCT ecoregions in dry washes, plains, valley bottoms, mountain slopes, streambanks, and ridges, generally in well-drained, sandy to loamy soils. Often occurs and is codominant with bitterbrush (*Purshia tridentata*). Sagebrush (*Artemisia tridentata*, pictured above) is the quintessential shrub of the Great Basin Desert. Fire plays an important role in maintaining healthy sagebrush stands, and fire intervals of 30–70 years are typical. Increased fire frequency or severity, however, may prove deleterious as sagebrush does not sprout after fire and is totally reliant on an established seedbank or adjacent plants to recolonize a burn. When fires are too frequent or severe, the seedbank is depleted, and the landscape generally becomes dominated by weeds. Disturbance, especially from cattle or vehicles, leads to an increase of invasive, nonnative plants.

RABBITBRUSH SCRUBS

Rabbitbrush Scrubs are more common in the intermountain states but appear along the CA PCT as well, most often in the southern Sierra Nevada. California stands are dominated by subspecies of rubber rabbitbrush (*Ericameria nauseosa*, pictured above), many of which have extensive ranges throughout the state. Casting a gray-green hue on the landscape, this community stands out from the more common stands of Sagebrush Scrubs, Pinyon-Juniper Woodlands, and forest associations. Habitat characteristics include well-drained soils in valleys, alluvial fans, and pediments at the base of slopes. Soils, usually of high clay content, may "self-till," shrinking and swelling with the wet-dry precipitation cycles emblematic of California. Rabbitbrush Scrubs have a reputation for being a disturbance-follower, thriving on abandoned (tilled) agricultural property, overgrazed lands, burned areas, and along roadways.

PCT SECTIONS:
All
ELEVATION:
Below 12,000 ft.

BLACK BUSH SCRUBS

PCT SECTIONS:
1–2 & 8
ELEVATION:
Below 6000 ft.

Of all the desert-affiliated plant communities along the CA PCT, perhaps none is more dominated by a single species than is Black Bush Scrub. On dry, well-drained slopes and ridges, black bush (*Coleogyne ramosissima*, pictured above) forms a monoculture of low, intricately branched, dark grayish green shrubs. While quite common in the Mojave Desert and western Sonoran Desert of California, the only known stands of Black Bush Scrubs along the PCT occur in the San Felipe Valley region of San Diego County and just north of Kelso Valley in Kern County, separated by about 520 trail miles! Black bush grows in shallow, often calcareous soils with a well-developed crusty caliche layer. Some mature stands may exceed 500 years in age. These ancient stands have not fared well with increased fire frequency in recent years. The shallow-rooted plants rarely survive a burn, and post-fire recovery, which may take decades, is limited to germination of seeds cached by rodents.

CALIFORNIA PRAIRIES

Prairies along the CA PCT are associated with valleys and foothills mixed with oaks or shrubs, or open, treeless expanses. They also include native annual species such as California poppies (*Eschscholzia californica*), lupines (*Lupinus*), phacelias (*Pacelia* spp.) and popcorn flowers (*Plagiobothrys* spp.), all pictured above. With increasing elevation, prairies generally transition into woodlands or chaparrals. Unfortunately, because of intensive grazing, agriculture, and human development, California Prairies mostly consist of nonnative annual grasses and herbs such as wild oats (*Avena* spp.), bromes (*Bromus* spp.), star-thistles (*Centaurea* spp.), and filarees (*Erodium* spp.). Fire can have positive effects on this habitat by reducing nonnative species, especially grasses and their thatch buildup, allowing native plants to germinate. Fire was likely infrequent in California Prairies due to the low occurrence of lightning strikes, but grasslands close to habitation by Indigenous peoples were likely burned to attract wildlife with a proliferation of lush, new vegetation the following spring.

PCT SECTIONS:
1–8 & 18–19
ELEVATION:
Below 4000 ft.

JOSHUA TREE WOODLANDS

PCT SECTIONS:
4-9
ELEVATION:
Below 7000 ft.

Joshua tree (*Yucca brevifolia*, pictured above) has an extensive range throughout the Mojave Desert and is encountered along the Mojave Desert–influenced segments of the CA PCT. Though it rarely dominates a plant community, in denser stands this small tree becomes structurally significant. Joshua Tree Woodlands range along the PCT from sandy flats, such as those in the Antelope Valley, to elevations as high as 7000 ft. on the transmontane slopes of the San Bernardino Mountains and eastern Sierra Nevada and Tehachapi Mountains. They intergrade at lower elevations with Creosote Bush Scrubs and at higher elevations with Pinyon-Juniper Woodlands. Joshua Tree Woodlands, especially in Kern County, are subject to habitat degradation due to grazing, recreational activities, altered fire regimes, and more recently by the rapid sprawl of renewable energy development.

PINYON-JUNIPER WOODLANDS

Pinyon-Juniper Woodlands take on many forms across the southwestern US but are especially symbolic of the vast Great Basin Desert. Along the CA PCT, several combinations occur; the most common involves singleleaf pinyon pine (*Pinus monophylla*, pictured above) and California juniper (*Juniperus californica*). This plant community occupies the mid-elevation transmontane slopes of the southern Sierra Nevada and Southern California Mountains ecoregions, where precipitation is 9–17 in. annually. In the Peninsular Ranges, Parry pinyon (*P. quadrifolia*) is added to this plant community. Pinyon pines and junipers have slow growth rates and are poorly adapted to fire. Over the past several decades, land management agencies have cleared Pinyon-Juniper Woodlands for the benefit of range and fire management programs. Environmental groups, tribal leaders, and other conservationists have argued that removing these trees is harmful to this storied plant community.

PCT SECTIONS:
1–10
ELEVATION:
Below 8500 ft.

OAK WOODLANDS

PCT SECTIONS:
1–10 & 16–24
ELEVATION:
Below 7000 ft.

Oaks can be found on every section of the CA PCT, and in this community, oaks are the dominant tree. Oak Woodlands commonly intermix with Pinyon-Juniper Woodlands, Foothill Chaparrals, Lower Montane Coniferous Forests, and Montane Chaparrals. Fire is an important component in maintaining most Oak Woodlands. Frequent, low to moderately intense fires create openings for seedlings and sprouts. There's evidence that Indigenous peoples maintained stands of oaks for acorn production by having frequent, low intensity fires. The most common oak here is canyon live oak (*Quercus chrysolepis*, pictured above).

FOOTHILL CHAPARRALS

Foothill Chaparrals are the major vegetation type at lower elevations of the various mountain ranges. As you hike the CA PCT, Foothill Chaparrals tend to be the first shrub-dominated community you'll encounter above California Prairies, and as you gain elevation, they transition into woodlands or Lower Montane Coniferous Forests. Although Foothill Chaparrals are dominated by shrubs, they can include small trees. Dominant species include chamise and red shank (*Adenustema* spp.). manzanitas (*Arctostaphylos* spp.), and ceanothuses (*Ceanothus* spp.). Fire intervals in this community may vary from 10 to 100+ years. Many of the dominant shrubs can sprout following fire, but frequent high intensity burns can eliminate chaparral altogether. Competition from nonnative plants, following disturbances such as fires or manual clearing, can also hinder the return of native chaparral species.

PCT SECTIONS: 1–6 & 8 **ELEVATION:** Below 6000 ft.

MONTANE CHAPARRALS

PCT SECTIONS:
All
ELEVATION:
Below 11,000 ft.

This mountain community is typified by dry, brushy areas between stands of trees. It may include some of the same species that occur in Foothill Chaparrals, as well as shrubs requiring the increase in precipitation associated with the montane zone. Dominant species include manzanitas (*Arctostaphylos* spp.), ceanothuses (*Ceanothus* spp.), and chinquapins (*Crysolepsis* spp.). As you continue to gain elevation above timberline, Montane Chaparrals and associated Subalpine Coniferous Forests transition into Alpine Communities. Fire interval range is 20–75+ years. Although many of the dominant shrubs can sprout following fire, frequent or high intensity fires can eliminate chaparral completely. After burning, rocky sites tend to stay shrub-dominated, while other, less harsh sites can eventually convert into coniferous forest as long as the fire-return interval is long enough for trees to become dominant.

LOWER MONTANE CONIFEROUS FORESTS

onifers are a quintessential part of the PCT experience as one hikes above the scrubs, woodlands, and chaparrals. At lower elevations, Lower Montane Coniferous Forests (aka mixed coniferous forests) transition into woodlands or shrub-dominated habitats. The upper limits of this community are not always clear as you transition into a preponderance of dominant trees associated with Upper Montane Coniferous Forests. Moister sites tend to favor white fir (*Abies concolor*), sugar pine (*Pinus lambertiana*), and Douglas-fir (*Pseudotsuga menziesii*). Fire is an important component of this community, especially when pines dominate. With livestock grazing and fire exclusion, pine stands can be replaced by more shade-tolerant trees like white fir and Douglas-fir. Climate change is linked to altered fire frequency and intensity, and more and more, forest fires result in complete stand replacements. In other words, forests along the trail may never return to tree-dominated communities. Loss of seed banks and viable sprouting material, generally drier conditions (climate change), and competition from nonnative plants are major factors working against coniferous forests returning along recently burned portions of the trail.

PCT SECTIONS:
All
ELEVATION:
Below 8800 ft.

UPPER MONTANE CONIFEROUS FORESTS

PCT SECTIONS:
3–5 & 10–24
ELEVATION:
Below 11,200 ft.

As you transition out of Lower Montane Coniferous Forests by gaining elevation or by moving onto cooler, moister slopes (often north-facing), red fir (*Abies magnifica*), lodgepole pine (*Pinus contorta* subsp. *murrayana*), and/or mountain hemlock (*Tsuga mertensiana*) become more dominant in the landscape. Lodgepole pines tend to occupy cold, moist habitats near meadows, lakes, and streams; red firs prefer slopes where winter snow accumulations are deep (to 20 ft.). For lodgepole pines, large stand fires tend to happen at long intervals, sometimes several hundred years between events. Lodgepole pines establish after burns with wind-dispersed seeds; surface fires tend to happen every 20–30 years. Red firs have a different relationship with fire; surface fires mostly occur at intervals of 10–65 years. Intense, large fires are very rare since fuels are often moist and compact, or just very sparse.

SUBALPINE CONIFEROUS FORESTS

As you continue going up in elevation, this is the last plant community containing conifers. It is a boreal forest, bordering Alpine Communities and forming the timberline ecotone. Elfin, weather-battered, stunted trees that look like shrubs (aka krummholz) are common on exposed ridges within this community. Lightning strikes are also common, but fires are generally restricted to one or few trees. The shrub and herbaceous layers are mostly open and sparse, slowing the spread of fire. Foxtail pines (*Pinus balfouriana*) occur with the whitebark pines (*Pinus albicaulis*), which are the quintessential tree occupying this zone from the southern Sierra Nevada to the Klamath Mountains. Whitebark pine seeds are mostly scattered by Clark's nutcrackers and squirrels. Summer climate is mild, with maximum temperatures normally not exceeding 65°F.

PCT SECTIONS:
3–5 & 10–24
ELEVATION:
Above 8000 ft.

ALPINE COMMUNITIES

PCT SECTIONS:
10–15 & 18
ELEVATION:
Above timberline
(over 9500 ft.)

Besides the desert communities, plants in these communities, which include snowbank margins, talus and scree slopes, and meadows, face some of the harshest conditions along the PCT. Extreme wind, cold, lingering snow, and generally thin, rocky soils limit plant diversity mostly to low, tufted perennials (aka cushion plants). Plants can also seek protection from the elements by growing in protected rock crevices, between rocks, and at the base of boulders. Dominant species include Sierra columbine (*Aquilegia pubescens*), sedges (*Carex* spp.), and paintbrushes (*Castilleja* spp.). Lightning strikes are common, generally striking rock without causing any fires. Summer climate is very mild, with maximum temperatures normally not exceeding 60°F. The optimum growing season is limited to 4–7 weeks in summer, but hard frosts can happen year-round!

PACIFIC CREST TRAIL

SECTIONS 1–11

SECTION 1

MILE 0–77.3

SOUTHERN PENINSULAR RANGES

CLOCKWISE | Creosote bush scrub habitat in San Felipe Valley near Scissors Crossing, Mile 76.3. Dominant yellow annual is needle goldfields (*Lasthenia gracilis*). At 2240 ft., this is the lowest elevation in Section 1 of the CA PCT. / Parry's jujube (*Ziziphus parryi*), Mile 73.7, attains a height of 15 ft. along the trail. / Fingertips (*Dudleya edulis*) growing on granitic rock slabs just south of Morena Lake, Mile 19. / Parry pinyon (*Pinus quadrifolia*) atop windswept crest of the Laguna Mountains, Mile 43.5.

LENGTH: 77.3 miles, US/Mexico Border south of Campo (elev. 2925 ft.) to Highway 78 at Scissors Crossing (elev. 2259 ft.)

PREDOMINANT PLANT COMMUNITIES: Wetland-Riparian Communities, Creosote Bush Scrubs, Sonoran Mixed Woody Scrubs, Sagebrush Scrubs, California Prairies, Foothill Chaparrals, Oak Woodlands, Montane Chaparrals, Lower Montane Coniferous Forests

ECOREGIONS SOUTH TO NORTH: Southern California/Northern Baja Coast (Diegan Western Granitic Foothills and Morena/Boundary Mountain Chaparral), Southern California Mountains (Southern California Lower Montane Shrub and Woodland and Southern California Montane Coniferous Forest); Sonoran Basin and Range (Western Sonoran Mountain Woodland and Shrubland)

PLACES AND PLANTS OF INTEREST

San Diego County is a well-known US biodiversity hotspot, containing an astounding 2500 native plant species. Traversing numerous plant communities from the interior coastal valleys to arid desert regions of San Diego County, Section 1 of the CA PCT intercepts many of these species.

Hauser Mountain and Creek, mixed chaparral and wildflowers, Mile 2–20. The chamise and mixed chaparral assemblages along this stretch of trail are unique to the PCT, as they contain species typical of the coastal and interior foothills of southern San Diego

County and northern Baja, Mexico. For example, fingertips (*Dudleya edulis*) reaches its easternmost range here, clinging to the granitic slabs south of Morena Lake at Mile 19. In spring, look for Campo clarkia (*Clarkia delicata*) at Campo Creek, Mile 2.5, and again in the Hauser Creek drainage, Mile 15.

Though limited in California to the interior southern San Diego County, robust herbaceous perennial sticky geraea (*Geraea viscida*) can be seen in the foothill chaparrals south of Mt. Laguna. Look for occurrences at Mile 3 (at railroad crossing) northwest of Campo, and at Mile 30.5 just east of Kitchen Creek.

Laguna Mountains, montane chaparrals and coniferous forests, Mile 42–58. Winding along the precipitous crest of the Laguna Mountains just east of the Sunrise Highway and overlooking the Borrego Desert below, the PCT bisects the southernmost stands of lower montane coniferous forests in California. Dominated by Jeffrey pine (*Pinus jeffreyi*), Coulter pine (*P. coulteri*), and ponderosa pine (*P. ponderosa*), as well as black oak (*Quercus kelloggii*) and incense cedar (*Calocedrus decurrens*), fires are common in these forests opening up areas to rapid succession by chaparral species.The suite of species found along this stretch includes the uncommon Parry pinyon (*P. quadrifolia*) at Mile 43–44 and two rarities, velvety false-lupine (*Thermopsis californica* var. *semota*) at Mile 46–48 and San Diego sunflower (*Hulsea californica*) at Mile 53–57.

San Felipe Valley from Rodriquez Canyon to Scissors Crossing, Mile 68–77. This stretch of Section 1 descends the steep escarpment of the Laguna Mountains through Anza Borrego State Park, an abrupt transition from the southern Peninsular Ranges into the Sonoran Desert at San Felipe Valley. Along the trail one encounters unusual combinations of montane chaparrals, California juniper woodlands, and mixed woody scrubs, culminating in creosote bush scrubs and mesquite woodlands at Highway 78. Many of the species along the trail here are affiliated with the Sonoran Desert and occur in California only in this region, including the impressively thorny Parry's jujube (*Ziziphus parryi*), mouse's eye (*Bernardia incana*), shrubby brickellbush (*Brickellia frutescens*), and desert agave (*Agave deserti* var. *deserti*). The flora in this zone is comprised of a high percentage of ephemeral annual plants and after rainy winters the spring wildflower displays can be spectacular. Summer thunderstorms are also common here, and can activate a second bloom of annuals (summer annuals) in late summer and early fall.

SECTION 2

MILE 77.3–151.9

CENTRAL PENINSULAR RANGES

LENGTH: 74.6 miles, Highway 78 at Scissors Crossing (elev. 2259 ft.) to Highway 74 at Santa Rosa Summit (elev. 4906 ft.)

PREDOMINANT PLANT COMMUNITIES: Wetland-Riparian Communities, Creosote Bush Scrubs, Sonoran Mixed Woody Scrubs, Sagebrush Scrubs, California Prairies, Foothill Chaparrals, Oak Woodlands, Montane Chaparrals, Lower Montane Coniferous Forests

ECOREGIONS SOUTH TO NORTH: Southern California Mountains (Southern California Lower Montane Shrub and Woodland); Sonoran Basin and Range (Western Sonoran Mountain Woodland and Shrubland)

PLACES AND PLANTS OF INTEREST

Section 2 begins in the San Felipe Valley, San Diego County, gradually rising in elevation while traversing the eastern mountains and valleys of the central Peninsular Ranges. While the trail meanders northward, PCT hikers experience a mosaic of diverse vegetation types that typify the sharp transition between the western Sonoran Desert and the eastern Peninsular Ranges.

San Felipe Hills, enriched succulent scrub and desert wildflowers, Mile 78–82. From Scissors Crossing at Highway 78, the PCT again enters the Anza Borrego Desert State Park, and quickly ascends the rocky desert slopes of the southern San Felipe Hills. For several miles, hikers encounter impressive succulent diversity, shrubs

OVERLEAF, CLOCKWISE | Desert agave (*Agave deserti* var. *deserti*) and various cacti in Sonoran mixed woody scrub, overlooking the San Felipe Valley, Mile 77.9. / Hidden among the barrel cactuses in this section is fish hook cactus (*Mammillaria dioica*). / Dense chaparrals and oak woodlands near Coombs Peak (Bucksnort Mountain), Mile 129. Candle-like lily stalks are those of chaparral yucca (*Hesperoyucca whipplei*). / Chaparral dominated by red shank (*Adenostoma sparsifolium*), Mile 118.4. / Agua Caliente Creek north of Warner Springs, Mile 111.8. The pink annual in foreground is fringed linanthus (*Linanthus dianthiflorus*).

that can't be found elsewhere on the PCT, and, on years of sufficient rainfall, striking displays of annuals. Featured succulents include California barrel cactus (*Ferocactus cylindraceus*), Engelmann's hedgehog cactus (*Echinocereus engelmannii*), and Mojave yucca (*Yucca schidigera*).

Warner Springs area, valley grasslands and woodlands, Mile 109–112. Few places along the PCT are quite like Warner Springs, aka Kupa after the Indigenous peoples who once occupied the expansive valley. Majestic groves of oak, cottonwood, sycamore, willow, and ash can be found along the many watercourses, including Agua Caliente Creek, that filter into the valley. And though centuries of livestock grazing have taken a toll on the meadows and perennial grasslands that once thrived here, some areas have recovered and still offer spectacular wildflower blooms that include California dandelion (*Malacothrix californica*), fringed linanthus (*Linanthus dianthiflorus*), and miniature lupine (*Lupinus bicolor*). At Mile 110.2, look for the regional endemics Engelmann oak (*Quercus engelmannii*) and cane cholla (*Cylindropuntia californica* var. *parkeri*).

Chaparral dominated by red shank (*Adenostoma sparsifolium*), Mile 117–120. Compared to chamise (*Adenostoma fasciculatum*), its more ubiquitous cousin, red shank is somewhat patchy along the PCT, limited to the Peninsular Ranges. This stretch of trail, adjacent to Lost Valley Road, highlights some of the denser stands we've seen along the PCT.

Coombs Peak (Bucksnort Mountain) region, Mile 128–130. At 6193 ft. elevation, the unheralded Coombs Peak, one of the tallest peaks in San Diego County, supports small stands of conifers, including Coulter pine (*Pinus coulteri*). Also look for Parry's beargrass (*Nolina parryi*) and the rare Orcutt's linanthus (*Linanthus orcuttii*). Munz's mariposa lily (*Calochortus palmeri* var. *palmeri*), Mile 151.6, makes a cameo appearance just south of Highway 74 on Lookout Mountain, growing with sagebrush (*Artemisia tridentata*), Parry pinyon (*P. quadrifolia*), red shank, and Palmer oak (*Quercus palmeri*).

SECTION 3

MILE 151.9–209.5

NORTHERN PENINSULAR RANGES— SAN JACINTO MOUNTAINS

CLOCKWISE | Looking southward at the dramatic escarpment of the northeastern San Jacinto Mountains. Brittlebush (*Encelia farinosa*) dominates the trail here, close to where it crosses Interstate 10. / View to south of the San Jacinto Mountains from Snow Creek village, Mile 207. / California corn lily (*Veratrum californicum*) growing in the Skunk Cabbage Meadow complex, southeast of Mile 180. / Palmer oak (*Quercus palmeri*) lines the trail at the southern end of Section 3, Mile 152–153.

LENGTH: 57.6 miles, Highway 74 at Santa Rosa Summit (elev. 4906 ft.) to Interstate 10 near Cabazon (elev. 1335 ft.)

PREDOMINANT PLANT COMMUNITIES: Wetland-Riparian Communities, Creosote Bush Scrubs, Sonoran Mixed Woody Scrubs, Saltbush Scrubs, Sagebrush Scrubs, California Prairies, Oak Woodlands, Montane Chaparrals, Lower Montane Coniferous Forests, Upper Montane Coniferous Forests, Subalpine Coniferous Forests

ECOREGIONS SOUTH TO NORTH: Southern California Mountains (Southern California Lower Montane Shrub and Woodland, Southern California Montane Coniferous Forest, and Southern California Subalpine); Sonoran Basin and Range (Upper Coachella Valley and Hills and Western Sonoran Mountains)

PLACES AND PLANTS OF INTEREST

Section 3 of the CA PCT encompasses the San Jacinto Mountains, the northernmost and most prominent range in the Peninsular Ranges. Sandwiched between the coastal valleys to the west and the hot Sonoran Desert to the east, the lofty San Jacinto Mountains form an ecological sky island that harbors more than a dozen endemic, or near-endemic, plant species. In addition, at least 40 plant species reach their southern distributional limit in the range. Though much of the southern end of the San Jacinto has recently

burned, Section 3 quickly rises to 9000 ft. (or 10,834 ft. if you hike the San Jacinto Peak alternative) and much of it is still dominated by montane forest communities. At its northern terminus, the trail abruptly descends 2 vertical miles to an elevation of 1000 ft. at the San Gorgonio River near Interstate 10, the hottest, driest, and perhaps windiest, stretch of the PCT!

Palmer oak (*Quercus palmeri*) and Parry pinyon (*Pinus quadrifolia*), Mile 152. At the Pines to Palms Highway (Highway 74) near Santa Rosa Summit, the trail immediately enters a stand of Palmer oak and Parry pinyon, accompanied by sagebrush (*Artemisia tridentata*), red shank (*Adenostoma sparsifolium*), and Jeffrey pine (*Pinus jeffreyi*). This is one of the few locations along the PCT to see Palmer oak with its spiny leaf margins and broad and corky acorn cups. A number of rare herbaceous species also occur here, including southern jewelflower (*Streptanthus campestris*) and California beardtongue (*Penstemon californicus*). This site is also the southernmost occurrence of Burlew's onion (*Allium burlewii*).

Coulter pine (*Pinus coulteri*), Forbes Saddle, Mile 166.5. This locality is particularly interesting because Forbes Saddle has burned several times in the last century, and yet various sizes and ages of Coulter pines are evident here. Sporting the world's largest and heaviest pine cones, Coulter pine is more fire-adapted than most pines, as its thick, protective cones remain sealed shut until fire toasts the cone thus releasing its seeds.

Tahquitz Creek to Saddle Junction, montane meadows, Mile 177–180. Though impacted by a century of overgrazing, the meadow complex in this region remains of great significance to botanists, containing species not found elsewhere in the Peninsular Ranges, such as alpine shootingstar (*Primula tetrandra*), lemon lily (*Lilium parryi*), and California corn lily (*Veratrum californicum*). Skunk Cabbage Meadow is named for the corn lilies there.

Base of Snow Creek Canyon, Sonoran mixed woody scrubs, Mile 202–207. Snow Creek Canyon is one of the few places on earth where a vertical displacement of 2 miles occurs over such a short horizontal distance. Here, vegetation rapidly transitions to various diverse scrub types, supporting a number of species unique to this hot Sonoran Desert crossing of the PCT among them Bigelow's ragged rock flower (*Crossosoma bigelovii*), jojoba (*Simmondsia chinensis*), and desert willow (*Chilopsis linearis*).

SECTION 4

MILE 209.5–342

SAN BERNARDINO MOUNTAINS

LENGTH: 132.5 miles, Interstate 10 near Cabazon (elev. 1335 ft.) to Interstate 15 near Cajon Junction (elev. 2995 ft.)

PREDOMINANT PLANT COMMUNITIES: Wetland-Riparian Communities, Creosote Bush Scrubs, Sonoran Mixed Woody Scrubs, Mojave Mixed Woody Scrubs, Sagebrush Scrubs, California Prairies, Joshua Tree Woodlands, Pinyon-Juniper Woodlands, Oak Woodlands, Foothill Chaparrals, Montane Chaparrals, Lower Montane Coniferous Forests, Upper Montane Coniferous Forests

ECOREGIONS SOUTH TO NORTH: Southern California Mountains (Arid Montane Slopes, Southern California Lower Montane Shrub and Woodland, and Southern California Montane Coniferous Forest); Sonoran Basin and Range (Upper Coachella Valley and Hills); Mojave Basin and Range (Western Mojave Basins)

OVERLEAF, CLOCKWISE |
Looking southward across Big Bear Valley at San Gorgonio Peak from the PCT at Bertha Ridge, Mile 276. / Brittlebush (*Encelia farinosa*) lights up the trail in early morning, east of Cabazon, Mile 211. / Pebble plain habitat north of Baldwin Lake, Mile 267.5. / Looking to the southwest at San Gorgonio Peak from the PCT at Onyx Peak, Mile 252 (elev. 8700 ft.). / California sycamore (*Platanus racemosa*) along lower Deep Creek, near Mile 310.

PLACES AND PLANTS OF INTEREST

Section 4 of the CA PCT traverses the entire length of the San Bernardino Mountains, the tallest range in southern California. From the south, the trail begins in the Sonoran Desert at Interstate 10 at 1335 ft., the hottest and driest stretch of the CA PCT. It then climbs steadily into forested montane zones, cresting at about 8700 ft. at Onyx Summit, and then slowly descends to Interstate 15 near Cajon Junction at 2995 ft., where vegetation transitions into the Mojave Desert. Along this route, hikers will experience one of the great North American biodiversity hotspots. Of all the PCT sections, none can rival the high diversity and endemism of Section 4 plant species.

Cabazon to the North Fork of Mission Creek, mixed woody scrubs, Mile 212–225. This stretch of trail passes through numerous life zones that exemplify both the Sonoran and southern Mojave Desert biomes. It also bisects the moist canyons containing the Whitewater River and the West and North forks of Mission Creek. Recent floristic inventories have documented more than 500 plant species along this stretch, including such common desert taxa as creosote bush (*Larrea tridentata*), brittlebush (*Encelia farinosa*), and catclaw (*Senegalia greggii*). This area also marks the northwestern distributional limit for many Sonoran Desert species in California, such as Parry's jujube (*Ziziphus parryi*), and it is the only locality along the PCT to see the rare Joshua tree poppy (*Eschscholzia androuxii*).

Mission Springs to Onyx Summit, upper montane coniferous forests, Mile 240–252. This is the highest stretch of the PCT in the San Bernardino Mountains, generally staying above an elevation of 8000 ft. Though somewhat rain-shadowed by San Gorgonio Peak just to the west, the forest associations here are quite diverse with at least 9 conifer species including limber pine (*Pinus flexilis*), impressive old-growth stands of sugar pine (*P. lambertiana*), and Sierra juniper (*Juniperus grandis*) near Coon Creek Jumpoff. Many rare plants are found in the understory, including Mill Creek alumroot (*Heuchera parishii*), Big Bear Valley phlox (*Phlox dolichantha*), and Big Bear Valley woollypod (*Astragalus leucolobus*).

Highway 18 to Polique Canyon, pebble plain habitat, Mile 266–279. The San Bernardino Mountains mark the southern extent of glaciation in California. With post-glacial drying of the region, quartzite pebbles were pushed to the surface in the clay soils by frost heaving, leaving a substrate that trees were unable to colonize. The resultant opening among the lower montane coniferous forests and pinyon-juniper woodlands supports a unique plant community comprised of many endemic species (found nowhere else), most of which are matted perennials or tiny annuals. Indeed, the pebble plains of the San Bernardino Mountains are renowned among botanists as perhaps the single most significant hotspot for endemism in California, supporting at least 17 rare, threatened, or endangered plant species.

The best-developed pebble plain habitat can be found in the Big Bear and Holcomb Valley areas, or are for conservation management purposes, deliberately avoided by the PCT. However, as the trail traverses to the north of Baldwin and Big Bear lakes, one encounters numerous ridgetop flats and forest openings with well-developed pebble plains. Hikers should take extra care to avoid impacting this incredibly fragile habitat, but along the trail it's easy to spot some of the iconic rare species, including Parish's rockcress (*Boechera parishii*), little purple monkeyflower (*Erythranthe purpurea*), Big Bear Valley sandwort (*Eremogone ursina*), ashgray paintbrush (*Castilleja cinerea*), silver-haired ivesia (*Ivesia argyrocoma* var. *argyrocoma*), and Baldwin Lake linanthus (*Linanthus killipii*).

Mojave River Tributaries, riparian woodlands and chaparrals, Mile 310–330. The PCT zig-zags through the headwaters of the Mojave River, paralleling extensive riparian woodlands at Deep Creek and again west of Silverwood Lake that are dominated by Fremont's cottonwood (*Populus fremontii*), red willow (*Salix laevigata*), California sycamore (*Platanus racemosa*), and Durango root (*Datisca glomerata*). The Deep Creek watershed is designated as a National Wild and Scenic River. The stretch along Summit Valley passes through chaparral habitats that are heavily influenced by the Mojave Desert. This is one of the few places along the PCT where typically coastal chaparral species such as chamise (*Adenostoma fasciculatum*) and hollyleaf cherry (*Prunus ilicifolia*) grow alongside desert species such as gray amsonia (*Amsonia tomentosa*) and desert almond (*P. fasciculata*).

SECTION 5

MILE 342–444

LENGTH: 102 miles, Interstate 15 at Cajon Junction (elev. 2995 ft.) to Soledad Canyon near Acton (elev. 2237 ft.)

PREDOMINANT PLANT COMMUNITIES: Wetland-Riparian Communities, Sagebrush Scrubs, California Prairies, Pinyon-Juniper Woodlands, Oak Woodlands, Foothill Chaparrals, Montane Chaparrals, Lower Montane Coniferous Forests, Upper Montane Coniferous Forests, Subalpine Coniferous Forests

ECOREGIONS SOUTH TO NORTH: Southern California Mountains (Arid Montane Slopes, Southern California Lower Montane Shrub and Woodland, Southern California Montane Coniferous Forest, and Southern California Subalpine)

OVERLEAF, CLOCKWISE | View of Mt. Baldy from the slopes of Mt. Baden-Powell, San Gabriel Mountains, Mile 375. / Limber pine (*Pinus flexilis*) forest atop Mt. Baden-Powell. / Rocky slopes at Kratka Ridge, Mile 389.5. / Looking west at Mt. Baden-Powell from Blue Ridge, Mile 368.1.

PLACES AND PLANTS OF INTEREST

Section 5 of the CA PCT traverses the entire length of the San Gabriel Mountains of the Transverse Ranges, an east-to-west oriented range and one of the highest in southern California. From the east, the PCT commences at Cajon Junction along Interstate 15 (roughly elev. 3000 ft.), where vegetation is greatly influenced by the Mojave Desert to the north, as well as the maritime chaparrals and scrubs from the Los Angeles basin to the south. The trail quickly climbs onto several connecting ridgelines, and generally follows the crest of the range, remaining over 6000 ft. for about 50 miles, reaching its highest point atop Mt. Baden-Powell (elev. 9399 ft.).

Ralston Peak to Lone Pine Canyon, post-fire foothill chaparrals, Mile 344–348. Just west of the Interstate 15 crossing, the PCT traverses the Miocene-age sandstone beds at the base of Ralston Peak. Shearing along the San Andreas Fault has resulted in the tilting and re-exposure of these formations. Vegetation along this stretch of trail is recovering from recent fire, and the wildflower blooms are spectacular. Look for an abundance of tree poppy (*Dendromecon rigida*), showy penstemon (*Penstemon spectabilis*), California flannelbush (*Fremontodendron californicum*), and poodle-dog bush (*Eriodictyon parryi*). Avoid touching poodle-dog bush: it causes a severe rash (contact dermatitis) in some people!

Blue Ridge, montane chaparrals and coniferous forests, Mile 357–368. This segment of the trail winds along the Blue Ridge, just north of Mt. Baldy and south of the town of Wrightwood, passing through various vegetation assemblages dominated by mixed conifers and montane chaparral species. In late spring look for the rare San Gabriel linanthus (*Linanthus concinnus*) and pinewoods missionbells (*Fritillaria pinetorum*).

Mt. Baden-Powell, subalpine zone, Mile 378. At 9399 ft., Mt. Baden-Powell is the highest point along the PCT in southern California. Generally, above 8500 ft., hikers will encounter open stands of windswept limber pine (*Pinus flexilis*). This subalpine zone harbors several species unique to the San Gabriel Mountains, including lamb's horns (*Cycladenia humilis*) and woolly mountainparsley (*Oreonana vestita*).

Kratka Ridge, rock gardens, Mile 386–391. Rock outcrops and crevices are host to some of the more showy plants in the montane zones of San Gabriel Mountains. And this rocky stretch of the PCT at Kratka Ridge showcases many colorful rock-loving species. Here, look for urn-flowered alumroot (*Heuchera caespitosa*), Parish's catchfly (*Silene parishii*), California fuchsia (*Epilobium canum*), longstalk phacelia (*Phacelia longipes*), and the rare gray monardella (*Monardella australis* subsp. *cinerea*).

SECTION 6

MILE 444–517.6

WESTERN TRANSVERSE RANGES

CLOCKWISE | Vasquez Rocks Natural Area, Mile 453.4. / Looking south at the Liebre Mountains, Mile 516. California poppy (*Eschscholzia californica*) blankets the desert floor at the western edge of Antelope Valley near Neenach. / Maritime-influenced chaparrals and woodlands along the PCT in San Francisquito Canyon, Mile 478.2.

LENGTH: 73.6 miles, Soledad Canyon near Acton (elev. 2237 ft.) to Highway 138 (elev. 3026 ft.)

PREDOMINANT PLANT COMMUNITIES: Wetland-Riparian Communities, Sagebrush Scrubs, California Prairies, Oak Woodlands, Foothill Chaparrals, Montane Chaparrals, Lower Montane Coniferous Forests

ECOREGIONS SOUTH TO NORTH: Southern California Mountains (Arid Montane Slopes, Southern California Lower Montane Shrub and Woodland, and Southern California Montane Coniferous Forest)

PLACES AND PLANTS OF INTEREST

Section 6 of the CA PCT traverses the westernmost Transverse Ranges, a series of smaller ranges (generally less than 5500 ft. elevation) collectively referred to as the Sierra Pelona Mountains. From east to west the trail climbs out of the Santa Clara River in Soledad Canyon passing through the scenic Vasquez Rocks Natural Area. It then continues westward traversing the Liebre Mountains paralleling the San Andreas Fault, until it spills into the far western Mojave Desert in Antelope Valley, at Highway 138, near Neenach.

Soledad Canyon, subalkaline clay soils, Mile 444.2. Just above the riparian woodlands of the Santa Clara River, the PCT briefly passes through ashy-colored clay soils. Here, we can observe the lovely

prickly phlox (*Linanthus californicus*) and Mojave paintbrush (*Castilleja plagiotoma*), a regional endemic.

Vasquez Rocks Natural Area, juniper-dominated chaparral, Mile 451–454. Just east of the town of Agua Dulce, the PCT crosses through the Vasquez Rocks of western film and Star Trek fame. These uplifted and inclined breccia and conglomerate formations date back to the Oligocene Epoch (beginning 40 million years ago). Vegetation is dominated by California juniper (*Juniperus californica*), hollyleaf cherry (*Prunus ilicifolia*), green ephedra (*Ephedra viridis*), and chaparral yucca (*Hesperoyucca whipplei*). It is a veritable medley of species associated with both the arid montane slopes to the north and the maritime chaparrals to the south. At about Mile 451, look for short-joint beavertail cactus (*Opuntia basilaris* var. *brachyclada*).

San Francisquito to Lake Elizabeth Canyons, woodlands and chaparrals, Mile 478–486. This stretch of trail connects two riparian corridors containing diverse woodlands comprised of numerous oak and willow species, bigcone Douglas-fir (*Pseudotsuga macrocarpa*), Coulter pine (*Pinus coulteri*), and California sycamore (*Platanus racemosa*). Chamise (*Adenostoma fasciculatum*), manzanita, and scrub oaks dominate the slopes and ridges here, along with many showy herbaceous perennials, including Fremont's bushmallow (*Malacothamnus fremontii*) and Grinnell's beardtongue (*Penstemon grinnellii*).

Liebre Mountains near Three Points, Mile 492–510. This is a very interesting stretch of the CA PCT in that it marks the northern terminus of the Southern California Mountains and the last chance to see many species that have been along the PCT since the Mexico border, including toyon (*Heteromeles arbutifolia*), sugar bush (*Rhus ovata*), and Eastwood manzanita (*Arctostaphylos glandulosa*). The region is also ecologically distinct from those ranges to the south, as the plant associations exhibit characteristics of the coastal and interior mountains of central California. Here we see woodlands comprised of California buckeye (*Aesculus californica*), foothill pine (*Pinus sabiniana*), and even scattered occurrences of valley oak (*Quercus lobata*).

SECTION 7

MILE 517.6–566.5

ANTELOPE VALLEY AND TEHACHAPI MOUNTAINS

LENGTH: 48.9 miles, Highway 138 (elev. 3026 ft.) to Highway 58 (elev. 3821 ft.)

PREDOMINANT PLANT COMMUNITIES: Creosote Bush Scrubs, Saltbush Scrubs, Sagebrush Scrubs, Rabbitbrush Scrubs, California Prairies, Joshua Tree Woodlands, Pinyon-Juniper Woodlands, Oak Woodlands, Lower Montane Coniferous Forests

ECOREGIONS SOUTH TO NORTH: Mojave Basin and Range (Western Mojave Basins); Sierra Nevada (Eastern Sierran Mojavean Slopes and Tehachapi Mountains)

PLACES AND PLANTS OF INTEREST

The southern half of this relatively short section spans the Mojave Desert in Antelope Valley, while the northern half traverses the arid eastern slopes of the Tehachapi Mountains of the Sierra Nevada. This region is ecologically unique in California as several major geographic subdivisions form a knot here. Vegetation associations reflect this tangle, as species with affiliations to the Mojave Desert, Sierra Nevada, Transverse Ranges, Coast Ranges, and San Joaquin Valley all come together. Unfortunately, the recent sprawl of land uses, especially energy development, has had a profound impact on the quality of the ecosystem here, perhaps more so than any other section of the PCT.

Antelope Valley, saltbush and creosote bush scrubs, Mile 518–530. This relatively flat stretch is comprised of low-diversity scrub,

OVERLEAF, CLOCKWISE |
Looking westward at ridgeline dotted with foothill pine (*Pinus sabiniana*) and wind turbines, above Cameron Creek, from Mile 564.2. Yellow flowers are Bigelow's tickseed (*Leptosyne bigelovii*). / Pale-yellow layia (*Layia heterotricha*), looking rare enough in an ocean of Great Valley phacelia (*Phacelia ciliata*). / Foothill pine (*Pinus sabiniana*) on ridge above Oak Creek Canyon, Mile 551. / Mixed desert scrub at the foot of Tehachapi Mountains, Mile 534.6.

typified by saltbush (*Atriplex*), creosote bush (*Larrea tridentata*), and spiny hopsage (*Grayia spinosa*). In places the trail skirts around land developed for solar or agriculture. With abundant winter precipitation, however, colorful annual blooms may occur along this stretch and none more spectacular than those dominated by California poppy (*Eschscholzia californica*), the most celebrated wildflower in Antelope Valley.

Alluvial fans, Joshua tree woodlands, and mixed scrubs, Mile 534–538. The PCT follows the Cottonwood Creek watershed into low foothills of the Tehachapi Mountains, weaving around enormous wind turbines along the way. Shrub diversity increases here, with the most prominent additions being Joshua tree (*Yucca brevifolia*) and Mojave yucca (*Y. schidigera*). Annual diversity is also fairly high, including such species as thistle sage (*Salvia carduacea*) and broad-flowered gilia (*Gilia latiflora*). Also look for the rare Lemmon's syntrichopappus (*Syntrichopappus lemmonii*).

Ridgeline south of Oak Creek Canyon, juniper woodlands and sagebrush scrubs, Mile 548–554. This represents PCT's high point in Section 7, attaining an elevation of just over 6000 ft. The trail meanders through mosaics of scrubs (on south-facing slopes) and woodlands (north-facing slopes). The scrub community is a mix of sagebrush (*Artemisia tridentata*), desert bitterbrush (*Purshia tridentata* var. *glandulosa*), Mojave kingcup cactus (*Echinocereus mojavensis*), and herbaceous perennials such as the beautiful Mojave beardtongue (*Penstemon incertus*). The woodlands are comprised of scattered singleleaf pinyon pine (*Pinus monophylla*) and foothill pine (*P. sabiniana*) but are largely dominated by California juniper (*Juniperus californica*) and Tucker oak (*Quercus john-tuckeri*).

Cameron Canyon, rabbitbrush scrub, Mile 565. The slopes along the trail here are heavily disturbed by grazing but feature stands of rubber rabbitbrush (*Ericameria nauseosa*) and, in rainy years, the rare pale-yellow layia (*Layia heterotricha*).

SECTION 8

MILE 566.5–652

PIUTE AND SCODIE MOUNTAINS

LENGTH: 85.5 miles, Highway 58 (elev. 3821 ft.) to Highway 178 at Walker Pass (elev. 5271 ft.)

PREDOMINANT PLANT COMMUNITIES: Sagebrush Scrubs, Rabbitbrush Scrubs, Black Bush Scrubs, California Prairies, Joshua Tree Woodlands, Pinyon-Juniper Woodlands, Oak Woodlands, Montane Chaparrals, Lower Montane Coniferous Forests

ECOREGIONS SOUTH TO NORTH: Sierra Nevada (Eastern Sierran Mojavean Slopes, Eastern Sierra Great Basin Slopes, Tehachapi Mountains, and Southern Sierra Lower Montane Forest and Woodland)

PLACES AND PLANTS OF INTEREST

Section 8 marks the beginning of the trail's journey north through the Sierra Nevada. At the south, the section begins at Highway 58 and climbs quickly, holding an elevation of 5000–6000 ft. until it reaches the Piute Mountains. It then angles to the northeast into the Kaivah Wilderness and traverses the crest of the Scodie Mountains to Highway 178 at Walker Pass. In terms of the flora, this region marks a swift transition from south to north. More than 100 species in this guidebook, many of them affiliated with desert regions, reach their northernmost distribution along the PCT in this section. By contrast, only a dozen or so reach their southern range in this section, as many southern Sierra Nevada montane species are also found in the Transverse Ranges.

PACIFIC CREST
NATIONAL SCENIC
TRAIL
SCODIE SEGMENT

Piute Mountains, tall conifers and fog, Mile 601–610. The PCT in the southern Sierra Nevada generally straddles the crest of the range at its eastern desert escarpment. But the Piute Mountains are an exception, being situated west of the crest where precipitation is enhanced, and where fog from the San Joaquin Valley is more prevalent. As a result, the mountain is a mosaic of montane meadows, oak woodlands, and pine forests dominated by ponderosa pine (*Pinus ponderosa*), Jeffrey pine (*P. jeffreyi*), and California black oak (*Quercus kelloggii*), resembling some of the forests in the San Bernardino Mountains 200 miles to the south. Interestingly, many rare species here also occur in the San Bernardino Mountains, such as the Tehachapi ragwort (*Packera ionophylla*), Transverse Range phacelia (*Phacelia exilis*), and pinewoods missionbells (*Fritillaria pinetorum*).

Pinyon Mountain, pinyon-juniper woodlands, Mile 620–622. This stretch epitomizes the tug-of-war between pinyon-juniper woodlands, Joshua tree woodlands, and various scrub communities. Here the pinyon-juniper woodlands win out, but only briefly. In spring, look here for the rare white pygmypoppy (*Canbya candida*).

Birds Spring Pass to Skinner Peak, Scodie Mountains, Webber's Joshua tree, Mile 630–635. The Joshua tree in this area has a distinctive shrubby form, with multiple stems (from underground rootstalks). Though not formally recognized as distinct from Joshua tree (*Yucca brevifolia*), this form has been called Webber's Joshua tree (var. *herbertii*). Also, look for the deep blue flowers of the rare Charlotte's phacelia (*Phacelia nashiana*).

North end of the Scodie Mountains to Walker Pass, pinyon-juniper woodlands, Mile 648–652. This stretch contains dense stands of singleleaf pinyon pine with scattered juniper. In fact, this marks the northernmost California juniper (*Juniperus californica*) along the PCT. Near Walker Pass, look for the lovely desert peach (*Prunus andersonii*) and mustang mint (*Monardella exilis*). One of the most spectacular flowers, Bigelow's tickseed (*Leptosyne bigelovii*), can turn entire hillsides yellow with thousands of blooms.

SECTION 9 | SIERRA NEVADA

MILE 652–704.7

LENGTH: 52.7 miles, Walker Pass (elev. 5271 ft.) to Kennedy Meadows BLM Campground (elev. 6151 ft.)

PREDOMINANT PLANT COMMUNITIES: Wetland-Riparian Communities, Sagebrush Scrubs, Joshua Tree Woodlands, Pinyon-Juniper Woodlands, Oak Woodlands, Montane Chaparrals, Lower Montane Coniferous Forests

ECOREGIONS SOUTH TO NORTH: Sierra Nevada (Eastern Sierra Great Basin Slopes)

PLACES AND PLANTS OF INTEREST

This southern portion of the Sierra Nevada is very much influenced by the Great Basin Desert. The woodlands, scrubs, and chaparrals are very similar to those you would find in desert mountain ranges east of the Sierra. Three wilderness areas (Owens Peak, Chimney Peak, and Dome Land) are located along this section of the PCT. Besides having Joshua trees, this area is also known for spectacular wildflower displays during years with favorable rain. Many of the flowers are associated with the Mojave and/or Great Basin Desert(s).

Parry's beargrass (*Nolina parryi*), Mile 657–661. This yucca-like plant is scattered on the east-facing, rocky slopes above and below the PCT.

OVERLEAF, CLOCKWISE | Kennedy Meadows and South Fork Kern River. / Parry's beargrass (*Nolina parryi*) on rocky, east-facing slopes. These plants do not die after flowering like the similar chaparral yucca (*Hesperoyucca whipplei*). / Rose-flowered larkspur (*Delphinium purpusii*), Mile 666.7. / Walker Pass, PCT crossing of Highway 178 with Joshua trees (*Yucca brevifolia*), singleleaf pinyon pine (*Pinus monophylla*), sagebrush (*Artemisia tridentata*), and desert bitterbrush (*Purshia tridentata* var. *glandulosa*) in the foreground.

Rose-flowered larkspur (*Delphinium purpusii*), Mile 666.7. A very rare larkspur known to occur in only two places along PCT Sections 8–9. This is the only pink larkspur in North America.

Owens Peak desertparsley (*Lomatium shevockii*), Mile 671.2. Look for this low-growing, purple-flowered perennial on gravelly slopes below the trail at this location. It occurs only in this section of the PCT.

Kern larkspur (*Delphinium hansenii* subsp. *kernense*), Mile 679.8. Look for this tall larkspur among boulders. The flowers are blue-purple to white.

Kennedy Meadows and South Fork Kern River, Mile 699.9–704.7. A large valley dominated by sagebrush (*Artemisia tridentata*) with the South Fork Kern River flowing from the north out the south end. Located just off the PCT, the Kennedy Meadows General Store offers hikers free camping at store, showers, laundry facilities, resupply packages, and outdoor movies during the summer on Saturday nights.

SECTION 10 | SIERRA NEVADA

MILE 704.7–878.8

CLOCKWISE | An alpine meadow along the shore of Sapphire Lake, Mile 842. / The majestic Sierra foxtail pine (*Pinus balfouriana* subsp. *austrina*) in Sequoia National Park. / Muir Hut (elev. 11,973 ft.) below Mt. Solomons, Mile 838.6. / Evolution Valley and Evolution Creek, Kings Canyon National Park. / Dollar Lake (elev. 10,222 ft.) with Painted Lady (back left) and Fin Dome (back right) taken by York in 1979, Mile 795.8.

LENGTH: 174.1 miles, Kennedy Meadows Campground (elev. 6151 ft.) to Lake Edison Ferry Trail (elev. 7899 ft.)

PREDOMINANT PLANT COMMUNITIES: Wetland-Riparian Communities, Sagebrush Scrubs, Pinyon-Juniper Woodlands, Oak Woodlands, Montane Chaparrals, Lower Montane Coniferous Forests, Upper Montane Coniferous Forests, Subalpine Coniferous Forests, Alpine Communities

ECOREGIONS SOUTH TO NORTH: Sierra Nevada (Eastern Sierra Great Basin Slopes, Southern Sierra Mid Montane Forests, Southern Sierra Upper Montane Forests, Southern Sierra Subalpine Forests, and Sierran Alpine)

PLACES AND PLANTS OF INTEREST

This section and Section 11 comprise nearly 238 trail miles of the PCT—with no road crossings. It's almost entirely within US Forest Service and National Park wilderness areas. Section 10 starts at the campground located at the north end of Kennedy Meadows, which is a large valley dominated by sagebrush (*Artemisia tridentata*) with the South Fork Kern River flowing from the north out the south end. Just a short distance along the PCT, at Mile 704.8, is South Sierra Wilderness with the northern boundary at Mile 725. Like Kennedy Meadows, many of the meadows in the southern portion of this section, such as Monache, are dominated by sagebrush. Other wilderness areas (south to north) include Golden Trout, Sequoia and Kings Canyon, and John Muir. Section 10 includes the highest point on the PCT at Forester Pass (elev. 13,153 ft.), Mile 779.5.

You can climb even higher if you add 17 miles to your trip and climb Mt. Whitney (elev. 14,505 ft.), the highest point in the lower 48 states. Section 10 also has more PCT miles of alpine communities than any of the other Sierran sections.

Pinyon-juniper woodlands in the Eastern Sierra Great Basin Slopes ecoregion, Mile 704–711. As you head north along the South Fork Kern River from Kennedy Meadows Campground, you will leave the pinyon-juniper woodlands behind for the last time on the PCT. Although this plant community has been the most dominant in the southern Sierra so far (applicable to northbound hikers), it disappears for good as you gain elevation and leave all desert influences.

Sequoia and Kings Canyon National Parks, Mile 753.9–856. These two parks, managed as one, are the crown jewels of the southern, high Sierra Nevada. Alpine lakes, spectacular peaks, deep river valleys, extensive uncut forests, granite everywhere, and some 1300 native plant species are just a few of the things that make this portion of the PCT so spectacular! Heading north through Sequoia National Park, the PCT intersects the John Muir Trail (JMT) at Mile 767. They're a mostly shared trail until they part ways in Tuolumne Meadows, Yosemite National Park. From Tuolumne Meadows, the JMT heads down to its northern terminus at Happy Isles, Yosemite Valley.

Mt. Whitney/Whitney Portal Trail, Mile 766–767. Mt. Whitney is 8.5 miles from the PCT. From the south, take a spur trail to the John Muir Trail (JMT). From the north, continue along the JMT to Mt. Whitney (elev. 14,505 ft.). The trails also have an option to continue down the east escarpment to Whitney Portal (16.6 trail miles from the PCT). Look for the following alpine plants along the trail or at the summit: cutleaf daisy (*Erigeron compositus*), cushion buckwheat (*Eriogonum ovalifolium*), Pacific hulsea (*Hulsea algida*), alpine mountainsorrel (*Oxyria digyna*), showy skypilot (*Polemonium eximium*), and gray chickensage (*Sphaeromeria cana*).

Sierra foxtail pine (*Pinus balfouriana* subsp. *austrina*), Mile 745–866. A majestic pine found in the subalpine zone only within this section of the PCT. It is mostly restricted to Sequoia and Kings Canyon National Parks. Its cousin, the Klamath foxtail pine (subsp. *balfouriana*), isn't encountered until Section 20, in the Klamath Mountains.

Muir Hut (John Muir Memorial Shelter) at Muir Pass, Mile 838.6. The hut was built in 1930 to honor John Muir. It serves as an emergency shelter and trail beacon when the trail is covered in snow. Look for the showy, yellow-flowered Lemmon's draba (*Draba lemmonii*) on the pass and down the northwest side.

Evolution Valley and Evolution Creek, Mile 846–851. A breathtaking valley with Evolution Creek meandering its way through an extensive meadow complex. Upper montane coniferous forests dominated by lodgepole pine (*Pinus contorta* subsp. *murrayana*) border the meadows.

Muir Trail Ranch and Blayney Meadows Hot Springs trail, Mile 857.7. Take this 2-mile trail, off the PCT, for the ranch (resupply point) and a soak in the hot springs. Please use care crossing the South Fork San Joaquin River to go over to the meadow and hot springs. The ranch has a cable car for its guests to cross the river.

Lake Edison Ferry Trail junction to Vermilion Valley Resort, Mile 878.8. If you decide not to use the ferry, and you're a northbound hiker, then take the Vermilion Valley Resort Trail (Mile 874.5) for 5 trail miles. Southbound hikers who want to skip the ferry ride can take the ferry trail and continue another 5 miles (from the ferry drop-off point) along the north shore to the resort.

SECTION 11 | SIERRA NEVADA

MILE 878.8–942.5

CLOCKWISE | Devils Postpile National Monument (near Mile 908.5). / On the PCT: York's son, Noah, and impressive clumps of shaggy lupine (*Lupinus covillei*) in a subalpine coniferous forest in Yosemite. / Lake Edison from the northeast shore.

LENGTH: 63.7 miles, Lake Edison Ferry Trail (elev. 7899 ft.) to Tuolumne Meadows, Yosemite National Park at Highway 120 (elev. 8596 ft.)

PREDOMINANT PLANT COMMUNITIES: Wetland-Riparian Communities, Sagebrush Scrubs, Oak Woodlands, Montane Chaparrals, Lower Montane Coniferous Forests, Upper Montane Coniferous Forests, Subalpine Coniferous Forests, Alpine Communities

ECOREGIONS SOUTH TO NORTH: Sierra Nevada (Southern Sierra Upper Montane Forests, Southern Sierra Subalpine Forests, and Sierran Alpine)

PLACES AND PLANTS OF INTEREST

If you started in Section 10, you haven't seen a road in 174 miles and this trend will continue until you get to Tuolumne Meadows in Yosemite National Park at the end of this section. Section 11 is spectacular in many of the ways that Section 10 is, with high granite peaks and cliffs, a plethora of glacier-carved lakes and canyons to 5000 ft. deep. It is a land of snow and ice. Of course, snow on the ground means few wildflowers to be found. You can either concentrate on trees and shrubs, or look for some early gems such as drabas (*Draba*), lewisias (*Lewisia*), or white pasqueflower (*Anemone occidentalis*). The geology does change when you get to Devils Postpile National Monument. It is of volcanic origin: pumice and andesite, which cooled 630,000 years ago, form the rock column cliff at the monument. Wilderness areas crossed include John Muir, Ansel Adams, and Yosemite National Park. The highest

point along the trail is Donohue Pass (elev. 11,073 ft.) at the southern boundary of Yosemite (Mile 929.5).

Lake Edison Ferry Trail junction to Vermilion Valley Resort, Mile 878.8. If you decide not to use the ferry, and you're a northbound hiker, then take the Vermilion Valley Resort Trail (Mile 874.5) for 5 trail miles. Southbound hikers who want to skip the ferry ride can take the ferry trail and continue another 5 miles (from the ferry drop-off point) along the north shore to the resort.

Reds Meadow Resort, Devils Postpile National Monument, and Agnew Meadow Trailhead, Mile 906.7–714.8. Supplies, showers, and shuttles to Mammoth Lakes if needed, are just some of the things that are just off the PCT through this area. There's also the option of taking the John Muir Trail for 14.1 miles as an alternate route to the west of PCT Mile 909–923. Look for pumice alpinegold (*Hulsea vestita* subsp. *vestita*) around Devils Postpile NM, a strikingly showy sunflower when seen against the area's open, gravelly soils.

Yosemite National Park, Mile 929.6–997.1. Sierran park well known for its waterfalls, granite cliffs, giant sequoias (at elevations below the PCT), and tenacious bears that love to find ways to get human food! Look for alpineflames (*Pyrrocoma apargioides*), a cool little sunflower, in the meadows. In Tuolumne Meadows there's a campground (including an area for PCT hikers), lodging, store, gas station, post office, and grill. Tuolumne Meadows is also the point where the John Muir Trail veers off to Happy Isles in Yosemite Valley.

SPECIES DESCRIPTIONS

CONIFERS

Abies concolor

white fir

PINACEAE PINE FAMILY

PCT Sections: All **Abundance:** Common **Height:** to 200 ft. **Habitat-Community:** Dry or moist soils from lower montane to subalpine coniferous forests **Elevation:** Below 10,200 ft. **Ecoregions:** All (except Mojave Basin and Range)

Ubiquitous tree found throughout the mountains of California and other western states. Bark on young trees is smooth, grayish; on mature trees, thick and furrowed with a yellowish inner layer. Needles 0.5–2.5 in. long, single, and tend to grow in 2 rows (2-ranked). Shaded needles usually flattened along their stem; those in the sun curve upward, much like red firs, but without the hockey stick–like bend just above the point of attachment. Seed cones, as with other true firs, sit erect on the upper branches and mature in a season; by maturity, they fall apart or are dismantled by squirrels and chickarees. Mixes with other conifers and fairly shade-tolerant, but young trees are easily killed by fire.

Abies magnifica

red fir

PINACEAE PINE FAMILY

PCT Sections: 9–24 **Abundance:** Common **Height:** to 190 ft. **Habitat-Community:** Upper montane coniferous forests subjected to cold winters and deep snow **Elevation:** 5000–9000 ft. **Ecoregions:** Sierra Nevada, Cascades, Klamath Mountains

Tree forming pure groves or a component of mixed stands mostly at mid-elevations in areas that receive large amounts of rain and snow. Bark of mature trees is thick and reddish. Needles 1–1.5 in. long, single, curved upward on stems, and not flat in cross section. Needles have an abrupt bend, resembling hockey sticks, just above the point of attachment. Seed cones 6–9 in. long and barrel-shaped with or without exserted bracts. Wolf lichens (*Letharia*) growing near the base of the trunk occur above the average winter snow depth, demarcating a vivid yellow "snow depth indicator" that is easy to observe as you hike through red fir stands. Young trees have a conical form (helps shed snow) and dense branching, making them popular Christmas trees. Aka silvertip fir.

Pinus monophylla

singleleaf pinyon pine

PINACEAE PINE FAMILY

PCT Sections: 1–10 **Abundance:** Common **Height:** to 60 ft. **Habitat-Community:** Dry slopes and ridges in pinyon-juniper woodlands **Elevation:** Below 9200 ft. **Ecoregions:** Southern California Mountains, Mojave Basin and Range, Sierra Nevada

Much-branched, rounded tree, often lacking a prominent central trunk. Bark red-brown and irregularly furrowed or cross-checked. Needles 1–2.5 in. long, single, curved, gray-green, and persisting 5–10 years. Seed cones 2–4 in. long and maturing in 2 years. A widespread and definitive tree of the Great Basin Desert, and the state tree of Nevada. The world's only 1-needled pine, forming extensive open woodlands in association with juniper and live oak along the southern sections of the PCT. The edible seeds (aka pinenuts) are important food sources for wildlife and people, both past and present. Hybridizes with *P. quadrifolia*.

Pseudotsuga macrocarpa

bigcone Douglas-fir

PINACEAE PINE FAMILY

PCT Sections: 1–6 **Abundance:** Locally common **Height:** to 120 ft. **Habitat-Community:** North-facing slopes and ravines, and mixed with hardwoods in chaparrals and lower montane coniferous forests **Elevation:** Below 7000 ft. **Ecoregions:** Southern California Mountains

Broad, strong-tapered conifer with large, drooping branches. Bark smooth gray on young trees, becoming rough and much darker when mature. Needles 0.5–2 in. long, evergreen, single, and bluish green with a pointed tip. Seed cones to 8 in. long, largest in the genus, with distinctive, exserted bracts. Typically survives fire, which is a common hazard in chaparral. Fire may scorch the needles on branches, but they soon resprout. The largest known specimen, with a trunk 8 ft. in diameter, occurs in the San Gabriel Mountains. Though not a useful timber tree, the species is highly aesthetic and valuable for watershed protection in fire-prone areas. Aka bigcone spruce.

Tsuga mertensiana

mountain hemlock

PINACEAE PINE FAMILY

PCT Sections: 10–24 **Abundance:** Locally common **Height:** to 150 ft. **Habitat-Community:** Moist slopes from lower montane to subalpine coniferous forests **Elevation:** Below 11,600 ft. **Ecoregions:** Sierra Nevada, Cascades, Klamath Mountains

Conical, spire-like tree with droopy tops, growing in areas with deep winter snows. Bark dark gray to reddish and thick with furrows on mature trees. Needles 0.4–0.8 in. long, dark green to blue-green, spirally arranged, and blunt-tipped. The leaf stalks remain after leaves fall, forming pegs along the stems. Seed cones 1–3 in. long, purple (young), composed of thin, leathery scales, and pendent from stems. Very susceptible to fires, which are now occurring more frequently in areas that previously stayed too moist to burn intensely. John Muir felt mountain hemlock (which he called hemlock spruce) was the most beautiful conifer. Easy to spot by looking for droopy treetops. Tolerates shade and lives for over 800 years.

▼ 2 NEEDLES

Pinus contorta subsp. *murrayana*

lodgepole pine

PINACEAE PINE FAMILY

PCT Sections: 3–5 & 10–24 **Abundance:** Common **Height:** to 100 ft. **Habitat-Community:** Dry slopes and ridges, meadows, and lakeshores in upper montane & subalpine coniferous forests **Elevation:** Below 11,000 ft. **Ecoregions:** Southern California Mountains, Sierra Nevada, Cascades, Klamath Mountains

Trees grow in mixed or pure stands; because of their tolerance for wet habitats, they are especially common around meadows and lakes. Bark orange to purple-brown, with thin, puzzle-piece scales. Needles 2–3 in. long, 2 per bundle, yellow-green, twisted, and sharp-pointed. Seed cones 1–2.5 in. long with scale tips having slender prickles. Flourishes in full sun, so even-aged stands usually represent areas that burned in the past. A prolific seeder, but unlike its cousins in the Rocky Mountains, its cones do not require fire to open. The quintessential PCT campsite tree and the only 2-needle pine along the trail. Shore pine (subsp. *contorta*), the other California subspecies, is restricted to coastal habitats.

Pinus coulteri

Coulter pine

PINACEAE PINE FAMILY

PCT Sections: 1–6 **Abundance:** Locally common **Height:** to 120 ft. **Habitat-Community:** Dry, rocky slopes with hardwoods in woodlands, chaparrals, and lower montane coniferous forests **Elevation:** Below 7000 ft. **Ecoregions:** Southern California Mountains

Long-needled pine with a broad crown. Bark dark gray-brown to nearly black and deeply furrowed. Needles 6–12 in. long, 3 per bundle, and stiff. Seed cones 8–16 in. long, drooping, persistent, dense, and serotinous, requiring fire or disturbance to release seeds. Known colloquially as widow-maker thanks to its massive cones, the heaviest of any pine in the world. In addition to being impressively hefty (up to 15 lbs.), the cones also feature large talon-like scales that are covered in a thick, sticky resin. Dense stands are found along the PCT at mid-elevations in the Peninsular and Transverse ranges.

Pinus jeffreyi

Jeffrey pine

PINACEAE PINE FAMILY

PCT Sections: All **Abundance:** Common **Height:** to 200 ft. **Habitat-Community:** Dry montane to subalpine coniferous forests, including serpentine and granitic soils **Elevation:** Below 10,000 ft. **Ecoregions:** All

Single-trunked tree with lower portion generally straight and clear of branches. Bark orange-brown (mature trees), thick, deeply furrowed, and vanilla- or pineapple-scented, especially in the sun. Needles 5–11 in. long, gray- to blue-green, and 3 per bundle. Like the bark, the needles have a sweet vanilla or pineapple smell when crushed. Seed cones 6–12 in. long, with inward-curving prickles that keep a cupped hand safe from being poked. Along the PCT, occurs in pure stands on serpentine soils or in mixed-conifer stands on other substrates. Can occur with ponderosa pine (*P. ponderosa*) but also grows at much higher elevations, especially on granitic rock outcrops. Tolerant of ground fires and bark beetles, if not stressed. Stressors include drought or lack of sun because of competition from shade-tolerant conifers. Crystallized sap of Jeffrey and ponderosa pines has historically been enjoyed as candy.

Pinus ponderosa

ponderosa pine

PINACEAE PINE FAMILY

PCT Sections: All **Abundance:** Common **Height:** to 220 ft. **Habitat-Community:** Dry slopes from oak woodlands to upper montane coniferous forests **Elevation:** Below 9000 ft. **Ecoregions:** All

Like Jeffrey pines, these iconic trees tend to have few lower branches because of self-pruning from shade intolerance. Bark on mature trees is thick with deeply furrowed, yellow-brown, flaky scales. Needles 4–10 in. long, yellow-green, and 3 per bundle. Seed cones 3–6.5 in. long, smaller than those of Jeffrey pines, and with sharp recurved prickles that poke your hand when squeezed. (The two pines are nicknamed "gentle Jeffrey" and "prickly ponderosa" as a way to remember the character differences of their cones.) Found throughout low-elevation conifer zones, but many have died, especially in the Sierra Nevada, during recent drought cycles. Weakened, drought-stressed trees are susceptible to bark beetles and diseases. Resin has historically been used for building and medicinal purposes.

Pinus sabiniana

foothill pine

PINACEAE PINE FAMILY

PCT Sections: 6–9 **Abundance:** Occasional **Height:** to 80 ft. **Habitat-Community:** Generally mixed with other conifers from oak woodlands to lower montane coniferous forests **Elevation:** Below 4500 ft. **Ecoregions:** Southern California Mountains, Sierra Nevada

Tree with a single (or multiple) crooked trunk. Needles 7–17 in. long, 3 per bundle, and gray-green, giving the trees a pale appearance and earning them their other common names, gray pine and ghost pine. Seed cones 6–10 in. long and extremely dense, weighing over 2 lbs. when green. Cones are mostly persistent and somewhat serotinous, requiring fire or other disturbance to release seeds. Historically, the seeds have been an important food source for Indigenous peoples.

▼ 4 NEEDLES

Pinus quadrifolia

Parry pinyon

PINACEAE PINE FAMILY

PCT Sections: 1–3 **Abundance:** Uncommon **Height:** to 45 ft. **Habitat-Community:** Dry slopes in woodlands and lower montane coniferous forests **Elevation:** Below 6500 ft. **Ecoregions:** Southern California Mountains

Small, round tree; fairly straight single trunk with the crown narrowly pyramidal when young. Bark initially light gray and smooth becoming red-brown and furrowed with age. Needles 1–3 in. long, mostly 4(5) per bundle, slightly curved, stiff, sharp, green to blue-green, and finely toothed. Seed cones 2–4.5 in. long and maturing in 2 years. The rarest pinyon pine in North America and one of the smallest in stature. Like many of the pinyon pines, the large, thin-shelled seeds are gathered for food by birds, rodents, and people. Plants in northern Baja California are nearly always with 5 needles, suggesting that the southern California plants with 4 (2 or 3) needles may be hybrids with *P. monophylla*.

▼ 5 NEEDLES

Pinus albicaulis

whitebark pine

PINACEAE PINE FAMILY

PCT Sections: 10–14 & 20–23 **Abundance:** Locally common **Height:** to 60 ft. **Habitat-Community:** Dry, open slopes and ridges in subalpine coniferous forests **Elevation:** 6000–12,200 ft. **Ecoregions:** Sierra Nevada, Klamath Mountains

Multi-trunked tree with smooth, gray-white bark. Needles 1.2–2.8 in. long, 5 per bundle. Seed cones 1.5–3.5 in. long, ovoid to round, and open after falling to the ground or when attacked by critters. Trees occur individually, in mixed stands with other subalpine trees, in small pure stands, or as shrub-like clumps on exposed slopes, especially at timberline. Their pinenuts (seeds) are allegedly as good or better than pinyon nuts; certainly, they are preferred over other conifers' by Clark's nutcrackers. The establishment of new seedlings is dependent on germination occurring within a forgotten or unused nutcracker's food cache. Interrelated threats of climate change, bark beetles, and disease have killed large numbers of whitebark pines in recent years.

Pinus balfouriana subsp. *austrina*

Sierra foxtail pine

PINACEAE PINE FAMILY

PCT Section: 10 **Abundance:** Rare **Height:** to 80 ft. **Habitat-Community:** Dry, open, granitic slopes and ridges in subalpine coniferous forests **Elevation:** 9000–11,000 ft. **Ecoregions:** Sierra Nevada

Largest and most majestic of the subalpine pines in the Sierra Nevada. Occurs individually, in small stands, or mixed with *P. albicaulis* and/or *P. monticola*. Needles 0.7–1.5 in. long, 5 per bundle, yellow-green, and tightly clustered along the branches like a fox tail (hence the common name). Seed cones 3.5–5 in. long and armed with prickles. Endemic to the southern Sierra Nevada, mostly in Sequoia and Kings Canyon National Parks. Klamath foxtail pine (subsp. *balfouriana*), endemic to the Klamath Mountains, has blue-green needles and gray-brown bark. Clark's nutcrackers, vociferous alpine birds, are often found foraging the cones of these and other 5-needle pines. Can live over 1500 years.

Pinus flexilis

limber pine

PINACEAE PINE FAMILY

PCT Sections: 3–5 & 9–13 **Abundance:** Locally common **Height:** to 65 ft. **Habitat-Community:** Dry, rocky slopes and ridges in upper montane & subalpine coniferous forests **Elevation:** Below 11,500 ft. **Ecoregions:** Southern California Mountains, Sierra Nevada

Aka Rocky Mountain pine (it's most widespread there), this hardy, contorted tree is found in the high mountains of southern California, clinging to the eastern crest of the ranges in pure stands or with *P. contorta* subsp. *murrayana*. Bark on mature trees is dark brown and cross-checked. Needles 1.5–3 in. long, 5 per bundle, spreading to upcurved, and persisting up to 6 years. Seed cones 3.5–7 in. long, mature in 2 years, and shedding seeds just prior to falling. Named for its limbs that bend but don't break against the forces of snow and wind. Some trees have been dated to 2000 years in age. Stunted and twisted krummholz forms occur near timberline; excellent examples can be found along the PCT atop Mt. Baden-Powell, in the San Gabriel Mountains, and on Olancha Peak in the southern Sierra Nevada.

Pinus lambertiana

sugar pine

PINACEAE PINE FAMILY

PCT Sections: 1–10 & 13–24 **Abundance:** Common **Height:** to 200 ft. **Habitat-Community:** Dry slopes and ridges from oak woodlands to subalpine coniferous forests **Elevation:** Below 9000 ft. **Ecoregions:** All

Largest of all pines on the PCT. Straight, single trunks with branches generally far above the base on mature trees. Sometimes the dominant tree in mixed conifer stands. Bark (mature trees) reddish to gray-brown, with puzzle-piece scales that flake off with age. Needles 2–4 in. long, 5 per bundle, and blue-green. Seed cones 10–20 in. long, shiny yellow-brown, generally straight, and cylindric. Very susceptible to white pine blister rust, an introduced disease. Mature specimens are easily recognized because of their large size, distinctive bark, and gigantic cones—the longest of all conifer species. The nuts are a delicacy but extremely difficult to get to unless you collect them after they fall from the cones. John Muir reportedly used sugar pine sap as a sweetener.

Pinus monticola

western white pine

PINACEAE PINE FAMILY

PCT Sections: 10–24 **Abundance:** Common **Height:** to 180 ft. **Habitat-Community:** Dry slopes and ridges in upper montane & subalpine coniferous forests **Elevation:** Below 11,000 ft. **Ecoregions:** Sierra Nevada, Cascades, Klamath Mountains

Grows in mixed stands from middle elevations to tree line in the subalpine zone. Bark (mature trees) brown to gray and broken into small squarish sections. Needles 1.5–4 in. long, 5 per bundle, and pale blue-green. Seed cones 4–10 in. long, light brown to yellowish, curved, and scales thin and flexible. Trees can live up to 600 years but are very susceptible to white pine blister rust.

▼ SCALE-LIKE LEAVES

Calocedrus decurrens

incense cedar

CUPRESSACEAE CYPRESS FAMILY

PCT Sections: All **Abundance:** Common **Height:** to 160 ft. **Habitat-Community:** Dry slopes and canyons, including serpentine soils, from oak woodlands to upper montane coniferous forests **Elevation:** Below 9000 ft. **Ecoregions:** All

Aromatic tree with single trunk and cone-shaped crown found mostly mixed with other conifers. Bark cinnamon-brown, deeply furrowed with age, fibrous, and fluted at the base of the trunk. Leaves 0.2–0.8 in. long and scale-like; resembling a wine glass in outline where the lateral leaves overlap with the leaves on the upper and lower surface of stems. Seed cones 0.7–1.3 in. long, duck bill–like, and pendent. Trees are known to live over 500 years, their thick bark providing protection from fire and disease. Historically used for fencing, roof shingles, pencils, furniture–and keeping moths from eating your favorite sweater: placing cedar disks or balls in a closet can keep hungry critters away.

Juniperus californica

California juniper

CUPRESSACEAE CYPRESS FAMILY

PCT Sections: 1–9 **Abundance:** Common **Height:** to 25 ft. **Habitat-Community**: Dry slopes and mesas in Joshua tree & pinyon-juniper woodlands **Elevation:** Below 5500 ft. **Ecoregions:** Southern California Mountains, Sonoran Basin and Range, Sierra Nevada

Shrubby, rounded tree; dioecious. Bark ashy gray and peeling in strips. Leaves scale-like, in whorls of 3, with an obvious central gland. Seed cones 0.3–0.5 in. across, blue (red-brown when mature) berries with whitish bloom. Perhaps the most drought-tolerant of all junipers, persisting with as little as 6 in. average annual precipitation. Plants have numerous medicinal uses and are a food source for wildlife and people. Look for it where the PCT intersects the desert foothills and dry ridges at lower elevations from San Diego to Kern County.

Juniperus communis

mountain juniper

CUPRESSACEAE CYPRESS FAMILY

PCT Sections: 11–17 & 20–24 **Abundance:** Occasional **Height:** to 3 ft. **Habitat-Community:** Dry, rocky openings and understories, including serpentine soils, in upper montane & subalpine coniferous forests **Elevation:** Below 11,000 ft.

Ecoregions: Sierra Nevada, Klamath Mountains

Aromatic shrub forming dense mats; dioecious. Leaves 0.2–0.5 in. long, awl-like, dark green with a white stripe on the upper surface, sharp-tipped, and 3 per whorl. Seed cones 0.2–0.5 in. across, blue-black berries with whitish bloom. Juniper berries are sweet and have been used for many things, including medicines, perfumes, marinades, and gin.

Juniperus grandis

Sierra juniper

CUPRESSACEAE CYPRESS FAMILY

PCT Sections: 4–5 & 8–16 **Abundance:** Locally common **Height:** to 80 ft. **Habitat-Community:** Dry, rocky slopes and outcrops from pinyon-juniper woodlands to subalpine coniferous forests **Elevation:** Below 10,000 ft. **Ecoregions:** Southern California Mountains, Sierra Nevada

Picturesque tree, especially when growing on exposed slopes where the weather-beaten trunks are twisted and the crowns manage only a sparse display of foliage; generally dioecious. Bark red-brown, thin, fibrous. Leaves scale-like, gray- to blue-green, and 3 (sometimes 4) per whorl. Seed cones 0.2–0.4 in. across, blue-gray berries with whitish bloom. Trees live over 3000 years and are drought-tolerant, surviving with as little as 8 in. of rain per year. Thin bark provides little protection from fires, and trees do not sprout after fire; regeneration is wholly dependent on birds and mammals dispersing seeds. Rare in the San Gabriel Mountains.

Sequoiadendron giganteum

giant sequoia

CUPRESSACEAE CYPRESS FAMILY

PCT Sections: 4–5 **Abundance:** Rare **Height:** to 280 ft. **Habitat-Commutnity:** Moist slopes and canyons in lower montane conifertous forests **Elevation:** Below 7500 ft. **Ecoregions:** Southern California Mountains

Majestic trees living over 3000 years, with few lower branches and thick, fibrous, orange-tan to cinnamon-red bark with deep furrows. Leaves 0.3 in. long, blue-green, sharp-tipped, awl-like. Seed cones 2–3 in. long, brown, and shaped like a mini barrel with wrinkled scales. Tolerant of fire, requiring periodic burning for seedling recruitment. The southern California populations of introduced trees are the only opportunity along the PCT to observe them; the natural southern Sierra groves are west of the trail in lower montane coniferous forests at 5000–8000 ft. elevation. John Muir (1838–1914) was instrumental in establishing Sequoia National Park to protect giant sequoias in the southern Sierra Nevada; as he wrote in 1901, "Any fool can destroy trees. They cannot run away; and if they could, they would still be destroyed–chased and hunted down as long as fun or a dollar could be got out of their bark hides. It took more than three thousand years to make some of the trees in these Western woods–trees that are still standing in perfect strength and beauty, waving and singing in the mighty forests of the Sierra. Through all the wonderful, eventful centuries God has cared for these trees, saved them from drought, disease, avalanches, and a thousand straining, leveling tempests and floods; but he cannot save them from fools–only Uncle Sam can do that."

TREES AND SHRUBS

SIMPLE LEAVES

▼ ALTERNATE

Rhus ovata

sugar bush

ANACARDIACEAE SUMAC FAMILY

PCT Sections: 1–6 **Abundance:** Common **Height:** to 20 ft. **Flowering:** March–May **Flower Color:** White to pale pink **Habitat-Community:** Slopes and valleys in foothill chaparrals and oak woodlands **Elevation:** Below 4500 ft. **Ecoregions:** Southern California Mountains

Large, rounded shrub with flexible stems and dark green, leathery foliage. Leaves 1–3 in. long, evergreen, alternate, ovoid, shiny, and often folded along the midrib. Flowers 0.4–0.6 in. across, clustered on stout branches, white- to pink-tinged, and partially enclosed by reddish sepals. Fruits 0.3–0.5 in. across, fleshy berries with a sticky skin. The edible fruit is used to make a drink similar to lemonade. Commonly associated with *Adenostoma fasciculatum* in the inland valleys and lower-elevation woodlands of southern California.

Acamptopappus sphaerocephalus

rayless goldenhead

ASTERACEAE SUNFLOWER FAMILY

PCT Sections: 1–7 **Abundance:** Locally common **Height:** 1–3 ft. **Flowering:** April–May **Flower Color:** Pale yellow to cream **Habitat-Community:** Sandy to gravelly plains and gentle slopes in creosote bush scrubs and Joshua tree and juniper woodlands and scrubs **Elevation:** Below 5600 ft. **Ecoregions:** Southern California Mountains, Sonoran/Mojave Basin and Range, Sierra Nevada

Inconspicuous, much-branched, low shrub or subshrub with erect green stems shredding and turning gray with age. Leaves 0.5–0.8 in. long, evergreen, alternate, erect and appressed (to stem), linear to spoon-shaped. Flowers in open, flat-topped clusters, disk only (rayless); globe-shaped involucres 0.3–0.5 in. across. Disk flowers 0.1–0.2 in. long, 13–27 per head, pale yellow to cream. Fruits achenes to 0.2 in. long with 20–25 bristles. Two varieties along the PCT, at lower desert crossings: var. *hirtellus* (short-hairy leaves) and var. *sphaerocephalus* (glabrous leaves). An often-overlooked representative of mixed scrub at mid-elevations in the California deserts. *Sphaerocephalus* is Greek for "sphere-headed."

Ambrosia dumosa

white bursage

ASTERACEAE SUNFLOWER FAMILY

PCT Sections: 1–4 & 7–8 **Abundance:** Locally common **Height:** 1–3 ft. **Flowering:** March–June **Flower Color:** Pale yellow **Habitat-Community:** Dry, sandy flats and washes in scrubs and Joshua tree woodlands **Elevation:** Below 4900 ft. **Ecoregions:** Sonoran/Mojave Basin and Range, Sierra Nevada

Low, multi-branched shrub of the California deserts; monoecious. Leaves 0.2–1.6 in. long, summer-deciduous, mostly alternate, pinnately lobed, soft-hairy. Plants have both pistillate flowers and staminate flowers, mixed along a spike-like stem. Male heads 0.1–0.2 in. across, rounded, and hairy. Female heads contain just 2 flowers. Fruits 0.2–0.4 in. across, rounded burs with 12–35 golden to purple-brown spines that inevitably stick to your socks. Occurs along the PCT only along the lower desert crossings and can dominate vast areas of the Mojave and western Sonoran deserts. *Ambrosia* is Greek for "food of the gods."

Ambrosia salsola

cheesebush

ASTERACEAE SUNFLOWER FAMILY

PCT Sections: 1–8 **Abundance:** Locally common **Height:** 2–4 ft. **Flowering:** March–May **Flower Color:** Pale yellow **Habitat-Community:** Dry, sandy flats, washes, and rocky slopes in scrubs and Joshua tree woodlands **Elevation:** Below 5500 ft. **Ecoregions:** Sonoran/Mojave Basin and Range, Sierra Nevada

Small shrub of California deserts; monoecious. Leaves 1–2 in. long, thread-like, summer-deciduous. Pistillate flowers and staminate flowers in different heads. Female heads contain just 1 flower, which becomes pearly white when in fruit; male heads have 5–15 flowers. Occurs along the PCT at desert crossings and in dry areas of the southeastern Sierra Nevada. The foliage has a pungent, cheese-like scent when crushed. Hybridizes with *A. dumosa*. Aka burrobrush.

Artemisia rothrockii

timberline sagebrush

ASTERACEAE SUNFLOWER FAMILY

PCT Sections: 4 & 9–14 **Abundance:** Locally common **Height:** 7–20 in. **Flowering:** July–September **Flower Color:** Pale yellow **Habitat-Community:** Meadows and rocky slopes from upper montane coniferous forests to alpine communities **Elevation:** 6500–10,200 ft. **Ecoregions:** Southern California Mountains, Sierra Nevada

Aromatic shrub with sticky and dark gray-green (sometimes white-hairy) foliage. Leaves 0.4–0.8 in. long, evergreen, alternate, generally covered with dense hairs, sticky, 0- or 3-lobed at tip. Flowers to 0.1 in. long, composite, 10–16 per head, disk only, pale yellow, in terminal clusters extending above the leaves. Fruits to 0.1 in. long, achenes with resinous glands. Restricted to high elevations and tends to be much smaller than its non-sticky cousin, *A. tridentata*.

Artemisia tridentata

sagebrush

ASTERACEAE SUNFLOWER FAMILY

PCT Sections: All **Abundance:** Common **Height:** 1.5–10 ft. **Flowering:** July–September **Flower Color:** Pale yellow **Habitat-Community:** Arid sites on desert and montane slopes and plateaus to subalpine coniferous forests **Elevation:** Below 10,500 ft. **Ecoregions:** All

Aromatic shrub growing in dry openings. Leaves 0.4–1.2 in. long, evergreen, alternate, covered with dense gray hairs, 3-lobed at tip. Flowers to 0.1 in. long, composite, disk only, pale yellow, in terminal clusters extending above the leaves. Fruits achenes with glands or sparse hairs. Most common sagebrush along the PCT. Other shrubby *Artemisia* spp. with 3-lobed leaves are rare along the trail, generally associated with unique substrates such as limestone/marble. Sagebrush does not respond well to frequent wildfires: it does not resprout. Plants generally live for 50 years but can survive to be over 100! The leaves are commonly used for smudging.

Baccharis salicifolia

mule fat

ASTERACEAE SUNFLOWER FAMILY

PCT Sections: 1–8 **Abundance:** Locally common **Height:** 5–15 ft. **Flowering:** March–October **Flower Color:** White to pale yellow **Habitat-Community**: Riparian woodlands, canyon bottoms, and slopes from scrubs to lower montane coniferous forests **Elevation:** Below 7500 ft. **Ecoregions:** Southern California Mountains, Sierra Nevada

Tall, relatively unbranched shrub forming thickets along intermittent and perennial watercourses along the PCT; dioecious. Leaves 3–7 in. long, evergreen, alternate, sticky resinous and gland-dotted, lance-shaped, with smooth (winter/spring flowering form) or fine-toothed (summer/fall flowering form) margins. Flowers composite, in flat-topped or pyramidal clusters with either female flowers (white) or male flowers (pale yellow). The genus name honors Bacchus, the Greek god of vegetation, wine, and ecstasy. The leafy shoots are important browse for mule deer (hence the common name).

Brickellia atractyloides

spearleaf brickellbush

ASTERACEAE SUNFLOWER FAMILY

PCT Sections: 1–4 **Abundance:** Locally common **Height:** 1–2 ft. **Flowering:** March–September **Flower Color:** Cream **Habitat-Community**: Dry rocky slopes and canyons in creosote bush scrubs, foothill chaparrals, and Joshua tree woodlands **Elevation:** Below 4500 ft. **Ecoregions:** Southern California Mountains, Sonoran/Mojave Basin and Range

Densely branched, aromatic, evergreen shrub with minutely glandular stems. Leaves 0.4–0.9 in. long, alternate (or opposite near base of stem), bright green, ovoid, prominently 3-veined, short-hairy and sometimes glandular, with sharp-toothed margins. Flowers composite, rayless, solitary on short, leafy branches. Disk flowers many per head; cylindric involucres 0.4–0.7 in. long with 3–4 rows of bright green (darker stripes) phyllaries. Fruits achenes to 0.2 in. long with 18–25 pappus bristles. Two varieties along the PCT: var. *arguta* (outer phyllary margins entire) is found on the desert flanks of the San Jacinto and southern San Bernardino Mountains; var. *odontolepis* (outer phyllary margins toothed) is restricted to San Diego County. The genus name honors Irish-born naturalist John Brickell (1748–1809).

Brickellia californica

California brickellbush

ASTERACEAE SUNFLOWER FAMILY

PCT Sections: 1–9 & 16–17 & 23–24 **Abundance:** Locally common **Height:** 2–6 ft. **Flowering:** June–November **Flower Color:** Pale yellow to green **Habitat-Community**: Dry rocky slopes and canyons from creosote bush scrubs to lower montane coniferous forests **Elevation:** Below 7800 ft. **Ecoregions:** Southern California Mountains, Sonoran/Mojave Basin and Range, Sierra Nevada, Klamath Mountains

Much-branched (from the base), sweet-scented shrub with short-hairy, gland-dotted stems. Leaves 0.4–3.5 in. long (petiole 0.2–2.4 in. long), evergreen, alternate (opposite at base), ovoid to triangular, fuzzy hairy, dark green, with lobed to toothed margins. Flowers composite, in leafy clusters, heads rayless; cylindric involucres 0.3–0.5 in. long with 5–6 rows of purple-tinged, glandular phyllaries. Disk flowers 0.2–0.4 in. long, pale yellow-green. Fruits achenes to 0.2 in. long with 24–30 pappus bristles. Often ranked among the the most fragrant plants in California.

Brickellia frutescens
shrubby brickellbush
ASTERACEAE SUNFLOWER FAMILY

PCT Sections: 1–2 **Abundance:** Rare **Height:** 1–2 ft. **Flowering:** March–June, October **Flower Color:** Purple to cream **Habitat-Community**: Dry, rocky (granitic) slopes, canyons, and sandy washes in creosote bush scrubs **Elevation:** Below 4700 ft. **Ecoregions:** Sonoran Basin and Range

Intricately branched, aromatic shrub with coarse-hairy, sparsely gland-dotted stems. Leaves 0.1–0.5 in. long, evergreen, alternate, gray-green, spoon-shaped, densely hairy, with smooth margins. Flowers composite, 1–3 heads at tips of branches, rayless, disk flowers many; cylindric involucre 0.4–0.5 in. long with 5–6 rows of sparsely long-hairy gland-dotted phyllaries, purple-tinged with stripes. Fruits achenes to 0.2 in. long with 26–30 bristles. Restricted in California to the San Diego County desert; observe it along the PCT in the San Felipe Valley and surrounding hills. It stands out from other brickellias by lacking toothed leaves. *Frutescens* is Latin for "shrub-like."

Chrysothamnus viscidiflorus
yellow rabbitbrush
ASTERACEAE SUNFLOWER FAMILY

PCT Sections: 3–17 **Abundance:** Locally common **Height:** 2–5 ft. **Flowering:** July–October **Flower Color:** Yellow **Habitat-Community:** Dry meadows, understories, and rocky slopes from pinyon-juniper woodlands to alpine communities **Elevation:** Below 12,500 ft. **Ecoregions:** Southern California Mountains, Sierra Nevada

Plants along the PCT typically have pale stem branches becoming white with age. Leaves 1–3 in. long, evergreen, alternate, linear, often wavy or twisted, and resinous, sticky to the touch. Flowers composite, 4–14 per head, disk only, yellow; narrowly cylindric involucres with 5 vertically lined-up rows of phyllaries. Fruits 0.1–0.2 in. long, hairy achenes with many pappus bristles. A highly variable and widespread shrub, with several subspecies in North and South America. It thrives in alkaline areas, or soils rich in calcium, making it a valuable species for revegetation of disturbed or depleted soils.

Encelia actoni
Acton encelia
ASTERACEAE SUNFLOWER FAMILY

PCT Sections: 1–8 **Abundance:** Locally common **Height:** to 4.5 ft. **Flowering:** March–July **Flower Color:** Yellow **Habitat-Community:** Gravelly hills and rocky slopes in creosote bush scrubs and Joshua tree & pinyon-juniper woodlands **Elevation:** Below 6000 ft. **Ecoregions:** Southern California Mountains, Sonoran/Mojave Basin and Range, Sierra Nevada

Multi-branched, rounded shrub or subshrub of arid, rocky landscapes. Leaves 1–2.5 in. long, drought-deciduous, alternate, oval to triangular, gray-green, sometimes woolly. Flowers composite, radiate heads 1–2 in. across, solitary at tips of elongated branches, daisy-like, with showy yellow rays. Fruits 0.2–0.3 in. long, achenes without awns or bristles. Named for the community of Acton, in the San Gabriel Mountains, a favored pit stop for PCT hikers.

Encelia farinosa

brittlebush

ASTERACEAE SUNFLOWER FAMILY

PCT Sections: 1–6 **Abundance:** Locally common **Height:** to 4.5 ft. **Flowering:** March–July **Flower Color:** Yellow **Habitat-Community:** Gravelly hills and rocky slopes in creosote bush scrubs and Joshua tree woodlands **Elevation:** Below 5000 ft. **Ecoregions:** Southern California Mountains, Sonoran/Mojave Basin and Range

Rounded, ubiquitous shrub across much of the Sonoran and Mojave deserts. Leaves 1–3 in. long, clustered near stem tips, drought-deciduous, alternate, diamond-shaped, silver-gray-hairy, and leathery. Flowers composite, in a branched inflorescence, heads 1.4–2.5 in. across, and radiate with showy yellow rays. Disk flowers brown-purple in some plants. Fruits 0.1–0.3 in. long, achenes without awns or bristles. Limited along the PCT to low desert crossings with an especially dominant stand at Snow Creek, at the base of the San Jacinto Mountains. Aka incienso: Spanish missionaries burned the dried sap as a fragrant incense.

Ericameria bloomeri

rabbitbush heathgoldenrod

ASTERACEAE SUNFLOWER FAMILY

PCT Sections: 9–23 **Abundance:** Occasional **Height:** to 2 ft. **Flowering:** July–October **Flower Color:** Yellow **Habitat-Community:** Open, rocky places in montane coniferous forests **Elevation:** Below 13,500 ft. **Ecoregions:** Sierra Nevada, Cascades, Klamath Mountains

Generally resinous, compact subshrub or shrub with ascending to erect stems. Leaves 1–3 in. long, drought-deciduous, alternate, thread-like to oblanceolate, point-tipped, and covered with white, generally woolly hairs. Flowers composite and in rounded clusters of radiate heads. Ray flowers 1–5 per head, 0.3–0.5 in. long, yellow. Disk flowers 4–14 per head, 0.2–0.4 in. long, yellow. Fruits 0.2–0.3 in. long, brown, hairy or not achenes with minutely barbed, tan or reddish bristles.

Ericameria brachylepis

boundary goldenbush

ASTERACEAE SUNFLOWER FAMLY

PCT Sections: 1–3 **Abundance:** Occasional **Height:** 2–6 ft. **Flowering:** September–December **Flower Color:** Yellow **Habitat-Community:** Rocky to gravelly slopes in scrubs, foothill chaparrals, and woodlands **Elevation:** Below 4600 ft. **Ecoregions:** Southern California Mountains

Aromatic, fall-flowering shrub with erect to spreading branches and green stems when young, becoming tan-brown (sometimes deciduous) with age. Leaves 0.4–1.1 in. long, drought-deciduous, alternate, crowded along stems, ascending, linear to thread-like, gland-dotted, and sparsely hairy. Flowers composite, in scattered heads at tips of stems, rayless; involucres 0.1–0.3 in. long with green-tipped phyllaries in 3–4 rows. Disk flowers 0.2–0.3 in. long, 6–16 per head, yellow. Fruits achenes topped with soft, white, barbed bristles. Best observed along the PCT in open, sunny chaparrals from the Mexican border to southern Riverside County. Plants have a distinctive lemony scent.

Ericameria cooperi

Cooper's goldenbush

ASTERACEAE SUNFLOWER FAMILY

PCT Sections: 4–8 **Abundance:** Rare **Height:** 1–3 ft. **Flowering:** March–June **Flower Color:** Yellow **Habitat-Community:** Gravelly slopes and sandy alluvium in creosote bush scrubs and Joshua tree woodlands **Elevation:** Below 5400 ft. **Ecoregions:** Southern California Mountains, Mojave Basin and Range, Sierra Nevada

Low, seasonally deciduous, densely branched shrub with short-hairy, resinous stems. Leaves 0.2–0.7 in. long, alternate, clustered near the bases of stems, longer and solitary near tips of stems, linear, and gland-dotted. Flowers composite, in rounded bunches of radiate heads; bell-shaped involucres 0.2 in. across with phyllaries in 4–5 rows. Ray flowers, corolla 0.2–0.5 in. long, 0–3, yellow. Disk flowers 0.1–0.2 in. long, 4–12 per head, yellow. Fruits achenes encircled by silky white hairs. Codominant at mid-elevations of the Mojave Desert. Found along the PCT from the Cajon Pass region to Walker Pass, Kern County. Hybridizes with *E. linearifolia*.

Ericameria cuneata

cliff goldenbush

ASTERACEAE SUNFLOWER FAMILY

PCT Sections: 1–16 **Abundance:** Occasional **Height:** to 3 ft. **Flowering:** September–December **Flower Color:** Yellow **Habitat-Community:** Granite outcrops from oak woodlands to upper montane coniferous forests **Elevation:** Below 9200 ft. **Ecoregions:** Southern California/Northern Baja Coast, Southern California Mountains, Mojave Basin and Range, Sierra Nevada

Densely branched, hairless shrub growing on cliffs. Leaves to 1 in. long, evergreen, alternate, wedge-shaped, deep green. Flowers to 0.2 in. long, composite, yellow, in rounded clusters of radiate heads containing 0–7 ray flowers and 7–70 disk flowers. Fruits 0.1–0.2 in. long, 4-angled, hairy brown achenes with minutely barbed bristles. First collected in Bear Valley (Sierra Nevada) in 1866, at 4500 ft. elevation. Look for the yellow flowers on cliffs during the fall, when most other shrubs are in fruit.

Ericameria discoidea

whitestem goldenbush

ASTERACEAE SUNFLOWER FAMILY

PCT Sections: 10–15 **Abundance:** Locally common **Height:** to 1.5 ft. **Flowering:** July–September **Flower Color:** Yellow **Habitat-Community:** Rocky slopes in subalpine coniferous forests and alpine communities **Elevation:** 7500–12,500 ft. **Ecoregions:** Sierra Nevada

Erect to spreading shrub with dense, silver-white hairs covering the stems. Leaves 0.5–1.5 in. long, deciduous, alternate, oval to lance-shaped, glandular, with wavy margins. Flowers 0.4–1 in. long, composite, 1 to several rayless heads at stem tips, 10–26 yellow disk flowers, and glandular phyllaries. Fruits to 0.3 in. long, hairy brown achenes with minutely barbed bristles. A very conspicuous shrub on rock outcrops and talus slopes in the alpine zone, especially in Section 10.

Ericameria linearifolia

narrowleaf goldenbush

ASTERACEAE SUNFLOWER FAMILY

PCT Sections: 1–10 **Abundance:** Common **Height:** 1–5 ft. **Flowering:** February–May **Flower Color:** Yellow **Habitat-Community:** Rocky or sandy slopes in deserts and woodlands from scrubs to lower montane coniferous forests **Elevation:** Below 6600 ft. **Ecoregions:** Southern California/Northern Baja Coast, Southern California Mountains, Mojave Basin and Range, Sierra Nevada

Showy shrub. Leaves 0.5–2 in. long, drought-deciduous, alternate, linear, gray-green, glandular, point-tipped, and sticky. Flowers 0.4 in. long, radiate, yellow, in a single head at stem tips. Fruits 0.1–0.2 in. long, compressed, silky-hairy achenes with white bristles. Populations increase in areas subjected to heavy grazing.

Ericameria nauseosa

rubber rabbitbrush

ASTERACEAE SUNFLOWER FAMILY

PCT Sections: All **Abundance:** Common **Height:** 2–6 ft. **Flowering:** July–October **Flower Color:** Yellow to white **Habitat-Community:** Slopes, valleys, meadows, and forest understories from scrubs to upper montane coniferous forests **Elevation:** Below 9800 ft. **Ecoregions:** All

Erect shrub with flexible, leafy or not stems and loosely to densely hairy foliage. Leaves 0.5–2.8 in. long, drought-deciduous, alternate, variable, thread-like to lance-shaped, and sometimes glandular but lacking resin pits. Flowers composite, heads in flat-topped to rounded clusters, rayless; involucres 0.3–0.7 in. long with phyllaries aligned vertically in 3–5 rows, generally forming a boat-like keel. Disk flowers 0.3–0.6 in. long, 5 per head. Fruits achenes with white pappus hairs. Ubiquitous, found in most vegetation associations across western North America. *Nauseosa* means "smelly," but we like the fragrance, likening it to pineapple.

Ericameria paniculata

black-banded rabbitbrush

ASTERACEAE SUNFLOWER FAMILY

PCT Sections: 1–4 **Abundance:** Locally common **Height:** 2–6 ft. **Flowering:** June–December **Flower Color:** Yellow **Habitat-Community:** Sandy washes in creosote bush scrubs and Joshua tree woodlands **Elevation:** Below 4800 ft. **Ecoregions:** Sonoran/Mojave Basin and Range

Sprawling to erect evergreen shrub with black-banded stems, the result of an infection by smut fungus (*Puccinia splendens*). Leaves 0.4–1.4 in. long, alternate, thread-like, hairless, and gland-dotted. Flowers composite, in large clusters of rayless heads, yellow; triangle-shaped involucres 0.3–0.5 in. long with lined-up phyllaries in 3–5 rows. Fruits tiny, hairy achenes. Very common along the San Gorgonio River crossing of the PCT in Riverside County.

Ericameria parishii

Parish's goldenbush

ASTERACEAE SUNFLOWER FAMILY

PCT Sections: 1–3 **Abundance:** Occasional **Height:** 4–12 ft. **Flowering:** July–October **Flower Color:** Yellow **Habitat-Community:** Dry slopes and open understories in foothill chaparrals and lower montane coniferous forests **Elevation:** Below 6500 ft. **Ecoregions:** Southern California Mountains

Large, woody (sometimes tree-like) shrub with gland-dotted stems. Leaves 0.8–2.8 in. long, evergreen, alternate, elliptic to lance-shaped, leathery, green, usually hairless, and gland-dotted in pits. Flowers composite, in dense clusters of rayless heads at stem tips, yellow, with cone-shaped involucres 0.2–0.3 in. long. Disk flowers 0.2–0.3 in. long, 8–18 per head, yellow. Fruits tiny, hairy, dull white to brown achenes. Best seen along the PCT in post-burn areas in the Peninsular Ranges, but may also turn up on the more maritime southern aspects of the San Gabriel Mountains.

Ericameria parryi

Parry's rabbitbrush

ASTERACEAE SUNFLOWER FAMILY

PCT Sections: 3–20 **Abundance:** Occasional **Height:** 0.3–3 ft. **Flowering:** August–September **Flower Color:** Yellow **Habitat-Community:** Dry openings and barrens from lower montane forests to alpine communities **Elevation:** Below 12,000 ft. **Ecoregions:** All

Sparsely branched, resinous subshrub or shrub with ascending to erect stems. Leaves 0.4–3.2 in. long, drought-deciduous, alternate, thread- to lance-like, and surfaces with fine white hairs. Flowers composite, in rounded clusters of rayless heads. Disk flowers 5–18 per head, 0.1–0.4 in. long, yellow. Fruits 0.1–0.3 in. long, hairy tan achenes with minutely barbed bristles. Six varieties occur in California. Populations can increase in areas of heavy grazing or other disturbance, but grazing animals are not too excited about munching down on most rabbitbrushes. Rabbits are not fond of eating them either, but the shrubs provide great places for critters to hide and hang out.

Ericameria pinifolia

pinebush

ASTERACEAE SUNFLOWER FAMILY

PCT Sections: 1–6 **Abundance:** Locally common **Height:** to 9 ft. **Flowering:** April–December **Flower Color:** Yellow **Habitat-Community:** Sandy to rocky soils in foothill chaparrals and woodlands **Elevation:** Below 6100 ft. **Ecoregions:** Southern California Mountains

Tall, shaggy shrub with green (gray-white with age), generally hairless, gland-dotted stems. Leaves 0.4–1.8 in. long, alternate, thread-like, green, with clusters of smaller leaves throughout the stem. Flowers composite, in elongated clusters of radiate heads at stem tips; triangular involucres 0.2–0.4 in. long with woolly phyllaries in 4–6 rows. Ray flowers 0.1–0.2 in. long, 10–30 per head, yellow. Disk flowers 0.2–0.4 in. long, 11–25 per head, yellow. Fruits 0.1–0.2 in. long, cylindric, striped, bright white or red achenes. Often found in disturbed soils in various habitats. At quick glance, the leaves resemble pine needles (hence the specific epithet, from the Latin *pinus*, "pine," *folium*, "leaf").

Ericameria suffruticosa

singlehead goldenbush

ASTERACEAE SUNFLOWER FAMILY

PCT Sections: 10–16 **Abundance:** Occasional **Height:** to 1 ft. **Flowering:** July–October **Flower Color:** Yellow **Habitat-Community:** Rocky slopes and ridges in subalpine coniferous forests **Elevation:** 7000–12,500 ft. **Ecoregions:** Sierra Nevada

Densely branched subshrub with spreading, stalked-glandular stems. Leaves 0.2–1.5 in. long, deciduous, alternate, linear to lance-shaped, glandular-hairy. Flowers composite, heads radiate, solitary or 2–3 per leafy cluster, with 2–3 rows of stalked-glandular phyllaries. Ray flowers 0.2–0.5 in. long, 1–8 per head, yellow. Disk flowers 0.3–0.4 in. long, 15–40 per head, yellow. Fruits 0.2–0.3 in. long, angled, hairy achenes with white to pale yellow, minutely barbed bristles. Originally described from the Blue Mountains of Oregon, so it might also occur in the Cascades and Klamath Mountains ecoregions.

Gutierrezia californica

California matchweed

ASTERACEAE SUNFLOWER FAMILY

PCT Sections: 1–7 **Abundance:** Locally common **Height:** to 3 ft. **Flowering:** July–November **Flower Color:** Yellow **Habitat-Community:** Dry, often rocky, slopes and ridges from California prairies to woodlands **Elevation:** Below 5000 ft. **Ecoregions:** All (except Cascades, Klamath Mountains)

Low, sprawling subshrub. Leaves 0.3–0.5 in. long, drought-deciduous, alternate, linear, gland-dotted, sticky, lacking petioles, and on thin stems that turn brown with age. Flowers composite, in 8–20 radiate heads at stem tips; bell-shaped involucres with 9–21 gland-dotted phyllaries. Ray flowers 0.1–0.3 in. long, 4–13 per head, yellow. Disk flowers to 0.2 in. long, 3–13 per head, yellow. Fruits to 0.1 in. long, hairy achenes with fine-toothed scales. Flowers during the hot season in desert zones of the PCT. May co-occur with *G. sarothrae* in the western Mojave Desert region. Leaves contain compounds that are toxic to livestock.

Gutierrezia sarothrae

broom matchweed

ASTERACEAE SUNFLOWER FAMILY

PCT Sections: 1–7 **Abundance:** Locally common **Height:** to 2 ft. **Flowering:** May–October **Flower Color:** Yellow **Habitat-Community:** Dry, gravelly flats from Joshua tree woodlands to upper montane coniferous forests **Elevation:** Below 9500 ft. **Ecoregions:** Southern California/Northern Baja Coast, Southern California Mountains, Mojave Basin and Range, Sierra Nevada

Low subshrub with brown lower stems that become green at the tips. Leaves 0.8–1.5 in. long and thread-like. Flowers composite, in clusters of 2–5 radiate heads at stem tips; cylindric involucres with 8–21 green-tipped phyllaries. Ray flowers 0.1–0.3 in. long, 2–7 per head, yellow. Disk flowers to 0.2 in. long, 2–8 per head, yellow. Fruits to 0.1 in. long, hairy achenes with fine-toothed scales. Found across most of western North America. May co-occur with *G. californica* in the western Mojave Desert region. *Sarothrae* is Greek for "broom."

Hazardia squarrosa

sawtooth goldenbush

ASTERACEAE SUNFLOWER FAMILY

PCT Sections: 1–6 **Abundance:** Occasional **Height:** 1–7 ft. **Flowering:** July–October **Flower Color:** Yellow **Habitat-Community:** Rocky slopes and mesas in scrubs, chaparrals, and woodlands **Elevation:** Below 5200 ft. **Ecoregions:** Southern California Mountains

Low, clumpy to tall shrub with branches having white hairs that often have a zig-zag shape, changing directions at the flowering nodes. Leaves 1–2 in. long, evergreen, alternate, oblong, leathery, with sharp-toothed margins. Flowers composite, in rayless heads 0.4–0.6 in. wide with 30–60 recurved phyllaries. Disk flowers 9–16 per head, yellow (red-tinged). Fruits to 0.3 in. long, hairless achenes with white to red-brown bristles. A mostly coastal species of southern California, *squarrosa* (from the Latin, "rough") refers to the sawtooth leaf margins. The Kumeyaay people boil the plant in water and use it for a healing bath to treat general aches and pains.

Lepidospartum squamatum

California scalebroom

ASTERACEAE SUNFLOWER FAMILY

PCT Sections: 2–8 **Abundance:** Locally common **Height:** to 9 ft. **Flowering:** August–November **Flower Color:** Yellow **Habitat-Community:** Sandy washes and stream terraces in creosote bush scrubs, foothill chaparrals, and Joshua tree woodlands **Elevation:** Below 5500 ft. **Ecoregions:** Southern California Mountains, Sierra Nevada

Large shrub, often wider than tall, with broom-like branches coated in woolly fibers. Leaves to 0.5 in. long, evergreen, alternate, spoon-shaped, erect, stubby, and hugging the stem. Flowers composite, in rayless heads 0.1–0.3 in. long, clustered at stem tips. Disk flowers 4–17 per head, yellow. Fruits to 0.2 in. long, achenes with white-brown bristles. Attracts bees, butterflies, tarantula hawk wasps, and other pollinators. In fruit, the flowers take on a cottony look; the heads disarticulate, and the achenes become wind-borne. Limited to dry arroyos and washes crossed by the PCT in southern California. Especially common at Cajon Junction along Interstate 15.

Tetradymia axillaris var. *longispina*

long-spined horsebrush

ASTERACEAE SUNFLOWER FAMILY

PCT Sections: 4–10 **Abundance:** Occasional **Height:** to 5 ft. **Flowering:** April–June **Flower Color:** Yellow **Habitat-Community:** Sandy to gravelly alluvium and wash terraces in scrubs and woodlands **Elevation:** Below 7200 ft. **Ecoregions:** Southern California Mountains, Sierra Nevada

Large shrub, often forming impenetrable thickets of spiny, white-hairy branches covered with spines at leaf nodes. Leaves 1–2 in. long, evergreen, alternate, thread-like, in clusters of 2–12 at the spines. Flowers composite, in rayless heads 0.6–1 in. wide; involucres with 5 hairy phyllaries and 5–7 disk flowers per head. Fruits to 0.2 in. long, long-white-hairy achenes with many pappus scales. The sharp spines, 0.7–1.2 in. long, were used as tattooing needles by Indigenous peoples.

Tetradymia canescens

gray horsebrush

ASTERACEAE SUNFLOWER FAMILY

PCT Sections: 4–10 & 12–15 **Abundance:** Locally common **Height:** 1–4 ft. **Flowering:** July–October **Flower Color:** Pale yellow **Habitat-Community:** Gravelly to rocky slopes from sagebrush scrubs to upper montane coniferous forests **Elevation:** Below 10,500 ft. **Ecoregions:** Southern California Mountains, Sierra Nevada

Multi-branched, woody shrub, often associated with *Artemisia tridentata*. Leaves 1–1.6 in. long, evergreen, alternate, lance-shaped, and woolly or silver-haired; shorter-lived leaves occur in clusters at the axils of main leaves. Flowers composite, in flat-topped clusters of rayless heads with 4 phyllaries covered in matted white hairs. Disk flowers 0.3–0.6 in. long, 4 per head, pale yellow. Fruits to 0.2 in. long, long-white-hairy achenes with many pappus scales. Plants are burn-resistant, sprouting actively after fire. *Tetradymia* (from the Latin, "four-sided") refers to the 4 phyllaries per flower head, common to many species in the genus.

Alnus incana subsp. *tenuifolia*

thinleaf alder

BETULACEAE BIRCH FAMILY

PCT Sections: 10–24 **Abundance:** Common **Height:** 6–30 ft. **Flowering:** February–March **Habitat-Community:** Streambanks and meadows in wetland-riparian communities **Elevation:** Below 8000 ft. **Ecoregions:** Sierra Nevada, Cascades, Klamath Mountains

Thicket-forming, multi-stemmed shrub or small tree with broad and spreading crown and bark without lenticels; monoecious. Leaves 1.5–4 in. long, deciduous, alternate, oval to ovoid, with double-toothed margins. Flowers pendent, separate male and female catkins, generally 4 stamens. Fruits round, unwinged nutlets formed in female catkins (cones); cone stalks are shorter than the cone. The cones make great decorations on Christmas gifts and wreaths. Thinleaf alder thickets are great places to find *Listera convallarioides* and other unusual plants.

Alnus rhombifolia

white alder

BETULACEAE BIRCH FAMILY

PCT Sections: 1–6 & 8–24 **Abundance:** Common **Height:** to 80 ft. **Flowering:** January–April **Habitat-Community:** Permanent streambanks in wetland-riparian communities **Elevation:** Below 7900 ft. **Ecoregions:** All (except Sonoran/Mojave Basin and Range)

Single-stemmed tree with mottled, thin, gray bark that becomes furrowed with age; monoecious. Leaves 1.5–3 in. long, deciduous, alternate, oval to diamond-shaped, with toothed margins. Flowers pendent, separate male and female catkins, 1–3 stamens. Fruits round, unwinged nutlets formed in female catkins (cones). An important if short-lived (usually <100 years) riparian tree, protecting watersheds and providing wildlife habitat.

Chilopsis linearis

desert willow

BIGNONIACEAE

TRUMPET-CREEPER FAMILY

PCT Sections: 1–4 **Abundance:** Rare **Height:** 5–23 ft. **Flowering:** April–October **Flower Color:** White, pink, or purple **Habitat-Community:** Washes and canyons in creosote bush scrubs and Joshua tree woodlands **Elevation:** Below 4500 ft. **Ecoregions:** Sonoran Basin and Range

Large shrub or small tree with dark gray bark and long branches of durable hardwood. Leaves 5–12 in. long, deciduous, alternate (opposite or whorled), willow-like, linear. Flowers irregular, fragrant, with 2-lobed upper lip and 3-lobed lower lip. Corollas 1–2.5 in. long, funnel- or bell-shaped, white to pink or purple, with jagged margins and throat with yellow and purple markings. Fruits 8–14 in. long, linear capsules that burst open in summer, sending winged seeds flying through the air. The only species in *Chilopsis*. Pollinated by bumblebees and carpenter bees and widely cultivated for its showy flowers and tolerance of hot, dry climates.

Eriodictyon californicum

California yerba santa

BORAGINACEAE BORAGE FAMILY

PCT Sections: 3–5 & 15–20 & 23–24 **Abundance:** Occasional **Height:** 3–10 ft. **Flowering:** April–July **Flower Color:** White to purple **Habitat-Community:** Dry, open slopes from oak woodlands to lower montane coniferous forests **Elevation:** Below 6000 ft. **Ecoregions:** Southern California Mountains, Sierra Nevada, Cascades, Klamath Mountains

Erect, open, strongly aromatic shrub with sticky stems. Leaves 1.5–6 in. long, evergreen, alternate, thick, elliptic, dark green above, pale green and hairy below, with smooth or toothed margins. Flowers 0.3–0.7 in. long, clustered at stem ends, white to purple, 5-parted, funnel-shaped. Fruits to 0.2 in. across, capsules opening along 4 valves. Leaves smell very pleasant when crushed; historically, they have been chewed or smoked as a tobacco substitute and made into a syrup to treat colds, coughs, and sore throats (*yerba santa* is Spanish for "sacred herb").

Eriodictyon crassifolium

thickleaf yerba santa

BORAGINACEAE BORAGE FAMILY

PCT Sections: 1–6 **Abundance:** Locally common **Height:** 3–9 ft. **Flowering:** April–July **Flower Color:** Lavender **Habitat-Community:** Canyons and slopes in chaparrals and woodlands **Elevation:** Below 6200 ft. **Ecoregions:** Southern California Mountains

Large shrub with densely hairy stems and foliage. Leaves 4–8 in. long, evergreen, alternate, dark green, lance-shaped, hairy (sometimes sticky to the touch), with coarsely toothed margins. Flowers 0.3–0.6 in. long, clustered at stem ends, lavender, 5-parted, funnel-shaped. *Crassifolium* means "thick leaf." Two varieties along the PCT: var. *nigrescens* is more common in the western Transverse Ranges; var. *crassifolium* is more prevalent to the south.

poodle-dog bush

Eriodictyon parryi

BORAGINACEAE BORAGE FAMILY

PCT Sections: 1–9 **Abundance:** Locally common **Height:** 2–8 ft. **Flowering:** May–August **Flower Color:** Lavender, blue, or purple **Habitat-Community:** Open, granitic soils in foothill chaparrals and lower montane coniferous forests **Elevation:** Below 7300 ft. **Ecoregions:** Southern California Mountains, Sierra Nevada

Strongly aromatic, taprooted subshrub, woody only at base, with glandular-sticky stems and foliage. Leaves 4–12 in. long, evergreen, alternate, bright green, linear to lance-shaped, with smooth or toothed margins. Flowers 0.3–0.5 in. long, clustered at stem ends, lavender, blue or purple, 5-parted, funnel- to urn-shaped, glandular. Fruits 0.1–0.2 in. long, densely glandular capsules. Often grows in areas disturbed by fire or landslides. The leaves are sometimes densely clustered along the stem, resembling a poodle (or Cleopatra, the carnivorous plant from the 1960s TV sitcom *The Addams Family*). Notorious among hikers as a plant to avoid: it can cause a severe rash, akin to poison oak! That said, it's also an attractive member of our California flora, valued for its role in post-fire erosion control.

hairy yerba santa

Eriodictyon trichocalyx

BORAGINACEAE BORAGE FAMILY

PCT Sections: 1–5 **Abundance:** Locally common **Height:** 2–6 ft. **Flowering:** April–July **Flower Color:** White to lavender **Habitat-Community:** Wooded slopes and mesas in chaparrals and lower montane coniferous forests **Elevation:** Below 7800 ft. **Ecoregions:** Southern California Mountains

Shrub with hairy or hairless branches becoming woody, especially at higher elevations. Leaves 3–6 in. long, evergreen, alternate, lance-shaped, sticky above, hairy below, typically with rolled-under margins. Flowers 0.3–0.4 in. long, clustered at stem tips, with white-hairy calyces and white (tinged lavender), bell-shaped, 5-parted corollas. Two varieties along the PCT: var. *lanatum*, with hairier leaves and stems, is confined to the southern Peninsular Ranges; var. *trichocalyx* occurs in the Transverse Ranges. *Trichocalyx* refers to the characteristic hairy (hair = trichome) sepals.

four-wing saltbush

Atriplex canescens

CHENOPODIACEAE GOOSEFOOT FAMILY

PCT Sections: 1–8 **Abundance:** Locally common **Height:** 2–6 ft. **Flowering:** June–August **Flower Color:** Pale yellow to brown **Habitat-Community:** Saline flats and gravelly slopes in scrubs and Joshua tree woodlands **Elevation:** Below 6100 ft. **Ecoregions:** Southern California Mountains, Sonoran/Mojave Basin and Range, Sierra Nevada

Stiff-branched shrub, as wide as tall; dioecious. Leaves 1.1–1.8 in. long, evergreen, alternate, linear to spoon-shaped, with smooth margins. Male flowers pale yellow (to brown), in elongated clusters 2–6 in. long. Female flowers minute, in elongated clusters 2–15 in. long. Fruits 0.1–0.3 in. wide, spherical, 1-seeded, with 4 distinctively toothed wings. Ubiquitous, ranging from California to Texas and South Dakota. *Canescens* ("to become gray or white") refers to its overall hue.

Grayia spinosa

spiny hopsage

CHENOPODIACEAE

GOOSEFOOT FAMILY

PCT Sections: 4–8 **Abundance:** Occasional **Height:** 2–5 ft. **Flowering:** March–June **Flower Color:** White to reddish brown **Habitat-Community:** Valley bottoms and gravelly slopes in scrubs and Joshua tree woodlands **Elevation:** Below 7200 ft. **Ecoregions:** Southern California Mountains, Mojave Basin and Range, Sierra Nevada

Rounded, multi-branched shrub with red-brown stems becoming dark gray and lined with age; monoecious. Lateral branches are stiff with spiny tips. Leaves 0.1–0.6 in. long, often winter-deciduous, alternate, spoon-shaped, green with white tips. Flowers in 1–few-flowered clusters at stem tips. Male flowers <0.1 in. across, with 4–5 stamens. Female flowers highly reduced, consisting of an ovary with 2 protruding stigmas. Fruits 0.3–0.5 in. across, elliptic, flattened, wing-like, clustered at stem tips and turning a showy bright pink to red in spring. The only species in *Grayia*.

Krascheninnikovia lanata

winterfat

CHENOPODIACEAE

GOOSEFOOT FAMILY

PCT Sections: 5–8 **Abundance:** Occasional **Height:** 1–4 ft. **Flowering:** May–July **Flower Color:** White to red-brown **Habitat-Community:** Valleys, sandy slopes, or clay soils in scrubs and woodlands **Elevation:** Below 7400 ft. **Ecoregions:** Southern California Mountains, Mojave Basin and Range, Sierra Nevada

Erect shrub with gray-woolly stems; monoecious. Leaves 0.4–1.6 in. long, evergreen or drought-deciduous, alternate, clustered in axils along stems, linear, white-hairy, with rolled-in margins. Flowers in dense spikes. Male flowers <0.1 in. across with 4 stamens. Female flowers highly reduced, densely white-hairy, consisting of an ovary with 2 protruding stigmas. Fruits 0.1 in. across, ovoid, white-hairy achenes. Extends from Canada to Mexico to Kansas, intercepting the CA PCT only in the Southern California Mountains, western Mojave Desert, and southern Sierra. This halophyte (salt-lover) thrives in alkaline soils and is an important forage plant for wildlife.

Crossosoma bigelovii

Bigelow's ragged rock flower

CROSSOSOMATACEAE

CROSSOSOMA FAMILY

PCT Sections: 3–4 **Abundance:** Rare **Height:** 1–5 ft. **Flowering:** February–April **Flower Color:** White to purple **Habitat-Community:** Dry, steep, rocky canyons and slopes in creosote bush scrubs **Elevation:** Below 4100 ft. **Ecoregions:** Sonoran Basin and Range

Intricately branched, thorny shrub that grows among (or hangs from) granitic rocks. Leaves 0.2–0.7 in. long, deciduous, alternate, clustered on stems, elliptic or spoon-shaped, gray-green with a waxy coating. Flowers 0.4–0.6 in. long, solitary, with 5 white-purple petals narrowing to a claw-like base. Stamens generally >10. Fruits 0.3–0.5 in. long, narrow pods, 1–3 per flower. Occurs along the PCT only on the lower slopes of the northern San Jacinto Mountains and adjacent southern flanks of the San Bernardino Mountains.

Glossopetalon spinescens

spiny greasebush

CROSSOSOMATACEAE
CROSSOSOMA FAMILY

PCT Sections: 4 & 21 **Abundance:** Rare **Height:** 3–10 ft. **Flowering:** April–May **Flower Color:** White **Habitat-Community:** Rocky, limestone or serpentine slopes and ridges from chaparrals to upper montane coniferous forests **Elevation:** Below 8000 ft. **Ecoregions:** Southern California Mountains, Klamath Mountains

Erect to spreading shrub with intricately branched, spiny stems. Leaves 0.2–0.7 in. long, deciduous, alternate, oblong to lance-shaped, gray-green, with smooth margins. Flowers 0.1–0.3 in. long, generally solitary in leaf axils, white, with 4–6 petals. Fruits to 0.2 in. long, ovoid capsules with 1–2 seeds.

Arbutus menziesii

Pacific madrone

ERICACEAE HEATH FAMILY

PCT Sections: 1 & 17–20 & 23–24 **Abundance:** Occasional **Height:** 25–130 ft. **Flowering:** March–May **Flower Color:** White to pink **Habitat-Community:** Dry, generally open slopes in woodlands, chaparrals, and lower montane coniferous forests **Elevation:** Below 5000 ft. **Ecoregions:** All (except Sonoran/Mojave Basin and Range)

Erect, single- or multi-stemmed tree with flaky, smooth (furrowed on older trees), red-brown bark. Leaves 3–5 in. long, 1.5–3 wide, evergreen, alternate, thick, oval to oblong, dark green above, white-green below, with smooth or toothed margins. Flowers to 0.3 in. long, white to pink, aromatic, urn-shaped. Fruits 0.2–0.5 in. across, spherical, orange to red berries, each with about 20 dark brown seeds. The berries are edible but bitter. Can live 400 to 500 years. Sprouts after fire, which helps maintain mycorrhizal diversity and hastens habitat recovery. *Arbutus* ("strawberry tree") is a reference to the brightly colored berries.

Arctostaphylos glandulosa

Eastwood manzanita

ERICACEAE HEATH FAMILY

PCT Sections: 1–6 **Abundance:** Common **Height:** to 9 ft. **Flowering:** January–May **Flower Color:** White to pink **Habitat-Community:** Gravelly slopes and ridges from chaparrals to upper montane coniferous forests **Elevation:** Below 6600 ft. **Ecoregions:** Southern California Mountains

Erect shrub with a hemispheric basal burl that sprouts from the root crown if burned. Twigs have short, sometimes glandular, stiff hairs. Leaves 0.9–2.1 in. long, elliptic to ovoid, bright green, often glandular. Flowers clustered at stem tips on hairy pedicels, corollas urn-shaped, 0.3–0.4 in. long, white to pink. Fruits 0.2–0.5 in. across, sticky or glandular-hairy round berries. Widespread with least 10 subspecies, 7 of which (some quite rare) occur along the PCT. The common name honors manzanita aficionado Alice Eastwood (1859–1953), curator at the California Academy of Sciences.

Arctostaphylos glauca

big berry manzanita

ERICACEAE HEATH FAMILY

PCT Sections: 1–7 **Abundance:** Common **Height:** 3–22 ft. **Flowering:** December–April **Flower Color:** White to pink **Habitat-Community:** Dry slopes and ridges in chaparrals, pinyon-juniper woodlands, and lower montane coniferous forests **Elevation:** Below 6400 ft. **Ecoregions:** Southern California Mountains, Sierra Nevada

Shrub or small tree with hairless twigs and no basal burl. Leaves 1.2–2.6 in. long, round to ovoid, gray-green, and white-wax-coated. Flowers clustered at stem tips on hairless pedicels, urn-shaped corollas 0.3–0.4 in. long, white to pink. Fruits 0.4–0.7 in. across (large for a manzanita), spherical, edible, and sparsely glandular. A long-lived species, easily exceeding 100 years in age, abstaining from fruit production until age 20. The shrub is allelopathic: chemical compounds released by its decomposing foliage inhibit the growth of other plants.

Arctostaphylos nevadensis

pinemat manzanita

ERICACEAE HEATH FAMILY

PCT Sections: 10–24 **Abundance:** Common **Height:** to 2 ft. **Flowering:** January–June **Flower Color:** White to pink **Habitat-Community:** Open slopes, rocky places, and flats from lower montane to subalpine coniferous forests **Elevation:** Below 10,000 ft. **Ecoregions:** Sierra Nevada, Cascades, Klamath Mountains

Trailing or mounded shrub with smooth, red bark under exfoliating strips and sparsely hairy stems. Leaves 0.4–1.2 in. long, evergreen, alternate, thick, lance-shaped to ovoid, hairless when mature, bright green, point-tipped, with smooth margins. Flowers 0.2 in. long, white to pink, urn-shaped, and clustered at stem tips. Fruits 0.3 in. across, spherical, hairless, brown-red berries. Another manzanita with no burl and therefore incapable of sprouting from its base after fire. The red blisters often found on the leaves are galls caused by aphids; when the gall matures and dries, the mature manzanita leaf gall aphid flies off to mate and start the cycle again.

Arctostaphylos patula

greenleaf manzanita

ERICACEAE HEATH FAMILY

PCT Sections: 3–24 **Abundance:** Common **Height:** to 6.5 ft. **Flowering:** January–June **Flower Color:** Pink **Habitat-Community:** Open slopes and flats from oak woodlands to subalpine coniferous forests **Elevation:** Below 11,000 ft. **Ecoregions:** Southern California Mountains, Mojave Basin and Range, Sierra Nevada, Cascades, Klamath Mountains

Burl-forming (sometimes absent or obscure), erect to spreading shrub with smooth, red-brown bark and hairy, golden-glandular stems. Leaves 1–2.5 in. long, evergreen, alternate, thick, round to ovoid, hairless, shiny green, point-tipped, with smooth margins. Flowers 0.2 in. long, pink, urn-shaped, and clustered at stem tips. Fruits 0.4 in. across, spherical, hairless, dark red-brown berries. Young, green berries can be made into a cider; a delicious hot tea is possible by steeping the flowers. Burl-forming populations sprout from base or roots after fire.

Arctostaphylos pungens

pointleaf manzanita

ERICACEAE HEATH FAMILY

PCT Sections: 1–5 **Abundance:** Locally common **Height:** to 9 ft. **Flowering:** February–April **Flower Color:** White to pink **Habitat-Community:** Dry slopes and ridges in chaparrals, pinyon-juniper woodlands, and lower montane coniferous forests **Elevation:** Below 7100 ft. **Ecoregions:** Southern California Mountains

Shrub with hairless twigs and lacking a basal burl. Leaves 0.8–2 in. long, erect, lance-shaped to ovoid, leathery, shiny green and hairless in age, and point-tipped (hence the common name). Flowers to 0.4 in. long, clustered at stem tips, white to pink, urn-shaped, with hairless pedicels. Fruits 0.3–0.5 in. across, spherical, hairy and glandless; seeds require disturbance by wildfire or other means before they can germinate. Ranges from California to Texas and northern Mexico. Of the 40 or so manzanita species in California, perhaps the most tolerant of hot, arid environments.

Arctostaphylos viscida

sticky whiteleaf manzanita

ERICACEAE HEATH FAMILY

PCT Sections: 7–8 & 14–24 **Abundance:** Common **Height:** to 12 ft. **Flowering:** January–April **Flower Color:** Pink to white **Habitat-Community:** Open slopes and flats in oak woodlands, chaparrals, and lower montane coniferous forests **Elevation:** Below 6000 ft. **Ecoregions:** Sierra Nevada, Cascades, Klamath Mountains

Erect shrub with smooth red-brown bark, sticky stems (especially when young), and no burl. Leaves 0.4–1 in. long, evergreen, alternate, thick, oval, hairless, white-waxy, round-tipped. with smooth or toothed margins. Flowers 0.2 in. long, pink to white, urn-shaped, and clustered at stem tips. Fruits 0.2–0.3 in. across, glandular-hairy or hairless red-brown berries. Young, green berries can be made into a cider or jelly.

Phyllodoce breweri

purple mountain heath

ERICACEAE HEATH FAMILY

PCT Sections: 4–5 & 10–20 **Abundance:** Occasional **Height:** to 1 ft. **Flowering:** June–August **Flower Color:** Pink to rose-purple **Habitat-Community:** Open forests, meadows, and moist, rocky slopes in subalpine coniferous forests and alpine communities **Elevation:** 6500–12,000 ft. **Ecoregions:** Southern California Mountains, Sierra Nevada, Cascades, Klamath Mountains

Matted shrub that can form extensive thickets with densely glandular stems. Leaves 0.2–1 in. long, evergreen, alternate, linear, blunt-tipped, with tightly rolled-under margins. Flowers to 0.3 in. long, clustered at stem ends, 5-parted, pink to rose-purple, fused petals, bell-shaped, with 10 stamens. Fruits spherical, glandular-hairy capsules. Phyllodoce is a sea nymph. William Henry Brewer (1828–1910) made the first voucher collections of this species on Mt. Hoffman, in Yosemite National Park, on 24 June 1863.

Rhododendron columbianum

western Labrador tea

ERICACEAE HEATH FAMILY

PCT Sections: 10–24 **Abundance:** Common **Height:** 1–7 ft. **Flowering:** May–August **Flower Color:** Creamy white **Habitat-Community:** Wet places in meadows, bogs, fens, and streambanks in wetland-riparian communities **Elevation:** Below 12,000 ft. **Ecoregions:** Sierra Nevada, Cascades, Klamath Mountains

Aromatic rhizomatous shrub with glandular-hairy stems. Leaves 1–3 in. long, evergreen, alternate, thick, elliptic (tightly rolled-under margins), dark green above, white-hairy below. Flowers 0.2–0.4 in. long, rounded clusters at stem ends, creamy white, 5-parted, widely cup-shaped, with 8–10 stamens. Fruits 0.3–0.4 in. across, elliptic, nodding capsules. Crushed leaves are pleasantly fragrant. Although known for a tea made from the leaves, the plant is toxic!

Rhododendron occidentale

California azalea

ERICACEAE HEATH FAMILY

PCT Sections: 1–3 & 11–24 **Abundance:** Common **Height:** 3–17 ft. **Flowering:** May–June **Flower Color:** White to pink **Habitat-Community:** Streambanks, meadows, springs, bogs, fens, and moist slopes in the understory of montane coniferous forests and wetland-riparian communities **Elevation:** Below 7000 ft. **Ecoregions:** Southern California/Northern Baja Coast, Sierra Nevada, Cascades, Klamath Mountains

Erect to spreading, loosely branched shrub with smooth to furrowed bark that can become peeling. Leaves 1–4 in. long, deciduous, alternate, elliptic, dark green above, pale green below, with hairy margins. Flowers 1–2.5 in. long, clustered at stem tips, white to pink, funnel-shaped, aromatic, and tinged with orange or yellow. Fruits 0.5 in. long, longer than wide, glandular-hairy capsules. Showy; planted extensively by gardeners. The foliage is reportedly toxic, which keeps it safe from hungry critters. Sprouts after fire or being damaged.

Vaccinium cespitosum

dwarf bilberry

ERICACEAE HEATH FAMILY

PCT Sections: 10–24 **Abundance:** Locally common **Height:** to 1 ft. **Flowering:** May–August **Flower Color:** White to pink **Habitat-Community:** Meadows and moist slopes from lower montane coniferous forests to alpine communities **Elevation:** Below 12,000 ft. **Ecoregions:** Sierra Nevada, Cascades, Klamath Mountains

Prostrate to erect, rhizomatous thicket-forming shrub. Leaves 0.5–1.3 in. long, deciduous, alternate, oval to elliptic (widest above middle), with fine-toothed margins. Flowers to 0.3 in. long, solitary in leaf axils, white to pink, 4–5-parted, urn-shaped, with 8 or 10 stamens. Fruits to 0.4 in. across, blue to purple-black, waxy or not berries. Known for tasty berries and beautiful fall color.

Vaccinium uliginosum
subsp. *occidentale*

western blueberry

ERICACEAE HEATH FAMILY

PCT Sections: 10–24 **Abundance:** Occasional **Height:** to 2.5 ft. **Flowering:** June–July **Flower Color:** Pink **Habitat-Community:** Meadows and moist slopes in upper montane & subalpine coniferous forests **Elevation:** Below 11,500 ft. **Ecoregions:** Sierra Nevada, Cascades, Klamath Mountains

Mat-forming shrub with prostrate or erect stems. Leaves 0.5–1 in. long, deciduous, alternate, oval to ovoid, with smooth margins. Flowers 0.2–0.3 in. long, 1 to few in leaf axils, white to pink, 4–5-parted, urn-shaped, with 8 or 10 stamens. Fruits 0.2–0.3 in. across, blue, waxy berries. The edible berries can be eaten fresh or dried and made into cakes or muffins.

Bernardia incana

mouse's eye

EUPHORBIACEAE SPURGE FAMILY

PCT Sections: 1–4 **Abundance:** Rare **Height:** 2–7 ft. **Flowering:** April–November **Flower Color:** Pale green to cream **Habitat-Community:** Gravelly or rocky slopes and canyons in creosote bush scrubs and pinyon-juniper woodlands **Elevation:** Below 5600 ft. **Ecoregions:** Southern California Mountains, Sonoran Basin and Range

Much-branched, shrubby spurge with clear sap, usually growing inconspicuously in the shade of rocks or other shrubs; dioecious. Leaves 0.3–1.3 in. long, deciduous, alternate, olive-green, slightly fleshy, oval, with star-shaped hairs and scalloped margins. Leaves turn yellow-orange before dropping. Male flowers in an elongated spike, with 3–4-parted calyces, 0 petals, and 4–22 stamens. Female flowers 0.1 in. long, solitary, pale green, with 5 sepals, superior ovary, and 3 distinctly and irregularly jagged styles. Fruits 0.3–0.6 in. long, rounded, 3-lobed woolly capsules with single-seeded carpels. Occurs sporadically along the PCT from the desert slopes of the Laguna Mountains to the San Felipe Hills.

Cercis occidentalis

western redbud

FABACEAE LEGUME FAMILY

PCT Sections: 1–2 & 4–9 & 18–20 & 23–24 **Abundance:** Occasional **Height:** to 25 ft. **Flowering:** February–May **Flower Color:** Red-purple to pink **Habitat-Community:** Dry slopes in chaparrals and oak woodlands **Elevation:** Below 6300 ft. **Ecoregions:** All (except Sonoran/Mojave Basin and Range)

Large shrub or small tree with rounded crown of erect, reddish stems. Leaves 1–4 in. long, deciduous, alternate, round, heart-shaped at the base, with smooth margins. Flowers 0.5 in. long, clustered along the stems, red-purple to pink, 5-parted, pea-like, with 10 stamens. Fruits 2–4 in. long, flat, brown to red-purple pods clustered along stems. The showy flowers appear in the early spring before the leaves unfold. Western redbud shows off again in the fall with its colorful foliage and fruits. Aka Judas tree, a reference to *C. siliquastrum*, a Middle Eastern species associated with the story of Judas.

Chrysolepis sempervirens

bush chinquapin

FAGACEAE OAK FAMILY

PCT Sections: 3–5 & 8–24 **Abundance:** Common **Height:** to 8 ft. **Flowering:** July–August **Habitat-Community:** Dry, rocky slopes from foothill chaparrals to subalpine coniferous forests **Elevation:** Below 12,000 ft. **Ecoregions:** Southern California Mountains, Sierra Nevada, Cascades, Klamath Mountains

Multi-stemmed shrub with conical crown, and thin, smooth, brown-gray bark; monoecious. Leaves 1–3 in. long, evergreen, alternate, thick, elliptic, golden below, with smooth margins and round tip. Flowers arranged in separate, aromatic (not in a good way), erect or spreading catkins in leaf axils; 0 petals. Fruits 1–2.5 in. across, brown, spherical, spiny burs with 1–3 nuts that take 2 years to mature. Can sprout after fire or being cut down. If you can get through the nasty armed burs, the mature nuts (about 0.3 in. across) taste sweet.

Quercus agrifolia

coast live oak

FAGACEAE OAK FAMILY

PCT Sections: 1–6 **Abundance:** Locally common **Height:** 20–70 ft. **Flowering:** February–April **Habitat-Community:** Dry valleys and slopes in woodlands, chaparrals, and lower montane coniferous forests **Elevation:** Below 5300 ft. **Ecoregions:** Southern California Mountains

Massive, multi-branched, gnarled tree with trunks up to 8 ft. in diameter; monoecious (like all oaks). Leaves 1–3 in. long, evergreen, alternate, oval, dark green, convex, with hair-tufted central veins. Male flowers have 4–10 stamens and form pendent catkins. Female flowers minute, in leaf axils, with 1 pistil. Fruits 1–1.7 in. long, acorns with cup-shaped, thin-scaled cap 0.5–0.8 in. wide. Acorns mature in 1 year. Two varieties along the PCT: var. *oxyadenia* (leaves densely hairy below) is most common in San Diego County; var. *agrifolia* (hairless leaves) is more widespread. Trees have been known to exceed 1000 years in age!

Quercus berberidifolia

scrub oak

FAGACEAE OAK FAMILY

PCT Sections: 1–6 **Abundance:** Common **Height:** 5–25 ft. **Flowering:** February–April **Habitat-Community:** Dry slopes in chaparrals **Elevation:** Below 6000 ft. **Ecoregions:** Southern California Mountains

Shrub to small tree with trunks up to 2 ft. across; monoecious. Leaves 0.6–1.3 in. long, evergreen, alternate, oblong to elliptic, shiny green, with spine-toothed margins. Male flowers have up to 10 stamens and form pendent catkins. Female flowers minute, in leaf axils, with 1 pistil. Fruits 0.6–1.3 in. long, ovoid acorns with thick, cup-shaped, bumpy cap 0.5–0.8 in. wide. Acorns mature in 1 year. The common name is applied to shrubby oaks in general; all are challenging to identify to species, and many commonly hybridize. The word *chaparral* is derived from the Spanish word for scrub oak, *chaparro*.

Quercus chrysolepis

canyon live oak

FAGACEAE OAK FAMILY

PCT Sections: 1–10 & 16–20 & 23–24 **Abundance:** Common **Height:** 15–70 ft. **Flowering:** May–June **Habitat-Community:** Canyon walls, dry slopes, cliffs, and rock outcrops from oak woodlands to upper montane coniferous forests **Elevation:** Below 9000 ft. **Ecoregions:** All (except Sonoran/Mojave Basin and Range)

Single- or multi-stemmed tree with dense, rounded crown and furrowed, gray-brown bark; monoecious. Leaves 1–4 in. long, evergreen, alternate, thick, elliptic to ovoid, golden hairs below (young leaves), with smooth or toothed margins. Flowers in drooping catkins (male) and generally solitary (female) flowers in leaf axils. Fruits 1–1.5 in. long, light brown, ovoid, round-tipped acorns with cup-shaped cap covered in golden hairs. Acorns take 2 years to mature and are edible once tannins are leached. Can sprout after fire, but trees are killed by frequent burning. An important wildlife tree for food, cover, and roosting. Its wood is used for furniture, pallets, flooring, and firewood. John Muir called this a "tough, rugged mountaineer of a tree."

Quercus cornelius-mulleri

desert scrub oak

FAGACEAE OAK FAMILY

PCT Sections: 1–4 **Abundance:** Locally common **Height:** 3–10 ft. **Flowering:** February–April **Habitat-Community:** Rocky or gravelly (granitic) ridges and slopes in scrubs, foothill chaparrals, and pinyon-juniper woodlands **Elevation:** Below 6300 ft. **Ecoregions:** Southern California Mountains, Sonoran Basin and Range

Densely branched shrub with gray-brown, fuzzy (when young) twigs; monoecious. Leaves 1.1–1.7 in. long, evergreen, leathery, oval, smooth or toothed margins, and distinctly bicolored: dull green and faintly hairy above, white and woolly (with star-shaped hairs obscuring all but the primary veins) below. Male flowers with up to 10 stamens in pendent catkins. Female flowers minute, in leaf axils, with 1 pistil. Fruits 0.8–1.3 in. long, cylindric to widely cone-shaped acorns with cup-shaped, non-bumpy cap 0.5–0.9 in. wide, maturing in 1 year. Described in 1981 and named after ecologist and oak specialist Cornelius Muller (1909–1997). Hybridizes with *Q. engelmannii* in the Peninsular Ranges, forming an intermediate form that is sometimes elevated to specific status as *Q. acutidens*.

Quercus engelmannii

Engelmann oak

FAGACEAE OAK FAMILY

PCT Sections: 1–3 **Abundance:** Rare **Height:** 15–75 ft. **Flowering:** April–May **Habitat-Community:** Dry slopes and valleys in foothill chaparrals and woodlands **Elevation:** Below 4200 ft. **Ecoregions:** Southern California Mountains

Tree forming a crown 30–60 ft. across, trunk 1–4 ft. in diameter, with narrowly furrowed, gray bark and hairy young twigs; monoecious. Leaves 1–2.4 in. long, evergreen, alternate, oblong, dull blue-green, hairless above, soft-hairy below, with smooth to wavy margins. Male flowers with up to 10 stamens in pendent catkins. Female flowers minute, in leaf axils, with 1 pistil. Fruits 0.7–1.1 in. long, oblong-cylindric acorns with thick, cup-shaped, bumpy cap 0.4–0.7 in. wide, maturing in 1 year. Its range once extended from the Pacific Coast to Arizona and Baja, but climatic drying has shrunk that. More than 90% of remaining specimens (some aged to 350 years) are in central San Diego County, near areas of rapid urbanization!

Quercus garryana

Oregon white oak

FAGACEAE OAK FAMILY

PCT Sections: 5–6 & 16–24 **Abundance:** Common **Height:** 3–90 ft. **Flowering:** April–May **Habitat-Community:** Exposed slopes, meadow edges, and valleys in oak woodlands, chaparrals, and lower montane coniferous forests **Elevation:** Below 7500 ft. **Ecoregions:** Southern California Mountains, Sierra Nevada, Cascades, Klamath Mountains

Shrub or tree with crooked branches and scaly, furrowed, thin, white-gray bark; monoecious. Leaves 3–4 in. long, deciduous, alternate, elliptic to ovoid, 5–9 rounded lobes, dark and shiny green above, with smooth or toothed margins. Male flowers in drooping catkins; 2–4 female flowers in leaf axils. Fruits 0.7–1.3 in. long, brown, ovoid, round-tipped acorns with wart-scaled, cup-shaped caps. Acorns take 1 year to mature and are edible after leaching the tannins. Can sprout after fire and is well adapted to frequent burning. An important wildlife tree for food, cover, and roosting. Known to live over 500 years.

Quercus john-tuckeri

Tucker oak

FAGACEAE OAK FAMILY

PCT Sections: 4–8 **Abundance:** Locally common **Height:** 6–18 ft. **Flowering:** February–April **Habitat-Community:** Dry slopes and mesas in foothill chaparrals and Joshua tree & pinyon-juniper woodlands **Elevation:** Below 6200 ft. **Ecoregions:** Southern California Mountains, Sierra Nevada

Evergreen shrub or small tree having gray to brown branches with fibrous-hairy young twigs; monoecious. Leaves 1–1.6 in. long, evergreen, alternate, leathery and thick, elliptic, with spine-toothed margins; leaves gray-green, slightly hairy above, pale green and hairy below, but hairs not obscuring the veins. Male flowers in pendent catkins with up to 10 stamens. Female flowers minute, in leaf axils, with 1 pistil. Fruits 0.8–1.2 in. long, maturing in 1 year, ovoid, point-tipped acorns with a hairless inner shell and cup-shaped, non-bumpy, thin caps 0.4–0.6 in. wide. Best found along the PCT at the desert transitions of the Transverse Ranges, where it hybridizes with *Q. berberidifolia*. Named after John M. Tucker (1916–2008), professor of botany at UC Davis and oak specialist.

Quercus kelloggii

California black oak

FAGACEAE OAK FAMILY

PCT Sections: 1–10 & 14–24 **Abundance:** Common **Height:** 30–80 ft. **Flowering:** May–June **Habitat-Community:** Dry slopes and valleys in oak woodlands, foothill chaparrals, and lower montane coniferous forests **Elevation:** Below 8000 ft. **Ecoregions:** All (except Sonoran/Mojave Basin and Range)

Tall, single-stemmed tree with crooked branches, broad-rounded crown, and checkered, furrowed, gray-black to black bark; monoecious. Leaves 3.5–8 in. long, deciduous, alternate, elliptic to ovoid, 7–9-lobed with bristle tips, dark and shiny green above, with sharp-toothed to lobed margins. Flowers in drooping male catkins, and 1–7 female flowers in leaf axils. Fruits 0.7–1.3 in. long, brown, oblong to ovoid, round-tipped acorns with thin scales on cup-shaped caps that cover about half the nut. Acorns take 2 years to mature and are edible once tannins are leached; highly prized for their flavor, they were extensively traded throughout California by Indigenous peoples. Trees are shade-tolerant when young, much less so when mature. Can sprout after fire; tolerant of low intensity burns. An important wildlife tree for food, cover, and roosting. Known to live over 500 years.

Quercus palmeri

Palmer oak

FAGACEAE OAK FAMILY

PCT Sections: 1–5 **Abundance:** Rare **Height:** 6–15 ft. **Flowering:** April–May **Flower Color:** Pale green to white **Habitat-Community:** Rocky slopes and mesas in foothill chaparrals, scrubs, and woodlands **Elevation:** Below 5000 ft. **Ecoregions:** Southern California Mountains

Spreading and rigid shrub or small tree with red-brown young twigs; monoecious. Leaves 0.4–1.2 in. long, evergreen, alternate, leathery and waxy, elliptic to round-ovoid, wavy, with spine-toothed margins; shiny olive-green above, gray-green, coated in glandular hairs below. Male flowers with up to 10 stamens in pendent catkins. Female flowers minute, in leaf axils, with 1 pistil. Fruits 0.8–1.2 in. long, maturing in 2 years, ovoid acorns with a hairy inner shell and bowl-shaped, non-bumpy, hairy caps 0.8–1.1 in. wide. Hybridizes with *Q. chrysolepis*. Look for a large population near the Highway 74 crossing in southern Riverside County. A clone in the Jurupa Mountains was recently estimated to be 13,000 years old!

Quercus vacciniifolia

huckleberry oak

FAGACEAE OAK FAMILY

PCT Sections: 10–24 **Abundance:** Common **Height:** to 5 ft. **Flowering:** May–July **Habitat-Community:** Cliffs, rocky slopes, and openings with shallow soils, including serpentine, from oak woodlands to subalpine coniferous forests **Elevation:** Below 10,000 ft. **Ecoregions:** Sierra Nevada, Cascades, Klamath Mountains

Low, spreading, flexible shrub with smooth gray bark; monoecious. Leaves 0.5–1.3 in. long, evergreen, alternate, thick, oblong, point- or round-tipped, with smooth or irregularly toothed margins. Male flowers in drooping catkins; generally solitary female flowers in leaf axils. Fruits 0.3–0.7 in. long, ovoid acorns with saucer-shaped caps covering about 25% of the nut. Acorns mature in 2 years and are edible once tannins are leached. This and manzanitas dominate montane chaparral in the Sierra Nevada, Cascades, and Klamath Mountains. Stems are commonly covered with insect galls.

Quercus wislizeni

interior live oak

FAGACEAE OAK FAMILY

PCT Sections: 1–9 **Abundance:** Common **Height:** 8–60 ft. **Flowering:** March–May **Flower Color:** Pale green to white **Habitat-Community:** Dry slopes and valleys in foothill chaparrals and lower montane coniferous forests **Elevation:** Below 6500 ft. **Ecoregions:** Southern California Mountains, Sierra Nevada

Shrub or tree with trunks up to 3 ft. in diameter and furrowed gray bark; monoecious. Leaves 0.9–2.2 in. long, evergreen, alternate, oblong to lance-shaped, hairless, shiny green above, yellow-green below, with spine-toothed to smooth margins. Male flowers with up to 10 stamens in drooping catkins; generally solitary female flowers with 1 pistil in leaf axils. Fruits 0.8–1.7 in. long, ovoid acorns with thick, cup-shaped, smooth cap 0.5–0.8 in. wide. Acorns mature in 2 years. Two varieties along the PCT: var. *frutescens* is the more common shrub form; var. *wislizeni* is the tree form.

Ribes cereum

wax currant

GROSSULARIACEAE

GOOSEBERRY FAMILY

PCT Sections: 3–5 & 9–24 **Abundance:** Common **Height:** 2–5 ft. **Flowering:** June–July **Flower Color:** Green-white or white to pink **Habitat-Community:** Forest openings and dry, rocky slopes from lower montane coniferous forests to alpine communities **Elevation:** Below 13,000 ft. **Ecoregions:** Southern California Mountains, Sierra Nevada, Cascades, Klamath Mountains

Erect to spreading shrub with 0 nodal spines and glandular-hairy stems. Leaves 0.5–1 in. long, deciduous, alternate, aromatic, obscurely 3–5-lobed, roundish, hairy or hairless, with toothed margins. Flowers solitary or in dense, 2–8-flowered, drooping clusters, 5-parted, bell-shaped. Sepals to 0.1 in. long, recurved, green-white or white to pink. Petals to 0.1 in. long, < sepals, white to pink. Fruits 0.5 in. across, glandular-hairy (when young), bright red berries. Although the berries are bitter, they can be used in pies and breads.

Ribes indecorum

whiteflower currant

GROSSULARIACEAE

GOOSEBERRY FAMILY

PCT Sections: 1–5 **Abundance:** Common **Height:** 3–12 ft. **Flowering:** December–April **Flower Color:** White **Habitat-Community:** Canyons in dry soils in foothill chaparrals and woodlands **Elevation:** Below 6200 ft. **Ecoregions:** Southern California Mountains

Fragrant shrub with thick stems that are fuzzy and glandular in texture, lacking spines, and shredding, dark bark (older plants). Leaves 0.5–1.7 in. long, deciduous, alternate, dark green, wrinkly, divided into 3–5-toothed lobes (maple-like), often glandular-hairy. Flowers 0.1–0.2 in. long, 10–25, loosely scattered along stems, hypanthium nearly as wide as long, petal-like and spreading sepals, and minute white petals. Fruits 0.2–0.3 in. across, sticky, hairy, purple (mature) berries, which are edible and quite tasty when fresh. Oddly, *indecorum* means "unattractive" or "without decoration." Someone wasn't impressed!

Ribes lasianthum

alpine gooseberry

GROSSULARIACEAE

GOOSEBERRY FAMILY

PCT Sections: 5 & 8–15 **Abundance:** Occasional **Height:** 1–4 ft. **Flowering:** May–August **Flower Color:** Yellow **Habitat-Community:** Open, rocky slopes in upper montane & subalpine coniferous forests **Elevation:** 7000–10,000 ft. **Ecoregions:** Southern California Mountains, Sierra Nevada

Erect to spreading shrub with 1–3 nodal spines and rigid, intricately branched stems. Leaves 0.4–0.8 in. long, deciduous, alternate, obscurely 3–5-lobed, roundish, glandular-hairy, with toothed margins. Flowers solitary or 2–4 in erect clusters, 5-parted, bell-shaped. Sepals to 0.1 in. long, recurved, yellow. Petals to 0.1 in. long, < sepals, erect, yellow. Fruits 0.3 in. across, dark red, hairless berries. Plants tend to form thickets over granite rock. The berries can be eaten fresh, but they are much better made into pies, cobblers, jellies, and jams.

Ribes montigenum

mountain gooseberry

GROSSULARIACEAE

GOOSEBERRY FAMILY

PCT Sections: 3–5 & 10–24 **Abundance:** Locally common **Height:** to 2 ft. **Flowering:** June–July **Flower Color:** Yellow-green to pinkish and reddish **Habitat-Community:** Open, rocky slopes from upper montane coniferous forests to alpine communities **Elevation:** 6800–14,000 ft. **Ecoregions:** Southern California Mountains, Sierra Nevada, Cascades, Klamath Mountains

Open, straggly shrub with 1–5 nodal spines and stems armed with prickles. Leaves 0.5–1 in. long, deciduous, alternate, 5-lobed, roundish, glandular-hairy, with toothed margins. Flowers 4–10 per cluster, drooping, 5-parted, saucer-shaped. Sepals to 0.2 in. long, spreading, yellow-green to pinkish. Petals to 0.1 in. long, < sepals, erect, reddish. Fruits to 0.2 in. across, orange-red, glandular-bristly berries, which can be eaten fresh.

Ribes nevadense

Sierra currant

GROSSULARIACEAE

GOOSEBERRY FAMILY

PCT Sections: 1–8 & 10–24 **Abundance:** Common **Height:** 3–6 ft. **Flowering:** April–July **Flower Color:** Pink to reddish and white **Habitat-Community:** Streambanks, meadows, and understories from lower montane to subalpine coniferous forests and wetland-riparian communities **Elevation:** Below 9800 ft. **Ecoregions:** All (except Sonoran/Mojave Basin and Range)

Erect to spreading shrub with 0 nodal spines and openly branched stems. Leaves 1–3 in. long, deciduous, alternate, thin, 3–5-lobed, roundish, hairy or hairless, with toothed margins. Flowers 8–20 per cluster, 5-parted, bowl-shaped. Sepals 0.1–0.2 in. long, erect, pink to reddish. Petals to 0.1 in. long, < sepals, erect, white. Fruits 0.2–0.3 in. across, blue-black, waxy, glandular-hairy berries. The berries are bitter if eaten fresh, but they can be made into pies, cobblers, jellies, and jams. Flowers appear in early spring, after snowmelt.

Ribes quercetorum

rock gooseberry

GROSSULARIACEAE

GOOSEBERRY FAMILY

PCT Sections: 1–9 **Abundance:** Occasional **Height:** to 4 ft. **Flowering:** February–March **Flower Color:** Yellow to cream **Habitat-Community:** Underneath oaks on rocky slopes in foothill chaparrals and woodlands **Elevation:** Below 4500 ft. **Ecoregions:** Southern California/Northern Baja Coast, Southern California Mountains, Sierra Nevada

Arching, rounded shrub with 1(3) curved nodal spine and hairy stems. Leaves 0.4–0.8 in. long, alternate, 3–5-lobed, thin, glandular-hairy, with lobed margins. Flowers 2–3, in tight clusters, 5-parted, tube-shaped. Sepals to 0.1 in. long, recurved, yellow. Petals to 0.1 in. long, < sepals, erect, yellow to cream. Fruits 0.3 in. across, hairless black berries. Plants form rounded thickets. The berries can be eaten fresh, but they are much better made into pies, cobblers, jellies, and jams.

Ribes roezlii

Sierra gooseberry

GROSSULARIACEAE

GOOSEBERRY FAMILY

PCT Sections: All **Abundance:** Common **Height:** to 4 ft. **Flowering:** March–July **Flower Color:** Reddish and white **Habitat-Community:** Understories and open slopes from oak woodlands to upper montane coniferous forests **Elevation:** Below 8500 ft. **Ecoregions:** All (except Sonoran/Mojave Basin and Range)

Stout shrub with 1–3 nodal spines and hairy stems. Leaves 0.5–1 in. long, deciduous, alternate, 3- or 5-lobed, roundish, nonglandular and hairy or hairless, with toothed margins. Flowers solitary or paired, drooping, 5-parted, tubular, with erect white pistil. Sepals 0.2–0.4 in. long, recurved, reddish. Petals to 0.2 in. long, length < stamens, white. Fruits 0.5–0.8 in. across, glandular-bristly purple-red berries. The berries can be eaten fresh or made into a delicious jelly utilizing their natural pectin. Thick gloves are recommended to collect the berries!

Ribes velutinum

desert gooseberry

GROSSULARIACEAE

GOOSEBERRY FAMILY

PCT Sections: All (except 3 & 6) **Abundance:** Common **Height:** 2–6 ft. **Flowering:** April–June **Flower Color:** Yellow to white **Habitat-Community:** Open slopes in chaparrals, sagebrush scrubs, pinyon-juniper woodlands, and lower montane coniferous forests **Elevation:** Below 12,200 ft. **Ecoregions:** Southern California Mountains, Sierra Nevada, Cascades, Klamath Mountains

Spiny shrub with intricately branched stems and 1–3 spines, 0.3–1 in. long, at branching nodes. Flowers solitary or 2–4 per cluster, usually glandular-hairy, hypanthium about as wide as long, yellow sepals 0.2 in. long, and yellow to white petals 0.1 in. long. Fruits 0.2–0.4 in. across, edible berries, ripening yellow then turning red or purple. Intergrades with *R. quercetorum* in places.

Ribes viscosissimum

sticky currant

GROSSULARIACEAE

GOOSEBERRY FAMILY

PCT Sections: 8 & 11–24 **Abundance:** Locally common **Height:** 3–7 ft. **Flowering:** April–July **Flower Color:** Greenish or pinkish and white **Habitat-Community:** Streambanks, openings, and understories from lower montane to subalpine coniferous forests and wetland-riparian communities **Elevation:** Below 10,000 ft. **Ecoregions:** Sierra Nevada, Cascades, Klamath Mountains

Erect, straggly shrub with 0 nodal spines and aromatic foliage. Leaves 1–3 in. long, deciduous, alternate, thick, 3–5-lobed, roundish, glandular-hairy, with toothed margins. Flowers 6–17 per cluster, erect or drooping, 5-parted, bell-shaped. Sepals to 0.3 in. long, spreading or recurved, greenish or pinkish. Petals to 0.1 in. long, < sepals, erect, white. Fruits 0.4–0.5 in. across, hairless or glandular-hairy blue-black berries, which are bitter and best left on the shrub!

Umbellularia californica

California bay

LAURACEAE LAUREL FAMILY

PCT Sections: 1–6 & 16–17 **Abundance:** Rare **Height:** to 100 ft. **Flowering:** November–May **Flower Color:** Yellow to green **Habitat-Community:** Canyons and shaded slopes in foothill chaparrals and woodlands **Elevation:** Below 6500 ft. **Ecoregions:** Southern California Mountains, Sierra Nevada

Shade-tolerant, single- or multi-branched tree with a dome-shaped crown and trunk to 10 ft. across. Bark green to reddish brown, somewhat furrowed with age. Leaves 2–5 in. long, evergreen, alternate, aromatic, lance-shaped to narrowly ovoid, shiny dark green, with smooth margins. Flowers clustered in heads, with 6 petal-like tepals (instead of petals or sepals) and 9 stamens. Tepals 0.1–0.3 in. long, yellow to green. Fruits 0.8–1.3 in. across, olive-shaped, green (aging purple) berries. Under the fleshy leathery skin of the fruit is a thin-shelled pit (bay nut), resembling that of its close relative, the avocado. Bay nuts can be roasted and ground for coffee or broken open to reveal the edible seeds. All plant parts contain a camphor-like volatile oil that has medicinal, therapeutic, and irritating qualities– the fragrance can cause a headache lasting for days! A common coastal tree of California and Oregon; perhaps best observed along the PCT atop the Laguna Mountains in San Diego County.

Fremontodendron californicum

California flannelbush

MALVACEAE MALLOW FAMILY

PCT Sections: 1–9 **Abundance:** Locally common **Height:** 5–18 ft. **Flowering:** April–July **Flower Color:** Yellow to orange **Habitat-Community:** Open slopes in foothill chaparrals and woodlands **Elevation:** Below 7400 ft. **Ecoregions:** Southern California Mountains, Sierra Nevada

Fast-growing, broadleaf, wide-crowned shrub that puts on a spectacular late-spring bloom. Leaves 0.5–2.8 in. long, evergreen, alternate, palmately lobed, olive- to gray-green, with a leathery, fuzzy texture, like flannel (hence the common name). Flowers 1.3–2.4 in. across, 0 petals, 5 sepals, somewhat succulent, yellow to orange. Fruits 1–2 in. long, partially enclosed by drying sepals, wedge-shaped capsules with 2–3 seeds. Avoid touching: the shrub's bristly hairs can break off under the skin, causing irritation!

Malacothamnus densiflorus

many-flowered bushmallow

MALVACEAE MALLOW FAMILY

PCT Sections: 1–3 **Abundance:** Occasional **Height:** to 7 ft. **Flowering:** May–October **Flower Color:** Pale pink to purple **Habitat-Community:** Open slopes and mesas in foothill chaparrals and oak woodlands **Elevation:** Below 6100 ft. **Ecoregions:** Southern California/Northern Baja Coast, Southern California Mountains

Endemic shrub of the Peninsular Ranges and northwestern Baja California, with slender, multi-branched, greenish stems covered in yellowish, star-shaped hairs. Leaves 1.2–2.8 in. wide, evergreen, alternate, thick to leathery, round to ovoid, palmately veined, shaggy-haired below. Flowers 10–15 per cluster, scattered along stems. Petals 0.4–0.9 in. long, 5, pale pink to purple. Outer calyx bracts longer than greenish (mostly lacking star-shaped hairs) calyx. Fruits 0.2–0.3 in. long, ovoid capsules. As with many species in *Malacothamnus* (from the Greek, "soft shrub"), plants most commonly occur in early-successional, post-burn areas.

Malacothamnus fasciculatus

chaparral bushmallow

MALVACEAE MALLOW FAMILY

PCT Sections: 2–6 **Abundance:** Occasional **Height:** to 15 ft. **Flowering:** April–October **Flower Color:** Pale pink to purple **Habitat-Community:** Open slopes and mesas in chaparrals **Elevation:** Below 4500 ft. **Ecoregions:** Southern California Mountains

Fast-growing, short-lived shrub with multi-branched, slender stems covered in white, star-shaped hairs. Leaves 0.9–2.7 in. wide, evergreen, alternate, thick to leathery, round to ovoid, palmately veined, with star-shaped hairs on both surfaces. Flowers 3–7 per cluster at branch tips. Petals 0.4–0.7 in. long, 5, pale pink to purple. Outer calyx bracts highly reduced, much shorter than gray-green calyx covered in star-shaped hairs. Fruits 0.2–0.3 in. long, ovoid capsules. Like most *Malacothamnus* spp., plants are post-fire opportunists, often growing in dense colonies. *Fasciculatus* (from the Latin, "clustered," "bundled") refers to the flowers.

Malacothamnus fremontii

Fremont's bushmallow

MALVACEAE MALLOW FAMILY

PCT Sections: 4–9 **Abundance:** Locally common **Height:** 3–8 ft. **Flowering:** May–July **Flower Color:** Pale pink to purple **Habitat-Community:** Open slopes and mesas in foothill chaparrals and woodlands **Elevation:** Below 7400 ft. **Ecoregions:** Southern California Mountains, Sierra Nevada

Erect shrub with stout branches and felt-like stems densely coated in white, star-shaped hairs. Leaves 1.3–3.4 in. wide, evergreen, alternate, thick to leathery, round to ovoid, palmately veined, and star-shaped to shaggy white-hairy. Flowers form rounded buds, 3–5 per cluster at branch tips. Petals 0.5–0.8 in. long, 5, pale pink to purple. Outer calyx bracts about half as long as calyx. Fruits 0.2–0.3 in. long, ovoid capsules. Plants are post-fire opportunists, often growing in dense colonies. *Malacothamnus* is highly variable; all 12 species occur in California or northwestern Mexico.

Dendromecon rigida

tree poppy

PAPAVERACEAE POPPY FAMILY

PCT Sections: 1–8 & 14–19 **Abundance:** Locally common **Height:** 3–9 ft. **Flowering:** April–June **Flower Color:** Yellow **Habitat-Community:** Dry slopes and washes in foothill chaparrals and woodlands **Elevation:** Below 5800 ft. **Ecoregions:** Southern California Mountains, Sierra Nevada

Showy shrub of sandy soils that can rapidly colonize and become temporarily dominant in recently burned areas. Leaves 1.5–4.5 in. long, evergreen, alternate, rigid and somewhat leathery, narrowly lance-shaped, bright green, with minutely toothed margins. Flowers 1–3 in. across, solitary at the tips of branches, with 4 yellow petals and many stamens. Fruits 2–4 in. long, linear, cylindric capsules that open from base. Seeds require exposure to fire for germination. The common name is a translation of *Dendromecon* (from the Greek *dendron*, "tree," *mekon*, "poppy").

Platanus racemosa

California sycamore

PLATANACEAE SYCAMORE FAMILY

PCT Sections: 1–6 **Abundance:** Locally common **Height:** to 110 ft. **Flowering:** February–April **Flower Color:** Maroon to green **Habitat-Community:** Streambanks, floodplains, springs, canyons, and valleys from California prairies to lower montane coniferous forests and wetland-riparian communities **Elevation:** Below 5700 ft. **Ecoregions:** Southern California/Northern Baja Coast, Southern California Mountains

Majestic, generally riparian tree with trunk 2–5 ft. across and massive horizontal branches that can be as widely spreading as the tree is tall; monoecious. Bark smooth, mottled, an attractive white, gray, and pale brown patchwork of peeling plates becoming darker with age. Leaves 9–13 in. wide, deciduous, alternate, palmately 3-5-lobed (maple-like), soft-hairy, turning yellow to orange-red in fall. Flowers in dangling chains of 2–7 spherical heads. Male flowers minute, 3–6 petals, 0 sepals, and 3–6 stamens. Female flowers with a red-tipped style, maroon stigma, and usually 0 petals and sepals. Fruits 0.8–1.2 in. across, woolly maroon-red achenes. In *Pilgrim at Tinker Creek*, Annie Dillard confides that her poet-friend Rosanne Coggeshall considered *sycamore* "the most intrinsically beautiful word in the English language." Hard to argue with that.

Eriogonum fasciculatum

California buckwheat

POLYGONACEAE BUCKWHEAT FAMILY

PCT Sections: 1–9 **Abundance:** Common **Height:** 1–5 ft. **Flowering:** All year **Flower Color:** White to pink **Habitat-Community:** Gravelly alluvium and rocky slopes in scrubs, foothill chaparrals, and pinyon-juniper woodlands **Elevation:** Below 7500 ft. **Ecoregions:** Southern California Mountains, Sierra Nevada

Compact, rounded shrub, usually wider than tall, found throughout the southwestern US and northwest Mexico. Leaves 0.5–1.5 in. long, evergreen, alternate, in clusters along the stem nodes, typically leathery. Flowers in compact or loose heads. Tepals 0.1–0.2 in. long, 6, white to pink, elliptic to spoon-shaped, generally hairy. Fruits <0.1 in. long, hairless achenes. Two of the 4 varieties that occur along the PCT are common: var. *polifolium* (leaves hairy on both sides; mostly flat margins) is found on desert slopes and in mountains at higher elevations; var. *foliolosum* (leaves hairy above; rolled-under margins) occurs on the coastal sides of ranges, at lower elevations. A nectar food plant for butterflies and bees, and an important source of honey in California, commonly seeded/planted along highways/roads.

Eriogonum microthecum

slender buckwheat

POLYGONACEAE BUCKWHEAT FAMILY

PCT Sections: 3–5 & 7–9 & 12–13 **Abundance:** Locally common **Height:** 0.5–4 ft. **Flowering:** July–September **Flower Color:** White (cream), yellow, or pink **Habitat-Community:** Gravelly alluvium, rocky slopes, and scree, from sagebrush scrubs and pinyon-juniper woodlands to subalpine coniferous forests **Elevation:** Below 10,500 ft. **Ecoregions:** Southern California Mountains, Sierra Nevada

Matted or erect shrub or subshrub with hairy or hairless stems. Leaves 0.1–0.5 in. long, 1 per node or clustered, lance-shaped to elliptic, often woolly, with generally rolled-under margins. Flowers in flat-topped clusters with forked branches. Tepals 0.1–0.2 in. long, 6, oblong, hairless, white (cream), yellow, or pink. Fruits <0.1 in. long, tiny, brown, hairless achenes (*Microthecum* is Greek for "small seed"). Several varieties along the PCT, from the matted clumping var. *alpinum* of the high Sierra to var. *simpsonii*, a sprawling shrub of the eastern San Bernardino Mountains. The rare var. *corymbosoides* in the Transverse Ranges has distinctive brown flowers.

Polygonum shastense

Shasta knotweed

POLYGONACEAE BUCKWHEAT FAMILY

PCT Sections: 10–18 **Abundance:** Locally common **Height:** to 1.5 ft. **Flowering:** July–September **Flower Color:** Pink or white **Habitat-Community:** Rocky ridges and slopes in upper montane & subalpine coniferous forests **Elevation:** 6800–11,200 ft. **Ecoregions:** Sierra Nevada, Cascades, Klamath Mountains

Prostrate to ascending, gnarled, wiry subshrub with brown, generally angled stems. Leaves 0.2–1 in. long, deciduous, alternate, thick, oval to lance-shaped, with rolled-under, smooth margins. Flowers 0.2–0.4 in. long, 2–6 per cluster, in leaf axils, bell-shaped, with 8 stamens and 6 petal-like tepals. Tepals fused at base, pink or white, dark midveins, and partially overlapping lobes. Fruits to 0.2 in. long, narrowly ovoid, shiny, brown achenes.

Ceanothus cordulatus

mountain whitethorn

RHAMNACEAE BUCKTHORN FAMILY

PCT Sections: 3–5 & 8–19 **Abundance:** Common **Height:** 2–5 ft. **Flowering:** May–June **Flower Color:** White **Habitat-Community:** Open slopes and rocky places from lower montane to subalpine coniferous forests **Elevation:** Below 9500 ft. **Ecoregions:** Southern California Mountains, Sierra Nevada, Cascades

Flat-topped, thicket-forming shrub with gray-green, thorn-like stems. Leaves to 1.3 in. long, evergreen, alternate, gray-blue, 3-veined, oval, soft-hairy below, with smooth (toothed) margins. Flowers white in dense, head-like clusters. Sepals and petals small and 5-parted. Fruits 0.1–0.2 in. across, 3-ridged (at tip) capsules without horns. As with many *Ceanothus* spp., populations generally increase after fire. Aka snowbush, referring to its growing in places with deep snow accumulations and its snow-like appearance when in full bloom.

Ceanothus integerrimus

deerbrush

RHAMNACEAE BUCKTHORN FAMILY

PCT Sections: 1–8 & 10 & 13–24 **Abundance:** Common **Height:** to 13 ft. **Flowering:** May–June **Flower Color:** White to blue (pink) **Habitat-Community:** Open slopes from woodlands and chaparrals to upper montane coniferous forests **Elevation:** Below 7000 ft. **Ecoregions:** All (except Sonoran/Mojave Basin and Range)

Densely branched shrub with a flat top and flexible stems. Leaves 0.5–2.5 in. long, deciduous, alternate, 3-veined, oval, with generally smooth margins. Flowers white to blue (pink), in dense, head-like clusters. Sepals and petals small and 5-parted. Fruits 0.1–0.3 in. across, sticky, smooth to 3-ridged (at tip) capsules without horns. Seeds are triggered to germinate by fire. For hikers feeling ripe: a fragrant, soapy lather can be made from the flowers.

Ceanothus leucodermis

chaparral whitethorn

RHAMNACEAE BUCKTHORN FAMILY

PCT Sections: 1–8 **Abundance:** Common **Height:** to 15 ft. **Flowering:** April–June **Flower Color:** Blue, lavender, or white **Habitat-Community:** Sandy to gravelly slopes in foothill chaparrals and woodlands **Elevation:** Below 6500 ft. **Ecoregions:** Southern California Mountains, Sierra Nevada

Thorny (twigs becoming sharp-tipped with age) shrub with a waxy, gray-white bark that is somewhat hairy. Leaves 1–1.9 in. long, evergreen, alternate, oval, generally white-wax-coated above, with prominent veins, early-deciduous stipules, and sometimes toothed and glandular margins. Flowers in elongated clusters at stem tips, blue, lavender, or white. Sepals and petals 0.1 in. across, 5-parted. Fruits 0.2 in. across, sticky, 3-ridged (at tip) capsules without horns. *Leucodermis* (from the Latin, "white skin") refers to the distinctive bark.

Ceanothus palmeri

Palmer ceanothus

RHAMNACEAE BUCKTHORN FAMILY

PCT Sections: 1–3 **Abundance:** Locally common **Height:** to 15 ft. **Flowering:** February–June **Flower Color:** White to pale blue or lilac **Habitat-Community:** Dry slopes in woodlands and montane chaparrals **Elevation:** Below 6300 ft. **Ecoregions:** Southern California Mountains

Thick-trunked shrub with green, not-thorn-like branches. Leaves 0.6–1.6 in. long, typically deciduous, alternate, elliptic, thin, hairless, shiny green, with 1 main vein at the base and smooth margins. Flowers in showy, elongated clusters at stem tips, white to pale blue or lilac. Sepals and petals 0.2 in. across, 5-parted. Fruits 0.2–0.4 in. across, sticky, 3-lobed capsules without horns and sometimes ridged (at tip), bulging outwardly. Limited along the PCT to the Peninsular Ranges of Riverside and San Diego counties.

Ceanothus velutinus

tobacco brush

RHAMNACEAE BUCKTHORN FAMILY

PCT Sections: 10–24 **Abundance:** Common **Height:** to 20 ft. **Flowering:** March–July **Flower Color:** White **Habitat-Community:** Open, generally rocky slopes from foothill chaparrals to upper montane coniferous forests **Elevation:** Below 10,000 ft. **Ecoregions:** Sierra Nevada, Cascades, Klamath Mountains

Large, aromatic (walnut, balsam, or cinnamon) shrub sometimes growing in dense thickets, especially dominant after fire. Leaves to 3 in. long, evergreen, alternate, 3-veined, broadly elliptic, sticky above and velvety below, with toothed margins. Flowers in open clusters, white. Sepals and petals small, 5-parted. Fruits 0.1–0.2 in. across, sticky, smooth to 3-ridged (at tip) capsules without horns. Long-lived (200+ years) seeds are triggered to germinate by fire. On a hot day, the leaves emit an odor that can be overwhelming; they make a good tea and have historically been used for tobacco.

Frangula californica

California coffeeberry

RHAMNACEAE BUCKTHORN FAMILY

PCT Sections: 1–9 & 14–24 **Abundance:** Common **Height:** 5–17 ft. **Flowering:** May–August **Flower Color:** Greenish **Habitat-Community:** Sandy or rocky slopes, including serpentine and carbonate soils, from woodlands and foothill chaparrals to upper montane coniferous forests **Elevation:** Below 7500 ft. **Ecoregions:** All (except Sonoran/ Mojave Basin and Range)

Erect, hardy shrub with flexible stems. Leaves 1–3 in. long, evergreen, alternate, elliptic, with toothed margins. Flowers in rounded clusters, greenish, stalked. Sepals and petals small, 5-parted, petal length < sepals. Fruits 0.5 in. across, black to red, berry-like stone fruits with 2–3 stones (seeds). The dry-roasted seeds are an excellent coffee substitute. Sprouts after fire. The edible fruits are a known laxative, so some restraint is advised unless you are looking for that kind of help!

Rhamnus ilicifolia

hollyleaf redberry

RHAMNACEAE BUCKTHORN FAMILY

PCT Sections: 1–10 & 23–24 **Abundance:** Locally common **Height:** to 12 ft. **Flowering:** March–June **Flower Color:** Yellow **Habitat-Community:** Dry slopes from scrubs to lower montane coniferous forests **Elevation:** Below 6900 ft. **Ecoregions:** Southern California Mountains, Sierra Nevada, Klamath Mountains

Shrub with stiff, ascending branches, hairless to finely hairy twigs, and gray bark; generally dioecious. Leaves 0.9–1.8 in. long, evergreen, alternate, deep green, somewhat concave, ovoid to round, thick, hairless above and hairy below, with sharp-toothed margins. Flowers 1–6 in clusters along branches in twig axils. Sepals 0.1 in. long, inconspicuous, yellow, 4-parted; 0 petals. Fruits 0.2–0.3 in. across, 2-stoned, red (when mature), berry-like stone fruits. *Ilicifolia* (from the Latin *ilici*, "holly," *folia*, "leaves") describes the foliage.

Ziziphus parryi

Parry's jujube

RHAMNACEAE BUCKTHORN FAMILY

PCT Sections: 1–4 **Abundance:** Occasional **Height:** 5–15 ft. **Flowering:** February–April **Flower Color:** Pale green to white **Habitat-Community:** Slopes and valleys, often among boulders, in foothill chaparrals and woodlands **Elevation:** Below 4100 ft. **Ecoregions:** Southern California Mountains, Sonoran Basin and Range

Conspicuous shrub with smooth bark and brown to gray twigs that form impressive thorns 0.8–1.3 in. long. Leaves 0.5–1.1 in. long, deciduous, alternate, clustered on short shoots, spoon-shaped, hairless, olive-green, with smooth margins. Flowers in small groups of 2–4, 5-parted, with hypanthium 0.1 in. across, yellow-green sepals, and white petals (often absent at maturity). Fruits 0.4–1 in. long, berry-like 1-seeded drupes, elliptic, beaked, drying orange- or red-brown. The sweetly aromatic fruits are edible but can be bitter; the Cahuilla eat them fresh or dry and grind them into flour. Spot this along the PCT at the lower desert crossings in San Diego and Riverside counties.

Adenostoma fasciculatum

chamise

ROSACEAE ROSE FAMILY

PCT Sections: 1–6 **Abundance:** Common **Height:** to 10 ft. **Flowering:** April–June **Flower Color:** Cream to white **Habitat-Community:** Dry slopes and flats in foothill chaparrals and woodlands **Elevation:** Below 6000 ft. **Ecoregions:** Southern California/Northern Baja Coast, Southern California Mountains

Erect, much-branched shrub and a dominant member of California chaparral. Leaves 0.2–0.4 in. long, evergreen, alternate, stiff, sickle-shaped, borne on the stems in fascicles (hence the specific epithet). Flowers 0.2–0.3 in. across, in dense clusters at stem tips, with 5-lobed calyces, 5 cream to white petals, and 15 (5 groups of 3) stamens. Fruits achene-like with 1–5 stones (seeds). Chamise has a close adaptive relationship with fire. Its basal burl sprouts after burning, and its resinous wood is easily ignited; in fact, *chama* (Portuguese for "flame") is the basis for its common name.

Adenostoma sparsifolium

red shank

ROSACEAE ROSE FAMILY

PCT Sections: 1–3 **Abundance:** Locally common **Height:** to 18 ft. **Flowering:** July–September **Flower Color:** Cream to white **Habitat-Community:** Dry slopes and flats in foothill chaparrals and woodlands **Elevation:** Below 6400 ft. **Ecoregions:** Southern California/Northern Baja Coast, Southern California Mountains

Tree-like shrub with notably shredding, red-brown bark. Leaves 0.2–1 in. long, evergreen, alternate, linear, glandular, and (as the specific epithet suggests) sparse on the stems, not clustered as they are on *A. fasciculatum*. Flowers 0.2–0.3 in. across, in open clusters at stem tips, with 5-lobed calyces, 5 cream to white petals, and 10 (5 groups of 2) stamens. Fruits achene-like with 1 stone (seed). Sprouts vigorously after fire from its root crown, which may extend 6 ft. underground. Exceptional stands are encountered along the PCT from Mile 1 in San Diego County northward to the San Jacinto Mountains. Aka ribbonwood for its peeling bark.

western serviceberry

Amelanchier alnifolia

ROSACEAE ROSE FAMILY

PCT Sections: 4 & 10–24 **Abundance:** Common **Height:** 3–25 ft. **Flowering:** June–July **Flower Color:** White **Habitat-Community:** Moist sites from scrubs and chaparrals to upper montane coniferous forests **Elevation:** Below 8800 ft. **Ecoregions:** Southern California Mountains, Sierra Nevada, Cascades, Klamath Mountains

Shrub to small tree with hairless twigs. Leaves 0.7–1.5 in. long, deciduous, alternate, with margins toothed on upper half. Flowers clustered at branch tips, each with 4–5 styles. Petals 0.3–0.6 in. long, white, 5-parted, generally twisted. Fruits 0.2–0.5 in. across, fleshy, reddish to dark purple berries. Caution: the seeds are toxic when fresh. Fruits are dried or used fresh for jams, jellies, wine, and pies. Common name is based on a Scottish serviceberry species, whose early flowers mark the beginning of thaw, when burial services are able to resume for the year. Aka Saskatoon berry.

pale-leaved serviceberry

Amelanchier utahensis

ROSACEAE ROSE FAMILY

PCT Sections: All **Abundance:** Common **Height:** to 20 ft. **Flowering:** April–June **Flower Color:** White **Habitat-Community:** Rocky habitats from scrubs and chaparrals to upper coniferous forests **Elevation:** Below 11,100 ft. **Ecoregions:** Southern California Mountains, Sierra Nevada, Cascades, Klamath Mountains

Shrub to small tree with generally hairy stems. Leaves 0.5–1 in. long, deciduous, alternate, with margins toothed on upper half. Flowers clustered at branch tips, each with 2–4(5) styles. Petals 0.2–0.4 in. long, white, 5-parted, generally twisted. Fruits 0.2–0.4 in. across, reddish to dark purple berries. Caution: the seeds are toxic, especially when fresh. Fruits are dried or used fresh for jams, jellies, wine, and pies.

birchleaf mountain mahogany

Cercocarpus betuloides

ROSACEAE ROSE FAMILY

PCT Sections: 1–9 & 18–19 & 23–24 **Abundance:** Occasional **Height:** 3–23 ft. **Flowering:** March–June **Flower Color:** Greenish **Habitat-Community:** Rocky, shrubby slopes or open forests from foothill chaparrals to upper montane coniferous forests **Elevation:** Below 8200 ft. **Ecoregions:** All

Shrub to small tree with smooth gray to brown bark. Leaves 0.5–1 in. long, evergreen, alternate, birch-like, with toothed margins. Flowers small, aromatic, bell-shaped, greenish, scattered along stems generally in clusters of 2–3; 0 petals. Fruits 1–4 in. long, achenes with long, feathery tails, giving fruiting specimens a fuzzy appearance. Achene tails attach to foraging wildlife fur as a dispersal mechanism. Long-lived, like all mahogany species.

Cercocarpus ledifolius

mountain mahogany

ROSACEAE ROSE FAMILY

PCT Sections: 4–24 **Abundance:** Occasional **Height:** 3–33 ft. **Flowering:** March–June **Flower Color:** Greenish **Habitat-Community:** Rocky, shrubby slopes or open forests from sagebrush scrubs to subalpine coniferous forests **Elevation:** Below 10,500 ft. **Ecoregions:** Southern California Mountains, Sierra Nevada, Cascades, Klamath Mountains

Shrub to small, twisted tree with furrowed, reddish or gray bark. Leaves 0.5–1 in. long, evergreen, alternate, leathery, elliptic, with smooth margins. Flowers small, bell-shaped, greenish, scattered along stems generally in clusters of 1–3; 0 petals. Fruits 2–3 in. long, achenes with long, feathery tails. The extremely hard wood of mahogany species was historically used for arrow shafts, spears, and digging sticks.

Heteromeles arbutifolia

toyon

ROSACEAE ROSE FAMILY

PCT Sections: 1–6 **Abundance:** Common **Height:** to 25 ft. **Flowering:** May–August **Flower Color:** White **Habitat-Community:** Canyons and dry slopes in oak woodlands, foothill chaparrals, and lower montane coniferous forests **Elevation:** Below 4800 ft. **Ecoregions:** Southern California/Northern Baja Coast, Southern California Mountains

Large shrub or small tree with showy berries that mature in the fall and persist well into winter. Leaves 2–4 in. long, evergreen, alternate, leathery, glossy green, elliptic, with sharp-toothed margins. Flowers 0.2–0.4 in. across, in flat-topped terminal clusters; 5 minute sepals, 5 white petals, and 10 stamens. Fruits 0.2–0.4 in. across, bright red (yellow) elliptic berries. Extends along the Pacific Coast from Baja California to British Columbia. The official native plant of the City of Los Angeles: it's rumored that Hollywood got its name due to toyon's resemblance to holly. With the added help of a sweetener, the berries can be eaten raw, steamed, toasted, or boiled, or made into a cider.

Holodiscus discolor

oceanspray

ROSACEAE ROSE FAMILY

PCT Sections: All **Abundance:** Common **Height:** to 20 ft. **Flowering:** May–September **Flower Color:** White to cream **Habitat-Community:** Open, rocky slopes or moist places from oak woodlands to alpine communities **Elevation:** Below 13,000 ft. **Ecoregions:** All

Shrub with generally hairy, shredding (when mature) stems and red-gray bark. Leaves 0.5–3 in. long, deciduous, alternate, oval to wedge-shaped, prominently veined, lobed, with toothed margins. Flowers small, in many-branched, arching clusters reminiscent of spray from waves smashing into a rocky shoreline. Petals 0.1 in. long, white, 5-parted, length slightly > sepals. Fruits 0.1 in. long, light brown, hairy achenes. The wood is very strong, used for making bows, arrow shafts, and wooden pegs for construction before the advent of nails. The high-elevation var. *microphyllus* has smaller leaves (blade <1.5 in. long) and is found on open, rocky alpine slopes. Aka ironwood.

Prunus andersonii

desert peach

ROSACEAE ROSE FAMILY

PCT Sections: 8–9 **Abundance:** Occasional **Height:** 2–6 ft. **Flowering:** March–May **Flower Color:** Pink to whitish **Habitat-Community:** Dry, rocky slopes in Joshua tree & pinyon-juniper woodlands **Elevation:** Below 7200 ft. **Ecoregions:** Sierra Nevada

Tangled shrub with sharp, spiny branches and showy pink flowers. Leaves 1–1.4 in. long, deciduous, alternate, clustered in bright green fascicles, lance-shaped, with toothed margins. Flowers 1–2 per cluster, densely spread across stems, with 5 deep pink to rose (sometimes white) petals, 0.3–0.6 in. long, and many whisker-like stamens. Fruits 0.4–0.8 in. long, ovoid, fuzzy, berry-like drupes becoming red-orange and splitting with age, revealing heart-shaped stone. Can sprout vegetatively from rhizomes, forming large clonal masses covering several acres. Best observed along the PCT in the southern Sierra, from the Piute Range to Kennedy Meadows.

Prunus emarginata

bitter cherry

ROSACEAE ROSE FAMILY

PCT Sections: All **Abundance:** Common **Height:** 3–30 ft. **Flowering:** April–July **Flower Color:** White **Habitat-Community:** Streambanks, open forests, and rocky slopes from chaparrals to upper montane coniferous forests and wetland-riparian communities **Elevation:** Below 9200 ft. **Ecoregions:** All

Shrub or small tree, often forming thickets. Bark smooth, reddish to gray, covered with lenticels. Leaves 0.5–3 in. long, deciduous, alternate, clustered, oval, with 1–2 glands (at leaf base), fine-toothed margins, and wedge-shaped base. Flowers 0.1–0.3 in. long, 3–12 per cluster, white, 5-parted, saucer-shaped, with many stamens and 1 pistil. Fruits 0.3–0.5 in. across, red to dark purple, hairless berry-like drupes (stone fruits). Not edible—the common name says it all! Early mountaineers made a medicinal tonic by soaking the cherries in brandy or whiskey. The fruits are popular with birds even before they ripen.

Prunus fasciculata

desert almond

ROSACEAE ROSE FAMILY

PCT Sections: 1–8 **Abundance:** Occasional **Height:** 2–8 ft. **Flowering:** March–May **Flower Color:** White to pale yellow **Habitat-Community:** Dry washes and canyons in creosote bush scrubs and woodlands **Elevation:** Below 6100 ft. **Ecoregions:** Southern California Mountains, Sonoran/Mojave Basin and Range, Sierra Nevada

Intricately branched, rounded shrub with somewhat thorny branches; dioecious. Leaves 0.2–0.9 in. long, deciduous, alternate, clustered, linear to spoon-shaped, sparsely soft-hairy. Flowers 1–2 per cluster, along branches among the leaves, with 5 hairless sepals and 5 white petals 0.1–0.2 in. long. Male flowers have 10–15 stamens; female flowers have 1 pistil. Fruits 0.4 in. long, a pale-brown-hairy, thin-fleshed, ovoid, berry-like drupe; the almond-like seed contains cyanide and is not edible. Occurs along the PCT at lower desert crossings and in washes on the arid sides of mountain ranges. In early spring, plants are often adorned with the webby nests of tent caterpillars (*Malacosoma*).

Prunus fremontii

desert apricot

ROSACEAE ROSE FAMILY

PCT Sections: 1–2 **Abundance:** Occasional **Height:** 3–12 ft. **Flowering:** January–March **Flower Color:** White to light pink **Habitat-Community:** Dry, rocky slopes in scrubs and pinyon-juniper woodlands **Elevation:** Below 4800 ft. **Ecoregions:** Sonoran Basin and Range

Thorny shrub limited along the PCT to the desert flanks of the Peninsular Ranges of southern California. Leaves 0.3–1.2 in. long, deciduous, alternate, glossy green, ovoid to round, with toothed margins. Flowers 1–3 per cluster, scattered among the leaves, with 5 gland-toothed sepals and 5 spoon-shaped petals, white to pinkish, 0.1–0.4 in. long. Fruits 0.3–0.7 in. across, fuzzy, apricot-like drupes becoming yellow and splitting open in age to reveal the stone. The fruits contain cyanide but with processing were an important food for the Cahuilla.

Prunus ilicifolia

hollyleaf cherry

ROSACEAE ROSE FAMILY

PCT Sections: 1–6 **Abundance:** Common **Height:** 4–25 ft. **Flowering:** April–May **Flower Color:** White to pale yellow **Habitat-Community:** Dry canyons and slopes in foothill chaparrals and woodlands **Elevation:** Below 6100 ft. **Ecoregions:** Southern California Mountains

Long-lived, drought-tolerant shrub to tree with stiff, woody branches. Leaves 1.1–2.2 in. long, evergreen, alternate, thick, shiny green, widely spoon-shaped, with toothed margins. Flowers ≥15 per cluster at stem tips with 5 white to yellowish petals 0.1 in. long. Fruits 0.5–1.1 in. long, ovoid, red to purple-black berry-like drupes with a fleshy pulp containing a single stone. Abundant along the California coast but ranges as far east as Joshua Tree National Park. *Prunus* means "plum" in Greek.

Prunus virginiana var. demissa

western chokecherry

ROSACEAE ROSE FAMILY

PCT Sections: 1–7 & 13–24 **Abundance:** Common **Height:** 3–50 ft. **Flowering:** March–June **Flower Color:** White **Habitat-Community:** Streambanks, moist slopes, and open forests from oak woodlands to upper montane coniferous forests and wetland-riparian communities **Elevation:** Below 9500 ft. **Ecoregions:** All

Shrub or small tree often forming thickets. Bark smooth, reddish to gray-brown, covered with lenticels. Leaves 2.5–3.5 in. long, deciduous, alternate, broadly oval, point-tipped, with 2 glands (on petiole at leaf base) and fine-toothed margins. Flowers to 0.3 in. long, ≥12 per cluster, white, 5-parted, saucer-shaped, with many stamens and 1 pistil. Fruits to 0.5 in. across, hairless, red to black berry-like drupes (stone fruits). Although the cherries are edible, they can induce a choking sensation—common names can be important! When made into jam, the cherries are often mixed with apples as a way to remove the astringency. The stems are popular browse for wildlife, and birds cherish the fruits.

Purshia tridentata var. *glandulosa*

desert bitterbrush

ROSACEAE ROSE FAMILY

PCT Sections: 1–9 **Abundance:** Common **Height:** 3–8 ft. **Flowering:** March–May **Flower Color:** White to pale yellow **Habitat-Community:** Dry, rocky slopes in foothill chaparrals and woodlands **Elevation:** Below 8900 ft. **Ecoregions:** Southern California/Northern Baja Coast, Southern California Mountains, Sierra Nevada

Spreading to erect, many-branched shrub with generally glandular-hairy stems and strongly aromatic flowers. Leaves 0.5–1 in. long, mostly deciduous, alternate, wedge-shaped, 3-lobed, sparsely hairy above, with rolled-under margins. Flowers to 0.3 in. long, solitary, white to pale yellow, 5-parted, with many stamens and 1–2 pistils. Fruits 0.5 in. long, spindle-shaped, red-brown, hairy achenes. The nitrogen-rich foliage and bitter-tasting fruits of this and var. *tridentata* are a valuable food source for critters and birds. Often used for restoration projects; plants sprout after low to moderately intense fires.

Purshia tridentata var. *tridentata*

antelope bitterbrush

ROSACEAE ROSE FAMILY

PCT Sections: 1–10 & 13–22 **Abundance:** Common **Height:** 3–8 ft. **Flowering:** February–July **Flower Color:** White to pale yellow **Habitat-Community:** Dry, rocky slopes from scrubs and chaparrals to subalpine coniferous forests **Elevation:** Below 8000 ft. **Ecoregions:** All (except Sonoran/Mojave Basin and Range)

Spreading to erect, many-branched shrub with nonglandular-hairy stems and strongly aromatic flowers. Leaves 0.5–1 in. long, mostly deciduous, alternate, wedge-shaped, 3-lobed, hairy, with rolled-under margins. Flowers to 0.3 in. long, solitary, white to pale yellow, 5-parted, with many stamens and 1–2 pistils. Fruits 0.5 in. long, spindle-shaped, red-brown, hairy achenes. Often stunted on exposed slopes, at higher elevations, but the distinctive sagebrush-like leaves remain a good identification characteristic.

Rubus parviflorus

western thimbleberry

ROSACEAE ROSE FAMILY

PCT Sections: 1–5 & 10–24 **Abundance:** Common **Height:** to 6 ft. **Flowering:** March–August **Flower Color:** White to pinkish **Community/Habitat:** Moist forest openings and understories from woodlands to upper montane coniferous forests **Elevation:** Below 9000 ft. **Ecoregions:** All (except Sonoran/Mojave Basin and Range)

Erect, rhizomatous, sometimes thicket-forming shrub with gray, shredding bark. Leaves 2–6 in. long, deciduous, alternate, maple-like, 3-7-lobed, hairy, with toothed margins. Flowers 0.5–1 in. long, 4–7 in clusters, white to pinkish, 5-parted, saucer-shaped, with many stamens and >30 pistils. Fruits to 0.5 in. across, red, finely hairy, thimble-like berries. Fruits are not bad fresh but are more often dried and eaten with other berries. *Parviflorus* (from the Latin, "small-flowered") is not very apt.

Spiraea splendens

rose meadowsweet

ROSACEAE ROSE FAMILY

PCT Sections: 10–24 **Abundance:** Common **Height:** to 3 ft. **Flowering:** June–September **Flower Color:** Pink **Community/Habitat:** Streambanks, lakeshores, meadows, and moist, rocky slopes, including serpentine, from lower montane coniferous forests to alpine and wetland-riparian communities **Elevation:** Below 11,200 ft. **Ecoregions:** Sierra Nevada, Cascades, Klamath Mountains

Erect rhizomatous shrub with hairy or hairless brown stems. Leaves 0.5–3 in. long, deciduous, alternate, thin, ovoid, hairy or hairless, round-tipped, with fine-toothed margins above midleaf. Flowers to 0.1 in. long, flat-topped clusters, pink, 5-parted, with >15 stamens and 5 pistils. Fruits to 0.1 in. long, pod-like follicles that can persist long after leaves have dropped in the fall. The wood has been used to make various tools, including hooks for drying food.

Thamnosma montana

turpentine-broom

RUTACEAE RUE FAMILY

PCT Sections: 1–4 **Abundance:** Uncommon **Height:** 1–3 ft. **Flowering:** February–May **Flower Color:** Purple **Habitat-Community:** Dry slopes and valleys in creosote & black bush scrubs and Joshua tree woodlands **Elevation:** Below 5100 ft. **Ecoregions:** Sonoran/Mojave Basin and Range

Desert shrub or subshrub with straight, broom-like, yellow-green stems speckled with orange resin glands. Leaves 0.2–0.7 in. long, summer-deciduous, alternate, spoon-shaped, with smooth margins, usually appearing only after significant rains. Flowers scattered along stems, with 4 minute green sepals and 4 gland-dotted royal purple petals, fused at the base, forming a tube 0.3–0.5 in. long; petal tips curve outward. Fruits leathery, gland-dotted capsules with 2 nearly separate rounded lobes, resembling miniature tangerines; indeed, when scrunched and sniffed, they smell like citrus. The exclusive food plant for black swallowtails (*Papilio polyxenes coloro*). Occurs along the low-elevation desert portions of the PCT.

Populus fremontii

Fremont's cottonwood

SALICACEAE WILLOW FAMILY

PCT Sections: 1–9 **Abundance:** Locally common **Height:** 10–90 ft. **Flowering:** March–April **Flower Color:** Cream to yellow-green **Habitat-Community:** Moist or wet soils in canyons, valleys, and streambanks in wetland-riparian communities **Elevation:** Below 6300 ft. **Ecoregions:** Southern California Mountains, Sierra Nevada

Large tree with wide crown and trunk up to 11 ft. in diameter; dioecious. Bark smooth when young, becoming gray and deeply fissured with whitish cracks. Leaves 1.3–2.8 in. long, deciduous, alternate, bright green turning yellow-orange each October–November, triangular to heart-shaped, with coarsely scalloped margins. Flowers in yellow-green, pendent catkins 1–4 in. long, with 8–60 stamens and 2–3 large, 2-lobed stigmas per flower. Fruits 0.1–0.5 in. across, spherical, densely spaced (along the drooping catkin) capsules. Cottonwoods are named for their seeds, which have a tuft of cotton-like hair to aid in their wind dispersal.

Populus tremuloides

quaking aspen

SALICACEAE WILLOW FAMILY

PCT Sections: 4–5 & 9–23 **Abundance:** Locally common **Height:** 20–80 ft. **Flowering:** April–June **Habitat-Community:** Streambanks, moist, open slopes, and meadows in wetland-riparian communities **Elevation:** Below 10,000 ft.
Ecoregions: Southern California Mountains, Sierra Nevada, Cascades, Klamath Mountains

Single-stemmed tree with long, clear trunk, rounded crown, and smooth, green-white bark becoming furrowed with age; dioecious. Leaves 1–3 in. long, deciduous, alternate, round to ovoid, hairless, point-tipped, green above and pale green with white coating below, with wavy margins and flat petioles. Flowers in catkins 1.5–4 in. long, blooming before leaves emerge, 6–14 stamens per flower, hairless ovary, hairy catkin scales. Fruits 0.1–0.5 in. long, hairless capsules with silk-haired seeds. Very well known for its spectacular fall foliage display. Individual trees may live 100–200 years, but they mostly reproduce from an extensive root system connecting clones. Clonal groves are estimated to be thousands of years old. The leaves quiver and quake when wind hits the flat petioles (hence the common name). The wood has been used for boards, furniture, and to make pulp. Important habitat and forage plant for deer, elk, and beaver.

Populus trichocarpa

black cottonwood

SALICACEAE WILLOW FAMILY

PCT Sections: 3–5 & 8–24 **Abundance:** Locally common **Height:** to 160 ft. **Flowering:** February–April **Habitat-Community:** Streambanks in wetland-riparian communities **Elevation:** Below 10,000 ft. **Ecoregions:** Southern California Mountains, Sierra Nevada, Cascades, Klamath Mountains

Single-stemmed tree with spreading crown and furrowed gray-brown bark; dioecious. Leaves 3–6 in. long, deciduous, alternate, ovoid (or narrower), hairless, point-tipped, green above and pale green with white coating below, with wavy margins and round (in cross section) petioles. Flowers in catkins 3–4 in. long, blooming before leaves emerge, 30–50 stamens per flower, 2–4 stigmas, hairy ovary, hairy catkin scales that drop off early. Fruits 0.1–0.5 in. long, hairless capsules with silk-haired seeds. Sprouts after fire or flood damage. The wood has been used for boards and to make pulp. Historic uses include medicines, shampoo from the ash, basketry, glue, and paint. Sweetly aromatic in the spring when the leaves first appear and the buds are covered in sticky resin.

Salix eastwoodiae

mountain willow

SALICACEAE WILLOW FAMILY

PCT Sections: 10–24 **Abundance:** Common **Height:** 2–13 ft. **Flowering:** May–July **Habitat-Community:** Streambanks, meadows, and moist slopes from lower montane coniferous forests to alpine and wetland-riparian communities **Elevation:** Below 12,500 ft. **Ecoregions:** Sierra Nevada, Cascades, Klamath Mountains

Shrub with yellowish or red to purple-brown stems and solitary (margins generally fused) bud scales; dioecious. Leaves 1–4 in. long, deciduous, alternate, elliptic, densely hairy, no white coating on surfaces, generally point-tipped, with toothed or smooth margins. Flowers in catkins 0.5–2 in. long, blooming as leaves emerge, 2 stamens per flower, hairy ovary, hairy brown or black catkin scales. Fruits hairy capsules of seeds with basal tuft of hairs. Willow stems and wood have many historic and current uses. The active ingredient in aspirin, salicylic acid, was originally synthesized from willow sap.

Salix exigua

narrowleaf willow

SALICACEAE WILLOW FAMILY

PCT Sections: All (except 11–12) **Abundance:** Locally common **Height:** 5–20 ft. **Flowering:** March–June **Flower Color:** Green to yellow **Habitat-Community:** Springs, canyon seeps, streambanks, and lakeshores in wetland-riparian communities **Elevation:** Below 8200 ft. **Ecoregions:** All

Streamside shrub or small, multi-branched tree growing in clonal thickets; dioecious. Stems generally flexible, twigs yellow to brown. Leaves 1.5–6 in. long, deciduous, alternate, linear, fine-silky hairy, with short petioles and smooth to slender-toothed margins. Flowers in catkins 1–3 in. long, blooming as or after leaves emerge, 2 stamens per flower, hairless ovary, hairy catkin scales. Fruits 0.1–0.3 in. long, 2-valved capsules of seeds with basal tuft of hairs. Ranges from Alaska to Mexico. Two common varieties along the CA PCT hybridize prolifically: var. *hindsiana* (appressed hairs) dominates the coastal side of ranges; var. *exigua* (spreading hairs) occurs in the desert-side regions.

Salix gooddingii

Goodding's black willow

SALICACEAE WILLOW FAMILY

PCT Sections: 1–9 **Abundance:** Locally common **Height:** to 90 ft. **Flowering:** March–April **Flower Color:** Yellow to green **Habitat-Community:** Washes, moist valleys, streambanks, and lakeshores in wetland-riparian communities **Elevation:** Below 6500 ft. **Ecoregions:** Southern California Mountains, Sierra Nevada

Riparian tree with a broad, rounded crown, trunk to 30 in. across, bark thick, furrowed, dark, shredding (with age); dioecious. Dark brown branches and slender, velvety red-brown to yellowish green twigs. Leaves 2.8–5.7 in. long, deciduous, alternate, stipules leaf-like, linear to narrowly elliptic, satiny green on both surfaces, with toothed margins; yellow fall color. Flowers in drooping catkins 1.5–3.2 in. long, blooming as leaves emerge, 4–6 stamens per flower, hairy or hairless ovary, and hairy, tan catkin scales. Fruits hairy or hairless capsules with silky, white-hairy seeds.

Salix laevigata

red willow

SALICACEAE WILLOW FAMILY

PCT Sections: 1–9 & 16–19 **Abundance:** Locally common **Height:** to 60 ft. **Flowering:** December–June **Flower Color:** Yellow to green **Habitat-Community:** Seeps, canyons, streambanks, and brackish waters in wetland-riparian communities **Elevation:** Below 6400 ft. **Ecoregions:** Southern California Mountains, Sierra Nevada, Cascades

Attractive tree with a broad, rounded crown and usually branching-at-base trunk to 25 in. across; dioecious. Bark dark and furrowed with age. Twigs tan to red-brown, brittle, hairy becoming hairless, with free bud scale margins. Leaves 2.4–7.8 in. long, deciduous, alternate, lance-shaped, glossy green above, white wax-coated and hairy below, with leaf-like stipules, scalloped margins, and petioles with glands (dark bumps). Flowers in drooping catkins 1.6–4 in. long, blooming after leaves fully formed, 5 stamens per flower, hairless ovary, and hairy, tan catkin scales. Fruits 2-valved capsules with silky, white-hairy seeds. *Laevigata* (from the Latin, "smooth") refers to the leaves. Hybridizes with *S. gooddingii*.

Salix lasiandra

Pacific willow

SALICACEAE WILLOW FAMILY

PCT Sections: All **Abundance:** Locally common **Height:** 3–40 ft. **Flowering:** March–April **Habitat-Community:** Streambanks, lakeshores, seeps, and wet meadows in wetland-riparian communities **Elevation:** Below 9000 ft. **Ecoregions:** All

Shrub with brownish stems and solitary (margins fused) bud scales; dioecious. Leaves 2–7 in. long, deciduous, alternate, lance-shaped, hairy or hairless, white-coated below, generally long and curved toward the pointed tip, with toothed margins. Petioles generally with conspicuous glands. Flowers in catkins 1–4 in. long, blooming as leaves emerge, 3–6 stamens per flower, hairless ovary, and hairy, yellowish catkin scales. Fruits 0.2–0.4 in. long, hairless capsules of seeds with basal tuft of hairs. Willows are a common component of wetland and stream restoration projects.

Salix lasiolepis

arroyo willow

SALICACEAE WILLOW FAMILY

PCT Sections: 1–19 & 23 **Abundance:** Common **Height:** 5–40 ft. **Flowering:** January–June **Habitat-Community:** Streambanks, lakeshores, seeps, and wet meadows in wetland-riparian communities **Elevation:** Below 8900 ft. **Ecoregions:** All

Shrub or small tree with yellowish to red-brown stems and solitary (margins fused) bud scales; dioecious. Leaves 2–5 in. long, deciduous, alternate, lance-shaped, hairy or hairless, white-coated below, point- or round-tipped, with toothed or smooth margins. Flowers in catkins 1–3.5 in. long, blooming before leaves emerge, 2 stamens per flower, hairless ovary, and hairy, blackish catkin scales. Fruits 0.1–0.2 in. long, hairless capsules of seeds with basal tuft of hairs. Occurs from coastal sand dunes through the mountains and into deserts.

Salix lutea

yellow willow

SALICACEAE WILLOW FAMILY

PCT Sections: 3–5 & 8–10 **Abundance:** Locally common **Height:** to 16 ft. **Flowering:** March–May **Flower Color:** Yellow to green **Habitat-Community:** Streambanks and meadows in wetland-riparian communities **Elevation:** Below 9600 ft. **Ecoregions:** Southern California Mountains, Sierra Nevada

Erect shrub often forming clonal thickets along creeks; dioecious. Yellowish, hairy or hairless, smooth stems sometimes white-coated with sparkling wax crystals. Young twigs red-brown or brownish. Leaves 1.7–3.8 in. long, deciduous, alternate, elliptic to lance-shaped, glossy or dull above, hairy or hairless below, somewhat white-waxy, with leaf-like stipules and smooth to fine-toothed or gland-studded margins. Flowers in catkins 1–2 in. long, blooming before or with leaves, 2 stamens per flower, hairless ovary, and sparsely hairy, brown to tan catkin scales. Fruits hairless capsules with silky, white-hairy seeds. As with most willows, reproduces both vegetatively (from stem pieces) and sexually by wind dispersal. Most common along the PCT at creek crossings in the San Bernardino Mountains. *Lutea* ("yellow") refers to the branches.

Salix orestera

gray-leafed Sierra willow

SALICACEAE WILLOW FAMILY

PCT Sections: 10–16 **Abundance:** Locally common **Height:** to 6 ft. **Flowering:** April–July **Habitat-Community:** Streambanks and meadows in wetland-riparian communities **Elevation:** Below 13,100 ft. **Ecoregions:** Sierra Nevada

Shrub with yellow- to red-brown stems and solitary (margins fused) bud scales; dioecious. Leaves 1–4 in. long, deciduous, alternate, narrowly elliptic, densely hairy, white coating below, point- or round-tipped, with generally smooth margins. Flowers in catkins 0.8–2.2 in. long, blooming as leaves emerge, 2 stamens per flower, long-silky ovary, and hairy, dark brown catkin scales. Fruits hairy capsules of seeds with basal tuft of hairs.

Salix petrophila

Arctic willow

SALICACEAE WILLOW FAMILY

PCT Sections: 10–13 **Abundance:** Locally common **Height:** 1–4 in. **Flowering:** July–August **Habitat-Community:** Rocky slopes and meadows in subalpine coniferous forests and alpine communities **Elevation:** 5500–13,100 ft. **Ecoregions:** Sierra Nevada

Low-growing, trailing shrub with yellow-green to yellow-brown, hairy stems and solitary (margins fused) bud scales; dioecious. Leaves 0.7–1.7 in. long, deciduous, alternate, oval or lance-shaped to ovoid, hairy, white coating below or absent, point- or round-tipped, with smooth margins. Flowers in catkins 1–3 in. long, blooming as leaves emerge, 2 stamens per flower, hairy ovary, and hairy, tan or brown catkin scales. Fruits hairy capsules of seeds with basal tuft of hairs. This cute little willow forms carpets in the alpine zone.

Salix scouleriana

Scouler's willow

SALICACEAE WILLOW FAMILY

PCT Sections: 3–5 & 8–24 **Abundance:** Common **Height:** 3–40 ft. **Flowering:** February–June **Habitat-Community:** Lakeshores, streambanks, open slopes, and disturbed places from oak woodlands to subalpine coniferous forests and wetland-riparian communities **Elevation:** Below 10,000 ft. **Ecoregions:** Southern California Mountains, Sierra Nevada, Cascades, Klamath Mountains

Multi-stemmed shrub or small tree with yellowish to brown stems and solitary (margins fused) bud scales; dioecious. Leaves 1–4 in. long, deciduous, alternate, oval or lance- to spoon-shaped, hairy or hairless, point- or round-tipped, with rolled-under, toothed, or smooth margins. Flowers in catkins 1–2.5 in. long, blooming before leaves emerge, 2 stamens per flower, hairy ovary, and hairy, brown or blackish catkin scales. Fruits hairy capsules of seeds with basal tuft of hairs. Often found along roads and on dry slopes away from obvious sources of water.

Lycium andersonii

Anderson boxthorn

SOLANACEAE NIGHTSHADE FAMILY

PCT Sections: 1–8 **Abundance:** Occasional **Height:** to 7 ft. **Flowering:** March–May **Flower Color:** White to violet **Habitat-Community:** Gravelly slopes and sandy, silty flats in creosote bush scrubs and Joshua tree woodlands **Elevation:** Below 4700 ft. **Ecoregions:** Southern California Mountains, Sonoran/Mojave Basin and Range, Sierra Nevada

Densely branched shrub covered in thin spines up to 1 in. long. Leaves 0.4–0.9 in. long, drought-deciduous, alternate or clustered along stems, linear to spoon-shaped, rounded in cross section, and succulent. Flowers solitary in the forks of branches, short, hairless calyces, funnel-shaped, white to violet corollas 0.3–0.6 in. long with a white to yellowish tube, and petals fused to near tips with 4–5 spreading lobes. Fruits 0.1–0.2 in. across, round, bright red or orange berries. Found at lower desert crossings of the PCT, primarily in Riverside and San Diego counties. The berries can be eaten fresh (only when ripe) or dried. They are also enjoyed by birds and mammals.

Lycium cooperi

Cooper boxthorn

SOLANACEAE NIGHTSHADE FAMILY

PCT Sections: 1–2 & 4–8 **Abundance:** Occasional **Height:** to 9 ft. **Flowering:** March–May **Flower Color:** Green-white and violet **Habitat-Community:** Gravelly slopes and sandy flats/washes in creosote & black bush scrubs and Joshua tree woodlands **Elevation:** Below 5400 ft. **Ecoregions:** Southern California Mountains, Sonoran/Mojave Basin and Range, Sierra Nevada

Thick-branched shrub with stout branch spines 1–3 in. long. Leaves 0.4–1.3 in. long, drought-deciduous, alternate or clustered along stems, oblong to spoon-shaped, glandular-hairy, generally flattened and somewhat succulent. Flowers solitary in the forks of branches, narrowly bell-shaped, 4–5-lobed calyces 0.3–0.6 in. long, and funnel-shaped, white to violet corollas 0.3–0.6 in. long with a green-white tube 0.4–0.6 in. long and 4–5 spreading, violet-tinged lobes. Fruits 0.2–4 in. across, round, bright orange or yellow berries that look like mini tomatoes; they can be eaten fresh (only when ripe) or dried and are also enjoyed by birds and mammals. Named after zoologist and surgeon James G. Cooper (1830–1902), who made significant botanical discoveries across the California deserts.

Styrax redivivus

California snowdrop bush

STYRACACEAE STORAX FAMILY

PCT Sections: 2 & 4–5 & 16–19 **Abundance:** Rare **Height:** to 8 ft. **Flowering:** April–June **Flower Color:** White **Habitat-Community:** Open slopes or understories in woodlands, chaparrals, and lower montane coniferous forests **Elevation:** Below 6300 ft. **Ecoregions:** Southern California/Northern Baja Coast, Southern California Mountains, Sierra Nevada, Cascades

Shrub with stiff, gray stems. Leaves 0.7–3.5 in. long, deciduous, opposite, roundish, shiny green above and generally gray-hairy below, with smooth margins. Flowers solitary or in drooping clusters, with 4–10 bell-shaped petals, ≤20 stamens, and bright yellow anthers; sweet-scented like an orange-flower. Calyces 6–9-lobed, brown-yellow. Petals 0.5–1 in. long, fused, white. Fruits 1.2–2.4 in. across, round, hairy, tan capsules. It is easily spotted along the trail after the flowers fall, covering the ground in a white blanket of "snowdrops."

Vitis californica

California wild grape

VITACEAE GRAPE FAMILY

PCT Sections: 7–8 & 16–19 & 23–24 **Abundance:** Occasional **Height:** Vine **Flowering:** May–June **Flower Color:** Yellowish **Habitat-Community:** Canyons and streambanks in oak woodlands, chaparrals, lower montane coniferous forests, and wetland-riparian communities **Elevation:** Below 5600 ft. **Ecoregions:** Sierra Nevada, Cascades, Klamath Mountains

Climbing, woody vine to 50 ft. long with tendrils opposite leaves and peeling bark; monoecious. Leaves 3–6 in. wide, deciduous, alternate, roundish, 0–5-lobed, hairy, with toothed margins. Flowers minute, many in elongate clusters. Petals 5, aromatic, yellowish. Fruits to 0.3 in. across, hairless, white-wax-coated purple berries. The grapes are delicious fresh or dried in the sun. Emergency water is possible from vines if cut at the top first and then at the bottom to allow them to drain. If you are really brave, you can try to make water-bottle wine from the fruits!

▼ OPPOSITE, WHORLED, OR BASAL

Agave deserti var. *deserti*

desert agave

AGAVACEAE CENTURY PLANT FAMILY

PCT Sections: 1–2 **Abundance:** Rare **Height:** 1–3 ft. **Flowering:** May–July **Flower Color:** Yellow **Habitat-Community:** Gravelly slopes, sandy flats, and washes in creosote bush & Sonoran mixed woody scrubs **Elevation:** Below 4200 ft. **Ecoregions:** Sonoran Basin and Range

Succulent perennial that suckers prolifically, forming many short-stemmed, gray-green, basal leaf rosettes per individual plant. Leaves 10–25 in. long, lance-shaped, fleshy, blue-waxy-coated, with sharp spines along the margins and tip. Flowers 1.2–2.6 in. long, bell-shaped, and densely clustered (12–48 per cluster) on tall, erect stems with branches 4–8 in. long. Flowers 6-parted, lobes 0.5–0.9 in. long, yellow, and stamens long-exserted. Fruits capsules 1.3–2.8 in. long. Plants take 20–40 years to reach maturity, flower once, and then the flowering basal rosette dies. As a key dietary supplement, Indigenous peoples harvest, boil, and roast the leaves and artichoke-like heads.

Hesperoyucca whipplei

chaparral yucca

AGAVACEAE CENTURY PLANT FAMILY

PCT Sections: 1–9 **Abundance:** Common **Height:** 20–40 in. **Flowering:** April–June **Flower Color:** White to cream **Habitat-Community:** Gravelly slopes and sandy flats in foothill chaparrals, woodlands, and lower montane coniferous forests **Elevation:** Below 6800 ft. **Ecoregions:** Southern California Mountains, Sierra Nevada

Perennial from a primary basal rosette of ≥100 long stiff leaves, often with numerous secondary rosettes. Leaves 10–40 in. long, evergreen, gray-green, rigid, fibrous, sharp-pointed, with finely toothed margins. Flowers in the hundreds on densely branched stalks 2–12 ft. long, 2 ft. wide. Flowers 1.3–1.7 in. long, 6-parted in 2 petal-like whorls, white to cream, sometimes purple-tinged, and fleshy. Fruits 1.2–2 in. long, ovoid, 3-chambered capsules with many dull black seeds. Takes 5–7 years to reach maturity and flower, at which point the rosette dies; the plant may then put its energy into its secondary rosettes. It also sprouts after a burn, an adaptation lacking in other yuccas. A yucca moth, *Tegeticula maculata*, is the sole pollinator.

Yucca brevifolia

Joshua tree

AGAVACEAE

CENTURY PLANT FAMILY

PCT Sections: 4–9 **Abundance:** Common **Height:** to 50 ft. **Flowering:** March–June **Flower Color:** White **Habitat-Community:** Open slopes and valleys in desert scrubs and woodlands **Elevation:** Below 6500 ft. **Ecoregions:** Mojave Basin and Range, Sierra Nevada

Erect, small, twisted, generally single-stemmed tree with rosettes of leaves at branch ends. Bark of mature trees is gray to red-brown and fissured. Leaves 8–14 in. long, evergreen, whorled, thick, fibrous, sword-shaped, with toothed margins. Flowers 1.5–2.8 in. long, bell-shaped, densely clustered on erect stems, and mostly open at night. Tepals 1.5–2.8 in. long, 6-parted (3 sepals, 3 petals), white; sepals and petals fused half their length. Fruits 0.2–0.4 in. long, many-seeded capsules, spongy or leathery (when young). An important plant for night lizards and many other wildlife species. Pollination is completely dependent upon the silver-gray, night-flying yucca moth (*Tegeticula antithetica*), which deposits a ball of gathered pollen and eggs on the flowers. The larvae survive on the maturing seeds, but they eat only a portion of them before boring out of the fruit. The twisted forms reminded early Mormon explorers of the biblical Joshua, with his arms extending out from his sides. Artwork for U2's *The Joshua Tree* album included a Joshua tree located just west of Death Valley National Park. The seeds are edible, and an alcoholic beverage can be made from the buds and flowers.

Yucca schidigera

Mojave yucca

AGAVACEAE

CENTURY PLANT FAMILY

PCT Sections: 1–4 **Abundance:** Common **Height:** 3–18 ft. **Flowering:** March–May **Flower Color:** White to cream **Habitat-Community:** Rocky slopes and gravelly alluvium in scrubs, foothill chaparrals, and Joshua tree woodlands **Elevation:** Below 6100 ft. **Ecoregions:** Southern California Mountains, Sonoran Basin and Range

Evergreen shrub with basal crown of whorled, bayonet-like leaves or aboveground branching, sometimes forming a single-trunk "tree." Bark on older plants corky, palm tree–like, gray-brown; younger stems covered in old leaves. Leaves 1–5 ft. long, 1–2 in. wide, evergreen, thick, linear, yellowish green, fibrous, spine-tipped, with shredding margins. Flowers 1–2.3 in. long, pendent, 6-parted in 2 petal-like whorls, white to cream, with pistil 0.8–1.2 in. long. Fruits 2.2–4.5 in. long, drooping, cylindric, fleshy, berry-like capsules. Seed production is entirely dependent on pollination by *Tegeticula yuccasella*, another yucca moth. It can also reproduce via root-sprouting, forming massive clonal rings, some estimated to be over 2000 years old. Indigenous peoples eat the fruits and make blankets, shoes, soap, and rope with its leaves.

Bahiopsis parishii

Parish goldeneye

ASTERACEAE SUNFLOWER FAMILY

PCT Sections: 1–4 **Abundance:** Locally common **Height:** to 4 ft. **Flowering:** February–June **Flower Color:** Yellow **Habitat-Community:** Canyons and dry, rocky slopes in creosote bush scrubs and Joshua tree woodlands **Elevation:** Below 5200 ft. **Ecoregions:** Sonoran Basin and Range

Much-branched, desert shrub branching mainly from the base. Leaves 0.4–1.6 in. long, mostly opposite (except on young stems), prominently 3-veined, triangular-ovate, glossy green to lightly hairy. Flowers in heads 1.5–2.5 in. across, composite, rays often slightly arched with white tips. Disk flowers to 0.2 in. long, many per head, yellow. Fruits achenes to 0.2 in. long with long and short scales.

Lonicera conjugialis

purpleflower honeysuckle

CAPRIFOLIACEAE

HONEYSUCKLE FAMILY

PCT Sections: 10–24 **Abundance:** Locally common **Height:** 2–7 ft. **Flowering:** May–August **Flower Color:** Dark red **Habitat-Community:** Streambanks and moist slopes from lower montane to subalpine coniferous forests and wetland-riparian communities **Elevation:** Below 10,500 ft. **Ecoregions:** Sierra Nevada, Cascades, Klamath Mountains

Slender, erect shrub. Leaves 0.7–3 in. long, deciduous, opposite, thin, elliptical, hairy, with smooth margins. Flowers to 0.3 in. long, paired in leaf axils, fragrant, irregular, 5-lobed, 2-lipped, dark red, with lobes longer than the tubes. Fruits to 0.5 in. across, paired, bright red berries. The showy berries are toxic, but birds love them!

Lonicera interrupta

chaparral honeysuckle

CAPRIFOLIACEAE

HONEYSUCKLE FAMILY

PCT Sections: 3–9 & 13 & 18–22 **Abundance:** Locally common **Height:** to 9 ft. **Flowering:** April–June **Flower Color:** Pale yellow to cream **Habitat-Community:** Moist canyons in woodlands and chaparrals **Elevation:** Below 7200 ft. **Ecoregions:** Southern California Mountains, Sierra Nevada, Cascades, Klamath Mountains

Erect, woody shrub with long sprawling branches. Leaves 0.8–1.2 in. long, evergreen, opposite, often fused around the stem, elliptic, round-tipped. Flowers 0.3–0.5 in. long, forming "interrupted" spikes, irregular, strongly 2-lipped, deeply divided, pale yellow to cream. Prominent stamens extend from rolled-back corolla lips. Fruits 0.4–0.6 in. across, round, red berries. Berries are toxic! *Lonicera* honors German physician and herbalist Johann Lonitzer (1499–1569).

Lonicera involucrata

twinberry honeysuckle

CAPRIFOLIACEAE

HONEYSUCKLE FAMILY

PCT Sections: 10–24 **Abundance:** Locally common **Height:** 1–17 ft. **Flowering:** May–August **Flower Color:** Yellow or reddish-tinged **Habitat-Community:** Streambanks, lakeshores, and moist slopes in montane coniferous forests and wetland-riparian communities **Elevation:** Below 9500 ft. **Ecoregions:** Sierra Nevada, Cascades, Klamath Mountains

Erect shrub with shredding gray bark. Leaves 2–5.5 in. long, deciduous, opposite, thin, elliptic, hairy below (young leaves), with smooth, hairy margins. Flowers 0.5–0.7 in. long, paired in leaf axils, fragrant, irregular, 5-lobed, 2-lipped, yellow or reddish-tinged, lobes shorter than the tubes. Fruits to 0.4 n. across, fused in pairs, black berries. The berries are toxic, but birds love them!

Lonicera subspicata var. *denudata*

Johnston's honeysuckle

CAPRIFOLIACEAE

HONEYSUCKLE FAMILY

PCT Sections: 1–6 **Abundance:** Locally common **Height:** to 7 ft. **Flowering:** June–July **Flower Color:** Pale yellow **Habitat-Community:** Moist canyons and slopes in chaparrals **Elevation:** Below 5800 ft. **Ecoregions:** Southern California Mountains

Fragrant-flowered, twining shrub, often reclining on other shrubs for support. Leaves 0.4–1.7 in. long, evergreen, opposite, upper short-petioled, roundish, and usually wider than long. Flowers 0.4–0.6 in. long, in spikes, often glandular-hairy, pale yellow, irregular, strongly 2-lipped, with stamens long-exserted. Fruits 0.3–0.5 in. across, red or yellow, round berries. Honeysuckle derives its name from the edible sweet nectar within the tube of its flowers—but its fruits are toxic to humans!

Symphoricarpos mollis

creeping snowberry

CAPRIFOLIACEAE

HONEYSUCKLE FAMILY

PCT Sections: All (except 8–9) **Abundance:** Occasional **Height:** to 3 ft. **Flowering:** April–June **Flower Color:** Pink to reddish **Habitat-Community:** Slopes, ridges, and openings in chaparrals, woodlands, and montane coniferous forests **Elevation:** Below 9000 ft. **Ecoregions:** All (except Sonoran/Mojave Basin and Range)

Low-growing, sprawling shrub with branches often rooting at the nodes. Leaves 0.2–1.2 in. long, deciduous, opposite, hairless to soft-hairy. Flowers 0.2–0.3 in. long, in groups of 2–8 on tips of stems, 1–2 per leaf axil, pink or reddish, bell- or funnel-shaped, 5-lobed, lobes hairy on the inside and half as long as the tube. Fruits 0.3–0.4 in. across, round, white to pink berries. Berries are not toxic but are distasteful, much like eating soap. *Mollis* (from the Latin, "soft") refers to the texture of its leaves.

Symphoricarpos rotundifolius

roundleaf snowberry

CAPRIFOLIACEAE

HONEYSUCKLE FAMILY

PCT Sections: 1–22 **Abundance:** Occasional **Height:** to 4 ft. **Flowering:** May–June **Flower Color:** Pink or white **Habitat-Community:** Rocky slopes or openings from lower montane to subalpine coniferous forests **Elevation:** 5000–10,000 ft. **Ecoregions:** All (except Sonoran/Mojave Basin and Range)

Trailing to erect shrub with shredding bark on old stems. Leaves 0.5–1 in. long, deciduous, opposite, thin, oval to elliptic, with fine, soft hairs on both surfaces. Flowers 0.2–0.4 in. long, 1–2 per leaf axil, pink or white, narrowly bell-shaped, 5-lobed, lobes 25% as long as the tube. Fruits to 0.5 in. across, white berries. Foliage is an important food source for deer. The berries are toxic!

Cornus nuttallii

mountain dogwood

CORNACEAE DOGWOOD FAMILY

PCT Sections: 1–5 & 15–24 **Abundance:** Common **Height:** 7–40 ft. **Flowering:** April–July **Flower Color:** White to pinkish **Habitat-Community:** Streambanks, moist slopes, and understories in montane coniferous forests and wetland-riparian communities **Elevation:** Below 6500 ft. **Ecoregions:** All (except Sonoran/Mojave Basin and Range)

Shade-tolerant, single-stemmed tree with smooth to ridged, brownish bark. Leaves 1.5–5 in. long, deciduous, opposite, oval to ovoid, with smooth to wavy margins and prominent veins curving toward the leaf tip as they approach the margins. Flowers green-white and clustered in spherical heads subtended by showy, white to pinkish bracts, 1–3 in. long, which are often mistaken for petals. Fruits to 0.5 in. long, elliptic, red, bitter-tasting, berry-like stone fruits. Sprouts after fire and is relatively drought-tolerant. The wood has historically been made into piano keys and golf club heads. Provides spectacular shows twice yearly, in spring with its white flower-like bracts and with a profusion of red foliage in fall.

Cornus sericea

American dogwood

CORNACEAE DOGWOOD FAMILY

PCT Sections: All **Abundance:** Locally common **Height:** 5–16 ft. **Flowering:** May–July **Flower Color:** White **Habitat-Community:** Moist canyons and slopes from chaparrals to upper montane coniferous forests and wetland-riparian communities **Elevation:** Below 8400 ft. **Ecoregions:** All

Large shrub, forming dense thickets with dark red or purple branches (especially when young). Leaves 2–5 in. long, 1–3 in. wide, deciduous, opposite, lance-shaped to ovoid, hairless to rough-hairy, with 4–7 pairs of veins. Flowers many in head-like clusters, 4-lobed calyces, and 4 white petals 0.1–0.2 in. long. Fruits white to cream, rounded drupes (berries) 0.3–0.4 in. across. Two subspecies along the PCT: subsp. *sericea*, hairless to silky hairy with short petals (0.1 in. long), is uncommon in southern California; subsp. *occidentalis*, rough-hairy with petals twice as long, is found throughout the state. *Sericea* (from the Latin, "silky") refers to the texture of the leaves.

Cassiope mertensiana

white heather

ERICACEAE HEATH FAMILY

PCT Sections: 10–24 **Abundance:** Occasional **Height:** to 1 ft. **Flowering:** July–August **Flower Color:** White to pink **Habitat-Community:** Rocky, moist slopes (where snow lingers into the summer) in subalpine coniferous forests and alpine communities **Elevation:** 5900–11,500 ft. **Ecoregions:** Sierra Nevada, Cascades, Klamath Mountains

Erect or low-growing shrub with dark green, scale-like leaves. Leaves to 0.3 in. long, evergreen, opposite, thick, and overlapping like roof shingles. Flowers 0.2–0.3 in. long, solitary in leaf axils at branch ends, 4–5-parted, white to pink, nodding, bell-shaped. Fruits to 0.2 in. across, spherical 5-chambered capsules with several seeds in each chamber. Often forms dense mats on granite outcrops. John Muir's favorite plant!

Kalmia polifolia

swamp laurel

ERICACEAE HEATH FAMILY

PCT Sections: 10–24 **Abundance:** Occasional **Height:** to 3 ft. **Flowering:** May–August **Flower Color:** Pink to rose-purple **Habitat-Community:** Bogs, fens, lake edges, and wet meadows from upper montane coniferous forests to alpine communities **Elevation:** 7000–12,000 ft. **Ecoregions:** Sierra Nevada, Cascades, Klamath Mountains

Spreading shrub with stems rooting (if in contact with soil) and dark green foliage. Leaves 0.5–1.5 in. long, evergreen, opposite, thick, linear to oval or oblong, hairless above, gray-hairy below, with rolled-under margins. Flowers 0.2–0.5 in. long, clustered at stem ends, 5-parted, pink to rose-purple, with 10 stamens and 1 pistil. Petals fused at base and cup-shaped. Fruits 0.2 in. across, spherical, hairless capsules. As bees land, the flower's filaments spring into action, releasing the anthers from depressions in the petals; pollen then covers the bees' underparts. Caution: contains andromedo-toxin, a poisonous neurotoxin.

Garrya flavescens

ashy silktassel

GARRYACEAE SILKTASSEL FAMILY

PCT Sections: 1–9 **Abundance:** Locally common **Height:** to 9 ft. **Flowering:** February–April **Flower Color:** Gray-green to white **Habitat-Community:** Shaded slopes in scrubs, chaparrals, and woodlands **Elevation:** Below 7500 ft. **Ecoregions:** Southern California Mountains, Sierra Nevada

Lanky, evergreen shrub; dioecious. Leaves 1–3 in. long, opposite, oval, leathery (manzanita-like), with smooth margins. Flowers in pendent, catkin-like tassels 2–6 in. long, and wind-pollinated. Male flowers 0.1 in. long, 3 per bract. Female flowers 0.1–0.2 in. long, 1–3 per bract. Fruits spherical, ashy gray (aging dark), densely hairy 2-seeded berries. An infusion of the leaves is used as a laxative and for stomachaches by southwestern Indigenous peoples.

Garrya fremontii

Fremont's silktassel

GARRYACEAE SILKTASSEL FAMILY

PCT Sections: 1–3 & 12–24 **Abundance:** Common **Height:** to 10 ft. **Flowering:** January–April **Flower Color:** Yellowish **Habitat-Community:** Open, dry slopes, including serpentine soils, in oak woodlands, chaparrals, and lower montane coniferous forests **Elevation:** Below 7000 ft. **Ecoregions:** Southern California, Sierra Nevada, Cascades, Klamath Mountains

Erect shrub with gray bark and generally sparsely hairy stems; dioecious. Leaves 1.5–3 in. long, evergreen, opposite, thick, oval to elliptic, hairless when mature, with smooth margins. Flowers in drooping tassels, with yellowish bract-like sepals, 0 petals, and 4 stamens. Fruits purple or black, hairless or sparsely hairy (near tip) berries. Popular landscape plant, thanks to its evergreen nature, showy catkins, and resistance to pests and diseases.

Garrya veatchii

canyon silktassel

GARRYACEAE SILKTASSEL FAMILY

PCT Sections: 1–5 **Abundance:** Locally common **Height:** to 6 ft. **Flowering:** February–April **Flower Color:** White to olive-cream **Habitat-Community:** Open slopes and ridges in chaparrals **Elevation:** Below 5800 ft. **Ecoregions:** Southern California Mountains

Evergreen shrub branching from base; dioecious. Leaves 1–4 in. long, opposite, narrowly ovoid, flat to wavy, densely woolly below, sometimes with rolled-under margins. Flowers in pendent, catkin-like tassels 1–3 in. long, and wind-pollinated. Male flowers 0.1 in. long, 3 per bract. Female flowers 0.1–0.2 in. long, 1–3 per bract. Fruits spherical, ash-gray, densely hairy, 2-seeded berries. Look for dense populations around the Interstate 15 crossing.

Jamesia americana var. *rosea*

rosy-petalled cliffbush

HYDRANGEACEAE
HYDRANGEA FAMILY

PCT Sections: 10–11 **Abundance:** Rare **Height:** 1.5–6 ft. **Flowering:** May–September **Flower Color:** Pink **Habitat-Community:** Open, rocky slopes and cliffs in subalpine coniferous forests and alpine communities **Elevation:** 6800–12,100 ft. **Ecoregions:** Sierra Nevada

Erect, multi-stemmed shrub with shreddy grayish or reddish bark and generally hairy stems. Leaves 0.5–2 in. long, deciduous, opposite, oblong to round, hairy or hairless above, densely hairy below, with toothed margins. Flowers solitary or clustered at stem ends, 5-parted, fragrant, with 10 stamens and 3–5 styles. Sepals to 0.2 in. long, green, fused at base, erect. Petals 0.2–0.3 in. long, pink. Fruits to 0.5 in. long, cone-shaped capsules with many seeds. Pretty cool to see this in its rocky habitat. Most alpine shrubs have white or yellow flowers, so when you spot pink blooms on a shrub growing out of the rocks with its bark peeling off, you know that you have come upon a botanical treasure!

Philadelphus lewisii

wild mock orange

HYDRANGEACEAE
HYDRANGEA FAMILY

PCT Sections: 5 & 16–24 **Abundance:** Locally common **Height:** to 10 ft. **Flowering:** May–July **Flower Color:** White **Habitat-Community:** Dry slopes and canyons in oak woodlands, chaparrals, and lower montane coniferous forests **Elevation:** Below 4500 ft. **Ecoregions:** Southern California Mountains, Sierra Nevada, Cascades, Klamath Mountains

Erect, loosely branched shrub with red to brown flaky bark. Leaves 1.2–3.5 in. long, deciduous, opposite, oval to ovoid, hairy or hairless, 3-veined from base, with smooth or toothed margins. Flowers solitary or scattered at stem ends, 4–5-parted, fragrant, with many stamens and 4-lobed style. Sepals 0.1–0.3 in. long, green, fused at base, spreading to erect. Petals 0.3–0.5 in. long, white. Fruits to 0.4 in. long, oval capsules with many seeds. The strong wood does not warp or crack if treated properly, hence its historical use for bows, arrows, combs, netting shuttles, and knitting needles. The leaves and flowers create a cleansing lather when rubbed vigorously.

Condea emoryi

desert lavender

LAMIACEAE MINT FAMILY

PCT Sections: 1–3 **Abundance:** Occasional **Height:** 3–13 ft. **Flowering:** January–May **Flower Color:** Violet **Habitat-Community:** Dry, gravelly or sandy canyons and washes in scrubs and foothill chaparrals **Elevation:** Below 5300 ft. **Ecoregions:** Southern California/Northern Baja Coast, Southern California Mountains

Aromatic multi-stemmed evergreen shrub covered with branched white hairs. Leaves 0.4–1.2 in. long, opposite, ovoid to roundish, white-haired, with shallowly toothed margins. Flowers 10–15, clustered in leaf axils, subtended by leaf-like bracts, irregular. Corollas 0.2–0.3 in. long, 2-lipped, violet, with 4 exserted stamens. Fruits 4 angled nutlets. A favored plant of honeybees.

Salvia apiana

white sage

LAMIACEAE MINT FAMILY

PCT Sections: 1–6 **Abundance:** Locally common **Height:** 2–6 ft. **Flowering:** March–August **Flower Color:** White to lavender **Habitat-Community:** Dry slopes in scrubs and foothill chaparrals **Elevation:** Below 5100 ft. **Ecoregions:** Southern California Mountains

Aromatic evergreen shrub and iconic member of coastal sage scrub habitats. Leaves 1.2–3.5 in. long, opposite, widely lance-shaped, grayish, with scalloped margins and oily hairs that when rubbed produce a strong minty aroma. Flowers borne on long stalks extending 2–3 ft. above the leaves. Corollas irregular, 0.8–1.3 in. long, white to pale lavender, upper lip 0.1 in. long, lower lip 0.3 in. long and upcurved, with 2 stamens extending well beyond tube. Fruits 4 ovoid to oblong, shiny light brown nutlets 0.1 in. long. *Salvia* (from the Latin, "to heal") refers to the plants' many medicinal properties. *Apiana* (from the Latin *apis*, "bees") reflects the attractiveness of the flowers to bees, especially bumblebees. Popular (and overcollected!) for smudging; please smudge with common alternatives, such as *Artemisia tridentata*.

Salvia dorrii

purple sage

LAMIACEAE MINT FAMILY

PCT Sections: 4–9 **Abundance:** Occasional **Height:** to 2.5 ft. **Flowering:** May–June **Flower Color:** Dark blue **Habitat-Community:** Rocky slopes in scrubs, woodlands, and lower montane coniferous forests **Elevation:** 2500–8800 ft. **Ecoregions:** Southern California Mountains, Mojave Basin and Range, Sierra Nevada

Erect, mounded, fragrant (minty) shrub with rigid, white, scurfy stems. Leaves 0.1–1.2 in. long, clustered on short shoots, deciduous, opposite, thick, oval to spoon-shaped, silver-hairy, round-tipped, with smooth margins. Flowers 0.3–0.6 in. long, forming round-bracted clusters, 5-parted, irregular, 2-lipped, with purple-green to rose bracts, 2 stamens, and forked style. Petals fused, tube 0.2–0.5 in. long, dark blue (purple to rose or white), upper lip to 0.1 in. long, lower lip < upper lip. Fruits 4 ovoid to oblong, gray to red-brown nutlets to 0.2 in. long. This desert sage is a treat for your eyes and nose.

Salvia mellifera

black sage

LAMIACEAE MINT FAMILY

PCT Sections: 1–6 **Abundance:** Rare **Height:** 2–5 ft. **Flowering:** March–June **Flower Color:** Pale blue to lavender **Habitat-Community:** Dry slopes in foothill chaparrals **Elevation:** Below 4300 ft. **Ecoregions:** Southern California Mountains

Aromatic evergreen shrub with erect glandular stems. Leaves 1–2.7 in. long, opposite, oblong, green and hairless above, hairy below. Flowers in clusters scattered along stem tips, with 2 stamens and style barely exserted. Corollas 0.9–1.2 in. long, pale blue to lavender, irregular, 2-lipped, upper lip 2-lobed, lower lip 3-lobed. Fruits 4 ovoid to oblong, shiny brown nutlets 0.1 in. long. Readily hybridizes with *S. apiana* and other salvias. Plants can sprout from the root crown and rapidly reoccupy burn areas. Common in coastal sage scrub, making only a brief cameo appearance in coast-influenced areas of the PCT, such as in Soledad Canyon and Vasquez Rocks in the western Transverse Ranges.

Salvia pachyphylla

blue sage

LAMIACEAE MINT FAMILY

PCT Sections: 2–5 & 8–9 **Abundance:** Occasional **Height:** 1–3 ft. **Flowering:** May–October **Flower Color:** Blue-violet to rose **Habitat-Community:** Dry slopes in foothill chaparrals, pinyon-juniper woodlands, and lower montane coniferous forests **Elevation:** Below 8800 ft. **Ecoregions:** Southern California Mountains, Sierra Nevada

Low-growing shrub often rooting at the nodes giving the plant a sprawling appearance. Leaves 1–2.6 in. long, evergreen, opposite, leathery, spoon-shaped, with smooth, wavy margins. Flowers densely clustered, 2–5 per stem, irregular, calyx bracts rose-colored. Corollas 0.7–1 in. long, blue-violet, with 2 stamens and style exserted. Fruits generally 4 per flower, ovoid to oblong, shiny tan to brown nutlets 0.1 in. long. Known for many medicinal properties, including a potential for suppressing cancer cell growth. Occurs along the PCT in the San Bernardino Mountains and in the southern Sierra Nevada.

Trichostema lanatum

woolly bluecurls

LAMIACEAE MINT FAMILY

PCT Sections: 1–5 **Abundance:** Locally common **Height:** to 5 ft. **Flowering:** March–July **Flower Color:** Blue to pink or white **Habitat-Community:** Dry slopes and ridges in foothill chaparrals **Elevation:** Below 5300 ft. **Ecoregions:** Southern California/Northern Baja Coast, Southern California Mountains

Aromatic evergreen subshrub with erect, glandular-hairy to woolly stems. Leaves 1.3–3 in. long, opposite, linear, green and hairless above, gray-hairy below, with rolled-under margins. Flowers clustered in leaf axils, irregular, 2-lipped, hairy, blue to lavender, corolla tube 0.4–0.6 in. long, 4 obvious stamens 1–1.6 in. long. Fruits 4 small, hairy, irregularly ridged nutlets. A fire-follower: seeds require stimulus from chemicals in smoke to germinate. Hummingbirds are its primary pollinators, but bees are also frequent visitors. Used to treat rheumatism and as a disinfectant.

Parish's bluecurls

Trichostema parishii

LAMIACEAE MINT FAMILY

PCT Sections: 1–5 **Abundance:** Common **Height:** 1–3.5 ft. **Flowering:** March–July **Flower Color:** Blue to lavender **Habitat-Community:** Dry slopes and ridges in foothill chaparrals **Elevation:** Below 6100 ft. **Ecoregions:** Southern California/Northern Baja Coast, Southern California Mountains

Aromatic evergreen subshrub with erect, glandular-hairy stems. Leaves 1.3–2.7 in. long, opposite, linear, green and hairy above, gray-hairy below, with rolled-under margins. Flowers clustered in leaf axils, irregular, 2-lipped, hairy, blue to lavender, corolla tube 0.1–0.3 in. long, 4 obvious stamens 0.7–1.1 in. long. Fruits 4 small, hairy, irregularly ridged nutlets. Seeds require stimulus from chemicals in smoke to germinate. Hummingbirds are the primary pollinators.

desert olive

Forestiera pubescens

OLEACEAE OLIVE FAMILY

PCT Sections: 3–9 **Abundance:** Occasional **Height:** to 20 ft. **Flowering:** March–May **Flower Color:** Yellow or green **Habitat-Community:** Streambanks, canyons, and washes from scrubs to lower montane coniferous forests and wetland-riparian communities **Elevation:** Below 6600 ft. **Ecoregions:** Southern California Mountains, Sierra Nevada

Mounded shrub or small tree with smooth, light gray stems, generally forming thickets in moist drainages; dioecious. Leaves 0.6–1.8 in. long, deciduous, opposite or clustered, lance-shaped to ovoid, shiny green, hairless, with smooth to slightly toothed margins. Flowers generally appear before the leaves and eventually cluster among them. Male flowers 0.1–0.3 in. long, 1–5 per bud, yellow, 4 stamens. Female flowers 0.1–0.3 in., 1–8 per bud, green. Fruits 0.2–0.4 in. long, elliptic, blue-black olive-like drupes, often produced in abundance. Edible to humans, coveted by birds and small mammals. The genus name honors André R. Forestier (1736–1812), French physician and botany teacher.

rock bush monkeyflower

Diplacus calycinus

PHRYMACEAE LOPSEED FAMILY

PCT Sections: 8–9 **Abundance:** Occasional **Height:** to 2.5 ft. **Flowering:** March–June **Flower Color:** Pale yellow to white **Habitat-Community:** Rocky slopes, cliffs, and boulders in scrubs and woodlands **Elevation:** Below 7200 ft. **Ecoregions:** Sierra Nevada

Erect subshrub with glandular-hairy stems. Leaves 1–2 in. long, drought-deciduous, opposite, narrowly elliptic, hairless, with toothed or rolled-under margins. Flowers 2 per upper stem nodes, irregular, 5-lobed, 2-lipped, with 4 stamens and 1 pistil. Petals fused, tube-throat 1.4–1.7 in. long, pale yellow to white. Fruits 1–1.4 in. long, elliptical capsules with many seeds. When observed straight on, the flowers appear to be smiling back.

Diplacus longiflorus

southern bush monkeyflower

PHRYMACEAE LOPSEED FAMILY

PCT Sections: 1–6 **Abundance:** Locally common **Height:** to 4 ft. **Flowering:** March–June **Flower Color:** Yellow-orange **Habitat-Community:** Rock outcrops and crevices in chaparrals and oak woodlands **Elevation:** Below 6500 ft. **Ecoregions:** Southern California Mountains

Sticky, evergreen shrub or subshrub found on boulder slopes. Leaves 2–4 in. long, opposite, narrowly elliptic or lance-shaped, bright green, with branched, star-like hairs below and often with toothed margins. Petals 5, irregular, fused into a 2-lipped corolla, yellow-orange, tube-throat 1.4–3.1 in. long. Fruits 0.7–1.2 in. long, capsules with many dark seeds. The leaves produce chemicals that deter herbivores, which helps the plant retain water in dry environments.

Keckiella antirrhinoides

chaparral beardtongue

PLANTAGINACEAE

PLANTAIN FAMILY

PCT Sections: 1–4 **Abundance:** Occasional **Height:** 3–16 ft. **Flowering:** April–June **Flower Color:** Yellow **Habitat-Community:** Rocky slopes in scrubs, foothill chaparrals, and woodlands **Elevation:** Below 4800 ft. **Ecoregions:** Southern California Mountains

Robust shrub with snapdragon-like flowers. Leaves 0.3–0.8 in. long, drought-deciduous, opposite, lance-shaped, hairless to hairy, with smooth margins. Flowers in long, terminal clusters, irregular, brilliant yellow (aging black). Corolla tube 0.7–1 in. long with a widely expanded throat 0.2–0.4 in. long. Upper corolla lip 0.3–0.6 in. long with 2 joined lobes; lower lip with 3 lobes that arch downward and densely yellow-hairy staminode obviously exserted. Fruits ovoid many-seeded capsules. Two varieties come together along the PCT in the Peninsular Ranges: var. *antirrhinoides* (calyx <0.3 in. long; sepals broad) and var. *microphylla* (calyx >0.3 in. long; sepals lance-shaped).

Keckiella breviflora

bush beardtongue

PLANTAGINACEAE

PLANTAIN FAMILY

PCT Sections: 5–9 & 11–17 **Abundance:** Common **Height:** 2–7 ft. **Flowering:** April–July **Flower Color:** White to pink and purple- or pink-lined **Habitat-Community:** Dry, rocky slopes from oak woodlands to upper montane coniferous forests **Elevation:** Below 9200 ft. **Ecoregions:** Southern California Mountains, Sierra Nevada, Cascades

Erect to spreading shrub with slender, gray-green stems. Leaves 0.5–1.5 in. long, drought-deciduous, opposite, lance-shaped, gray-green, with toothed margins. Flowers 0.5–0.7 in. long, many in open clusters at stem ends, irregular, 5-lobed, 2-lipped, with 4 stamens, 1 staminode, and 1 pistil. Petals fused, tube-throat to 0.3 in. long, white to pink and purple- or pink-lined. Fruits many-seeded capsules. The original 1837 description was based on material grown in England from seed suspected to be collected in Monterey County.

Keckiella rothrockii
Rothrock's keckiella

PLANTAGINACEAE PLANTAIN FAMILY

PCT Sections: 3 & 8–9 **Abundance:** Rare **Height:** 1–3 ft. **Flowering:** June–August **Flower Color:** Pale yellow to brown-cream **Habitat-Community:** Exposed ridges and canyons in sagebrush scrubs, pinyon-juniper woodlands, and montane coniferous forests **Elevation:** Below 9400 ft. **Ecoregions:** Southern California Mountains, Sierra Nevada

Low-growing shrub with generally unbranched, green, short-hairy or nearly hairless stems. Leaves 0.3–0.8 in. long, drought-deciduous, opposite or clustered in 3s, sessile, lance-shaped to ovoid, green to gray-hairy, sometimes with slightly toothed margins at the tip. Flowers scattered along stem tips, irregular, calyx 0.2–0.3 in. long. Corollas 5-lobed, 2-lipped, hairy outer surface, dull brown-yellow, sometimes reddish or purple-lined, expanded throat 0.3–0.5 in. long, upper lip projecting 0.2 in., with 4 stamens, 1 staminode, and 1 pistil. Fruits ovoid, many-seeded capsules. The rare var. *jacintensis*, endemic to the San Jacinto Mountains, has hairless leaves and slightly smaller corollas; look for it along the PCT at Fuller Ridge and Saddle Junction. The more widespread var. *rothrockii* of the Sierra Nevada has leaves with a dense covering of short hairs. Named for Joseph T. Rothrock (1839–1922), who studied under Asa Gray at Harvard.

Keckiella ternata
scarlet keckiella

PLANTAGINACEAE PLANTAIN FAMILY

PCT Sections: 1–6 **Abundance:** Locally common **Height:** 3–12 ft. **Flowering:** May–September **Flower Color:** Red **Habitat-Community:** Shaded or exposed slopes and canyons in foothill chaparrals and woodlands **Elevation:** Below 6700 ft. **Ecoregions:** Southern California/Northern Baja Coast, Southern California Mountains

Attractive shrub with wispy, spreading, waxy stems. Leaves 1.8–2.7 in. long, opposite or in whorls of 3, spoon- to lance-shaped, curved downward, with toothed margins. Corollas 0.8–1.3 in. long, aromatic, irregular, red, tubular, with 2-lobed upper lip 0.3–0.4 in. long and 3-lobed lower lip. Fruits ovoid, many-seeded capsules. The red flowers attract hummingbirds and butterflies. *Ternata* (from the Latin, "in clusters of three") refers to the stem leaves.

Penstemon incertus
Mojave beardtongue

PLANTAGINACEAE PLANTAIN FAMILY

PCT Sections: 7–9 **Abundance:** Locally common **Height:** 1–3 ft. **Flowering:** May–July **Flower Color:** Violet to purple **Habitat-Community:** Sandy slopes and washes in sagebrush scrubs and woodlands **Elevation:** Below 6700 ft. **Ecoregions:** Sierra Nevada

Attractive, rounded shrub or subshrub with intricately branched, blue- to white-waxy stems. Leaves 2–3 in. long, opposite, linear, hairless, gray-green, with rolled-up margins. Flowers several per node, borne on a glandular stem, with 4 stamens, 1 hairy staminode, and 1 pistil. Corollas irregular, 1–1.6 in. long, violet to purple, 5-lobed, 2-lipped; throat 0.5 in. wide, glandular on the outside. Fruits ovoid, lumpy capsule with many, angled seeds. Observe this California endemic along the PCT from Antelope Valley to the southern Sierra Nevada. *Penstemon* ("almost thread," a reference to the staminode) is the largest genus of flowering plants endemic to North America.

Eriogonum wrightii

bastardsage

POLYGONACEAE BUCKWHEAT FAMILY

PCT Sections: 1–14 **Abundance:** Locally common **Height:** to 3 ft. **Flowering:** June–October **Flower Color:** White to pink or rose **Habitat-Community:** Rocky places from scrubs, woodlands, and chaparrals to subalpine coniferous forests **Elevation:** Below 12,000 ft. **Ecoregions:** Southern California/Northern Baja Coast, Southern California Mountains, Sierra Nevada

Matted to erect subshrub or shrub with white, hairy stems. Leaves to 1.2 in. long, 1 in. wide, deciduous, basal (whorled) and few along lower stem, oval to lance-shaped, hairy or hairless, occasionally with rolled-under margins. Flowers to 0.2 in. long, clustered along stems, small, 6-parted, cup-shaped, subtended by cup-like involucre, with 9 stamens. Tepals fused at base, white to pink or rose, hairless, shorter than stamens. Fruits to 0.1 in. across, hairless brown achenes. Usually a shrub of deserts or desert-like places. Most wild buckwheats are non-shrubby perennials or annuals, with few exceptions in California; you have to appreciate their ability to flourish in some of the state's harshest environments.

Ceanothus crassifolius

hoaryleaf ceanothus

RHAMNACEAE BUCKTHORN FAMILY

PCT Sections: 1–6 **Abundance:** Rare **Height:** to 10 ft. **Flowering:** January–April **Flower Color:** White **Habitat-Community:** Sandy to gravelly slopes and ridges in foothill chaparrals **Elevation:** Below 3800 ft. **Ecoregions:** Southern California Mountains

Erect, spreading shrub with long branches and white or tan fuzzy twigs (especially when young). Leaves 0.5–1 in. long, evergreen, opposite, leathery, widely spoon-shaped, deep green and hairless above, densely white-hairy below, with widely spaced, prominently toothed margins. Flowers in dense clusters 0.5–0.9 in. wide, scattered along stem tips, small, 5-parted, 0.2 in. across, white. Fruits 0.2–0.4 in. across, 3-lobed, short-horned capsules. Best observed along the PCT near Cajon Junction and in the Soledad Canyon region of the western San Gabriel Mountains.

Ceanothus cuneatus

buckbrush

RHAMNACEAE BUCKTHORN FAMILY

PCT Sections: 1–8 & 14–24 **Abundance:** Common **Height:** to 8 ft. **Flowering:** February–April **Flower Color:** White, blue, or lavender **Habitat-Community:** Open slopes and rocky soils, including serpentine, from oak woodlands to lower montane coniferous forests **Elevation:** Below 6000 ft. **Ecoregions:** All

Densely branched shrub with rigid, brown to grayish stems. Leaves 0.2–1.3 in. long, evergreen, opposite, wedge-shaped, 1-veined, with smooth or toothed margins. Flowers in dense, rounded clusters, fragrant, small, 5-parted, white, blue, or lavender. Fruits 0.1–0.3 in. across, ridged (at tip), short-horned capsules. York's favorite springtime fragrance is produced by flowering patches of buckbrush. The spring foliage provides forage for deer, and the fruits are great for birds.

Ceanothus pauciflorus

Mojave buckthorn

RHAMNACEAE BUCKTHORN FAMILY

PCT Sections: 1–9 **Abundance:** Occasional **Height:** 2–6 ft. **Flowering:** March–May **Flower Color:** White **Habitat-Community:** Gravelly slopes and mesas in scrubs, foothill chaparrals, and pinyon-juniper woodlands **Elevation:** Below 7600 ft. **Ecoregions:** Southern California Mountains, Sierra Nevada

Erect, intricately branched shrub with pale gray to white, short-hairy stems. Leaves 0.2–0.9 in. long, evergreen, opposite, leathery, oval, mostly hairless, with smooth to 3-5-toothed margins. Flowers in dense clusters 0.4–0.8 in. wide, scattered along stem tips, small, 5-parted, white. Fruits 0.2–0.3 in. across, 3-ridged (at tip) capsules with 0 to minute horn per lobe. Extends into the southern Sierra Nevada.

Ceanothus perplexans

cupped-leaf ceanothus

RHAMNACEAE BUCKTHORN FAMILY

PCT Sections: 1–5 **Abundance:** Occasional **Height:** 3–9 ft. **Flowering:** March–May **Flower Color:** White to pale blue **Habitat-Community:** Gravelly soils in chaparrals, pinyon-juniper woodlands, and lower montane coniferous forests **Elevation:** Below 6800 ft. **Ecoregions:** Southern California Mountains

Erect, densely branched shrub with pale gray-waxy, short-hairy to hairless stems. Leaves 0.4–0.9 in. long, evergreen, opposite, leathery, elliptic, mostly hairless, with 6–11 sharp teeth along margins. Flowers in dense clusters 0.5–0.9 in. wide, scattered along stem tips, small, 5-parted, white to pale blue. Fruits 0.2–0.3 in. across, 3-ridged (at tip) capsules with 0 to minute horn per lobe.

Ceanothus pinetorum

Kern ceanothus

RHAMNACEAE BUCKTHORN FAMILY

PCT Sections: 9–10 **Abundance:** Rare **Height:** 0.5–3 ft. **Flowering:** May–July **Flower Color:** Blue **Habitat-Community:** Open places, generally in rocky or gravelly, granitic soils from lower montane to subalpine coniferous forests **Elevation:** 5400–9000 ft. **Ecoregions:** Sierra Nevada

Densely branched, mounded shrub with red-brown stems; low branches can root at nodes. Leaves 0.5–1 in. long, <2 times longer than wide, evergreen, opposite, widely elliptic to roundish, shiny green above, pale green below, 1-veined, with 9–15 spines along margins. Flowers clustered at leaf axils and stem ends, small, 5-parted, blue. Fruits 0.2–0.4 in. across, ridged (at tip) or smooth, horned capsules. California endemic with populations occurring hundreds of miles apart between the southern Sierra and the Klamath Mountains. Populations in the Klamath Mountains are not known to grow along the PCT.

Coleogyne ramosissima

black bush

ROSACEAE ROSE FAMILY

PCT Sections: 1–2 & 8 **Abundance:** Occasional **Height:** to 5 ft. **Flowering:** April–June **Flower Color:** Pale yellow **Habitat-Community:** Gravelly soils in creosote & black bush scrubs and Joshua tree woodlands **Elevation:** Below 6100 ft. **Ecoregions:** Southern California Mountains, Sonoran Basin and Range, Sierra Nevada

Intricately branched, long-lived shrub with dark gray-green, spine-tipped branches. Leaves 0.2–0.7 in. long, opposite in clusters, narrowly spoon-shaped, short-hairy, gray-green. Flowers solitary at branch tips, with 0 petals (a unique feature among roses), 20–25 stamens, and 4 spreading, leathery, pale yellow (often red underneath) sepals 0.2–0.3 in. long. Fruits 0.2–0.3 in. long, crescent-shaped reddish achenes. Found along the PCT in the San Felipe Valley region in San Diego County, and just north of Kelso Valley in Kern County. The only species in *Coleogyne*.

Nolina parryi

Parry's beargrass

RUSCACEAE
BUTCHER'S-BROOM FAMILY

PCT Sections: 1–4 & 8–9 **Abundance:** Rare **Height:** 3–8 ft. **Flowering:** May–June **Flower Color:** White **Habitat-Community:** Rocky slopes in creosote & black bush scrubs, foothill chaparrals, and Joshua tree woodlands **Elevation:** Below 5900 ft. **Ecoregions:** Southern California Mountains, Sonoran Basin and Range, Sierra Nevada

Burly plant with aboveground, sometimes branching, woody trunks to 2 ft. across and leaf clusters to 6 ft. across; dioecious. Leaves 1.5–3.7 ft. long, 0.8–1.6 in. wide, clustered in crowns of 80–220, sword-like, bases much expanded, with minutely saw-toothed but not shredding margins. Flowers 1.8–2.4 in. long, densely clustered on tall, branched stalks, 6-parted in 2 petal-like whorls, white. Fruits 0.4–0.7 in. long, papery 3-chambered capsules with red-brown seeds. One of the largest species in the genus, which is named after 18th-century French arboriculturist C. Nolin. Impressive stands can be seen along the PCT in Kern County near Walker Pass, or on desert slopes of the Peninsular Ranges.

Acer glabrum

mountain maple

SAPINDACEAE SOAPBERRY FAMILY

PCT Sections: 3–4 & 8–24 **Abundance:** Common **Height:** 3–30 ft. **Flowering:** April–June **Flower Color:** Green-yellow **Habitat-Community:** Slopes and canyons in montane coniferous forests **Elevation:** Below 9000 ft. **Ecoregions:** Southern California Mountains, Sierra Nevada, Cascades, Klamath Mountains

Erect, single-stemmed shrub to small tree with reddish or whitish, hairless stems. Leaves 1–2 in. long, deciduous, opposite, heart-shaped, 3–5-lobed, with toothed margins. Flowers in rounded clusters of 2–10, 4–6-parted, saucer-shaped, generally with 10 stamens, appearing with leaves. Flowers on a plant may be of one kind or a combination of bisexual, male only, or female only. Sepals to 0.1 in. long, green-yellow, fused. Petals to 0.1 in. long, free, green-yellow. Fruits 0.4–1 in. across, hairless double samaras aging green-brown, with obliquely angled (<90°) wings. Historically used to make snowshoe frames and ceremonial paddles.

Acer macrophyllum

bigleaf
maple

SAPINDACEAE SOAPBERRY FAMILY

PCT Sections: 1–7 & 16–24 **Abundance:** Common **Height:** 50–100 ft. **Flowering:** March–June **Flower Color:** Green-yellow **Habitat-Community:** Streambanks, slopes, and canyons in oak woodlands, chaparrals, lower montane coniferous forests, and wetland-riparian communities **Elevation:** Below 5000 ft. **Ecoregions:** All (except Sonoran/Mojave Basin and Range)

Erect, single-stemmed tree with ridged, gray-brown bark. Leaves 3–6 in. long, deciduous, opposite, roundish, 3–5-lobed, with wavy margins. Flowers in elongated, drooping clusters of 10–50, 4–6-parted, saucer-shaped, with 7–9 stamens, appearing with or after leaves. Flowers on a plant may be of one kind or a combination of bisexual or male only. Sepals to 0.1 in. long, green-yellow, fused. Petals to 0.1 in. long, free, green-yellow. Fruits 1.2–2.4 in. across, hairy double samaras aging orange-brown, with obliquely angled (<90°) wings. Sprouted seeds are edible. Historically used to make canoe paddles. Sprouts after fire or being cut.

Simmondsia chinensis

jojoba

SIMMONDSIACEAE JOJOBA FAMILY

PCT Sections: 1–4 **Abundance:** Occasional **Height:** to 7 ft. **Flowering:** March–May **Flower Color:** Green to yellow **Habitat-Community:** Washes and gravelly slopes in creosote bush scrubs, foothill chaparrals, and woodlands **Elevation:** Below 4700 ft. **Ecoregions:** Southern California Mountains, Sonoran Basin and Range

Stout, evergreen shrub with stiff, hairy (especially when young) branches; dioecious. Leaves 0.8–1.6 in. long, opposite, oval, thick, gray-green waxy. Male flowers in axillary clusters, 0 petals, 5 green sepals 0.1–0.2 in. long, 8–12 stamens. Female flowers singular, 0 petals, 5 green sepals 0.4–0.8 in. long, yellow anthers. Fruits 0.5–1 in. long, ovoid, leathery capsules (nuts). Harvested commercially for many contemporary uses, particularly oils from its seeds. Found along the PCT in abundance in the San Felipe Valley of San Diego County and at the northern base of the San Jacinto Mountains at Snow Creek.

Phoradendron bolleanum

Bollean
mistletoe

VISCACEAE MISTLETOE FAMILY

PCT Sections: 1–9 & 14–18 **Abundance:** Occasional **Height:** 1–2 ft. **Flowering:** June–August **Flower Color:** Yellow to green **Habitat-Community:** Pinyon-juniper woodlands, chaparrals, and montane coniferous forests **Elevation:** Below 7600 ft. **Ecoregions:** Southern California Mountains, Sierra Nevada, Cascades

Multi-branched, aerial, hemiparasitic (on conifers) subshrub with brittle olive-green stems; dioecious. Leaves 0.4–1.1 in. long, evergreen, opposite, spoon-shaped to oblong, hairless, green to rusty olive. Flowers 0.2 in. long, 3-parted perianth, in spikes. Male flowers 6–20 per spike. Female flowers 2 per spike. Fruits 0.1–0.3 in. across, shiny, stemless, white to pink (sometimes red) berries. Specializes on *Juniperus*, *Hesperocyparis*, and sometimes *Abies concolor*, sending modified roots into the cells of its host. *Phoradendron* (from the Greek *phor*, "thief," *dendron*, "tree") is an apt nod to its nutrient-robbing lifestyle. The berries are eaten and dispersed by birds, but all mistletoe foliage and fruits are toxic to humans!

Phoradendron californicum

desert
mistletoe

VISCACEAE MISTLETOE FAMILY

PCT Sections: 1–4 **Abundance:** Rare **Height:** 1–4 ft.
Flowering: January–April **Flower Color:** Yellow
to green **Habitat-Community:** Washes and sandy
areas in creosote bush scrubs and woodlands
Elevation: Below 4500 ft. **Ecoregions:** Sonoran
Basin and Range

Hemiparasitic subshrub, appearing on host plants as leafless, multi-branching, rock-star hairdos with red to greenish brown stems (sometimes hairy at the tips); dioecious. Leaves <0.1 in. long, 0 or scale-like, evergreen, opposite. Flowers <0.2 in. long, 3-parted perianth, in spikes. Male flowers 6–14 per spike. Female flowers 2 per spike. Fruits 0.1–0.2 in. across, stemless, orange-red to white berries. The berries are eaten by the phainopepla bird, which disperses the indigestible seeds at the next bathroom stop, on some unsuspecting host. Specializes on *Senegalia greggii*, *Prosopis*, *Parkinsonia*, and *Simmondsia chinensis*. Found only at lower desert crossings of the PCT, primarily in Riverside and San Diego counties. Caution: foliage and fruits are toxic!

Phoradendron juniperinum

juniper
mistletoe

VISCACEAE MISTLETOE FAMILY

PCT Sections: 3–5 & 8–24 **Abundance:** Common
Height: 8–30 in. **Flowering:** July–September
Flower Color: Yellow-green **Habitat-Community:**
Woodlands and lower montane coniferous forests
Elevation: 5600–8500 ft. **Ecoregions:** Southern
California Mountains, Sierra Nevada, Cascades,
Klamath Mountains

Erect or pendent hemiparasitic shrub with green to yellow-green, hairless stems that are woody toward the base; dioecious. Leaves to 0.1 in. long, evergreen, opposite, 4-ranked, scale-like, fused in pairs. Flowers minute, 3-parted perianth. Fruits to 0.2 in. across, hairless, pink-white, 1-seeded berries. Specializes on *Calocedrus decurrens* and *Juniperus*. Birds eat the berries and spread the sticky seeds from tree to tree. Caution: foliage and fruits are toxic!

Phoradendron leucarpum

bigleaf
mistletoe

VISCACEAE MISTLETOE FAMILY

PCT Sections: 1–9 **Abundance:** Occasional **Height:**
1–3 ft. **Flowering:** January–September **Flower
Color:** Yellow to green **Habitat-Community:**
Wetland-riparian communities, chaparrals, and
woodlands **Elevation:** Below 5900 ft. **Ecoregions:**
Southern California Mountains, Sierra Nevada

Multi-branched, hemiparasitic subshrub, forming large green orbs of brittle stems; dioecious. Leaves 0.7–2.5 in. long, evergreen, opposite, widely spoon-shaped to round, green. Flowers <0.3 in. long, 3-parted perianth, in spikes. Male flowers 25–35 per spike. Female flowers 6–15 per spike. Fruits 0.1–0.3 in. across, stemless, shiny white (sometimes pink-tinged) berries. Two subspecies along the PCT: subsp. *macrophyllum* is commonly hosted by *Platanus racemosa*, *Fraxinus*, and *Salix*; subsp. *tomentosum* specializes on *Quercus*. Commercially harvested in North America as a surrogate for European mistletoe (*Viscum album*) and used in Christmas decorations and for kissing under. Caution: foliage and fruits are toxic!

▼ ALTERNATE

Rhus aromatica

skunkbrush

ANACARDIACEAE SUMAC FAMILY

PCT Sections: 1–8 & 18–24 **Abundance:** Common **Height:** 1–8 ft. **Flowering:** March–May **Flower Color:** Pale yellow **Habitat-Community:** Rocky or disturbed places from chaparrals, scrubs, and woodlands to lower montane coniferous forests **Elevation:** Below 7200 ft. **Ecoregions:** All

Diffusely branched shrub with a strong skunky odor when stems or leaves are crushed. Leaves deciduous, alternate, palmate, with 3(5) leaflets. Leaflets 0.5–2 in. long, base tapered to a rounded tip, shiny green above, hairy below, with toothed or lobed margins. Flowers clustered, 5-parted, small, pale yellow. Fruits 0.2–0.3 across, sticky-haired red-orange berries, edible but tart. Foliage is similar to poison oak's, but skunkbrush's terminal leaflet tapers to the point of attachment and lacks a stalk. Sprouts after fire.

Toxicodendron diversilobum

western poison oak

ANACARDIACEAE SUMAC FAMILY

PCT Sections: 1–7 & 15–20 & 23–24 **Abundance:** Locally common **Height:** to 15 ft. (vine to 60 ft.) **Flowering:** April–June **Flower Color:** Pale yellow **Habitat-Community:** Moist, wooded slopes in foothill chaparrals and oak woodlands **Elevation:** Below 6000 ft. **Ecoregions:** Southern California Mountains, Sierra Nevada, Cascades, Klamath Mountains

Gangly, deciduous shrub or woody vine that often utilizes larger trees for support. Leaflets 1–5 in. long, compound (usually in 3s), oblong, leathery, shiny, resinous, unlobed or lobed, resembling an oak leaf, bright red in fall. Flowers 0.1–0.3 in. across, borne on nodding stems, 5-parted, with greenish sepals and pale-yellow petals. Fruits 0.2–0.3 in. across, round, white, berry-like drupes. Perhaps the most disparaged of all plants along the PCT: the surface oil urushiol, abundant in its leaves and fruits, causes a rash in 80% of humans; resistance generally dwindles with recurrent exposure. When burned, as in a campfire or brush pile, it becomes especially toxic, affecting even those who thought they were immune. Seeds dispersed by birds.

Eriophyllum confertiflorum

golden yarrow

ASTERACEAE SUNFLOWER FAMILY

PCT Sections: 1–10 **Abundance:** Common **Height:** to 2 ft. **Flowering:** April–August **Flower Color:** Yellow **Habitat-Community:** Gravelly hills and rocky slopes from Joshua tree woodlands to upper montane coniferous forests **Elevation:** Below 9000 ft. **Ecoregions:** Southern California Mountains, Sonoran/Mojave Basin and Range, Sierra Nevada

Tidy, rounded shrub or clumping subshrub, woody only at the base, with branches persistently hairy. Leaves 1–2 in. long, alternate, deeply 3–5- to many-lobed, densely white-hairy. Flowers composite, in dense, flat-topped clusters of 3–30. Flowering heads 0.3–0.4 in. across with both yellow ray and disk flowers. Fruits achenes to 0.2 in. long with white pappus scales. *Eriophyllum* means "woolly-leaved" in Latin. The common name distinguishes it from the similar (but white) flowers of *Achillea millefolium*.

Senecio flaccidus var. *monoensis*

Mono ragwort

ASTERACEAE SUNFLOWER FAMILY

PCT Sections: 1–8 **Abundance:** Occasional **Height:** to 4 ft. **Flowering:** March–October **Flower Color:** Yellow **Habitat-Community:** Sandy washes, alluvial plains, and rocky slopes in scrubs and woodlands **Elevation:** Below 6500 ft. **Ecoregions:** Southern California Mountains, Sierra Nevada

Fast-growing, short-lived subshrub from a woody taproot that quickly colonizes disturbed areas or washes following flood events. Stems few-branched, green, photosynthetic. Leaves 1–4 in. long, thread-like, often pinnately lobed, usually hairless. Flowers composite, in radiate, showy heads 3–4 in. across. Involucres 0.3–0.5 in. long, bell-shaped, with 13–25 generally black-tipped phyllaries of equal length. Disk flowers 45–55 per head, ray flowers 10–22 per head, yellow. Fruits 0.1–0.2 in. long, densely hairy achenes with white bristles. An important host plant for native bee and wasp pollinators. *Senecio* (from the Latin, "old man") refers to the white pappus.

Berberis aquifolium

Oregon grape

BERBERIDACEAE

BARBERRY FAMILY

PCT Sections: 1–8 & 13–24 **Abundance:** Common **Height:** to 10 ft. **Flowering:** February–April **Flower Color:** Yellow **Habitat-Community:** Open, mostly rocky slopes from oak woodlands to upper montane coniferous forests **Elevation:** Below 8600 ft. **Ecoregions:** All (except Sonoran/Mojave Basin and Range)

Creeping or erect shrub with glossy, spiny leaves. Leaves to 10 in. long, evergreen, alternate, pinnate, with 5–9 leaflets. Leaflets to 3 in. long, thick, round to elliptical, with central vein and spine-toothed margins. Flowers 30–60 per cluster, yellow, bowl-shaped, with 9 sepals, 6 petals, and 6 stamens. Fruits to 0.3 in. across, blue to purple berries with a white-waxy coating. Roots reportedly toxic, with spines that can lead to infections. The tart berries are edible in small quantities but more popularly used to make jelly and wine.

Peritoma arborea

bladderpod

CLEOMACEAE

SPIDERFLOWER FAMILY

PCT Sections: 1–4 & 6–8 **Abundance:** Occasional **Height:** 2–6 ft. **Flowering:** All year **Flower Color:** Yellow **Habitat-Community:** Washes, sandy slopes, and mesas in scrubs and foothill chaparrals **Elevation:** Below 4500 ft. **Ecoregions:** Southern California Mountains, Sierra Nevada

Malodorous shrub with tan stems, preferring disturbed habitats. Leaves 0.4–1.3 in. long, compound, with 3 lance-shaped to oblong, sometimes short-hairy leaflets 1–2 in. long; petiole 0.4–1.2 in. long. Flowers 0.4–0.7 in. long, irregular, with 4 green sepals, 4 yellow petals, and exserted stamens. Three varieties along the PCT: var. *globosa* (round pod) is most common in Tehachapi Mountains and the western Mojave Desert crossing; var. *angustata* (spindle-shaped pod) is most common near the Interstate 15 and 10 crossings; var. *arborea* (ovoid pod) is most common in San Diego and Riverside counties.

Amorpha californica

California false indigo

FABACEAE LEGUME FAMILY

PCT Sections: 3–6 **Abundance:** Occasional **Height:** 3–12 ft. **Flowering:** May–July **Flower Color:** Purple **Habitat-Community:** Open slopes and drainages from foothill chaparrals to lower montane coniferous forests **Elevation:** Below 7800 ft. **Ecoregions:** Southern California Mountains

Tall, erect, long-branched shrub with gland-dotted, hairy stems. Leaves to 12 in. long, pinnate, armed with spiny bristles. Leaflets 0.8–1.3 in. long, 11–27, oval, bright green, glandular. Flowers 0.5–0.7 in. long, arranged in long spikes at stem tips, irregular, just the banner and 10 protruding stamens. Fruits small, usually 1-seeded legume pods. *Amorpha* (from the Greek, "without form") refers to the 1-petaled flowers, a departure from the usual pea-like flowers of the Fabaceae. Widely scattered along the PCT from the San Jacinto to the San Gabriel Mountains.

Lupinus albifrons

silver bush lupine

FABACEAE LEGUME FAMILY

PCT Sections: 1–9 & 14–24 **Abundance:** Common **Height:** 1–3 ft. **Flowering:** March–June **Flower Color:** Violet to lavender **Habitat-Community:** Dry slopes and plateaus from scrubs to upper montane coniferous forests **Elevation:** Below 10,000 ft. **Ecoregions:** All (except Sonoran/Mojave Basin and Range)

Spreading to erect subshrub with a woody base. Leaves alternate, usually clustered near base, palmate. Leaflets 0.5–3.5 in. long, 6–10, silver-hairy. Flowers 0.4–0.7 in. long, in spike-like clusters 5–16 in. long, irregular, violet to lavender with a yellow banner spot. Fruits 1.2–2 in. long, hairy pea pods with 4–9 tan-mottled seeds. Plants were thought to rob the soil (hence *Lupinus*, "wolfish"), but they in fact obtain nitrogen from air surrounding the roots. Alkaloid toxins make this and many lupines resistant to forage.

Lupinus excubitus

grape soda lupine

FABACEAE LEGUME FAMILY

PCT Sections: 5–10 **Abundance:** Occasional **Height:** 2–6 ft. **Flowering:** April–June **Flower Color:** Violet to lavender **Habitat-Community:** Dry washes and sandy slopes in Mojave mixed woody scrub and Joshua tree & pinyon-juniper woodlands **Elevation:** Below 5400 ft. **Ecoregions:** Southern California Mountains, Mojave Basin and Range, Sierra Nevada

Tall, erect, woody subshrub with hairy stems. Leaves alternate, palmate. Leaflets 0.4–3.2 in. long, 7–10, silver-hairy. Flowers 0.4–0.7 in. long, whorled in spike-like clusters 4–28 in. long, irregular, violet to lavender, hairy banner back, and persistent through winter. Fruits 1.2–2 in. long, silky pea pods with 5–8 yellow-brown-mottled seeds. Look for it in Antelope Valley northward to the southern Sierra Nevada (Walker Pass to Kennedy Meadows).

Prosopis glandulosa

honey mesquite

FABACEAE LEGUME FAMILY

PCT Sections: 1–4 **Abundance:** Occasional **Height:** to 20 ft. **Flowering:** April–August **Flower Color:** Green to white or yellow **Habitat-Community:** Sandy alkali flats and washes in scrubs **Elevation:** Below 4000 ft. **Ecoregions:** Southern California Mountains, Sonoran/Mojave Basin and Range

Large, spiny shrub, often as wide as tall, with long, arching branches. Stem spines 0.2–1.7 in. long and opposite. Leaves 2-pinnate, secondary leaflets 0.5–1.2 in. long, 14–24, oblong. Flowers 0.1–0.2 in. long, numerous in spike-like clusters 2–4 in. long, irregular, greenish, with short-lobed bell-shaped calyces, inconspicuous petals, and 10 stamens extending much beyond the calyx. Fruits 2–8 in. long, linear pods, narrowed between the seeds, hairless. Roots are capable of penetrating 200 ft. in search of groundwater. Indigenous peoples use this as a medicinal plant, food source (pods and flowers), building and tool material, and fuel. Confined along the PCT to desert crossings at springs, washes, and canyon seeps.

Psorothamnus arborescens

indigo bush

FABACEAE LEGUME FAMILY

PCT Sections: 3–4 **Abundance:** Rare **Height:** to 4 ft. **Flowering:** April–May **Flower Color:** Violet to blue **Habitat-Community:** Sandy flats, slopes, and washes in creosote bush scrubs **Elevation:** Below 3200 ft. **Ecoregions:** Sonoran Basin and Range

Many-branched, thorny, sweet-scented desert shrub with usually hairless tan stems. Leaves deciduous, alternate, pinnate, silky-hairy. Leaflets 0.1–0.7 in. long, 5 or 7, and generally continuous with the axis. Flowers 0.2–0.3 in. long, in terminal spikes, irregular, brilliant indigo-blue; calyces gland-dotted with unequal lobes. Fruits 0.2–0.3 in. long, pea pods dotted with large, yellow glands. Found along the PCT only at the Coachella Valley crossing from Snow Creek to Whitewater Canyon.

Senegalia greggii

catclaw

FABACEAE LEGUME FAMILY

PCT Sections: 1–4 **Abundance:** Locally common **Height:** to 14 ft. **Flowering:** April–July **Flower Color:** Pale yellow to cream **Habitat-Community:** Rocky slopes and sandy washes in creosote bush & Sonoran mixed woody scrubs **Elevation:** Below 4400 ft. **Ecoregions:** Sonoran Basin and Range

Deep-rooted woody shrub armed with thorny hooked prickles. Leaves to 1 in. long, deciduous, 2-pinnate, appearing in spring before the flowers. Secondary leaflets 0.2–0.3 in. long, 3–6 pairs, ovoid, somewhat hairy. Flowers in solitary spikes of hundreds at branch tips, irregular, minute, pale yellow to cream. Fruits 3–6 in. long, flattened and often twisted pea pods, constricted between seeds. Common across the deserts of the southwestern US. Frequently hosts *Phoradendron californicum* but rarely succumbs to it. Seeds are not edible: they contain cyanogenic glycoside, which is toxic to humans! Aka wait-a-minute bush.

Dasiphora fruticosa

shrubby cinquefoil

ROSACEAE ROSE FAMILY

PCT Sections: 10–24 **Abundance:** Locally common **Height:** to 4 ft. **Flowering:** June–September **Flower Color:** Yellow **Habitat-Community:** Open slopes or moist places, including serpentine soils, from upper montane coniferous forests to alpine communities **Elevation:** 6500–13,000 ft. **Ecoregions:** Sierra Nevada, Cascades, Klamath Mountains

Multi-stemmed shrub with shredding red-brown bark. Leaves deciduous, alternate, pinnate, with 3–7 linear to oval leaflets 0.2–1 in. long. Flowers 0.2–0.5 in. long, clustered at the ends of stems, 5-petaled, yellow to pale yellow. Fruits dry, strawberry-like receptacles with many, hairy achenes to 0.1 in. long. Sometimes the dominant shrub in rocky, subalpine to alpine habitats. Increases in areas with heavy grazing since animals are not too excited about munching on it. Aka yellow rose.

Rosa californica

California wild rose

ROSACEAE ROSE FAMILY

PCT Sections: 1–10 **Abundance:** Occasional **Height:** to 8 ft. **Flowering:** February–November **Flower Color:** Pink **Habitat-Community:** Moist areas and streambanks in wetland-riparian communities **Elevation:** Below 6600 ft. **Ecoregions:** Southern California Mountains, Sierra Nevada

Fragrant-flowered, thicket-forming, prickly shrub or woody vine. Leaves deciduous, alternate, odd-pinnate, with 5 or 7 leaflets. Leaflets, terminal blade 0.7–2.2 in. long, ovoid, generally widest at or below the middle, with saw-toothed margins. Flowers 2–3 in. across, open-faced, flat, with 5 pink petals and >20 orange to yellow stamens and pistils. Fruits 0.3–0.7 in. long, red, ovoid, berry-like achenes (hips) with persistent, fleshy sepals; they remain on the plant throughout winter, providing food for birds and bears at a time when forage is scarce. Rose hips are an excellent source of vitamin C, but they can be dry and unpleasant when eaten fresh. A delicious, fruity tea is a better way to enjoy them: chop or steep the hips and sweeten with honey for a drink that tastes like punch. They also make a good jam.

Rosa woodsii

Woods' rose

ROSACEAE ROSE FAMILY

PCT Sections: 4–5 & 8–19 **Abundance:** Occasional **Height:** 3–7 ft. **Flowering:** May–August **Flower Color:** Pink **Habitat-Community:** Moist places from woodlands to subalpine coniferous forests and wetland-riparian communities **Elevation:** Below 10,900 ft. **Ecoregions:** Southern California Mountains, Sierra Nevada, Cascades

Thicket-forming, pleasantly aromatic shrub with straight, thin thorns or (rarely) unarmed. Leaves deciduous, alternate, pinnate, with 5–9 leaflets. Leaflets 0.5–2 in. long, oval to ovoid, with toothed margins and nonglandular teeth tips. Flowers 0.5–1 in. long, solitary or 2–5 per cluster, 5-parted, pink, saucer-shaped, with many stamens and 20–35 pistils. Fruits to 0.5 in. across, red, berry-like achenes (hips) with persistent sepals. Occurs at higher elevations than other roses along the PCT.

Rubus leucodermis

whitebark raspberry

ROSACEAE ROSE FAMILY

PCT Sections: 3–5 & 10–24 **Abundance:** Common **Height:** to 6.5 ft. **Flowering:** April–July **Flower Color:** White **Habitat-Community:** Forest openings and disturbed places in montane coniferous forests **Elevation:** Below 9200 ft. **Ecoregions:** Southern California Mountains, Sierra Nevada, Cascades, Klamath Mountains

Arching, mounded shrub with thick, curved thorns. Leaves deciduous, alternate, palmate, with 3–5 leaflets. Leaflets 1–3 in. long, lance-shaped to ovoid, woolly below, with double-toothed margins. Flowers to 0.3 in. long, 3–10 per cluster, 5-parted, white, bowl-shaped, with many stamens and generally >30 pistils. Fruits to 0.5 in. across, red-purple to black, finely hairy berries. The "blackcap" fruits are delicious treats in the summer!

Rubus ursinus

California blackberry

ROSACEAE ROSE FAMILY

PCT Sections: 1–6 & 16–24 **Abundance:** Common **Height:** to 20 ft. long **Flowering:** February–July **Flower Color:** White **Habitat-Community:** Forest openings and disturbed places in woodlands, chaparrals, and lower montane coniferous forests **Elevation:** Below 6600 ft. **Ecoregions:** All (except Sonoran/Mojave Basin and Range)

Viny, straggling shrub with round stems and thin, straight prickles; generally dioecious, sometimes with bisexual flowers. Leaves deciduous, alternate, palmate, with 3 leaflets. Leaflets 1–3 in. long, oval to ovoid, hairy or hairless, point-tipped, with double-toothed margins. Flowers to 0.3 in. long, solitary or 2–5 per cluster, 5-parted, white, saucer-shaped, with many stamens and >30 pistils. Fruits to 0.5 in. across, oval to roundish, black, hairless berries. The berries are delicious fresh or made into jams and pies. A healthy tea can be made from the fresh leaves.

Sorbus californica

California mountain ash

ROSACEAE ROSE FAMILY

PCT Sections: 10–24 **Abundance:** Locally common **Height:** 3–13 ft. **Flowering:** May–July **Flower Color:** White **Habitat-Community:** Moist places from lower montane to subalpine coniferous forests **Elevation:** Below 14,100 ft. **Ecoregions:** Sierra Nevada, Cascades, Klamath Mountains

Erect shrub with gray-brown stems. Leaves deciduous, alternate, pinnate, with 7–11 leaflets. Leaflets 1–1.5 in. long, oblong to ovoid, shiny above, point-tipped, with toothed margins. Flowers 0.5–1 in. long, many in clusters, 5-parted, white, with 15–20 stamens and 1–5 pistils. Fruits to 0.4 in. across, wax-coated red berries. The edible berries are mostly used to make jelly; as an old remedy for dandruff, they were rubbed into the scalp. Caution: do not confuse mountain ash with the highly poisonous *Actaea rubra*.

▼ OPPOSITE, WHORLED, OR BASAL

Sambucus nigra subsp. *caerulea*

blue elderberry

ADOXACEAE MUSKROOT FAMILY

PCT Sections: All **Abundance:** Common **Height:** 3–20 ft. **Flowering:** March–July **Flower Color:** White **Habitat-Community:** Well-drained sites near streams and forest openings from scrubs and chaparrals to upper montane coniferous forests **Elevation:** Below 10,000 ft. **Ecoregions:** All

Shrub or small tree with gray or brown bark that furrows with age. Leaves deciduous, opposite, pinnate, with 3–9 elliptical leaflets. Leaflets 1–6 in. long, point-tipped, with fine-toothed margins. Flowers in flat-topped clusters, small, white, 5-petaled. Fruits to 0.2 in. across, dark blue berries with white-waxy bloom. Fire stimulates sprouting and seed germination. Stems historically used to make flute-like musical instruments. Famous for its berries being made into jam, jelly, juice, and wine. A delightful juice can be made by soaking the flowers in lightly sweetened water.

Sambucus racemosa

red elderberry

ADOXACEAE MUSKROOT FAMILY

PCT Sections: 10–18 & 22–24 **Abundance:** Common **Height:** 3–25 ft. **Flowering:** July–August **Flower Color:** White to cream **Habitat-Community:** Moist places, streambanks, meadows, and openings from woodlands to subalpine coniferous forests **Elevation:** Below 12,000 ft. **Ecoregions:** Sierra Nevada, Cascades, Klamath Mountains

Shrub or small tree with red-brown bark. Leaves deciduous, opposite, pinnate, with 5–7 elliptical leaflets. Leaflets 1.5–5 in. long, point-tipped, with fine-toothed margins. Flowers in pyramidal to spherical clusters, small, white to cream, 5-petaled. Fruits to 0.2 in. across, red or black berries without white-waxy bloom. Raw berries are not edible! With some exceptions, red berries on shrubs or trees in the mountains are mostly bitter and generally toxic!

Fraxinus latifolia

Oregon ash

OLEACEAE OLIVE FAMILY

PCT Sections: 2–3 & 5 & 8 & 16–19 & 23–24
Abundance: Occasional **Height:** to 40 ft.
Flowering: March–May **Flower Color:** Green
Habitat-Community: Streambanks, canyons, and washes in wetland-riparian communities
Elevation: Below 5500 ft. **Ecoregions:** Southern California Mountains, Sierra Nevada, Cascades, Klamath Mountains

Single-stemmed, deciduous tree with trunk to 2 ft. across and broad to narrow crown; dioecious. Bark rough, gray, furrowed; branches hairless or long-shaggy-hairy. Leaves 5–14 in. long, opposite, pinnate, with 5–7 generally sessile (lateral only), elliptic to ovoid leaflets 3–7 in. long. Flowers in small, axillary clusters; 0 petals. Male flowers 4-toothed with 2 anthers. Female flowers minute, irregularly cut, with stigma <0.1 in. long. Fruits samaras; as they fall, they spin like miniature helicopters, increasing the distance dispersed. Known to live to 250 years old. Intergrades with *F. velutina* in Kern County.

Fraxinus velutina

velvet ash

OLEACEAE OLIVE FAMILY

PCT Sections: 1–9 **Abundance:** Occasional **Height:** to 40 ft. **Flowering:** March–April **Flower Color:** Green **Habitat-Community:** Streambanks, canyons, and washes in wetland-riparian communities **Elevation:** Below 5500 ft. **Ecoregions:** Southern California Mountains, Sierra Nevada

Small, deciduous tree of watercourses along the PCT, with velvet-downy young branches and a trunk to 2 ft. across; dioecious. Bark rough, gray-brown, furrowed. Leaves 4–10 in. long, opposite, stiff-leathery, pinnate, with 5–7 stalked, lance-shaped leaflets 1.5–2 in. long. Flowers in small, axillary clusters; 0 petals. Male flowers minute, with 2 anthers. Female flowers to 0.1 in. long, green, with stigma 0.1–0.2 in. long. Fruits samaras. Intergrades with *F. latifolia* in Kern County. No surprise, *velutina* is Latin for "velvety."

Clematis lasiantha

pipestem

RANUNCULACEAE
BUTTERCUP FAMILY

PCT Sections: 1–6 & 16–19 **Abundance:** Common **Height:** Vine **Flowering:** January–July **Flower Color:** White **Habitat-Community:** Streambanks in chaparrals, lower montane coniferous forests, and wetland-riparian communities **Elevation:** Below 6500 ft. **Ecoregions:** Southern California/ Northern Baja Coast, Southern California Mountains, Sierra Nevada, Cascades

Woody vine with climbing or sprawling, hairy (especially when young) stems. Leaves deciduous, opposite, pinnate, with 3–5 leaflets. Leaflets 0.5–2.5 in. long, ovoid, hairy below, 2–3-lobed, with toothed to smooth margins. Flowers 0.4–0.8 in. long, solitary or in clusters of 3–5, with 0 petals and many stamens and pistils. Petal-like sepals 4, white, hairy. Fruits ovoid, hairy, elongated achenes with a feathery style. Originally collected from San Diego and subsequently described by Thomas Nuttall (1786–1859).

Clematis ligusticifolia
virgin's bower
RANUNCULACEAE
BUTTERCUP FAMILY

PCT Sections: 1–9 & 19–20 **Abundance:** Common **Height:** Vine **Flowering:** March–September **Flower Color:** White **Habitat-Community:** Streambanks and moist slopes from chaparrals and oak woodlands to upper montane coniferous forests **Elevation:** Below 7900 ft. **Ecoregions:** Southern California/Northern Baja Coast, Southern California Mountains, Sierra Nevada, Cascades

Woody vine, climbing on shrubs and trees as high as 40 ft. Leaves deciduous, opposite, pinnate, with 5–7 leaflets. Leaflets 1–3 in. long, lance-shaped to ovoid, hairy below, 3-lobed, with toothed to smooth margins. Flowers to 0.5 in. long, 7–20 per cluster, with 0 petals and many stamens and pistils. Petal-like sepals 4, white, hairy. Fruits oval, hairy, elongated achenes with a feathery style. The common name is most likely associated with the biblical story of the Holy Family's seeking shelter under a wild clematis during their flight to Egypt.

Clematis pauciflora
few-flowered clematis
RANUNCULACEAE
BUTTERCUP FAMILY

PCT Sections: 1–4 **Abundance:** Occasional **Height:** to 9 ft. **Flowering:** January–June **Flower Color:** White to cream **Habitat-Community:** Dry slopes in scrubs and foothill chaparrals **Elevation:** Below 4500 ft. **Ecoregions:** Southern California/Northern Baja Coast, Southern California Mountains

Woody vine, sprawling through other shrubs. Leaves opposite, pinnate, borne every 1–2 in. at stem nodes. Leaflets 0.5–1.8 in. long, 3–5, dark green, 3-lobed. Flowers 1–3 per axil, white to cream, hairy above, with petal-like sepals 0.3–0.6 in. long, 0 petals, 40–50 stamens, and 30–40 pistils. Fruits hairless achenes with a long, plume-like style. *Pauciflora* means "few-flowered" in Latin.

Aesculus californica
California buckeye
SAPINDACEAE SOAPBERRY FAMILY

PCT Sections: 5–6 **Abundance:** Rare **Height:** 10–35 ft. **Flowering:** May–August **Flower Color:** White to pale rose **Habitat-Community:** Dry slopes, canyons, and along streams in oak woodlands and foothill chaparrals **Elevation:** Below 5500 ft. **Ecoregions:** Southern California Mountains

Sweet-scented, multi-trunked, deciduous tree or large shrub with a crown as broad as high. Bark gray, cracked, often coated with lichens. Leaves opposite, palmately compound, 5–7 leaflets; petiole 1–4 in. long. Leaflets 2.4–6.7 in. long, oblong to lance-shaped, bright green, with fine-toothed margins. Flowers in dense spike-like "candles" 4–8 in. long at the tips of erect branches. Petals 0.6–0.9 in. long, 4, fused at base, white to pale rose, with 5–7 exserted stamens. Fruits 2–3 in. long, 1–2 per stem tip, fig-shaped capsules with a large, round, orange-brown seed (or nut) 0.8–2.8 in. long. The seeds, the largest of any temperate (non-tropical) plant, are toxic to humans! Although widely distributed throughout the state, it intercepts the PCT only in the far western Transverse Ranges, a region influenced by a more maritime climate.

Larrea tridentata

creosote bush

ZYGOPHYLLACEAE CALTROP FAMILY

PCT Sections: 1–8 **Abundance:** Locally common **Height:** 3–12 ft. **Flowering:** March–October **Flower Color:** Yellow **Habitat-Community:** Dry slopes and plains in creosote & black bush scrubs and Joshua tree woodlands **Elevation:** Below 4700 ft. **Ecoregions:** Southern California Mountains, Sonoran/Mojave Basin and Range, Sierra Nevada

Dominant, long-lived, drought-tolerant evergreen shrub, whose brittle, gray branches have swollen nodes. Leaves opposite, 1-compound, with 2 leaflets fused at the base. Leaflets 0.3–0.8 in. long, lance-shaped, curved, waxy, resinous, green to rust-yellow. Flowers 0.6–1 in. across, solitary in leaf axils, 5-parted, with unequal sepals and early-deciduous, clawed, twisted, yellow petals. Fruits 0.1–0.2 in. across, 5-lobed capsules obscured by silky white hairs. The large round galls that often occur on plants are a reaction to creosote gall midges (*Asphondyila*). As plants approach the century mark, older branches die and new ones emerge along the plant's perimeter, eventually forming a ring of stem crowns around the original plant. The oldest clonal ring, "King Clone" in Lucerne Valley, has been radio-carbon dated to 11,700 years old—one of the oldest living organisms on earth. Following desert rains, plants exhibit a distinctive but pleasing, tar-like odor, thanks to the activation of their carbonaceous chemical oils, from which the common name derives.

NO OBVIOUS LEAVES

Ephedra aspera

boundary ephedra

EPHEDRACEAE EPHEDRA FAMILY

PCT Sections: 1–3 **Abundance:** Locally common **Height:** to 4 ft. **Habitat-Community:** Dry, sandy to gravelly flats in creosote bush & Sonoran mixed woody scrubs **Elevation:** Below 6500 ft. **Ecoregions:** Southern California Mountains, Sonoran Basin and Range

Highly branched, rounded shrub with long gray twigs maturing yellow-gold and becoming cracked and fissured with age; dioecious. Leaves scale-like bracts 0.1–0.2 in. long, in pairs at nodes. Cones develop on plants in spring. Male plants have yellow pollen cones, several per node. Female plants have seed cones 0.2–0.3 in. long, with 1 smooth or roughened seed. Found along the PCT at the lower desert crossings of southern California. Most common in the San Felipe Valley of San Diego County. A mildly stimulating tea can be made from the stems.

Ephedra californica

desert tea

EPHEDRACEAE EPHEDRA FAMILY

PCT Sections: 1–7 **Abundance:** Locally common **Height:** to 5 ft. **Habitat-Community:** Washes and sandy soils in creosote bush scrubs and Joshua tree woodlands **Elevation:** Below 4500 ft. **Ecoregions:** Southern California Mountains, Sonoran/Mojave Basin and Range

Spindly shrub with photosynthetic stems that become yellow and woody (at the base) with age; dioecious. Leaves reduced to tiny bracts 0.1–0.3 in. long in whorls of 3 along the stem. Male plants have orange-yellow pollen cones, several per node, that become papery with age. Female plants have seed cones with 1 smooth, dark brown seed. The twigs are commonly brewed for medicinal properties.

Ephedra nevadensis

Nevada ephedra

EPHEDRACEAE EPHEDRA FAMILY

PCT Sections: 4–9 **Abundance:** Occasional **Height:** to 4.5 ft. **Habitat-Community:** Dry, rocky slopes and hills in creosote bush scrubs and woodlands **Elevation:** Below 6000 ft. **Ecoregions:** Southern California Mountains, Sierra Nevada

Multi-branched shrub, rarely seen in valleys or sandy flats, with pale, bluish green twigs, rarely purely green like other ephedras; dioecious. Leaves opposite, reduced to small bracts 0.1–0.2 in. long at nodes. Male plants have pollen cones that when mature release microsporangia into the air. In late spring, seed cones on female plants produce smooth, dark brown seeds, split into pairs. Primarily wind-pollinated, with male plants growing in dry areas and female plants in wetter sites, an arrangement that increases seed production. Known for its medicinal qualities; Indigenous peoples make a tea from the stems. Aka Mormon tea, cowboy tea, Brigham tea.

Ephedra viridis

green ephedra

EPHEDRACEAE EPHEDRA FAMILY

PCT Sections: 4–9 **Abundance:** Locally common **Height:** to 5 ft. **Habitat-Community:** Dry, rocky slopes and canyon walls in creosote bush and sagebrush scrubs and pinyon-juniper woodlands **Elevation:** Below 7000 ft. **Ecoregions:** Southern California Mountains, Sierra Nevada

Shrub with long, erect branches and bright green, photosynthetic, broom-like twigs; dioecious. Leaves in pairs at each node, reduced to small bracts 0.2–0.3 in. long. Male plant pollen cones are bright yellow when mature. In early summer, seed cones on female plants produce elongated, dark brown seeds, in pairs. Along the PCT, it can be found from the Transverse Ranges northward to Kennedy Meadows in the southern Sierra. Its medicinal uses are many, including treatment for the common cold. But because the plant is also toxic, it should not be ingested without a doctor's recommendation! Aka mountain joint fir.

CACTI

Cylindropuntia californica var. *parkeri*

cane cholla

CACTACEAE CACTUS FAMILY

PCT Sections: 1–5 **Abundance:** Occasional **Height:** to 8 ft. **Flowering:** April–July **Flower Color:** Yellow to yellow-green **Habitat-Community**: Canyons and mesas in foothill chaparrals and woodlands **Elevation:** Below 5900 ft. **Ecoregions:** Southern California Mountains

Erect, narrow, mostly unbranched cactus with stems that have tubercles 3–5 times longer than wide. Spines 0.9–1.6 in. long, yellow to yellow-brown. Flowers 1–1.4 in. across, yellow-green with purple-tipped inner perianth segments. Fruits leathery to slow-drying with 0–many spines and white (when dry) seeds to 0.3 in. long. Native to the coastal foothills and mountains of southern California and northern Baja California. Densely spined plants along the PCT at Scissor's Crossing in San Diego County are hybrids between it and *C. ganderi*.

Cylindropuntia echinocarpa

silver cholla

CACTACEAE CACTUS FAMILY

PCT Sections: 3–6 **Abundance:** Locally common **Height:** to 5 ft. **Flowering:** March–June **Flower Color:** Yellow-green **Habitat-Community**: Gravelly, open flats or sandy slopes in creosote bush scrubs and Joshua tree woodlands **Elevation:** Below 5100 ft. **Ecoregions:** Southern California Mountains, Sonoran Basin and Range, Sierra Nevada

Densely branched cactus with a short, single trunk and short terminal stems. Tubercles 0.5 in. long and 0.7 in. wide, each with up to 20 straight, yellowish spines 1–2 in. long. Flowers 1–2 in. across, yellow-green. Fruits dry with many spines and white (when dry) seeds to 0.2 in. long. Reproduces mainly through seeds but also asexually, when dropped stem segments take root in the soil. Short branches and rounded tubercles help distinguish it from other chollas. Occurs along the PCT only at the lower desert crossings.

Echinocereus engelmannii

Engelmann's hedgehog cactus

CACTACEAE CACTUS FAMILY

PCT Sections: 1–4 **Abundance:** Occasional **Height:** 1–3 ft. **Flowering:** May–June **Flower Color:** Purple to magenta **Habitat-Community:** Rocky slopes in creosote bush scrubs and Joshua tree & pinyon-juniper woodlands **Elevation**: Below 5900 ft. **Ecoregions:** Southern California Mountains, Sonoran/Mojave Basin and Range

Our common form grows in loose clumps of up to 20 shaggy-spined, thick stems, each with 10–13 ribs. Flowers 2–3 in. across, funnel- to bell-shaped, purple to brilliant magenta or "strawberry" in color. Fruits 0.8–1.2 in. across, spherical, densely spiny, with black seeds to 0.1 in. long. Typically delays flowering until 2–3 stems are developed, which may take 10 years. Look for it in the Anza-Borrego region and other desert crossings. The genus name comes from the Greek *echinos* ("hedgehog") and the Latin *cereus* ("candle").

Echinocereus mojavensis

Mojave kingcup cactus

CACTACEAE CACTUS FAMILY

PCT Sections: 4 **Abundance:** Rare **Height:** 1–3 ft. **Flowering:** April–July **Flower Color:** Red to orange-red **Habitat-Community:** Rocky slopes from scrubs to lower montane coniferous forests **Elevation**: Below 9000 ft. **Ecoregions:** Southern California Mountains

Attractive hedgehog cactus, forming clusters of as many as 400 cylindrical stems. Stems, variously armed with twisted spines, are tightly squeezed together to form a contiguous dome or mound, sometimes up to 8 ft. across. Flowers 2–3 in. long, funnel-shaped, succulent, with red to orange-red tepals. Fruits 0.7–1 in. long, generally spherical, covered in minutely hairy spines. In a good year, the mound may be completely blanketed by tomato-red flowers, creating one of the most striking displays of any plant in the California flora. Pollinated by hummingbirds. Limited on the PCT to the scrubs, woodlands, and lower montane coniferous forests of eastern San Bernardino Mountains. Aka Mojave mound cactus.

Ferocactus cylindraceus

California barrel cactus

CACTACEAE CACTUS FAMILY

PCT Sections: 1–4 **Abundance:** Locally common **Height:** to 8 ft. **Flowering:** April–June **Flower Color:** Yellow to orange-red **Habitat-Community:** Rocky, desert slopes in scrubs **Elevation:** Below 4800 ft. **Ecoregions:** Southern California Mountains, Sonoran Basin and Range

Single-stemmed cactus, forming a column to 20 in. across. Column ribs are prominent, numbering 20–30 in mature plants. Ribs are armed with 10–32 spines per areole; the 4 larger central spines are reddish, and the largest is up to 6 in. long. Flowers 1.6–2.5 in. across, funnel-shaped, yellow to orange-red with maroon on the outside. Fruits hairless/spineless, opening by pore near base, yellow, with pitted black seeds to 0.1 in. long. Lives up to 100 years. To avoid freezing, plants grow leaning to the south to keep the growing tips of the stems warm. Excellent stands occur on the PCT in the Anza-Borrego region; elsewhere plants are increasingly threatened by collectors and habitat clearing for renewable energy. *Ferocactus* means "fierce cactus" in Latin.

Opuntia basilaris var. *basilaris*

beavertail cactus

CACTACEAE CACTUS FAMILY

PCT Sections: 1–4 & 7–10 **Abundance:** Occasional **Height:** to 3.5 ft. **Flowering:** March–June **Flower Color:** Red to pink-magenta **Habitat-Community:** Sandy to rocky soils in desert scrubs and pinyon-juniper woodlands **Elevation:** Below 7200 ft. **Ecoregions:** Southern California Mountains, Sonoran Basin and Range, Sierra Nevada

Low-growing, "prickly-pear" cactus comprised of several to dozens of blue-gray platyclades, each to about 8 in. long and more than 5 times as wide as thick, typically with glochids, not spines. Flowers 1.9–3.2 in. across, showy, deep magenta. Fruits 0.7–1.6 in. long, dry at maturity, green and purple (aging tan), generally hairy, with up to 76 areoles and spherical seeds to 0.4 in. long. Like all *Opuntia* spp., the flowers have thigmotactic anthers that, upon being gently poked by bee or human, curl up and deposit their pollen. Occurs at the lower desert crossings and in the eastern San Bernardino Mountains.

Opuntia basilaris
var. brachyclada

short-joint
beavertail

CACTACEAE CACTUS FAMILY

PCT Sections: 4–6 **Abundance:** Rare **Height:** to 2.5 ft. **Flowering:** April–July **Flower Color:** Red to pink-magenta **Habitat-Community:** Sandy to rocky soils in woodlands **Elevation**: Below 6500 ft. **Ecoregions:** Southern California Mountains

Low-growing, densely branched cactus with pads that are cylindric rather than flattened, no more than 2 times wider than they are thick. Flowers 1.7–2.9 in. across, showy, pink-magenta. Fruits 0.7–1.6 in. long, dry at maturity, green and purple (aging tan), generally hairy, with up to 76 areoles and spherical seeds to 0.4 in. long. Plants are pollinated by native bees or moths. Endemic to the Transverse Ranges. Restricted along the PCT to the eastern San Gabriel Mountains and western San Bernardino Mountains. One other variety along the PCT: var. *treleasei*, a rare and endangered taxon with spiny pads, occurs in the Tehachapi Mountains. The Latin *brachy* ("short") alludes to its dwarf growth form.

Opuntia phaeacantha

brown-spined
prickly-pear

CACTACEAE CACTUS FAMILY

PCT Sections: 1–7 **Abundance:** Occasional **Height:** to 5 ft. **Flowering:** May–July **Flower Color:** Yellow to orange-green **Habitat-Community:** Gravelly to rocky soils in chaparrals and woodlands **Elevation**: Below 6800 ft. **Ecoregions:** Southern California Mountains

Sprawling cactus to 10 ft. wide, with long, erect to horizontal stems of large interconnected pads. Pads 5–13 in. across, flattened, obovate, gray-green. Spines to 3 in. long, 1–4 per areole, dark brown; pads are otherwise hairless/spineless. Flowers 1.5–2.6 in. long, generally yellow with a reddish base. Fruits 1.6–3.2 in. long, reddish purple. Widespread, ranging east as far as Kansas. The edible fruit (aka cactus fig or tuna) has a mild pear or watermelon flavor. *Phaeacantha* (from the Greek *phaios*, "dusky", *akantha*, "thorn") refers to the spines.

WILDFLOWERS

▼ COMPOSITE / RAY AND DISK FLOWERS

Achillea millefolium

common yarrow

ASTERACEAE SUNFLOWER FAMILY

PCT Sections: All **Abundance:** Common **Height:** 1–6 ft. **Flowering:** April–September **Flower Color:** White (pink) **Habitat-Community:** Dry or moist, well-drained openings from scrubs, chaparrals, and woodlands to alpine communities **Elevation:** Below 12,000 ft. **Ecoregions:** All

Erect perennial with aromatic, fern-like foliage. Leaves basal and alternate, pinnately lobed, hairy. Flowers in flat-topped clusters; involucres bell-shaped with 3–4 rows of phyllaries. Ray flowers minute, 5–8, white (pink). Disk flowers to 0.1 in. long, 15–40, white to pink. Fruits to 0.1 in. long, flattened, hairless achenes without pappus. Historically used to treat headaches, colds, toothaches, bruises, upset stomachs, and other ailments. The genus name honors Greek warrior Achilles, who used yarrow to staunch bloody wounds.

Erigeron compositus

cutleaf daisy

ASTERACEAE SUNFLOWER FAMILY

PCT Sections: 4 & 10–24 **Abundance:** Locally common **Height:** 1–6 in. **Flowering:** April–September **Flower Color:** White to pink or lavender **Habitat-Community:** Rocky, generally granitic slopes, outcrop crevices, and sandy soils from lower montane coniferous forests to alpine communities **Elevation:** 6500–13,150 ft. **Ecoregions:** Southern California Mountains, Sierra Nevada, Cascades, Klamath Mountains

Compact, tufted perennial with glandular, generally leafless stems. Leaves 0.5–2 in. long, basal, spoon-shaped, deeply lobed, hairy, with unusual doubly-lobed margins. Flowers solitary, radiate (sometimes discoid at high elevation) heads on leafless stems; involucres cup-shaped with equal, purple-tipped, hairy, minutely glandular phyllaries. Ray flowers 0.2–0.5 in. long, (0)30–60, white to pink or lavender. Disk flowers many per head, funnel-shaped, yellow. Fruits to 0.1 in. long, oblong, hairy achenes with 12–15 bristles.

Erigeron coulteri

large mountain fleabane

ASTERACEAE SUNFLOWER FAMILY

PCT Sections: 9–18 **Abundance:** Locally common **Height:** 3–18 in. **Flowering:** July–September **Flower Color:** White **Habitat-Community:** Moist slopes, seeps, streambanks, and wet meadows in wetland-riparian communities **Elevation:** Below 11,200 ft. **Ecoregions:** Sierra Nevada, Cascades

Erect perennial, sometimes forming large colonies, with hairy upper stems. Leaves 2–5 in. long, widely oblong, hairy above, clasping, with smooth or toothed margins. Flowers 1(4) per stem; involucres hemispheric, 0.2–0.4 in. long, with equal, minutely glandular phyllaries, hairy with black cross-walls. Ray flowers 0.3–1 in. long, 45–140, white. Disk flowers many per head, funnel-shaped, yellow. Fruits to 0.1 in. long, oblong, 2–4-ribbed, hairy achenes with 20–25 bristles.

Erigeron lonchophyllus

shortray boreal daisy

ASTERACEAE SUNFLOWER FAMILY

PCT Sections: 4 & 9–13 **Abundance:** Occasional **Height:** 1–8 in. **Flowering:** July–August **Flower Color:** White or pale lavender **Habitat-Community:** Moist meadows and streambanks from sagebrush scrubs to subalpine coniferous forests and wetland-riparian communities **Elevation:** 5900–11,700 ft. **Ecoregions:** Southern California Mountains, Sierra Nevada

Erect annual or perennial with solitary or tufted, slender, hairy stems. Leaves 1–2.5 in. long, linear to narrowly spoon-shaped, hairy or generally hairless, with hairy margins. Flowers many per stem, with unequal, hairy, purple-tipped phyllaries. Ray flowers to 0.1 in. long, 25–50, barely > involucre, white or pale lavender. Disk flowers many per head, funnel-shaped, yellow. Fruits to 0.1 in. long, hairy achenes with 20–30 bristles and generally fewer, smaller outside bristles.

Erigeron vagus

rambling fleabane

ASTERACEAE SUNFLOWER FAMILY

PCT Sections: 10–13 **Abundance:** Occasional **Height:** 1–6 in. **Flowering:** June–August **Flower Color:** White to pink **Habitat-Community:** Talus in alpine communities **Elevation:** 10,800–14,500 ft. **Ecoregions:** Sierra Nevada

Tufted perennial with glandular, leafless stems arising from a basal rosette. Leaves 0.4–1.2 in. long, basal, spoon-shaped, deeply 3-lobed at tip, hairy, glandular. Flowers in solitary heads on leafless stems; involucres hemispheric with equal, purple-tipped, hairy, minutely glandular phyllaries. Ray flowers 0.1–0.3 in. long, 25–35, white to pink. Disk flowers many per head, funnel-shaped, yellow. Fruits to 0.1 in. long, oblong, hairy achenes with 16–20 pappus bristles.

Layia glandulosa

white layia

ASTERACEAE SUNFLOWER FAMILY

PCT Sections: 1–9 **Abundance:** Locally common **Height:** 5–20 in. **Flowering:** February–July **Flower Color:** White **Habitat-Community:** Open, sandy or gravelly soils in creosote bush scrubs, chaparrals, and woodlands **Elevation:** Below 7800 ft. **Ecoregions:** Southern California Mountains, Sonoran/Mojave Basin and Range, Sierra Nevada

Erect, few-branched, spicy-scented annual with dark purple, glandular stems. Leaves 1–4 in. long, alternate, linear to spatula-shaped, dark glandular. Flowers in solitary heads at stem tips; involucres bell-shaped, 0.1–0.4 in. across, with cobwebby phyllaries 0.2–0.5 in. long. Ray flowers 0.1–0.9 in. long, 3–14 per head, white to cream. Disk flowers 0.1–0.3 in. long, many per head, yellow. Fruits achenes, ray fruits hairless, disk fruits woolly with 10–15 pappus scales. The genus name honors British naturalist George Tradescant Lay (1799–1845), who botanized in California, Hawaii, and Alaska. Aka whitedaisy tidytips.

Layia heterotricha

pale-yellow layia

ASTERACEAE SUNFLOWER FAMILY

PCT Sections: 7–8 **Abundance:** Rare **Height:** 5–30 in. **Flowering:** April–June **Flower Color:** Cream to pale yellow **Habitat-Community:** Open, clayey or sandy soils in sagebrush scrubs and pinyon-juniper woodlands **Elevation:** Below 5800 ft. **Ecoregions:** Sierra Nevada

Erect, few-branched, sweet-scented annual with hollow stems covered in dark, glandular hairs. Leaves 2–5 in. long, alternate, sessile and often clasping the stem, elliptic to ovoid, with minutely toothed margins on lower leaves. Flowers in solitary heads at stem and branch tips; involucres hemispheric, 0.3–0.6 in. across, with keeled (especially at base) phyllaries 0.3–0.5 in. long. Ray flowers 0.2–1 in. long, 7–13 per head, cream to pale yellow. Disk flowers many per head, yellow. Fruits achenes, ray fruits hairless, disk fruits hairy with 14–20 feather-like bristles. The plant's scent is reminiscent of apples or bananas. Endemic to west-central California, reaching its easternmost range at the PCT, east of the town of Tehachapi. Threatened by grazing, wind energy, agricultural conversion, and rural development.

Syntrichopappus lemmonii

Lemmon's syntrichopappus

ASTERACEAE SUNFLOWER FAMILY

PCT Sections: 4–8 **Abundance:** Rare **Height:** 1–4 in. **Flowering:** April–May **Flower Color:** White **Habitat-Community:** Sandy to gravelly soils on flats and mesas in foothill chaparrals, sagebrush scrubs, and Joshua tree & pinyon-juniper woodlands **Elevation:** Below 5000 ft. **Ecoregions:** Southern California Mountains, Mojave Basin and Range, Sierra Nevada

Tiny, upright annual with hairy (hairless in age) stems. Leaves 0.1–0.3 in. long, mostly alternate, linear to spoon-shaped, with smooth margins. Flowers in solitary heads at stem and branch tips, with reddish peduncles and 5–8 phyllaries. Ray flowers 0.2 in. long, 1 per phyllary, lower surface white with pink. Disk flowers 10–20 per head, hairless, yellow. Fruits hairless achenes with 0–many bristles. Endemic to just a few counties in central-southern California, typically occurring in small localized populations.

▼ COMPOSITE / RAY FLOWERS ONLY

Hieracium albiflorum

white-flowered hawkweed

ASTERACEAE SUNFLOWER FAMILY

PCT Sections: 1–5 & 9–24 **Abundance:** Common **Height:** 1–3 ft. **Flowering:** May–June **Flower Color:** White **Habitat-Community:** Dry slopes and shaded openings in montane coniferous forests **Elevation:** Below 10,800 ft. **Ecoregions:** All (except Sonoran/Mojave Basin and Range)

Erect annual with milky sap and hairy stems. Leaves 3–7 in. long, mostly basal, spoon- to lance-shaped, long-hairy, with smooth to toothed margins. Flowers 3–50+ heads per stem with bell-shaped involucres 0.2–0.5 in. long. Ray flowers 15–30, white. Fruits to 0.2 in. long, achenes with dull white or tan bristles. The genus name derives from the Greek *hierax* ("hawk"). Ancient Greeks believed that hawks would tear apart a plant they knew as hieracion to clear their eyesight with the juice. The only white hawkweed along the PCT.

Malacothrix saxatilis var. *tenuifolia*

cliff desertdandelion

ASTERACEAE SUNFLOWER FAMILY

PCT Sections: 4–7 **Abundance:** Rare **Height:** 1–3 ft. **Flowering:** May–August **Flower Color:** White **Habitat-Community:** Gravelly to rocky substrates in foothill chaparrals and oak woodlands **Elevation:** Below 6000 ft. **Ecoregions:** Southern California Mountains, Sierra Nevada

Long-stemmed perennial with sparsely leafy, hairless stems and milky sap. Leaves 2–5 in. long, mostly cauline, 1–2 pinnately lobed with narrow, generally toothed segments. Flowers in heads at stem and branch tips; involucres 0.4–0.6 in. long with lance-shaped, generally sparsely hairy phyllaries. Ray flowers 0.6–0.9 in. long, many per head, tips slightly toothed, white. Fruits to 0.1 in. long, minutely spiny achenes with a toothed pappus. Five varieties of *M. saxatilis* are scattered across west-central California (some quite rare); this is the only one that occurs along the PCT. *Saxatilis* means "living among rocks" in Latin.

Rafinesquia californica

California chicory

ASTERACEAE SUNFLOWER FAMILY

PCT Sections: 1–8 **Abundance:** Occasional **Height:** 8–45 in. **Flowering:** April–July **Flower Color:** White **Habitat-Community:** Openings in foothill chaparrals, Sonoran/Mojave mixed woody scrubs, and oak woodlands **Elevation:** Below 5200 ft. **Ecoregions:** Southern California Mountains, Sierra Nevada

Erect (sometimes branched near flowers), elegant-flowered annual with hairless stems and milky sap. Leaves 1–5 in. long, basal and alternate, spoon-shaped, pinnately lobed, hairless. Cauline leaves reduced, clasping, with smooth or toothed margins. Flowers generally solitary heads on stems; involucres 0.4–0.8 in. long with 8–14 reflexed outer phyllaries and 7–20 lance-linear inner phyllaries (translucent margins). Ray flowers 15–30 per head, surpassing the phyllaries by 0.2–0.4 in., white sometimes with purple veins, tips slightly toothed. Fruits 0.4–0.6 in. long, achenes with feather-like bristles. Especially common in recent burns.. *Rafinesquia* honors brilliant naturalist and eccentric genius Constantine Samuel Rafinesque (1783–1840).

Rafinesquia neomexicana

desert chicory

ASTERACEAE SUNFLOWER FAMILY

PCT Sections: 1–4 & 6–8 **Abundance:** Locally common **Height:** 6–24 in. **Flowering:** February–June **Flower Color:** White **Habitat-Community:** Sandy to gravelly soils in creosote bush scrubs, black bush scrubs, and Joshua tree woodlands **Elevation:** Below 5000 ft. **Ecoregions:** Sonoran/Mojave Basin and Range, Sierra Nevada

Erect, showy annual with hairless stems and milky sap, often growing through and supported by shrubs, generally branched near flowers. Leaves 2–9 in. long, basal and alternate, pinnately lobed. Cauline leaves reduced, clasping. Flowers generally solitary heads on stems; involucres 0.7–1.1 in. long with phyllaries purple-tinged on midribs. Ray flowers 20–40 per head, surpassing phyllaries by 0.6–0.9 in., 5-toothed tips, white sometimes with purple veins. Fruits 0.4–0.6 in. long, achenes with feather-like bristles. The species was first described from New Mexico (hence the specific epithet).

Anaphalis margaritacea

pearly everlasting

ASTERACEAE SUNFLOWER FAMILY

PCT Sections: 4 & 10–24 **Abundance:** Common **Height:** 0.5–3 ft. **Flowering:** July–October **Flower Color:** White phyllaries (yellowish flowers) **Habitat-Community:** Openings, meadows, and disturbed slopes from chaparrals and woodlands to subalpine coniferous forests **Elevation:** Below 10,500 ft. **Ecoregions:** Southern California Mountains, Sierra Nevada, Cascades, Klamath Mountains

Erect, loosely clumped, unbranched perennial with white-hairy stems. Leaves 1–6 in. long, alternate, linear to lance-shaped, sparsely hairy above, white-woolly below, generally clasping bases, with rolled-under margins. Flowers tightly clustered, male and female disk flowers generally in different heads, yellowish, with bright white phyllaries to 0.3 in. long. Fruits to 0.1 in. long, stalk-based, hairy or hairless achenes with deciduous white bristles. The long-lasting flower heads are commonly used in flower arrangements. Rubbing the foliage softens hands.

Antennaria corymbosa

meadow pussytoes

ASTERACEAE SUNFLOWER FAMILY

PCT Sections: 10–15 **Abundance:** Common **Height:** 2–6 in. **Flowering:** April–August **Flower Color:** White **Habitat-Community:** Streambanks and meadows from upper montane coniferous forests to alpine and wetland-riparian communities **Elevation:** 6200–10,500 ft. **Ecoregions:** Sierra Nevada

Loosely matted, slender perennial with white-hairy stems; generally dioecious. Leaves to 0.9 in. long, alternate, spoon-shaped, gray-hairy, with smooth margins. Flowers 3–7 heads per cluster, white to yellow or red disk flowers to 0.2 in. long with densely hairy white phyllaries to 0.2 in. long, each with a black-brown spot near base. Fruits to 0.1 in. long, achenes with bristles.

Antennaria dimorpha

low pussytoes

ASTERACEAE SUNFLOWER FAMILY

PCT Sections: 4–5 & 8–10 & 14–15 & 20 **Abundance:** Occasional **Height:** 1–3 in. **Flowering:** May–July **Flower Color:** Cream to white **Habitat-Community:** Ridgetops, flats, and dry, gravelly openings in sagebrush scrubs, pinyon-juniper woodlands, and montane coniferous forests **Elevation:** Below 10,200 ft. **Ecoregions:** Southern California Mountains, Sierra Nevada, Klamath Mountains

Matted perennial with branches from a thick base; dioecious. Leaves 0.3–0.5 in. long, basal and alternate, linear to spoon-shaped, gray-hairy. Flowers in solitary heads tucked into the leaves, with narrow phyllaries in several series. Female flowers 0.3–0.4 in. long, involucres 0.4–0.5 in. long, cream to white. Male flowers 0.1–0.2 in. long, involucres 0.2–0.3 in. long, cream to dingy brown. Fruits 0.4–0.6 in. long, achenes with barbed bristles. Co-occurs with numerous rare endemics on the pebble plains of the San Bernardino Mountains, but its distribution extends to Alberta, Canada.

Antennaria media

alpine pussytoes

ASTERACEAE SUNFLOWER FAMILY

PCT Sections: 4 & 10–24 **Abundance:** Common **Height:** 2–6 in. **Flowering:** July–August **Flower Color:** White **Habitat-Community:** Rocky slopes or ridges and meadows in subalpine coniferous forests and alpine communities **Elevation:** 5900–12,800 ft. **Ecoregions:** Southern California Mountains, Sierra Nevada, Cascades, Klamath Mountains

Densely matted perennial with many stolons; generally dioecious. Leaves to 0.8 in. long, alternate, linear to spoon-shaped, white- to gray-hairy, with smooth margins. Flowers 2–7 heads per cluster; white to yellow or red disk flowers to 0.2 in. long with black-green to brown-tipped, woolly (at base) phyllaries to 0.3 in. long. Fruits to 0.1 in. long, achenes with bristles. North America's version of the European edelweiss.

Antennaria microphylla

littleleaf pussytoes

ASTERACEAE SUNFLOWER FAMILY

PCT Sections: 3–4 & 10–24 **Abundance:** Common **Height:** 3–12 in. **Flowering:** April–July **Flower Color:** White **Habitat-Community:** Dry meadows from upper montane coniferous forests to alpine communities **Elevation:** 5900–12,800 ft. **Ecoregions:** Southern California Mountains, Sierra Nevada, Cascades, Klamath Mountains

Matted perennial with stalked glands on the upper stem; generally dioecious. Leaves to 1 in. long, alternate, linear to spoon-shaped, gray-hairy, with smooth margins. Flowers 6–13 heads per cluster; white to yellow or red disk flowers to 0.2 in. long with green, whitish-tipped, woolly (at base) phyllaries to 0.3 in. long. Fruits to 0.1 in. long, achenes with bristles.

Antennaria rosea

rosy pussytoes

ASTERACEAE SUNFLOWER FAMILY

PCT Sections: 3–4 & 9–24 **Abundance:** Common **Height:** 3–16 in. **Flowering:** June–August **Flower Color:** White **Habitat-Community:** Ridges, rocky slopes, and meadow edges from upper montane coniferous forests to alpine communities **Elevation:** 4000–12,200 ft. **Ecoregions:** Southern California Mountains, Sierra Nevada, Cascades, Klamath Mountains

Matted perennial with white-hairy stems; generally dioecious. Leaves to 1.6 in. long, alternate, linear to spoon-shaped, gray-hairy, with smooth margins. Flowers 3–16 heads per cluster; white to yellow or red disk flowers to 0.2 in. long with green, white to rose, or brown-tipped, woolly (at base) phyllaries to 0.3 in. long. Fruits to 0.1 in. long, achenes with bristles. The involucre is generally rose-tipped.

Chaenactis alpigena

southern Sierra pincushion

ASTERACEAE SUNFLOWER FAMILY

PCT Sections: 10–14 **Abundance:** Rare **Height:** to 3 in. **Flowering:** July–September **Flower Color:** White to pink **Habitat-Community:** Rocky or sandy, open slopes and ridges from upper montane coniferous forests to alpine communities **Elevation:** 7200–12,800 ft. **Ecoregions:** Sierra Nevada

Stout, tufted to matted, multi-stemmed perennial with woolly stems. Leaves 0.4–1.4 in. long, basal and alternate, deeply lobed, fern-like, gland-pitted, hairy, with lobed margins. Flowers a solitary head per stem, white to pink, 8–70 disk flowers per head, to 0.3 in. long with glandless, silky phyllaries to 0.5 in. long in 1–2 equal series. Fruits to 0.3 in. long, achenes with 10–20 pappus scales. Aka Sharsmith pincushion.

Chaenactis artemisiifolia

white pincushion

ASTERACEAE SUNFLOWER FAMILY

PCT Sections: 1–2 **Abundance:** Locally common **Height:** 1–3 ft. **Flowering:** April–July **Flower Color:** White **Habitat-Community:** Sandy or gravelly, granitic soils in foothill chaparrals and oak woodlands **Elevation:** Below 5100 ft. **Ecoregions:** Southern California/Northern Baja Coast, Southern California Mountains

Robust annual, single-stemmed below, branched above, with powdery white stems. Leaves 1–5 in. long, basal and alternate, triangular in outline, 3–4-pinnate, white-hairy. Flowers in 3–20 heads per stem, with shaggy, hairy phyllaries 0.3–0.4 in. long. Disk flowers 0.2–0.3 in. long, radial, white. Fruits 0.2–0.3 in. long, compressed achenes with 0 or 10 small pappus scales. Common along the PCT in San Diego County in foothill chaparral, especially in recent burns between Campo and Kitchen Creek. The highly divided leaves resemble some *Artemisia* spp. (hence the specific epithet). The anthers and curly styles protrude high above the flower heads (hence the common name).

Chaenactis douglasii

dusty-maidens

ASTERACEAE SUNFLOWER FAMILY

PCT Sections: 8–24 **Abundance:** Occasional **Height:** 6–24 in. **Flowering:** May–September **Flower Color:** White to pinkish **Habitat-Community:** Rocky outcrops and open slopes from sagebrush scrubs, chaparrals, and woodlands to subalpine coniferous forests **Elevation:** Below 11,500 ft. **Ecoregions:** Sierra Nevada, Cascades, Klamath Mountains

Stout, ascending, single- or multi-stemmed perennial with cobwebby or short-hairy stems. Leaves 0.5–6 in. long, basal and alternate, elliptic, deeply lobed (generally 5–9 pairs of major lobes), fern-like, gland-pitted, hairy, with lobed margins. Flowers solitary or many heads per cluster, with 8–70 white to pinkish disk flowers per head, to 0.3 in. long, with glandular-hairy phyllaries to 0.7 in. long in 1–2 equal series. Fruits to 0.3 in. long, achenes with 10–20 pappus scales. Dusty-maidens is found throughout North America.

Chaenactis fremontii

Fremont pincushion

ASTERACEAE SUNFLOWER FAMILY

PCT Sections: 1–9 **Abundance:** Locally common **Height:** 4–16 in. **Flowering:** February–May **Flower Color:** White **Habitat-Community:** Sandy or gravelly soils in creosote bush & Sonoran/Mojave mixed woody scrubs and Joshua tree & pinyon-juniper woodlands **Elevation:** Below 5200 ft. **Ecoregions:** Southern California Mountains, Sierra Nevada

Erect, few-branched (from the base) annual with green (becoming hairless and sometimes purplish with age) stems. Leaves 0.4–2.8 in. long, basal or alternate along the stem, withering with age, linear, pinnately lobed with cylindric, fleshy, usually hairless lobes. Flowers in 1–5 heads per stem, radiant, white, with stiff, acute, sparsely hairy phyllaries 0.3–0.4 in. long. Inner disk flowers, corolla 0.2–0.3 in. long. Outer disk flowers irregular, radiant, 0.3–0.4 in. long with 3–5 flaring lobes. Fruits 0.1–0.3 in. long, achenes with pappus of 4 scales. One of the more dominant spring wildflowers in the Mojave Desert, and a food source for the desert tortoise (*Gopherus agassizii*). The genus name (from the Greek *chaino*, "to gape," *aktis*, "a ray") refers to the shape of the peripheral ring of enlarged disk flowers in some species.

Chaenactis parishii

Parish's chaenactis

ASTERACEAE SUNFLOWER FAMILY

PCT Sections: 1–3 **Abundance:** Rare **Height:** 8–22 in. **Flowering:** May–July **Flower Color:** White to pale pink **Habitat-Community:** Rocky to sandy soils in foothill chaparrals, oak woodlands, and lower montane coniferous forests **Elevation:** Below 7800 ft. **Ecoregions:** Southern California Mountains

Erect, conspicuous perennial or subshrub, branching primarily from the base, with stems covered by a felt-like coat of hairs. Leaves 1–2 in. long, triangular in outline, pinnately lobed, white-hairy. Flowers in 1–3 heads per stem; phyllaries shaggy hairy, 0.4–0.5 in. long, with recurved tips. Disk flowers 0.3 in. long, symmetric, white. Fruits 0.2–0.3 in. long, achenes with pappus scales. Confined to the Peninsular Ranges of southern California and northern Baja, Mexico. If you're fortunate, you might get a glimpse of it along the PCT in the San Jacinto Mountains, and in San Diego County in the Laguna and Bucksnort Mountains. Named after Samuel B. Parish (1838–1928).

Chaenactis santolinoides

santolina pincushion

ASTERACEAE SUNFLOWER FAMILY

PCT Sections: 4–9 **Abundance:** Occasional **Height:** 4–18 in. **Flowering:** May–August **Flower Color:** White to pink **Habitat-Community:** Scree and rocky slopes in montane chaparrals, oak & pinyon-juniper woodlands, and montane coniferous forests **Elevation:** Below 9400 ft. **Ecoregions:** Southern California Mountains, Sierra Nevada

Attractive, low-growing, sometimes matted perennial with densely white-woolly herbage, thinning and becoming purple-tinted with age. Leaves 1.2–4.8 in. long in a crowded basal rosette, persistent, cylindric, 1–2-pinnate, with overlapping, twisted, white- or gray-woolly lobes. Flowers in solitary heads with glandular-hairy, obtuse phyllaries 0.3–0.4 in. long. Disk flowers 0.2–0.3 in. long, white to pinkish. Fruits 0.1–0.3 in. long, achenes with 10–16 pappus scales in 4 series. A regional endemic, scattered along the PCT in the Transverse Ranges and southern Sierra Nevada. The specific epithet references its likeness to members of *Santolina*, a genus of small Mediterranean shrubs.

Chaenactis stevioides

desert pincushion

ASTERACEAE SUNFLOWER FAMILY

PCT Sections: 1–9 **Abundance:** Common **Height:** 3–15 in. **Flowering:** February–June **Flower Color:** White **Habitat-Community:** Sandy or gravelly plains and hillsides in creosote & black bush scrubs and Joshua tree & pinyon-juniper woodlands **Elevation:** Below 6500 ft. **Ecoregions:** Southern California Mountains, Sonoran/Mojave Basin and Range, Sierra Nevada

Few-branched, ubiquitous desert annual, cobwebby-hairy near the stem tips. Leaves 0.5–3.2 in. long, basal or alternate, elliptic in outline, 1–2-pinnate with 4–8 pairs of cobwebby-hairy lobes. Flowers in 3–20+ heads per stem, radiant; phyllaries 0.2–0.3 in. long, glandular, cobwebby, with rounded or blunt tips. Disk flowers 0.2–0.3 in. long; inner disk flowers white to cream, irregular; outer radiant disk flowers 0.3 in. long with flaring lobes, white (sometimes pink-tinged). Fruits achenes with pappus of 4 scales. Perhaps the most widespread native annual in arid regions of the western US.

Chaenactis xantiana

Mojave pincushion

ASTERACEAE SUNFLOWER FAMILY

PCT Sections: 4–9 **Abundance:** Locally common **Height:** 4–18 in. **Flowering:** March–July **Flower Color:** White to cream **Habitat-Community:** Sandy or gravelly hillsides in foothill chaparrals, Mojave mixed woody scrubs, and oak & pinyon-juniper woodlands **Elevation:** Below 7400 ft. **Ecoregions:** Southern California Mountains, Sierra Nevada

Few-branched annual of desert transitional regions, with gray-cobwebby stems becoming hairless with age. Leaves 1.2–2.8 in. long, basal or alternate, elliptic in outline, pinnately lobed with succulent, gray-green lobes in 1–2 pairs. Flowers in 1–7 heads per stem; phyllaries 0.4–0.8 in. long, thick, hairless or short-hairy, with recurved, purple-tinged tips. Disk flowers 0.2–0.4 in. long, symmetric, white (sometimes dirty cream). Fruits 0.2–0.4 in. long, achenes with pappus of 8 scales in 2 series. Common in burns. The specific epithet honors Hungarian zoologist John Xantus de Vesey (1825–1894).

Cirsium cymosum

peregrine thistle

ASTERACEAE SUNFLOWER FAMILY

PCT Sections: 10–24 **Abundance:** Locally common **Height:** 2–5 ft. **Flowering:** April–July **Flower Color:** White **Habitat-Community:** Rocky soils, including serpentine, in oak woodlands, chaparrals, and lower montane coniferous forests **Elevation:** Below 6900 ft. **Ecoregions:** Sierra Nevada, Cascades, Klamath Mountains

Large, branched perennial with cobwebby herbage. Leaves 4–8 in. long, cobwebby or becoming hairless, with spine-tipped lobes. Flowers 0.8–1.3 in. long, 1–few heads per stem in flat-topped clusters. Disk flowers white; phyllaries spine-margined, with spine to 0.2 in. long at tip. Fruits to 0.3 in. long, achenes with many bristles. As with most thistles, the flowers are usually pollinated by bumblebees and other flying insects. Nectar-loving ants are repelled by the cobwebby hairs.

Cirsium scariosum

elk thistle

ASTERACEAE SUNFLOWER FAMILY

PCT Sections: 1–4 & 10–21 **Abundance:** Occasional **Height:** 5–40 in. **Flowering:** May–August **Flower Color:** White to purple **Habitat-Community:** Moist, rocky soils, including serpentine, and wet places from scrubs to subalpine coniferous forests **Elevation:** Below 11,500 ft. **Ecoregions:** All (except Sonoran/Mojave Basin and Range)

Biennial or short-lived perennial from a basal rosette, with hairy or hairless stems (when present) and foliage. Leaves 4–16 in. long, hairy or hairless, with tapered or spiny-winged petioles and spine-tipped lobes. Flowers 0.8–1.6 in. long, in densely clustered heads. Disk flowers white to purple; phyllaries spine-margined, hairless, with spine to 0.5 in. long at tip. Fruits to 0.3 in. long, achenes with many bristles. Stemless and stemmed plants are often found together, glowing like angels when their hairs and spines are backlit. The flowers are food for elk and other foraging critters (hence the common name). Aka meadow thistle.

Iva axillaris

povertyweed

ASTERACEAE SUNFLOWER FAMILY

PCT Sections: 4–9 **Abundance:** Occasional **Height:** 6–20 in. **Flowering:** April–October **Flower Color:** White **Habitat-Community:** Seasonally wet soils, saline habitats, springs, and roadsides from creosote bush scrubs to lower montane coniferous forests and wetland-riparian communities **Elevation:** Below 8200 ft. **Ecoregions:** Southern California Mountains, Mojave Basin and Range, Sierra Nevada

Erect, foul-smelling perennial, branched at base, with glandular herbage. Leaves 0.2–1.7 in. long, opposite on lower stem, alternate near stem ends, elliptic to spoon-shaped, somewhat succulent, minutely hairy, gland-dotted. Flowers in solitary heads in axils; involucres nodding, hemispheric, with fused, gray-green phyllaries. Disk flowers 4–20 per head, white. Pistillate flowers inconspicuous, 3–8 per head, white. Fruits 0.1 in. long, pear-shaped achenes. Grows in clonal colonies throughout the US and Canada. Weedy in nature, it's often seen in moist, disturbed areas or agricultural fields. The huge volume of pollen it produces is infamous for contributing to hay fever—*achoo!*

Logfia filaginoides

California cottonrose

ASTERACEAE SUNFLOWER FAMILY

PCT Sections: 1–9 **Abundance:** Common **Height:** 1–12 in. **Flowering:** February–May **Flower Color:** Cream to pale yellow **Habitat-Community:** Dry, gravelly to rocky openings in creosote bush scrubs, foothill chaparrals, and Joshua tree & pinyon-juniper woodlands **Elevation:** Below 5700 ft. **Ecoregions:** Southern California Mountains, Sierra Nevada

Erect annual, with cobwebby, gray-green to purplish, sometimes forked stems. Leaves 0.2–0.7 in. long, alternate, sessile, linear to spoon-shaped, hairy. Flowers in heads in small clusters along stems, enclosed by glossy bracts; involucres with 0 phyllaries. Pistillate flowers cream to pale yellow, 7–13 per head (with pappus) in the outer ring, and 14–35 per head in the inner ring. Disk flowers 4–7 per head, 4-lobed, red to purple. Fruits to 0.1 in. long, achenes with many bristles. The most common native *Logfia* along the PCT. *Logfia* is an anagram of *Filago*, the genus that once included it.

Palafoxia arida

desert
Spanish needle

ASTERACEAE SUNFLOWER FAMILY

PCT Sections: 3–4 **Abundance:** Locally common
Height: 8–35 in. **Flowering:** February–October
Flower Color: White to pink **Habitat-Community:**
Sandy flats and dunes in creosote bush scrubs
Elevation: Below 3200 ft. **Ecoregions:** Sonoran
Basin and Range

Hardy, upright, branched annual with herbage covered in glands and rough, stiff hairs. Leaves 0.1–0.4 in. long, opposite on lower stem, alternate above, sessile, lance-shaped, green to gray-green, rough to the touch. Flowers in flat-topped clusters; involucres 0.2–0.4 in. across with linear, glandular phyllaries. Disk flowers 10–40 per head, white to light pink, with pink to purple anthers. Fruits 0.4–0.6 in. long, hairy achenes with pappus scales. Common across the California deserts but occurs only along a 20-mile stretch of the PCT, on both sides of the Interstate 10 crossing west of Coachella Valley. Named in honor of Spanish general José Rebolledo de Palafox y Melzi (1776–1847).

Porophyllum gracile

odora

ASTERACEAE SUNFLOWER FAMILY

PCT Sections: 1–2 **Abundance:** Occasional **Height:** 10–28 in. **Flowering:** February–October **Flower Color:** White to purple **Habitat-Community:** Rocky to sandy slopes and washes in creosote bush & Sonoran mixed woody scrubs and foothill chaparrals **Elevation:** Below 5000 ft. **Ecoregions:** Southern California/Northern Baja Coast, Southern California Mountains, Sonoran Basin and Range

Erect to ascending, pungent-scented perennial with gray-green, wax-coated stems dotted with purple glands. Leaves 0.4–2 in. long, linear, glandular. Flowers in 1–few heads per stem; involucres 0.4–0.7 in. long, cylindric, with 5 purple-glandular phyllaries. Disk flowers 0.3–0.4 in. long, 20–30 per head, white to purple, with purple anthers. Fruits cylindric achenes with many bristles. Its list of ethnobotanical and medicinal uses is long, from treatment of toothaches and the common cold to aiding in childbirth. Look for it in foothill chaparral in far southern San Diego County and (more likely) the desert crossings near Anza-Borrego State Park. *Porophyllum* ("pore-leaved") refers to the gland-dotted leaves.

Sphaeromeria cana

gray
chickensage

ASTERACEAE SUNFLOWER FAMILY

PCT Sections: 10–12 **Abundance:** Locally common
Height: 3–40 in. **Flowering:** July–September
Flower Color: White **Habitat-Community:** Shaded
understories, talus slopes, and rocky outcrops
in montane coniferous forests **Elevation:** Below
6500 ft. **Ecoregions:** Sierra Nevada, Cascades,
Klamath Mountains

Branched perennial or subshrub with silky stems covered with forked hairs and resin glands. Leaves 0.4–1.6 in. long, alternate, mostly on the stem, hairy, gland-dotted, with smooth margins. Flowers in 1–12 heads in dense clusters, with male and female disk flowers in same head and phyllaries in 2–3 graduated series. Female flowers 4–15 around head margin, white, with narrowly tubular corollas. Disk flowers 30–50, white, with hairy corolla lobes. Fruits to 0.1 in. long, cylindric achenes without pappus. Plants can have a sage-like odor.

Hooveria parviflora

smallflower soap plant

AGAVACEAE AGAVE FAMILY

PCT Sections: 1–2 **Abundance:** Rare **Height:** 2–6 ft. **Flowering:** May–August **Flower Color:** White to pink **Habitat-Community:** Sandstone or decomposed granite soils, especially in burns, in foothill chaparrals and Sonoran mixed woody scrubs **Elevation:** Below 3500 ft. **Ecoregions:** Southern California/Northern Baja Coast, Southern California Mountains

Ascending to erect perennial from a basal rosette and a large (2–3 in. wide) scaly bulb. Leaves 4–9 in. long, basal, ascending or flopped on the ground, linear, green, with wavy margins. Flowers on stalks 2–6 ft. tall with thread-like pedicels 0.1–0.3 in. long. Tepals 0.3 in. long, 6-parted (3 sepals, 3 petals) in 2 petal-like whorls, free, spreading from base, white to pale pink, with yellow anthers. Fruits 0.1–0.2 in. long, 3-chambered capsules. Occurs along the PCT only in the interior chaparral of San Diego County and, curiously, in San Felipe Valley near Anza-Borrego State Park. The Kumeyaay people use the bulbs for food, soap, glue, fish poison, and brushes.

Allium burlewii

Burlew's onion

ALLIACEAE ONION FAMILY

PCT Sections: 8–9 **Abundance:** Rare **Height:** 1–4 in. **Flowering:** April–July **Flower Color:** White (aging pale purple) **Habitat-Community:** Sandy or gravelly soils, including serpentine, in montane coniferous forests **Elevation:** Below 9200 ft. **Ecoregions:** Sierra Nevada

Perennial with somewhat flat stems and 1 leaf per plant. Leaves flat, solitary, 1–2 times stem length. Flowers 8–20 in head-like cluster at stem tip, symmetric. Tepals to 0.4 in. long, 6-parted (3 sepals, 3 petals), white (pink-tinged at base) aging pale purple, ovoid, dark-veined, with smooth margins. Fruits to 0.2 in. long, capsules with generally 6 black seeds to 0.1 in. long. *Allium* is the Latin word for garlic (*A. sativum*).

Allium haematochiton

red-skinned onion

ALLIACEAE ONION FAMILY

PCT Sections: 1–6 **Abundance:** Occasional **Height:** 4–16 in. **Flowering:** March–May **Flower Color:** White to rose **Habitat-Community:** Open, sandy to rocky soils in canyons and on dry slopes in California prairies, chaparrals, and oak woodlands **Elevation:** Below 4000 ft. **Ecoregions:** Southern California/Northern Baja Coast, Southern California Mountains, Sierra Nevada

Erect perennial from a cluster of shiny red-brown bulbs with bright green (sometimes reddish at base) stems. Leaves 4–12 in. long, upright, 4–6 per stem, narrow, flat, green. Flowers 10–30 per plant, borne in heads, on pedicels 0.4–1.2 in. long. Tepals 0.3 in. long, 6-parted (3 sepals, 3 petals) in 2 whorls, free, spreading from base, white (with a reddish midstripe) to rose with age; 6 stamens. Fruits 3-chambered capsules. Can form large clonal patches up to 3 ft. in diameter! The flower becomes papery and colorless at maturity, eventually concealing the fruits. *Haematochiton* (from the Latin, "blood coat") references the red skin of the bulb and emerging stem.

Allium lacunosum

pitted onion

ALLIACEAE ONION FAMILY

PCT Sections: 1–8 **Abundance:** Occasional **Height:** 4–15 in. **Flowering:** April–May **Flower Color:** White **Habitat-Community:** Open, sandy slopes and ridges in pinyon-juniper woodlands and montane coniferous forests **Elevation:** Below 6800 ft. **Ecoregions:** Southern California Mountains, Sierra Nevada

Garlic-scented perennial from a yellow-brown bulb. Leaves 3–20 in. long, basal, 2 per stem, linear, cylindric or flat, green. Flowers 10–35 per plant, borne in heads, on pedicels 0.3–1 in. long. Tepals 0.3 in. long, 6-parted (3 sepals, 3 petals) in 2 whorls, free, spreading from base, white with dark mid-veins; 6 stamens. Fruits 3-chambered capsules. Endemic to California. Two varieties along the PCT: var. *davisiae* (leaves longer than stem) from southern California and var. *kernense* (leaves shorter than stem) from the southern Sierra and Mojave Desert regions. Populations are often small and geographically isolated.

Allium marvinii

Yucaipa onion

ALLIACEAE ONION FAMILY

PCT Sections: 1–3 **Abundance:** Rare **Height:** 4–20 in. **Flowering:** March–May **Flower Color:** White **Habitat-Community:** Open, dry slopes and canyons in foothill chaparrals and oak woodlands **Elevation:** Below 4500 ft. **Ecoregions:** Southern California/Northern Baja Coast, Southern California Mountains

Ascending to erect perennial from many interconnected reddish bronze bulbs. Leaves 6–14 in. long, 4–6 per stem, basal, linear, flat. Flowers 10–30 per head on pedicels 0.3–0.6 in. long. Tepals 0.3 in. long, 6-parted (3 sepals, 3 petals) in 2 whorls, free, spreading from base, white with rose midveins; 6 stamens. Fruits 3-chambered capsules. Threatened by urbanization and altered fire regimes. Look for it along the PCT at Kitchen Creek in the southern Laguna Mountains or in the Bucksnort Mountains north of Warner Springs in San Diego County. The specific epithet honors Cornelius J. Marvin (1888–1944), chemist and rare-plant photographer.

Allium obtusum

red Sierra onion

ALLIACEAE ONION FAMILY

PCT Sections: 10–20 **Abundance:** Occasional **Height:** 1–7 in. **Flowering:** May–July **Flower Color:** White **Habitat-Community:** Sandy or gravelly, generally granitic soils from lower montane to subalpine coniferous forests **Elevation:** Below 12,000 ft. **Ecoregions:** Sierra Nevada, Cascades, Klamath Mountains

Perennial with slightly flattened stems and 1–2 leaves per plant. Leaves 1–4 times stem length, 1–2, flat. Flowers 6–30 in dense, head-like cluster at stem tip, symmetric. Tepals to 0.5 in. long, 6-parted (3 sepals, 3 petals), white, oblong, purplish-veined, blunt-tipped, with smooth margins. Fruits to 0.1 in. long, capsules with tiny black seeds. *Obtusum* refers to the blunt-tipped tepals. While hiking in granite, you are likely to smell this small onion before you see its white flowers.

Allium parryi

Parry's onion

ALLIACEAE ONION FAMILY

PCT Sections: 1 & 3–4 **Abundance:** Occasional **Height:** 2–8 in. **Flowering:** May–July **Flower Color:** White to pale pink **Habitat-Community:** Flats, gentle slopes, and openings in montane coniferous forests **Elevation:** Below 7000 ft. **Ecoregions:** Southern California Mountains

Small, inconspicuous onion with a reddish brown bulb. Leaves 3–10 in. long, basal, 1 per stem, cylindric. Flowers 10–50 per head on pedicels 0.2–0.8 in. long. Tepals 0.2–0.4 in. long, 6-parted (3 sepals, 3 petals) in 2 whorls, free, spreading from base, white with pink midveins; 6 stamens. Fruits 6-crested capsules. Occurs along the PCT in the Laguna Mountains of San Diego County and the Big Bear Lake region in the San Bernardino Mountains. The leaves are often shriveled (or munched) at time of flowering.

Calochortus albus

white fairy lantern

LILIACEAE LILY FAMILY

PCT Sections: 1 **Abundance:** Occasional **Height:** 8–30 in. **Flowering:** April–June **Flower Color:** White to pale pink **Habitat-Community:** Open or shaded areas and burns from oak woodlands to lower montane coniferous forests **Elevation:** Below 6200 ft. **Ecoregions:** Southern California/ Northern Baja Coast, Southern California Mountains

Perennial with unusual flowers and leafy, wax-coated stems. Basal leaves 12–26 in. long, lance-shaped; stem leaves 0.2–1 in. long, linear to lance-shaped, 2–6. Flowers 2–many per stem, nodding, globe-like (unlike most mariposa lilies), with free perianth segments. Tepals 0.4–1 in. long, 6-parted (3 sepals, 3 petals); sepals ovoid to lance-shaped, petals ovoid, white to pale pink. Fruits 0.8–1.6 in. long, winged, nodding capsules. Best seen along the PCT in the Laguna Mountains of San Diego County. *Calochortus* is Greek for "beautiful grass."

Calochortus invenustus

plain mariposa lily

LILIACEAE LILY FAMILY

PCT Sections: 1–5 & 8–12 **Abundance:** Locally common **Height:** 7–20 in. **Flowering:** May–August **Flower Color:** White or pale lavender **Habitat-Community:** Dry, granitic soils in montane coniferous forests **Elevation:** Below 9900 ft. **Ecoregions:** Southern California Mountains, Sierra Nevada

Erect, slender, generally unbranched perennial with white- to blue-waxy-coated herbage. Leaves to 8 in. long, basal and 1–2 on stem, linear to lance-shaped, channeled. Flowers 1–6 at stem tip, erect, symmetric. Tepals to 1.6 in. long, 6-parted (3 sepals, 3 petals), bell-shaped, white or pale lavender, sepals < petals, petals hairy at base. Fruits to 2.8 in. long, erect capsules with many flat seeds. The spotted petals resemble butterflies (hence *mariposa*, Spanish for "butterfly").

Calochortus leichtlinii

mountain mariposa lily

LILIACEAE LILY FAMILY

PCT Sections: 10–18 **Abundance:** Common **Height:** 7–24 in. **Flowering:** June–August **Flower Color:** White or pale lavender **Habitat-Community:** Dry, gravelly soils from lower montane to subalpine coniferous forests **Elevation:** Below 13,200 ft. **Ecoregions:** Sierra Nevada, Cascades

Erect, unbranched perennial with withering basal leaves. Leaves to 6 in. long, basal and 1–2 on stem, linear, flat. Flowers 1–5 at stem tip, erect, symmetric. Tepals to 1.6 in. long, 6-parted (3 sepals, 3 petals), bell-shaped, white or pale lavender, sepals < petals, petals hairy at base; heart-shaped anther bases where attached to the filament. Fruits to 2.4 in. long, erect capsules with many flat, dark brown seeds.

Toxicoscordion brevibracteatum

desert deathcamas

MELANTHIACEAE

FALSE-HELLEBORE FAMILY

PCT Sections: 4 & 7 **Abundance:** Occasional **Height:** 8–24 in. **Flowering:** April–June **Flower Color:** Cream to pale yellow **Habitat-Community:** Sandy soils, dunes, sand ramps, valleys, and flats in creosote bush scrubs and Joshua tree & pinyon-juniper woodlands **Elevation:** Below 6000 ft. **Ecoregions:** Southern California Mountains, Mojave Basin and Range

Erect perennial with hairless stems arising from a 2–3-in. bulb. Leaves to 12 in. long, basal and alternate, reduced up stem, linear, sometimes folded, with smooth and hairy margins. Flowers at stem and branch tips on spreading pedicels 0.5–1.5 in. long. Tepals 0.2–0.3 in. long, 6-parted (3 sepals, 3 petals), free, cream to pale yellow. Fruits 0.4–0.8 in. long, oblong capsules. The 12-syllable binomial is perhaps the biggest Latin mouthful of any species along the CA PCT. *Toxicoscordion* (from the Greek, "poisonous garlic") refers to the poisonous bulb. All parts of the plant are toxic and should not be ingested! Occurs along the PCT at the lower Mojave Desert segments, such as from Deep Creek to Cajon Junction in San Bernardino County.

Toxicoscordion venenosum

meadow deathcamas

MELANTHIACEAE

FALSE-HELLEBORE FAMILY

PCT Sections: 1–2 & 8–24 **Abundance:** Locally common **Height:** 6–28 in. **Flowering:** May–July **Flower Color:** White **Habitat-Community:** Moist meadows to dry, rocky soils from scrubs and woodlands to upper montane coniferous forests **Elevation:** Below 8600 ft. **Ecoregions:** Southern California/Northern Baja Coast, Sierra Nevada, Cascades, Klamath Mountains

Erect, unbranched perennial with hairless stems. Leaves to 16 in. long, to 0.4 in. wide, mostly basal and few along lower stem, grass-like. Flowers generally many, densely clustered from stem tip down, symmetric, with 6 stamens and 3-lobed style. Tepals to 0.3 in. long, 6-parted (3 sepals, 3 petals), ovoid, narrowed where attached, white with green to yellow gland dot near base. Fruits to 0.6 in. long, cylindric capsules with many brown seeds. The bulbs are extremely toxic (hence the genus name)! Plants often grow with camas (hence the common name).

Veratrum californicum

California corn lily

MELANTHIACEAE

FALSE-HELLEBORE FAMILY

PCT Sections: 3–5 & 10–24 **Abundance:** Common **Height:** 3–6 ft. **Flowering:** June–August **Flower Color:** White or greenish **Habitat-Community:** Moist meadows, streambanks, and forest edges from lower montane to subalpine coniferous forests and wetland-riparian communities **Elevation:** Below 11,500 ft. **Ecoregions:** Southern California Mountains, Sierra Nevada, Cascades, Klamath Mountains

Erect, stout perennial with hollow stems and large leaves. Leaves to 16 in. long, alternate, ovoid, hairy below. Flowers many on crowded, spreading to ascending branches, symmetric, with 6 stamens and 3 styles. Tepals to 0.6 in. long, 6-parted (3 sepals, 3 petals), oblong to widely spoon-shaped, white or greenish. Fruits to 1.2 in. long, ovoid, hairless or sparsely hairy capsules with many, generally winged seeds. *Veratrum* is Latin for "dark roots." All *Veratrum* spp. are toxic to humans and livestock!

Cephalanthera austiniae

phantom orchid

ORCHIDACEAE ORCHID FAMILY

PCT Sections: 4 & 14–24 **Abundance:** Rare **Height:** 7–22 in. **Flowering:** March–July **Flower Color:** White **Habitat-Community:** Shaded understories, rich in humus, in montane coniferous forests **Elevation:** Below 7300 ft. **Ecoregions:** Southern California Mountains, Sierra Nevada, Cascades, Klamath Mountains

Erect, white (aging yellowish to brown) perennial with leafless (bracts only) stems; mycoheterotrophic. Flowers 0.8 in. long, 10–20 in spike-like clusters along a single stem, irregular, with stamen and style fused into a column. Sepals 3, white, elliptic to spoon-shaped, curved over column. Petals 3, lateral 2 similar to sepals, and lowest forming white lip with yellow blotch and downcurved tip. Fruits erect capsules with many small seeds. *Cephalanthera* ("head-like anther") refers to the lip shape. Please do not disturb or try to collect this sensitive orchid: it can't survive away from its natural habitat!

Platanthera dilatata var. *leucostachys*

Sierra bog orchid

ORCHIDACEAE ORCHID FAMILY

PCT Sections: 1–5 & 10–24 **Abundance:** Common **Height:** 3–28 in. **Flowering:** May–September **Flower Color:** White **Habitat-Community:** Wet meadows, seeps, and streambanks in wetland-riparian communities **Elevation:** Below 11,200 ft. **Ecoregions:** Southern California Mountains, Sierra Nevada, Cascades, Klamath Mountains

Erect, stiff, unbranched perennial with leafy stems and fragrant (spicy-smelling) flowers. Leaves to 14 in. long, 1.2 in. wide, alternate, linear to lance-shaped. Flowers densely scattered along stem to tip, small, irregular, with stamen and style fused into a column. Sepals to 0.3 in. long, 3, white, petal-like, upper forming a hood with lateral petals. Petals to 0.3 in. long, 3, white, lowest forming a lance-shaped lip to 0.4 in. long with upcurved tip; curved spur to 0.6 in. long. Fruits ascending to erect capsules with many small seeds. *Platanthera* means "wide anther." The aromatic flowers have been described as a mix of mock orange (*Philadelphus*), cloves, and vanilla.

Spiranthes romanzoffiana

hooded ladies tresses

ORCHIDACEAE ORCHID FAMILY

PCT Sections: 3–4 & 10–24 **Abundance:** Occasional **Height:** 3–12 in. **Flowering:** May–September **Flower Color:** White **Habitat-Community:** Wet banks and meadows from lower montane to subalpine coniferous forests and wetland-riparian communities **Elevation:** Below 10,900 ft. **Ecoregions:** Southern California Mountains, Sierra Nevada, Cascades, Klamath Mountains

Erect, stout, unbranched perennial with hairless stems. Leaves to 5 in. long, mostly basal, linear to lance-linear. Flowers densely clustered and spirally arranged to stem tip, irregular, with stamen and style fused into a column. Sepals to 0.5 in. long, 3, white, narrowly lance-shaped, upper fused to petals forming a hood. Petals to 0.5 in. long, 3, white, upper 2 fused to sepal, lowest forming pouch-like lip. Fruits spreading to ascending capsules with many small seeds. *Spiranthes* means "coiled flowers." Named for Nikolai Romanzoff (1754–1826), a Russian patron of science. The common name refers to the braided-hair-like flowers.

Argemone munita

prickly poppy

PAPAVERACEAE POPPY FAMILY

PCT Sections: 4–8 **Abundance:** Occasional **Height:** 1–4 ft. **Flowering:** July–August **Flower Color:** White **Habitat-Community:** Sandy or gravelly soils and washes in chaparrals, woodlands, and lower montane coniferous forests **Elevation:** Below 9000 ft. **Ecoregions:** Southern California Mountains, Mojave Basin and Range, Sierra Nevada

Erect, stout, spiny perennial (or annual) with blue-green herbage and generally reddish prickles. Leaves 2–6 in. long, alternate, ovoid to spatula-shaped, toothed and lobed about half-way to midrib, prickly surfaces, mint green. Flowers 2–6 in. across, with 3 prickly sepals, 6 white, crinkled, ovoid petals 1–2 in. long, and 100–250 orange stamens. Fruits 1.2–2 in. long, prickly capsules. Bleeds a distinctive yellow sap that contains several poisonous alkaloids! *Munita* means "armed" in Latin.

Platystemon californicus

creamcups

PAPAVERACEAE POPPY FAMILY

PCT Sections: 1–8 **Abundance:** Locally common **Height:** 3–12 in. **Flowering:** March–May **Flower Color:** Cream or pale yellow **Habitat-Community:** Sandy to gravelly soils and burns in creosote bush scrubs, foothill chaparrals, and Joshua tree woodlands **Elevation:** Below 3500 ft. **Ecoregions:** Southern California Mountains, Sonoran/Mojave Basin and Range, Sierra Nevada

Erect, variable, variously long-hairy little annual with clear to orange sap. Leaves 1–4 in. long, mostly basal; stem leaves alternate if present. Flowers solitary from axils or stems, with 3 hairy sepals and many stamens with flat filaments. Petals 0.3–0.8 in. long, 6, hairy, cream (yellow base or tip or both). Fruits 0.4–0.6 in. long, narrowly ovoid capsules. Especially abundant along the southern segments of the PCT in recent burns.

Acanthoscyphus parishii

flowery puncturebract

POLYGONACEAE BUCKWHEAT FAMILY

PCT Sections: 4–5 **Abundance:** Occasional **Height:** 3–20 in. **Flowering:** June–October **Flower Color:** White **Habitat-Community:** Sandy to rocky substrates in montane coniferous forests **Elevation:** 5500–8500 ft. **Ecoregions:** Southern California Mountains

Erect, single-stemmed annual from a basal rosette, intricately branched above with waxy, hairless stems. Leaves 0.4–2.4 in. long, ovoid, hairless, green with a purple central vein or spot. Flowers in open clusters on reflexed pedicels, 6-parted, tepals 0.1–0.2 in. long, white to cream. Involucres with up to 30 teeth, each with a pronounced spike-like awn. Fruits to 0.1 in. long, brown to maroon, elliptic achenes. The only species in *Acanthoscyphus* (from the Latin, "thorn cup," referring to the very distinctive awns on the involucre). Two varieties along the PCT: var. *parishii* (13–30 awns per involucre) is the most common; var. *cienegensis* (7–10 awns) is restricted to the San Bernardino Mountains southeast of Big Bear Lake.

Bistorta bistortoides

western bistort

POLYGONACEAE
BUCKWHEAT FAMILY

PCT Sections: 3–4 & 9–24 **Abundance:** Locally common **Height:** 4–28 in. **Flowering:** July–September **Flower Color:** White or pale pink **Habitat-Community:** Wet meadows, streambanks, and moist slopes from lower montane to subalpine coniferous forests and wetland-riparian communities **Elevation:** Below 9900 ft. **Ecoregions:** Southern California Mountains, Sierra Nevada, Cascades, Klamath Mountains

Erect, multi-stemmed perennial from thick roots with hairless herbage. Leaves 1.6–12 in. long, mostly basal, oblong to lance-oblong or spoon-shaped, tapered to rounded base, with smooth margins. Flowers in spike-like heads at stem tips. Tepals to 0.2 in. long, 6-parted (3 sepals, 3 petals), fused in lower portion, white or pale pink, bell-shaped. Fruits to 0.2 in. long, angled, shiny, pale brown achenes. The roots and leaves are a food source when boiled.

Eriogonum angulosum

anglestem buckwheat

POLYGONACEAE
BUCKWHEAT FAMILY

PCT Sections: 4–9 **Abundance:** Locally common **Height:** 4–18 in. **Flowering:** March–October **Flower Color:** White to rose **Habitat-Community:** Sandy to clayey soils in creosote bush scrubs, foothill chaparrals, and woodlands **Elevation:** Below 5200 ft. **Ecoregions:** Southern California Mountains, Mojave Basin and Range, Sierra Nevada

Single-stemmed, 2-forked (at branching nodes) annual from a basal rosette with 6-ridged, woolly, leafy stems. Leaves 0.5–1.9 in. long, basal and alternate, spoon-shaped, woolly. Flowers clustered at ends of forked peduncles, with rose-red involucres. Tepals 6-parted (3 sepals, 3 petals), fused at base, white to rose, with dish-shaped tube. Fruits to 0.1 in. long, hairless achenes. Easily distinguished from other annual buckwheats along the PCT by its ridged stems (hence the common and scientific names), and one of only a handful of annual buckwheats with leafy stems. *Eriogonum* (from the Greek, "woolly knees") refers to the hairy stem nodes of the first named buckwheat. Among the largest genera in California's flora.

Eriogonum baileyi

Bailey's buckwheat

POLYGONACEAE

BUCKWHEAT FAMILY

PCT Sections: 4–9 **Abundance:** Locally common
Height: 4–16 in. **Flowering:** May–October
Flower Color: White **Habitat-Community:** Sandy
or gravelly soils in chaparrals, woodlands,
sagebrush scrubs, and montane coniferous
forests **Elevation:** Below 9300 ft. **Ecoregions:**
Southern California Mountains, Sierra Nevada

Erect, single-stemmed (forked at branching nodes) annual from a basal rosette with ascending, hairless or woolly branches. Leaves 0.2–0.8 in. long, basal, round to spoon-shaped, woolly, sometimes with wavy or crinkled margins. Flowers clustered along branches at regular intervals in sessile, ribbed involucres. Tepals 6-parted (3 sepals, 3 petals), minutely glandular, white. Fruits 0.1 in. long, hairless achenes. Two varieties along the PCT: var. *baileyi* (common; hairless inflorescence) and var. *praebens* (uncommon; woolly inflorescence). Most buckwheat species have edible seeds; the Kawaiisu people of southern California mash the seeds of this species into meal that is eaten dry or used in a beverage.

Eriogonum cithariforme

cithara buckwheat

POLYGONACEAE

BUCKWHEAT FAMILY

PCT Sections: 4–6 **Abundance:** Occasional
Height: 8–12 in. **Flowering:** May–October **Flower
Color:** White to rose **Habitat-Community:** Sandy
or gravelly soils in woodlands, sagebrush
scrubs, and lower montane coniferous forests
Elevation: Below 6800 ft. **Ecoregions:** Southern
California Mountains

Graceful, branched annual from a basal rosette with hairless or woolly herbage. Leaves 0.4–0.8 in. long, basal, sometimes alternate on stem, spoon-shaped to elliptic, woolly. Flowers clustered at branch tips in hairless, sessile, ribbed involucres 0.1 in. long. Tepals to 0.1 in. long, 6-parted (3 sepals, 3 petals), hairless, white to rose. Fruits to 0.1 in. long, hairless achenes. Two varieties along the PCT: var. *agninum* (uncommon; hairless inflorescence) and var. *cithariforme* (San Gabriel Mountains; woolly hairy inflorescence), both endemic to California.

Eriogonum davidsonii

Davidson's buckwheat

POLYGONACEAE

BUCKWHEAT FAMILY

PCT Sections: 1–9 **Abundance:** Common **Height:**
6–18 in. **Flowering:** May–September **Flower
Color:** White to pink **Habitat-Community:** Sandy
or gravelly soils from scrubs to lower montane
coniferous forests **Elevation:** Below 8200 ft.
Ecoregions: Southern California Mountains,
Mojave Basin and Range, Sierra Nevada

Erect annual from a basal rosette with hairless green stems. Leaves 0.4–0.8 in. across, basal, round, hairy; petiole 0.4–2 in. long, hairy. Flowers along straight or incurved branches in sessile, ribbed involucres 0.1–0.2 in. long. Tepals to 0.1 in. long, 6-parted (3 sepals, 3 petals), hairless, white to pink. Fruits to 0.1 in. long, hairless achenes. Widespread and exceedingly variable. Plants in the Southern California Mountains may have upturned branches.

Eriogonum deflexum

skeleton weed

POLYGONACEAE

BUCKWHEAT FAMILY

PCT Sections: 1–9 **Abundance:** Occasional **Height:** 6–30 in. **Flowering:** June–October **Flower Color:** White to pink **Habitat-Community:** Sandy to gravelly soils in disturbed areas in creosote bush & sagebrush scrubs and Joshua tree & pinyon-juniper woodlands **Elevation:** Below 8000 ft. **Ecoregions:** Southern California Mountains, Mojave Basin and Range, Sierra Nevada

Single-stemmed, erect annual from a basal rosette. Leaves 0.5–1.3 in. across, basal, round to heart-shaped, hairy below; petiole 0.4–2.8 in. long. Flowers arranged in a flat-topped inflorescence with some deflexed downward peduncles (hence the specific epithet), and hairless involucres 0.1 long. Tepals 0.1 in. long, 6-parted (3 sepals, 3 petals), hairless, white to pale pink. Fruits to 0.1 in. long, hairless achenes. Two varieties along the PCT: var. *baratum* (involucre >0.1 in. long; hollow stem) is by far the most common, especially on the eastern flanks of the Tehachapi Mountains and southern Sierra; var. *deflexum* (involucre <0.1 in. long; plant more flat-topped) shows up only at the lower desert crossings. Aka flat-topped buckwheat.

Eriogonum elongatum

longstem buckwheat

POLYGONACEAE BUCKWHEAT FAMILY

PCT Sections: 1–7 **Abundance:** Locally common **Height:** 2–4 ft. **Flowering:** July–November **Flower Color:** White to rose **Habitat-Community:** Sandy or clayey soils, or among rocks, in chaparrals and woodlands **Elevation:** Below 6200 ft. **Ecoregions:** Southern California Mountains, Sierra Nevada

Erect, tall, wand-like perennial with few branches below and green, hairy herbage. Leaves 0.4–1.2 in. long on stem but crowded at base, ovoid to elliptic. Flowers along branches and stems in sessile, hairy involucres 0.2–0.3 in. long. Tepals 0.1 in. long, 6-parted (3 sepals, 3 petals), hairless, white to rose. Fruits 0.1 in. long, hairless achenes. The stems have abundant chlorophyll and contribute to photosynthesis, a trait that is somewhat unusual in the genus. Ranges to the immediate coast but is equally abundant on the desert slopes of the Southern California Mountains.

Eriogonum gracile

slender buckwheat

POLYGONACEAE

BUCKWHEAT FAMILY

PCT Sections: 1–6 **Abundance:** Locally common **Height:** 6–20 in. **Flowering:** March–October **Flower Color:** White to pink or yellow **Habitat-Community:** Gravelly soils from California prairies to upper montane coniferous forests **Elevation:** Below 8000 ft. **Ecoregions:** Southern California/Northern Baja Coast, Southern California Mountains

Erect to sprawling annual with green to white, woolly (sometimes hairless) stems. Leaves 0.4–1.6 in. long, basal and alternate, ovoid to spoon-shaped; petiole 0.5–1.5 in. long. Flowers openly arranged along stems in sessile, appressed (to stem), hairy or hairless involucres 0.1–0.2 in. long. Tepals 0.1 in. long, 6-parted (3 sepals, 3 petals), hairless, white to pink or yellow. Fruits to 0.1 in. long, hairless achenes. Plants of the Transverse Ranges have hairy flowering branches (var. *gracile*); those of the Peninsular Ranges are hairless (var. *incultum*). The yellow-flowered form, more typical of the central coast of California, occurs along the PCT in the western Transverse Ranges (west of Vasquez Rocks).

Eriogonum kennedyi

Kennedy's buckwheat

POLYGONACEAE

BUCKWHEAT FAMILY

PCT Sections: 4–5 & 8–9 **Abundance:** Occasional **Height:** 2–6 in. **Flowering:** July–September **Flower Color:** White to rose **Habitat-Community:** Open, sandy or loose, gravelly soils on flats and ridges in pinyon-juniper woodlands, sagebrush scrubs, and montane coniferous forests **Elevation:** Below 11,500 ft. **Ecoregions:** Southern California Mountains, Sierra Nevada

Matted (4–16 in. across) prostrate perennial with naked (leafless), unbranched, hairy stems. Leaves 0.1–0.4 in. long, basal, tightly clustered, spoon-shaped, hairy, sometimes with rolled-under margins. Flowers within hairless or hairy involucres 0.1–0.2 in. long, clustered in compact heads, lacking peduncles, 3–7 per cluster. Tepals to 0.2 in. long, 6-parted (3 sepals, 3 petals), hairless, white to pink or rose. Fruits to 0.2 in. long, hairless achenes. Named for Kern County naturalist and merchant William Ledlie Kennedy (1827–1887).

Eriogonum latens

Inyo buckwheat

POLYGONACEAE

BUCKWHEAT FAMILY

PCT Sections: 10–11 **Abundance:** Occasional **Height:** 4–16 in. **Flowering:** June–August **Flower Color:** White to pale yellow **Habitat-Community:** Open, gravelly soils from pinyon-juniper woodlands to alpine communities **Elevation:** 8500–11,200 ft. **Ecoregions:** Sierra Nevada

Multi- to single-stemmed perennial with generally hairless stems. Leaves to 1.4 in. long, basal, roundish to spoon-shaped, short hairy, with smooth margins. Flowers in dense heads at stem tips with hairy involucres to 0.3 in. long and 5–8 teeth. Tepals to 0.3 in. long, 6-parted (3 sepals, 3 petals), fused at base into a cylindrical tube, white to pale yellow, hairy. Fruits to 0.2 in. long, hairless achenes. *Latens* ("hidden," "secret") could describe its habitat, which is sometimes steep or hard to access.

Eriogonum lobbii

Lobb's wild buckwheat

POLYGONACEAE

BUCKWHEAT FAMILY

PCT Sections: 10–24 **Abundance:** Common **Height:** 2–8 in. **Flowering:** June–August **Flower Color:** White to rose **Habitat-Community:** Open, gravelly or sandy soils from upper montane coniferous forests to alpine communities **Elevation:** Below 12,500 ft. **Ecoregions:** Sierra Nevada, Cascades, Klamath Mountains

Decumbent, sometimes matted perennial with hairy herbage. Leaves to 2 in. long, basal, roundish, short-hairy, with smooth margins. Flowers in dense, spherical heads at stem tips with short-hairy involucres to 0.5 in. long and 6–10, generally recurved teeth. Tepals to 0.3 in. long, 6-parted (3 sepals, 3 etals), fused at base into a cylindric tube, white to rose, hairless. Fruits to 0.3 in. long, hairless achenes. Look for ball-like flower heads sprawled along the ground!

Eriogonum maculatum

spotted buckwheat

POLYGONACEAE BUCKWHEAT FAMILY

PCT Sections: 1–9 **Abundance:** Common **Height:** 4–12 in. **Flowering:** April–November **Flower Color:** White to yellow or reddish **Habitat-Community:** Open, gravelly or sandy soils in scrubs and woodlands **Elevation:** Below 8200 ft. **Ecoregions:** All (except Cascades, Klamath Mountains)

Erect, multi-stemmed annual with hairy herbage. Leaves to 1.6 in. long, basal and cauline, spoon-shaped to oblong, short-hairy, with wavy or rolled-under margins. Flowers in scattered clusters at stem tips with glandular-hairy involucres to 0.1 in. long and roundish lobes. Tepals to 0.1 in. long, 6-parted (3 sepals, 3 petals), fused at base, glandular-hairy, white to yellow or reddish, with rose-purple spot. Fruits to 0.1 in. long, hairless achenes. *Maculatum* refers to the spotted tepals, which make this buckwheat one of the easiest to identify along the CA PCT!

Eriogonum nudum

naked buckwheat

POLYGONACEAE BUCKWHEAT FAMILY

PCT Sections: 3–24 **Abundance:** Common **Height:** 0.5–5 ft. **Flowering:** May–October **Flower Color:** White, yellow, or pink **Habitat-Community:** Open, rocky to sandy soils from woodlands to alpine communities **Elevation:** Below 12,500 ft. **Ecoregions:** Southern California Mountains, Sierra Nevada, Cascades, Klamath Mountains

Erect, multi-branched perennial with hairy or hairless, leafless stems. Leaves to 2.4 in. long, basal, variously shaped, hairy or hairless above, felt-like below, with generally wavy margins. Flowers in scattered head-like or hemispheric clusters at stem tips with involucres to 0.3 in. long and 5–8 teeth. Tepals to 0.2 in. long, 6-parted (3 sepals, 3 petals), fused at base, hairy or hairless, white, yellow, or pink. Fruits to 0.2 in. long, hairless achenes. The most common buckwheat along the PCT; just look for the tall, leafless stems. Of the 14 varieties found in CA, half of them occur along the CA PCT

Eriogonum ovalifolium

cushion buckwheat

POLYGONACEAE BUCKWHEAT FAMILY

PCT Sections: 4 & 10–18 **Abundance:** Common **Height:** to 8 in. **Flowering:** April–September **Flower Color:** White, yellow, or pink **Habitat-Community:** Open, rocky to sandy soils from woodlands to alpine communities **Elevation:** Below 13,800 ft. **Ecoregions:** Southern California Mountains, Sierra Nevada, Cascades

Densely matted perennial with generally hairy, short flowering stems. Leaves to 2.4 in. long, basal, narrow to roundish, felt-like to hairy, with generally wavy margins. Flowers in scattered pom-pom-like heads at the tips of stems with involucres to 0.3 in. long and 5 erect teeth. Tepals to 0.3 in. long, 6-parted (3 sepals, 3 petals), sepals much wider than petals, fused at base, hairless, white, yellow, or pink. Fruits to 0.1 in. long, hairless achenes. Wild buckwheats are excellent bee and butterfly plants. Only 3 of the 8 varieties found in CA occur along the CA PCT. Variety *vineum* is extremely rare and occurs only in the San Bernadino Mountains.

Eriogonum plumatella

yucca buckwheat

POLYGONACEAE BUCKWHEAT FAMILY

PCT Sections: 1–8 **Abundance:** Occasional **Height:** 10–35 in. **Flowering:** April–October **Flower Color:** White to cream **Habitat-Community:** Open, sandy or gravelly soils in creosote bush & Sonoran/Mojave mixed woody scrubs and Joshua tree & pinyon-juniper woodlands **Elevation:** Below 5500 ft. **Ecoregions:** Southern California Mountains, Sonoran/Mojave Basin and Range, Sierra Nevada

Erect perennial or subshrub, leafy below, with hairy or hairless (sometimes in the same population), gray-green stems. Leaves 0.3–0.6 in. long, basal and alternate, short-petioled, spoon-shaped, woolly. Flowers arranged in branched, flat-topped fountain-like spikes of 1 per node; erect, sessile involucres 0.1 in. long. Tepals 0.1 in. long, 6-parted (3 sepals, 3 petals), hairless, white to cream or pale yellow. Fruits 0.1 in. long, hairless achenes. Occurs at low desert crossings of the PCT, such as in the San Felipe Valley in San Diego County. *Plumatella* (from the Latin, "small-feathered") refers to the flowering branches.

Eriogonum polypodum

foxtail buckwheat

POLYGONACEAE BUCKWHEAT FAMILY

PCT Sections: 10 **Abundance:** Rare **Height:** 2–6 in. **Flowering:** July–August **Flower Color:** White **Habitat-Community:** Sandy soils in subalpine coniferous forests **Elevation:** Below 13,800 ft. **Ecoregions:** Sierra Nevada

Matted, hairy-stemmed perennial; dioecious. Leaves to 0.4 in. long, basal, ovoid, felt-like, with rolled-under margins. Flowers in spherical heads or openly branched at the tips of short stems with hairy involucres to 0.2 in. long and 5–7 spreading teeth. Tepals to 0.2 in. long, 6-parted (3 sepals, 3 petals), fused at base into a cylindrical tube, hairless, white. Fruits to 0.2 in. long, hairless achenes. Aka Tulare County buckwheat. Along or near PCT at mile 761–776.

Eriogonum roseum

wand buckwheat

POLYGONACEAE BUCKWHEAT FAMILY

PCT Sections: 5–10 & 23–24 **Abundance:** Locally common **Height:** 6–32 in. **Flowering:** May–November **Flower Color:** White to pink or red **Habitat-Community:** Sandy or gravelly soils in sagebrush scrubs, oak & pinyon-juniper woodlands, and montane chaparrals **Elevation:** Below 6900 ft. **Ecoregions:** Southern California Mountains, Sierra Nevada, Klamath Mountains

Erect, few-branched, lanky annual with variously hairy herbage. Leaves 0.4–1.2 in. long, basal and alternate, spoon-shaped to ovoid, white-hairy; petiole 0.4–1.6 in. long. Flowers on open, elongated branches in sessile, appressed, hairy involucres 0.1–0.3 in. long. Tepals 0.1 in. long, 6-parted (3 sepals, 3 petals), hairless, white to pink or red, occasionally yellow. Fruits to 0.1 in. long, hairless achenes. Occurs with *E. elongatum* along Sections 5–7.

hoary buckwheat

Eriogonum saxatile

POLYGONACEAE

BUCKWHEAT FAMILY

PCT Sections: 1–6 & 8–10 **Abundance:** Locally common **Height:** 2–6 in. **Flowering:** May–October **Flower Color:** White, pinkish, or yellowish **Habitat-Community:** Gravelly or sandy soils from pinyon-juniper woodlands to subalpine coniferous forests **Elevation:** Below 11,200 ft. **Ecoregions:** Southern California/Northern Baja Coast, Southern California Mountains, Sierra Nevada

Clumped perennial with white-hairy herbage. Leaves to 1 in. long, mostly basal, roundish, felt-like, often with brownish margins. Flowers in scattered clusters along stems with hairy or felt-like involucres to 0.2 in. long and 5–6 teeth. Tepals to 0.3 in. long, 6-parted (3 sepals, 3 petals), fused at base into a cylindrical, generally winged tube, hairless, white, pinkish, or yellowish. Fruits to 0.2 in. long, hairless achenes. *Saxatile* means "living among rocks" in Latin.

spurry buckwheat

Eriogonum spergulinum

POLYGONACEAE

BUCKWHEAT FAMILY

PCT Sections: 8–24 **Abundance:** Common **Height:** 2–16 in. **Flowering:** June–September **Flower Color:** White to pinkish **Habitat-Community:** Open, gravelly or sandy flats and gentle slopes from lower montane to subalpine coniferous forests **Elevation:** Below 11,500 ft. **Ecoregions:** Sierra Nevada, Cascades, Klamath Mountains

Erect annual with hairy and glandular or hairless stems. Leaves to 1.6 in. long, basal and cauline, linear, short-hairy, sometimes with rolled-under margins. Flowers in scattered clusters at stem tips with hairless involucres to 0.1 in. long and 4 teeth. Tepals to 0.2 in. long, 6-parted (3 sepals, 3 petals), fused at base, hairy or hairless, white to pinkish with darker midveins. Fruits to 0.1 in. long, hairless achenes. The small flowers resemble spurries in Caryophyllaceae (hence the common name).

Thurber's buckwheat

Eriogonum thurberi

POLYGONACEAE

BUCKWHEAT FAMILY

PCT Sections: 1–6 **Abundance:** Common **Height:** 3–16 in. **Flowering:** All year **Flower Color:** White to red **Habitat-Community:** Sandy to gravelly flats and slopes in Sonoran/Mojave mixed woody scrubs, oak & pinyon-juniper woodlands, and sagebrush scrubs **Elevation:** Below 4200 ft. **Ecoregions:** Southern California Mountains, Sierra Nevada, Klamath Mountains

Low, spreading, single-stemmed annual, branching above, with glandless to sparsely glandular stems. Leaves 0.3–1.7 in. long, basal, oblong to ovoid, white-hairy, with wavy margins; petiole 0.4–1.2 in. long. Flowers in an open inflorescence with erect, straight peduncles 0.2–1 in. long and minutely glandular-hairy involucres to 0.1 in. long. Tepals to 0.1 in. long, 6-parted (3 sepals, 3 petals), glandular-hairy with a tuft of long white hairs, white with greenish to reddish midribs. Fruits to 0.1 in. long, hairless achenes. The specific epithet honors American horticulturalist George Thurber (1821–1890).

Sidotheca emarginata
white-margined oxytheca

POLYGONACEAE

BUCKWHEAT FAMILY

PCT Sections: 3 **Abundance:** Rare **Height:** to 12 in.
Flowering: February–August **Flower Color:** White
to pink **Habitat-Community:** Gravelly soils on
slopes and ridges in pinyon-juniper woodlands,
montane chaparrals, and montane coniferous
forests **Elevation:** Below 8200 ft. **Ecoregions:**
Southern California Mountains

Single-stemmed annual from a rosette with erect to spreading upper branches and glandular stems. Leaves 0.6–3 in. long, basal, spoon-shaped. Flowers arranged in open inflorescences; glandular peduncles 0.2–1.2 in. long; involucres 0.1–0.3 in. long, 3–6-flowered, reddish, cup-shaped, 5-lobed, hairless, with distinctive white margin and awns to 0.1 in. long at tip of each lobe. Tepals 0.1–0.2 in. long, 6-parted (3 sepals, 3 petals), with 3–5 fringed linear lobes, white to pink. Fruits to 0.1 in. long, hairless achenes. This narrow endemic is restricted to the San Jacinto and Santa Rosa Mountains of Riverside County. Look for it along the PCT just north of the Highway 74 crossing. The genus name (from the Greek, "star case") alludes to the involucre awns.

Sidotheca trilobata
three-lobed oxytheca

POLYGONACEAE

BUCKWHEAT FAMILY

PCT Sections: 1–6 **Abundance:** Locally common
Height: 3–20 in. **Flowering:** April–September
Flower Color: White to pink **Habitat-Community:**
Sandy flats, slopes, and burns in foothill &
montane chaparrals, oak & pinyon-juniper
woodlands, and sagebrush scrubs **Elevation:**
Below 6500 ft. **Ecoregions:** Southern
California Mountains

Spreading, erect to prostrate annual, single-stemmed from rosette, branches spreading above. Leaves 0.4–2 in. long, mostly basal, linear to oblanceolate. Peduncles erect to spreading, sparsely glandular; involucres 0.2–0.3 in. long, deeply divided, both olive-green and red, glandular, 5-toothed, awn-tipped, awn up to 0.1 in. long. Flowers radial, 3–5 per involucre, 0.1–0.2 in. long, 6-lobed perianth, 3-lobed tepals, white to pink. Fruits <0.1 in. long, hairless achenes. Aka three-lobed starry puncturebract.

Maianthemum racemosum
large false Solomon's seal

RUSCACEAE

BUTCHER'S-BROOM FAMILY

PCT Sections: 3–4 & 11–24 **Abundance:** Common
Height: 1–3 ft. **Flowering:** March–July **Flower
Color:** White **Habitat-Community:** Streambanks
and moist, open understories and slopes in
montane coniferous forests and wetland-riparian
communities **Elevation:** Below 6600 ft.
Ecoregions: Southern California Mountains,
Sierra Nevada, Cascades, Klamath Mountains

Erect, unbranched perennial with hairless to finely hairy herbage. Leaves to 8 in. long, >5, alternate, ovoid to oblong, petioles generally lacking, ascending (<90°) along stem. Flowers tightly clustered along branches at stem tip, >20, symmetric, with 6 stamens and 3 stigmas. Tepals to 0.1 in. long, 6-parted (3 sepals, 3 petals), narrowly ovoid, generally erect, white. Fruits to 0.3 in. long, red (purple-dotted) berries with 1–3 brown seeds; berries are edible but not very palatable. *Maianthemum* ("May flower") refers to peak bloom month.

Maianthemum stellatum

little false Solomon's seal

RUSCACEAE

BUTCHER'S-BROOM FAMILY

PCT Sections: 1–5 & 8–24 **Abundance:** Common **Height:** 11–28 in. **Flowering:** April–June **Flower Color:** White **Habitat-Community:** Streambanks and moist, open slopes from woodlands and chaparrals to upper montane coniferous forests and wetland-riparian communities **Elevation:** Below 7900 ft. **Ecoregions:** Southern California Mountains, Sierra Nevada, Cascades, Klamath Mountains

Erect, unbranched perennial with hairless to finely hairy, arching (above middle) stems. Leaves to 6.7 in. long, >5, alternate, lance-shaped to oblong, at right angles along stem, petioles lacking. Flowers scattered along stem to tip, 5–15, symmetric, starry-looking, with 6 stamens and 3 stigmas. Tepals to 0.3 in. long, 6-parted (3 sepals, 3 petals), oblong to lance-shaped, spreading, white. Fruits to 0.4 in. long, red-purple to black berries with 1–3 brown seeds; berries are edible but not very palatable. Aka star Solomon's seal.

Muilla coronata

crowned muilla

THEMIDACEAE BRODIAEA FAMILY

PCT Sections: 4–9 **Abundance:** Rare **Height:** 1–2 in. **Flowering:** March–June **Flower Color:** White or bluish **Habitat-Community:** Open flats and slopes in scrubs and woodlands **Elevation:** Below 5300 ft. **Ecoregions:** Southern California Mountains, Mojave Basin and Range, Sierra Nevada

Small, onion-like perennial. Leaves to 7 in. long, 1–2, basal, grass-like. Flowers 2–10 in an open, hemispheric cluster, ascending to erect, symmetric, with 6 stamens and 3-lobed stigma. Tepals to 0.3 in. long, 6-parted (3 sepals, 3 petals), white or bluish, spreading, petals wider than sepals. Fruits to 0.3 in. across, spherical, 3-angled capsules with angled black seeds. *Muilla* is a backward anagram of *Allium*, the onion genus, a humorous reference to its similar flowers.

Mullia maritima

common muilla

THEMIDACEAE BRODIAEA FAMILY

PCT Sections: 1–8 **Abundance:** Common **Height:** 4–20 in. **Flowering:** March–June **Flower Color:** White to green-white **Habitat-Community:** Ridges and flats in chaparrals and woodlands **Elevation:** Below 7300 ft. **Ecoregions:** Southern California/Northern Baja Coast, Southern California Mountains, Sierra Nevada

Slender, unbranched perennial with a hairless stem. Leaves 6–24 in. long, basal, 3–10 per plant, thread-like. Flowers generally 4–20 in an open, hemispheric cluster, ascending to erect, symmetric, with 6 stamens (with thread-like filaments) and 3-lobed stigma. Tepals 0.1–0.3 in. long, 6-parted (3 sepals, 3 petals), free to their base, white to green-white. Fruits to 0.3 in. long, 3-angled capsules. Looks like an onion but lacks the scent.

Triteleia hyacinthina

white brodiaea

THEMIDACEAE BRODIAEA FAMILY

PCT Sections: 4–5 & 13–24 **Abundance:** Locally common **Height:** 1–2 ft. **Flowering:** March–July **Flower Color:** White **Habitat-Community:** Dry slopes, vernally wet meadows, and seeps from woodlands to upper montane coniferous forests **Elevation:** Below 6600 ft. **Ecoregions:** Southern California Mountains, Sierra Nevada, Cascades, Klamath Mountains

Erect, unbranched perennial with smooth to hairy stems. Leaves to 16 in. long, 0.9 in. wide, keeled, basal. Flowers clustered at stem tip, ascending to erect, symmetric, with 6 stamens and 3-lobed stigma. Tepals to 0.7 in. long, 6-parted, petals and sepals similar, white (sometimes bluish), in a bowl-shaped tube with ascending to spreading lobes. Fruits erect, 3-angled capsules with sharp-angled, black-crusted seeds. *Triteleia* ("3 complete") is a reference to its members having 3 sepals and 3 petals. Herbage and flowers lack an onion scent. Aka fool's onion.

Triantha occidentalis

western false-asphodel

TOFIELDIACEAE

FALSE-ASPHODEL FAMILY

PCT Sections: 10–24 **Abundance:** Common **Height:** 12–32 in. **Flowering:** July–September **Flower Color:** White **Habitat-Community:** Wet meadows, bogs, fens, and seeps in wetland-riparian communities **Elevation:** Below 10,200 ft. **Ecoregions:** Sierra Nevada, Cascades, Klamath Mountains

Erect, unbranched perennial with densely glandular-hairy stems. Leaves to 8 in. long, 0.3 in. wide, mostly basal, linear. Flowers densely clustered at stem tip, ascending to erect, symmetric, with 6 stamens and 3 styles. Tepals to 0.3 in. long, 6-parted (3 sepals, 3 petals), white, oblong-ovoid, spreading, petals narrower than sepals. Fruits erect, red, 3-lobed capsules to 0.4 in. long with tailed, red-brown seeds. Recently discovered to be carnivorous: insects stuck to the glandular stems die and are subsequently absorbed into the plant. Bog plants can have difficulty absorbing nitrogen, but not if they are munching down on bugs! Plants are toxic! Aka sticky false-asphodel.

▼ 4 PETALS

Anelsonia eurycarpa

broad-podded anelsonia

BRASSICACEAE MUSTARD FAMILY

PCT Sections: 10–13 **Abundance:** Rare **Height:** 0.5–2 in. **Flowering:** June–July **Flower Color:** White to purplish **Habitat-Community:** Rocky slopes and ridges in alpine communities **Elevation:** 5200–13,500 ft. **Ecoregions:** Sierra Nevada

Tufted, multi-branched perennial with hairy, leafless stems. Leaves 0.4–0.6 in. long, basal, linear to widely spoon-shaped, with smooth margins. Flowers in head-like clusters, erect sepals to 0.2 in. long, white to purplish petals 0.2–0.3 in. long. Fruits 0.6–1.2 in. long, hairless point-tipped siliques with 10–24 hairy, flat seeds. *Eurycarpa* means "well-formed fruit," referring to how large the fruits are for such as small plant!

Athysanus pusillus

common sandweed

BRASSICACEAE MUSTARD FAMILY

PCT Sections: 1–8 **Abundance:** Occasional **Height:** 2–12 in. **Flowering:** February–May **Flower Color:** White **Habitat-Community:** Sandy to rocky slopes and flats in Sonoran/Mojave mixed woody scrubs, foothill chaparrals, and oak woodlands **Elevation:** Below 6200 ft. **Ecoregions:** Southern California Mountains, Sierra Nevada

Erect, spindly annual with hooked hairs. Leaves 0.1–1 in. long, mostly basal, spoon-shaped to oblong, with slightly toothed margins. Flowers scattered along one side of stem, erect sepals (falling off early), and white petals 0.1–0.2 in. long. Fruits round, flattened, downwardly reflexed silicles with distinctive hooked (or branched) hairs. Like many species in the mustard family, responds to early winter rains, without which it may not germinate.

Boechera lyallii

Lyall's rockcress

BRASSICACEAE MUSTARD FAMILY

PCT Sections: 9–24 **Abundance:** Rare **Height:** 1–6 in. **Flowering:** June–August **Flower Color:** Whitish to purplish **Habitat-Community:** Rocky outcrops and gravelly soils in alpine communities **Elevation:** 6500–12,800 ft. **Ecoregions:** Sierra Nevada, Cascades, Klamath Mountains

Erect perennial from a woody base, with single hairless stem from a basal rosette. Leaves 0.4–1.2 in. long, basal (hairy) and along stems, narrowly spoon-shaped, with smooth margins. Flowers at stem tips, with hairless and erect pedicels, hairless sepals, and whitish to purplish petals 0.2–0.4 in. long. Fruits 1.2–2.2 in. long, to 0.1 in. wide, erect, hairless siliques with generally 2 rows of seeds.

Boechera pygmaea

Tulare County rockcress

BRASSICACEAE MUSTARD FAMILY

PCT Sections: 10 **Abundance:** Rare **Height:** 1–3 in. **Flowering:** May–July **Flower Color:** White **Habitat-Community:** Open, gravelly or sandy flats in subalpine coniferous forests **Elevation:** 6800–11,200 ft. **Ecoregions:** Sierra Nevada

Erect, many-stemmed perennial from a woody base, with rosette of leaves and old leaf bases. Leaves 0.4–0.8 in. long, basal and alternate, linear, hairy, with smooth margins. Flowers 2–5 at stem tips, with hairy and erect to ascending pedicels, hairy sepals, and white petals 0.1–0.2 in. long. Fruits 0.5–1.3 in. long, 0.1–0.2 in. wide, erect to ascending, hairless siliques with 1 row of seeds. Look for this gem at Mile 730-744.

Boechera stricta

Drummond's rockcress

BRASSICACEAE MUSTARD FAMILY

PCT Sections: 10–16 **Abundance:** Occasional
Height: 0.5–3 ft. **Flowering:** May–August
Flower Color: White **Habitat-Community:**
Open, gravelly slopes and meadows from
lower montane to subalpine coniferous forests
and wetland-riparian communities **Elevation:**
5900–11,200 ft. **Ecoregions:** Sierra Nevada

Erect, 1-4-stemmed biennial or short-lived perennial with basal rosette and hairy to hairless stems. Leaves 1–2.8 in. long, basal and alternate, linear, generally hairy, with smooth margins. Flowers 8–80 at stem tips, with hairless and erect pedicels, hairless sepals, and white (aging pale lavender) petals 0.2–0.5 in. long. Fruits 1.5–4 in. long, to 0.2 in. wide, erect, hairless siliques with 2 rows of seeds. Scottish botanist Thomas Drummond (1793–1835) made 750 plant and 150 bird collections in North America.

Cardamine breweri

Brewer's bittercress

BRASSICACEAE MUSTARD FAMILY

PCT Sections: 4 & 9–20 **Abundance:** Locally
common **Height:** 2–24 in. **Flowering:** May–July
Flower Color: White **Habitat-Community:**
Wet places from lower montane to subalpine
coniferous forests and wetland-riparian
communities **Elevation:** Below 10,500 ft.
Ecoregions: Southern California Mountains,
Sierra Nevada, Cascades, Klamath Mountains

Decumbent to erect, unbranched to branched perennial with mostly hairless stems. Leaves 1–5.3 in. long, 3–8, alternate, pinnately compound, with 3–5 ovate to round (terminal) leaflets and lobed to toothed margins. Flowers in elongated clusters at stem tips, sepals to 0.2 in. long, white petals 0.1–0.3 in. long. Fruits 0.6–1.4 in. long, to 0.1 in. wide, erect siliques with 1 row of 14–28 seeds. The only *Cardamine* along the PCT without rhizome leaves.

Cardamine californica

milkmaids

BRASSICACEAE MUSTARD FAMILY

PCT Sections: 1–5 & 16–24 **Abundance:** Common
Height: 8–24 in. **Flowering:** January–May
Flower Color: White or pinkish **Habitat-Community:** Shaded sites in woodlands and
lower montane coniferous forests **Elevation:**
Below 4600 ft. **Ecoregions:** All (except Sonoran/
Mojave Basin and Range)

Erect, unbranched perennial with rhizome leaves (coming from an underground attachment to the roots) and mostly hairless stems. Leaves 1–5.3 in. long, alternate, pinnately compound, rhizome leaflets generally 3(7), stem leaflets 2–5, ovate to round or lance-shaped with smooth to lobed margins. Flowers in elongated clusters at stem tips, sepals to 0.2 in. long, white petals 0.3–0.6 in. long. Fruits 0.6–2.4 in. long, to 0.1 in. wide, ascending siliques with 1 row of 12–22 seeds. Found at lower elevations throughout California.

Caulanthus hallii

Hall's caulanthus

BRASSICACEAE MUSTARD FAMILY

PCT Sections: 2–3 **Abundance:** Rare **Height:** 8–40 in. **Flowering:** March–May **Flower Color:** White to cream **Habitat-Community:** Dry, rocky to gravelly hills in Sonoran mixed woody scrubs, chaparrals, and pinyon-juniper woodlands **Elevation:** Below 6000 ft. **Ecoregions:** Southern California Mountains

Erect, bristly, few-branched annual with somewhat hollow stems. Basal leaves 1–6 in. long, spoon-shaped, with pinnately lobed or toothed margins. Stem leaves reduced in size up the stem, alternate, petioled, lance-shaped, with unlobed bases. Flowers in elongated spikes at stem tip, 4-parted, with erect yellow sepals and white to cream petals 0.3–0.5 in. long. Fruits 3–6 in. long, spreading, cylindric, linear, purplish, usually hairless siliques. Limited to northern San Diego and southern Riverside counties. Look for it along the PCT at Mile 78 in the San Felipe Hills.

Caulanthus lasiophyllus

California mustard

BRASSICACEAE MUSTARD FAMILY

PCT Sections: 1–8 **Abundance:** Common **Height:** 8–32 in. **Flowering:** March–June **Flower Color:** White **Habitat-Community:** Sandy, alluvial flats and washes on gravelly to rocky slopes in creosote bush scrubs, foothill chaparrals, and Joshua tree & pinyon-juniper woodlands **Elevation:** Below 4600 ft. **Ecoregions:** Southern California Mountains, Sonoran/Mojave Basin and Range, Sierra Nevada

Erect, thin-stemmed annual with sparsely to densely hairy stems branched at inflorescence. Leaves 1–5 in. long, basal (early withering) and alternate, green, erect, lance-shaped to oblong, pinnately lobed to toothed (stem leaves). Flowers in elongated spikes at stem tip, 4-parted, with erect sepals and white petals 0.1–0.2 in. long. Fruits 1–2 in. long, narrow, ascending to strongly descending, straight to curved outward, slightly flattened, hairless siliques. A dominant annual, especially in desert zones, during years with abundant early winter rains. *Lasiophyllus* is Latin for "woolly-leaved."

Caulanthus major

slender wild cabbage

BRASSICACEAE MUSTARD FAMILY

PCT Sections: 4–5 **Abundance:** Occasional **Height:** 10–40 in. **Flowering:** May–July **Flower Color:** White to purple **Habitat-Community:** Rocky to gravelly slopes and forest margins in sagebrush scrubs, pinyon-juniper woodlands, and lower montane coniferous forests **Elevation:** Below 8800 ft. **Ecoregions:** Southern California Mountains

Attractive perennial from a woody base, with smooth, hairless, somewhat hollow stems. Basal leaves 1–4 in. long, spatula-shaped, with smooth to toothed margins. Stem leaves alternate, reduced, linear without lobed bases, hairless. Flowers in elongated spikes at stem tip, 4-parted, with white to cream, hairy, erect sepals and white to pale purple, dark-veined, recurved petals 0.5–0.7 in. long. Fruits 2–5 in. long, narrow, erect to ascending, straight to curved, hairless siliques. Most common in the Great Basin Desert but edges onto the PCT along the northeastern flanks of the San Bernardino and San Gabriel Mountains.

Caulanthus simulans

Payson's jewelflower

BRASSICACEAE MUSTARD FAMILY

PCT Sections: 1–3 **Abundance:** Occasional **Height:** 6–26 in. **Flowering:** March–June **Flower Color:** White to cream **Habitat-Community:** Dry, rocky to gravelly hills in Sonoran mixed woody scrubs, chaparrals, and oak & pinyon-juniper woodlands **Elevation:** Below 6800 ft. **Ecoregions:** Southern California Mountains

Erect, bristly, few-branched annual with conspicuously spreading-hairy stems. Basal leaves 1–3 in. long, spoon-shaped, pinnately lobed or toothed. Stem leaves reduced in size up the stem, alternate, sessile, ovoid, with lobed bases and toothed margins. Flowers in elongated spikes at stem tip, 4-parted, with erect yellow sepals and white to cream petals 0.4–0.6 in. long. Fruits 1–3 in. long, reflexed (sometimes spreading), cylindric, linear, purplish, usually hairless siliques. Restricted to San Diego and Riverside counties.

Draba breweri

cushion draba

BRASSICACEAE MUSTARD FAMILY

PCT Sections: 10–12 **Abundance:** Locally common **Height:** 1–6 in. **Flowering:** July–August **Flower Color:** White **Habitat-Community:** Open, rocky slopes and ridges in subalpine coniferous forests and alpine communities **Elevation:** 10,100–13,500 ft. **Ecoregions:** Sierra Nevada

Tufted, few- to many-stemmed perennial. Leaves 0.1–1 in. long, mostly basal, 0–6 alternate along stems, narrowly to widely spoon-shaped, hairy. Flowers in clusters of 5–24 at stem tip, sepals to 0.1 in. long, white petals to 0.1 in. long. Fruits 0.1–0.4 in. long, to 0.1 in. wide, lance-shaped to oblong or linear, twisted, hairy siliques, with 28–40 seeds and minute style.

Draba cuneifolia

wedgeleaf draba

BRASSICACEAE MUSTARD FAMILY

PCT Sections: 1–8 **Abundance:** Occasional **Height:** 2–12 in. **Flowering:** January–May **Flower Color:** White **Habitat-Community:** Rocky slopes, gravelly plains and washes in Sonoran/Mojave mixed woody scrubs and Joshua tree & pinyon-juniper woodlands **Elevation:** Below 6500 ft. **Ecoregions:** Southern California Mountains, Sierra Nevada

Annual with a cluster of thick basal leaves, bolting one or more erect stems covered with hairs. Leaves 0.4–1.3 in. long, mainly basal, 0–6 much reduced along stem, spoon-shaped to ovoid, toothed, hairy. Flowers 10–70 at stem tip, 4-parted, white petals 0.1–0.2 in. long. Fruits 0.2–0.6 in. long, linear to elliptic or ovoid, flat, not twisted, hairless to hairy siliques.

Lepidium fremontii

desert pepperweed

BRASSICACEAE MUSTARD FAMILY

PCT Sections: 4–8 **Abundance:** Occasional **Height:** 1–3 ft. **Flowering:** March–June **Flower Color:** White **Habitat-Community:** Sandy flats and gravelly hillsides in creosote bush scrubs, Mojave mixed woody scrubs, and Joshua tree & pinyon-juniper woodlands **Elevation:** Below 6500 ft. **Ecoregions:** Southern California Mountains, Mojave Basin and Range, Sierra Nevada

Intricately branched perennial or subshrub with tangled, hairless gray stems. Leaves 1–4 in. long, seasonally deciduous, pinnately lobed (3–9 lobes) with thread-like, hairless segments. Flowers densely clustered, 4-parted, with spoon-shaped white petals 0.1–0.2 in. long. Fruits 0.2–0.3 in. across, oblong to round silicles with a notched tip and exserted style. Unremarkable for much of the year but quite distinctive in full bloom. Common across the mid-elevations of the Mojave Desert, intersecting the PCT only along the Mojave-influenced segments, including the Antelope Valley crossing.

Nasturtium officinale

watercress

BRASSICACEAE MUSTARD FAMILY

PCT Sections: All **Abundance:** Occasional **Height:** 5–30 in. **Flowering:** March–November **Flower Color:** White **Habitat-Community:** Streams, springs, marshes, lake margins, and other non-brackish shallow, slow-running waters in wetland-riparian communities **Elevation:** Below 10,500 ft. **Ecoregions:** All (except Sonoran/Mojave Basin and Range)

Fast-growing, generally decumbent, few-branched perennial with hollow green stems and hairless herbage. Leaves 1–6 in. long, alternate, pinnate, with 3–9 ovoid leaflets. Flowers scattered at stem tip, 4-parted, with white petals 0.1–0.2 in. long. Fruits 0.4–0.8 in. long, linear to slightly club-shaped siliques. Among the first leafy vegetables eaten by humans worldwide, now found in many grocery stores. The genus name (from the Latin *nasus tortus*, "twisted nose") refers to the contortions human noses go through in response to the sharp, peppery smell of the seeds.

Thysanocarpus curvipes

sand fringepod

BRASSICACEAE MUSTARD FAMILY

PCT Sections: All (except 21–22) **Abundance:** Common **Height:** 5–25 in. **Flowering:** February–June **Flower Color:** White to pale purple **Habitat-Community:** Rocky slopes, washes, and meadows in creosote bush scrubs, California prairies, foothill chaparrals, and woodlands **Elevation:** Below 7800 ft. **Ecoregions:** All

Slender, usually single-stemmed annual with hairless to hairy (on lower) stems. Leaves 1–3 in. long, basal and alternate, spatula- to lance-shaped, with smooth to wavy-toothed margins; reduced stem leaves with lobed bases clasping the stem. Flowers openly scattered along branch and stem tips, 4-parted, with small (exceeding the sepals), white, purple-tinged petals. Fruits 0.1–0.3 in. across, pendent, round, flattened, variously hairy, disk-like siliques with smooth or lobed margins, sometimes with small holes.

Thysanocarpus laciniatus

narrow-leaved fringepod

BRASSICACEAE MUSTARD FAMILY

PCT Sections: 1–9 **Abundance:** Common **Height:** 6–24 in. **Flowering:** March–May **Flower Color:** White to purple-tinged **Habitat-Community:** Rocky slopes, washes, and ridges in creosote bush scrubs, foothill chaparrals, and woodlands **Elevation:** Below 6100 ft. **Ecoregions:** Southern California Mountains, Mojave Basin and Range, Sierra Nevada

Wiry annual with waxy, hairless herbage and generally a single stem from base. Leaves 1–3 in. long, alternate, spoon-shaped to elliptic or linear, smooth to pinnately lobed, with upper leaves not clasping the stem. Flowers scattered along branch and stem tips, 4-parted, with small (exceeding the sepals), white, purple-tinged petals. Fruits 0.1–0.3 in. across, pendent, disk-like, roundish, flattened, variously hairy siliques with smooth to deeply toothed or fringed margins (hence *laciniatus*, from the Latin, "deeply cut").

Turritis glabra

tower rockcress

BRASSICACEAE MUSTARD FAMILY

PCT Sections: 1–6 & 8–24 **Abundance:** Common **Height:** 1–4 ft. **Flowering:** March–July **Flower Color:** White (purplish) **Habitat-Community:** Shaded places, rocky outcrops, and meadows in woodlands, chaparrals, and lower montane coniferous forests **Elevation:** Below 9200 ft. **Ecoregions:** All (except Sonoran/Mojave Basin and Range)

Erect, 1–few-branched biennial or short-lived perennial with basal rosette and hairy, white-waxy upper stems. Leaves 1–5 in. long, basal and alternate, lance- to spoon-shaped or ovoid, with generally branched hairs and smooth to toothed margins. Flowers in much-elongated clusters at stem tips, erect sepals to 0.2 in. long, white (purplish) petals 0.2–0.4 in. long. Fruits 1–5 in. long, 0.1 in. wide, erect, 4-angled, hairless siliques with 2 rows of seeds per chamber. *Turritis* ("tower") refers to the pyramidal shape formed by overlapping leaves and fruits.

Euphorbia albomarginata

rattlesnake sandmat

EUPHORBIACEAE SPURGE FAMILY

PCT Sections: 1–9 **Abundance:** Common **Height:** 1–2 in. **Flowering:** April–November **Flower Color:** White to dark red **Habitat-Community:** Washes, sandy to gravelly plains and dunes in creosote bush scrubs, Joshua tree & pinyon-juniper woodlands, and chaparrals **Elevation:** Below 7200 ft. **Ecoregions:** Southern California Mountains, Sonoran/Mojave Basin and Range, Sierra Nevada

Prostrate, many-branched, hairless annual forming spherical mats covering the ground; monoecious. Leaves 0.1–0.3 in. long, usually opposite, round to ovoid. Cyathium contains 4 crescent-shaped nectary glands enclosing many minute male flowers and 1 female flower, all lacking petals. Nectary glands dark red to burgundy, each with a white, petal-like gland appendage (hence *albomarginata*, "white-margined"). Fruits 3-lobed, ovoid capsules. Long used as a folk remedy to treat snakebites; it is medically ineffective, but the common name remains. The milky white sap is poisonous. *Euphorbia* is derived from Euphorbos, Greek physician to King Juba II of Numidia, who married the daughter of Antony and Cleopatra.

Euphorbia polycarpa

smallseed sandmat

EUPHORBIACEAE SPURGE FAMILY

PCT Sections: 1–8 **Abundance:** Occasional **Height:** 1–7 in. **Flowering:** February–November **Flower Color:** White and dark red **Habitat-Community:** Dry, sandy to gravelly slopes and flats in scrubs **Elevation:** Below 4000 ft. **Ecoregions:** Southern California Mountains, Sonoran/Mojave Basin and Range, Sierra Nevada

Densely matted perennial with much-branched stems and hairless or hairy herbage containing a milky sap; monoecious. Leaves 0.1–0.4 in. long, opposite, round to ovoid. Flowers usually 1 per node, each cyathium containing a bell-shaped involucre and 4 dark burgundy or black nectary glands with white to red, petal-like appendages of equal size. Male flowers obscure, 15–32; female flower 1. Fruits 3-lobed, hairless or sparsely short-hairy capsules. Occurs along the low desert segments of the PCT, becoming scarce in the Antelope Valley and surrounding ranges farther north. In the right conditions, plants may live for decades, forming compact mounds that become woody at the base.

Euphorbia serpillifolia

thyme-leafed spurge

EUPHORBIACEAE SPURGE FAMILY

PCT Sections: 1–5 & 8 & 15–24 **Abundance:** Occasional **Height:** 2–15 in. **Flowering:** July–October **Flower Color:** White to reddish **Habitat-Community:** Dry flats in sagebrush scrubs, Sonoran/Mojave mixed woody scrubs, foothill chaparrals, pinyon-juniper woodlands, and lower montane coniferous forests **Elevation:** Below 7600 ft. **Ecoregions:** All (except Southern California/Northern Baja Coast)

Matted to ascending, branched summer annual with hairless or hairy herbage; monoecious. Leaves 0.2–0.7 in. long, opposite, oblong to spoon-shaped, with finely toothed (especially near tip) margins. Flowers solitary at stem nodes, each cyathium containing a bell-shaped involucre, 4 nectary glands, and 4 white, petal-like appendages enclosing 5–18 obscure male flowers and 1 pistillate flower. Fruits 3-lobed, ovoid capsules. Subsp. *hirtella* (hairy leaves) is nearly endemic to southern California and the southern Sierra Nevada. Subsp. *serpillifolia* (hairless leaves) is scattered along the full length of the CA PCT, except for the high Sierra.

Frasera neglecta

pine green gentian

GENTIANACEAE GENTIAN FAMILY

PCT Sections: 4–5 **Abundance:** Rare **Height:** 8–20 in. **Flowering:** May–July **Flower Color:** White to pale green **Habitat-Community:** Dry, open slopes and meadow margins in oak woodlands and montane coniferous forests **Elevation:** Below 8000 ft. **Ecoregions:** Southern California Mountains

Erect, many-stemmed perennial, often from 1–many rosettes, with hairless herbage. Basal leaves 1–8 in. long, whorled in rosette, linear to lance-shaped, narrowly white-margined; stem leaves opposite with clasping base. Flowers in dense clusters along the stem, 4-parted, calyces 0.2–0.3 in. long (sepals fused at base), corollas rotate with green-white (purple-streaked) lobes 0.3–0.7 in. long. Fruits 2-valved, many-seeded capsules. Best seen along the PCT north of Big Bear Lake.

Frasera parryi

Coahuila frasera

GENTIANACEAE GENTIAN FAMILY

PCT Sections: 1–4 **Abundance:** Occasional **Height:** 2–5 ft. **Flowering:** April–July **Flower Color:** White to pale green **Habitat-Community:** Dry openings in foothill chaparrals and oak woodlands **Elevation:** Below 6000 ft. **Ecoregions:** Southern California Mountains

Erect, showy-flowered perennial with 1–2 stems bolting from a rosette and hairless herbage. Basal leaves 2–10 in. long, whorled in rosette, strap-shaped, wavy white-margined; stem leaves opposite, reduced, linear to lance-shaped. Flowers in open clusters at branch and stem tips, 4-parted, calyces 0.3–0.7 in. long (sepals fused at base), corollas rotate with green-white (purple-speckled) lobes 0.4–0.8 in. long. Fruits 2-valved, many-seeded capsules. Can be locally common in burn areas. Best seen along the PCT at the transition from chamise chaparral to the lower montane zones from Campo to the southern San Jacinto Mountains.

Frasera tubulosa

Kern green gentian

GENTIANACEAE GENTIAN FAMILY

PCT Sections: 8–10 **Abundance:** Rare **Height:** 2–44 in. **Flowering:** July–August **Flower Color:** White **Habitat-Community:** Open understories and gravelly soils in montane coniferous forests **Elevation:** Below 8900 ft. **Ecoregions:** Sierra Nevada

Erect perennial with 1 hairless stem. Leaves to 3.5 in. long, basal and whorled, spoon-shaped or linear-oblong, with smooth white margin and pointed tip. Flowers in elongated clusters. Calyces to 0.5 in. long with 4 lance-shaped lobes. Corollas to 0.5 in. long, white with blue veins, bell-shaped, with 4 oblong to spoon-shaped lobes, each with 1 ovoid nectary pit (green blotch with fringed extensions) at the base of the inner surface. Fruits many-seeded capsules. Look for this jewel at Mile 646–647.5, 721.5–722, and 728–728.5.

Calyptridium umbellatum

pussypaws

MONTIACEAE

MINER'S LETTUCE FAMILY

PCT Sections: 3–5 & 9–24 **Abundance:** Common **Height:** to 24 in. **Flowering:** May–October **Flower Color:** White **Habitat-Community:** Open, sandy or gravelly soils from lower montane coniferous forests to alpine communities **Elevation:** Below 14,100 ft. **Ecoregions:** Southern California Mountains, Sierra Nevada, Cascades, Klamath Mountains

Spreading to ascending perennial from a basal rosette. Leaves 0.6–2.8 in. long. Flowers in dense clusters on 1 flowering stem per plant. Sepals to 0.3 in. long, 2, translucent, round. Petals 0.1–0.3 in. long, 4, white, fused at tips. Fruits to 0.1 in. long, capsules with 1–8 black seeds. Chipmunks relish the seeds, carrying hundreds in their cheek pouches as they forage. The fused petal tips form a cap over the fruit (hence *Calyptridium*, "capped").

Chylismia claviformis

browneyes

ONAGRACEAE

EVENING-PRIMROSE FAMILY

PCT Sections: 3–9 **Abundance:** Locally common **Height:** 6–20 in. **Flowering:** March–May **Flower Color:** White to pale yellow **Habitat-Community:** Sandy to gravelly alluvium, especially in washes, in creosote bush scrubs, Mojave mixed woody scrubs, and Joshua tree woodlands **Elevation:** Below 5500 ft. **Ecoregions:** Sonoran/Mojave Basin and Range, Sierra Nevada

Erect, few-branched desert annual bolting from a basal rosette with hairless to hairy stems. Leaves 2–8 in. long, generally basal (reduced and alternate along stem, if present), narrowly elliptic to lance-shaped, irregularly pinnately lobed, with gray-green mottling. Flowers at branch and stem tips, nodding, opening at dawn, 4-parted, with erect sepals, 8 stamens, and rounded stigma. Petals 0.2–0.3 in. long, white to pale yellow, often with brown ("eyes") or reddish spots at base. Fruits 0.3–1.5 in. long, straight, ascending, cylindric capsules. Some of the 8 subspecies in California are yellow-flowered; subsp. *claviformis* (hairless) and subsp. *aurantiaca* (hairy), both white-flowered, are most common on the PCT.

Epilobium ciliatum

fringed willowherb

ONAGRACEAE

EVENING-PRIMROSE FAMILY

PCT Sections: All **Abundance:** Locally common **Height:** 8–40 in. **Flowering:** May–October **Flower Color:** White to pink **Habitat-Community:** Moist soils, springs, shaded streambanks, meadows, and ponds in wetland-riparian communities **Elevation:** Below 12,600 ft. **Ecoregions:** All (except Sonoran/Mojave Basin and Range)

Erect, loosely clumped, widespread perennial with somewhat fleshy, hairy (in lines) stems. Leaves 1–5 in. long, alternate, lance-shaped to ovoid, maintaining size up the stem. Flowers clustered at stem and branch tips, 4-parted, with erect sepals 0.1–0.3 in. long, 8 stamens, and club-shaped stigma. Petals 0.2–0.6 in. long, notched ("fringed") or 2-lobed, white to pink Fruits 1–4 in. long, slender, cylindric, straight capsules with hair-tufted seeds. *Ciliatum* (from the Latin, "hairy") refers to fine marginal hairs that cast a silvery glow along the edges of the seed pods and buds.

Oenothera californica

California evening-primrose

ONAGRACEAE

EVENING-PRIMROSE FAMILY

PCT Sections: 1–9 **Abundance:** Occasional **Height:** 4–30 in. **Flowering:** April–June **Flower Color:** White **Habitat-Community:** Sandy to gravelly soils from Mojave mixed woody scrubs to lower montane coniferous forests **Elevation:** Below 7600 ft. **Ecoregions:** Southern California Mountains, Mojave Basin and Range, Sierra Nevada

Decumbent to ascending, large-flowered perennial with peeling stems and hairless or hairy herbage. Leaves 1–2.5 in. long, alternate, lance-shaped, smooth to pinnately lobed, green to gray-green; young plants have basal rosettes. Flowers nodding in bud, opening in the evening, 4-parted, with erect sepals 0.1–0.3 in. long, 8 stamens, and deeply lobed stigma. Petals 0.7–1.5 in. long, white with a yellow base. Fruits 1.2–2.2 in. long, narrowly cylindric capsules. Two subspecies along the PCT: subsp. *californica* (green leaves with wavy-margins) and subsp. *avita* (gray-green leaves with pinnately lobed margins).

Oenothera cespitosa

fragrant evening-primrose

ONAGRACEAE

EVENING-PRIMROSE FAMILY

PCT Sections: 4 **Abundance:** Rare **Height:** 4–12 in. **Flowering:** April–August **Flower Color:** White **Habitat-Community:** Sandy to gravelly soils in pinyon-juniper woodlands and montane coniferous forests **Elevation:** Below 7700 ft. **Ecoregions:** Southern California Mountains

Night-blooming perennial from a densely clustered rosette and woody base with coarsely hairy or sometimes glandular herbage. Leaves 2–13 in. long, basal, spoon-shaped, green, with toothed to pinnately lobed margins. Flowers tucked among leaves, 4-parted, with sepals 0.7–2 in. long, 8 stamens, and deeply lobed stigma. Petals 0.8–2.2 in. long, white with a yellow base. Fruits 1.1–2.5 in. long, elliptic to narrowly ovoid, bumpy capsules. Common throughout the western US, but found along the PCT only in the eastern San Bernardino Mountains. The botanical term *cespitose* means "growing in dense tufts," referring to the dense cluster of leaves.

Oenothera deltoides subsp. *deltoides*

birdcage evening-primrose

ONAGRACEAE

EVENING-PRIMROSE FAMILY

PCT Sections: 3–7 **Abundance:** Occasional **Height:** 6–24 in. **Flowering:** March–May **Flower Color:** White **Habitat-Community:** Sandy soils, including dunes, in creosote bush scrubs, Mojave mixed woody scrubs, foothill chaparrals, and Joshua tree woodlands **Elevation:** Below 3600 ft. **Ecoregions:** Sonoran/Mojave Basin and Range

Decumbent to ascending, large-flowered annual with stout, peeling stems that eventually arch up, forming a birdcage-like structure. Leaves 2–6 in. long, in loose basal rosettes and alternate, spoon-shaped, gray-green, smooth-margined to pinnately lobed. Flowers in leaf axils, nodding in bud, opening in the evening, 4-parted, with sepals 0.3–1.2 in. long, 8 stamens, and deeply lobed stigma. Petals 0.7–1.7 in. long, white with a yellow base. Fruits 0.8–2.3 in. long, cylindric, linear, slightly curved capsules. This celebrated annual of desert dunes, found throughout the southwestern US, is infrequent along the PCT, observable only along the lowest desert crossings from northern Riverside to Kern County. Some of the dry remnant basket- or birdcage-like structures are so perfectly symmetrical that they may actually function as a cage for birds!

Dicentra nevadensis

Tulare County bleeding heart

PAPAVERACEAE POPPY FAMILY

PCT Sections: 9–10 **Abundance:** Rare **Height:** 7–18 in. **Flowering:** June–August **Flower Color:** White to yellowish or pinkish **Habitat-Community:** Meadows and rocky slopes from upper montane coniferous forests to alpine communities **Elevation:** 7200–10,200 ft. **Ecoregions:** Sierra Nevada

Clustered, many-stemmed perennial with hairless stems and generally white- to blue-waxy-coated foliage. Leaves 6–10 in. long, basal, 2-divided into oblong, fern-like leaflets. Flowers irregular, nodding, heart-shaped, in clusters of 2–20 at stem tips. Sepals 2, generally shed after flower. Petals 0.5–0.7 in. long, 4, white to yellowish or pinkish, outer free and pouched at base, inner fused at tips. Fruits to 0.8 in. long, oblong capsules with few seeds. *Dicentra* (from the Greek, "twice-spurred") refers to the outer petals. Occurs only in the southern high Sierra, mostly in the Sequoia and Kings Canyon National Parks region and west of the PCT.

Plantago patagonica

woolly plantain

PLANTAGINACEAE

PLANTAIN FAMILY

PCT Sections: 1–4 **Abundance:** Occasional **Height:** 2–7 in. **Flowering:** March–July **Flower Color:** White **Habitat-Community:** Sandy to rocky substrates in foothill chaparrals and Joshua tree & pinyon-juniper woodlands **Elevation:** Below 6500 ft. **Ecoregions:** Southern California Mountains

Ascending to erect, small, tufted annual with velvety herbage. Leaves 1–4 in. long, basal, linear to spoon-shaped, soft-hairy, pale green. Flowers crowded in short, dense spikes, with linear bracts and deeply 4-lobed, fused-at-base calyces. Corollas symmetric or irregular, petals fused into a cylindric tube, with 4 spreading, opaque white lobes and 4 stamens. Fruits 2-seeded capsules. Ranges across the Americas: described in the late 1700s from a specimen collected in Patagonia.

Galium aparine

common bedstraw

RUBIACEAE MADDER FAMILY

PCT Sections: All **Abundance:** Common **Height:** 12–30 in. **Flowering:** April–June **Flower Color:** White **Habitat-Community:** Shaded areas from chaparrals to upper montane coniferous forests **Elevation:** Below 8000 ft. **Ecoregions:** All

Straggling, vine-like, few-branched annual, climbing through and clinging to other plants by small cleaver-like prickles, and 4-sided stems. Leaves 0.5–2 in. long, in whorls of 6–8, spaced along stem, linear to spoon-shaped, and green. Flowers on small branches from leaf axils, 0 sepals, fused-at-base corolla with 4 white, spreading lobes to 0.1 in. long, 4 stamens, and 1 pistil. Fruits 0.1 in. across, 2-chambered, and densely bristly with hooked prickles that cling like VELCRO® to clothes and animal fur. The leaves and stems can be cooked as a leaf vegetable. Certain bedstraws were used to curdle milk, hence *Galium* (from *gala*, "milk").

▼ 5 PETALS / SYMMETRIC COROLLAS

Amaranthus fimbriatus

fringed amaranth

AMARANTHACEAE

AMARANTH FAMILY

PCT Sections: 1–4 **Abundance:** Occasional **Height:** 10–30 in. **Flowering:** July–November **Flower Color:** White to pink **Habitat-Community:** Sandy to rocky soils in creosote bush & Sonoran mixed woody scrubs and pinyon-juniper woodlands **Elevation:** Below 5400 ft. **Ecoregions:** Southern California Mountains, Sonoran Basin and Range

Erect, few-branched summer annual with green to purple, hairless stems; monoecious. Leaves 0.8–2.4 in. long, alternate, linear; petiole 0.3–1.6 in. long. Flowers on leafy, elongated, spike-like stalks, white to pink. Male flowers (at tips of flowering stalks) 5-parted with 3 stamens. Female flowers 0.1 in. long, 5-parted, spreading to reflexed, fan-shaped, with minutely toothed margins. Fruits tiny, wrinkled, 1-seeded utricles. Found along the PCT in the lower desert crossings; locally common after a productive summer thunderstorm. Amaranths have a long history of uses in Indigenous cultures; this species has been used as a nutritious food crop (especially the seeds) and for dyes and oils. *Amaranthus* (from the Greek *marantos*, "unfading") refers to the long-lasting flowers.

Angelica breweri

Brewer's angelica

APIACEAE CARROT FAMILY

PCT Sections: 10–18 **Abundance:** Locally common **Height:** 3–6 ft. **Flowering:** June–September **Flower Color:** White **Habitat-Community:** Open, wooded slopes in montane coniferous forests **Elevation:** Below 9900 ft. **Ecoregions:** Sierra Nevada, Cascades

Erect perennial with generally hairy herbage. Leaves 2–3-pinnately compound, generally hairy, with lance-shaped, tooth-margined leaflets 2.4–4 in. long. Flowers symmetric, with 5 free, white petals, in open, head-like clusters with 20–50 rays to 4 in. long. Fruits to 0.5 in. long, hairy, winged. *Angelica* refers to the medicinal properties of some of its members.

Angelica capitellata

ranger's button

APIACEAE CARROT FAMILY

PCT Sections: 3–5 & 10–19 **Abundance:** Locally common **Height:** 2–6 ft. **Flowering:** July–August **Flower Color:** White or purplish **Habitat-Community:** Wet places and slopes from lower montane to subalpine coniferous forests and wetland-riparian communities **Elevation:** Below 11,500 ft. **Ecoregions:** Southern California Mountains, Sierra Nevada, Cascades

Erect, branched perennial with enlarged leaf sheaths along the stems. Leaves 1–2-pinnately compound, generally hairy, with lance-shaped, lobe- to tooth-margined leaflets 1–5 in. long. Flowers symmetric, with many bractlets and 5 free, spoon-shaped, white or purplish petals, in open, head-like clusters with 4–18 rays to 4 in. long. Fruits to 0.3 in. long, hairy, winged. Caution: all plant parts are very poisonous! Aka swamp white heads.

Angelica lineariloba

Sierra angelica

APIACEAE CARROT FAMILY

PCT Sections: 9–11 **Abundance:** Locally common **Height:** 2–6 ft. **Flowering:** June–August **Flower Color:** White or pinkish **Habitat-Community:** Moist habitats and open, gravelly soils from sagebrush scrubs to subalpine coniferous forests **Elevation:** 5500–10,900 ft. **Ecoregions:** Sierra Nevada

Erect perennial with hairy or hairless stems. Leaves 2–3-pinnately compound, hairy or hairless, with linear, smooth-margined leaflets 0.8–4 in. long. Flowers symmetric, with 5 free, white or pinkish petals, in open, head-like clusters with 20–40 rays to 3 in. long. Fruits to 0.5 in. long, hairless in age, winged. Caution: the herbage and roots are toxic. Aka poison angelica.

Angelica tomentosa

woolly angelica

APIACEAE CARROT FAMILY

PCT Sections: 3–5 & 20–24 **Abundance:** Locally common **Height:** 2–7 ft. **Flowering:** June–August **Flower Color:** White **Habitat-Community:** Moist, generally shaded habitats, including serpentine, in chaparrals and lower montane coniferous forests **Elevation:** Below 7900 ft. **Ecoregions:** Southern California Mountains, Klamath Mountains

Erect perennial with hairy or hairless stems and foliage with blue- to white-waxy coating. Leaves 2–3-pinnately compound, hairy or hairless, with lance-shaped to ovoid, smooth- or tooth-margined leaflets 0.8–5 in. long. Flowers symmetric, with 5 free, white petals, in open, head-like clusters with 20–60 rays to 4 in. long. Fruits to 0.4 in. long, hairy or hairless, winged.

Bowlesia incana

hoary bowlesia

APIACEAE CARROT FAMILY

PCT Sections: 1–7 **Abundance:** Occasional **Height:** 5–25 in. **Flowering:** March–April **Flower Color:** White to pale green **Habitat-Community:** Slopes and flats, usually in shade of rocks or shrubs, in Sonoran mixed woody scrubs, foothill chaparrals, and Joshua tree woodlands **Elevation:** Below 4500 ft. **Ecoregions:** Southern California Mountains, Sonoran/Mojave Basin and Range, Sierra Nevada

Spreading, mostly unbranched, slight annual with thin, white-hairy stems. Leaves 0.3–1.2 in. wide, generally opposite, roundish or kidney-shaped, covered in star-shaped hairs, 5–9-lobed; petiole 1–5 in. long. Flowers clustered in small heads, 5-parted, with minute green sepals. Petals to 0.1 in. long, free, ovoid, white to pale green or yellow. Fruits tiny and inflated, with 1 seed. Best observed at lower elevations of the PCT in the Peninsular Ranges. The genus name honors Irish writer William Bowles (1720–1780).

Daucus pusillus

American wild carrot

APIACEAE CARROT FAMILY

PCT Sections: 1–2 & 5–6 **Abundance:** Locally common **Height:** 5–35 in. **Flowering:** April–June **Flower Color:** White **Habitat-Community:** Rocky to sandy soils in foothill chaparrals and oak woodlands **Elevation:** Below 5300 ft. **Ecoregions:** Southern California/Northern Baja Coast, Southern California Mountains

Decumbent or erect, 0–few-branched annual with fine, downward-arching hairs covering the stems. Leaves 1–4 in. long, alternate, feathery, pinnately dissected into bristly-hairy, linear segments; petiole 2–6 in. long. Flowers 5-parted, 30–60 per dense, hemispheric cluster surrounded by 5–8 leaf-like bracts. Petals to 0.1 in. long, free, white. Fruits 0.1–0.2 in. long, elliptic, armed with bristles and prickles, and with a distinctive carrot-like scent. The only *Daucus* sp. native to the US. It does produce edible carrots, but be careful: it can be mistaken for several of its poisonous relatives! The nonnative Queen Anne's lace (*D. carota*) is mostly absent from the CA PCT and tends to have some purple flowers.

Heracleum maximum

cow parsnip

APIACEAE CARROT FAMILY

PCT Sections: 4–5 & 9–24 **Abundance:** Common **Height:** 3–10 ft. **Flowering:** June–July **Flower Color:** White **Habitat-Community:** Moist, open or shaded areas, including streambanks, from woodlands and chaparrals to subalpine coniferous forests and wetland-riparian communities **Elevation:** Below 9600 ft. **Ecoregions:** Southern California Mountains, Sierra Nevada, Cascades, Klamath Mountains

Erect, stout perennial with hollow, hairy stems and aromatic foliage. Leaves 8–20 in. long, roundish, pinnately compound, hairy, with 3 round to ovoid, tooth-margined leaflets 0.8–5 in. long. Flowers symmetric, with 5 free, spoon-shaped, white petals, in open, hemispheric clusters with 15–30 rays to 4 in. long. Fruits to 0.5 in. long, hairy, thin-winged. A genus of large plants, appropriately named for Hercules.

Ligusticum grayi

Gray's lovage

APIACEAE CARROT FAMILY

PCT Sections: 10–24 **Abundance:** Common **Height:** 3–36 in. **Flowering:** June–September **Flower Color:** White **Habitat-Community:** Meadows, bogs, and openings from lower montane to subalpine coniferous forests and wetland-riparian communities **Elevation:** Below 10,900 ft. **Ecoregions:** Sierra Nevada, Cascades, Klamath Mountains

Erect perennial. Stems hairless, with 0–few leaves. Leaves 4–10 in. long, oval to triangular, 2-pinnately compound, hairless, with ovoid, tooth-margined leaflets 0.4–1.6 in. long. Flowers symmetric, with minute sepals and 5 free, white petals, in open, hemispheric clusters with 5–18 rays to 2 in. long. Fruits to 0.2 in. long and narrowly winged. Lovage ("love-parsley") is an old translation of the first *Ligusticum* sp.

Lomatium macrocarpum

bigseed biscuitroot

APIACEAE CARROT FAMILY

PCT Sections: 8 & 15–24 **Abundance:** Common **Height:** 4–20 in. **Flowering:** February–June **Flower Color:** White, yellowish, or purple **Habitat-Community:** Open, gravelly soils, including serpentine, from woodlands and chaparrals to subalpine coniferous forests **Elevation:** Below 9900 ft. **Ecoregions:** Sierra Nevada, Cascades, Klamath Mountains

Perennial with short stems and finely hairy herbage. Leaves 1–6 in. long, 3-pinnately lobed, with linear to spoon-shaped, smooth-margined lobes to 0.3 in. long. Flowers symmetric, with many bractlets and 5 free, white, yellowish, or purple petals, in open, hemispheric clusters with 5–25 rays to 3.3 in. long. Fruits to 0.8 in. long, generally hairy, with wings wider than body. *Lomatium* (from the Greek *loma*, "bordered") refers to the prominent, marginal fruit wings. The Apiaceae has many poisonous plants: do not eat any part of a lomatium.

Lomatium nevadense

Nevada lomatium

APIACEAE CARROT FAMILY

PCT Sections: 4–6 & 8–10 & 12 **Abundance:** Locally common **Height:** 4–18 in. **Flowering:** April–July **Flower Color:** White to cream **Habitat-Community:** Sandy soils in sagebrush scrubs, Joshua tree & pinyon-juniper woodlands, and montane coniferous forests **Elevation:** Below 9500 ft. **Ecoregions:** Southern California Mountains, Sierra Nevada

Gray-hairy perennial with leaves emerging from base. Leaves 1.5–4 in. long, generally 2-pinnately dissected into crowded, small, oblong-ovoid, pointed, densely short-hairy segments; petiole 1.5–2.5 in. long. Flowers to 0.1 in. across, 8–22 in hemispheric clusters, with 5 white to cream petals and elongated, purplish stamens. Fruits 0.3–0.5 in. long, flattened, disk-like, hairy or hairless, ovoid to round, with wings about equal to body in width. The most common variety along the PCT, var. *parishii*, has a hairless fruit. Caution: do not eat any part of a lomatium.

Oreonana clementis

pygmy mountainparsley

APIACEAE CARROT FAMILY

PCT Sections: 9–11 **Abundance:** Rare **Height:** 1–3 in. **Flowering:** July–August **Flower Color:** White **Habitat-Community:** Rocky places in subalpine coniferous forests and alpine communities **Elevation:** 4900–13,200 ft. **Ecoregions:** Sierra Nevada

Cushion-forming, stemless perennial with gray-hairy herbage. Leaves 0.6–1.4 in. long, ovoid, gray-hairy, pinnately lobed, with smooth-margined lobes to 0.1 in. long. Flowers symmetric, in spheric clusters with 5–15 rays to 0.3 in. long, with fused bractlets, 5 yellow sepals, 5 free white petals, and purple anthers. Fruits to 0.2 in. long, hairy or hairless, with equal, thread-like ribs.

Osmorhiza berteroi

mountain sweetcicely

APIACEAE CARROT FAMILY

PCT Sections: 1–5 & 13–24 **Abundance:** Common **Height:** 1–4 ft. **Flowering:** March–August **Flower Color:** White **Habitat-Community:** Shaded understories and disturbed places in montane coniferous forests **Elevation:** Below 9200 ft. **Ecoregions:** All (except Sonoran/Mojave Basin and Range)

Erect, 1–few-branched, leafy perennial with hairy herbage. Leaves 2–8 in. across, widely ovoid to spoon-shaped, hairy, 2-pinnately compound; leaflets 0.8–3.2 in. long, lance-shaped to round, with lobed or toothed margins. Flowers symmetric, with 5 free, white petals, in hemispheric clusters with 3–8 rays to 4.7 in. long. Fruits to 1 in. long, linear, hairy, and slender-beaked.

Perideridia bolanderi

Bolander's yampah

APIACEAE CARROT FAMILY

PCT Sections: 10–22 **Abundance:** Locally common **Height:** 0.5–3 ft. **Flowering:** June–August **Flower Color:** White **Habitat-Community:** Meadows and open slopes from scrubs and woodlands to subalpine coniferous forests and wetland-riparian communities **Elevation:** Below 9100 ft. **Ecoregions:** Sierra Nevada, Cascades, Klamath Mountains

Erect, branched perennial with few stem leaves. Leaves 4–8 in. long, ovoid, hairless, 2-pinnately lobed, with thread-like to narrowly elliptic, tooth-margined lobes 0.8–3.2 in. long. Flowers symmetric, in hemispheric clusters with 9–23 rays to 0.8 in. long, with 8–12 bracts, 4–10 membranous bractlets, 5 sepals, and 5 free, white petals. Fruits to 0.3 in. long, narrowly elliptic, hairless, with thread-like ribs. *Yampah* is the Shoshone word for *Perideridia* spp. Much larger terminal leaf lobe than other yampahs.

Perideridia parishii subsp. *latifolia*

wide-leaved Parish's yampah

APIACEAE CARROT FAMILY

PCT Sections: 1 & 3 & 5 & 10–23 **Abundance:** Common **Height:** 0.5–3 ft. **Flowering:** July–August **Flower Color:** White **Habitat-Community:** Meadows and open forests from lower montane to subalpine coniferous forests and wetland-riparian communities **Elevation:** 6500–11,200 ft. **Ecoregions:** All (except Sonoran/Mojave Basin and Range)

Erect perennial with few stem leaves and hairless, green herbage. Leaves 4–8 in. long, ovoid, hairless, pinnately compound, with 1–3 pairs of lance-shaped, smooth-margined leaflets 0.8–5 in. long. Flowers symmetric, with 6–8 bractlets, 5 sepals, and 5 free, white petals, in hemispheric clusters with 12–14 rays to 1.8 in. long. Fruits to 0.2 in. long, ovoid to roundish, hairless, with thread-like ribs.

Perideridia pringlei

adobe yampah

APIACEAE CARROT FAMILY

PCT Sections: 5–7 **Abundance:** Occasional **Height:** 14–32 in. **Flowering:** April–June **Flower Color:** White **Habitat-Community:** Sandy to clayey soils on grassy slopes in California prairies, sagebrush scrubs, and oak & pinyon-juniper woodlands **Elevation:** Below 5800 ft. **Ecoregions:** Southern California Mountains, Sierra Nevada

Erect, wand-like perennial with hairless herbage. Leaves 1–2 pinnate, with cylindric, linear leaflets 0.2–3.5 in. long. Flowers in whorls of head-like clusters, with 5 calyx lobes and 5 white petals 0.1 in. long. Fruits 0.2–0.4 in. long, linear to oblong, with thread-like ribs. The seeds can be used in seasoning, resembling caraway seeds in flavor. In grassy meadows, plants can mimic sedges, grasses, and rushes, remaining unnoticed until they flower.

Asclepias eriocarpa

woollypod milkweed

APOCYNACEAE DOGBANE FAMILY

PCT Sections: 1–9 **Abundance:** Occasional **Height:** 10–30 in. **Flowering:** May–October **Flower Color:** White to cream **Habitat-Community:** Open, dry areas in foothill chaparrals, sagebrush scrubs, and oak & pinyon-juniper woodlands **Elevation:** Below 6300 ft. **Ecoregions:** Southern California Mountains, Sierra Nevada

Erect perennial with densely white-hairy stems and milky sap. Leaves to 6 in. long, opposite or 3–4 per whorl, elliptic, lance-shaped, or ovoid, thickly white-hairy, with tapered bases and sometimes wavy margins. Flowers in head-like clusters at tips of branches, 5-parted, with small, obscured calyx lobes. Petals reflexed to ascending, white to cream tinged pink, with cream and purple-tinged hoods slightly exceeded by the anther head. Fruits 2–3 in. long, erect, woolly, pod-like follicles with seeds bearing a cluster of silky white hairs. Milkweeds are known for their medicinal qualities, but this species is poisonous! The specific epithet is from the Greek *erion* ("wool") and *carpos* ("fruit").

Asclepias vestita

woolly milkweed

APOCYNACEAE DOGBANE FAMILY

PCT Sections: 4–5 & 8 **Abundance:** Occasional **Height:** 12–30 in. **Flowering:** April–June **Flower Color:** Cream to violet **Habitat-Community:** Dry plains and hillsides in foothill chaparrals and Joshua tree & pinyon-juniper woodlands **Elevation:** Below 4400 ft. **Ecoregions:** Southern California Mountains, Sierra Nevada

Erect or sprawling, branched-from-base, robust perennial with densely hairy stems and milky sap. Leaves 2–3 in. long, opposite, densely hairy (less so with age), with rounded bases and tapered tips. Flowers in head-like clusters, 5-parted, with small, obscured calyx lobes. Petals reflexed, cream to purple-tinged, with yellow-white hoods at same level as anther head. Fruits 2–3 in. long, 1 in. wide, erect, yellowish, fuzzy pod-like follicles with large seeds (to 0.4 in. long) covered in silky white hairs. Look for it in the Cajon Pass region. The specific epithet (from the Latin *vestio*, "dressed") is often applied to plants clothed in woolly hair.

Funastrum cynanchoides var. *hartwegii*

climbing milkweed

APOCYNACEAE DOGBANE FAMILY

PCT Sections: 1–4 **Abundance:** Occasional **Height:** 1–6 ft. **Flowering:** April–July **Flower Color:** Cream or white to purple **Habitat-Community:** Dry, sandy flats and canyons in foothill chaparrals, creosote bush scrubs, and Sonoran mixed woody scrubs **Elevation:** Below 5000 ft. **Ecoregions:** Southern California Mountains

Vine-like climbing perennial, often twining through shrubs, with hairless or sparsely short-hairy stems and milky sap. Leaves 1.2–2.4 in. long, opposite, lance-shaped, with lobed arrowhead-shaped bases. Flowers in head-like clusters along vining stems, 5-parted, with small, obscured calyx lobes. Corollas 0.1–0.3 in. across, with spreading, purple-pink or white lobes. Fruits 2.5–4.5 in. long, narrowly lance-shaped, pod-like follicles with hair-tufted seeds. Limited along the PCT to the lower desert crossings, such as lower Snow Creek Canyon, at the northern base of the San Jacinto Mountains. *Funastrum* (from the Latin *funis*, "rope") alludes to the twining stems.

Eremogone congesta

ballhead sandwort

CARYOPHYLLACEAE PINK FAMILY

PCT Sections: 10–24 **Abundance:** Locally common **Height:** 3–16 in. **Flowering:** April–August **Flower Color:** White **Habitat-Community:** Rocky outcrops and open, gravelly or sandy soils, including serpentine, in montane coniferous forests **Elevation:** Below 10,900 ft. **Ecoregions:** Sierra Nevada, Cascades, Klamath Mountains

Tufted perennial with woody base and glandular-hairy stems. Leaves 0.4–3 in. long, opposite, needle-like, and sharp-pointed. Flowers in dense hemispheric clusters, symmetric, with 5 sepals to 0.3 in. long and 5 free, white petals to 0.3 in. long. Fruits to 0.3 in. long, capsules with 4–8 red-brown seeds.

Eremogone ferrisiae

Ferris' sandwort

CARYOPHYLLACEAE PINK FAMILY

PCT Sections: 3 & 8–10 **Abundance:** Locally common **Height:** 8–16 in. **Flowering:** April–August **Flower Color:** White **Habitat-Community:** Gravelly or sandy soils from woodlands to upper montane coniferous forests **Elevation:** Below 9600 ft. **Ecoregions:** Southern California Mountains, Sierra Nevada

Tufted perennial with slightly woody base and glandular-hairy to hairless stems. Leaves 0.8–2.4 in. long, opposite, needle-like, and sharp-pointed. Flowers in open terminal clusters, symmetric, with 5 sepals to 0.2 in. long and 5 free, white petals to 0.4 in. long. Fruits to 0.3 in. long, capsules with 4–5 red-brown to black seeds.

Eremogone kingii var. *glabrescens*

King's compact sandwort

CARYOPHYLLACEAE PINK FAMILY

PCT Sections: 10–18 **Abundance:** Locally common **Height:** 0.5–8 in. **Flowering:** June–September **Flower Color:** White **Habitat-Community:** Open, rocky places from upper montane coniferous forests to alpine communities **Elevation:** Below 9600 ft. **Ecoregions:** Sierra Nevada, Cascades

Tufted perennial with woody base and glandular-hairy to hairless stems. Leaves 0.1–0.8 in. long, opposite, needle-like, and sharp-pointed. Flowers 1–many in open terminal clusters, symmetric, with 5 sepals to 0.2 in. long and 5 free, white petals to 0.4 in. long. Fruits to 0.3 in. long, capsules with 2–5 red-brown to dark purple or black seeds. The name honors Sir George King (1840–1909), a British botanist who served as superintendent of the Royal Botanic Garden.

desert sandwort

Eremogone macradenia

CARYOPHYLLACEAE PINK FAMILY

PCT Sections: 3–9 **Abundance:** Locally common **Height:** 8–16 in. **Flowering:** April–July **Flower Color:** White **Habitat-Community:** Open woodlands and rocky places, including carbonates, in scrubs, woodlands, and lower montane coniferous forests **Elevation:** Below 7300 ft. **Ecoregions:** Southern California Mountains, Sonoran/Mojave Basin and Range, Sierra Nevada

Tufted perennial with woody base and glandular-hairy to hairless stems. Leaves 0.8–2.4 in. long, opposite, needle-like, thick, and blunt to sharp-pointed. Flowers many in open terminal clusters, symmetric, with 5 sepals to 0.3 in. long and 5 free, white petals to 0.4 in. long; flowering stems erect to ascending. Fruits to 0.3 in. long, capsules with 4–9 red-brown to black seeds.

Big Bear Valley sandwort

Eremogone ursina

CARYOPHYLLACEAE PINK FAMILY

PCT Sections: 4 **Abundance:** Rare **Height:** 4–7 in. **Flowering:** May–June **Flower Color:** White **Habitat-Community:** Open, rocky or pebbly soils in pinyon-juniper woodlands and montane coniferous forests **Elevation:** 6200–7400 ft. **Ecoregions:** Southern California Mountains

Decumbent, low-tufted (to 1 ft. across) perennial with shiny, sometimes glandular-hairy stems. Leaves 0.2–0.4 in. long, opposite, needle-like, waxy, and sharp-pointed. Flowers in open terminal clusters, 5-parted, with rounded sepals, oval white petals 0.1–0.2 in. long, and 10 stamens with protruding purple anthers. Fruits 0.1–0.3 in. long, toothed capsules with 1–2 seeds. Endemic to the quartzite pebble plain habitat in the Big Bear Valley region. Threats include recreational activities, development, mining, and disturbance associated with fire suppression efforts. *Ursina* (from the Latin, "little bear") refers to its Big Bear Valley home.

Nuttall's sandwort

Minuartia nuttallii

CARYOPHYLLACEAE PINK FAMILY

PCT Sections: 4–5 & 9–24 **Abundance:** Locally common **Height:** 1–8 in. **Flowering:** May–August **Flower Color:** White **Habitat-Community:** Open, rocky slopes and sandy flats from scrubs and woodlands to alpine communities **Elevation:** Below 12,500 ft. **Ecoregions:** Southern California Mountains, Sierra Nevada, Cascades, Klamath Mountains

Matted perennial with woody base and glandular-hairy to hairless stems. Leaves 0.8–2.4 in. long, opposite, thread-like to oblong, thick, and blunt to sharp-pointed. Flowers many in open terminal clusters, symmetric, with 5 sepals to 0.3 in. long, 1–3-veined, and 5 free white petals to 0.4 in. long. Fruits to 0.3 in. long, capsules with 4–9 red-brown to black seeds. The genus name honors Spanish botanist J. Minuartia (1693–1768).

Pseudostellaria jamesiana

sticky
starwort

CARYOPHYLLACEAE PINK FAMILY

PCT Sections: 4 & 13–24 **Abundance:** Locally common **Height:** 1–8 in. **Flowering:** June–August **Flower Color:** White **Habitat-Community:** Meadows and dry understories, including serpentine soils, from sagebrush scrubs to upper montane coniferous forests **Elevation:** Below 8900 ft. **Ecoregions:** Southern California Mountains, Sierra Nevada, Cascades, Klamath Mountains

Ascending to erect perennial with single or branched, 4-angled, glandular-hairy (upper) stems. Leaves 0.6–6 in. long, opposite, linear to lance-shaped or oval, thick, and blunt to sharp-pointed. Flowers few at stem and branch tips, symmetric, with 5 sepals to 0.3 in. long and 5 free, white petals to 0.4 in. long; petals lobed for half their length. Fruits spheric capsules with 1–2 red-brown to brown seeds.

Silene antirrhina

sleepy
catchfly

CARYOPHYLLACEAE PINK FAMILY

PCT Sections: 1–6 **Abundance:** Occasional **Height:** 5–32 in. **Flowering:** April–August **Flower Color:** White to red **Habitat-Community:** Open areas and burns in foothill chaparrals, oak woodlands, and lower montane coniferous forests **Elevation:** Below 6200 ft. **Ecoregions:** Southern California Mountains

Slender annual with glandular upper stems. Leaves 0.4–1.2 in. long, opposite, needle-like, lance-linear, reduced in size up the stem. Flowers erect at stem and branch tips, 5-parted, with inflated, hairless, 10-veined calyces 0.2–0.4 in. long. Petals extending 0.1 in. beyond calyx, double-lobed, white to red. Fruits ovoid capsules. Sticky glands on the stems trap and kill insects, but the plant is unable to ingest their nutrients as carnivorous plants do. Found along the PCT in areas influenced by maritime climates, so look for it on the coastal side of the Southern California Mountains at lower elevations, especially in recently burned chaparral.

Silene bernardina

Palmer's
catchfly

CARYOPHYLLACEAE PINK FAMILY

PCT Sections: 9–22 **Abundance:** Locally common **Height:** 6–24 in. **Flowering:** June–August **Flower Color:** White, pink, or purple **Habitat-Community:** Rocky places from sagebrush scrubs and oak woodlands to alpine communities **Elevation:** Below 11,900 ft. **Ecoregions:** Sierra Nevada, Cascades, Klamath Mountains

Erect, few-branched perennial with glandular (throughout or upper) hairy stems. Leaves 0.8–3.1 in. long, opposite, linear to narrowly spoon-shaped, with smooth margins. Flowers few at stem tips and at leaf nodes, symmetric, with 5-lobed calyces to 0.6 in. long and 5 free, generally 4-lobed, white, pink, or purple petals to 0.3 in. long, with 2 appendages. Fruits ovoid, hairy capsules with many brown seeds. Plants do indeed catch flies and crawling insects with their sticky glands, especially on the upper stems, thus saving the flower nectar for butterflies.

Silene lemmonii

Lemmon's catchfly

CARYOPHYLLACEAE PINK FAMILY

PCT Sections: 1–5 & 10–24 **Abundance:** Locally common **Height:** 6–18 in. **Flowering:** May–September **Flower Color:** White-yellow to pink **Habitat-Community:** Open places, including serpentine soils, from woodlands to upper montane coniferous forests **Elevation:** Below 9200 ft. **Ecoregions:** All (except Sonoran/Mojave Basin and Range)

Decumbent to erect, few-branched perennial with short-hairy and glandular (upper) stems. Leaves 0.2–1.4 in. long, opposite, smaller on upper stem, oval to narrowly spoon-shaped, with smooth margins. Flowers few at stem tips and at leaf nodes, nodding, symmetric, with 5-lobed calyces to 0.4 in. long and 5 free, 4-lobed, white-yellow to pink petals to 0.3 in. long, with 2 appendages. Fruits oblong to ovoid, hairy capsules with many brown seeds. Named for John Lemmon (1832–1908), a California pioneer who taught school in Sierra Valley.

Silene menziesii

Menzies' campion

CARYOPHYLLACEAE PINK FAMILY

PCT Sections: 4 & 10–19 **Abundance:** Locally common **Height:** 2–8 in. **Flowering:** June–July **Flower Color:** White **Habitat-Community:** Moist understories, streambanks, and meadows from lower montane to subalpine coniferous forests and wetland-riparian communities **Elevation:** Below 9600 ft. **Ecoregions:** Southern California Mountains, Sierra Nevada, Cascades

Matted to erect, many-stemmed perennial with short-hairy and glandular (upper) stems. Leaves 0.8–2.4 in. long, opposite, smaller on upper stem, oval to lance-shaped, with smooth margins. Flowers few at stem tips and at upper leaf nodes, ascending to erect, symmetric, with 5-lobed calyces to 0.3 in. long and 5 free, generally 2-lobed white petals to 0.1 in. long, with 2 appendages. Fruits ovoid capsules with many black seeds. *Campion* is an old term meaning "champion," a reference to the flower garlands worn by victors in battle.

Silene sargentii

Sargent's catchfly

CARYOPHYLLACEAE PINK FAMILY

PCT Sections: 10–16 **Abundance:** Locally common **Height:** 4–6 in. **Flowering:** June–September **Flower Color:** White to red-purple **Habitat-Community:** Talus slopes and crevices in rocky outcrops in subalpine coniferous forests and alpine communities **Elevation:** 7800–12,500 ft. **Ecoregions:** Sierra Nevada

Decumbent to erect, many-stemmed perennial with short-hairy and glandular (upper) stems. Leaves 0.6–1.2 in. long, opposite, smaller on upper stem, fleshy, narrowly spoon-shaped to linear, with smooth margins. Flowers few at stem tips and at upper leaf nodes, ascending to erect, symmetric, with 5-lobed calyces to 0.6 in. long and 5 free, 2–6-lobed, white to red-purple petals to 0.2 in. long, with 2 appendages. Fruits ovoid, hairy capsules with many brown seeds. Named for Charles Sargent (1841–1927), first director of the Arnold Arboretum.

Stellaria longipes

meadow starwort

CARYOPHYLLACEAE PINK FAMILY

PCT Sections: 4 & 9–19 **Abundance:** Locally common **Height:** 4–6 in. **Flowering:** April–August **Flower Color:** White **Habitat-Community:** Streambanks, seeps, and meadows in wetland-riparian communities **Elevation:** Below 11,500 ft. **Ecoregions:** Southern California Mountains, Sierra Nevada, Cascades

Ascending to erect perennial with scattered hairs or hairless stems. Leaves 0.4–1.6 in. long, opposite, evenly spaced, fleshy, linear, with smooth margins. Flowers 1–7 at stem tips and at upper leaf nodes, ascending to erect, symmetric, with 5 sepals to 0.2 in. long and 5 free, 2-lobed (to base) white petals to 0.3 in. long. Fruits ovoid capsules with many red-brown seeds. *Stellaria* ("star") refers to the flower shape.

Dudleya edulis

fingertips

CRASSULACEAE STONECROP FAMILY

PCT Sections: 1 **Abundance:** Occasional **Height:** 5–15 in. **Flowering:** May–July **Flower Color:** White to cream **Habitat-Community:** Rocky (granite or sandstone) slopes, canyon walls, ledges, outcrops, and roadside cuts in foothill chaparrals and oak woodlands **Elevation:** Below 3900 ft. **Ecoregions:** Southern California/Northern Baja Coast

Charismatic succulent perennial, typically with 1–16 rosettes, 2–6 in. across, with hairless stems lightly covered in translucent white wax. Leaves 3–8 in. long, basal, evergreen, linear, cylindric (finger-like), erect, pale green, fleshy, with pointed tips (like long fingernails). Flowers 3–11 at branch tips in open displays, 5-parted, with white to cream, fused-at-base petals 0.3–0.4 in. long with pointed lobes. Fruits small follicles. The tips of the leaves often turn orange or red during the summer. Aka string bean plant. The specific epithet refers to the edibility of the leaves and stems, which are considered a delicacy (albeit with a chalky aftertaste). But given that all wild *Dudleya* spp. are threatened by poaching (and most are protected by law), we highly recommend not eating them.

Marah macrocarpa

chilicothe

CUCURBITACEAE GOURD FAMILY

PCT Sections: 1–6 **Abundance:** Locally common **Height:** 1–15 ft. (vine) **Flowering:** January–April **Flower Color:** White **Habitat-Community:** Washes and slopes in Sonoran mixed woody scrubs, foothill chaparrals, and oak woodlands **Elevation:** Below 3500 ft. **Ecoregions:** Southern California/ Northern Baja Coast, Sonoran Basin and Range, Southern California Mountains

Sprawling vine from a large tuberous root, twining through woody shrubs or small trees, with short-hairy herbage; monoecious. Leaves 2–5 in. across, alternate, palmately 5–7-lobed (like a maple leaf), and short-hairy. Flowers, staminate in spikes and pistillate 1 per node, 5-parted, with fused sepals. Petals 0.3–0.6 in. across, fused at base, somewhat cup-shaped, and white. Fruits 6–8 in. long, 2–3 in. wide, capsules covered in prickles (without hooks), bright green, ripening yellow. The tubers of this plant (aka manroot) can weigh up to 220 pounds! All plant parts have an unpleasant taste (*Marah* in Hebrew means "bitter").

Drosera rotundifolia

roundleaf sundew

DROSERACEAE SUNDEW FAMILY

PCT Sections: 10–21 **Abundance:** Rare **Height:** 2–14 in. **Flowering:** June–September **Flower Color:** White or pink **Habitat-Community:** Swamps, seeps, fens, bogs, and meadows in wetland-riparian communities **Elevation:** Below 8900 ft. **Ecoregions:** Sierra Nevada, Cascades, Klamath Mountains

Erect carnivorous perennial. Leaves 0.1–0.5 in. long, rosetted, roundish, covered with red, sticky, gland-tipped hairs that trap insects. Flowers symmetric, scattered along stem tips. Calyces to 0.3 in. long, 5-lobed, fused near base. Petals to 0.3 in. long, 5, generally free, white or pink. Fruits many-seeded capsules. Often found with sphagnum moss, which is pretty cool stuff when it comes to water absorption. The insects trapped and absorbed as food, such as mosquitoes, midges, and gnats, are the same critters that pollinate the flowers. The fresh leaves have been used to remove corns, warts, and bunions, so walk barefoot through a patch only if you are attempting to remove the ailments just listed!

Geranium richardsonii

Richardson's geranium

GERANIACEAE GERANIUM FAMILY

PCT Sections: 3–5 & 10–15 **Abundance:** Occasional **Height:** 6–30 in. **Flowering:** May–September **Flower Color:** White **Habitat-Community:** Moist soils, meadows, streambanks in wetland-riparian communities and montane & subalpine coniferous forests **Elevation:** Below 8600 ft. **Ecoregions:** Southern California Mountains, Sierra Nevada

Spreading to erect, few-branched perennial with soft-hairy stems. Leaves 2–5 in. across, alternate or opposite, 5–7-palmately lobed or divided, with diamond-shaped lobes. Flowers 1–2 at branch and stem tips, pedicels 0.7–1.4 in. long, 5-parted, with 10 stamens, sepals 0.3 in. long with pointed tips, and rounded, white (purple-veined) petals 0.7–0.8 in. long. Fruits 1-seeded, 0.1–0.2 in. wide with a long beak. The genus name (from the Greek *geranos*, "crane") refers to fruit's resemblance to a crane's bill. There are 422 species of geranium in the temperate regions of the world!

Limnanthes alba

white meadowfoam

LIMNANTHACEAE
MEADOWFOAM FAMILY

PCT Sections: 1 & 18–19 **Abundance:** Rare **Height:** 3–16 in. **Flowering:** April–June **Flower Color:** White to cream **Habitat-Community:** Moist soils, meadows, streambanks, and shaded understories in wetland-riparian communities, oak woodlands, and lower montane coniferous forests **Elevation:** Below 6500 ft. **Ecoregions:** Southern California Mountains, Cascades

Decumbent or erect annual with hairless herbage. Leaves 1–4 in. long, alternate, pinnate, with 5–11 linear to ovoid leaflets. Flowers solitary, 5-parted, in leaf axils, with 8 or 10 stamens. Corollas bell-shaped; petals 0.3–0.6 in. long, free, rounded, white (aging pink), sometimes cream-yellow at base, purple-veined. Fruits small, 1-seeded nutlets. Two of the 3 subspecies in California occur along the PCT: subsp. *parishii* is found in the Laguna Mountains of San Diego County; subsp. *versicolor* occurs near Burney, in Shasta County. *Limnanthes* (from the Greek, "marsh flower") refers to the habitat of the species.

Mentzelia involucrata

whitebract blazingstar

LOASACEAE LOASA FAMILY

PCT Sections: 1–4 **Abundance:** Occasional **Height:** 4–15 in. **Flowering:** January–May **Flower Color:** White to yellow **Habitat-Community:** Sandy to rocky soils in washes, canyons, and steep slopes in creosote bush & Sonoran mixed woody scrubs **Elevation:** Below 3200 ft. **Ecoregions:** Sonoran Basin and Range

Sprawling to erect, intricately branched, large-flowered annual with glossy, white to tan, sometimes hairy stems. Leaves 1–7 in. long, generally alternate, lance-shaped to ovoid, sometimes fleshy, with irregularly toothed margins. Flowers solitary on stems, 5-parted, with ovoid, translucent white bracts, 4–5 per flower, with 6–20-toothed green margins. Sepals 0.3–1 in. long and petals 0.8–2.5 in. long, shiny white to creamy yellow, orange-veined. Fruits 0.7–1 in. long, erect, broadly cylindric capsules with ridged, gray-white seeds. Found along the PCT only at the lower desert crossings at the base of the Peninsular Ranges.

Claytonia lanceolata

western springbeauty

MONTIACEAE

MINER'S LETTUCE FAMILY

PCT Sections: 4–5 & 12–24 **Abundance:** Locally common **Height:** 2–6 in. **Flowering:** May–July **Flower Color:** White or pink **Habitat-Community:** Gravelly soils, including serpentine, and meadows in upper montane & subalpine coniferous forests **Elevation:** Below 8600 ft. **Ecoregions:** Southern California Mountains, Sierra Nevada, Cascades, Klamath Mountains

Erect perennial with 1 short flowering stem and 0 or shriveled basal leaves. Leaves 0.4–2.8 in. long, mostly opposite, clasping, linear to wedge-shaped, and sharp-tipped. Flowers 3–15 in open clusters. Sepals to 0.3 in. long and 2. Petals 0.2–0.5 in. long, 5, white or pink, and free. Fruits to 0.2 in. long, capsules with 3–6 black seeds. Plants flower just as the snow is melting (hence their common name). The tuber-like roots taste much like a potato when cooked.

Claytonia parviflora

narrowleaf miner's lettuce

MONTIACEAE

MINER'S LETTUCE FAMILY

PCT Sections: All **Abundance:** Common **Height:** 3–15 in. **Flowering:** March–July **Flower Color:** White to pale pink **Habitat-Community:** Vernally moist or shaded soils in creosote bush scrubs, woodlands, chaparrals, and lower montane coniferous forests **Elevation:** Below 7400 ft. **Ecoregions:** All

Ubiquitous annual of moist, shaded sites with dense, succulent, hairless herbage. Basal leaves 1–7 in. long, linear to narrowly spoon-shaped; stem leaves fused into a disk 2 in. across, or free and diamond-shaped. Flowers 3–40 at stem and branch tips, with a single bract below flowers, 2 fleshy sepals, and generally 5, free, white to pink petals 0.1–0.3 in. long. Fruits to 0.2 in. long, 3-valved capsules. Forms a dense groundcover under shrubs and trees during years of abundant precipitation. As the common name implies, the green foliage does well in salads.

Parnassia palustris

California grass-of-Parnassus

PARNASSIACEAE

GRASS-OF-PARNASSUS FAMILY

PCT Sections: 4 & 10–24 **Abundance:** Locally common **Height:** 2–6 in. **Flowering:** July–October **Flower Color:** White **Habitat-Community:** Wet banks and meadows in wetland-riparian communities **Elevation:** Below 11,900 ft. **Ecoregions:** Southern California Mountains, Sierra Nevada, Cascades, Klamath Mountains

Erect, 1–many-stemmed perennial with hairless stems. Leaves 0.8–2 in. long, basal, ovoid, with tapered to heart-shaped base. Flowers 1 per stem. Calyx lobes to 0.4 in. long, 5, oblong. Petals 0.3–0.8 in. long, 5, white with yellow, green, or brownish veins, free, with smooth tips. Fruits to 0.5 in. long, capsules with many winged seeds. Mistakenly taken for a grass when Dioscorides described it from the slopes of Mt. Parnassus, Greece.

Aquilegia pubescens

Sierra columbine

RANUNCULACEAE

BUTTERCUP FAMILY

PCT Sections: 10–12 **Abundance:** Occasional **Height:** 6–20 in. **Flowering:** July–August **Flower Color:** White to yellow or pink **Habitat-Community:** Rocky soils in subalpine coniferous forests and alpine communities **Elevation:** 8500–12,000 ft. **Ecoregions:** Sierra Nevada

Tufted perennial with mostly glandular-hairy stems. Leaves alternate, 3-lobed or 1–2-pinnately compound with lobed leaflets to 1 in. long. Flowers 1–few along stem, spreading to erect, with 5 pistils and many stamens. Sepals to 1 in. long, 5, petal-like, white to yellow or pink. Petals 5, white to yellow, 0.3–0.8 in. long; spurs to 2 in. long, white to yellow or pink. Fruits, body to 1 in. long, beak to 0.5 in. long. *Aquilegia* refers to columbine's claw-like spurs. Pollinated by hawkmoths. Hybridizes with *A. formosa*.

Thalictrum sparsiflorum

fewflower meadow rue

RANUNCULACEAE

BUTTERCUP FAMILY

PCT Sections: 4 & 9–18 **Abundance:** Occasional **Height:** 2–6 ft. **Flowering:** July–August **Flower Color:** Green-white to purplish **Habitat-Community:** Moist understories and streambanks from lower montane to subalpine coniferous forests and wetland-riparian communities **Elevation:** Below 11,500 ft. **Ecoregions:** Southern California Mountains, Sierra Nevada, Cascades

Erect, slender perennial with stem and basal leaves. Leaves alternate, 2–4-pinnately compound with ultimate segments to 0.8 in. long, finely glandular-puberulent. Flowers in loose clusters at stem tips, petal-less, with 6–22 pistils and 10–20 stamens. Sepals to 0.2 in. long, generally 5, petal-like, green-white to purplish. Fruits to 0.3 in. long and strongly flattened. A tea made of the roots of meadow rues is used to treat colds.

Drymocallis glandulosa

sticky cinquefoil

ROSACEAE ROSE FAMILY

PCT Sections: 1–5 & 8–24 **Abundance:** Common **Height:** 6–32 in. **Flowering:** May–August **Flower Color:** White to yellow **Habitat-Community:** Shaded understories and moist places in wetland-riparian communities from lower montane coniferous forests to alpine communities **Elevation:** Below 12,400 ft. **Ecoregions:** All (except Sonoran/Mojave Basin and Range)

Erect, tufted perennial with glandular-hairy stems and foliage. Leaves alternate and pinnately compound with 5–9 widely oval, glandular-hairy leaflets to 2.2 in. long and toothed margins. Flowers in loose clusters at stem tips, with many pistils and generally 20–25 stamens. Sepals to 0.3 in. long, 5, spreading to recurved. Petals to 0.2 in. long, 5, roundish to oblong or spoon-shaped, white to yellow. Fruits tiny, red to brown, seed-like achenes.

Drymocallis lactea

Sierran woodbeauty

ROSACEAE ROSE FAMILY

PCT Sections: 3–5 & 9–24 **Abundance:** Common **Height:** 4–24 in. **Flowering:** May–September **Flower Color:** White or yellow **Habitat-Community:** Rocky, generally moist places in montane coniferous forests **Elevation:** Below 12,200 ft. **Ecoregions:** Southern California Mountains, Sierra Nevada, Cascades, Klamath Mountains

Erect, tufted perennial with generally glandular-hairy herbage and stems >10 in. tall. Leaves alternate and pinnately compound with 7–9 oval to spoon-shaped leaflets to 1.6 in. long with single-toothed margins. Flowers in narrow clusters along stem, with many pistils and generally 20–25 stamens. Sepals to 0.3 in. long, 5, narrow-tipped, generally < petals. Petals to 0.3 in. long, 5, oval, white or yellow. Fruits tiny, brown, seed-like achenes.

Fragaria vesca

woodland strawberry

ROSACEAE ROSE FAMILY

PCT Sections: 1–4 & 19–24 **Abundance:** Locally common **Height:** 1–6 in. **Flowering:** January–July **Flower Color:** White **Habitat-Community:** Partially shaded, moist understories in chaparral and lower montane coniferous forests **Elevation:** Below 6600 ft. **Ecoregions:** Southern California/Northern Baja Coast, Southern California Mountains, Cascades, Klamath Mountains

Erect, tufted perennial with generally glandular-hairy herbage. Leaves alternate, pinnately compound with 3 hairy, oblong to widely spoon-shaped leaflets to 2 in. long with single-toothed margins. Flowers 1–several per stem in open clusters above leaves, with many pistils and 20 stamens. Sepals to 0.3 in. long, 5, and generally < petals. Petals to 0.3 in. long, 5, widely spoon-shaped, white. Fruits to 0.6 in. across, strawberries. If you are lucky enough to find wild strawberries to eat, you will be amazed by how intense their flavor is, compared to cultivated varieties. The leaves make a good-tasting tea that is high in vitamin C.

Fragaria virginiana

mountain strawberry

ROSACEAE ROSE FAMILY

PCT Sections: 10–24 **Abundance:** Common **Height:** 1–5 in. **Flowering:** May–August **Flower Color:** White **Habitat-Community:** Meadows and openings from lower montane to subalpine coniferous forests **Elevation:** Below 10,900 ft. **Ecoregions:** Sierra Nevada, Cascades, Klamath Mountains

Matted perennial with thin leaves; generally dioecious. Leaves alternate, pinnately compound with 3 widely spoon-shaped leaflets, hairy below, blue-green and generally hairless above, to 3.1 in. long, with single-toothed margins. Flowers often 1 per stem in open clusters among leaves, with many pistils and 20 stamens. Sepals to 0.3 in. long, 5. Petals to 0.4 in. long, 5, roundish, white. Fruits to 0.6 in. across, strawberries. Its leaves, flowers, and fruits are edible.

Horkelia clevelandii

Cleveland's horkelia

ROSACEAE ROSE FAMILY

PCT Sections: 1–3 **Abundance:** Rare **Height:** 4–20 in. **Flowering:** May–August **Flower Color:** White **Habitat-Community:** Shaded or moist sites, meadows, streambanks, and understories in oak woodlands, montane coniferous forests, and wetland-riparian communities **Elevation:** Below 7800 ft. **Ecoregions:** Southern California Mountains

Spreading, tufted perennial with green, resinous-glandular, hairy stems. Leaves 2–6 in. long, mostly basal, densely hairy, fern-like, pinnate, with 6–12 wedge-shaped or oval leaflets (0.2–0.5 in. long) per side. Stem leaves alternate and reduced. Flowers 5–30 in an open cluster at stem tips, 5-parted, sepals slightly < petals, with 10 stamens and 10–50 pistils. Petals 0.2–0.3 in. long, widely spoon-shaped, white. Fruits tiny, seed-like achenes. Populations in San Diego County serve as the sole larval host plant for the endangered Laguna Mountains Skipper (*Pyrgus ruralis lagunae*). The specific epithet honors San Diego–based plant collector and lawyer Daniel Cleveland (1838–1929).

Horkelia fusca

smallflower horkelia

ROSACEAE ROSE FAMILY

PCT Sections: 9–24 **Abundance:** Locally common **Height:** 4–24 in. **Flowering:** May–September **Flower Color:** White or pink **Habitat-Community:** Meadows, openings, and rocky soils from lower montane to subalpine coniferous forests **Elevation:** Below 10,900 ft. **Ecoregions:** Sierra Nevada, Cascades, Klamath Mountains

Tufted or matted perennial with green to grayish herbage. Leaves fern-like, alternate, pinnately compound, with 9–19 hairy, wedge-shaped to round leaflets to 0.8 in. long and deep- to shallow-toothed margins, becoming fewer and smaller on the upper stems. Flowers 5–30 per cluster at stem tips, with 10–20 pistils and 10 stamens. Sepals to 0.1 in. long, 5, green to purple. Petals to 0.2 in. long, 5, wedge-shaped, white or pink. Fruits to 0.1 in. long, seed-like achenes. Johann Horkel (1769–1846) was a German plant physiologist.

Horkelia rydbergii
Rydberg's horkelia
ROSACEAE ROSE FAMILY

PCT Sections: 4–5 **Abundance:** Occasional **Height:** 4–25 in. **Flowering:** June–August **Flower Color:** White **Habitat-Community:** Shaded or moist sites, meadows, streambanks, and understories in oak woodlands, montane coniferous forests, and wetland-riparian communities **Elevation:** Below 8400 ft. **Ecoregions:** Southern California Mountains

Matted perennial with gray-green stems covered in ascending to appressed hairs. Leaves 2–8 in. long, fern-like, gray-green, mostly basal, pinnate, with 7–14 wedge-shaped or oval, densely hairy leaflets (0.2–0.6 in. long) per side. Stem leaves alternate and reduced. Flowers 8–40 in an open cluster at stem tips, 5-parted, sepals slightly < petals, with 10 stamens and 10–50 pistils. Petals 0.2 in. long, oblong to spoon-shaped, white. Fruits tiny, seed-like achenes. Look for it along the PCT at small stream crossings in the San Bernardino Mountains. The specific epithet honors Per Axel Rydberg (1860–1931), first curator of the New York Botanical Garden Herbarium.

Horkeliella purpurascens
purple false horkelia
ROSACEAE ROSE FAMILY

PCT Sections: 8–10 **Abundance:** Occasional **Height:** 6–24 in. **Flowering:** June–August **Flower Color:** White **Habitat-Community:** Meadow edges and streambanks, generally in partial shade, in montane coniferous forests and wetland-riparian communities **Elevation:** Below 9600 ft. **Ecoregions:** Sierra Nevada

Erect, tufted perennial with gray-hairy stems. Leaves basal (mostly) and alternate, fern-like, pinnately compound, with 30–60 leaflets divided into 2–8 spoon-shaped, hairy, round-tipped segments. Flowers few, scattered mostly at stem tips, with 25–50 pistils and 20 stamens. Sepals to 0.3 in. long, 5, lance-shaped, purplish. Petals to 0.3 in. long, 5, narrowly spoon-shaped, white, sometimes with purplish to reddish tinge. Fruits to 0.1 in. long, dark brown, gray-spotted achenes. *Horkeliella* is Latin for "small *Horkelia*."

Ivesia argyrocoma var. argyrocoma
silver-haired ivesia
ROSACEAE ROSE FAMILY

PCT Sections: 4 **Abundance:** Rare **Height:** 4–8 in. **Flowering:** April–July **Flower Color:** White **Habitat-Community:** Open, gravelly soils, pebble plains, and dry meadows in sagebrush scrubs, pinyon-juniper woodlands, and montane coniferous forests **Elevation:** Below 7200 ft. **Ecoregions:** Southern California Mountains

Small, clumped perennial with horizontal (often directly on ground), red-green, fuzzy-hairy stems. Leaves cylindric strips of overlapping leaflets, densely silver-hairy, pinnate, with 51–71 elliptic leaflets 0.1 in. long. Flowers 0.3–0.4 in. across, 5–15 per cluster, 5-parted, sepals slightly < petals, with 20 stamens and 1–8 pistils. Petals 0.1–0.2 in. long, white. Fruits to 0.1 in. long, smooth, brown achenes. Endemic to the pebble plains surrounding the Big Bear Valley region of the San Bernardino Mountains. Threatened by development, grazing, mining, and recreational activities. *Argyrocoma* means "silver-haired" in Latin.

Ivesia santolinoides
Sierra mousetail
ROSACEAE ROSE FAMILY

PCT Sections: 3–5 & 8–14 **Abundance:** Locally common **Height:** 6–16 in. **Flowering:** June–September **Flower Color:** White **Habitat-Community:** Gravelly slopes, ridges, and open flats from lower montane coniferous forests to alpine communities **Elevation:** Below 11,900 ft. **Ecoregions:** Southern California Mountains, Sierra Nevada

Erect, tufted perennial with silvery herbage. Leaves to 4 in. long, basal (mostly) and alternate, mousetail-like, pinnately compound, with 121–161 tiny overlapping leaflets, each with minutely 1–5-lobed margins. Flowers 30–200 in open clusters along stems, with 1 pistil and 15 stamens. Sepals to 0.1 in. long, 5. Petals to 0.1 in. long, 5, narrowly oval to roundish, white. Fruits to 0.1 in. long, mottled gray-brown, seed-like achenes. The genus name honors Eli Ives (1779–1861), a well-respected Yale professor and physician.

Heuchera caespitosa
urn-flowered alumroot
SAXIFRAGACEAE SAXIFRAGE FAMILY

PCT Sections: 4–6 **Abundance:** Rare **Height:** 4–15 in. **Flowering:** May–July **Flower Color:** White to pink-red **Habitat-Community:** Open, rocky substrates in montane coniferous forests **Elevation:** Below 7200 ft. **Ecoregions:** Southern California Mountains

Rock crevice–loving perennial with glandular-hairy stems. Leaves 0.4–1.6 in. across, mostly basal, round, shallowly 5-lobed, glandular-hairy; petiole 0.4–2.5 in. long. Flowers scattered along stems, 5-lobed, appearing symmetric but actually slightly bilateral, pink-red hypanthium + calyx 0.1–0.3 in., with 5 stamens and 1 pistil. Petals 0.1–0.3 in. long, slightly > calyx lobes, spoon-shaped, white. Fruits small, minutely spiny, red-brown capsules.

Heuchera micrantha
crevice alumroot
SAXIFRAGACEAE SAXIFRAGE FAMILY

PCT Sections: 8 & 14–17 & 19–24 **Abundance:** Locally common **Height:** 4–40 in. **Flowering:** April–July **Flower Color:** White petals **Habitat-Community:** Moist banks, rock outcrops, and cliffs in montane coniferous forests **Elevation:** Below 8200 ft. **Ecoregions:** Sierra Nevada, Klamath Mountains

Tufted perennial with generally leafless flowering stems. Basal leaves to 4.7 in. long, ovoid to oblong, shallowly 5-7-lobed, generally hairy, with lobed to toothed margins. Flowers cup-shaped, in small, scattered clusters at stem tips, with 1 pistil (2 styles) and 5 stamens. Calyx lobes to 0.1 in. long, 5, erect, green to red. Petals to 0.1 in. long, 5, spoon-shaped, white. Fruits to 0.2 in. long, capsules with tiny, spiny, red-brown seeds. Used by Indigenous peoples to relieve soreness and inflammation on cuts.

Heuchera parishii

Mill Creek alumroot

SAXIFRAGACEAE SAXIFRAGE FAMILY

PCT Sections: 4 **Abundance:** Rare **Height:** 2–11 in. **Flowering:** June–July **Flower Color:** White to pink-red **Habitat-Community:** Rocky slopes, boulder fields, and talus from lower montane coniferous forests to alpine communities **Elevation:** 5500–11,800 ft. **Ecoregions:** Southern California Mountains

Crevice-inhabiting perennial with sticky, glandular-hairy herbage. Leaves 0.2–1.6 in. across, mostly basal, kidney-shaped to broadly ovoid, shallowly 5-lobed, glandular-hairy; petiole 0.4–3.5 in. long. Flowers many in narrow spikes, 5-lobed, appearing symmetric but actually bilateral, hypanthium inflated on one side, with 5 stamens, 1 pistil, and pink calyces with green tips. Petals 0.1 in. long, unequal, white. Fruits small, minutely spiny, red-brown capsules. Endemic to the San Bernardino Mountains. Threatened by recreational activities and mining. The common name refers to the Mill Creek watershed, from which this species hails.

Heuchera rubescens

pink alumroot

SAXIFRAGACEAE SAXIFRAGE FAMILY

PCT Sections: 1–5 & 8–17 **Abundance:** Locally common **Height:** 3–22 in. **Flowering:** May–September **Flower Color:** White **Habitat-Community:** Rock outcrops and cliffs from pinyon-juniper woodlands to alpine communities **Elevation:** Below 13,200 ft. **Ecoregions:** Southern California/Northern Baja Coast, Southern California Mountains, Sierra Nevada

Tufted perennial with generally leafless flowering stems. Basal leaves to 2.4 in. long, ovoid to roundish, deeply 5–9-lobed, generally hairy, with lobed to toothed margins. Flowers cup-shaped, more or less symmetrical to irregular, in scattered, generally 1-sided clusters at stem tips, with 1 pistil (2 styles) and 5 stamens. Calyx lobes to 0.1 in. long, 5, erect, white to reddish. Petals to 0.3 in. long, 5, thread-like to narrowly spoon-shaped, white. Fruits to 0.2 in. long, capsules with tiny, spiny, red-brown seeds. The common name refers to the alum-like taste of the roots.

Lithophragma tenellum

slender woodland star

SAXIFRAGACEAE SAXIFRAGE FAMILY

PCT Sections: 4–5 & 16–18 **Abundance:** Occasional **Height:** 3–12 in. **Flowering:** April–July **Flower Color:** White to pale pink **Habitat-Community:** Shaded slopes from chaparrals to upper montane coniferous forests **Elevation:** Below 9500 ft. **Ecoregions:** Southern California Mountains, Sierra Nevada

Perennial with unbranched, sparsely hairy stems. Leaves mostly basal (in rosettes) and alternate, 3-lobed or divided, lobes with smaller lobes, and highly reduced stem leaves. Flowers 3–12 clustered at stem tip, hemispheric hypanthium, with 5 calyx lobes, 10 stamens, and 1 pistil. Petals 0.3–0.4 in. long, 5, white to pale pink, shallowly 5–7-lobed. Fruits tiny, smooth capsules. Widespread, ranging from California to Canada, to the Rocky Mountain states, and variable. Plants in the northern Sierra are just as likely to be pink as white. *Tenellum* is Latin for "quite delicate, dainty."

Micranthes aprica

Sierra saxifrage

SAXIFRAGACEAE SAXIFRAGE FAMILY

PCT Sections: 10–24 **Abundance:** Locally common **Height:** 2–6 in. **Flowering:** May–August **Flower Color:** White **Habitat-Community:** Moist, rocky openings and seasonally wet flats from upper montane coniferous forests to alpine communities **Elevation:** Below 11,900 ft. **Ecoregions:** Sierra Nevada, Cascades, Klamath Mountains

Single-stemmed perennial with leafless flowering stems and basal tufts of leaves. Leaves to 1.8 in. long, oval to oblong, hairless, smooth or with minutely toothed margin toward tip. Flowers generally in 1 head-like cluster at stem tip, with 2 pistils and 10 stamens. Calyx lobes to 0.1 in. long, 5, spreading to erect, ovoid. Petals to 0.1 in. long, 5, ovoid, white. Fruits to 0.2 in. long with 2 capsule-like structures containing many tiny seeds. *Micranthes* means "small flower."

Micranthes bryophora

bud saxifrage

SAXIFRAGACEAE SAXIFRAGE FAMILY

PCT Sections: 10–24 **Abundance:** Locally common **Height:** 1–10 in. **Flowering:** June–August **Flower Color:** White **Habitat-Community:** Sandy meadows, rocky ledges, moist gravelly soils from upper montane coniferous forests to alpine communities **Elevation:** Below 11,900 ft. **Ecoregions:** Sierra Nevada, Cascades, Klamath Mountains

Single-stemmed perennial with leafless, glandular-hairy flowering stems and basal tufts of leaves. Leaves to 1.6 in. long, fleshy, linear-oblong, smooth or with minute-toothed margin toward tip. Flowers scattered along stem, slightly irregular, with 2 pistils and 10 stamens; lower flowers replaced by bulblets. Calyx lobes to 0.1 in. long, 5, recurved, oblong. Petals to 0.2 in. long, 5, lance- to arrow-shaped, white, with 2 yellow to green spots at base. Fruits to 0.2 in. long, capsules with many tiny seeds.

Micranthes nidifica

peak saxifrage

SAXIFRAGACEAE SAXIFRAGE FAMILY

PCT Sections: 10–24 **Abundance:** Locally common **Height:** 4–20 in. **Flowering:** May–August **Flower Color:** White **Habitat-Community:** Wet meadows and moist slopes from lower montane to subalpine coniferous forests and wetland-riparian communities **Elevation:** Below 11,500 ft. **Ecoregions:** Sierra Nevada, Cascades, Klamath Mountains

Single-stemmed, few-branched perennial with leafless, glandular-hairy flowering stems and basal tufts of leaves. Leaves to 4 in. long, ovoid, with smooth or minutely toothed margins. Flowers in well-spaced, head-like (mostly so) clusters at stem tips, with 2 pistils and 10 stamens. Calyx lobes to 0.1 in. long, 5, ovoid to oblong, recurved. Petals to 0.1 in. long, 5, widely oblong to round, white. Fruits to 0.1 in. long, capsule-like follicles with many tiny seeds. *Nidifica* means "nest" in Latin, referring to the nest-like flower clusters.

Micranthes odontoloma

brook saxifrage

SAXIFRAGACEAE SAXIFRAGE FAMILY

PCT Sections: 10–24 **Abundance:** Occasional **Height:** 7–20 in. **Flowering:** July–August **Flower Color:** White **Habitat-Community:** Wet meadows and streambanks in wetland-riparian communities **Elevation:** Below 11,200 ft. **Ecoregions:** Sierra Nevada, Cascades, Klamath Mountains

Erect perennial with leafless, glandular-hairy flowering stems and basal tufts of leaves. Leaves to 2.8 in. wide, round, with sharply toothed, scalloped margins. Flowers openly scattered along stem, with 2 pistils and 10 stamens. Calyx lobes to 0.1 in. long, 5, ovoid to oblong, generally purplish, recurved. Petals to 0.2 in. long, 5, round to oblong, white, with 2 yellow to green spots at base. Fruits to 0.3 in. long, capsules with many tiny seeds.

Micranthes oregana

bog saxifrage

SAXIFRAGACEAE SAXIFRAGE FAMILY

PCT Sections: 9–24 **Abundance:** Locally common **Height:** 9–50 in. **Flowering:** June–August **Flower Color:** White **Habitat-Community:** Bogs, seeps, marshes, and lakeshores in wetland-riparian communities **Elevation:** Below 8200 ft. **Ecoregions:** Sierra Nevada, Cascades, Klamath Mountains

Erect, single-stemmed perennial with leafless, glandular-hairy flowering stems and basal tufts of leaves. Leaves to 10 in. long, linear to widely ovoid, with generally glandular-toothed margins. Flowers in open to congested clusters at stem tips, with 2 pistils and 10 stamens. Calyx lobes to 0.1 in. long, 5, ovoid, recurved. Petals to 0.2 in. long, 5, linear to oblong, white. Fruits to 0.2 in. long, capsule-like follicles, often purplish, with many tiny seeds.

Micranthes tolmiei

Tolmie's saxifrage

SAXIFRAGACEAE SAXIFRAGE FAMILY

PCT Sections: 10–18 **Abundance:** Occasional **Height:** to 5 in. **Flowering:** July–September **Flower Color:** White **Habitat-Community:** Moist, rock outcrops and rocky slopes from upper montane coniferous forests to alpine communities **Elevation:** 6500–11,800 ft. **Ecoregions:** Sierra Nevada, Cascades

Matted perennial with sprawling, leafy, finely glandular-hairy and generally reddish flowering stems. Leaves to 0.6 in. long, fleshy, densely clustered along stem, oblong to spoon-shaped, with smooth margins. Flowers in head-like clusters at stem tips, with 2 pistils and 10 stamens with club-shaped, petal-like filaments. Calyx lobes to 0.1 in. long, 5, ovoid, recurved. Petals to 0.2 in. long, 5, linear to oblong, white. Fruits to 0.2 in. long, capsule-like follicles, often purplish, with many tiny seeds. The red stems and fruits make it easy to spot and identify.

Pyrola dentata

toothed wintergreen

ERICACEAE HEATH FAMILY

PCT Sections: 4–5 & 10–24 **Abundance:** Locally common **Height:** to 1 ft. **Flowering:** June–August **Flower Color:** Whitish, pink, or greenish **Habitat-Community:** Understories in humus or sandy soils from oak woodlands to upper montane coniferous forests **Elevation:** Below 9600 ft. **Ecoregions:** Southern California Mountains, Sierra Nevada, Cascades, Klamath Mountains

Evergreen subshrub or perennial with numerous, blue-waxy coated, erect, basal leaves; partially myco-heterotrophic. Leaves to 5 in. long, round to ovoid or spoon-shaped or oval, blue-waxy coated above, with white veins and smooth to toothed margins. Flowers 1–20 scattered along stem, irregular, nodding, and flower bract half pedicel length or less. Sepals to 0.1 in. long, 5, free, triangle-shaped. Petals to 0.3 in. long, 5, free, whitish, pink, or greenish. Fruits many-seeded, pendent capsules. Although the term *wintergreen* was originally applied to ivy, it is also used for pyrolas, with their white-veined evergreen leaves.

Pyrola picta

white-veined wintergreen

ERICACEAE HEATH FAMILY

PCT Sections: 1–5 & 10–24 **Abundance:** Common **Height:** to 14 in. **Flowering:** June–August **Flower Color:** Whitish, pink, or greenish **Habitat-Community:** Moist to dry understories, sometimes in decomposed granite, in montane coniferous forests **Elevation:** Below 7900 ft. **Ecoregions:** All (except Sonoran/Mojave Basin and Range)

Evergreen subshrub or perennial with numerous basal leaves; partially mycoheterotrophic. Leaves to 6 in. long, ovoid to spoon-shaped or oval, white-veined above, with generally smooth margins. Flowers 5–25 scattered along stem, irregular, nodding, and flower bract half pedicel length. Sepals to 0.1 in. long, 5, free, triangle- to lance-shaped. Petals to 0.3 in. long, 5, free, whitish, pink, or greenish. Fruits many-seeded, pendent capsules. A healing poultice of the leaves is applied to sores or bruises.

Acmispon americanus

Spanish lotus

FABACEAE LEGUME FAMILY

PCT Sections: All **Abundance:** Common **Height:** 2–24 in. **Flowering:** April–October **Flower Color:** White or yellow to pink **Habitat-Community:** Disturbed sites from woodlands and chaparrals to subalpine coniferous forests **Elevation:** Below 7900 ft. **Ecoregions:** All (except Sonoran Basin and Range)

Prostrate to erect annual with hairy stems. Leaves alternate, pinnate, with 3 hairy, lance-shaped to oval leaflets 0.4–0.8 in. long. Flowers solitary along leafy stems, irregular (pea-like), consisting of a banner, keel, and wings. Calyces to 0.3 in. long, 5-lobed. Petals 0.2–0.4 in. long, 5, white or yellow to pink. Fruits to 1.2 in. long, flat pods with 3–8 seeds. Found throughout the North American continent (hence the specific epithet), especially along roadsides.

Astragalus bicristatus

crested milkvetch

FABACEAE LEGUME FAMILY

PCT Sections: 4–5 **Abundance:** Rare **Height:** 6–24 in. **Flowering:** May–August **Flower Color:** White to cream **Habitat-Community:** Gravelly to rocky soils in montane coniferous forests **Elevation:** 5700–8800 ft. **Ecoregions:** Southern California Mountains

Sprawling, branched perennial with minutely hairy herbage. Leaves 0.2–0.8 in. long, pinnate, with 11–23 widely spaced, narrowly oblong leaflets, the terminal leaflet jointed to the midrib. Flowers in spikes of 2–20, ascending, irregular (pea-like), consisting of a banner, keel, and wings, with 5 hairy calyx lobes. Petals 0.5–0.8 in. long, 5, white to cream, tinged purple. Fruits 0.8–1.8 in. long, 0.2–0.4 in. wide, pendent, leathery pods, sometimes mottled, becoming distinctly 4-sided, crescent-shaped, glossy (when mature). Endemic to the San Bernardino and San Gabriel Mountains (east of Mt. Baden-Powell).

Astragalus douglasii

Douglas milkvetch

FABACEAE LEGUME FAMILY

PCT Sections: 1–8 **Abundance:** Common **Height:** 1–3 ft. **Flowering:** April–August **Flower Color:** White to pale yellow **Habitat-Community:** Open, gravelly to rocky soils in montane chaparrals, oak & pinyon-juniper woodlands, and montane coniferous forests **Elevation:** Below 7400 ft. **Ecoregions:** Southern California Mountains, Sierra Nevada

Erect to sprawling, bushy perennial with leafy, minutely hairy stems. Leaves 2–7 in. long, pinnate, with 7–25 elliptic to ovoid leaflets 0.2–1 in. long. Flowers 10–30 along stem tips, spreading to ascending, irregular (pea-like), consisting of a banner, keel, and wings, with 5 green calyx lobes. Petals 0.4–0.6 in. long, 5, white to pale yellow. Fruits 2.5 in. long, 1.2 in. wide, inflated, leathery, sparsely hairy to hairless, shiny pods. Three varieties along the PCT: var. *douglasii* (pod longer than wide) is found in the western Transverse Ranges and southern Sierra; var. *parishii* (pod as wide as long; prostrate stems) occurs in the Peninsular Ranges and San Bernardino Mountains; var. *perstrictus* (pod as wide as long; stiffly erect stems) is rare, found along the PCT only from Campo to the southern Laguna Mountains in San Diego County.

Astragalus ertterae

Walker Pass milkvetch

FABACEAE LEGUME FAMILY

PCT Sections: 8–9 **Abundance:** Rare **Height:** 1–4 in. **Flowering:** April–May **Flower Color:** Whitish (cream) **Habitat-Community:** Open, sandy, granitic soils in woodlands **Elevation:** 5700–6300 ft. **Ecoregions:** Sierra Nevada

Prostrate perennial with base buried in sand and shaggy hairs along stems. Leaves 1–2.6 in. long, 4–5, alternate, pinnate, with 9–13 hairy, spoon-shaped, notch- or blunt-tipped leaflets to 0.5 in. long. Flowers 7–17 in crowded clusters, irregular (pea-like), consisting of a banner to 0.5 in. long, keel to 0.4 in. long, and wings. Calyces 5-lobed, hairy. Petals 5, whitish (cream). Fruits to 0.9 in. long, spreading, hairless 1-chambered pods. First described in 1987. Look for it in sandy soils at Mile 649–650.5. The specific epithet honors botanist Barbara Ertter, of the Jepson Herbarium.

Astragalus lentiginosus var. sierrae

Big Bear Valley milkvetch

FABACEAE LEGUME FAMILY

PCT Sections: 4 **Abundance:** Rare **Height:** 4–14 in. **Flowering:** April–August **Flower Color:** White **Habitat-Community:** Gravelly to rocky soils and dry meadows in sagebrush scrubs, pinyon-juniper woodlands, and montane coniferous forests **Elevation:** Below 10,400 ft. **Ecoregions:** Southern California Mountains

Loosely matted perennial with wide-branched stems and sparsely hairy herbage. Leaves 1–2 in. long, pinnate, with 15–21 distinctly crowded, ovoid leaflets 0.1–0.3 in. long. Flowers in crowded clusters of 5–15, irregular (pea-like), consisting of a banner 0.4–0.7 in. long, keel, and wings, with 5 hairy calyx lobes. Petals 5, white to pink-tinged. Fruits 0.7–1 in. long, 0.3–0.7 in. wide, inflated, plump-ovoid pods, papery, tan (purple-speckled), sparsely hairy. Endemic to the Big Bear Lake region. Threatened by urbanization, mining, and recreational activities.

Glycyrrhiza lepidota

wild licorice

FABACEAE LEGUME FAMILY

PCT Sections: 1–2 & 4–6 **Abundance:** Occasional **Height:** 16–40 in. **Flowering:** May–July **Flower Color:** White to pale green **Habitat-Community:** Seasonally moist, sandy or alkaline soils, springs, and streambanks in foothill chaparrals and Joshua tree & pinyon-juniper woodlands **Elevation:** Below 6200 ft. **Ecoregions:** Southern California Mountains

Erect, few-branched perennial with usually glandular-hairy stems. Leaves 4–6 in. long, pinnate, with 9–19 narrowly ovoid, gland-dotted leaflets 0.6–1.1 in. long. Flowers in dense spikes, irregular (pea-like), consisting of a banner, keel, and wings, with 5 unequal calyx lobes. Petals 0.4–0.7 in. long, 5, white to pale green or yellow. Fruits 0.6–0.8 in. long, oblong to elliptic burs (pods) covered in hooked bristles. Roots contain glycyrrhizin, a sweet compound that is used for medicinal purposes, or as a gel-forming agent to add flavor to foods. Herbage is toxic to both humans and livestock!

Lupinus microcarpus var. densiflorus

whitewhorl lupine

FABACEAE LEGUME FAMILY

PCT Sections: 1–8 **Abundance:** Occasional **Height:** 4–28 in. **Flowering:** April–June **Flower Color:** White, yellow, or purple **Habitat-Community:** Open areas in foothill chaparrals, sagebrush scrubs, and oak & pinyon-juniper woodlands **Elevation:** Below 5200 ft. **Ecoregions:** Southern California Mountains, Sierra Nevada

Erect, sometimes clumped annual with hollow stems, disk-like leaf at base, and hairy herbage. Leaves palmate, with 5–11 (usually 9), oblong to lance-shaped leaflets 0.4–2 in. long. Flowers whorled in a dense spike, irregular (pea-like), consisting of a banner, wings, and generally hairy keel, with 5 hairy calyx lobes. Petals 0.3–0.7 in. long, white to yellow or purple. Fruits 0.4–1.7 in. long, ovoid, hairy capsules, spreading outward. Occurs along the PCT with var. *microcarpus* (fruiting pods erect). *Microcarpus* is Latin for "small seeds."

Rupertia rigida

Parish's rupertia

FABACEAE LEGUME FAMILY

PCT Sections: 1 & 4 **Abundance:** Occasional **Height:** 14–30 in. **Flowering:** May–July **Flower Color:** White to pale yellow (cream) **Habitat-Community:** Open understories in oak woodlands, montane chaparrals, and lower montane coniferous forests **Elevation:** Below 7600 ft. **Ecoregions:** Southern California Mountains

Bushy perennial with a woody base, hairy stems, and slender, leafy branches. Leaves 1-pinnate, with 3 bright green, lance-shaped, hairy, glandular leaflets 1.4–2.9 in. long. Flowers in spikes at leaf axils, irregular (pea-like), consisting of a banner, keel, and wings; calyces swollen in fruit. Petals 0.6–0.7 in. long, white to pale yellow (usually cream). Fruits to 0.5 in. long, elliptic, glandular-hairy, golden-brown pods. Best seen along the PCT in the northern and eastern San Bernardino Mountains, and also atop the Laguna Mountains in San Diego County.

Trifolium monanthum

mountain carpet clover

FABACEAE LEGUME FAMILY

PCT Sections: 3–5 & 10–18 **Abundance:** Locally common **Height:** 1–8 in. **Flowering:** June–August **Flower Color:** White **Habitat-Community:** Meadows, streambanks, moist rocky slopes, and pine forests from lower montane coniferous forests to alpine and wetland-riparian communities **Elevation:** Below 12,800 ft. **Ecoregions:** Southern California Mountains, Sierra Nevada, Cascades

Slender, lax to erect perennial with hairless or hairy herbage. Leaves alternate, palmate, with 3 elliptic to widely spoon-shaped leaflets to 0.5 in. long. Flowers in 1–6-flowered heads, irregular (pea-like), consisting of a banner, keel, and wings. Calyces to 0.2 in. long, 5-lobed, the lobes = tube. Petals to 0.5 in. long, 5, white, sometimes lavender-tinged. Fruits 1–2-seeded pods. Often forms mats (hence the common name).

Viola macloskeyi

small white violet

VIOLACEAE VIOLET FAMILY

PCT Sections: 3–5 & 9–24 **Abundance:** Common **Height:** to 9 in. **Flowering:** March–September **Flower Color:** White **Habitat-Community:** Bogs, wet meadows, seeps, lakeshores, and streambanks in wetland-riparian communities **Elevation:** Below 11,900 ft. **Ecoregions:** Southern California Mountains, Sierra Nevada, Cascades, Klamath Mountains

Patch-forming, stemless perennial. Leaves to 2.6 in. long, basal, heart-shaped to ovoid, with smooth to wavy margins. Flowers irregular and solitary, with 5 stamens and 1 pistil, on peduncle to 8.3 in. long. Sepals to 0.4 in. long, 5, lance-shaped, hair-fringed. Petals 5, white, lower 3 purple-veined, lateral 2 hairy or hairless, lowest with base forming a minute spur. Fruits to 0.3 in. long, hairless capsules with small, tan seeds that are attractive to ants. It is believed that violets blooming in autumn foretell an epidemic.

Amsonia tomentosa

gray amsonia

APOCYNACEAE DOGBANE FAMILY

PCT Sections: 4 **Abundance:** Rare **Height:** 8–26 in. **Flowering:** March–May **Flower Color:** White to blue-green **Habitat-Community:** Sandy to gravelly slopes and flats in creosote bush scrubs and Joshua tree & pinyon-juniper woodlands **Elevation:** Below 5700 ft. **Ecoregions:** Southern California Mountains

Eye-catching perennial from a woody crown with 2 distinct types of herbage: one green and hairless, the other gray-woolly. Leaves 0.8–1.7 in. long, alternate, ovoid to lance-shaped, narrow at both ends, green or gray. Flowers densely clustered at stem tips, 5-parted, with erect calyx lobes. Corolla tube 0.5–0.8 in. long, funnel-shaped but narrowed just before the spreading, white lobes with blue to green tinge. Fruits 1.2–3 in. long, pod-like follicles distinctly constricted between the seeds. Look for it along the PCT in the lower Whitewater Canyon and Mojave River drainages of the San Bernardino Mountains.

Apocynum cannabinum

hemp dogbane

APOCYNACEAE DOGBANE FAMILY

PCT Sections: 1–10 & 16–24 **Abundance:** Occasional **Height:** 1–7 ft. **Flowering:** April–October **Flower Color:** White to green or pink **Habitat-Community:** Moist, sandy to gravelly soils in sagebrush scrubs, pinyon-juniper woodlands, and montane coniferous forests **Elevation:** Below 7200 ft. **Ecoregions:** Southern California Mountains, Sierra Nevada, Cascades, Klamath Mountains

Erect perennial with stiff reddish stems and milky sap, growing from spreading shoots. Leaves 2.1–3.3 in. long, opposite, ascending, lance-shaped, yellow-green, with white hairs below. Flowers clustered at stem tips, 5-parted, with erect calyx lobes. Corollas 0.1–0.2 in. long, fused about half the length, cylindric to urn-shaped, white with green or pink tinge. Fruits 2.5–3.6 in. long, slender, pod-like, pendent follicles. The white latex sap can cause skin blisters. Native to North America but can be weedy in places and difficult to eradicate.

Cryptantha barbigera

bearded cryptantha

BORAGINACEAE BORAGE FAMILY

PCT Sections: 1–8 **Abundance:** Common **Height:** to 15 in. **Flowering:** February–June **Flower Color:** White **Habitat-Community:** Open, sandy to rocky soils in creosote bush & Sonoran/Mojave mixed woody scrubs and Joshua tree & pinyon-juniper woodlands **Elevation:** Below 6000 ft. **Ecoregions:** Southern California Mountains, Sonoran/Mojave Basin and Range, Sierra Nevada

Erect to ascending, branching annual. Leaves 0.5–2 in. long, oblong to narrowly lance-shaped, green to gray-green, and bristly, white-hairy (especially on margins). Flowers usually in coiled (especially in bud) spikes, 5-parted, with coarsely hairy calyx lobes 0.2–0.4 in. long in fruit and tubular, bell-shaped corollas 0.1–0.4 in. with white, spreading lobes. Fruits 1–4 ovoid, bumpy nutlets. Two varieties occur: var. *barbigera* (flower 0.1–0.2 in. across) and var. *fergusoniae* (flower 0.2–0.4 in. across; calyx to 0.4 in. long in fruit; lance-shaped leaves; gray-green herbage). The latter is especially common along the Interstate 10 corridor.

Cryptantha cinerea var. *abortiva*

bownut cryptantha

BORAGINACEAE BORAGE FAMILY

PCT Sections: 4 **Abundance:** Rare **Height:** to 10 in. **Flowering:** May–August **Flower Color:** White **Habitat-Community:** Gravelly soils and openings in sagebrush scrubs, pinyon-juniper woodlands, and montane coniferous forests **Elevation:** 6000–10,400 ft. **Ecoregions:** Southern California Mountains

Sprawling to decumbent, low-growing perennial forming clumps to 15 in. across with leafy, hairy stems and ash-gray herbage. Leaves 1–3 in. long, alternate, linear to spoon-shaped, gray-green, hairy, nd bulbous-based bristly. Flowers in cylindric clusters, symmetric, 5-parted, with soft-white-hairy calyx lobes 0.1–0.2 in. long and tubular corollas 0.2–0.3 in. across with white, spreading lobes; the top of the corolla tube projects slightly above the base of the petal lobes, forming a pale yellow ring. Fruits 4 ovoid, shiny gray, smooth, strongly bowed nutlets 0.1 in. across with sharp-edged margins.

Cryptantha intermedia

common cryptantha

BORAGINACEAE BORAGE FAMILY

PCT Sections: 1–8 **Abundance:** Common **Height:** to 24 in. **Flowering:** April–July **Flower Color:** White **Habitat-Community:** Open, sandy to gravelly soils in foothill chaparrals, oak woodlands, and lower montane coniferous forests **Elevation:** Below 7200 ft. **Ecoregions:** Southern California/ Northern Baja Coast, Southern California Mountains, Sierra Nevada

Erect annual, mostly 1-stemmed at base, branched above, with slender stems and green, hairy herbage. Leaves 0.5–3.5 in. long, alternate, linear to lance-shaped, bright green, with erect to spreading hairs. Flowers in coiled spikes, typically in groups of 3 at the tips of branches, 5-parted, with hairy calyx lobes and short trumpet-shaped corollas 0.2–0.5 in. across with white, spreading lobes and pale green (aging yellow) tube and throat. Fruits 4 lance-shaped to narrowly ovoid, minutely to roughly bumpy nutlets to 0.1 in. long. Intermediate in appearance to other cryptanthas (hence the specific epithet) and (as the common name implies) perhaps the most common one along the PCT in southern California.

Cryptantha juniperensis

rigid cryptantha

BORAGINACEAE BORAGE FAMILY

PCT Sections: 4–8 **Abundance:** Locally common **Height:** to 15 in. **Flowering:** April–July **Flower Color:** White **Habitat-Community:** Open, sandy to gravelly soils in pinyon-juniper woodlands and lower montane coniferous forests **Elevation:** Below 7300 ft. **Ecoregions:** Southern California Mountains, Sierra Nevada

Erect to spreading annual, single-stemmed at base, branched above, with rough-hairy to finely bristly herbage. Leaves 0.5–2 in. long, alternate, mainly along stem, linear to spoon-shaped. Flowers on spikes at branch and stem tips, coiled in bud, elongating in fruit, well spaced, 5-parted, with bristly-hairy calyx lobes 0.2–0.3 in. long in fruit. Corollas 0.1–0.3 in. across, tubular, short trumpet-shaped, with pale green (aging yellow) tube and throat and white, spreading lobes. Fruits 3–4 lance-shaped to narrowly ovoid nutlets to 0.1 in. long, covered in minute, sharply pointed bumps. *Juniperensis* ("of junipers") refers to its propensity to grow in pinyon-juniper woodlands.

red-root cryptantha

Cryptantha micrantha

BORAGINACEAE BORAGE FAMILY

PCT Sections: 1–8 **Abundance:** Common **Height:** 1–7 in. **Flowering:** March–August **Flower Color:** White **Habitat-Community:** Sandy to gravelly soils in creosote bush scrubs, foothill chaparrals, Joshua tree & pinyon-juniper woodlands, and lower montane coniferous forests **Elevation:** Below 8500 ft. **Ecoregions:** Southern California Mountains, Sonoran/Mojave Basin and Range, Sierra Nevada

Diminutive, cushion-like annual with distinctively red to purple taproots, thread-like stems, and hairy herbage. Leaves 0.1–0.3 in. long, crowded around flowers, oblong to spoon-shaped. Flowers in axils of leaves or branch forks, 5-parted, with hairy calyx lobes 0.1 in. long in fruit. Corollas 0.1–0.3 in. across, tubular, short trumpet-shaped, with white, spreading lobes and prominent yellow appendages at base of lobes. Fruits 4 lance-shaped to narrowly ovoid, grainy to smooth nutlets to 0.1 in. long. The roots will dye one's skin when handled. Two varieties along the PCT: var. *micrantha* (plants wider than tall; corolla 0.1 in. across) is found along the lower desert crossings; var. *lepida* (plants taller than wide; corolla 0.1–0.3 in. across) occurs at higher elevations.

Tejon cryptantha

Cryptantha microstachys

BORAGINACEAE BORAGE FAMILY

PCT Sections: 1–8 **Abundance:** Common **Height:** 6–24 in. **Flowering:** April–June **Flower Color:** White **Habitat-Community:** Open, sandy to gravelly soils, especially burns, in foothill chaparrals, oak woodlands, and lower montane coniferous forests **Elevation:** Below 6500 ft. **Ecoregions:** Southern California/Northern Baja Coast, Southern California Mountains, Sierra Nevada

Erect, few-branched annual with thin, elongated stems and hairy to bristly herbage. Leaves 0.2–2.1 in. long, basal and alternate, linear to oblong, with coarse-hairy margins. Flowers in narrow spikes, coiled in bud, 5-parted, with calyx lobes to 0.1 in. long. Corollas 0.1–0.2 in. across, tubular, short trumpet-shaped, with white, spreading lobes and minute, yellow appendages at base of lobes. Fruits usually 1 lance-shaped, smooth, shiny nutlet to 0.1 in. long. Especially abundant in newly burned chaparral, where plants may reach 3 ft. in height! *Microstachys* (from the Latin, "small spike") refers to the thread-like flowering branches.

Cryptantha muricata

pointed cryptantha

BORAGINACEAE BORAGE FAMILY

PCT Sections: 1–10 & 14–15 **Abundance:** Common **Height:** 6–40 in. **Flowering:** March–August **Flower Color:** White **Habitat-Community:** Open areas and burns in foothill chaparrals, sagebrush scrubs, oak & pinyon-juniper woodlands, and montane coniferous forests **Elevation:** Below 8800 ft. **Ecoregions:** Southern California/ Northern Baja Coast, Southern California Mountains, Sierra Nevada

Erect, 1–several-stemmed annual with relatively stout, elongated stems and both soft and stiff, white-bristly hairs. Leaves 0.2–2 in. long, alternate, linear to spoon-shaped. Flowers in spikes at stem and branch tips, 5-parted, with calyx lobes to 0.2 in. long. Corollas 0.1–0.2 in. across, tubular, short trumpet-shaped with white, spreading lobes and pale yellow appendages at base of lobes. Fruits generally 4, ovoid or deltoid, coarsely sharp-bumpy nutlets to 0.1 in. long with a fin (dorsal ridge). Two varieties along the CA PCT: var. *jonesii*, most common at lower elevations on the coastal sides of the southern California Mountains, has a dominant central stem, branching in the upper half of plant, and smaller flowers and fruits; var. *denticulata*, found in more montane habitats, is shorter, has relatively larger flowers and fruits, and lacks a dominant central stem. *Muricata* (from the Latin, "surface roughened with pointed projections") refers to the bumpy nutlets.

Cryptantha pterocarya

wingnut cryptantha

BORAGINACEAE BORAGE FAMILY

PCT Sections: 1–10 **Abundance:** Common **Height:** 5–15 in. **Flowering:** March–June **Flower Color:** White **Habitat-Community:** Sandy soils in creosote bush & Mojave mixed woody scrubs, sagebrush scrubs, and Joshua tree & pinyon-juniper woodlands **Elevation:** Below 7000 ft. **Ecoregions:** Southern California Mountains, Sonoran/Mojave Basin and Range, Sierra Nevada

Ascending to erect, few- to many-stemmed annual with short-hairy, green to yellow-green herbage. Leaves 0.2–2 in. long, basal and alternate, linear to oblong below, lance-shaped above, with bulbous-based hairs. Flowers in coiled clusters at branch and stem tips, 5-parted, with broadly ovoid, constricted-above calyx lobes 0.1 in. long. Corollas to 0.1 in. across, white, and falling early. Fruits winged (or not) nutlets to 0.1 in. across. Three varieties along the PCT: var. *pterocarya* (3 nutlets with very broad wings; 1 nutlet not winged) is the most common; var. *purpusii* (3 nutlets with narrow knife-like wings; 1 nutlet not winged) occurs at higher elevations; var. *cycloptera* has 4 winged nutlets and yellowish green herbage.

Cryptantha similis

cushion cryptantha

BORAGINACEAE BORAGE FAMILY

PCT Sections: 4–8 **Abundance:** Locally common **Height:** 1–5 in. **Flowering:** March–June **Flower Color:** White **Habitat-Community:** Sandy to gravelly soils in creosote bush & sagebrush scrubs, Mojave mixed woody scrubs, and Joshua tree & pinyon-juniper woodlands **Elevation:** Below 6200 ft. **Ecoregions:** Southern California Mountains, Mojave Basin and Range, Sierra Nevada

Ascending, densely branched, cushion-like annual, wider than tall, up to 6 in. across, with short-hairy herbage. Leaves 0.1–0.4 in. long, crowded at the ends of branches, linear to spoon-shaped. Flowers in leaf axils or branch forks, 5-parted, with calyx lobes to 0.1 in. long. Corollas 0.1–0.3 in. across, white with bright yellow appendages at base of lobes. Fruits 3–4 triangular to ovoid, shiny nutlets to 0.1 in. across.

Eucrypta chrysanthemifolia

spotted hideseed

BORAGINACEAE BORAGE FAMILY

PCT Sections: 1–6 **Abundance:** Locally common **Height:** 8–32 in. **Flowering:** March–June **Flower Color:** White **Habitat-Community:** In shade of rocks or shrubs in chaparrals and Joshua tree & pinyon-juniper woodlands **Elevation:** Below 7100 ft. **Ecoregions:** Southern California Mountains, Sonoran/Mojave Basin and Range

Delicate, lemon-scented annual, growing erect or sprawling through rock crevices, with openly branched, glandular-sticky stems. Leaves 1–4 in. long, opposite on lower stem, alternate above, widely ovoid, green (sometimes white-spotted), and pinnately lobed with 7–12 toothed lobes. Flowers on pedicels that turn downward, 5-parted, with erect calyx lobes. Corollas 0.1–0.3 in. long, bell-shaped, white (sometimes purple-lined), hairy below, with spreading to erect lobes. Fruits small, bristly capsules with 6–8 seeds. Two varieties along the CA PCT: var. *chrysanthemifolia*, with a corolla tube extending beyond the sepal tips, occurs on the coastal side of the mountains; var. *bipinnatifida*, on the desert slopes, has a shorter corolla tube and more white-spotting on its leaves. *Eucrypta* (from the Greek, "well-hidden") refers to the seeds.

Heliotropium curassavicum var. *oculatum*

alkali heliotrope

BORAGINACEAE BORAGE FAMILY

PCT Sections: 1–8 **Abundance:** Occasional **Height:** 4–24 in. **Flowering:** March–October **Flower Color:** White **Habitat-Community:** Sandy or saline soils in washes and flats in California prairies, saltbush & creosote bush scrubs, and oak woodlands **Elevation:** Below 6800 ft. **Ecoregions:** All (except Cascades, Klamath Mountains)

Creeping, elegant-flowered perennial with fleshy, hairless herbage. Leaves 0.5–2.3 in. long, alternate, spoon-shaped, with smooth margins. Flowers in coiled spikes, 5-parted. Corollas 0.1–0.2 in. across, bell-shaped, with yellow tube, blue-purple throat, and white, spreading lobes. Fruits 4 smooth nutlets. Ranges throughout western North America. Often thought to be invasive or a weed of disturbed sites, a reputation aided perhaps in part by the generally negative perception of saline environments. *Heliotrope* (from the Greek *helios*, "sun," *trepein*, "to turn") suggests that flowers turn to face the sun throughout the course of the day.

Hesperochiron californicus

California hesperochiron

BORAGINACEAE BORAGE FAMILY

PCT Sections: 4 & 9–10 & 13–22 **Abundance:** Locally common **Height:** 2–5 in. **Flowering:** April–July **Flower Color:** White to bluish **Habitat-Community:** Wet meadows and moist flats in montane coniferous forests and wetland-riparian communities **Elevation:** Below 9500 ft. **Ecoregions:** Southern California Mountains, Sierra Nevada, Cascades, Klamath Mountains

Low-growing perennial with basal rosette of 6–8 leaves. Leaves to 3 in. long, ovoid, hairy below, generally hairy edges, with smooth margins. Flowers solitary at stem tip with 5 calyx lobes to 0.4 in. long. Corollas 0.4–1.2 in. long, to 0.8 in. across, 5-parted, petals fused below, bowl- to funnel-shaped, white with generally yellow throat; stamens within tube. Fruits to 0.5 in. long, hairy capsules. *Hesperochiron* ("western centaur") likely refers to a similar European plant.

Hesperochiron pumilus

dwarf hesperochiron

BORAGINACEAE BORAGE FAMILY

PCT Sections: 10–19 **Abundance:** Occasional **Height:** to 4 in. **Flowering:** April–July **Flower Color:** White to bluish **Habitat-Community:** Wet meadows, slopes, and flats from sagebrush scrubs to upper montane coniferous forests and wetland-riparian communities **Elevation:** Below 9900 ft. **Ecoregions:** Sierra Nevada, Cascades

Low-growing perennial with basal rosette of 2–10 leaves. Leaves to 2.8 in. long, oblong to spoon-shaped, generally hairless below, generally hairy edges, with smooth margins. Flowers 1–8 per plant, solitary at stem tips, with 5 calyx lobes to 0.4 in. long. Corollas 0.2–0.6 in. long, to 1.2 in. across, 5-parted, petals fused below, wheel-shaped, white with generally yellow throat; stamens within tube. Fruits to 0.5 in. long, ovoid, hairy capsules with many red-brown seeds.

Lappula redowskii

western stickseed

BORAGINACEAE BORAGE FAMILY

PCT Sections: 4 **Abundance:** Locally common **Height:** 8–32 in. **Flowering:** April–July **Flower Color:** White to pale blue **Habitat-Community:** Dry, open or disturbed areas in sagebrush scrubs, pinyon-juniper woodlands, and lower montane coniferous forests **Elevation:** Below 8500 ft. **Ecoregions:** Southern California Mountains

Erect, fuzzy-haired annual with green stems branched at base. Leaves 0.5–2.5 in. long, alternate, lower with petioles 0.4–0.8 in. long, ovoid; upper reduced, linear to oblong, sessile. Flowers along stem and branch tips, 5-parted, with tiny, inconspicuous, funnel-shaped, white to pale blue corollas 0.1 in. across. Fruits generally 4 concave nutlets 0.1 in. across with prickle-lined margins. *Lappula* (the Latin diminutive for *lappa*, "a bur") refers to the distinctive nutlets.

Nemophila spatulata

Sierra baby blue eyes

BORAGINACEAE BORAGE FAMILY

PCT Sections: 1–18 **Abundance:** Common **Height:** 4–12 in. **Flowering:** April–July **Flower Color:** White **Habitat-Community:** Meadows and slopes in montane coniferous forests **Elevation:** Below 10,500 ft. **Ecoregions:** Southern California/Northern Baja Coast, Southern California Mountains, Sierra Nevada, Cascades

Sprawling to ascending annual with shallowly lobed leaves. Leaves 0.2–1.2 in. long, opposite, spoon-shaped, appressed-hairy, pinnately lobed or toothed, with 3–5 shallow lobes. Flowers solitary on pedicels along stem with 5 calyx lobes to 0.2 in. long. Corollas 0.1–0.3 in. long, to 0.4 in. across, 5-parted, bowl-shaped, white to bluish (purple-blotched at corolla lobe tips). Fruits to 0.3 in. across, hairy brown capsules with shallow-pitted seeds.

Phacelia affinis

limestone phacelia

BORAGINACEAE BORAGE FAMILY

PCT Sections: 1–2 & 4–7 **Abundance:** Occasional **Height:** 2–12 in. **Flowering:** March–June **Flower Color:** White to lavender **Habitat-Community:** Gravelly or sandy soils in Sonoran/Mojave mixed woody scrubs, Joshua tree & pinyon-juniper woodlands, and lower montane coniferous forests **Elevation:** Below 8200 ft. **Ecoregions:** Southern California Mountains, Sierra Nevada

Erect, small, few-branched annual with short-hairy herbage. Leaves 0.4–2.5 in. long, oblong, either deeply lobed or divided into several lobed leaflets, sparsely hairy, and glandular. Flowers above leaves on stem and branch tips, with small, unequal calyx lobes and bell-shaped corollas 0.1–0.3 in. long with pale blue to lavender lobes. Fruits 0.2 in. across, capsules with 2–4 seeds. Causes light dermatitis (rash) in some people!

Phacelia brachyloba

shortlobe phacelia

BORAGINACEAE BORAGE FAMILY

PCT Sections: 1–6 **Abundance:** Locally common **Height:** 5–24 in. **Flowering:** April–June **Flower Color:** White to pink **Habitat-Community:** Open, sandy soils, especially recent burns, in foothill chaparrals and oak woodlands **Elevation:** Below 6800 ft. **Ecoregions:** Southern California Mountains

Aromatic, erect, few-branched annual with short-hairy, usually glandular herbage. Leaves 0.6–2 in. long, elliptic to spoon-shaped, deeply lobed to compound, with toothed segments. Flowers above leaves on stem and branch tips. Corollas funnel- to bell-shaped, 0.3–0.4 in. long, with yellow throat and white to pink, spreading lobes. Fruits 0.2 in. across, capsules with 10–25 seeds. Found in profusion after chaparral fires. Glandular hairs secrete oil droplets that cause an unpleasant skin rash in some people!

Phacelia egena
Kaweah River phacelia
BORAGINACEAE BORAGE FAMILY

PCT Sections: 5–6 & 8–9 **Abundance:** Locally common **Height:** 6–24 in. **Flowering:** March–August **Flower Color:** White **Habitat-Community:** Openings and streambanks in woodlands, chaparrals, and lower montane coniferous forests **Elevation:** Below 8200 ft. **Ecoregions:** Southern California Mountains, Sierra Nevada

Ascending perennial with densely stiff-hairy stems. Leaves 4–8 in. long, mostly basal, lance- to spoon-shaped, hairy; basal 7–11-lobed with prominent veins, stem leaves unlobed. Flowers in coiled clusters with 5 calyx lobes to 0.3 in. long. Corollas 0.2–0.4 in. long, 5-parted, bell-shaped, white; stamens exserted. Fruits to 0.1 in. across, hairy capsules with 1–2 pitted seeds.

Phacelia eisenii
Eisen's phacelia
BORAGINACEAE BORAGE FAMILY

PCT Sections: 9–14 **Abundance:** Occasional **Height:** 6–24 in. **Flowering:** May–July **Flower Color:** White to lavender **Habitat-Community:** Sandy or gravelly soils from lower montane to subalpine coniferous forests **Elevation:** Below 11,200 ft. **Ecoregions:** Sierra Nevada

Erect annual with leaves crowded at base of plant and hairy, glandular stems. Leaves 0.4–1 in. long, opposite on lower stem, elliptic to spoon-shaped, hairy and glandular, and generally unlobed. Flowers in coiled clusters with 5 calyx lobes to 0.1 in. long. Corollas 0.1–0.2 in. long, 5-parted, bell-shaped, white to lavender; stamens not exserted, and styles divided to or near the base. Fruits to 0.1 in. across, hairy capsules with 2–4 pitted seeds.

Phacelia hastata
mountain phacelia
BORAGINACEAE BORAGE FAMILY

PCT Sections: 4–5 & 10–23 **Abundance:** Common **Height:** 2–20 in. **Flowering:** May–September **Flower Color:** White to lavender **Habitat-Community:** Sandy or gravelly soils from sagebrush scrubs to alpine communities **Elevation:** Below 13,200 ft. **Ecoregions:** Southern California Mountains, Sierra Nevada, Cascades, Klamath Mountains

Decumbent to erect or mat-forming perennial with glandless to sparsely glandular stems and mostly basal leaves. Leaves 0.5–4.7 in. long, widely elliptic to lance-shaped, unlobed or 2–4-lobed or compound with 3–5 leaflets. Flowers in crowded, coiled clusters with 5 calyx lobes to 0.3 in. long. Corollas 0.1–0.3 in. long, 5-parted, urn- to bell-shaped, white to lavender; stamens exserted. Fruits to 0.2 in. across, hairy capsules with 1–3 pitted seeds. Generally shorter and matted, especially as you go up in elevation.

Phacelia hydrophylloides

waterleaf phacelia

BORAGINACEAE BORAGE FAMILY

PCT Sections: 11–18 **Abundance:** Common **Height:** 4–12 in. **Flowering:** June–September **Flower Color:** White to bluish **Habitat-Community:** Open slopes, flats, and meadows in montane coniferous forests **Elevation:** 4900–10,200 ft. **Ecoregions:** Sierra Nevada, Cascades

Decumbent to ascending perennial with hairy, generally not glandular stems. Leaves 0.6–2.4 in. long, oblong to ovoid, 1–2-lobed or with smooth margins. Flowers in dense heads at stem tips with 5 calyx lobes to 0.2 in. long. Corollas 0.2–0.3 in. long, 5-parted, bell-shaped, white to bluish; stamens exserted. Fruits to 0.3 in. across, hairy capsules with 3–8 pitted seeds.

Phacelia imbricata

imbricate phacelia

BORAGINACEAE BORAGE FAMILY

PCT Sections: 1–8 **Abundance:** Occasional **Height:** 8–45 in. **Flowering:** May–August **Flower Color:** White to lavender **Habitat-Community:** Gravelly to rocky slopes and ridges in chaparrals, oak & pinyon-juniper woodlands, and lower montane coniferous forests **Elevation:** Below 7800 ft. **Ecoregions:** Southern California Mountains, Sierra Nevada

Unbranched perennial with rosetted leaves and glandular-hairy stems. Leaves 2–6 in. long, mostly crowded at the base of plant, pale green, and pinnately lobed with 3–15 lance-shaped to ovoid segments (terminal the largest). Flowers in coiled spikes at branch and stem tips, 5-parted, glandular-hairy, with ovoid calyx lobes. Corollas cylindric to bell-shaped, 0.2–0.3 in. long, with white to lavender lobes and orange-red (as they mature) stamens. Fruits 0.1 in. across, bristly capsules with 1–3 seeds. Plants in the southern Sierra and western Transverse Ranges may be confused with *P. egena*. Two varieties along the CA PCT: var. *patula* (leaves with 3–7 segments) is most common in the montane zones of the Peninsular and eastern Transverse Ranges; var. *imbricata* (leaves with 7–15 segments) occurs in the far western Transverse Ranges and southern Sierra.

Phacelia longipes

longstalk phacelia

BORAGINACEAE BORAGE FAMILY

PCT Sections: 5–6 **Abundance:** Occasional **Height:** 4–20 in. **Flowering:** April–July **Flower Color:** White to pale lavender **Habitat-Community:** Rocky talus and open, gravelly slopes and ridges in montane chaparrals and coniferous forests **Elevation:** Below 7900 ft. **Ecoregions:** Southern California Mountains

Decumbent to erect, few-branched annual with soft, glandular-hairy herbage. Leaves 0.5–2.2 in. long, basal (mostly) and alternate, ovoid to round, glandular-hairy, with elongated petioles and wavy to toothed margins. Flowers clustered on elongated stem and branch tips, 5-parted, with linear calyx lobes. Corollas widely bell-shaped, 0.3–0.5 in. long, with white to lavender lobes and orange-red (as they mature) stamens. Fruits 0.2–0.3 in. across, glandular-hairy ovoid capsules. Best seen along the PCT in the San Gabriel Mountains from Gobblers Knob southeast of Wrightwood, westward to Pacifico Mountain. *Longipes* (from the Latin, "long foot") refers to the elongated inflorescence branches.

Mojave phacelia

Phacelia mohavensis

BORAGINACEAE BORAGE FAMILY

PCT Sections: 4–5 & 8 **Abundance:** Rare **Height:** 2–10 in. **Flowering:** April–August **Flower Color:** White to pale blue **Habitat-Community:** Sandy to gravelly soils in oak woodlands and montane coniferous forests **Elevation:** Below 7800 ft. **Ecoregions:** Southern California Mountains, Sierra Nevada

Small, erect, few-branched annual with minutely glandular-hairy stems. Leaves 0.4–1.6 in. long, alternate, linear to spoon-shaped, with smooth margins. Flowers in open, coiled spikes at branch and stem tips, 5-parted, with unequal-in-length, linear calyx lobes 0.1–0.2 in. long. Corollas bell-shaped, 0.2–0.3 in. long, white (aging pale blue) with 2 parallel translucent patches and yellow tubular throat; stamens exserted. Fruits 0.1–0.2 in. across, ovoid, glandular-hairy capsules with 4–8 seeds. Best seen along the PCT in the San Bernardino and Gabriel Mountains with a slight chance of encountering it in the Piute Mountains (southern Sierra).

changeable phacelia

Phacelia mutabilis

BORAGINACEAE BORAGE FAMILY

PCT Sections: 3–5 & 9–24 **Abundance:** Common **Height:** 4–24 in. **Flowering:** May–October **Flower Color:** White to lavender **Habitat-Community:** Ridges and open forest from lower montane to subalpine coniferous forests **Elevation:** Below 11,500 ft. **Ecoregions:** Southern California Mountains, Sierra Nevada, Cascades, Klamath Mountains

Decumbent to erect, biennial to short-lived perennial with hairy stems and mostly basal leaves. Leaves 0.8–7 in. long, ovoid to lance-shaped, hairy, and unlobed, 3-lobed, or compound with 3 leaflets (terminal being the largest). Flowers in crowded, coiled clusters with 5 calyx lobes to 0.2 in. long. Corollas 0.1–0.3 in. long, 5-parted, tubular to bell-shaped, white to lavender; stamens exserted. Fruits to 0.1 in. across, hairy capsules with 1–4 pitted seeds. *Mutabilis* means "changeable."

branching phacelia

Phacelia ramosissima

BORAGINACEAE BORAGE FAMILY

PCT Sections: 1–17 **Abundance:** Locally common **Height:** 1–5 ft. **Flowering:** April–October **Flower Color:** White to lavender or blue **Habitat-Community:** Rocky or sandy soils from sagebrush scrubs and chaparrals to upper montane coniferous forests **Elevation:** Below 12,500 ft. **Ecoregions:** Southern California/Northern Baja Coast, Southern California Mountains, Sierra Nevada, Cascades

Prostrate to ascending, multi-branched perennial with hairless or hairy, sometimes glandular stems. Leaves 1.5–8 in. long, oblong to widely ovoid, pinnately compound, with coarsely toothed to lobed leaflets. Flowers in open or dense, coiled clusters with 5 calyx lobes to 0.3 in. long. Corollas 0.1–0.3 in. long, 5-parted, funnel- to bell-shaped, white to lavender or blue; stamens exserted. Fruits to 0.2 in. across, hairy capsules with 2–4 pitted seeds. *Ramosissima* means "much branched."

Pholistoma membranaceum

white fiestaflower

BORAGINACEAE BORAGE FAMILY

PCT Sections: 1–8 **Abundance:** Occasional **Height:** 8–36 in. **Flowering:** February–May **Flower Color:** White **Habitat-Community:** Gravelly to rocky slopes in foothill chaparrals, Sonoran/Mojave mixed woody scrubs, and Joshua tree woodlands **Elevation:** Below 4600 ft. **Ecoregions:** Southern California Mountains, Sonoran/Mojave Basin and Range, Sierra Nevada

Erect, much-branched annual, often tangled through shrubs or in shade of rocks, with waxy, brittle stems covered with hooked prickles. Leaves 1–5 in. long, bright green, lower opposite, alternate along the upper stem, with narrow-winged petiole, not clasping, and deeply lobed or cut, usually linear lobes with rounded tips. Flowers generally 2–10 in clusters at branch and stem tips, 5-parted, with prickly calyx lobes. Corollas 0.1–0.3 in. long, 0.4 in. across, rotate, lobes white with a purple spot or streak. Fruits 0.1–0.2 in. across, capsules with 1–2 seeds. Found along the PCT where it traverses low-elevation desert slopes and (ironically) on the foggy coastal beach bluffs of San Diego County.

Plagiobothrys arizonicus

Arizona popcornflower

BORAGINACEAE BORAGE FAMILY

PCT Sections: 1–8 **Abundance:** Common **Height:** to 15 in. **Flowering:** February–May **Flower Color:** White **Habitat-Community:** Dry, coarse soils in washes and on flats and gentle slopes in creosote bush scrubs, foothill chaparrals, and pinyon-juniper woodlands **Elevation:** Below 6500 ft. **Ecoregions:** Southern California Mountains, Sonoran/Mojave Basin and Range, Sierra Nevada

Erect to ascending annual with reddish (especially near base) stems with spreading hairs. Leaves 0.6–2 in. long, basal in rosette and alternate, lance-shaped, green, with distinctive red margins and veins. Flowers in small clusters above leafy bracts, 5-parted, with spreading-hairy calyx to 0.2 in. long (curved over the developing fruit). Corollas to 0.2 in. across, broadly funnel-shaped, with white, spreading lobes and pale yellow appendages at throat. Fruits 0.1 in. across, generally 2 widely ovoid nutlets, erect, arched, strongly attached, ribbed and ridged, with scar on back side near middle. The herbage leaks a staining purple juice when crushed. The pale yellow corolla appendages turn white after successful pollination.

Plagiobothrys collinus

Cooper's popcornflower

BORAGINACEAE BORAGE FAMILY

PCT Sections: 1–5 **Abundance:** Common **Height:** to 14 in. **Flowering:** February–June **Flower Color:** White **Habitat-Community:** Dry, open, gravelly soils in foothill chaparrals, oak woodlands, and lower montane coniferous forests **Elevation:** Below 7500 ft. **Ecoregions:** Southern California Mountains

Prostrate to ascending annual with finely, soft-hairy to rusty-haired herbage. Leaves 0.4–1.2 in. long, rosetted and alternate, lance-shaped, olive- to silvery-green. Flowers in dense, elongated spikes that generally exceed leaves, 5-parted, and calyx 0.1 in. long (curved over the developing fruit). Corollas to 0.3 in. across, broadly funnel-shaped, with white, spreading lobes. Fruits 3–4 erect, ovoid nutlets to 0.1 in. across with net-like patterning and scar on back side near middle. *Collinus* (from Collatina, Roman goddess of hills) suggests it's hill-loving.

Calystegia longipes

Piute morning-glory

CONVOLVULACEAE

MORNING-GLORY FAMILY

PCT Sections: 1 & 5–9 **Abundance:** Locally common **Height:** 10–40 in. **Flowering:** May–July **Flower Color:** White to cream **Habitat-Community:** Rocky slopes and open areas in Sonoran/Mojave mixed woody scrubs and foothill chaparrals **Elevation:** Below 6600 ft. **Ecoregions:** Southern California Mountains, Sierra Nevada

Showy perennial, usually twining through shrubs, sometimes forming a bushy mat. Leaves 1.3–2.5 in. long, alternate, linear to arrowhead-shaped, with narrow basal lobes. Flowers generally 1 per leaf axil on long peduncles, 5-parted, with fused, white to pale cream or lavender petals 1.3–1.9 in. long. Fruits 4-seeded capsules. *Longipes* ("long-stalked") refers to the elongated peduncles.

Calystegia malacophylla

Sierra false bindweed

CONVOLVULACEAE

MORNING-GLORY FAMILY

PCT Sections: 6 & 8 & 15–20 **Abundance:** Locally common **Height:** 4–40 in. **Flowering:** June–August **Flower Color:** White **Habitat-Community:** Dry slopes from woodlands and chaparrals to upper montane coniferous forests **Elevation:** Below 7900 ft. **Ecoregions:** Southern California Mountains, Sierra Nevada, Cascades, Klamath Mountains

Decumbent to ascending perennial, often climbing on other vegetation, with generally brown- to gray-hairy herbage. Leaves 1–2.5 in. long, widely triangular to heart-shaped, with 2-tipped basal lobes. Flowers solitary along leafy stems with 5 sepals to 0.8 in. long and 5 short stamens. Corollas 0.8–1.8 in. long, 5-lobed, bell-shaped, symmetric, white. Fruits spheric capsules with generally 4 seeds.

Calystegia occidentalis

chaparral false bindweed

CONVOLVULACEAE

MORNING-GLORY FAMILY

PCT Sections: 1–8 & 16–24 **Abundance:** Occasional **Height:** 10–40 in. **Flowering:** May–August **Flower Color:** White to creamy yellow **Habitat-Community:** Canyons and dry slopes from oak woodlands to lower montane coniferous forests **Elevation:** Below 8200 ft. **Ecoregions:** Southern California Mountains, Sierra Nevada, Cascades, Klamath Mountains

Showy perennial, twisting and climbing through other plants, with fine-hairy herbage. Leaves 0.7–1.7 in. long, alternate, linear to narrowly lance-shaped or widely triangular, with distinct basal lobes. Flowers 1–4 per peduncle, 5-parted, with fused, white to creamy yellow petals 0.8–2.3 in. long. Fruits 4-seeded capsules. Hybridizes with *C. malacophylla* in Kern County. *Calystegia* is Greek for "hiding calyx" by bracts of some species.

Orthilia secunda

sidebells wintergreen

ERICACEAE HEATH FAMILY

PCT Sections: 3–4 & 10–24 **Abundance:** Common **Height:** to 8 in. **Flowering:** June–August **Flower Color:** Cream to green-white **Habitat-Community:** Understories in dry to moist soils from lower montane to subalpine coniferous forests **Elevation:** Below 10,500 ft. **Ecoregions:** Southern California Mountains, Sierra Nevada, Cascades, Klamath Mountains

Shrubby or not, evergreen perennial with leaves mostly near base; partially mycoheterotrophic. Leaves 0.6–2.4 in. long, alternate, narrowly ovoid, sometimes leathery, with toothed to smooth margins. Flowers along one side of arching stem. Sepals 5, fused. Corollas to 0.4 in. long, symmetric, 5-lobed, urn-shaped, cream to green-white. Fruits to 0.2 in. across, pendent, many-seeded capsules. Well known for its myriad therapeutic properties.

Pterospora andromedea

woodland pinedrops

ERICACEAE HEATH FAMILY

PCT Sections: 3–5 & 8–24 **Abundance:** Common **Height:** 1–3 ft. **Flowering:** June–August **Flower Color:** White, pink, or yellow **Habitat-Community:** Dry, deep humus in montane coniferous forests **Elevation:** Below 12,200 ft. **Ecoregions:** All (except Sonoran/Mojave Basin and Range)

Erect, nongreen, leafless perennial with scale-like bracts along sticky red-brown stems; mycoheterotrophic. Flowers pendent along upper half of stem. Sepals to 0.2 mm long, 5, and free. Corollas to 0.4 in. long, 5-lobed, symmetric, urn-shaped, and white, pink, or yellow. Fruits to 0.5 in. across, pendent many-seeded capsules. The flowers resemble pine resin dripping down a tree trunk (hence the common name).

Menyanthes trifoliata

buckbean

MENYANTHACEAE
BUCKBEAN FAMILY

PCT Sections: 10–22 **Abundance:** Occasional **Height:** to 18 in. **Flowering:** April–August **Flower Color:** White or pink **Habitat-Community:** Ponds, fens, bogs, wet meadows, and lakeshores in wetland-riparian communities **Elevation:** Below 10,500 ft. **Ecoregions:** Sierra Nevada, Cascades, Klamath Mountains

Prostrate to ascending, hairless perennial having rhizomes covered in old leaf bases (generally underwater). Leaves 1–2.5 in. long, alternate, palmate, with 3 oblong, smooth-margined leaflets. Flowers are clustered at the end of a single stalk. Calyx lobes to 0.2 mm long, 5, oblong. Corollas to 0.6 in. long, 5-lobed, symmetric, fused, funnel-shaped, hairy inside, and white (generally pink at tip) or pink. Fruits 2-valved, many-seeded capsules. Historically used to treat scurvy. It's a treat to see the showy flowers when they're held just inches above water, but you may have to back up and dry off your boots!

Abronia pogonantha

Mojave
sand verbena

NYCTAGINACEAE

FOUR O'CLOCK FAMILY

PCT Sections: 4–8 **Abundance:** Occasional **Height:** 4–18 in. **Flowering:** April–July **Flower Color:** White to pink **Habitat-Community:** Sandy flats and hillsides in creosote bush scrubs and Joshua tree & pinyon-juniper woodlands **Elevation:** Below 6200 ft. **Ecoregions:** Southern California Mountains, Mojave Basin and Range, Sierra Nevada

Decumbent to ascending, showy annual with glandular-hairy, reddish stems. Leaves 0.5–2.2 in. long, opposite, petiole to 1.5 in. long, lance-shaped to broadly ovoid, fleshy, glandular-hairy. Flowers 12–24 per hemispheric head, 5-parted, with peduncles 0.8–2.8 in. long and 5 thin leaf-like bracts at base of cluster. Corollas trumpet-shaped, red tube 0.4–0.8 in. long and white to pink lobes 0.3 in. long with irregularly lobed margins. Fruits 0.1–0.3 in. long, 2-winged anthocarps. Populations may have all white flowers, or all pink, or both colors mixed together. Occurs along the PCT in the Antelope Valley region of the Mojave Desert and the desert slopes of the Transverse Ranges and far southern Sierra.

Allophyllum integrifolium

white
false gilia

POLEMONIACEAE PHLOX FAMILY

PCT Sections: 4–5 & 12–18 **Abundance:** Occasional **Height:** 4–10 in. **Flowering:** April–June **Flower Color:** White to pale blue **Habitat-Community:** Open, rocky or sandy areas on ridgetops in oak woodlands and montane coniferous forests **Elevation:** Below 9000 ft. **Ecoregions:** Southern California Mountains, Sierra Nevada, Cascades

Generally unbranched annual with long-stalked, glandular-hairy stems. Leaves 0.3–0.8 in. long, alternate; lower unlobed and toothed, upper 3-lobed, with longest lobe 0.2–0.6 in. long. Flowers 0.3–0.5 in. long, 5-parted, funnel-shaped, with white to pale blue corolla lobes 0.1 in. long. Fruits 3–6-seeded, spherical capsules. *Integrifolium* means "with whole [unlobed] leaves."

Collomia linearis

narrowleaf
mountaintrumpet

POLEMONIACEAE PHLOX FAMILY

PCT Sections: 10–18 **Abundance:** Common **Height:** to 15 in. **Flowering:** May–August **Flower Color:** White to pink **Habitat-Community:** Open places from lower montane to subalpine coniferous forests **Elevation:** Below 12,000 ft. **Ecoregions:** Sierra Nevada, Cascades

Erect, 1-few-branched annual with hairy stems and generally glandular foliage. Leaves to 2.4 in. long, alternate, lance-shaped to linear, with smooth to toothed margins. Flowers 7–20 in heads at stem tips. Calyces to 0.3 in. long, 5-lobed, the lobes connected by a thin membrane with a water pitcher–like projection at the tip. Corollas to 0.6 in. long, funnel-shaped, white to pink. Fruits 1-seed-per-chamber capsules that explosively open to scatter the seeds. *Collomia* ("glue") refers to the sticky coat of wet seeds.

Modoc gilia

Gilia modocensis

POLEMONIACEAE PHLOX FAMILY

PCT Sections: 4–8 **Abundance:** Occasional **Height:** 4–14 in. **Flowering:** April–June **Flower Color:** White to lavender **Habitat-Community:** Open, sandy to rocky areas in sagebrush & rabbitbrush scrubs, Joshua tree & pinyon-juniper woodlands, and lower montane coniferous forests **Elevation:** Below 7500 ft. **Ecoregions:** Southern California Mountains, Sierra Nevada

Much-branched (from base) annual from a basal rosette with green stems that are cobwebby-hairy below, glandular above. Leaves 1–2 in. long, mostly basal, pinnately lobed, strap-shaped (wide central axis), woolly; stem leaves alternate, reduced, clasping. Flowers in open clusters at stem and branch tips, 5-parted, with black-glandular pedicels and glandular calyx 0.1–0.3 in. long with lobes wider than membrane. Corollas 0.3–0.5 in. long, purple to white tube included in calyx, bright yellow throat, white to lavender lobes; stamens and style exserted. Fruits 0.1–0.3 in. long, widely ovoid capsules with 15–30 seeds. Ranges from the CA PCT to Oregon and Idaho.

ballhead ipomopsis

Ipomopsis congesta

POLEMONIACEAE PHLOX FAMILY

PCT Sections: 11–24 **Abundance:** Locally common **Height:** 4–12 in. **Flowering:** May–September **Flower Color:** White **Habitat-Community:** Open, dry, rocky soils from sagebrush scrubs and woodlands to alpine communities **Elevation:** Below 12,200 ft. **Ecoregions:** Sierra Nevada, Cascades, Klamath Mountains

Decumbent to erect, matted to many-branched perennial with hairy to hairless stems. Leaves to 1.6 in. long, alternate, palmately or pinnately lobed, with spine-tipped ultimate lobe segments. Flowers in head-like terminal clusters. Calyces to 0.2 in. long, 5-lobed, bell-shaped, hairy, with lobes connected by a thin membrane. Corollas to 0.4 in. long, elongate-funnel-shaped, yellow tube, and white lobes. Fruits 1-2-seeded capsules.

many-flowered linanthus

Leptosiphon floribundus

POLEMONIACEAE PHLOX FAMILY

PCT Sections: 1–5 **Abundance:** Locally common **Height:** 4–18 in. **Flowering:** March–August **Flower Color:** White **Habitat-Community:** Open to shaded areas in oak woodlands and lower montane coniferous forests **Elevation:** Below 7500 ft. **Ecoregions:** Southern California Mountains

Much-branched perennial, sometimes forming loose mounds, with hairy or hairless herbage. Leaves opposite and deeply palmately dissected with 3 linear lobes 0.3–0.8 in. long. Flowers clustered, 5-parted, and tubular calyces 0.3–0.4 in. long with lobes connected by narrow translucent membranes. Corollas funnel-shaped, white tube 0.2–0.4 in. long, yellow throat, and white spreading lobes 0.2–0.4 in. long; stamens included to slightly exserted. Fruits 3-chambered capsules. Two subspecies along the PCT: subsp. *glabra* (leaf & calyx glabrous) and subsp. *floribundus* (leaf & calyx hairy). Dense populations in full bloom brighten the pine forest understory atop the Laguna Mountains in San Diego County.

Lemmon's linanthus

Leptosiphon lemmonii

POLEMONIACEAE PHLOX FAMILY

PCT Sections: 1–4 **Abundance:** Locally common **Height:** 2–6 in. **Flowering:** April–June **Flower Color:** White or cream **Habitat-Community:** Open, dry flats in foothill chaparrals and oak woodlands **Elevation:** Below 6000 ft. **Ecoregions:** Southern California Mountains

Low-growing, ascending to spreading annual, branched at base, with hairy herbage. Leaves opposite and palmately dissected with linear lobes 0.1–0.2 in. long. Flowers in heads, sessile, 5-parted, and calyces 0.2 in. long with lobes connected by a thin membrane. Corollas funnel-shaped, yellow tube 0.1 in. long, yellow or maroon throat, and white or cream, spreading lobes 0.1 in. long; stamens exserted from tube. Fruits 3-chambered capsules. Especially common from Warner Springs in San Diego County to the south end of the San Jacinto Mountains in Riverside County.

flax-flowered linanthus

Leptosiphon liniflorus

POLEMONIACEAE PHLOX FAMILY

PCT Sections: 1–4 & 6–7 **Abundance:** Occasional **Height:** 4–20 in. **Flowering:** April–June **Flower Color:** White to pale blue **Habitat-Community:** Open, dry flats in foothill chaparrals and oak woodlands **Elevation:** Below 5500 ft. **Ecoregions:** Southern California Mountains, Sierra Nevada

Ascending to erect, single-stemmed annual with thread-like, hairless to slightly hairy branches. Leaves opposite and palmately 3-lobed with linear lobes 0.2–1.3 in. long. Flowers 1–few at branch and stem tips, 5-parted, rotate, and hairy calyx 0.1–0.2 in. long with membrane wider than lobes. Corollas funnel-shaped, tube 0.1 in. long, yellow throat, and spreading, white or pale blue (purple-veined) lobes 0.3 in. long; stamens exserted. Fruits 3-chambered capsules. Emerges later in spring, after many other annuals (and non-native grasses) have dried up. It is so delicate that most pollinators must hover (rather than land) to obtain nectar from its flower. The veined flowers resemble flax (hence the common name).

Sierra Nevada leptosiphon

Leptosiphon oblanceolatus

POLEMONIACEAE PHLOX FAMILY

PCT Sections: 10–11 **Abundance:** Rare **Height:** 1–5 in. **Flowering:** July–August **Flower Color:** White **Habitat-Community:** Open flats near meadows in subalpine coniferous forests **Elevation:** 9100–12,200 ft. **Ecoregions:** Sierra Nevada

Erect, 1–few-branched annual with hairy herbage. Leaves to 0.6 in. long, opposite, palmately lobed, lobes blunt- to notch-tipped. Flowers in 1–few-flowered, head-like terminal clusters. Calyces to 0.2 in. long, 5-lobed, hairy, with lobes connected by a wide (≥ lobe width), thin membrane. Corollas to 0.5 in. long, narrowly funnel-shaped, white to pink tube, yellow throat, and blunt- to notch-tipped white lobes. Fruits 3-seeded capsules. *Leptosiphon* means "narrow tube," referring to the corolla tubes of many species.

Linanthus bigelovii
Bigelow's linanthus
POLEMONIACEAE PHLOX FAMILY

PCT Sections: 1–8 **Abundance:** Locally common **Height:** 2–8 in. **Flowering:** March–May **Flower Color:** White **Habitat-Community:** Sandy to gravelly washes and hillsides in creosote bush scrubs and woodlands **Elevation:** Below 5400 ft. **Ecoregions:** Southern California Mountains, Sonoran/Mojave Basin and Range, Sierra Nevada

Erect, wiry annual with thread-like, nearly leafless, glossy, hairless stems. Leaves 0.4–1.2 in. long, opposite, linear, hairless. Flowers sessile in leaf axils, 5-parted, opening at night. Calyces tubular, hairless, 0.3–0.5 in. long, with lobes connected by a wide (≥ lobe width), thin membrane. Corollas funnel-shaped, tube 0.2 in. long, white with purple-tinged lobes 0.3 in. long. Fruits 3-chambered capsules. During the day, when flowers are coiled up, it closely resembles *L. dichotomus*.

Linanthus concinnus
San Gabriel linanthus
POLEMONIACEAE PHLOX FAMILY

PCT Sections: 5 **Abundance:** Rare **Height:** 1–7 in. **Flowering:** May–June **Flower Color:** White **Habitat-Community:** Gravelly to scree slopes in montane chaparrals, sagebrush scrubs, and montane coniferous forests **Elevation:** Below 9000 ft. **Ecoregions:** Southern California Mountains

Ascending, slender annual, branched above, with glandular-hairy stems. Leaves opposite and deeply 3–5-lobed with linear lobes 0.3–0.6 in. long. Flowers sessile, 5-parted, tubular. Calyces glandular, 0.4 in. long, with lobes connected by a wide (≥ lobe width), translucent membrane. Corollas funnel-shaped, tube 0.1 in. long, and white (dark purple-lined at base), spreading lobes 0.2–0.4 in. long. Fruits 3-chambered capsules. This attractive, day-flowering endemic of the San Gabriel Mountains is threatened primarily by recreational activities. Limited along the PCT to the trail segment extending from Blue Ridge above Wrightwood, westward to Mt. Pacifico.

Linanthus dichotomus
eveningsnow
POLEMONIACEAE PHLOX FAMILY

PCT Sections: 1–9 **Abundance:** Locally common **Height:** 2–10 in. **Flowering:** April–June **Flower Color:** White **Habitat-Community:** Sandy to gravelly soils, especially burns, in foothill chaparrals, Sonoran/Mojave mixed woody scrubs, and woodlands **Elevation:** Below 6200 ft. **Ecoregions:** Southern California Mountains, Sonoran/Mojave Basin and Range, Sierra Nevada

Erect to spreading, much-branched, thread-like annual with hairless and waxy herbage. Leaves opposite at branching nodes, 3–7 linear lobes 0.4–0.9 in. long. Flowers clustered at branch and stem tips, 5-parted, tubular. Calyces hairless, 0.3–0.6 in. long, with lobes connected by a wide (≥ lobe width), translucent membrane. Corollas funnel-shaped, tube 0.3–0.4 in. long, and white (purple-tinged) lobes 0.4–0.7 in. long. Fruits cylindric capsules with 15–28 seeds. Flowers open only at night, casting a snow-like glow upon the ground (hence the common name). *Dichotomus* ("divided in pairs") refers to the forked branching pattern.

Linanthus inyoensis

Inyo gilia

POLEMONIACEAE PHLOX FAMILY

PCT Sections: 9–10 **Abundance:** Locally common **Height:** 4–12 in. **Flowering:** April–July **Flower Color:** White **Habitat-Community:** Open, sandy flats from sagebrush scrubs and woodlands to upper montane coniferous forests **Elevation:** 6200–8600 ft. **Ecoregions:** Sierra Nevada

Erect, branched annual with white-hairy lower stems. Leaves to 0.3 in. long, alternate, spoon-shaped to ovoid, with smooth to toothed margins. Flowers 2 per stem. Calyces to 0.2 in. long, 5-lobed, with lobes connected by a narrow (≤ lobe width), thin membrane. Corollas to 0.3 in. long, narrowly funnel-shaped, yellow tube and throat, and short-pointed, white lobes. Fruits 30–45-seeded capsules.

Linanthus killipii

Baldwin Lake linanthus

POLEMONIACEAE PHLOX FAMILY

PCT Sections: 4 **Abundance:** Rare **Height:** 2–6 in. **Flowering:** May–June **Flower Color:** White **Habitat-Community:** Dry, open, gravelly soils in sagebrush scrubs, pinyon-juniper woodlands, and lower montane coniferous forests **Elevation:** 5300–7800 ft. **Ecoregions:** Southern California Mountains

Erect, diminutive annual, branched above, with hairy herbage. Leaves opposite and deeply lobed, with linear lobes 0.1–0.4 in. long. Flowers clustered at branch and stem tips, open during the day, sessile, 5-parted, tubular, with hairless calyces 0.3 in. long. Corollas funnel-shaped, yellow throat and tube 0.2 in. long, and white (red-spotted at base) lobes 0.2 in. long. Fruits ovoid capsules with 6–12 seeds. Endemic to the quartz-rich, pebble plains of the Big Bear Valley region of the San Bernardino Mountains. Threatened by urbanization, fire management, and recreational activities. It is named in honor of Ellsworth Paine Killip (1890–1968), curator of the botany department at the US National Museum (now the Smithsonian).

Linanthus pungens

granite prickly phlox

POLEMONIACEAE PHLOX FAMILY

PCT Sections: 3–5 & 8–24 **Abundance:** Common **Height:** 4–12 in. **Flowering:** May–September **Flower Color:** White or pink **Habitat-Community:** Rock outcrops and open, rocky slopes from scrubs and woodlands to alpine communities **Elevation:** 5500–13,200 ft. **Ecoregions:** Southern California Mountains, Sierra Nevada, Cascades, Klamath Mountains

Low, branched perennial with generally glandular-hairy stems. Leaves to 0.6 in. long, alternate, palmately 3–7-lobed, with sharp-tipped lobes. Flowers clustered at stem tips and open mostly in the evening. Calyces to 0.4 in. long, unequally 5-lobed, with lobes connected by a wide (> lobe width), thin membrane. Corollas to 1 in. long, funnel-shaped, white to pink tube and throat, and white or pink lobes with dark shading on outside edge. Fruits 15–30-seeded capsules. Its shrubby form is noticeable on rocky slopes.

Saltugilia australis
southern woodland gilia
POLEMONIACEAE PHLOX FAMILY

PCT Sections: 1–6 **Abundance:** Occasional **Height:** 3–20 in. **Flowering:** March–June **Flower Color:** White to pale pink **Habitat-Community:** Dry openings in gravelly or clayey soils in foothill chaparrals and oak woodlands **Elevation:** Below 4000 ft. **Ecoregions:** Southern California/Northern Baja Coast, Southern California Mountains

Erect, slender annual, branched above, with hairless to glandular herbage. Leaves basal in an erect rosette, 2–3 pinnately lobed, with linear lobes 1–6 in. long; stem leaves alternate, reduced. Flowers generally solitary at branch and stem tips, 5-parted, tubular, with hairless calyces 0.1–0.2 in. long. Corollas 0.2–0.4 in. long, tube included in calyx, white throat, and white lobes. Fruits ovoid capsules with 21–39 seeds. Plants in this genus differ from those in *Gilia* by having translucent hairs and basal leaves that are minutely glandular.

Datura wrightii
Jimson weed
SOLANACEAE NIGHTSHADE FAMILY

PCT Sections: 1–8 **Abundance:** Occasional **Height:** 1–5 ft. **Flowering:** April–October **Flower Color:** White **Habitat-Community:** Sandy to gravelly soils in washes and disturbed areas in creosote bush scrubs, foothill chaparrals, and Joshua tree & pinyon-juniper woodlands **Elevation:** Below 6800 ft. **Ecoregions:** All (except Cascades, Klamath Mountains)

Vigorous perennial forming mounds up to 6 ft. across with white-hairy stems. Leaves 3–8 in. long, alternate, short-petioled, ovoid, dark green, with smooth to lobed margins. Flowers often nodding, 5-parted, fused, trumpet-shaped, with calyces 0.3–0.5 in. long and white corollas 6–8 in. long. Fruits 1–1.3 in. long, prickly capsules. The sweetly scented flowers open at night, attracting large hawkmoths. Aka sacred datura: it contains alkaloids, including atropine and hyoscine, and although its narcotic and hallucinogenic properties have been utilized in rituals by Indigenous peoples, modern-day experimentations have resulted in numerous deaths!

Nicotiana attenuata
coyote tobacco
SOLANACEAE NIGHTSHADE FAMILY

PCT Sections: All (except 11–14) **Abundance:** Occasional **Height:** 1–4 ft. **Flowering:** May–October **Flower Color:** White to cream **Habitat-Community:** Sandy areas, burns, and disturbed soils in chaparrals, oak & pinyon-juniper woodlands, and lower montane coniferous forests **Elevation:** Below 9200 ft. **Ecoregions:** All

Erect, fast-growing annual, single-stemmed or branched and bushy, with glandular-hairy herbage. Leaves 1–4 in. long, alternate, mostly concentrated at stem base, elliptic to lance-shaped, with smooth margins. Flowers nodding, 5-parted, tubular, calyces 0.2–0.4 in. long, and corollas 0.8–1.2 in. long with pale green tube and white lobes. Fruits 0.3–0.5 in. long, many-seeded capsules. This western US native is a bit weedy in its ability to colonize disturbed areas; it is increasingly abundant along recently burned sections of the trail. *Nicotiana* was named by Linnaeus in 1753 for Jean Nicot (1530–1600), the French ambassador to Portugal.

Valeriana californica

California valerian

VALERIANACEAE VALERIAN FAMILY

PCT Sections: 10–24 **Abundance:** Locally common **Height:** 10–20 in. **Flowering:** June–August **Flower Color:** White **Habitat-Community:** Generally moist places in upper montane & subalpine coniferous forests and wetland-riparian communities **Elevation:** Below 12,200 ft. **Ecoregions:** Sierra Nevada, Cascades, Klamath Mountains

Perennial with hairy or hairless stems and mostly basal leaves. Leaves to 5 in. long, basal (mostly) and opposite, compound or 3–9-lobed with the terminal lobe > lateral lobes and smooth to toothed margins. Flowers clustered at leaf axils and stem tips. Calyx lobes 5–15, curved inward, feather-like in age. Corollas to 0.2 in. long, funnel-shaped, white, with 1 pistil and 3 stamens. Fruits to 0.3 in. long, hairy or hairless achenes. *Valeriana* ("strength") is either a reference to its Old World use in medicine or to the Roman emperor Valerian. Used by Indigenous peoples in California to cure stomach problems.

▼ 5 FUSED PETALS / IRREGULAR COROLLAS

Nemacladus longiflorus

longflower threadplant

CAMPANULACEAE
BELLFLOWER FAMILY

PCT Sections: 1–5 & 8 **Abundance:** Locally common **Height:** 2–8 in. **Flowering:** April–June **Flower Color:** White **Habitat-Community:** Sandy to gravelly flats and washes in foothill chaparrals, woodlands, and lower montane coniferous forests **Elevation:** Below 7800 ft. **Ecoregions:** Southern California Mountains, Mojave Basin and Range, Sierra Nevada

Slender, thread-like, much-branched annual with shiny, brownish purple stems. Leaves 0.1–0.6 in. long, basal, spoon-shaped to ovoid, hairy, with smooth to finely scalloped margins. Flowers scattered along zig-zag branches on S-shaped pedicels, 5-parted, irregular, and inverted (upside-down). Corollas 0.1–0.4 in. long, white (deep pink lower surface), 2-lipped, fused halfway to base, cylindric tube with a distinctive, orange-spotted throat, 2 erect upper lobes, and 3 spreading lower lobes. Fruits 0.1–0.2 in. long, capsules with narrow ends. *Nemacladus* (from the Greek, "thread-like branch") is an apt name.

Monardella exilis

mustang mint

LAMIACEAE MINT FAMILY

PCT Sections: 4–10 **Abundance:** Locally common **Height:** 3–14 in. **Flowering:** April–September **Flower Color:** White to pale purple **Habitat-Community:** Sandy soils in washes and on alluvial fans in creosote bush scrubs and Joshua tree & pinyon-juniper woodlands **Elevation:** Below 6600 ft. **Ecoregions:** Southern California Mountains, Mojave Basin and Range, Sierra Nevada

Erect, simple or branched annual with 4-angled, short-hairy stems. Leaves 0.6–1.4 in. long, opposite, lance-shaped, green, short-hairy, with obvious petioles. Flowers in compact clusters at tips of stems, 5-lobed, with ovoid, pale green (purple-tinged) outer bracts 0.4–0.8 in. wide, long-hairy. Corollas 0.4 in. long, irregular, 2-lipped, white, with erect 2-lobed upper lip and recurved 3-lobed lower lip, lobes gland-tipped. Fruits 4 ovoid nutlets. During years of high winter precipitation, this aromatic annual may form an extensive groundcover in openings among shrubs. *Exilis* means "small and slender."

Monardella nana

little monardella

LAMIACEAE MINT FAMILY

PCT Sections: 1–3 **Abundance:** Occasional **Height:** 2–12 in. **Flowering:** May–August **Flower Color:** White to cream **Habitat-Community:** Dry, gravelly to rocky slopes and crevices in Sonoran mixed woody scrubs, chaparrals, and lower montane coniferous forests **Elevation:** Below 8200 ft. **Ecoregions:** Southern California Mountains

Matted to prostrate perennial or subshrub with short, leafy stems covered with recurved or spreading hairs. Leaves 0.3–1.1 in. long, opposite, ovoid to round, hairless to short-hairy, with obvious petioles. Flowers in compact clusters at tips of stems, 5-lobed. Calyces white, ovoid, long-hairy, resembling leaves, usually with green outer bracts 0.4–1.4. wide; contrasting middle bracts are conspicuously white (rose- or purple-tinged). Corollas 0.6–1.2 in. long, irregular, fused into a long, cylindric tube, generally 2-lipped, with 5 white to cream, narrow, elongated, spreading lobes. Fruits 4 small, ovoid nutlets. This attractive mint is highly variable, with many subspecies and varieties. Look for it along the PCT atop the San Jacinto and Laguna Mountains.

Stachys albens

whitestem hedgenettle

LAMIACEAE MINT FAMILY

PCT Sections: 3–11 **Abundance:** Occasional **Height:** 1–7 ft. **Flowering:** March–July **Flower Color:** White to pale pink-blue **Habitat-Community:** Moist soils, meadows, swamps, seeps, and streambanks in wetland-riparian communities from oak woodlands to subalpine coniferous forests **Elevation:** Below 10,200 ft. **Ecoregions:** Southern California Mountains, Sierra Nevada

Erect perennial with cobwebby stems and fuzzy leaves. Leaves 1–6 in. long, opposite, petioled, lance-shaped to ovoid, soft long-hairy, with toothed margins. Flowers in interrupted clusters along spikes, 5-lobed, with bell-shaped calyces to 0.3 in. long. Corollas 0.3–0.5 in. long, irregular, 2-lipped, white to pink, upper lip 0.1–0.3 in. long, and lower lip longer, 3-lobed, with central lobe being the largest. Fruits 4 small nutlets. Endemic to California. This mint-scented herb is not related to stinging nettle, so if you touch it, don't worry—be happy!

Castilleja attenuata

valley tassels

OROBANCHACEAE
BROOMRAPE FAMILY

PCT Sections: 1–2 & 7–8 **Abundance:** Occasional **Height:** 4–20 in. **Flowering:** March–May **Flower Color:** White to pale purple **Habitat-Community:** Heavy soils, open grassy areas, and dry meadows in wetland-riparian communities, California prairies, and foothill chaparrals **Elevation:** Below 5200 ft. **Ecoregions:** Southern California Mountains, Sierra Nevada

Erect, few-branched annual with spreading-hairy stems; hemiparasitic. Leaves 0.8–2.4 in. long, alternate, and 0–3-lobed with linear lobes. Flowers in delicate, spike-like stalks, irregular, white, with 3-lobed bracts 0.6–1.4 in. long, and unequally 4-lobed calyces 0.4–0.8 in. long (divided half the length). Corollas 0.4–1.1 in. long, 2-lipped, upper lip 2-lobed with a fused beak, lower lip white (with purple dots), reduced, pouched. Fruits 0.3–0.5 in. long, ovoid capsules. Common species of California's Central Valley, found along the PCT only as a disjunct occurrence in San Diego and Kern counties. Look for it near Lake Morena, north of Warner Springs, and the Tehachapi Mountains.

Cordylanthus nevinii

Nevin's bird's beak

OROBANCHACEAE

BROOMRAPE FAMILY

PCT Sections: 1 & 3–5 **Abundance:** Locally common **Height:** 8–30 in. **Flowering:** July–September **Flower Color:** White to purple **Habitat-Community:** Open areas and burns in oak woodlands and montane coniferous forests **Elevation:** Below 8000 ft. **Ecoregions:** Southern California Mountains

Ascending to erect, wispy annual, densely coated in glandular hairs with gray-green (red-purple-tinged) herbage; hemiparasitic. Leaves 0.2–1.3 in. long, alternate, sessile, linear, sometimes 3-lobed. Flowers in loose clusters of 1–3, irregular, with 3-lobed outer bracts 0.2–0.4 in. long and sheath-like calyces 0.4–0.6 in. long. Corollas 0.5–0.8 in. long, tubular, 2-lipped, upper lip white to purple-streaked, beaked, lower lip forming a pouch 0.2–0.3 in. wide. Fruits small, ovoid capsules. All bird's beaks are hemiparasitic on the roots of neighboring trees, shrubs, and perennials. Named after Joseph Cook Nevin (1835–1913), who collected in both China and California.

Antirrhinum coulterianum

Coulter's snapdragon

PLANTAGINACEAE

PLANTAIN FAMILY

PCT Sections: 1–6 **Abundance:** Locally common **Height:** 5–45 in. **Flowering:** April–July **Flower Color:** White to pale lavender **Habitat-Community:** Open areas and burns from California prairies to lower montane coniferous forests **Elevation:** Below 8400 ft. **Ecoregions:** Southern California/Northern Baja Coast, Southern California Mountains

Erect, stalky, fleshy annual, sometimes supported by other plants. Leaves 1–4 in. long, basal and alternate, linear to lance-shaped. Flowers in spikes, irregular, densely glandular-hairy, with 5-parted (upper lobes longest) calyces. Corollas 0.4–0.5 in. long, white to lavender, short-tubular, 2-lipped, upper lip 2-lobed, lower lip swollen (closing throat). Fruits 0.2–0.4 in. long, ovoid capsules. Frequently colonizes recent burns, especially in interior chaparral, where it's most abundant.

Loeseliastrum schottii

Schott's calico

POLEMONIACEAE PHLOX FAMILY

PCT Sections: 1–4 & 6–7 **Abundance:** Occasional **Height:** 1–5 in. **Flowering:** March–June **Flower Color:** White, pale yellow, or pink **Habitat-Community:** Dry washes in sandy to gravelly alluvium in creosote bush & sagebrush scrubs and Joshua tree & pinyon-juniper woodlands **Elevation:** Below 5600 ft. **Ecoregions:** Southern California Mountains, Sonoran/Mojave Basin and Range, Sierra Nevada

Cute but prickly annual with clustered, reddish, white-hairy stems. Leaves 0.3–1.2 in. long, generally alternate, spoon-shaped, and pinnately lobed with sharply bristle-tipped lobes. Flowers above leaf-like bracts, irregular, 5-lobed, with equal, bristle-tipped calyx lobes. Corollas 0.3–0.6 in. long, fused at base, white, pale yellow, or pink (maroon-streaked lobe bases), weakly to strongly 2-lipped, 3–4-lobed upper lip 0.1–0.3 in. long, and 1–2-lobed lower lip (slightly shorter than upper). Fruits small capsules. Look for it along the CA PCT at the lower desert crossings.

Lewisia glandulosa

Sierra lewisia

MONTIACEAE

MINER'S LETTUCE FAMILY

PCT Sections: 10–12 **Abundance:** Occasional **Height:** 1–2.5 in. **Flowering:** July–September **Flower Color:** White, pink, or reddish **Habitat-Community:** Rock outcrops, crevices in canyon walls, granitic sands, and wet meadows in alpine communities **Elevation:** 9800–13,200 ft. **Ecoregions:** Sierra Nevada

Fleshy perennial with many, rosetted leaves. Leaves 0.8–4 in. long, basal, thread-like to narrowly lance-shaped, with smooth margins. Flowers 1–2 per stem, in or above the leaves. Sepals to 0.2 in. long, 2, with gland-toothed (red to dark) margins. Petals to 0.3 in. long, 6–8, white, pink, or reddish, and free. Fruits to 0.6 in. long, capsules with up to 24 dark, generally shiny seeds. *Lewisia* honors Meriwether Lewis (1774–1809), of the Lewis and Clark Expedition.

Lewisia nevadensis

Nevada lewisia

MONTIACEAE

MINER'S LETTUCE FAMILY

PCT Sections: 4 & 9–24 **Abundance:** Locally common **Height:** 1–4 in. **Flowering:** May–August **Flower Color:** White or pale pink **Habitat-Community:** Sandy or gravelly soils and meadows from lower montane coniferous forests to alpine and wetland-riparian communities **Elevation:** Below 9900 ft. **Ecoregions:** Southern California Mountains, Sierra Nevada, Cascades, Klamath Mountains

Fleshy perennial with few to many, open-rosetted leaves. Leaves 1.2–5 in. long, basal, thread-like to narrowly lance-shaped, with smooth margins. Flowers 1–3 per stem, generally above the leaves. Sepals to 0.6 in. long, 2, with smooth or toothed margins. Petals 0.4–0.8 in. long, 5–10, white or pale pink, and free. Fruits to 0.4 in. long, capsules with 20–50 dark, generally shiny seeds.

Lewisia rediviva

bitterroot

MONTIACEAE

MINER'S LETTUCE FAMILY

PCT Sections: 3–5 & 7–9 & 21 **Abundance:** Rare **Height:** 1–3 in. **Flowering:** March–June **Flower Color:** White to pink or lavender **Habitat-Community:** Rocky to sandy soils in woodlands and montane coniferous forests **Elevation:** Below 7800 ft. **Ecoregions:** Southern California Mountains, Sierra Nevada, Klamath Mountains

Ground-hugging perennial with a simple or branched base. Leaves 0.1–2.1 in. long, in basal rosettes, linear, thick, succulent. Flowers 1.5–2.6 in. across, symmetric, with 6–9 sepals and 10–19 white to pink or lavender petals 0.8–1.3 in. long (> sepals). Fruits ovoid capsules with 6–20 seeds. First collected by Meriwether Lewis in the Bitterroot Mountains of Montana; it remains the state flower of Montana. *Rediviva* (from the Latin, "revived") refers to the plant's ability to regenerate from dry and seemingly dead roots.

Lewisia triphylla

threeleaf lewisia

MONTIACEAE

MINER'S LETTUCE FAMILY

PCT Sections: 10–24 **Abundance:** Occasional **Height:** 1–4 in. **Flowering:** May–August **Flower Color:** White or pinkish **Habitat-Community:** Moist, sandy or gravelly soils and meadows from lower montane to subalpine coniferous forests and wetland-riparian communities **Elevation:** Below 11,200 ft. **Ecoregions:** Sierra Nevada, Cascades, Klamath Mountains

Perennial with leaves that wither before flowering. Leaves 1.2–5 in. long, 2–5 along stem, opposite, thread-like or linear, with smooth margins. Flowers 1–25 per stem and generally 1–several stems per plant. Sepals to 0.2 in. long, 2, with smooth or toothed margins. Petals 0.2–0.3 in. long, 5–9, white or pinkish, and free. Fruits to 0.2 in. long, capsules with 8–25 dark, generally shiny seeds. The only lewisia along the PCT that lacks basal leaves.

Canbya candida

white pygmypoppy

PAPAVERACEAE POPPY FAMILY

PCT Sections: 4–8 **Abundance:** Rare **Height:** 2–12 in. **Flowering:** March–June **Flower Color:** White **Habitat-Community:** Sandy soils, dunes, alluvial fans, and washes in creosote bush scrubs and Joshua tree woodlands **Elevation:** Below 4500 ft. **Ecoregions:** Southern California Mountains, Mojave Basin and Range, Sierra Nevada

Clumped, diminutive annual with mostly hairless herbage. Leaves 0.2–0.4 in. long, in basal clumps, linear to oblong, somewhat fleshy, with smooth margins. Flowers 0.3 in. across, symmetric, with 3 sepals, 5–7 white petals 0.1–0.2 in. long, and many yellow stamens. Fruits to 0.1 in. across, capsules. Germinates only in years of abundant winter rains. Easily overlooked but satisfying when found along the PCT at the lower Mojave Desert crossings.

Actaea rubra

red baneberry

RANUNCULACEAE

BUTTERCUP FAMILY

PCT Sections: 4 & 10–24 **Abundance:** Locally common **Height:** 7–40 in. **Flowering:** May–September **Flower Color:** White or purple-green **Habitat-Community:** Streambanks and deep soils from lower montane to subalpine coniferous forests and wetland-riparian communities **Elevation:** Below 9200 ft. **Ecoregions:** Southern California Mountains, Sierra Nevada, Cascades, Klamath Mountains

Ascending to erect, 1–few-stemmed, branched perennial with sparsely hairy stems. Leaves to 24 in. long, alternate, 1–3-pinnately compound, with lance-shaped to ovoid or roundish, tooth-margined leaflets to 3.5 in. long. Flowers many in clustered spikes at stem tips, with many stamens. Sepals to 0.2 in. long, 3–5, petal-like, white or purple-green. Petals to 0.2 in. long, 4–10, spoon-shaped, white, dropping soon after flowering. Fruits to 0.4 in. across, red or white berries. The word *bane* is Anglo-Saxon for "murderous." Caution: the entire plant, including berries, is toxic!

Anemone occidentalis

white pasqueflower

RANUNCULACEAE

BUTTERCUP FAMILY

PCT Sections: 10–23 **Abundance:** Locally common **Height:** 4–30 in. **Flowering:** May–September **Flower Color:** White **Habitat-Community:** Open, rocky soils from lower montane coniferous forests to alpine communities **Elevation:** Below 10,500 ft. **Ecoregions:** Sierra Nevada, Cascades, Klamath Mountains

Clumped, 1–few-stemmed perennial with stout, hairy herbage. Leaves alternate, 2–3-pinnately lobed, with terminal leaflet to 0.3 in. long and linear leaflet segments to 0.1 in. wide. Flowers mostly 1 at stem tips, with 0 petals, many pistils, and 150–200 stamens. Sepals to 1.2 in. long, ≥0.4 in. wide, 5–7, petal-like, white with pale blue, soft-hairy lower surface. Fruits in spherical heads to 0.2 in. long with feathery, shaggy-hairy curved beaks to 2 in. long. The mophead-like fruit clusters are easy to spot long after the flowers (which open as the snow is melting) are gone. Aka Einstein heads.

Caltha leptosepala

marsh marigold

RANUNCULACEAE

BUTTERCUP FAMILY

PCT Sections: 10–24 **Abundance:** Locally common **Height:** 3–19 in. **Flowering:** May–July **Flower Color:** White **Habitat-Community:** Marshes, meadows, bogs, and fens in wetland-riparian communities **Elevation:** Below 10,900 ft. **Ecoregions:** Sierra Nevada, Cascades, Klamath Mountains

Clumped, 1–few-stemmed perennial with fleshy, hairless herbage, growing in spreading colonies. Leaves to 3.5 in. across, basal, roundish to heart-shaped, with wavy, toothed margins. Flowers 1–4 at stem tips, with 0 petals, many pistils, and 150–200 stamens. Sepals to 0.6 in. long, 5–11, petal-like, white. Fruits to 0.7 in. long, straight- or curved-beak follicles. Look for the flowers at or near ground level.

YELLOW

▼ COMPOSITE / RAY AND DISK FLOWERS

Arnica chamissonis

Chamisso arnica

STERACEAE SUNFLOWER FAMILY

PCT Sections: 4 & 9–19 **Abundance:** Locally common **Height:** 1–3 ft. **Flowering:** June–August **Flower Color:** Yellow **Habitat-Community:** Moist places and rocky slopes from lower montane to subalpine coniferous forests **Elevation:** 5900–11,500 ft. **Ecoregions:** Southern California Mountains, Sierra Nevada, Cascades, Klamath Mountains

Erect, single-stemmed perennial with stems glandular-hairy at tip. Leaves 2–12 in. long, 4–10 pairs along stem, opposite, lance-shaped, hairy, with smooth or toothed margins. Flowers 3–10 heads per cluster, with bell-shaped, hair-tufted (near tip) involucres 0.3–0.6 in. long. Ray flowers 0.4–0.8 in. long, 13 per head, yellow. Disk flowers to 0.2 in. long, many per head, cylindric, densely soft-hairy, yellow. Fruits to 0.3 in. long, cylindric, 5–10-veined, hairy or hairless achenes with many brown bristles. Tallest arnica along the CA PCT. Arnicas are one of the few composites with opposite leaves; all can be used externally as an antiseptic.

Arnica cordifolia

heartleaf arnica

ASTERACEAE SUNFLOWER FAMILY

PCT Sections: 10–24 **Abundance:** Common **Height:** 6–24 in. **Flowering:** May–August **Flower Color:** Yellow **Habitat-Community:** Meadows and understories from lower montane to subalpine coniferous forests and wetland-riparian communities **Elevation:** Below 11,200 ft. **Ecoregions:** Sierra Nevada, Cascades, Klamath Mountains

Erect, single- to few-stemmed, unbranched perennial with glandular-hairy stems. Leaves 1–4.5 in. long, 2–4 pairs along stem, opposite, heart-shaped, hairy, with smooth or toothed margins. Flowers 1–5 heads per cluster, with bell-shaped, white-hairy involucres 0.5–1.2 in. long. Ray flowers to 1.2 in. long, 6–13 per head, yellow. Disk flowers many per head, cylindric, densely soft-hairy, glandular, yellow. Fruits to 0.4 in. long, cylindric, 5–10-veined, hairy or glandular achenes with many white bristles.

Arnica lanceolata subsp. prima

clasping arnica

ASTERACEAE SUNFLOWER FAMILY

PCT Sections: 10–24 **Abundance:** Occasional **Height:** 20–32 in. **Flowering:** July–September **Flower Color:** Yellow **Habitat-Community:** Moist places, especially streambanks, from lower montane to subalpine coniferous forests and wetland-riparian communities **Elevation:** 7200–11,500 ft. **Ecoregions:** Sierra Nevada, Cascades, Klamath Mountains

Erect, single-stemmed, branched perennial with glandular-hairy stems on upper portion. Leaves 1.5–5 in. long, 4–10 pairs along stem, opposite, oval to lance-shaped, hairy, with toothed margins. Flowers 3–10 heads per cluster, with bell-shaped, hairy involucres 0.3–0.6 in. long; phyllaries evenly hairy and acute at the tips. Ray flowers to 0.8 in. long, 7–17 per head, yellow. Disk flowers to 0.2 in. long, many per head, soft-hairy, yellow. Fruits to 0.4 in. long, hairy achenes with many brown bristles.

Arnica latifolia

broadleaf arnica

ASTERACEAE SUNFLOWER FAMILY

PCT Sections: 11–16 & 22–24 **Abundance:** Common **Height:** 1–2 ft. **Flowering:** June–August **Flower Color:** Yellow **Habitat-Community:** Moist places, including streambanks, in upper montane & subalpine coniferous forests and wetland-riparian communities **Elevation:** 5900–7800 ft. **Ecoregions:** Sierra Nevada, Klamath Mountains

Erect, single-stemmed, unbranched perennial with glandular-hairy or hairless stems, often growing in clusters. Leaves 0.8–6 in. long, 2–4 pairs along stem, opposite, round to lance-shaped, hairy to hairless at maturity, with toothed margins. Flowers 1–5 heads per cluster, with hemispheric, glandular-hairy involucres 0.2–0.7 in. long. Ray flowers to 1.2 in. long, 8–15 per head, yellow. Disk flowers many per head, cylindric, sparsely soft-hairy, yellow. Fruits to 0.4 in. long, cylindric, hairy or glandular achenes with many white bristles.

Arnica mollis

hairy arnica

ASTERACEAE SUNFLOWER FAMILY

PCT Sections: 10–24 **Abundance:** Common **Height:** 6–24 in. **Flowering:** June–September **Flower Color:** Yellow **Habitat-Community:** Meadows and streambanks in upper montane & subalpine coniferous forests and wetland-riparian communities **Elevation:** 8200–11,500 ft. **Ecoregions:** Sierra Nevada, Cascades, Klamath Mountains

Erect, single- to multi-stemmed, generally unbranched perennial with glandular-hairy stems. Leaves 1.5–8 in. long, 3–5 pairs along stem, opposite, elliptic, hairy, with smooth or toothed margins. Flowers 1–7 per cluster, with bell-shaped, soft-hairy involucres 0.4–0.6 in. long. Ray flowers to 1.2 in. long, 10–22 per head, yellow. Disk flowers many per head, cylindric, glandular, densely soft-hairy, yellow. Fruits to 0.3 in. long, cylindric, glandular-hairy achenes with many brown pappus bristles.

Arnica nevadensis

Sierra arnica

ASTERACEAE SUNFLOWER FAMILY

PCT Sections: 10–24 **Abundance:** Locally common **Height:** 4–12 in. **Flowering:** July–August **Flower Color:** Yellow **Habitat-Community:** Meadows and forest understories from upper montane coniferous forests to alpine communities **Elevation:** 5000–9900 ft. **Ecoregions:** Sierra Nevada, Cascades, Klamath Mountains

Erect, single- to multi-stemmed, unbranched perennial with glandular-hairy stems. Leaves 1.2–3.2 in. long, 2–3 pairs along stem, opposite, widely oval to round, hairy, with generally smooth margins. Flowers 1–3 per cluster, with cup-shaped, stalked-glandular, hairy involucres 0.4–0.7 in. long. Ray flowers to 0.8 in. long, 6–14 per head, yellow. Disk flowers many per head, cylindric, glandular, yellow. Fruits to 0.4 in. long, cylindric, glandular or hairy achenes with many brown to white bristles.

Arnica ovata

sticky leaf arnica

ASTERACEAE SUNFLOWER FAMILY

PCT Sections: 10–24 **Abundance:** Rare **Height:** 4–20 in. **Flowering:** June–October **Flower Color:** Yellow **Habitat-Community:** Moist, rocky or shaded slopes from lower montane to subalpine coniferous forests **Elevation:** 5900–11,800 ft. **Ecoregions:** Sierra Nevada, Cascades, Klamath Mountains

Erect, single- to multi-stemmed, unbranched perennial with glandular-hairy or hairless stems. Leaves 1.5–3 in. long, 2–4 pairs along stem, opposite, elliptic or ovoid to triangular, hairy or glandular surfaces, with toothed margins. Flowers 1–5 per cluster, with bell-shaped, soft-hairy, glandular involucres 0.4–0.6 in. long. Ray flowers to 0.8 in. long, 8–16 per head, yellow. Disk flowers many per head, cylindric, soft-hairy, yellow. Fruits to 0.3 in. long, cylindric, glandular-hairy achenes with many tan to brown pappus bristles.

Balsamorhiza deltoidea

deltoid balsamroot

ASTERACEAE SUNFLOWER FAMILY

PCT Sections: 6–9 & 15–17 & 19–20 & 24
Abundance: Common **Height:** 1–3 ft. **Flowering:** April–July **Flower Color:** Yellow **Habitat-Community:** Open slopes and meadows from scrubs, woodlands, and chaparrals to upper montane coniferous forests **Elevation:** Below 7800 ft. **Ecoregions:** Southern California Mountains, Sierra Nevada, Klamath Mountains

Erect perennial with glandular-hairy stems, clumped basal leaves, and reduced stem leaves, often growing in colonies. Leaves 8–24 in. long, opposite or alternate, widely spear-shaped, thinly hairy, with smooth to toothed margins. Flowers 1–2 per stem, with bell-shaped, glandular, long-hairy involucres 0.4–1.5 in. long. Ray flowers to 2 in. long, 13–21 per head, yellow. Disk flowers to 0.3 in. long, many per head, cylindric to narrowly bell-shaped, yellow. Fruits to 0.3 in. long, 3–4-angled oblong achenes without pappus. The hearts of the roots are edible, but please do not dig up and destroy these beautiful sunflowers unless it's an emergency!

Balsamorhiza sagittata

arrowleaf balsamroot

ASTERACEAE SUNFLOWER FAMILY

PCT Sections: 4 & 8–18 **Abundance:** Common **Height:** 0.5–3 ft. **Flowering:** May–August **Flower Color:** Yellow **Habitat-Community:** Sandy openings in sagebrush scrubs, woodlands, and lower montane coniferous forests **Elevation:** Below 8500 ft. **Ecoregions:** Southern California Mountains, Sierra Nevada, Cascades

Erect perennial with glandular-hairy stems, clumped basal leaves, and reduced stem leaves, often growing in large colonies. Leaves 8–24 in. long, opposite or alternate, widely triangular with heart-shaped base, densely gray-hairy (mostly when young), with smooth margins. Flowers 1–3 per stem, with bell-shaped, glandular, velvety involucres 0.4–1 in. long. Ray flowers to 2 in. long, yellow. Disk flowers to 0.3 in. long, many per head, cylindric to narrowly bell-shaped, yellow. Fruits to 0.4 in. long, 3–4-angled oblong achenes without pappus. The hearts of the roots are edible, but please, no wild harvesting unless it's an emergency!

Eriophyllum ambiguum

beautiful woolly sunflower

ASTERACEAE SUNFLOWER FAMILY

PCT Sections: 2–3 & 5 & 7–9 **Abundance:** Locally common **Height:** 3–15 in. **Flowering:** March–June **Flower Color:** Yellow **Habitat-Community:** Open, dry sites, washes, and sandy plains in creosote bush scrubs and Joshua tree & pinyon-juniper woodlands **Elevation:** Below 7600 ft. **Ecoregions:** Southern California Mountains, Sierra Nevada

Woolly-stemmed, erect to ascending, branched annual. Leaves 0.8–1.6 in. long, spoon-shaped, smooth to shallowly 3-lobed, and hairy. Flowers 1 per stem, peduncle 0.5–3 in. long, and involucres 0.2–0.3 in. long with 6–10 phyllaries. Ray flowers 0.1–0.4 in. long, 6–10 per head, tips slightly toothed, yellow. Disk flowers many per head, most commonly hairy, yellow. Fruits to 0.1 in. long, hairy achenes with 0 or 6–10 pappus scales. A species of the southern Sierra Nevada and western Mojave Desert, found along the PCT in the San Jacinto Mountains.

Eriophyllum lanatum

common woolly sunflower

ASTERACEAE SUNFLOWER FAMILY

PCT Sections: 4–5 & 10–24 **Abundance:** Common **Height:** 4–40 in. **Flowering:** May–August **Flower Color:** Yellow **Habitat-Community:** Rocky or sandy soils from sagebrush scrubs, woodlands, and chaparrals to alpine communities **Elevation:** Below 11,500 ft. **Ecoregions:** Southern California Mountains, Sierra Nevada, Cascades, Klamath Mountains

Erect perennial or subshrub with densely woolly stems. Leaves 0.4–3 in. long, alternate, unlobed to 2-pinnately compound, linear to oval, densely gray-hairy (mostly when young), with smooth to toothed margins. Flowers 1–5 heads per stem, with bell-shaped to hemispheric involucres 0.2–0.5 in. long. Ray flowers to 0.8 in. long, 5–15 per head, yellow. Disk flowers to 0.2 in. long, many per head, cylindric to narrowly bell-shaped, yellow. Fruits to 0.2 in. long, glandular or hairy achenes with 0–12 pappus scales. Occurs throughout California in many habitats.

Eriophyllum wallacei

Wallace's woolly sunflower

ASTERACEAE SUNFLOWER FAMILY

PCT Sections: 1–9 **Abundance:** Common **Height:** 1–6 in. **Flowering:** February–July **Flower Color:** Yellow **Habitat-Community:** Washes and sandy plains in creosote bush scrubs and Joshua tree & pinyon-juniper woodlands **Elevation:** Below 7800 ft. **Ecoregions:** Southern California Mountains, Sierra Nevada

Tiny, often tufted annual with cobwebby-hairy stems. Leaves 0.3–0.9 in. long, alternate, spoon-shaped, smooth to 3-lobed at the tips, hairy. Flowers with bell-shaped involucres 0.2–0.3 in. long and 5–10 phyllaries. Ray flowers 0.1–0.2 in. long, 5–10 per head, tips slightly toothed, yellow. Disk flowers many per head, sometimes minutely hairy, yellow. Fruits club-shaped achenes with 0–few pappus scales.

Euthamia occidentalis

western goldenrod

ASTERACEAE SUNFLOWER FAMILY

PCT Sections: 1–9 & 13–19 **Abundance:** Common **Height:** 3–6 ft. **Flowering:** July–November **Flower Color:** Yellow **Habitat-Community:** Meadows and streambanks in wetland-riparian communities **Elevation:** Below 7600 ft. **Ecoregions:** Southern California/Northern Baja Coast, Southern California Mountains, Sierra Nevada, Cascades

Erect, single- or multi-stemmed perennial with hairless stems and grass-like leaves. Leaves to 4 in. long, alternate, linear at midstem, resin-dotted, with rough margins. Flowers many heads per stem; involucres 0.1–0.2 in. long with sticky, resinous phyllaries in 3–5 graduated series. Ray flowers to 0.1 in. long, 15–28 per head, yellow. Disk flowers to 0.2 in. long, 6–18 per head, yellow. Fruits to 0.1 in. long, hairy achenes with 25–45 bristles in 2 series, outer < inner. Goldenrods have been used historically to cure various ailments.

Whitney's goldenbush

Hazardia whitneyi

ASTERACEAE SUNFLOWER FAMILY

PCT Sections: 10–17 & 20–24 **Abundance:** Occasional **Height:** 8–20 in. **Flowering:** July–September **Flower Color:** Yellow **Habitat-Community:** Rocky, open slopes and serpentine soils in montane coniferous forests **Elevation:** Below 10,000 ft. **Ecoregions:** Sierra Nevada, Klamath Mountains

Ascending, multi-stemmed perennial with hairy stems and sharp-toothed leaves. Leaves 1–2 in. long, alternate, widely oblong to spoon-shaped, hairy, glandular, with toothed margins. Flowers in single radiate or discoid head per stem; bell-shaped involucres 0.2–0.5 in. long with glandular, sometimes recurved phyllaries in 4–6 graduated series. Ray flowers 0.2–0.3 in. long, (0)5–18 per head, yellow. Disk flowers to 0.4 in. long, 15–30 per head, yellow. Fruits to 0.4 in. long, hairless achenes with 20–60 brown bristles.

Bigelow's sneezeweed

Helenium bigelovii

ASTERACEAE SUNFLOWER FAMILY

PCT Sections: 3–5 & 10–24 **Abundance:** Common **Height:** 1–4 ft. **Flowering:** June–September **Flower Color:** Yellow **Habitat-Community:** Meadows, fens, bogs, lakeshores, and streambanks in wetland-riparian communities **Elevation:** Below 11,200 ft. **Ecoregions:** Southern California Mountains, Sierra Nevada, Cascades, Klamath Mountains

Erect, mostly unbranched perennial with hairy or hairless stems and showy flower heads. Leaves 4–10 in. long, alternate, linear or oblong to spoon- or lance-shaped, hairy or hairless, with smooth margins. Flowers 1–20 dome-shaped heads per stem, with hairy, basally fused phyllaries in 2 equal series. Ray flowers 0.5–1 in. long, 14–20 per head, drooping, yellow (in California). Disk flowers to 0.4 in. long, 250–500+ per head, yellow to brown or purple. Fruits to 0.1 in. long, hairy achenes with 6–8 awn-tipped pappus scales. Often forms large colonies. *Helenium* honors Helen of Troy. The dried flowers and leaves were used as a snuff to induce sneezing (hence the common name), as a way to clear colds, headaches, and evil spirits.

common sunflower

Helianthus annuus

ASTERACEAE SUNFLOWER FAMILY

PCT Sections: 1–9 & 12–15 **Abundance:** Locally common **Height:** to 10 ft. **Flowering:** June–October **Flower Color:** Yellow **Habitat-Community:** Disturbed places from California prairies to upper montane coniferous forests **Elevation:** Below 6600 ft. **Ecoregions:** Southern California/Northern Baja Coast, Southern California Mountains, Sonoran Basin and Range, Sierra Nevada

Tall, showy annual with stiff-hairy stems. Leaves 4–16 in. long, mostly alternate, widely lance-shaped to triangular-ovoid, bristly below, sometimes gland-dotted. Flowers 1–9 per stem; involucres 0.6–1.6 in. across with phyllaries 0.5–1 in. long. Ray flowers 0.2–2 in. long, 13–30+ per head, yellow. Disk flowers many per head, yellow or red to purple. Fruits to 0.6 in. long, achenes with pappus scales. Found throughout California, especially along roads, across to eastern North America. Flowers are thought to turn during the day to face the sun (hence *Helianthus*, from the Greek *helios*, "sun," *anthos*, "flower"). *Annuus* is Latin for "annual."

Helianthus gracilentus

slender sunflower

ASTERACEAE SUNFLOWER FAMILY

PCT Sections: 1–6 **Abundance:** Occasional **Height:** 2–6 ft. **Flowering:** April–October **Flower Color:** Yellow **Habitat-Community:** Hillside slopes and sunny ridges in chaparrals and oak woodlands **Elevation:** Below 6300 ft. **Ecoregions:** Southern California Mountains

Perennial with stiff-hairy stems from a thick taproot. Leaves 2.5–4.4 in. long, opposite or alternate near branch tips, lance-shaped, bristly gland-dotted below, dark green. Flowers 1–5 per stem; involucres 0.5–0.9 in. across with unequal phyllaries 0.2–0.4 in. long. Ray flowers 0.6–0.9 in. long, 13–21 per head, yellow. Disk flowers many per head, yellow or red. Fruits to 0.2 in. long, achenes with pappus scales. Most common along the PCT in San Diego and Riverside counties; infrequent elsewhere.

Hemizonella minima

opposite-leaved tarweed

ASTERACEAE SUNFLOWER FAMILY

PCT Sections: 3–5 & 8–24 **Abundance:** Common **Height:** to 8 in. **Flowering:** April–July **Flower Color:** Yellow **Habitat-Community:** Meadows, open forest, and serpentine soils from oak woodlands to upper montane coniferous forests **Elevation:** Below 8500 ft. **Ecoregions:** Sierra Nevada, Cascades, Klamath Mountains

Small, slender, many-branched annual with hairs below and glands on upper stems. Leaves to 1 in. long, alternate/clustered (lower stem) and opposite (upper stem), linear, hairy and glandular-hairy, with smooth to toothed margins. Flowers 1–few heads per stem, with 3–5 phyllaries, each enclosing a ray fruit. Ray flowers to 0.1 in. long, 3–5 per head, yellow. Disk flowers to 0.1 in. long, 1–2 per head, yellow. Fruits to 0.1 in. long, generally hairy achenes with no pappus. *Hemizonella* ("smaller than *Hemizonia*," from *hemi* "half," *zone*, "girdle," "belt") refers to the way the phyllaries half enclose the fruits.

Heterotheca grandiflora

telegraph weed

ASTERACEAE SUNFLOWER FAMILY

PCT Sections: 1–4 **Abundance:** Occasional **Height:** 1–7 ft. **Flowering:** June–October **Flower Color:** Yellow **Habitat-Community:** Streambeds, sandy flats, and disturbed areas in foothill chaparrals and oak woodlands **Elevation:** Below 3900 ft. **Ecoregions:** Southern California Mountains

Tall annual or perennial with bristly and glandular stems. Leaves 1–3 in. long, basal in rosettes and alternate, clasping the lower stem, ovoid to lance-shaped, lobed or toothed, and becoming glandular near the flowering branches. Flowers few to many in flat-topped clusters; involucres 0.2–0.5 in. long, glandular, with 4–6 series of phyllaries. Ray flowers 0.2–0.3 in. long, 25–40 per head, bright yellow. Disk flowers 30–75 per head, yellow. Fruits hairless or minutely hairy achenes, with 0 pappus on ray fruits and long, white bristles on disk fruits. Found along the PCT at the lower-elevation segments in southern California, often in disturbed areas.

Heterotheca sessiliflora

sessileflower false goldenaster

ASTERACEAE SUNFLOWER FAMILY

PCT Sections: 2–8 **Abundance:** Locally common **Height:** 10–28 in. **Flowering:** June–October **Flower Color:** Yellow **Habitat-Community:** Sandy or disturbed soils in foothill chaparrals, oak woodlands, and wetland-riparian communities **Elevation:** Below 6600 ft. **Ecoregions:** Southern California Mountains, Sierra Nevada

Decumbent to erect, branching-above perennial with bristly and glandular stems. Leaves 0.7–1.3 in. long, basal and alternate, generally lacking petioles, spoon-shaped, white-hairy, with flat to wavy margins. Flowers many in flat-topped clusters, composite, radiate; involucres 0.3–0.6 in. long, hairy, glandular, with 4–6 series of phyllaries. Ray flowers 0.3–0.6 in. long, 4–24 per head, bright yellow. Disk flowers 20–50 per head, yellow. Fruits hairy achenes with white bristles. *Heterotheca* (from the Latin, "different ovaries") refers to the dissimilar achenes of the ray and disk flowers; but in this species, the achenes are actually quite similar.

Hulsea algida

Pacific hulsea

ASTERACEAE SUNFLOWER FAMILY

PCT Sections: 10–14 **Abundance:** Locally common **Height:** 4–16 in. **Flowering:** July–August **Flower Color:** Yellow **Habitat-Community:** Rocky or sandy slopes and ridges in alpine communities **Elevation:** 9800–14,100 ft. **Ecoregions:** Sierra Nevada

Erect, single-stemmed perennial with hairy, glandular stems. Leaves to 6 in. long, basal (mostly) and alternate, linear, hairy, folded upward, with toothed margins. Flowers 1(2) heads per stem, with glandular phyllaries in 2–3 graduated series. Ray flowers to 0.6 in. long, 25–60 per head, yellow. Disk flowers to 0.4 in. long, many per head, yellow. Fruits to 0.4 in. long, hairy black achenes with pappus scales. *Algida* ("cold") refers to the ridges and slopes above timberline where you can see this flashy sunflower, first found by John Muir atop Mt. Lyell in 1872.

Hulsea californica

San Diego sunflower

ASTERACEAE SUNFLOWER FAMILY

PCT Sections: 1–2 **Abundance:** Rare **Height:** 1–4 ft. **Flowering:** May–August **Flower Color:** Yellow **Habitat-Community:** Open areas on slopes and ridges in chaparrals and oak woodlands **Elevation:** Below 6500 ft. **Ecoregions:** Southern California Mountains

Clumpy biennial with greenish gray to reddish woolly stems. Leaves 2–4 in. long, basal or alternate, scoop-shaped, becoming smaller up the stem, white-cobwebby, with mostly smooth margins. Flowers 2–5 per plant at stem tips, composite, radiate; involucres 0.6–1.1 in. long with lance-linear phyllaries 0.3–0.7 in. long. Ray flowers 0.6–0.9 in. long, 22–40 per head, bright yellow. Disk flowers many per head, deep yellow. Fruits silky achenes with pappus scales. Most individuals appear haggard and scruffy, like they just woke up. Endemic to the southern Peninsular Ranges. Look for it along the PCT in the Bucksnort and Laguna Mountains, especially in burns or chaparral and woodland clearings.

Hulsea vestita subsp. *vestita*

pumice alpinegold

ASTERACEAE SUNFLOWER FAMILY

PCT Sections: 9–11 **Abundance:** Rare **Height:** 4–16 in. **Flowering:** May–October **Flower Color:** Yellow **Habitat-Community:** Rocky slopes and ridges from sagebrush scrubs to subalpine coniferous forests **Elevation:** 7900–11,200 ft. **Ecoregions:** Sierra Nevada

Erect, sometimes leafless perennial with woolly herbage. Leaves to 3.2 in. long, basal (mostly) and alternate, spoon-shaped, woolly below, with smooth-margined basal leaves. Flowers 1–2 heads per stem, with densely woolly, red-tipped phyllaries in 2–3 graduated series. Ray flowers to 0.4 in. long, 9–32 per head, generally yellow. Disk flowers to 0.4 in. long, many per head, yellow. Fruits to 0.3 in. long, hairy achenes with pappus scales.

Lagophylla ramosissima

common hareleaf

ASTERACEAE SUNFLOWER FAMILY

PCT Sections: 1–7 & 16–19 **Abundance:** Common **Height:** 1–6 in. **Flowering:** April–October **Flower Color:** Yellow **Habitat-Community:** Open, generally hard, dry soils from California prairies to lower montane coniferous forests **Elevation:** Below 7300 ft. **Ecoregions:** Southern California/ Northern Baja Coast, Southern California Mountains, Sierra Nevada, Cascades

Erect, branched annual with hairy stems and glandular foliage. Leaves opposite on lower stem, alternate above, oblong to linear or spoon-shaped, gray-hairy, with smooth to toothed margins. Flowers in tightly or openly clustered heads, with long-hairy, glandular involucres to 0.3 in. long with 1 series of 5 phyllaries, each enveloping a ray ovary. Ray flowers to 0.3 in. long, 5 per head, yellow (red- to purple-veined below). Disk flowers 6 per head, yellow, with triangular lobes and purple anthers. Ray fruits generally compressed, hairless black achenes without pappus; disk fruits absent. *Lagophylla* ("hare leaf") refers to the softly furry leaves. Tends to flower later than surrounding vegetation, making the yellow flowers easier to spot.

Lasthenia californica subsp. *californica*

California goldfields

ASTERACEAE SUNFLOWER FAMILY

PCT Sections: 1–8 **Abundance:** Locally common **Height:** 6–24 in. **Flowering:** February–June **Flower Color:** Yellow **Habitat-Community:** Open areas from California prairies to lower montane coniferous forest, often in alkali or clay soils **Elevation:** Below 6000 ft. **Ecoregions:** Southern California Mountains, Sierra Nevada

Erect, delicate, few-branched annual with hairless or slightly hairy stems. Leaves 0.4–3.2 in. long, opposite, linear to lance-shaped. Flowers generally 1 per stem tip, composite, radiate; involucres hairy, hemispheric, 0.2–0.7 in. long, with 4–13 phyllaries in 1 series. Ray flowers 0.2–0.5 in. long, 6–13 per head, bright yellow. Disk flowers many per head, yellow to orange. Fruits to 0.1 in. long, achenes with 1–7 awn-tipped pappus scales. Found in large numbers with abundant rainfall, turning a landscape golden-yellow (hence the common name). The genus is named for Lasthenia, an Athenian girl who dressed as a boy in order to attend Plato's lectures.

royal goldfields

Lasthenia coronaria

ASTERACEAE SUNFLOWER FAMILY

PCT Sections: 1–4 **Abundance:** Occasional **Height:** 4–16 in. **Flowering:** February–June **Flower Color:** Yellow **Habitat-Community:** Open areas in California prairies, Sonoran mixed woody scrubs, and foothill chaparrals **Elevation:** Below 4900 ft. **Ecoregions:** Southern California Mountains

Sweet-scented, erect, mostly unbranched annual with bare or variously hairy and glandular stems. Leaves 0.7–2.5 in. long, opposite, deeply dissected or 1–2-pinnately lobed with linear, generally glandular-hairy lobes. Flowers generally 1 per stem tip; involucres hairy, hemispheric, 0.2–0.3 in. long, with 6–14 free phyllaries in 1 series. Ray flowers 0.2–0.4 in. long, 6–15 per head, bright yellow. Disk flowers many per head, yellow to orange. Fruits hairy achenes with pappus scales. Especially common in the lower Snow Creek drainage, at the northern base of the San Jacinto Mountains, where it grows among *Larrea tridentata* and *Simmondsia chinensis*.

needle goldfields

Lasthenia gracilis

ASTERACEAE SUNFLOWER FAMILY

PCT Sections: 1–8 **Abundance:** Common **Height:** 4–16 in. **Flowering:** February–June **Flower Color:** Yellow **Habitat-Community:** Openings in scrubs, foothill chaparrals, and woodlands **Elevation:** Below 5200 ft. **Ecoregions:** Southern California Mountains, Sierra Nevada

Erect, openly branched annual with hairless or hairy stems. Leaves 0.4–2.8 in. long, opposite, linear, hairless to hairy, with smooth margins. Flowers generally 1 per stem tip; involucres hairy, bell-shaped or hemispheric, 0.2–0.4 in. long, with 4–13 free phyllaries in 1 series. Ray flowers 0.2–0.4 in. long, 6–13 per head, bright yellow. Disk flowers many per head, yellow to orange. Fruits to 0.1 in. long, achenes with 4 distinct, opaque white pappus scales. The most common goldfields along the PCT, forming a springtime groundcover across many habitats, including desert zones.

coastal tidytips

Layia platyglossa

ASTERACEAE SUNFLOWER FAMILY

PCT Sections: 1–8 **Abundance:** Occasional **Height:** 5–18 in. **Flowering:** February–July **Flower Color:** Yellow (white tips) **Habitat-Community:** Openings and disturbed areas from California prairies to lower montane coniferous forests **Elevation:** Below 6300 ft. **Ecoregions:** Southern California Mountains, Sierra Nevada

Erect annual with stout, glandular stems. Leaves 0.5–3.5 in. long, alternate (sometimes opposite), linear to spoon-shaped, lacking petioles and usually with lobed lower leaves. Flowers generally 1 per stem tip; involucres 0.2–0.6 in. across with phyllaries interlocked by cottony hairs. Ray flowers 0.2–0.9 in. long, 5–18 per head, bright yellow with lobed, white tips. Disk flowers many per head, yellow to brown, with dark purple anthers. Fruits flattened achenes with bristles or bristle-like scales. This showy daisy is often used in commercial wildflower seed mixes and dispersed along roadsides. *Platyglossa* (from the Greek, "broad-tongued") alludes to the shape of the ray flowers.

Leptosyne bigelovii
Bigelow's tickseed
ASTERACEAE SUNFLOWER FAMILY

PCT Sections: 4–9 **Abundance:** Common **Height:** 5–15 in. **Flowering:** February–June **Flower Color:** Yellow **Habitat-Community:** Dry, sandy to gravelly soils in scrubs, chaparrals, and woodlands **Elevation:** Below 6200 ft. **Ecoregions:** Southern California Mountains, Sierra Nevada

Erect, showy annual with hairless stems. Leaves 0.8–3.1 in. long, basal, 1–2-pinnately divided with linear, shiny, fleshy segments. Flowers 1 head per stem; involucres cylindric with square base, with linear outer phyllaries and ovoid inner phyllaries. Ray flowers 0.2–1 in. long, 5–13 per head, slightly lobed tips, bright yellow. Disk flowers many per head, yellow to orange. Fruits hairy-margined dark achenes. The disk fruits are shaped like ticks (hence the common name).

Madia elegans
common madia
ASTERACEAE SUNFLOWER FAMILY

PCT Sections: All **Abundance:** Common **Height:** to 8 ft. **Flowering:** May–October **Flower Color:** Yellow **Habitat-Community:** Open or disturbed sites mostly in clayey soils, including serpentine, from scrubs, woodlands, and chaparrals to subalpine coniferous forests **Elevation:** Below 11,200 ft. **Ecoregions:** All

Erect, aromatic, leafy annual with hairy and glandular-hairy (especially on the upper stem) herbage. Leaves 1–8 in. long, opposite and alternate, linear to lance-shaped, hairy and generally glandular, with mostly smooth margins. Flowers many heads per stem in flat-topped clusters; involucres to 0.5 in. long, hairy and glandular-hairy, with 1 series of phyllaries having erect or reflexed tips. Ray flowers to 0.8 in. long, 2–22 per head, yellow (often maroon at base). Disk flowers to 0.2 in. long, 25–80+ per head, yellow, with yellow to brown or purple anthers. Ray fruits compressed or 3-angled hairless achenes without pappus; disk fruits absent. Flowers generally open late in the day and close next morning after sunlight reaches them.

Madia gracilis
grassy tarweed
ASTERACEAE SUNFLOWER FAMILY

PCT Sections: All **Abundance:** Common **Height:** to 3 ft. **Flowering:** April–July **Flower Color:** Lemon yellow **Habitat-Community:** Open or disturbed sites and meadows, including serpentine soils, from scrubs to lower montane coniferous forests **Elevation:** Below 8200 ft. **Ecoregions:** All

Erect, slender, aromatic, leafy annual with hairy and glandular-hairy (especially on the upper stem) herbage. Leaves 0.4–6 in. long, opposite and alternate, linear, hairy and glandular, with mostly smooth margins. Flowers many heads per stem in elongated clusters, not showy; involucres to 0.4 in. long, spheric to urn-shaped, glandular-hairy, with 1 series of phyllaries having erect or reflexed tips. Ray flowers to 0.3 in. long, 3–10 per head, lemon yellow. Disk flowers to 0.2 in. long, 2–16+ per head, yellow, with purple anthers. Ray fruits compressed, hairless achenes without pappus; disk fruits similar. *Gracilis* means "slender" or "graceful."

Packera bernardina

San Bernardino ragwort

ASTERACEAE SUNFLOWER FAMILY

PCT Sections: 4 **Abundance:** Rare **Height:** 6–16 in. **Flowering:** May–July **Flower Color:** Yellow **Habitat-Community:** Dry, gravelly or rocky areas and open areas in duff in sagebrush scrubs and montane coniferous forests **Elevation:** 5500–7400 ft. **Ecoregions:** Southern California Mountains

Erect perennial from a branched, woody base with 1 woolly (becoming hairless with age) stem per basal leaf rosette. Leaves 0.4–1.1 in. long, basal and alternate. Basal leaves spatula-like, woolly, with petioles 2–4 in. long and toothed or smooth margins. Cauline leaves reduced, lacking petioles, linear to spoon-shaped. Flowers 1 per stem, with 13–21 woolly green phyllaries 0.2–0.3 in. long. Ray flowers 0.3–0.4 in. long, 8 or 13 per head, yellow. Disk flowers 35–50 per head, yellow. Fruits hairless achenes with sharp bristles. Restricted to the pebble plains of the Big Bear Lake region. Threatened by grazing, mining, and recreational activities.

Packera cana

woolly ragwort

ASTERACEAE SUNFLOWER FAMILY

PCT Sections: 9–20 **Abundance:** Common **Height:** 4–12 in. **Flowering:** May–August **Flower Color:** Yellow **Habitat-Community:** Open, rocky sites and outcrop crevices, including serpentine soils, from woodlands to subalpine coniferous forests **Elevation:** Below 11,500 ft. **Ecoregions:** Sierra Nevada, Cascades, Klamath Mountains

Erect, 1–few-stemmed, woolly perennial with mostly basal leaves. Leaves to 2+ in. long, basal rosettes and alternate on stem, oval, densely woolly, with smooth to toothed margins. Flowers 8–15 heads per stem in flat-topped clusters, with 13 or 21 woolly phyllaries to 0.3 in. long and few, reduced, green outer phyllaries. Ray flowers to 0.4 in. long, 8–13 per head, yellow. Disk flowers 35–50+ per head, bell-shaped to tubular, yellow. Fruits to 0.2 in. long, cylindric, hairless achenes with white bristles. *Cana* ("hoary") describes its herbage quite well.

Packera ionophylla

Tehachapi ragwort

ASTERACEAE SUNFLOWER FAMILY

PCT Sections: 4–5 & 7–8 **Abundance:** Rare **Height:** 6–14 in. **Flowering:** June–August **Flower Color:** Yellow **Habitat-Community:** Dry, rocky slopes in pinyon-juniper woodlands and montane coniferous forests **Elevation:** Below 9300 ft. **Ecoregions:** Southern California Mountains, Sierra Nevada

Erect, taprooted perennial with cobwebby (glabrous with age) stems. Leaves basal and alternate. Basal leaves 0.4–1.2 in. long, spatula-like, pinnately lobed into 1–3 pairs of toothed segments, with petioles 2–5 in. long. Stem leaves petioled or not and reduced up the stem. Flowers openly clustered at stem tips, composite, radiate, with 13 or 21 densely hairy phyllaries 0.2–0.3 in. long. Ray flowers 0.3–0.4 in. long, 8–13 per head, yellow. Disk flowers 60–75 per head, yellow. Fruits hairless achenes with sharp bristles. Threatened by grazing, mining, and development.

Packera werneriifolia

hoary ragwort

ASTERACEAE SUNFLOWER FAMILY

PCT Sections: 10–13 **Abundance:** Common **Height:** 4–12 in. **Flowering:** July–August **Flower Color:** Yellow **Habitat-Community:** Dry, rocky habitats in alpine communities **Elevation:** 9800–11,000 ft. **Ecoregions:** Sierra Nevada

Erect, 1–few-stemmed, hairy perennial with mostly basal leaves. Leaves 0.6–1.6 in. long, basal rosettes and (few) alternate on stem, lance-shaped to oval, short-petioled or not, hairy, with smooth to toothed margins with rolled-under edges. Flowers 1–8 radiate or discoid heads per cluster, with 13 or 21 green (red-tipped) phyllaries to 0.4 in. long and few, reduced, green outer phyllaries. Ray flowers to 0.4 in. long, 0–13 per head, yellow. Disk flowers 30–50+ per head, bell-shaped to tubular, yellow. Fruits to 0.1 in. long, cylindric, hairless achenes with white bristles.

Pectis papposa var. *papposa*

cinchweed

ASTERACEAE SUNFLOWER FAMILY

PCT Sections: 1–4 **Abundance:** Locally common **Height:** 1–8 in. **Flowering:** July–November **Flower Color:** Yellow **Habitat-Community:** Sandy flats and hillsides in creosote bush & Sonoran mixed woody scrubs **Elevation:** Below 5500 ft. **Ecoregions:** Southern California Mountains, Sonoran Basin and Range

Aromatic, much-branched annual forming low mounds. Leaves 0.4–0.8 in. long, opposite, linear, with gland-dotted margins. Flowers densely clustered at stem tips; gland-dotted involucres 0.2–0.4 in. across with 8 phyllaries 0.1–0.2 in. long. Ray flowers 0.1–0.3 in. long, 8 per head, yellow. Disk flowers to 0.1 in. long, 6–14 per head, yellow to orange. Fruits to 0.2 in. long, achenes with feather-like bristles. The definitive summer annual of the California deserts; an opportunist with a long-lived seedbank that germinates and rapidly blooms immediately after abundant warm-season rains, forming vast yellow carpets at lower desert crossings of the PCT in late summer or early fall.

Pentachaeta aurea subsp. *aurea*

golden-rayed pentachaeta

ASTERACEAE SUNFLOWER FAMILY

PCT Sections: 1–4 **Abundance:** Rare **Height:** 4–14 in. **Flowering:** March–July **Flower Color:** Yellow **Habitat-Community:** Grassy openings and ridgetops in chaparrals and lower montane coniferous forests **Elevation:** Below 6800 ft. **Ecoregions:** Southern California Mountains

Showy annual from a slender taproot. Stem erect, sometimes glabrous or short-hairy, green to reddish. Leaves 0.5–2 in. long, alternate, mostly crowded at base, linear, sparsely hairy. Flowers to 22 heads per plant; involucres 0.1–0.3 in. long with elliptic, translucent-margined phyllaries in 2–3 series. Ray flowers 0.2–0.5 in. long, 14–52 per head, yellow to brown-orange. Disk flowers 30–90 per head, 5-lobed, yellow. Fruits generally hairy and compressed achenes with 5(8) bristles. Endemic to southern California and northern Baja. Occurs along the PCT in several spots, including atop the Laguna Mountains. *Pentachaeta* (from the Greek, "five bristles") describes the pappus.

Pyrrocoma apargioides

alpineflames

ASTERACEAE SUNFLOWER FAMILY

PCT Sections: 10–15 **Abundance:** Occasional
Height: 2–7 in. **Flowering:** July–September
Flower Color: Yellow **Habitat-Community:**
Rocky slopes, meadows, and forest opening
from upper montane coniferous forests to
alpine communities **Elevation:** 7200–12,500 ft.
Ecoregions: Sierra Nevada

Decumbent to ascending, single-stemmed perennial. Leaves 1–4 in. long, mostly basal (few reduced stem leaves), thick, linear, hairless, with toothed margins. Flowers in solitary heads; involucres hairless, hemispheric, to 0.4 in. long, with green-tipped phyllaries in 3–4 graduated series. Ray flowers to 0.6 in. long, 11–40 per head, yellow. Disk flowers to 0.6 in. long, 45–90 per head, yellow. Fruits to 0.3 in. long, 3-angled hairless achenes with 15–60 tan bristles. *Pyrrocoma* ("red hair") refers to the tan pappus bristles of many species.

Rudbeckia californica

California coneflower

ASTERACEAE SUNFLOWER FAMILY

PCT Sections: 10–16 **Abundance:** Occasional
Height: 2–4 ft. **Flowering:** July–August **Flower
Color:** Yellow **Habitat-Community:** Meadows and
seeps in wetland-riparian communities **Elevation:**
Below 8600 ft. **Ecoregions:** Sierra Nevada

Erect, stout perennial with a single hairless stem. Leaves 4–24 in. long, lance-shaped to ovoid or oval, hairy below, with smooth or toothed margins. Flowers a solitary head; hairless, disk-shaped involucres to 0.8 in. long with phyllaries in 1–3 graduated or equal series. Ray flowers 0.8–2.4 in. long, 8–21 per head, generally reflexed, yellow. Disk flowers to 0.2 in. long, many in a cone-shaped head, green-yellow. Fruits to 0.2 in. long, generally 4-angled hairless achenes with crown of pappus scales. The seeds are an important traditional food of Indigenous peoples.

Senecio californicus

California ragwort

ASTERACEAE SUNFLOWER FAMILY

PCT Sections: 1–6 **Abundance:** Occasional **Height:**
4–20 in. **Flowering:** March–June **Flower Color:**
Yellow **Habitat-Community:** Sandy or clayey soils
in openings among shrubs in foothill chaparrals
and Sonoran mixed woody scrubs **Elevation:**
Below 4200 ft. **Ecoregions:** Southern California
Mountains, Sonoran Basin and Range

Erect, fragile annual with solitary or branched, usually hairless stems. Leaves 1–3 in. long, alternate, evenly spaced along stem, dentate, with toothed margins and clasping bases with ear-like lobes. Flowers 1–15+ in open clusters; bell-shaped involucres with 21 black-tipped phyllaries 0.2–0.3 in. long. Ray flowers 0.3–0.6 in. long, 10–15 per head, yellow. Disk flowers 45–55 per head, yellow-orange. Fruits stiff-hairy achenes with barbed bristles. Mature ragworts have somewhat ragged-looking leaves (hence the common name).

Senecio fremontii

dwarf mountain ragwort

ASTERACEAE SUNFLOWER FAMILY

PCT Sections: 4 & 10–23 **Abundance:** Occasional **Height:** 4–12 in. **Flowering:** June–September **Flower Color:** Yellow **Habitat-Community:** Open, rocky slopes or sandy soils in subalpine coniferous forests and alpine communities **Elevation:** 8200–13,200 ft. **Ecoregions:** Southern California Mountains, Sierra Nevada, Cascades, Klamath Mountains

Erect, 2–many-stemmed perennial with hairless, often purplish stems. Leaves to 1.6 in. long, fleshy, lance- to spoon-shaped, hairless, with smooth to toothed margins. Flowers 1–13 heads per stem in flat-topped clusters, with 8 or 13 hairless phyllaries to 0.4 in. long and few, reduced outer phyllaries. Ray flowers to 0.5 in. long, 8 per head, yellow. Disk flowers 40–50 per head, bell-shaped to tubular, yellow. Fruits to 0.2 in. long, cylindric, hairless achenes with white pappus bristles (hence *Senecio*, "old man"). *Wort* ("plant") is frequently applied to plants with medicinal or culinary uses.

Senecio integerrimus

lambstongue ragwort

ASTERACEAE SUNFLOWER FAMILY

PCT Sections: 9–24 **Abundance:** Common **Height:** 4–28 in. **Flowering:** April–August **Flower Color:** Yellow **Habitat-Community:** Dry openings from sagebrush scrubs to subalpine coniferous forests **Elevation:** Below 11,900 ft. **Ecoregions:** Sierra Nevada, Cascades, Klamath Mountains

Erect, stout, single-stemmed perennial with hairy stems and thick basal leaves. Leaves 2.4–10 in. long, lance-shaped to roundish, generally hairy, with smooth to toothed margins. Flowers 6–15+ heads per stem in flat-topped clusters, with 13 or 21 green- or black-tipped phyllaries to 0.5 in. long and few, reduced outer phyllaries. Ray flowers to 0.6 in. long, (0)5 per head, yellow. Disk flowers 35–45 per head, bell-shaped to tubular, yellow. Fruits to 0.1 in. long, cylindric, generally hairless achenes with white pappus bristles.

Senecio scorzonella

Sierra ragwort

ASTERACEAE SUNFLOWER FAMILY

PCT Sections: 10–18 **Abundance:** Occasional **Height:** 4–20 in. **Flowering:** July–August **Flower Color:** Yellow **Habitat-Community:** Dry openings and meadows from oak woodlands to subalpine coniferous forests and wetland-riparian communities **Elevation:** Below 11,500 ft. **Ecoregions:** Sierra Nevada, Cascades

Erect, 1–4-stemmed perennial with hairy herbage. Leaves 1.5–5 in. long, lance- to spoon-shaped, hairy, with toothed margins. Flowers 5–24+ radiate or discoid heads per stem in flat-topped clusters, with generally 13, hairy or becoming hairless, black-tipped phyllaries to 0.2 in. long and few, reduced outer phyllaries. Ray flowers to 0.4 in. long, (0)5+ per head, yellow. Disk flowers 10–20 per head, bell-shaped to tubular, yellow. Fruits to 0.1 in. long, cylindric, hairless achenes with white bristles. Be aware that rayless plants can be hard to identify.

Senecio triangularis

arrowleaf ragwort

ASTERACEAE SUNFLOWER FAMILY

PCT Sections: 3–5 & 10–24 **Abundance:** Common **Height:** 1–5 ft. **Flowering:** June–September **Flower Color:** Yellow **Habitat-Community:** Meadows, bogs, fens, and streambanks in wetland-riparian communities **Elevation:** Below 10,900 ft. **Ecoregions:** Southern California Mountains, Sierra Nevada, Cascades, Klamath Mountains

Erect, tall, 1–many-stemmed perennial with hairy or hairless herbage and showy flower clusters. Leaves 2–8 in. long, arrow-shaped, with toothed margins. Flowers 10–60 heads per stem, with 8–21 generally all-green phyllaries to 0.4 in. long and few, reduced, black-tipped outer phyllaries. Ray flowers to 0.6 in. long, 8 per head, yellow. Disk flowers 35–45 per head, bell-shaped to tubular, yellow. Fruits to 0.2 in. long, cylindric, hairless achenes with white bristles. Some senecios contain alkaloids, which are harmful to livestock, wildlife, and people, but stock animals find this species palatable.

Solidago confinis

southern goldenrod

ASTERACEAE SUNFLOWER FAMILY

PCT Sections: 1–8 **Abundance:** Locally common **Height:** 1–6 ft. **Flowering:** May–October **Flower Color:** Yellow **Habitat-Community:** Moist soils, springs, streambanks, and shaded understories in wetland-riparian communities, oak woodlands, and montane coniferous forests **Elevation:** Below 7800 ft. **Ecoregions:** Southern California Mountains, Sierra Nevada

Multi-stemmed, hairless perennial branching from a thick, woody base. Leaves 2–10 in. long, alternate, lance-shaped, longest near base of stem, hairless, with smooth margins. Flowers in club-shaped clusters of many heads; bowl-shaped involucres 0.1 in. long with translucent (midrib is enlarged and obvious) phyllaries in 3–4 series. Ray flowers to 0.1 in. long, 3–13 per head, yellow. Disk flowers 10–20 per head, yellow. Fruits to 0.1 in. long, hairy achenes. Thomas Edison and Henry Ford experimented with *Solidago* spp., known for their resinous qualities, to produce rubber for automobile tires!

Solidago elongata

west coast Canada goldenrod

ASTERACEAE SUNFLOWER FAMILY

PCT Sections: 8–24 **Abundance:** Locally common **Height:** 1–5 ft. **Flowering:** May–October **Flower Color:** Yellow **Habitat-Community:** Meadows, bogs, fens, and streambanks in wetland-riparian communities **Elevation:** Below 9200 ft. **Ecoregions:** Sierra Nevada, Cascades, Klamath Mountains

Erect, tall, branched perennial with hairy herbage and showy flower clusters. Leaves 2–6 in. long, largest at midstem, none at or near stem base, lance-shaped, 3-veined, with toothed margins. Flowers heads many per stem in elongated clusters, with phyllaries in 3–5 strongly graduated series. Ray flowers to 0.1 in. long, 8–15 per head, yellow. Disk flowers to 0.2 in. long, 5–12 per head, yellow. Fruits to 0.1 in. long, hairy achenes with 25–45 bristles. *Solidago* ("to make whole," "strengthen") refers to the medicinal properties of some goldenrods.

Solidago multiradiata

northern goldenrod

ASTERACEAE SUNFLOWER FAMILY

PCT Sections: 10–24 **Abundance:** Locally common **Height:** 2–20 in. **Flowering:** June–September **Flower Color:** Yellow **Habitat–Community:** Meadows and moist slopes from lower montane coniferous forests to alpine and wetland-riparian communities **Elevation:** Below 13,000 ft. **Ecoregions:** Sierra Nevada, Cascades, Klamath Mountains

Erect, clumped perennial with generally hairless stems and mostly basal foliage. Leaves 2–5 in. long, largest at base, linear to spoon-shaped, with toothed margins. Flowers heads many per stem in flat- to round-topped clusters, with phyllaries in 3–5 almost equal series. Ray flowers to 0.2 in. long, 12–18 per head, yellow. Disk flowers to 0.2 in. long, 12–35 per head, yellow. Fruits to 0.1 in. long, hairy achenes with 25–45 bristles. Most frequent in alpine meadows.

Syntrichopappus fremontii

yellowray Fremont's gold

ASTERACEAE SUNFLOWER FAMILY

PCT Sections: 5–8 **Abundance:** Locally common **Height:** 1–4 in. **Flowering:** March–June **Flower Color:** Yellow **Habitat–Community:** Sandy to gravelly soils in creosote bush & Mojave mixed woody scrubs and Joshua tree & pinyon-juniper woodlands **Elevation:** Below 7800 ft. **Ecoregions:** Southern California Mountains, Mojave Basin and Range, Sierra Nevada

Low-growing, woolly annual with short branches. Leaves 0.1–0.8 in. long, alternate or opposite, spoon-shaped, cobwebby-hairy, smooth to 3-lobed. Flowers 1 head per stem tip; involucres cylindric with 5–8 hardened, woolly phyllaries. Ray flowers 0.1–0.2 in. long, 1 per phyllary, 3-lobed, yellow. Disk flowers 10–30 per head, yellow. Fruits short-hairy achenes with many bristles.

Wyethia mollis

woolly mule-ears

ASTERACEAE SUNFLOWER FAMILY

PCT Sections: 10–19 **Abundance:** Locally common **Height:** 12–20 in. **Flowering:** May–July **Flower Color:** Yellow **Habitat–Community:** Dry, rocky slopes, meadows, and forest openings from lower montane to subalpine coniferous forests **Elevation:** Below 11,200 ft. **Ecoregions:** Sierra Nevada, Cascades

Erect, leafy perennial with hairy herbage, especially when young. Leaves 7–9 in. long, basal and alternate, narrowly elliptic to spoon-shaped, glandular and densely hairy, with smooth margins. Flowers solitary or 2–3 heads per stem; involucres bell-shaped, with equal phyllaries in 2–3 series. Ray flowers to 1.8 in. long, 6–15 per head, yellow. Disk flowers to 0.4 in. long, 35–150+ per head, yellow. Fruits to 0.5 in. long, hairy achenes with pappus of minute scales. The seeds are edible.

Wyethia ovata

southern
mule-ears

ASTERACEAE SUNFLOWER FAMILY

PCT Sections: 1–2 & 5 & 7–9 **Abundance:** Occasional **Height:** 5–20 in. **Flowering:** May–September **Flower Color:** Yellow **Habitat-Community:** Open areas and shaded understories in California prairies, oak woodlands, and lower montane coniferous forests **Elevation:** Below 8500 ft. **Ecoregions:** Southern California Mountains, Sierra Nevada

Showy, sprawling perennial from a woody base, with branched, glandular-hairy (sticky) stems. Leaves 0.3–0.9 in. long, alternate, elliptic to broadly ovoid, soft-silky hairy. Flower heads tucked among leaves; bell-shaped involucre 0.7–0.9 in. across with 4–6 phyllaries 1–2 in. long. Ray flowers 0.3–0.8 in. long, 5–8 per head, yellow. Disk flowers many per head, yellow. Fruits 0.4–0.5 in. long, hairless achenes with short pappus scales. Of the 10 *Wyethia* spp. that occur in California, only this extends into Mexico (hence the "southern" of the common name). Best seen on the PCT atop the Laguna Mountains in San Diego County, or in the Piute Mountains in Kern County. The genus name honors Pacific Northwest explorer Nathaniel J. Wyeth (1802–1856).

▼ COMPOSITE / RAY FLOWERS ONLY

Agoseris glauca

pale
agoseris

ASTERACEAE SUNFLOWER FAMILY

PCT Sections: 8–19 **Abundance:** Occasional **Height:** 7–24 in. **Flowering:** April–August **Flower Color:** Yellow **Habitat-Community:** Moist places from scrubs and woodlands to subalpine coniferous forests **Elevation:** 4600–8200 ft. **Ecoregions:** Sierra Nevada, Cascades

Erect or decumbent perennial with basal leaves, milky sap, and naked flowering stems. Leaves 4–12 in. long, lance-shaped, softly white-hairy or hairless with a white coating, with toothed to lobed margins. Flowers a solitary head on leafless stem; involucres 0.4–0.8 in. long with 2–3 equal series of phyllaries. Ray flowers 0.4–0.7 in. long, 15–150 per head, yellow. Fruits 0.2–0.5 in. long, beaked achenes with 2 series of white bristles.

Agoseris monticola

mountain
agoseris

ASTERACEAE SUNFLOWER FAMILY

PCT Sections: 9–24 **Abundance:** Occasional **Height:** 1–10 in. **Flowering:** July–August **Flower Color:** Yellow **Habitat-Community:** Meadows and rocky slopes from lower montane coniferous forests to alpine communities **Elevation:** 5000–12,500 ft. **Ecoregions:** Sierra Nevada, Cascades, Klamath Mountains

Decumbent to prostrate perennial with basal leaves, milky sap, and naked flowering stems. Leaves 1–4 in. long, spatula-shaped, white-hairy or hairless, with generally toothed to lobed margins. Flowers a solitary head on leafless stem; involucres 0.4–0.8 in. long with 2–3 equal series of generally red-blotched phyllaries. Ray flowers 0.2–0.4 in. long, 10–40 per head, yellow. Fruits 0.2–0.5 in. long, beaked achenes with 2 series of white bristles.

Agoseris retrorsa

spearleaf agoseris

ASTERACEAE SUNFLOWER FAMILY

PCT Sections: All **Abundance:** Common **Height:** 4–26 in. **Flowering:** April–August **Flower Color:** Yellow **Habitat-Community:** Dry slopes and ridges from scrubs to lower montane coniferous forests **Elevation:** Below 6000 ft. **Ecoregions:** All

Erect perennial with basal leaves, milky sap, and hairy, stout, naked flowering stems. Leaves to 14 in. long, linear to elliptic, soft-hairy, spear-tipped, with generally deeply lobed margins, lobes mostly pointing toward base. Flowers a solitary head on leafless stem; involucres 0.8–1.2 in. long with 3 equal series of generally red-blotched phyllaries. Ray flowers 0.2–0.6 in. long, 10–100 per head, yellow. Fruits 0.8–1.3 in. long, beaked achenes with 4–6 series of white bristles.

Anisocoma acaulis

scalebud

ASTERACEAE SUNFLOWER FAMILY

PCT Sections: 1–9 **Abundance:** Locally common **Height:** 3–25 in. **Flowering:** March–June **Flower Color:** Pale yellow to cream **Habitat-Community:** Washes and sandy plains in creosote bush scrubs and Joshua tree & pinyon-juniper woodlands **Elevation:** Below 7400 ft. **Ecoregions:** Southern California Mountains, Sierra Nevada

Attractive, naked-stemmed annual with matted foliage and milky sap. Leaves 0.1–0.2 in. long, basal, and pinnately lobed with toothed, sometimes hairy lobes. Flowers 1 head per stem, peduncle 2–8 in. long; hairless involucres 0.8–1.2 in. long with often red-tipped, transparent-margined phyllaries in 4–5 series. Ray flowers 0.8–1.3 in. long, 35–45 per head, tips slightly toothed, pale yellow to cream. Fruits 10–15-veined achene with 10 feather-like bristles. The only species in *Anisocoma*. Common name describes the appearance of the flower bud.

Calycoseris parryi

yellow tackstem

ASTERACEAE SUNFLOWER FAMILY

PCT Sections: 1–8 **Abundance:** Locally common **Height:** 4–24 in. **Flowering:** April–May **Flower Color:** Yellow **Habitat-Community:** Washes and sandy plains in creosote bush & Sonoran/ Mojave mixed woody scrubs and Joshua tree & pinyon-juniper woodlands **Elevation:** Below 6500 ft. **Ecoregions:** Southern California Mountains, Sierra Nevada

Erect annual with 1–3 stems dotted with red glands. Leaves 0.2–0.6 in. long, basal (mostly) and alternate, pinnately lobed. Flowers 1–few heads per stem; involucres 0.6–0.8 in. long with gland-dotted phyllaries in several series. Ray flowers 0.7–1.1 in. long, 20–35 per head, tips slightly toothed, pale yellow to yellow. Fruits brown or gray achenes with smooth bristles 0.3–0.4 in. long. Found along the PCT where it traverses desert slopes and flats in southern California. *Calycoseris* is characterized by the tack-shaped gland hairs on the upper stems, a trait which gives this and the only other species in the genus their common name.

Crepis acuminata

long-leaved hawksbeard

ASTERACEAE SUNFLOWER FAMILY

PCT Sections: 4–24 **Abundance:** Occasional **Height:** 8–28 in. **Flowering:** May–August **Flower Color:** Yellow **Habitat-Community:** Ridges and open slopes in gravelly to sandy soils from sagebrush scrubs to subalpine coniferous forests **Elevation:** Below 10,800 ft. **Ecoregions:** Southern California Mountains, Sierra Nevada, Cascades, Klamath Mountains

Erect, branched perennial with milky sap. Leaves 5–16 in. long, basal and alternate, elliptic to lance-shaped, minutely hairy, with sharp-pointed lobes and long, tapering tip. Flowers 30–100+ heads per stem, flat-topped clusters; involucres 0.3–0.6 in. long, cylindric to bell-shaped, hairy or hairless. Ray flowers 5–10 per head, yellow. Fruits 0.2–0.4 in. long, cylindric achenes with 80–150 hair-like bristles.

Crepis nana

dwarf alpine hawksbeard

ASTERACEAE SUNFLOWER FAMILY

PCT Sections: 4–5 & 10–13 **Abundance:** Occasional **Height:** 1–4 in. **Flowering:** May–September **Flower Color:** Yellow **Habitat-Community:** Talus slopes and ridges from upper montane coniferous forests to alpine communities **Elevation:** 6500–13,200 ft. **Ecoregions:** Southern California Mountains, Sierra Nevada

Erect or ascending, hairless, branched or unbranched perennial with milky sap and mostly basal leaves. Leaves 0.4–2 in. long, round to spoon-shaped, hairless, purplish, with smooth to toothed margins. Flowers generally 5–10 heads per stem, elongated clusters; involucres 0.4–0.5 in. long, cylindric, hairless, dark green to black or purple. Ray flowers 9–12 per head, yellow. Fruits to 0.3 in. long, cylindric, golden-brown achenes with 80–150 white, hair-like bristles. *Nana* means "small." This cool little hawksbeard is the only hairless *Crepis* sp. along the CA PCT.

Crepis occidentalis

largeflower hawksbeard

ASTERACEAE SUNFLOWER FAMILY

PCT Sections: 4 & 12–23 **Abundance:** Common **Height:** 2–16 in. **Flowering:** May–July **Flower Color:** Yellow **Habitat-Community:** Ridges and open slopes in gravelly soils, including serpentine, from sagebrush scrubs to upper montane coniferous forests **Elevation:** Below 8200 ft. **Ecoregions:** Southern California Mountains, Sierra Nevada, Cascades, Klamath Mountains

Erect, densely gray-hairy, leafy, branched perennial with milky sap. Leaves to 12 in. long, smaller above, elliptic or spoon-shaped, gray-hairy and stalked-glandular, with pinnately lobed or sharp-toothed margins. Flowers 12–30 heads per stem, flat-topped clusters; involucres 0.4–0.8 in. long, cylindric, glandular-hairy. Ray flowers 9–40 per head, yellow. Fruits 0.2–0.4 in. long, cylindric achenes with hair-like bristles. *Crepis* is Greek for "slipper" and possibly refers to the fruits.

Hieracium horridum

shaggy hawkweed

ASTERACEAE SUNFLOWER FAMILY

PCT Sections: 3–5 & 9–24 **Abundance:** Common **Height:** 1–3 ft. **Flowering:** June–October **Flower Color:** Yellow **Habitat-Community:** Crevices in granite rock outcrops and rocky slopes from lower montane coniferous forests to alpine communities **Elevation:** Below 11,500 ft. **Ecoregions:** Southern California Mountains, Sierra Nevada, Cascades, Klamath Mountains

Erect annual with hairy stems and milky sap. Leaves 3–4 in. long, oblong, densely long-hairy, with smooth margins. Flowers many per stem; involucres 0.2–0.4 in. long, cylindric to bell-shaped, hairy. Ray flowers 6–15 per head, yellow. Fruits to 0.1 in. long, achenes with brown bristles. *Hieracium* is from the Greek *hierax* ("hawk"): ancient Greeks believed hawks cleared their eyesight with the juice of a plant called hieracion. The only hawkweed along the CA PCT with long, shaggy hairs.

Malacothrix californica

California dandelion

ASTERACEAE SUNFLOWER FAMILY

PCT Sections: 1–8 **Abundance:** Locally common **Height:** 6–20 in. **Flowering:** March–May **Flower Color:** Pale yellow **Habitat-Community:** Washes and sandy plains in California prairies, Sonoran/ Mojave mixed woody scrubs, foothill chaparrals, and oak woodlands **Elevation:** Below 5300 ft. **Ecoregions:** Southern California Mountains, Sierra Nevada

Erect, unbranched annual with sparsely woolly herbage and milky sap. Leaves basal, 0.6–2.8 in. long, pinnately lobed, thread-like, cobwebby at base. Flowers in solitary heads on bare stems; involucres 0.4–0.7 in. across with long, tangle-haired (at base) phyllaries in several series. Ray flowers 0.7–1 in. long, many per head, tips slightly toothed, pale yellow. Fruits 0.2 in. long, achenes with pappus of outer teeth and 2 bristles. Can form carpets of flowers along the PCT (such as in Warner Valley of San Diego County) during years of abundant precipitation. *Malacothrix* (from the Greek *malakos*, "soft," *thrix*, "hair") refers to the plant's woolliness, especially on its phyllaries.

Malacothrix clevelandii

Cleveland's dandelion

ASTERACEAE SUNFLOWER FAMILY

PCT Sections: 1–7 **Abundance:** Locally common **Height:** 5–20 in. **Flowering:** March–June **Flower Color:** Pale yellow **Habitat-Community:** Open areas in California prairies, Sonoran/Mojave mixed woody scrubs, foothill chaparrals, and oak woodlands **Elevation:** Below 5100 ft. **Ecoregions:** Southern California Mountains, Sierra Nevada

Erect annual, branched above, with hairless stems and milky sap. Leaves 0.5–2.2 in. long, basal and alternate, lance-linear, hairless, with toothed or lobed margins, and highly reduced and more toothed up the stem. Flowers in clusters at stem tips; involucres 0.2–0.3 in. long with hairless, lance-shaped phyllaries. Ray flowers 0.4–0.6 in. long, many per head, tips slightly toothed, pale yellow. Fruits to 0.1 in. long, achenes with pappus of needle-like outer teeth and 1 bristle. Most common in cleared or disturbed chaparral, especially post-wildfire areas.

desert dandelion

Malacothrix glabrata

ASTERACEAE SUNFLOWER FAMILY

PCT Sections: 1–8 **Abundance:** Common **Height:** 5–20 in. **Flowering:** March–June **Flower Color:** Pale yellow **Habitat-Community:** Sandy or gravelly flats and hillsides in creosote bush & Sonoran/Mojave mixed woody scrubs, foothill chaparrals, and Joshua tree woodlands **Elevation:** Below 6200 ft. **Ecoregions:** Southern California Mountains, Sonoran/Mojave Basin and Range, Sierra Nevada

Erect, much-branched annual with hairless herbage and milky sap. Leaves 1.5–4.2 in. long, basal and alternate, hairless, thread-like and deeply lobed with linear segments to 1.5 in. long. Flowers 1–few in clusters at stem tips; involucres 0.4–0.6 in. long with sometimes sparsely hairy, lance-shaped phyllaries. Ray flowers 0.7–1 in. long, many per head, tips slightly toothed, pale yellow. Fruits 0.2 in. long, achenes with pappus of outer teeth and 1–5 bristles. Flower heads may have an orange or red central "button" of immature flowers. A dominant annual across the California deserts in years of abundant precipitation.

nodding microseris

Microseris nutans

ASTERACEAE SUNFLOWER FAMILY

PCT Sections: 10–24 **Abundance:** Common **Height:** 4–25 in. **Flowering:** April–July **Flower Color:** Yellow **Habitat-Community:** Moist, rocky meadows and open slopes from sagebrush scrubs to upper montane coniferous forests **Elevation:** Below 9800 ft. **Ecoregions:** Sierra Nevada, Cascades, Klamath Mountains

Erect, short-lived perennial with basal leaves, milky sap, and leafy (near base) flowering stems. Leaves 2–12 in. long, linear, with smooth to lobed margins. Flowers from nodding bud to solitary head on a leafy (toward base) stem; involucres 0.3–0.9 in. long with a series of black-hairy phyllaries. Ray flowers much longer than involucre, 13–75 per head, yellow. Fruits 0.1–0.3 in. long, achenes with 15–30 bristle-tipped pappus scales.

alpine prairie dandelion

Nothocalais alpestris

ASTERACEAE SUNFLOWER FAMILY

PCT Sections: 10–17 & 20–24 **Abundance:** Rare **Height:** 1–18 in. **Flowering:** July–September **Flower Color:** Yellow **Habitat-Community:** Dry meadows, rocky outcrops and slopes, and ridges from lower montane coniferous forests to alpine communities **Elevation:** 4300–11,800 ft. **Ecoregions:** Sierra Nevada, Klamath Mountains

Erect perennial with basal leaves, milky sap, and hairless (below flower head), naked, unbranched flowering stems. Leaves 2–10 in. long, narrow to widely oval, generally hairless, with toothed to lobed margins. Flowers a solitary head on leafless stem; involucres 0.4–0.8 in. long with a series of fine-spotted phyllaries. Ray flowers 0.2–0.3 in. long, 13–many per head, yellow (reddish lower surface). Fruits 0.2–0.4 in. long, beakless achenes with 30–50 white bristles.

Uropappus lindleyi

silver puffs

ASTERACEAE SUNFLOWER FAMILY

PCT Sections: 1–9 & 16–19 **Abundance:** Common **Height:** 6–15 in. **Flowering:** March–May **Flower Color:** Pale yellow **Habitat-Community:** Open places, especially grassy areas, in oak woodlands, chaparrals, and lower montane coniferous forests **Elevation:** Below 7600 ft. **Ecoregions:** All

Erect annual with milky sap. Leaves basal, stem leaves alternate if present, 2–12 in. long, linear, hairy, with smooth to lobed margins with pointed tip. Flowers a solitary head per stem with 3–4 series of phyllaries that reflex in fruit. Ray flowers to 0.4 in. long, 5–many per head, pale yellow above, reddish below. Fruits 0.3–0.7 in. long, hairy black achenes with 5 bristle-tipped pappus scales. The flowers open in the morning and close by afternoon, showing the reddish side of the rays.

▼ COMPOSITE / DISK FLOWERS ONLY

Ambrosia acanthicarpa

annual bursage

ASTERACEAE SUNFLOWER FAMILY

PCT Sections: 1–9 **Abundance:** Occasional **Height:** 1–3 ft. **Flowering:** July–November **Flower Color:** Pale yellow **Habitat-Community:** Sandy plains and disturbed areas in scrubs, chaparrals, and woodlands **Elevation:** Below 7400 ft. **Ecoregions:** Southern California/Northern Baja Coast, Southern California Mountains, Sierra Nevada

Erect, aromatic summer annual with a few-branched central stem and gray-green, coarsely hairy herbage; monoecious. Leaves 0.4–3.1 in. long, opposite, simple to 1–3-pinnately divided, triangular in outline, deep green. Male flowering heads 0.1–0.2 in. across, few to many in spike-like clusters, pale yellow to translucent. Female flowering heads 0.1–0.2 in. across and 1-flowered. Fruits 0.2–0.3 in. across, spurs armed with up to 30 twisted spines or wings. Weedy, ranging throughout western North America. Responds quickly to summer precipitation, lining the trail in late summer or fall and filling one's socks with clinging burs. Has a spiny fruit (*carpa* in Latin), like those in *Acanthus* (hence the specific epithet). Aka ragweed. Nearly 50% of pollen-related allergies in the US are caused by ragweeds!

Ambrosia psilostachya

western ragweed

ASTERACEAE SUNFLOWER FAMILY

PCT Sections: 1–6 **Abundance:** Occasional **Height:** 1–4 ft. **Flowering:** June–November **Flower Color:** Pale yellow **Habitat-Community:** Sandy soils and disturbed areas in chaparrals and oak woodlands **Elevation:** Below 5500 ft. **Ecoregions:** Southern California/Northern Baja Coast, Southern California Mountains

Erect perennial, growing in colonial clumps, with few-branched, straw-colored stems and coarsely hairy or bristly herbage; monoecious. Leaves 1–5 in. long, opposite, lance-shaped to ovoid, 1–3-pinnately lobed or divided, hairy, resin-dotted. Male flowering heads 0.1–0.2 in. across, many in spike-like clusters, pale yellow to translucent. Female flowering heads 0.1–0.2 in. across, 1-flowered, clustered in leaf axils. Fruits 0.1–0.2 in. across, burs armed with up to 7 straight spines. Occurs throughout North America and used by Indigenous peoples, including the Kumeyaay of San Diego County, for several medicinal purposes.

Artemisia douglasiana

California mugwort

ASTERACEAE SUNFLOWER FAMILY

PCT Sections: 1–19 & 23–24 **Abundance:** Common **Height:** 2–8 ft. **Flowering:** May–November **Flower Color:** Pale yellow **Habitat-Community:** Openings and understories, generally in drainages, from scrubs to lower montane coniferous forests **Elevation:** Below 7200 ft. **Ecoregions:** All

Multi-stemmed, erect, aromatic perennial with hairy stems. Leaves 0.5–6 in. long, alternate, narrowly elliptic to wedge-shaped, white-hairy, unlobed or 3–5-lobed. Flowers, many heads per cluster, erect to nodding along stems, pale yellow. Female (5–9 per head) and bisexual (6–25 per head) disk flowers to 0.1 in. long, both types within the same head, with gray-hairy involucres. Fruits to 0.1 in. long, hairless achenes without pappus. An important medicinal plant, with many uses; the leaves can be chewed to relieve a toothache or applied topically to soothe the itchy rash caused by poison oak. Ingesting too much mugwort can cause health problems, too, so please use sparingly!

Artemisia dracunculus

tarragon

ASTERACEAE SUNFLOWER FAMILY

PCT Sections: 1–17 **Abundance:** Common **Height:** 1–5 ft. **Flowering:** August–October **Flower Color:** Pale yellow **Habitat-Community:** Openings and meadows, especially disturbed places, from woodlands and chaparrals to upper montane coniferous forests **Elevation:** Below 11,200 ft. **Ecoregions:** Southern California/Northern Baja Coast, Southern California Mountains, Sierra Nevada

Multi-stemmed, erect, odorless or aromatic perennial with hairless stems. Leaves 0.4–2.8 in. long, alternate, linear, hairless, bright green, unlobed to few-lobed. Flowers, many heads per cluster, nodding along stems, pale yellow. Female (14–25 per head) and bisexual (8–20 per head) disk flowers within the same head, with hairless involucres. Fruits to 0.1 in. long, hairless achenes without pappus. Tarragon has long been used for medicinal purposes, fragrance, and flavoring foods.

Artemisia norvegica
subsp. *saxatilis*

boreal sagebrush

ASTERACEAE SUNFLOWER FAMILY

PCT Sections: 10–14 & 22–24 **Abundance:** Occasional **Height:** 6–24 in. **Flowering:** July–September **Flower Color:** Yellow **Habitat-Community:** Exposed, tundra-like, rocky slopes and ridges from upper montane coniferous forests to alpine communities **Elevation:** 7500–12,500 ft. **Ecoregions:** Sierra Nevada, Klamath Mountains

Multi-stemmed, erect, mildly aromatic perennial with hairy stems. Leaves 2.5–6 in. long, alternate, 1–2-pinnately compound, hairy to hairless, with linear lobes. Flowers, many heads per spike-like cluster, nodding along stems, yellow (red-tinged). Female (6–12 per head) and bisexual (30–80 per head) disk flowers within the same head; involucres hairy, black-margined. Fruits to 0.1 in. long, hairless achenes without pappus. *Saxatilis* is Latin for "living among rocks," describing the habitat perfectly.

Chaenactis glabriuscula
yellow pincushion
ASTERACEAE SUNFLOWER FAMILY

PCT Sections: 1–8 **Abundance:** Locally common **Height:** 4–24 in. **Flowering:** February–July **Flower Color:** Yellow to orange **Habitat-Community:** Sandy or gravelly soils in chaparrals, woodlands, and lower montane coniferous forests **Elevation:** Below 7300 ft. **Ecoregions:** Southern California Mountains, Sierra Nevada

Erect, few-branched annual with green and cobwebby stems becoming purple-red and hairless with age. Leaves 0.5–2.4 in. long, basal or alternate, 1–2-pinnately dissected, ovoid in outline, lobes linear and cylindric, and somewhat fleshy. Flowers a solitary head per stem with glandular-hairy phyllaries to 0.3 in. long, >25 per involucre. Disk flowers yellow; inner disk flowers, corolla 0.1–0.2 in. long; outer disk flowers 0.2–0.3 in. wide, slightly irregular, 5-lobed. Fruits to 0.4 in. long, achenes with pappus of 4 scales. Highly variable: var. *glabriuscula* is the common variety on the PCT; var. *lanosum*, a woolly hairy plant, occurs in the Transverse Ranges. The genus name (from the Greek *chaino*, "to gape," *aktis*, "a ray") refers to the shape of the outer ring of florets in some species.

Doellingeria breweri
Brewer's aster
ASTERACEAE SUNFLOWER FAMILY

PCT Sections: 9–18 & 22–23 **Abundance:** Occasional **Height:** 4–12 in. **Flowering:** July–September **Flower Color:** Yellow **Habitat-Community:** Moist meadows and open slopes from lower montane to subalpine coniferous forests **Elevation:** Below 10,500 ft. **Ecoregions:** Sierra Nevada, Klamath Mountains

Erect, branched perennial with glandular or short-hairy stems and well-distributed foliage. Leaves 0.8–2 in. long, alternate, narrowly lance- to spoon-shaped, hairless to glandular-hairy, with smooth to toothed margins. Flowers few per cluster, with short- to glandular-hairy, equal or unequal phyllaries in 3–6 series. Disk flowers many per head, yellow. Fruits 1–2-ribbed achenes with 1 series of pappus bristles.

Erigeron aphanactis var. congestus
rayless shaggy fleabane
ASTERACEAE SUNFLOWER FAMILY

PCT Sections: 4 **Abundance:** Locally common **Height:** 3–9 in. **Flowering:** May–September **Flower Color:** Yellow to gold **Habitat-Community:** Gravelly or rocky plains and slopes in pinyon-juniper woodlands and lower montane coniferous forests **Elevation:** Below 8100 ft. **Ecoregions:** Southern California Mountains

Compact perennial, forming loose mats 4–12 in. across, with white-hairy, glandular stems. Leaves 1.5–2.8 in. long, basal or alternate along a short stem, narrowly spoon-shaped, stiff hairy, with smooth margins. Flowers in 1 head per stem, button-like; involucres 0.1–0.3 in. long and twice as wide, with 15–30 coarsely hairy, glandular phyllaries. Disk flower tube abruptly inflated to throat, yellow to gold (usually aging reddish or purple). Fruits achenes with pappus of 12–17 narrow bristles or scales. The only concentration in California is in the San Bernardino Mountains pebble plains habitat, in the vicinity of Big Bear Lake.

Eriophyllum pringlei

Pringle's woolly sunflower

ASTERACEAE SUNFLOWER FAMILY

PCT Sections: 1–2 & 4–9 **Abundance:** Locally common **Height:** 1–3 in. **Flowering:** February–July **Flower Color:** Yellow **Habitat-Community:** Sandy to gravelly plains and ridgetops in Sonoran/Mojave mixed woody scrubs and Joshua tree & pinyon-juniper woodlands **Elevation:** Below 6800 ft. **Ecoregions:** Southern California Mountains, Sierra Nevada

Diminutive "belly-plant" annual with short, spreading, woolly stems. Leaves 0.1–0.5 in. long, alternate, wedge-shaped, densely woolly hairy, with rolled-under margins and 3-lobed tips. Flower heads in leafy clusters; involucres 0.1–0.3 in. long with 6–8 phyllaries. Disk flowers 10–20 per head, minutely glandular, yellow. Fruits short-hairy achenes with minute pappus scales. Occurs along most desert crossings and slopes of the PCT.

Geraea viscida

sticky geraea

ASTERACEAE SUNFLOWER FAMILY

PCT Sections: 1 **Abundance:** Rare **Height:** 1–3 ft. **Flowering:** May–July **Flower Color:** Yellow **Habitat-Community:** Slopes and valleys in scrubs, chaparrals, and woodlands **Elevation:** Below 5500 ft. **Ecoregions:** Southern California/Northern Baja Coast, Southern California Mountains

Several-stemmed (from base), few-branched perennial with bristly and sticky-glandular stems. Leaves 1.2–3.5 in. long, alternate, ovoid to oblong, slightly hairy. Flowers 1–few heads in flat-topped clusters; involucres 0.4–0.7 in. long with wide, glandular, sticky phyllaries. Disk flowers 0.2–0.3 in. long, yellow. Fruits 0.4 in. long, achenes with pappus awns. Endemic to southern San Diego County and Baja, Mexico. Look for it along the PCT between Campo and the southern base of the Laguna Mountains. The genus name (from the Greek *geraios*, "old") refers to the white, bristly-haired involucre.

Hymenopappus filifolius var. *lugens*

Columbia cutleaf

ASTERACEAE SUNFLOWER FAMILY

PCT Sections: 3–4 **Abundance:** Rare **Height:** 8–32 in. **Flowering:** May–September **Flower Color:** Yellow to cream **Habitat-Community:** Gravelly to rocky slopes and ridges in pinyon-juniper woodlands and montane chaparrals & coniferous forests **Elevation:** Below 8300 ft. **Ecoregions:** Southern California Mountains

Erect, 1–few-stemmed perennial with nearly leafless, hairless or woolly hairy stems at the axils. Leaves 1–8 in. long, basal and cauline (0–3, much reduced), simple to 2-pinnately dissected into linear segments 0.2–2.1 in. long, thinly to densely cobwebby-hairy, gland-dotted. Flower heads in clusters of 3–8 at stem tips, with phyllaries 0.2–0.4 in. long, half as wide. Disk flowers 0.2–0.3 in. long, 10–70 per head, yellow to cream. Fruits hairy achenes with 12–22 pappus scales. Best seen along the PCT in the San Bernardino and San Jacinto Mountains.

Lessingia glandulifera
var. *glandulifera*

sticky lessingia

ASTERACEAE SUNFLOWER FAMILY

PCT Sections: 1–9 **Abundance:** Locally common **Height:** 4–16 in. **Flowering:** May–October **Flower Color:** Yellow **Habitat-Community:** Sandy or gravelly soils in foothill chaparrals, woodlands, and lower montane coniferous forests **Elevation:** Below 6900 ft. **Ecoregions:** Southern California Mountains, Sierra Nevada

Erect to decumbent, multi-branched annual with glandular, slightly hairy stems. Leaves 0.1–0.8 in. long, basal and alternate, spoon-shaped, with knobby glands on margins. Flowers in scattered heads along stems, yellow, radiant, with many glandular phyllaries in 4–8 series. Disk flowers 12–30 per head; inner disk flowers 0.1–0.2 in. long; outer radiant disk flowers 0.2–0.3 in. across, irregular, 5-lobed. Fruits to 0.2 in. long, achenes with long bristles. Two other varieties occur on the PCT: var. *peirsonii* (hairy but not glandular phyllaries) is limited to the western Transverse Ranges and southern Sierra; var. *tomentosa* (hairy leaves and stems) is extremely rare, limited to the Warner Springs region of San Diego County!

Orochaenactis thysanocarpha

California mountain pincushion

ASTERACEAE SUNFLOWER FAMILY

PCT Sections: 8–10 **Abundance:** Rare **Height:** 0.5–10 in. **Flowering:** June–September **Flower Color:** Yellow **Habitat-Community:** Gravelly slopes and dry meadows in upper montane & subalpine coniferous forests **Elevation:** 5200–12,500 ft. **Ecoregions:** Sierra Nevada

Spreading to erect, simple or branched annual with hairy and glandular stems. Leaves 0.4–1.5 in. long, lower opposite and upper alternate, linear to narrowly spoon-shaped, glandular and hairy, with smooth margins. Flower heads in small clusters at stem tips with 4–7 purple phyllaries in 1 series. Disk flowers to 0.2 in. long, 4–9 per head, yellow. Fruits to 0.2 in. long, club-shaped achenes with 11–17 pappus scales. *Orochaenactis* means "mountain *Chaenactis*." The only annual pincushion in the southern high Sierra.

Raillardella argentea

silky raillardella

ASTERACEAE SUNFLOWER FAMILY

PCT Sections: 4 & 10–18 **Abundance:** Locally common **Height:** 1–6 in. **Flowering:** July–September **Flower Color:** Yellow **Habitat-Community:** Dry, open, generally gravelly sites in subalpine coniferous forests and alpine communities **Elevation:** 5900–12,800 ft. **Ecoregions:** Southern California Mountains, Sierra Nevada, Cascades

Tufted, erect perennial with generally naked flowering stems and silky-hairy herbage. Leaves 0.3–3 in. long, basal, oblong, silky-hairy, with smooth to toothed margins. Flowers in solitary head at stem tip, with 0 phyllaries and 5–15 generally fused, phyllary-like bracts. Disk flowers 7–26 per head, yellow. Fruits linear, hairy black achenes with 16–30 pappus scales. Often found growing in large colonies of silver and gold!

Raillardella scaposa

stem raillardella

ASTERACEAE SUNFLOWER FAMILY

PCT Sections: 10–18 **Abundance:** Locally common **Height:** 2–16 in. **Flowering:** June–September **Flower Color:** Yellow **Habitat-Community:** Dry to wet, open, rocky, and sandy or gravelly places, including dry meadow borders, in upper montane & subalpine coniferous forests **Elevation:** 6500–11,500 ft. **Ecoregions:** Sierra Nevada, Cascades

Tufted, erect perennial with generally naked flowering stems and green herbage. Leaves 0.4–6 in. long, basal, linear to ovoid, green and glandular, with smooth margins. Flowers a solitary discoid or radiate head per stem, with 0–7 phyllaries and 8–20 generally fused, phyllary-like bracts. Ray flowers to 1 in. long, 0–7 per head, yellow. Disk flowers to 0.5 in. long, 7–44 per head, yellow. Fruits linear, hairy black achenes with (0)8–30 pappus scales. Often grows near *R. argentea*.

▼ NO PETALS AND 5 SEPALS

Croton californicus

California croton

EUPHORBIACEAE SPURGE FAMILY

PCT Sections: 1–4 **Abundance:** Locally common **Height:** 10–35 in. **Flowering:** April–July **Flower Color:** Pale yellow **Habitat-Community:** Washes, sandy plains, and dunes in creosote bush scrubs and Joshua tree & pinyon-juniper woodlands **Elevation:** Below 3200 ft. **Ecoregions:** Southern California Mountains, Sonoran/Mojave Basin and Range

Erect or decumbent perennial or subshrub with star-shaped hairs on herbage; dioecious. Leaves 1–2 in. long, alternate, elliptic to narrowly oblong. Male flowers with numerous stamens and 5 yellow sepals fused half-way into cup-shaped calyx 0.2 in. across. Female flowers 0.1 in. long with 5 sepals. Fruits 3-lobed, rounded capsules. Found along the PCT at the lower desert segments such as in San Felipe Valley or adjacent Interstate 10 near Cabazon. The genus name (from the Greek *krotos*, "tick") refers to the shape of the seeds. Speaking of which, seeds are best left uneaten: they are known to be violent purgatives.

▼ 3 OR 6 PETALS/TEPALS

Iris hartwegii

rainbow iris

IRIDACEAE IRIS FAMILY

PCT Sections: 4 & 16–19 **Abundance:** Locally common **Height:** 2–12 in. **Flowering:** May–June **Flower Color:** Pale to gold-yellow **Habitat-Community:** Open understories in lower montane coniferous forests **Elevation:** Below 7600 ft. **Ecoregions:** Southern California Mountains, Sierra Nevada, Cascades

Clustered perennial with mostly round stems. Leaves to 0.6 in. wide, mostly basal, 1–4 alternate and reduced on stem, 2-ranked, flat. Flowers 2–3 at stem tips, symmetric. Tepals to 2.8 in. long, pale to gold-yellow with lavender veining, and sepals wider than petals. Fruits to 1.2 in. long, capsules with brown seeds. *Iris* is Greek for "rainbow." The specific epithet honors German botanist Karl Hartweg (1812–1871), who made collections in California in 1846-47.

Sisyrinchium elmeri

Elmer's golden-eyed grass

IRIDACEAE IRIS FAMILY

PCT Sections: 10–22 **Abundance:** Occasional **Height:** to 10 in. **Flowering:** May–August **Flower Color:** Yellow **Habitat-Community:** Wet meadows in wetland-riparian communities **Elevation:** Below 8900 ft. **Ecoregions:** Sierra Nevada, Cascades, Klamath Mountains

Tufted perennial with slender, winged stems. Leaves to 0.1 in. wide, basal and alternate, grass-like, 2-ranked, flat. Flowers at stem and branch tips. Tepals to 0.4 in. long, yellow, and sepals and petals alike. Fruits to 0.3 in. long, capsules. *Sisyrinchium* (from the Latin and Greek, "pig snout") refers to swine uprooting plants for food.

Calochortus concolor

goldenbowl mariposa lily

LILIACEAE LILY FAMILY

PCT Sections: 1–4 **Abundance:** Occasional **Height:** 12–26 in. **Flowering:** May–July **Flower Color:** Yellow **Habitat-Community:** Open or shaded areas in decomposed granite, especially in recent burns, from oak woodlands to lower montane coniferous forests **Elevation:** Below 8000 ft. **Ecoregions:** Southern California/Northern Baja Coast, Southern California Mountains

Stout, erect perennial with waxy stems. Leaves 4–8 in. long, basal, withering at flowering, linear, white-waxy. Flowers 1–7 in open cluster at stem tip, bell-shaped, with 6 yellow tepals and 6 stamens. Sepals 3, ovoid to lance-shaped, 0.4–0.6 in. long. Petals 1.2–2 in. long, 3, widely spatula-shaped, with dark red blotch at base and hairy nectary surface. Fruits 2–3 in. long, erect capsules. Mostly confined to the Peninsular Ranges with a few occurrences along the PCT at the southern flanks of the San Bernardino Mountains. The only yellow-flowered mariposa lily in its range.

Lilium parryi

lemon lily

LILIACEAE LILY FAMILY

PCT Sections: 3–5 **Abundance:** Rare **Height:** 2–6 ft. **Flowering:** June–September **Flower Color:** Yellow **Habitat-Community:** Open or shaded areas in meadows and along streambanks in wetland-riparian communities and montane coniferous forests **Elevation:** Below 8200 ft. **Ecoregions:** Southern California Mountains

Erect, highly fragrant perennial from a scaly, elongated bulb to 4 in. long. Leaves 3–12 in. long, 1–5-whorled along the stem or alternate in young plants, linear. Flowers 2.8–4.3 in. long, spreading or nodding at stem tip, slightly irregular, trumpet-like with 6 spoon-shaped, recurved, yellow tepals. Stamens 6, magenta- or orange-brown. Fruits 1.5–2.4 in. long, erect capsules. Threatened by collecting, altered hydrology, recreational activities, and grazing.

Narthecium californicum

California bog asphodel

NARTHECIACEAE

BOG ASPHODEL FAMILY

PCT Sections: 10–24 **Abundance:** Locally common **Height:** 7–24 in. **Flowering:** July–August **Flower Color:** Yellow **Habitat-Community:** Wet meadows and streambanks, including serpentine soils, in wetland-riparian communities **Elevation:** Below 8600 ft. **Ecoregions:** Sierra Nevada, Cascades, Klamath Mountains

Erect, slender, unbranched perennial. Leaves to 12 in. long, grass-like, mostly basal and few (smaller) on stem, linear, hairless. Flowers many along stem tip, 6-parted (3 sepals, 3 petals), symmetric, with 6 stamens, woolly filaments, and 3-lobed style. Tepals to 0.4 in. long, sepals and petals alike, yellow, lance-linear, recurved to erect. Fruits to 0.5 in. long, capsules with bristle-tipped brown seeds. *Narthecium* ("bone-breaker") derives from the belief that sheep grazing the plants developed weak bones.

Eriogonum incanum

frosted buckwheat

POLYGONACEAE

BUCKWHEAT FAMILY

PCT Sections: 10–16 **Abundance:** Common **Height:** to 10 in. **Flowering:** June–September **Flower Color:** Yellow **Habitat-Community:** Open, rocky or sandy soils from upper montane coniferous forests to alpine communities **Elevation:** 6800–13,200 ft. **Ecoregions:** Sierra Nevada

Matted perennial with hairy stems; dioecious. Leaves to 0.6 in. long, basal, oblong to ovoid, densely white-hairy, with smooth margins. Flowers in open or tight head-like clusters at stem tips with hairy involucres to 0.1 in. long and 5–8 teeth. Tepals to 0.2 in. long, 6-parted, fused at base forming a cylindric tube, yellow, hairless. Fruits to 0.2 in. long, achenes with sparsely hairy tips. Male plants have tighter head-like clusters of flowers; the clusters on female plants are more open and scattered.

Eriogonum inflatum

desert trumpet

POLYGONACEAE

BUCKWHEAT FAMILY

PCT Sections: 1–8 **Abundance:** Occasional **Height:** 1–3 ft. **Flowering:** July–November **Flower Color:** Yellow **Habitat-Community:** Gravelly or rocky soils in saltbush & creosote bush scrubs and Joshua tree & pinyon-juniper woodlands **Elevation:** Below 5500 ft. **Ecoregions:** Southern California Mountains, Sonoran/Mojave Basin and Range, Sierra Nevada

Erect, hollow-stemmed perennial with gray-green, hairless to wax-coated stems. Leaves 0.8–2.2 in. long, basal, oblong or rounded, short-hairy, green. Flowers on spreading to erect branches, with erect peduncles 0.2–0.7 in. long and hairless involucres to 0.1 in. long. Tepals to 0.2 in. long, 6-parted, yellow. Fruits to 0.1 in. long, hairless achenes. Seen at lower desert crossings along the PCT—and in numerous films and TV shows, including *The Big Lebowski* and *Star Trek*. Indigenous peoples use the inflated stems as both a drinking tube and smoking pipe. The inflation is partly a function of available moisture: the drier the year, the less inflated the stems. When leaves wilt, the stems take over primary photosynthetic functions and CO_2 builds up within them, causing the phenomenon.

Eriogonum marifolium

marum-leaf wild buckwheat

POLYGONACEAE BUCKWHEAT FAMILY

PCT Sections: 11–24 **Abundance:** Common **Height:** 2–16 in. **Flowering:** June–August **Flower Color:** Yellow **Habitat-Community:** Open, rocky or sandy soils in upper montane & subalpine coniferous forests **Elevation:** Below 10,200 ft. **Ecoregions:** Sierra Nevada, Cascades, Klamath Mountains

Matted perennial with hairy or hairless stems; dioecious. Leaves to 1.2 in. long, basal, oval to ovoid, nearly hairless above, hairy below, with smooth margins. Flowers in clusters at stem tips with hairy or hairless involucres to 0.2 in. long and 5–6 teeth. Male plants have tighter head-like flower clusters; those on female plants are more open and scattered. Tepals to 0.3 in. long, 6-parted, yellow, hairless, fused at base forming a cylindric tube. Fruits to 0.2 in. long, achenes with sparsely hairy tips.

Eriogonum pusillum

yellow turbans

POLYGONACEAE BUCKWHEAT FAMILY

PCT Sections: 1–8 **Abundance:** Occasional **Height:** 2–12 in. **Flowering:** February–October **Flower Color:** Yellow to red **Habitat-Community:** Sandy to gravelly soils in creosote bush scrubs and Joshua tree & pinyon-juniper woodlands **Elevation:** Below 6600 ft. **Ecoregions:** Southern California Mountains, Sonoran/Mojave Basin and Range, Sierra Nevada

Desert annual, branched above, with basal rosette of leaves and hairless stems. Leaves 0.3–1 in. wide, round to ovoid, woolly, with plane or wavy margins; petiole 0.4–1.2 in. long. Flowers on spreading stems, with erect to curvy peduncles 0.5–2 in. long and glandular involucres. Tepals 0.1 in. long, 6-parted, yellow becoming rusty red. Fruits to 0.1 in. long, hairless achenes. Found along the PCT only at lower desert crossings, such as the transition between Antelope Valley and the Tehachapi Mountains. *Pusillum* is Latin for "small" or "weak."

Eriogonum rosense

rosy buckwheat

POLYGONACEAE BUCKWHEAT FAMILY

PCT Sections: 10–13 **Abundance:** Rare **Height:** 1–5 in. **Flowering:** July–September **Flower Color:** Bright yellow to red-yellow **Habitat-Community:** Open, sandy or gravelly soils from lower montane coniferous forests to alpine communities **Elevation:** 7500–13,200 ft. **Ecoregions:** Sierra Nevada

Mat-forming perennial with leafless, glandular-hairy stems. Leaves 0.1–0.7 in. long, basal, oval to spoon-shaped, densely hairy and glandular, with smooth margins. Flowers in dense, head-like clusters at stem tips with 3–6 hairy, glandular involucres to 0.2 in. long and 5–8 erect teeth. Tepals to 0.2 in. long, 6-parted, mostly free to base, sometimes glandular, bright yellow to red-yellow. Fruits to 0.1 in. long, hairless achenes. Flowers are sometimes rosy-yellow.

Eriogonum umbellatum

sulphur buckwheat

POLYGONACEAE BUCKWHEAT FAMILY

PCT Sections: 2–6 & 8–24 **Abundance:** Common **Height:** to 3 ft. **Flowering:** June–October **Flower Color:** Yellow, white, or red **Habitat-Community:** Rocky, gravelly, or sandy soils, including serpentine, from scrubs and woodlands to alpine communities **Elevation:** Below 11,900 ft. **Ecoregions:** All (except Sonoran/Mojave Basin and Range)

Matted or openly growing perennial or subshrub, generally lacking leaf-like bracts midway up the main flowering stem. Leaves to 0.3 in. long, basal or lower stem, felt-like, hairy or hairless. Flowers in clusters of spherical heads at stem tips with felt-like, hairy or hairless involucres to 0.3 in. long and 6–12 reflexed lobes. Tepals to 0.5 in. long, 6-parted, fused at base into a cylindrical tube, hairless, yellow, white, or red. Fruits to 0.3 in. long, hair-tipped achenes. Twenty-five subspecies occur in California.

Bloomeria crocea

common goldenstar

THEMIDACEAE BRODIAEA FAMILY

PCT Sections: 1–8 **Abundance:** Occasional **Height:** 8–28 in. **Flowering:** April–June **Flower Color:** Yellow to orange **Habitat-Community:** Sandy to clayey soils from California prairies to lower montane coniferous forests **Elevation:** Below 6000 ft. **Ecoregions:** Southern California/ Northern Baja Coast, Southern California Mountains, Sierra Nevada

Perennial with generally 1 naked, cylindric, rigid stem arising from a corm. Leaves 3–8 in. long, basal, usually 1, linear to lance-shaped, flattened, with parallel veins. Flowers 10–35 in open, head-like cluster, 6-parted, symmetric, with pedicels to 3 in. long, 6 stamens, and 3-lobed stigma. Tepals 0.2–0.5 in. long, free (no obvious tube), yellow to golden-orange. Fruits to 0.3 in. long, spherical capsules. Look for this showy wildflower in the chaparral segments (especially burns) of the PCT in southern California.

Triteleia ixioides

prettyface

THEMIDACEAE BRODIAEA FAMILY

PCT Sections: 10–20 **Abundance:** Locally common **Height:** 4–12 in. **Flowering:** May–July **Flower Color:** Yellow **Habitat-Community:** Forest edges in moist gravel or sand in lower montane coniferous forests **Elevation:** Below 9900 ft. **Ecoregions:** Sierra Nevada, Cascades, Klamath Mountains

Ascending, unbranched perennial with smooth or hairy stems. Leaves to 10 in. long, 0.6 in. wide, basal, linear. Flowers clustered at stem tip, ascending to erect, symmetric, with 6 stamens, fork-tipped filaments, and 3-lobed stigma. Tepals to 1 in. long, 6-parted, yellow (aging bluish) with dark midvein, in a funnel-shaped tube with spreading lobes, sepals and petals alike. Fruits erect, 3-angled capsules with sharp-angled, black-crusted seeds. *Triteleia* ("three complete") refers to the 3 sepals and 3 petals. *Ixioides* suggests plants are "like *Ixia*," a genus in the Iridaceae native to South Africa.

Triteleia montana

Sierra brodiaea

THEMIDACEAE
BRODIAEA FAMILY

PCT Sections: 11–18 **Abundance:** Locally common **Height:** 2–10 in. **Flowering:** June–July **Flower Color:** Yellow **Habitat-Community:** Open understories and ridges, generally in granitic gravel, in montane coniferous forests **Elevation:** Below 9900 ft. **Ecoregions:** Sierra Nevada, Cascades

Ascending, unbranched perennial with hairy stems. Leaves to 12 in. long, 0.2 in. wide, basal, linear. Flowers clustered at stem tip, ascending to erect, symmetric, with 6 stamens and 3-lobed stigma. Tepals to 0.7 in. long, 6-parted, yellow (aging purple) with dark midvein, in a narrowly funnel-shaped tube with spreading lobes, petals similar to sepals. Fruits erect, 3-angled capsules with sharp-angled, black-crusted seeds. Since they love open ridges, you will generally find plants in places with spectacular views! Aka mountain triteleia.

▼ 4 PETALS

Barbarea orthoceras

American yellowrocket

BRASSICACEAE MUSTARD FAMILY

PCT Sections: 1–6 & 9–24 **Abundance:** Common **Height:** 6–24 in. **Flowering:** February–July **Flower Color:** Yellow **Habitat-Community:** Meadows, streambanks, and moist, rocky places from lower montane to subalpine coniferous forests and wetland-riparian communities **Elevation:** Below 11,200 ft. **Ecoregions:** All (except Sonoran/Mojave Basin and Range)

Erect biennial to perennial with woody base and hairless, angled stems. Leaves 0.6–5 in. long, pinnately lobed, with ovoid terminal lobes much larger than the 1–4 pairs of lateral lobes. Flowers in elongated clusters at stem tips with sepals to 0.2 in. long and yellow petals 0.2–0.3 in. long. Fruits 1–1.8 in. long, erect to ascending, cylindric, hairless siliques with 24–36 ovoid to oblong seeds. *Barbarea* is named after a 4th-century saint; species were formerly called Saint Barbara's cress.

Descurainia incana

soft mountain tansymustard

BRASSICACEAE MUSTARD FAMILY

PCT Sections: 3–4 & 9–24 **Abundance:** Occasional **Height:** 0.5–4 ft. **Flowering:** May–September **Flower Color:** Yellow **Habitat-Community:** Meadows and open places from lower montane to subalpine coniferous forests **Elevation:** Below 11,500 ft. **Ecoregions:** Southern California Mountains, Sierra Nevada, Cascades, Klamath Mountains

Erect biennial with hairy, leafy, many-branched (upper) stems. Leaves 0.6–5 in. long, lance-shaped to ovoid, smooth-margined and pinnately lobed, with linear to oblong or lance-shaped lobes 0.1–0.6 in. long. Flowers in elongated displays at stem tips with sepals to 0.1 in. long and yellow petals to 0.8 in. long. Fruits 0.2–0.6 in. long, to 0.1 in. wide, erect, linear, hairless siliques with 14–22 seeds in 1 row. The genus name honors French botanist F. Descourain (1658–1740).

Descurainia pinnata

western tansymustard

BRASSICACEAE MUSTARD FAMILY

PCT Sections: 1–9 **Abundance:** Common **Height:** 10–25 in. **Flowering:** February–June **Flower Color:** Yellow **Habitat-Community:** Dry, sandy soils in washes and hillsides in scrubs, chaparrals, and woodlands **Elevation:** Below 7800 ft. **Ecoregions:** Southern California Mountains, Sierra Nevada

Variously branched annual with hairless to hairy stems. Leaves 1–6 in. long, reduced up the stem, spoon-shaped in outline, 1–2-pinnate, segments smooth or toothed. Flowers scattered along stems and branches, 4-parted, erect, with yellow to white petals 0.1 in. long and yellow, purple, or rose sepals. Fruits 0.1–0.6 in. long, hairless, distinctly club-shaped siliques. Several varieties in California: var. *glabra* (hairless inflorescence) is most common on the PCT. As with many mustard family species, the leaves are edible in small quantities.

Draba corrugata

southern California draba

BRASSICACEAE MUSTARD FAMILY

PCT Sections: 4–5 **Abundance:** Rare **Height:** 2–5 in. **Flowering:** June–July **Flower Color:** Yellow **Habitat-Community:** Rocky slopes, talus, and shaded understories in montane coniferous forests **Elevation:** 6400–11,200 ft. **Ecoregions:** Southern California Mountains

Cushion-forming biennial or short-lived perennial with hairy herbage. Leaves 0.5–1 in. long, basal overlapping, 6–10 reduced and alternate on stem, narrowly spoon-shaped, hairy, with smooth margins. Flowers 10–67 per plant along branch and stem tips, 4-parted, with yellow petals 0.1–0.2 in. long. Fruits 0.2–0.9 in. long, elliptic, distinctly twisted, hairy siliques. Limited in California to the San Bernardino and San Gabriel Mountains; also occurs in northern Baja.

Draba lemmonii

Lemmon's draba

BRASSICACEAE MUSTARD FAMILY

PCT Sections: 10–13 **Abundance:** Locally common **Height:** 1–6 in. **Flowering:** July–August **Flower Color:** Yellow **Habitat-Community:** Open rocky slopes, outcrops, and rocky meadows in subalpine coniferous forests and alpine communities **Elevation:** 10,000–13,200 ft. **Ecoregions:** Sierra Nevada

Tufted perennial from a basal rosette. Leaves 0.1–0.7 in. long, narrowly to widely spoon-shaped, hairy. Flowers in dense clusters of 4–21 at stem tips, with sepals to 0.1 in. long and yellow petals to 0.3 in. long. Fruits 0.1–0.4 in. long, to 0.2 in. wide, ovoid, generally twisted, hairy capsules with 10–16 seeds and minute style. Look for it at or near timberline in the Sierra Nevada.

Erysimum capitatum

western wallflower

BRASSICACEAE MUSTARD FAMILY

PCT Sections: All **Abundance:** Common **Height:** 0.5–4 ft. **Flowering:** March–July **Flower Color:** Yellow to orange **Habitat-Community:** Open places, including serpentine soils, from woodlands and chaparrals to subalpine coniferous forests **Elevation:** Below 13,200 ft. **Ecoregions:** All

Erect biennial or short-lived perennial with 1–few stems from a basal rosette. Leaves 1–6 in. long, linear to spoon-shaped, hairy, with smooth to toothed margins. Flowers in dense clusters at stem tips, with sepals to 0.5 in. long and yellow to orange petals 0.5–1 in. long. Fruits 1.4–6 in. long, to 0.2 in. wide, spreading-ascending hairy capsules not constricted between the 54–82 seeds. The plant juice of wallflowers has been used to induce blisters to treat various ailments.

Erysimum perenne

Sierra wallflower

BRASSICACEAE MUSTARD FAMILY

PCT Sections: 9–24 **Abundance:** Common **Height:** 15–26 in. **Flowering:** May–August **Flower Color:** Yellow **Habitat-Community:** Open, gravelly or sandy soils, including serpentine, from upper montane coniferous forests to alpine communities **Elevation:** 6500–13,200 ft. **Ecoregions:** Sierra Nevada, Cascades, Klamath Mountains

Erect, aromatic perennial with 1–few stems from a basal rosette. Leaves 1–2 in. long, spoon-shaped, hairy, with smooth to toothed margins. Flowers in clusters at stem tips, with sepals to 0.5 in. long and yellow petals 0.6–0.9 in. long. Fruits 1.5–5.5 in. long, to 0.1 in. wide, spreading-ascending hairy siliques constricted between the 26–44 seeds.

Physaria kingii subsp. *bernardina*

San Bernardino Mountains bladderpod

BRASSICACEAE MUSTARD FAMILY

PCT Sections: 4 **Abundance:** Rare **Height:** 2–8 in. **Flowering:** May–June **Flower Color:** Yellow **Habitat-Community:** Dry slopes and flats and forest margins in sagebrush scrubs and montane coniferous forests **Elevation:** 6200–8000 ft. **Ecoregions:** Southern California Mountains

Perennial, usually angled laterally rather than erect, branched from base, with hairy stems. Basal leaves diamond-shaped or oblong, 0.9–2.5 in. long; stem leaves alternate, reduced, spatula- or spoon-shaped. Flowers densely clustered at stem tips, 4-parted, with spatula-shaped yellow petals 0.3–0.6 in. long. Fruits 0.1–0.3 in. long, round to pear-shaped silicles with rounded tip and styles 0.2–0.3 in. long. Limited to a few occurrences in the Big Bear Lake region, this federally endangered species is protected by law. If observed along the PCT, be very careful not to trample or otherwise disturb.

Stanleya pinnata var. *pinnata*

desert
prince's plume

BRASSICACEAE MUSTARD FAMILY

PCT Sections: 1–8 **Abundance:** Occasional **Height:** 1–5 ft. **Flowering:** June–August **Flower Color:** Yellow **Habitat-Community:** Open sites, seeps, and alkali-rich soils in chaparrals, Joshua tree & pinyon-juniper woodlands, and lower montane coniferous forests **Elevation:** Below 9200 ft. **Ecoregions:** Southern California Mountains, Sierra Nevada

Showy perennial or woody-based subshrub with many erect, hairless, white-waxy stems. Leaves 2–6 in. long, 1–2 in. wide, pinnately lobed with many lance-shaped segments; uppermost stem leaves are smooth-margined (unlobed). Flowers in very dense clusters at stem tips, 4-parted, with yellow petals 0.5–0.9 in. long. Fruits 1.2–3.5 in. long, spreading, narrowly linear siliques, flattened, sometimes curvy. Often associated with alkali springs or gypsum-rich soils, which frequently harbor other unique plants. The genus name honors ornithologist E. S. Stanley (1775–1851).

Streptanthus bernardinus

Laguna
Mountains
jewelflower

BRASSICACEAE MUSTARD FAMILY

PCT Sections: 1 & 3–4 **Abundance:** Rare **Height:** 10–35 in. **Flowering:** June–August **Flower Color:** Pale yellow to cream **Habitat-Community:** Dry, gravelly slopes and flats in chaparrals and montane coniferous forests **Elevation:** Below 7900 ft. **Ecoregions:** Southern California Mountains

One- to few-branched perennial with a woody base and hairless stems. Leaves 1–4 in. long, basal and alternate, basal leaves spoon-shaped, with short-hairy petioles. Stem leaves sessile, reduced up the stem, ovoid, with smooth margins. Flowers openly scattered at stem and branch tips, 4-parted, with bell-shaped, pale yellow (appearing inflated) calyces enclosing all but the tips of the petals. Petals 0.3–0.5 in. long, spatula-shaped, white to cream. Fruits 0.2–0.5 in. long, to 0.1 in. wide, ascending to spreading, flattened, smooth siliques.

Tropidocarpum gracile

dobie pod

BRASSICACEAE MUSTARD FAMILY

PCT Sections: 1–8 **Abundance:** Occasional **Height:** 5–18 in. **Flowering:** March–May **Flower Color:** Yellow **Habitat-Community:** Dry, sandy to gravelly flats and washes in foothill chaparrals, creosote bush scrubs, and Joshua tree woodlands **Elevation:** Below 4900 ft. **Ecoregions:** Southern California Mountains, Sierra Nevada

Sprawling to decumbent annual with long- and short-hairy stems (short hairs are forked). Leaves 1–4 in. long, forming basal rosettes (largest leaves) and alternate, 3–8-pinnately-lobed, stem leaves reduced and green becoming reddish with age. Flowers mostly clustered toward stem tip, 4-parted, with erect, green sepals. Petals 0.1–0.3 in. long, yellow (occasionally purple-tinged). Fruits 1–3 in. long, linear, flat, purplish, short-hairy siliques. This peculiar mustard often grows in small local populations and can be mistaken as a waif or weed. Flowers open for only a few hours at midday. *Tropidocarpum* means "keeled-fruit" in Greek.

Euphorbia lurida

woodland spurge

EUPHORBIACEAE SPURGE FAMILY

PCT Sections: 1–5 **Abundance:** Occasional **Height:** 8–25 in. **Flowering:** April–July **Flower Color:** Pale golden-yellow to green **Habitat-Community:** Dry slopes, flats, and shaded understories in pinyon-juniper woodlands and montane coniferous forests **Elevation:** Below 9000 ft. **Ecoregions:** Southern California Mountains

Erect, many-branched, hairless perennial; monoecious. Leaves 0.2–0.8 in. long, usually alternate, spoon-shaped to oblong. Flowers are grouped in head-like clusters at tips of branches, each containing a 4-parted cyathium. Nectary glands (golden-yellow to green) enclose many minute male flowers and 1 female flower, all lacking petals. Fruits 3-lobed, rounded capsules. Most common along the PCT in the San Bernardino and San Jacinto Mountains. The plant's sap was used as a purgative (hence the common name, from the old French *espurge*, "to purge").

Camissonia campestris

Mojave suncup

ONAGRACEAE
EVENING-PRIMROSE FAMILY

PCT Sections: 4–8 **Abundance:** Locally common **Height:** 3–12 in. **Flowering:** March–May **Flower Color:** Yellow **Habitat-Community:** Dry, sandy to gravelly flats and washes in creosote bush & Mojave mixed woody scrubs, foothill chaparrals, and Joshua tree & pinyon-juniper woodlands **Elevation:** Below 6400 ft. **Ecoregions:** Southern California Mountains, Mojave Basin and Range, Sierra Nevada

Erect or decumbent, often curving, slender-stemmed annual with peeling, hairless stems. Leaves 0.2–1.2 in. long, alternate, linear to narrowly elliptic, with finely toothed margins. Flowers nodding, with 4 reflexed sepals, connected in pairs, 0.1–0.3 in. long, with 8 stamens, ball-like stigma, and inferior ovary. Petals 0.2–0.7 in. long, 4, yellow fading red-orange. Fruits 0.8–1.7 in. long, cylindric, sessile capsules that are narrowed between swollen seeds. This straggly-looking little plant tends to grow in full sun. *Campestris* (from the Latin, "of the fields") refers to its propensity to grow in open, flat landscapes.

Camissonia pusilla

little wiry suncup

ONAGRACEAE
EVENING-PRIMROSE FAMILY

PCT Sections: 4–9 **Abundance:** Occasional **Height:** 2–9 in. **Flowering:** May–June **Flower Color:** Yellow **Habitat-Community:** Dry, sandy to gravelly soils in sagebrush scrubs and Joshua tree & pinyon-juniper woodlands **Elevation:** Below 7000 ft. **Ecoregions:** Southern California Mountains, Sierra Nevada

Erect, slender annual with hairy, sometimes glandular stems. Leaves 0.4–1.2 in. long, alternate, sessile, linear, with sparsely toothed margins. Flowers nodding, with 4 reflexed, free (not connected in pairs) sepals 0.1 in. long, 8 stamens, ball-like stigma, and inferior ovary. Petals 0.1–0.15 in. long, 4, yellow fading red-orange, with 2 basal spots. Fruits 0.7–1.4 in. long, cylindric, straight or wavy, linear to thread-like capsules that are narrowed between swollen seeds. Widespread in the Great Basin Desert, making only a limited appearance along the PCT near Walker Pass to Kennedy Meadows, in the southern Sierra (occasional), and on the desert slopes of the Transverse Ranges (scarce).

Camissonia strigulosa

contorted evening-primrose

ONAGRACEAE

EVENING-PRIMROSE FAMILY

PCT Sections: 1–8 **Abundance:** Common **Height:** 5–20 in. **Flowering:** March–June **Flower Color:** Yellow **Habitat-Community:** Dry, sandy to gravelly soils in California prairies, chaparrals, and woodlands **Elevation:** Below 6600 ft. **Ecoregions:** Southern California Mountains, Sierra Nevada

Slender, sprawling annual with hairy, wiry, peeling stems turning raspberry red with age. Leaves 0.3–1.5 in. long, alternate, sessile, linear to narrowly elliptic, light green becoming reddish with age, with finely toothed margins. Flowers nodding, with 4 reflexed, free (not connected in pairs) sepals 0.1–0.2 in. long, 8 stamens, ball-like stigma, and inferior ovary. Petals 0.1–0.3 in. long, 4, yellow. Fruits 0.7–2 in. long, cylindric, straight or coiled, linear to thread-like capsules that are narrowed between swollen seeds. Omnipresent in the montane chaparral of southern California; also occurs on coastal dunes far from the PCT!

Camissoniopsis bistorta

California suncup

ONAGRACEAE

EVENING-PRIMROSE FAMILY

PCT Sections: 1–6 **Abundance:** Locally common **Height:** 12–32 in. **Flowering:** March–June **Flower Color:** Yellow **Habitat-Community:** Clayey to gravelly soils in California prairies, foothill chaparrals, and oak woodlands **Elevation:** Below 3500 ft. **Ecoregions:** Southern California/Northern Baja Coast, Southern California Mountains

Decumbent to ascending, showy annual with 1-many stems and short-hairy herbage. Leaves 0.6–3.3 in. long, in basal rosette and alternate, spoon-shaped (basal) to lance-shaped (cauline), densely hairy, aging reddish, with wavy margins. Flowers 0.7–1 in. across, generally along one side of stem tips, with 4 reflexed (partially fused at tips) sepals, 8 stamens, ball-like stigma, and inferior ovary. Petals 0.2–0.6 in. long, 4, yellow with bright red spot at base. Fruits 1–1.8 in. long, cylindric, linear, 4-sided, straight or coiled, thick-based capsules. Most common along the PCT in southern California where the trail bisects coastal-influenced woodlands and chaparral at lower elevations. *Bistorta* (from the Latin, "twice-twisted") refers to the fruiting capsule.

Camissoniopsis hirtella

hairy suncup

ONAGRACEAE

EVENING-PRIMROSE FAMILY

PCT Sections: 1–7 **Abundance:** Common **Height:** 6–24 in. **Flowering:** March–August **Flower Color:** Yellow **Habitat-Community:** Sandy to gravelly soils in chaparrals, woodlands, and lower montane coniferous forests **Elevation:** Below 7300 ft. **Ecoregions:** Southern California/Northern Baja Coast, Southern California Mountains, Sierra Nevada

Decumbent to erect annual with hairy green (aging orange-brown) stems. Leaves 0.4–2.4 in. long, in basal rosette and alternate, spoon-shaped (basal) to ovoid and clasping (stem), densely hairy, red with age, with wavy margins. Flowers in nodding spike with lowest generally opening first, with 4 reflexed (partially fused at tips) sepals, 8 stamens, nearly ball-like stigma, and inferior ovary. Petals to 0.2 in. long, 4, yellow, sometimes with red spots at base. Fruits 0.5–1.1 in. long, cylindric, linear, 4-sided, straight or coiled capsules. A common plant on the PCT throughout southern California. *Hirtella* (from the Latin *hirtus*, "bristly") refers to the stiff hairs that cover this plant.

Camissoniopsis pallida

pale yellow suncup

ONAGRACEAE

EVENING-PRIMROSE FAMILY

PCT Sections: 1–9 **Abundance:** Occasional **Height:** 4–16 in. **Flowering:** March–August **Flower Color:** Yellow **Habitat-Community:** Sandy to gravelly soils in Sonoran/Mojave mixed woody scrubs, foothill chaparrals, and Joshua tree & pinyon-juniper woodlands **Elevation:** Below 5800 ft. **Ecoregions:** Southern California Mountains, Sierra Nevada

Decumbent to ascending, desert annual with gray, hairy stems. Leaves 0.4–2.2 in. long, in basal rosette and alternate, narrowly lance-shaped (basal) to elliptic (cauline), green. Flowers nodding on spike with lowest generally opening first, with 4 reflexed sepals, 8 stamens, ball-like stigma, and inferior ovary. Petals 0.1–0.5 in. long, 4, pale yellow, sometimes with red spots at base. Fruits 0.4–1.1 in. long, cylindric, linear, 4-sided, often highly coiled capsules. Two subspecies along the PCT: subsp. *pallida* (petals 0.1–0.2 in. long) is most common; subsp. *hallii* (petals 0.3–0.5 in. long) is limited to the eastern San Bernardino Mountains, where the two intergrade extensively. *Pallida* (from the Latin, "pale") refers to the flower.

Eulobus californicus

California suncup

ONAGRACEAE

EVENING-PRIMROSE FAMILY

PCT Sections: 1–6 **Abundance:** Locally common **Height:** 4–16 in. **Flowering:** March–June **Flower Color:** Yellow **Habitat-Community:** Sandy to gravelly slopes and washes in creosote bush & Sonoran mixed woody scrubs, foothill chaparrals, and woodlands **Elevation:** Below 4200 ft. **Ecoregions:** Southern California Mountains, Sonoran/Mojave Basin and Range

Erect, few-branched, sparse-flowered annual, bolting from a basal rosette, with minutely hairy herbage. Leaves 2–10 in. long, basal and alternate, narrowly elliptic, irregularly pinnately lobed, much reduced up the stem, mottled gray-green. Flowers widely spaced, opening at dawn, with 4 reflexed sepals, 8 stamens, rounded stigma, and inferior ovary. Petals 0.2–0.6 in. long, 4, yellow fading orange-red, speckled with red at base. Fruits 1.6–4.2 in. long, slender, cylindric, reflexed, 4-sided, straight capsules. *Eulobus* (from the Greek, "well lobed") refers to the prominently lobed basal leaves.

Oenothera elata

tall evening-primrose

ONAGRACEAE

EVENING-PRIMROSE FAMILY

PCT Sections: All **Abundance:** Occasional **Height:** 2–6 ft. **Flowering:** May–September **Flower Color:** Yellow **Habitat-Community:** Moist soils, springs, meadows, ponds, and streambanks in chaparrals, oak woodlands, wetland-riparian communities, and lower montane coniferous forests **Elevation:** Below 9500 ft. **Ecoregions:** All

Erect, few-branched biennial with reddish, stout, peeling stems and short-hairy, glandular herbage. Leaves 2–10 in. long, in loose basal rosettes and alternate, spoon- to lance-shaped, with smooth to toothed margins. Flowers in dense, showy spikes, with 4 reflexed sepals 0.8–1.8 in. long (aging red), 8 stamens, deeply lobed stigma, and inferior ovary. Petals 1.1–2.1 in. long, 4, yellow fading red-orange. Fruits 0.8–2.7 in. long, cylindric, narrowly lance-shaped, straight capsules. The only yellow-flowered *Oenothera* along the PCT. Flowers open just before sunset and remain open until about noon the following day.

Ehrendorferia chrysantha
golden eardrops

PAPAVERACEAE POPPY FAMILY

PCT Sections: 1–9 **Abundance:** Occasional **Height:** 2–6 ft. **Flowering:** April–September **Flower Color:** Yellow **Habitat-Community:** Dry slopes and valleys in foothill chaparrals, oak & pinyon-juniper woodlands, and lower montane coniferous forests **Elevation:** Below 7200 ft. **Ecoregions:** Southern California/Northern Baja Coast, Southern California Mountains, Sierra Nevada

Erect, tall, few-branched perennial with blue-green-waxy, hairless stems. Leaves 6–12 in. long, basal and alternate, 2–3-pinnately dissected into fern-like segments. Flowers many on stem and branch tips, irregular, with 2 sepals and 6 stamens. Petals 4, golden-yellow; the outer 2 petals are pouched at the base and their tips curve outward from the 2 central petals. Fruits 0.6–0.8 in. long, elliptic capsules. Most common in recent burns.

Eschscholzia androuxii
Joshua tree poppy

PAPAVERACEAE POPPY FAMILY

PCT Sections: 4 **Abundance:** Rare **Height:** 6–16 in. **Flowering:** March–May **Flower Color:** Yellow **Habitat-Community:** Coarse, sandy to gravelly slopes and washes in creosote bush & Sonoran/Mojave mixed woody scrubs and Joshua tree woodlands **Elevation:** Below 4500 ft. **Ecoregions:** Southern California Mountains, Sonoran/Mojave Basin and Range

Erect to spreading annual with waxy green stems. Leaves 1–5 in. long, basal and alternate, basal foliage compact, ternately dissected, reduced above, waxy green. Flowers 1–few on stem and branch tips, with 2 sepals, 4 yellow (conspicuous darkened basal spot) petals 0.4–1 in. long, and 20–35 stamens. Fruits 0.1–0.3 in. long, capsules. The specific epithet honors University of California Riverside botanists Tasha La Doux and this guidebook's co-author, André. Look for this recently discovered species along the PCT north of Interstate 15 as the trail climbs the desert slopes upward into the San Bernardino Mountains.

Eschscholzia caespitosa
tufted poppy

PAPAVERACEAE POPPY FAMILY

PCT Sections: 1–9 & 14–17 **Abundance:** Occasional **Height:** 2–12 in. **Flowering:** March–August **Flower Color:** Yellow **Habitat-Community:** Open, shrubby places in chaparral and lower montane coniferous forests **Elevation:** Below 5900 ft. **Ecoregions:** Southern California/Northern Baja Coast, Southern California Mountains, Sierra Nevada

Multi-stemmed, erect annual with hairless stems. Leaves 1–4-lobed into narrow obtuse or acute segments. Flowers 1 per stem, with 2 fused sepals and yellow (occasionally orange at base) petals 0.4–1 in. long. Fruits 1.5–3.2 in. long, oblong capsules with many seeds. The genus is named for Russian surgeon and botanist J.F.G. von Eschscholtz (1793–1831).

Eschscholzia glyptosperma

desert
gold poppy

PAPAVERACEAE POPPY FAMILY

PCT Sections: 7–9 **Abundance:** Occasional
Height: 3–12 in. **Flowering:** March–May **Flower Color:** Yellow **Habitat-Community:** Sandy to gravelly soils on slopes and alluvium in creosote bush scrubs, Mojave mixed woody scrubs, and Joshua tree woodlands **Elevation:** Below 5000 ft. **Ecoregions:** Mojave Basin and Range, Sierra Nevada

Compact annual with leafless, hairless, blue-green-waxy stems. Leaves 1–4 in. long, basal, deeply 3-ternately dissected into fern-like segments. Flowers solitary on stems from nodding bud, with 2 sepals and many stamens. Petals 0.4–1 in. long, 4, yellow. Fruits 0.2–0.3 in. long, capsules. This poppy is easily identified by having only basal leaves. Though common throughout the Mojave Desert, it appears along the PCT only in the lower-elevation segments of Kern County.

Eschscholzia minutiflora

pygmy
poppy

PAPAVERACEAE POPPY FAMILY

PCT Sections: 1–8 **Abundance:** Locally common
Height: 4–16 in. **Flowering:** March–May **Flower Color:** Yellow **Habitat-Community:** Sandy to gravelly slopes and plains in creosote bush & Sonoran/Mojave mixed woody scrubs and Joshua tree woodlands **Elevation:** Below 6300 ft. **Ecoregions:** Southern California Mountains, Sonoran/Mojave Basin and Range, Sierra Nevada

Erect to spreading annual with thin, hairless, blue-green-waxy stems. Leaves 1–5 in. long, basal and alternate, much reduced above, 1–4-pinnately dissected, with segments widened to the tip. Flowers generally 1–few at stem tips from nodding and short-pointed bud, with 2 sepals, 4 yellow petals 0.2–0.3 in. long, and many stamens. Fruits 0.1–0.3 in. long, capsules. Several subspecies, the rarer ones having larger flowers; the smaller-flowered subsp. *minutiflora* is most common along the PCT. Look for it along the trail at the lower desert crossings from the southern Sierra to the Borrego Desert of San Diego County.

Galium andrewsii

phloxleaf
bedstraw

RUBIACEAE MADDER FAMILY

PCT Sections: 1–7 **Abundance:** Common **Height:** 2–5 in. **Flowering:** April–June **Flower Color:** Yellow to pale green **Habitat-Community:** Sandy to loamy soils from oak woodlands to lower montane coniferous forests **Elevation:** Below 8000 ft. **Ecoregions:** Southern California Mountains, Sierra Nevada

Matted (usually <8 in. across), cushion-like perennial with intricately branched, green, hairless stems; dioecious. Leaves 0.2–0.6 in. long, in whorls of 4 spaced along stem, linear or needle-like, keeled and pointed at tip. Male flowers in few-flowered clusters, female flowers 1 per leaf axil; 4 stamens, 1 pistil, and 4 spreading corolla lobes to 0.1 in. long, yellow to pale green. Fruits deeply 2-lobed, each lobe about 0.1 in. across and hairy. Resembles a robust moss. The specific epithet honors botanist Timothy Langdon Andrews (1819–1908).

Galium angustifolium

narrowleaf bedstraw

RUBIACEAE MADDER FAMILY

PCT Sections: 1–9 **Abundance:** Common **Height:** 1–3 ft. **Flowering:** March–July **Flower Color:** Yellow to pale red **Habitat-Community:** Cliffs, canyons, and washes from oak woodlands to lower montane coniferous forests **Elevation:** Below 8700 ft. **Ecoregions:** Southern California Mountains, Sierra Nevada

Much-branched perennial or subshrub with a woody base and hairless to hairy, 4-sided stems; dioecious. Leaves 0.1–0.8 in. long, in whorls of 4 spaced along stem, linear to lance-shaped, and point-tipped. Male flowers 0.1 in. across, female flowers radial; 4 stamens, 1 pistil, and 4 spreading corolla lobes to 0.1 in. long, yellow to pale red. Fruits 0.1–0.2 in. across, 2-chambered, bristly, white to tawny; in female plants, bristly white hairs are present on the developing fruits. At least 6 subspecies occur along the PCT, several of limited distribution and conservation concern; subsp. *angustifolium* is quite common.

Galium porrigens var. *porrigens*

climbing bedstraw

RUBIACEAE MADDER FAMILY

PCT Sections: 1–6 **Abundance:** Common **Height:** 1–6 ft. **Flowering:** May–August **Flower Color:** Pale yellow to red **Habitat-Community:** Among shrubs in foothill chaparrals, oak woodlands, and lower montane coniferous forests **Elevation:** Below 6500 ft. **Ecoregions:** Southern California/Northern Baja Coast, Southern California Mountains

Perennial vine (sometimes woody near base) with recurved hairs along stems that help it cling to other shrubs for support; dioecious. Leaves 0.1–0.7 in. long, in whorls of 4 spaced along stem, oblong to ovoid, point-tipped. Flowers 0.1 in. across, radial, with 4 spreading, pale yellow to red corolla lobes to 0.1 in. long. Fruits 0.1 in. across, 2-chambered, with translucent white hairs. Quite common in newly burned chaparral, where, lacking a nearby shrub to twine on, plants may develop as self-supporting, multi-branched little subshrubs rather than vines. The Rubiaceae contains more than 600 genera, including *Coffea*, the source of coffee.

▼ 5 PETALS / SYMMETRIC COROLLAS

Cymopterus terebinthinus

turpentine cymopterus

APIACEAE CARROT FAMILY

PCT Sections: 7–20 **Abundance:** Locally common **Height:** 4–20 in. **Flowering:** April–June **Flower Color:** Yellow **Habitat-Community:** Rocky or sandy soils, including serpentine, from oak woodlands to subalpine coniferous forests **Elevation:** Below 11,500 ft. **Ecoregions:** Sierra Nevada, Cascades, Klamath Mountains

Erect, stout perennial with short stems and shiny, yellow- to gray-green herbage. Leaves 0.6–7 in. long, finely divided into linear segments with pointed tips. Flowers symmetric, with linear bractlets, 5 sepals, and 5 free, yellow petals, in open, hemispheric clusters with 3–24 rays to 3 in. long. Fruits to 0.4 in. across with equal sets of wings. Plants have a strong turpentine odor, as you may have guessed from the common name.

California lomatium

Lomatium californicum

APIACEAE CARROT FAMILY

PCT Sections: 5–8 **Abundance:** Occasional **Height:** 1–4 ft. **Flowering:** March–April **Flower Color:** Yellow **Habitat-Community:** Brushy slopes and openings in woodlands, chaparrals, and lower montane coniferous forests **Elevation:** Below 5900 ft. **Ecoregions:** Southern California Mountains, Sierra Nevada

Erect, hairless perennial with blue- or white-wax-coated herbage. Leaves 4–12 in. across, 1–2-pinnately compound, with relatively few (for a lomatium) wedge- to widely spoon-shaped leaflets 0.8–2 in. long with lobed or toothed margins. Flowers symmetric, with 5 free, yellow petals, in open, hemispheric clusters with 8–20 rays to 3 in. long. Fruits to 0.6 in. long, hairless, with thickened wings narrower than body. The Apiaceae has many poisonous plants: do not eat any part of a lomatium.

shiny biscuitroot

Lomatium lucidum

APIACEAE CARROT FAMILY

PCT Sections: 1–5 **Abundance:** Occasional **Height:** 6–40 in. **Flowering:** April–May **Flower Color:** Yellow **Habitat-Community:** Valleys, ridgetops, and burns in foothill chaparrals and oak woodlands **Elevation:** Below 4600 ft. **Ecoregions:** Southern California /Northern Baja Coast, Southern California Mountains

Somewhat fleshy perennial with hairless and green herbage; monoecious. Leaves 1–5 in. long, 1.5–5 in. wide, triangular, 1–2-ternate with ovoid, toothed, generally 3-lobed leaflets 0.5–2.1 in. long. Flowers in clusters of hemispheric heads, 10–20 rays, unisexual, female at head margins and male throughout head with elongated curving-inward stamens. Petals 5, yellow. Fruits 0.4–0.7 in. long, flattened, ovoid to round, hairless, with thickened wings much wider than body. Occurs along the PCT in the southern Peninsular Ranges and in the Cajon Pass region, especially in recent burns. Caution: do not eat any part of a lomatium.

Mojave desertparsley

Lomatium mohavense

APIACEAE CARROT FAMILY

PCT Sections: 1–9 **Abundance:** Locally common **Height:** 5–20 in. **Flowering:** April–May **Flower Color:** Yellow to purplish **Habitat-Community:** Valleys and ridgetops in sandy soils in creosote bush & Sonoran/Mojave mixed woody scrubs and Joshua tree & pinyon-juniper woodlands **Elevation:** Below 6600 ft. **Ecoregions:** Southern California Mountains, Mojave Basin and Range, Sierra Nevada

Stemless perennial with leaves emerging from plant base and gray-hairy herbage. Leaves 1–5 in. long, crowded into many small lance-linear segments, densely short-hairy, gray. Flowers in clusters of hemispheric heads, 8–18 rays, hairy, with elongated, yellowish stamens. Petals 5, yellow to purplish. Fruits 0.2–0.5 in. long, flattened, ovoid to round, short-hairy, with wings wider than body. Common throughout the western Mojave Desert. Skirts the PCT along the desert slopes of the southern California and southern Sierra Nevada Mountains. Plants are increasingly harvested from the wild for herbal uses. Caution: do not eat any part of a lomatium.

Lomatium multifidum

carrotleaf biscuitroot

APIACEAE CARROT FAMILY

PCT Sections: 3–24 **Abundance:** Locally common **Height:** 1–5 ft. **Flowering:** April–July **Flower Color:** Yellow or reddish **Habitat-Community:** Rocky soils and shaded slopes from lower montane to subalpine coniferous forests **Elevation:** Below 9900 ft. **Ecoregions:** Southern California Mountains, Sierra Nevada, Cascades, Klamath Mountains

Erect perennial with tall stems and hairy or hairless, fern-like foliage. Leaves 6–14 in. across, triangular-ovoid to round, pinnate, with widely linear lobes to 0.3 in. long and smooth margins. Flowers symmetric, with many linear bractlets and 5 free, yellow or reddish petals, in open, hemispheric clusters with 10–30 rays to 4 in. long. Fruits to 0.6 in. long, hairless, with thick wings wider than body. Caution: do not eat any part of a lomatium.

Oreonana vestita

woolly mountainparsley

APIACEAE CARROT FAMILY

PCT Sections: 4–5 **Abundance:** Rare **Height:** 2–6 in. **Flowering:** March–July **Flower Color:** Yellow **Habitat-Community:** Open, rocky slopes and ridgetops in coarse gravel and talus in upper montane & subalpine coniferous forests **Elevation:** 6200–11,100 ft. **Ecoregions:** Southern California Mountains

Cushion-forming perennial with white-hairy herbage. Leaves 0.7–2.1 in. long, basal, tightly clustered, ovoid, pinnately dissected into many ovoid to round segments 0.1–0.3 in. long; petiole 0.8–4 in. long. Flowers crowded in ball-shaped heads 0.8–2.1 in. across, tucked in among the leaves, with 10–25 rays, 0 (occasionally 5) calyces, and 5 yellow or sometimes maroon petals. Fruits 0.2–0.3 in. long, disk-like, oval, hairy. Endemic to the Transverse Ranges. Best observed along the PCT atop Mt. Baden-Powell to Kratka Ridge in the high San Gabriel Mountains. *Oreonana* means "mountain dwarf" in Latin.

Osmorhiza occidentalis

western sweetcicely

APIACEAE CARROT FAMILY

PCT Sections: 11–24 **Abundance:** Locally common **Height:** 1–4 ft. **Flowering:** March–July **Flower Color:** Yellow **Habitat-Community:** Shaded understories, meadows, streambanks, and seeps from oak woodlands to upper coniferous forests and wetland-riparian communities **Elevation:** Below 10,500 ft. **Ecoregions:** Sierra Nevada, Cascades, Klamath Mountains

Erect, 1–few-stemmed, leafy perennial with fine-hairy or hairless herbage. Leaves 4–8 in. long, elliptic to ovoid, 2-pinnately compound, with lance-shaped to ovoid leaflets 0.8–4 in. long with toothed margins. Flowers symmetric with 5 free, yellow petals, in hemispheric clusters with 5–12 rays to 3 in. long. Fruits to 0.9 in. long, linear, hairless, slender-beaked. The crushed roots emit a sweet odor (hence the common name).

Sanicula crassicaulis

Pacific blacksnakeroot

APIACEAE CARROT FAMILY

PCT Sections: 1–5 & 19–20 & 23–24 **Abundance:** Common **Height:** 1–4 ft. **Flowering:** February–May **Flower Color:** Yellow **Habitat-Community:** Open or partially shaded slopes in woodlands, chaparrals, and lower montane coniferous forests **Elevation:** Below 5000 ft. **Ecoregions:** Southern California/Northern Baja Coast, Southern California Mountains, Klamath Mountains

Erect, thick perennial with hairless green herbage. Leaves 1–5 in. long, round, palmately lobed, lobes 3–5 with sharp teeth. Flowers in spheric clusters, symmetric, with 5 bracts < heads, minute sepals, and 5 free, yellow petals; anthers and stigmas obviously exserted. Fruits to 0.2 in. long, roundish, covered with stout prickles. Plants, especially the roots, were believed to have curative properties (hence *Sanicula*, "to heal"). The palmately lobed leaves are unique among sanicles along the CA PCT.

Sanicula graveolens

Sierra sanicle

APIACEAE CARROT FAMILY

PCT Sections: 1 & 4 & 13–24 **Abundance:** Locally common **Height:** 2–18 in. **Flowering:** February–June **Flower Color:** Yellow **Habitat-Community:** Forest openings and rocky soils, including serpentine, in montane coniferous forests **Elevation:** Below 8600 ft. **Ecoregions:** All (except Sonoran/Mojave Basin and Range)

Erect, widely spreading perennial with hairless, aromatic, green or purplish foliage. Leaves 0.6–1.6 in. long, ovoid, 2–3-pinnately compound, the stalked leaflets with toothed to lobed margins. Flowers in spheric clusters, symmetric, with 6–10 fused-at-base bracts < heads, minute fused sepals, and 5 free, yellow petals; anthers and stigmas obviously exserted. Fruits to 0.2 in. long, ovoid to roundish, covered with stout (some hooked) prickles. Plants are strongly odorous, especially when the leaves are crushed (hence *graveolens*, "strong smelling").

Sanicula tuberosa

turkey pea

APIACEAE CARROT FAMILY

PCT Sections: 1–6 & 13–22 **Abundance:** Locally common **Height:** 2–31 in. **Flowering:** February–July **Flower Color:** Yellow **Habitat-Community:** Rocky or gravelly soils from woodlands and chaparrals to upper montane coniferous forests **Elevation:** Below 8900 ft. **Ecoregions:** All (except Sonoran/Mojave Basin and Range)

Erect, slender perennial with hairless, white-waxy, green to purple foliage. Leaves 0.8–5 in. long, triangular to ovoid, 2–3-pinnately compound, the leaflets with smooth to lobed margins. Flowers 6–10 in spheric clusters, symmetric, with fused bracts < heads, minute fused sepals, and 5 free, yellow petals; anthers and stigmas obviously exserted. Fruits to 0.2 in. long, ovoid to roundish, covered with warty bumps (not prickles). The common name likely refers to the weird fruits.

southern tauschia

Tauschia arguta

APIACEAE CARROT FAMILY

PCT Sections: 1–6 **Abundance:** Occasional **Height:** 12–28 in. **Flowering:** April–June **Flower Color:** Yellow **Habitat-Community:** Gravelly to rocky soils in foothill chaparrals, Sonoran/ Mojave mixed woody scrubs, and oak woodlands **Elevation:** Below 5000 ft. **Ecoregions:** Southern California/Northern Baja Coast, Southern California Mountains

Short-stemmed perennial with white-hairy herbage. Leaves 4–6.5 in. long (petiole 2.5–8 in. long), leathery, white-hairy, oblong to ovoid, 1-pinnate, with ovoid, sharply tooth-margined leaflets 1.2–2.8 in. long. Flowers in dense clusters of hemispheric heads, with 12–25 rays, 5 calyces, and 5 yellow petals. Fruits 0.2–0.4 in. long, oblong, with prominent longitudinal ribs.

Parish's tauschia

Tauschia parishii

APIACEAE CARROT FAMILY

PCT Sections: 1–9 **Abundance:** Occasional **Height:** 8–18 in. **Flowering:** May–July **Flower Color:** Yellow **Habitat-Community:** Slopes, ridges, and shaded understories in chaparrals, oak & pinyon-juniper woodlands, and lower montane coniferous forests **Elevation:** Below 8000 ft. **Ecoregions:** Southern California Mountains, Sierra Nevada

Low-growing, stemless perennial with waxy, hairless foliage. Leaves 3.5–6 in. long (petiole 2–6 in. long), often waxy, leathery, oblong to ovoid, 2-pinnate; leaflets 0.8–1.6 in. long with narrow, tooth-margined segments. Flowers in open, hemispheric heads, with 12–18 rays, 5 calyces, and 5 yellow petals. Fruits 0.2–0.4 in. long, oblong, with prominent longitudinal ribs. The leaves have a sweet parsley-like aroma.

Parish's catchfly

Silene parishii

CARYOPHYLLACEAE PINK FAMILY

PCT Sections: 3–5 **Abundance:** Occasional **Height:** 4–15 in. **Flowering:** May–September **Flower Color:** Yellow to cream **Habitat-Community:** Moist drainages and open rocky to gravelly slopes in upper montane & subalpine coniferous forests **Elevation:** 6000–10,300 ft. **Ecoregions:** Southern California Mountains

Ascending to erect, many-branched perennial with short-hairy above, often glandular throughout stems. Leaves 0.7–2.5 in. long, opposite, lance-shaped to ovoid, reduced in size on upper stem, and somewhat thick and leathery. Flowers 1–few at stem tips, 5-parted; fused sepals with 10-veined, short-glandular-hairy lobes 0.9–1.2 in. long. Petals, extending 0.3–0.4 in. beyond calyx, yellow to white, 6-lobed, with 2 appendages. Fruits ovoid to elliptic capsules with many brown seeds. Endemic to the higher elevations of the San Jacinto, San Bernardino, and San Gabriel Mountains, sometimes appearing above tree line. Its yellow flowers and leathery leaves are unique among the southern California *Silene* spp.

Crocanthemum aldersonii
Alderson's rush-rose
CISTACEAE ROCK-ROSE FAMILY

PCT Sections: 1–2 **Abundance:** Occasional **Height:** 12–25 in. **Flowering:** March–June **Flower Color:** Bright yellow **Habitat-Community:** Slopes and canyons in foothill chaparrals **Elevation:** Below 3900 ft. **Ecoregions:** Southern California/Northern Baja Coast, Southern California Mountains

Erect, showy perennial or subshrub with hairless to sparsely branched-hairy stems. Leaves 0.4–0.9 in. long, alternate, deciduous, linear to lance-shaped. Flowers 1–few at stem and branch tips, with 12–36 orange-yellow stamens and 5 sepals (outer 2 narrower). Petals 5, bright yellow, ovoid, 0.3–0.5 in. long. Fruits small capsules with 7–12 seeds. Sprouts by the thousands after a fire. Look for it along the PCT from the Mexico border to Lake Moreno, and in the hills surrounding Warner Springs. *Crocanthemum* is Greek for "yellow flower."

Dudleya abramsii subsp. abramsii
Abrams' liveforever
CRASSULACEAE STONECROP FAMILY

PCT Sections: 1 & 8–9 **Abundance:** Rare **Height:** 2–12 in. **Flowering:** May–July **Flower Color:** Pale yellow **Habitat-Community:** Rocky to gravelly soils, outcrops, and crevices in chaparrals and oak woodlands **Elevation:** Below 6200 ft. **Ecoregions:** Southern California Mountains, Sierra Nevada

Rock-loving, succulent perennial with 1–several, tightly clustered leaf rosettes 2–6 in. across. Leaves 0.6–4.3 in. long, basal, drying in summer but not deciduous, oblong, base sometimes reddish, succulent, and waxy. Flowers clustered at stem and branch tips, fleshy bracted, 5-parted, fused near base, symmetric, with triangular sepals to 0.2 in. long and pale yellow petals 0.3–0.7 in. long. Fruits erect to spreading, small follicles. Look for it along the PCT on granitic slabs from Campo to Mt. Laguna in San Diego County, and again in the Walker Pass region of the southern Sierra.

Dudleya abramsii subsp. affinis
San Bernardino Mountains dudleya
CRASSULACEAE STONECROP FAMILY

PCT Sections: 4 **Abundance:** Rare **Height:** 1–8 in. **Flowering:** May–July **Flower Color:** Pale yellow **Habitat-Community:** Rocky to gravelly soils in pinyon-juniper woodlands and lower montane coniferous forests **Elevation:** 5800–8100 ft. **Ecoregions:** Southern California Mountains

Succulent perennial with 1–several clustered leaf rosettes 1–2.5 in. across. Leaves 0.8–1.7 in. long, basal, sometimes summer deciduous, elliptic, triangular, or spoon-shaped, thick, waxy. Flowers clustered at stem and branch tips, fleshy bracted, 5-parted, fused near base, symmetric. Petals 0.2–0.4 in. long, pale yellow. Fruits small follicles. Endemic to the eastern San Bernardino Mountains, often affiliated with quartzite or calcareous substrates.

Dudleya abramsii subsp. *calcicola*

limestone liveforever

CRASSULACEAE

STONECROP FAMILY

PCT Sections: 7–9 **Abundance:** Rare **Height:** 2–7 in. **Flowering:** April–August **Flower Color:** Pale yellow **Habitat-Community:** Rocky, limestone or granite outcrops in woodlands and chaparrals **Elevation:** Below 8600 ft. **Ecoregions:** Sierra Nevada

Succulent perennial with 1–50 leafy rosettes and stems to 0.8 in. wide. Leaves 0.4–2.4 in. long, lance-shaped to cylindric, acute-tipped. Flowers in open, 2–8-flowered clusters at stem tips, symmetric. Calyces to 0.3 in. long, 5-lobed, fused near base. Corollas to 0.6 in. long, 5-lobed, fused at base, pale yellow. Fruits many-seeded follicles.

Dudleya cymosa

canyon liveforever

CRASSULACEAE

STONECROP FAMILY

PCT Sections: 3–9 & 12–16 **Abundance:** Locally common **Height:** 1–12 in. **Flowering:** March–July **Flower Color:** Yellow to red **Habitat-Community:** Rocky outcrops and talus slopes in woodlands, chaparrals, and lower montane coniferous forests **Elevation:** Below 8900 ft. **Ecoregions:** Southern California Mountains, Sierra Nevada

Succulent, evergreen perennial with 1–many leafy rosettes and stems to 1.4 in. wide. Leaves 0.6–6.7 in. long, spoon-shaped, acute- to point-tipped. Flowers in open, 2–10-flowered clusters at stem tips, symmetric. Calyces to 0.2 in. long, 5-lobed, fused near base. Corollas to 0.6 in. long, 5-lobed, fused at base, yellow to red. Fruits many-seeded follicles. Well respected and revered by rock climbers throughout the Sierra. As climbers are inching their way up granite cracks and walls, canyon liveforevers are idly hanging out, watching out-of-place humans use all their concentration to survive the next climbing move!

Dudleya lanceolata

lanceleaf liveforever

CRASSULACEAE

STONECROP FAMILY

PCT Sections: 3–6 **Abundance:** Occasional **Height:** 2–10 in. **Flowering:** April–July **Flower Color:** Golden-yellow to red **Habitat-Community:** Rocky soils, ledges, and outcrops in foothill chaparrals and oak & pinyon-juniper woodlands **Elevation:** Below 5000 ft. **Ecoregions:** Southern California Mountaiuns

Succulent perennial. Leaves 2–16 in. long, clustered at base in a rosette 2–9 in. across, lance-shaped to oblong, fleshy, green or powdery gray. Flowers in open, many-flowered clusters at stem and branch tips, 5-parted, fused near base, symmetric, with rusty red sepals and golden-yellow to red petals 0.4–0.7 in. long. Fruits small follicles. Varies greatly in size of parts and flower color. Occurs along the PCT at lower-elevation segments, such as near Cajon Junction at Interstate 15, and on the southeastern flanks of the San Bernardino Mountains, where plants are intermediate to *D. saxosa*. Threatened by collecting: all *Dudleya* spp. are coveted ornamental plants for rock gardens.

Dudleya saxosa subsp. *aloides*

desert dudleya

CRASSULACEAE

STONECROP FAMILY

PCT Sections: 1–4 **Abundance:** Occasional **Height:** 3–12 in. **Flowering:** April–June **Flower Color:** Yellow to pale green **Habitat-Community:** Rocky soils, ledges, and outcrops in Sonoran mixed woody scrubs, foothill chaparrals, and pinyon-juniper woodlands **Elevation:** Below 5500 ft. **Ecoregions:** Southern California Mountains, Sonoran Basin and Range

Attractive, succulent perennial with 1–4 basal leaf rosettes 3–9 in. across. Leaves 2–6 in. long, lance-shaped to oblong, fleshy, pale waxy coated, maturing green. Flowers in open clusters at stem and branch tips, 5-parted, fused near base, symmetric, with reddish sepals and golden-yellow to pale green petals 0.3–0.7 in. long. Fruits small follicles. Most common along the PCT in the desert transition of the Peninsular Ranges, where it hybridizes with *D. lanceolata*. *Saxosa* (from the Latin *saxum*, "rocky") references its preferred habitat.

Sedum lanceolatum

spearleaf stonecrop

CRASSULACEAE

STONECROP FAMILY

PCT Sections: 10–23 **Abundance:** Common **Height:** 1–8 in. **Flowering:** May–August **Flower Color:** Yellow **Habitat-Community:** Rocky outcrops and talus slopes, including carbonate, in upper montane & subalpine coniferous forests **Elevation:** 5900–9200 ft. **Ecoregions:** Sierra Nevada, Cascades, Klamath Mountains

Succulent perennial with leafy rosettes and ascending stems. Leaves 0.2–1.2 in. long, linear to ovoid, point-tipped. Flowers in dense, 3–24-flowered, head-like clusters at stem tips, symmetric. Calyces 5-lobed and fused near base. Petals to 0.3 in. long, 5, free or fused at base, yellow with reddish midribs. Fruits erect, many-seeded pods. The genus name (from the Latin *sedere*, "to sit") refers to the way many of the species "sit" on rocks.

Sedum obtusatum

Sierra stonecrop

CRASSULACEAE

STONECROP FAMILY

PCT Sections: 10–17 **Abundance:** Common **Height:** 1–9 in. **Flowering:** May–August **Flower Color:** Yellow to pale yellow or white **Habitat-Community:** Rocky outcrops and slopes from lower montane coniferous forests to alpine communities **Elevation:** Below 12,200 ft. **Ecoregions:** Sierra Nevada

Succulent perennial with mats of leafy rosettes and shiny or white-wax-coated stems and leaves. Leaves 0.2–1.3 in. long, oval to spoon-shaped, rounded or obtuse to notch-tipped. Flowers in dense, 8–60-flowered, flat-topped clusters at stem tips, symmetric. Calyces to 0.2 in. long, 5-lobed, fused near base. Petals to 0.4 in. long, 5, free or fused at base, yellow to pale yellow or white. Fruits erect, many-seeded pods. The common, high-elevation stonecrop of the Sierra (hence the common name).

Sedum spathulifolium

broadleaf stonecrop

CRASSULACEAE

STONECROP FAMILY

PCT Sections: 3–6 & 10–24 **Abundance:** Common **Height:** 2–8 in. **Flowering:** April–August **Flower Color:** Yellow **Habitat-Community:** Shaded, rocky outcrops from woodlands and chaparrals to upper montane coniferous forests **Elevation:** Below 8200 ft. **Ecoregions:** Southern California Mountains, Sierra Nevada, Cascades, Klamath Mountains

Succulent perennial with matted rosettes of much larger outer leaves and blue-wax-coated stems and leaves. Leaves 0.4–0.9 in. long, spoon-shaped, rounded or obtuse-tipped. Flowers along 3 main branch tips in 5–48-flowered flat-topped clusters, symmetric. Calyces 5-lobed, fused near base. Petals to 0.4 in. long, 5, free or fused at base, yellow. Fruits erect, many-seeded pods.

Hypericum anagalloides

tinker's penny

HYPERICACEAE

ST. JOHN'S WORT FAMILY

PCT Sections: 1–4 & 9–24 **Abundance:** Common **Height:** 1–12 in. **Flowering:** May–September **Flower Color:** Yellow **Habitat-Community:** Meadows, marshes, seeps, springs, streambanks, and lakeshores in wetland-riparian communities **Elevation:** Below 10,600 ft. **Ecoregions:** All (except Sonoran/Mojave Basin and Range)

Lax to decumbent perennial with matted roots and hairless stems. Leaves to 0.6 in. long, opposite, oblong to roundish or linear, and clear- to green-gland-dotted. Flowers 1–many at stem tips. Calyces to 0.2 in. long, fused near base, with 5 unequal, lance-shaped to ovoid lobes. Petals to 0.2 in. long, equal to calyx lobes, 5, yellow to salmon. Fruits many-seeded capsules. *Hypericum* ("above pictures") alludes to an early use: plants were placed above shrines to repel evil spirits.

Hypericum scouleri

Scouler's St. Johnswort

HYPERICACEAE

ST. JOHN'S WORT FAMILY

PCT Sections: 1–5 & 9–24 **Abundance:** Common **Height:** 7–28 in. **Flowering:** June–September **Flower Color:** Yellow **Habitat-Community:** Meadows, streambanks, and moist slopes in chaparrals, lower montane coniferous forests, and wetland-riparian communities **Elevation:** Below 9700 ft. **Ecoregions:** All (except Sonoran/ Mojave Basin and Range)

Erect perennial with few, hairless stems. Leaves to 1.2 in. long, opposite, ovoid to widely oblong, clasping base, with black-dotted margins. Flowers 3–25 per stem. Calyces to 0.2 in. long, fused near base, with 5 oblong to ovoid, black-dotted lobes. Petals to 0.5 in. long, 5, black-dotted yellow. Fruits many-seeded capsules with 3 lobes. Easily confused with its non-native cousin *H. perforatum*.

Mentzelia albicaulis

whitestem blazingstar

LOASACEAE LOASA FAMILY

PCT Sections: 1–9 **Abundance:** Common **Height:** 3–20 in. **Flowering:** March–July **Flower Color:** Yellow **Habitat-Community:** Sandy to gravelly soils in creosote bush & Sonoran/Mojave mixed woody scrubs and Joshua tree & pinyon-juniper woodlands **Elevation:** Below 7100 ft. **Ecoregions:** Southern California Mountains, Sonoran/Mojave Basin and Range, Sierra Nevada

Erect to spreading, variously branched, ubiquitous annual with white, hairless or short-hairy stems. Leaves 1–4 in. long, generally alternate, pinnately lobed lower, reduced upper, smooth to lobed, sandpaper-like hairy. Flowers few in open clusters at branch and stem tips, with inferior ovary and lance-shaped to ovoid, 3-toothed to smooth, occasionally white-based green bracts. Perianth 5-parted, with free, glossy yellow, golden orange-based petals 0.1–0.2 in. long. Fruits 0.3–1.1 in. long, narrowly cylindric, variously curved capsules with many irregularly shaped, tan to dark-mottled seeds. Highly variable and among the most common annuals in the western US, ranging from British Columbia to Mexico but limited along the PCT to the desert slopes and crossings. *Albicaulis* (from the Latin, "white-stemmed") is not so specific: many *Mentzelia* spp. have white stems.

Mentzelia congesta

united blazingstar

LOASACEAE LOASA FAMILY

PCT Sections: 4–10 **Abundance:** Locally common **Height:** 4–20 in. **Flowering:** April–July **Flower Color:** Pale yellow **Habitat-Community:** Sandy to gravelly soils in Joshua tree & pinyon-juniper woodlands and lower montane coniferous forests **Elevation:** Below 8600 ft. **Ecoregions:** Southern California Mountains, Mojave Basin and Range, Sierra Nevada

Erect to spreading, variously-branched, sticky annual, often in dense, isolated populations, with tan, hairless or short-hairy stems. Leaves 1–3 in. long, generally alternate, pinnately lobed lower, reduced upper, smooth to lobed, and sandpaper-like, sticky hairy. Flowers in dense clusters at stem and branch tips, with inferior ovary and widely ovoid, toothed to lobed bracts with the lower 75% distinctively white-membranous and green-margined. Perianth 5-parted, with free, pale yellow, orange-based petals 0.1–0.3 in. long. Fruits 0.1–0.3 in. long, erect, cylindric, straight capsules with many, irregularly ridged, tan to dark-mottled seeds. Found along the PCT at the mid-elevations of southern California and in Antelope Valley.

Mentzelia dispersa
bushy blazingstar
LOASACEAE LOASA FAMILY

PCT Sections: All **Abundance:** Locally common **Height:** 4–22 in. **Flowering:** May–August **Flower Color:** Yellow **Habitat-Community:** Sandy to rocky soils in chaparrals, oak & pinyon-juniper woodlands, and montane coniferous forests **Elevation:** Below 10,200 ft. **Ecoregions:** All

Erect, small-flowered annual, sometimes intricately branching above, with thin, short-hairy, greenish tan stems. Leaves 1–3 in. long, generally alternate, smooth to pinnately toothed (lobed) lower, upper mostly smooth and reduced, glossy green, short-hairy. Flowers clustered at branch and stem tips, with inferior ovary and ovoid, smooth to slightly lobed, entirely green bracts. Perianth 5-parted, with free, glossy yellow petals 0.1–0.2 in. long. Fruits 0.3–0.9 in. long, erect, narrowly cylindric, curved capsules with prism-shaped, tan to dark-mottled seeds. Widespread throughout the western US. *Mentzelia* spp. have sticky hairs that enable plants to gain support on other plants; these may also aid in "hitchhiker dispersal," where the maturing fruit catches a ride on a passing animal or hiker (hence the alternative common name, stickleaf).

Mentzelia laevicaulis
giant blazingstar
LOASACEAE LOASA FAMILY

PCT Sections: 3–6 & 9–10 & 17–24 **Abundance:** Occasional **Height:** 10–40 in. **Flowering:** May–October **Flower Color:** Yellow **Habitat-Community:** Sandy to rocky slopes and roadsides in oak & pinyon-juniper woodlands and montane coniferous forests **Elevation:** Below 9500 ft. **Ecoregions:** Southern California Mountains, Sierra Nevada, Cascades, Klamath Mountains

Erect, showy, large-flowered biennial or perennial (in rosette stage), branched above, with straight, glossy white, sometimes short-hairy stems. Leaves 1–8 in. long, generally basal and alternate, lance-shaped, smooth to pinnately toothed (lobed) basal, reduced upper. Flowers few at stem tips, with inferior ovary, many stamens to 2 in. long, and lance-shaped, smooth to deeply lobed, green bracts. Perianth star-shaped, 5-parted, with free, long, pointed sepals. Petals 1.6–3.2 in. long, bright yellow. Fruits 0.6–1.1 in. long, erect, cylindric capsules with saucer-shaped winged seeds. Widespread throughout the western US but rarely seen in large numbers. The star-like flowers can measure 5 in. across, closing up in the evening and reopening in morning light. *Laevicaulis* is Latin for "smooth-stemmed."

Mentzelia micrantha
chaparral blazingstar
LOASACEAE LOASA FAMILY

PCT Sections: 4–6 **Abundance:** Locally common **Height:** 5–30 in. **Flowering:** April–June **Flower Color:** Yellow **Habitat-Community:** Open, sandy soils in burns or disturbed areas in chaparrals and oak woodlands **Elevation:** Below 6600 ft. **Ecoregions:** Southern California Mountains

Erect, sticky, branched, small-flowered annual with thin stems and short-hairy herbage. Leaves 1–7 in. long, generally alternate, ovoid to lance-shaped, glossy, with irregularly toothed or lobed margins. Flowers with many stamens and inferior ovary; bracts ovoid, smooth to toothed, somewhat concealing the flowers, green. Petals 0.1–0.2 in. long, 5, glossy yellow, free. Fruits 0.2–0.5 in. long, cylindric, erect to curved capsules with prism-shaped, triangular, tan to dark-mottled seeds. Especially abundant along the PCT in recent burns near Cajon Pass and in the Liebre Mountains.

Mentzelia veatchiana

Veatch's blazingstar

LOASACEAE LOASA FAMILY

PCT Sections: 1–9 **Abundance:** Common **Height:** 3–20 in. **Flowering:** March–June **Flower Color:** Yellow to orange **Habitat-Community:** Sandy soils in chaparrals, creosote bush scrubs, Joshua tree & pinyon-juniper woodlands, and lower montane coniferous forests **Elevation:** Below 7800 ft. **Ecoregions:** Southern California Mountains, Sonoran/Mojave Basin and Range, Sierra Nevada

Erect annual with sticky-hairy stems. Leaves to 7 in. long, alternate, sessile, lance-shaped, pinnately lobed, smooth to toothed, reduced on upper stem. Flowers 1–few at stem tips, with inferior ovary and ovoid, toothed, sometimes white-based, green bracts. Perianth 5-parted; petals free, yellow to orange with distinctive orange-red bases, 0.2–0.3 in. long. Fruits 0.3–1.2 in. long, erect to curved capsules with cone-shaped, irregularly angled seeds. Notoriously variable, intergrading with at least 4 other species.

Chorizanthe watsonii

fivetooth spineflower

POLYGONACEAE
BUCKWHEAT FAMILY

PCT Sections: 4–9 **Abundance:** Occasional **Height:** 1–6 in. **Flowering:** April–August **Flower Color:** Pale yellow **Habitat-Community:** Sandy or rocky soils in Mojave mixed woody scrubs, sagebrush scrubs, montane chaparrals, and Joshua tree & pinyon-juniper woodlands **Elevation:** Below 7700 ft. **Ecoregions:** Southern California Mountains, Mojave Basin and Range, Sierra Nevada

Inconspicuous, horizontal to erect annual, branched at base, with brittle, woolly stems, green turning yellow-brown. Leaves 0.1–0.6 in. long, basal, linear to lance-shaped, densely hairy. Flowers at stem and branch tips, sessile with 2 awned bracts and 9 stamens; involucres 0.2 in. long, tubular, 5-ribbed (each rib with a hooked awn), green turning yellow. Tepals to 0.1 in. long, 5-parted, yellow. Fruits achenes to 0.1 in. long. Occurs along the PCT from desert scrubs in the Mojave to montane zones of the San Bernardino Mountains (e.g., near Baldwin Lake).

Ranunculus cymbalaria

Rocky Mountain buttercup

RANUNCULACEAE
BUTTERCUP FAMILY

PCT Sections: 1–5 & 8–17 **Abundance:** Locally common **Height:** 1–8 in. **Flowering:** May–August **Flower Color:** Pale yellow **Habitat-Community:** Streambanks, marshes, and ponds in muddy soils in wetland-riparian communities **Elevation:** Below 10,500 ft. **Ecoregions:** Southern California/ Northern Baja Coast, Southern California Mountains, Sierra Nevada

Creeping perennial spreading by strawberry-like stolons with clusters of leaves. Leaves to 1.5 in. long, alternate, oblong to heart-shaped or roundish, with wavy to toothed margins. Flowers 1–many at stem tip, with many pistils and stamens. Sepals to 0.3 in. long, 5, spreading, greenish yellow. Petals to 0.3 in. long, 5. Fruits to 0.1 in. long with straight beak. *Ranunculus* (from the Latin *rana*, "frog") alludes to buttercups' affinity for wet habitats.

Drymocallis pseudorupestris

woodbeauty

ROSACEAE ROSE FAMILY

PCT Sections: 10–24 **Abundance:** Occasional **Height:** 2–10 in. **Flowering:** July–September **Flower Color:** Pale yellow to white **Habitat-Community:** Rocky outcrops and soils in subalpine coniferous forests and alpine communities **Elevation:** 7500–12,800 ft. **Ecoregions:** Sierra Nevada, Cascades, Klamath Mountains

Tufted to matted perennial with glandular-hairy stems, especially near base. Leaves to 3.5 in. long, alternate, pinnately compound with 7–9 oval to spoon-shaped or round leaflets to 0.8 in. long, with toothed margins. Flowers with many pistils and generally 20–25 stamens on spreading branches along stem. Sepals to 0.3 in. long, 5. Petals to 0.4 in. long, 5, widely spoon-shaped, pale yellow to white. Fruits tiny, pale brown, seed-like achenes.

Geum macrophyllum

largeleaf avens

ROSACEAE ROSE FAMILY

PCT Sections: 4 & 10–24 **Abundance:** Locally common **Height:** 7–43 in. **Flowering:** May–August **Flower Color:** Yellow **Habitat-Community:** Meadows and streambanks in wetland-riparian communities **Elevation:** Below 10,900 ft. **Ecoregions:** Southern California Mountains, Sierra Nevada, Cascades, Klamath Mountains

Tufted perennial with bristly-hairy stems. Leaves to 18 in. long, alternate, deeply lobed to pinnately compound with 5–9 leaflets to 4 in. long and 3-lobed, toothed margins. Flowers 3–16 in open clusters at stem tips, with many pistils, >20 stamens, and densely hairy, glandular pedicels. Sepals to 0.2 in. long, 5, recurved. Petals to 0.3 in. long, 5, roundish, yellow. Fruits to 0.2 in. long, generally glandular, seed-like achenes with hooked-styles (for attaching to socks or fur). Well known to Indigenous peoples for its various medicinal properties.

Ivesia gordonii

alpine ivesia

ROSACEAE ROSE FAMILY

PCT Sections: 10–23 **Abundance:** Occasional **Height:** 2–8 in. **Flowering:** June–September **Flower Color:** Yellow **Habitat-Community:** Open, dry, rocky ridges and slopes, including serpentine soils, in subalpine coniferous forests and alpine communities **Elevation:** 5900–11,500 ft. **Ecoregions:** Sierra Nevada, Cascades, Klamath Mountains

Sprawling to erect, tufted perennial with hairy, generally glandular, sometimes red stems. Leaves to 3.2 in. long, basal (mostly) and alternate, pinnately compound with 21–33 glandular, oblong to spoon-shaped leaflets to 0.2 in. long and 4-8-lobed margins. Flowers 10–20 in head-like clusters at stem tips, with generally 2–4 pistils and 5 stamens. Sepals to 0.2 in. long, 5. Petals to 0.2 in. long, 5, narrowly spoon-shaped, yellow. Fruits to 0.1 in. long, mottled brown, seed-like achenes. The genus name honors Eli Ives (1779–1861), a well-respected Yale professor and practicing physician.

Ivesia lycopodioides

clubmoss mousetail

ROSACEAE ROSE FAMILY

PCT Sections: 10–13 **Abundance:** Locally common **Height:** 1–12 in. **Flowering:** June–September **Flower Color:** Yellow **Habitat-Community:** Open, rocky areas and wet meadows in wetland-riparian communities and from upper montane coniferous forests to alpine communities **Elevation:** 7500–13,500 ft. **Ecoregions:** Sierra Nevada

Sprawling to erect, tufted perennial with hairy or hairless stems and foliage. Leaves to 2.8 in. long, basal (mostly) and alternate, pinnately compound with 21–71 thick, overlapping leaflets to 0.3 in. long and 4–10-lobed margins. Flowers 3–20 in generally 1 head-like cluster at stem tips, with generally 5–15 pistils and 5 stamens. Sepals to 0.2 in. long, 5. Petals to 0.2 in. long, 5, widely spoon-shaped, yellow. Fruits to 0.1 in. long, pale, seed-like achenes.

Ivesia muirii

granite mousetail

ROSACEAE ROSE FAMILY

PCT Sections: 10–14 **Abundance:** Occasional **Height:** 2–6 in. **Flowering:** July–August **Flower Color:** Yellow **Habitat-Community:** Open, rocky areas from upper montane coniferous forests to alpine communities **Elevation:** 9500–13,200 ft. **Ecoregions:** Sierra Nevada

Ascending to erect, tufted perennial with silvery stems and foliage. Leaves to 2 in. long, basal (mostly) and alternate, mousetail-like, pinnately compound with 51–81 thick, overlapping, tiny leaflets and minutely 3-lobed margins. Flowers 10–20 in generally 1–few, head-like clusters at stem tips, with 1–4 pistils and 5 stamens. Sepals to 0.1 in. long, 5, = to petals. Petals to 0.1 in. long, 5, narrowly oblong to spoon-shaped, yellow. Fruits to 0.1 in. long, red-spotted, seed-like achenes.

Ivesia pygmaea

dwarf mousetail

ROSACEAE ROSE FAMILY

PCT Sections: 10 **Abundance:** Occasional **Height:** 1–6 in. **Flowering:** July–September **Flower Color:** Yellow **Habitat-Community:** Open, rocky, granitic soils in alpine communities **Elevation:** 8800–13,200 ft. **Ecoregions:** Sierra Nevada

Sprawling to erect, matted perennial with green stems and foliage. Leaves to 4 in. long, basal (mostly) and alternate, pinnately compound with 21–31 overlapping, widely spoon-shaped leaflets to 0.2 in. long and 5–8-lobed margins. Flowers 5–10 in dense to open, head-like clusters at stem tips, with 10–30 pistils and 10 stamens. Sepals to 0.2 in. long, 5. Petals to 0.2 in. long, 5, widely spoon-shaped, yellow. Fruits to 0.1 in. long, pale, seed-like achenes.

Ivesia shockleyi

sky mousetail

ROSACEAE ROSE FAMILY

PCT Sections: 10–14 **Abundance:** Locally common **Height:** to 6 in. **Flowering:** June–August **Flower Color:** Yellow **Habitat-Community:** Rocky soils in subalpine coniferous forests and alpine communities **Elevation:** 8800–13,200 ft. **Ecoregions:** Sierra Nevada

Spreading, matted, much-branched perennial with green, densely glandular herbage. Leaves to 3.2 in. long, basal (mostly) and alternate, pinnately compound, with 11–21 overlapping leaflets to 0.2 in. long and 3-5-lobed margins. Flowers 2–10 in open clusters along stems, with 2–6 pistils and 5 stamens. Sepals to 0.1 in. long, 5. Petals to 0.1 in. long, 5, spoon-shaped, yellow. Fruits to 0.1 in. long, light brown, seed-like achenes.

Potentilla breweri

Brewer's cinquefoil

ROSACEAE ROSE FAMILY

PCT Sections: 10–24 **Abundance:** Locally common **Height:** 4–16 in. **Flowering:** June–September **Flower Color:** Yellow **Habitat-Community:** Meadows and moist, rocky soils from lower montane coniferous forests to alpine communities **Elevation:** Below 12,200 ft. **Ecoregions:** Sierra Nevada, Cascades, Klamath Mountains

Sprawling to ascending, tufted perennial with hairy herbage. Leaves to 6 in. long, alternate, pinnately compound with 7–15 oval leaflets to 0.8 in. long and deeply palmate-toothed margins. Flowers 3–15 on ascending branches at stem tips, with 15–25 pistils and generally 20 stamens. Sepals to 0.3 in. long, 5. Petals to 0.4 in. long, 5, yellow. Fruits to 0.1 in. long, brown, seed-like achenes.

Potentilla drummondii

Drummond's cinquefoil

ROSACEAE ROSE FAMILY

PCT Sections: 10–24 **Abundance:** Locally common **Height:** 6–24 in. **Flowering:** June–August **Flower Color:** Yellow **Habitat-Community:** Meadows in upper montane & subalpine coniferous forests and wetland-riparian communities **Elevation:** Below 9900 ft. **Ecoregions:** Sierra Nevada, Cascades, Klamath Mountains

Erect, tufted perennial with slightly hairy herbage. Leaves to 10 in. long, alternate, pinnately compound with 5–9 leaflets to 2 in. long and unevenly 7–15-toothed margins. Flowers 3–15 on ascending branches at stem tips, with 15–25 pistils and generally 20 stamens. Sepals to 0.3 in. long, 5. Petals to 0.4 in. long, 5, yellow. Fruits to 0.1 in. long, brown, seed-like achenes.

Potentilla flabellifolia

fanleaf cinquefoil

ROSACEAE ROSE FAMILY

PCT Sections: 10–24 **Abundance:** Locally common **Height:** 4–12 in. **Flowering:** July–September **Flower Color:** Yellow **Habitat-Community:** Moist meadows in wetland-riparian communities **Elevation:** 5500–12,200 ft. **Ecoregions:** Sierra Nevada, Cascades, Klamath Mountains

Loosely clustered perennial with hairless or hairy stems. Leaves to 4.7 in. long, alternate, generally hairless, pinnately compound with 3 leaflets to 1.2 in. long and shallowly 7–15-toothed margins. Flowers 1–5 on ascending branches at stem tips, with 15–25 pistils and generally 20 stamens. Sepals to 0.2 in. long, 5. Petals to 0.4 in. long, 5, yellow. Fruits to 0.1 in. long, brown or reddish, seed-like achenes.

Potentilla gracilis

slender cinquefoil

ROSACEAE ROSE FAMILY

PCT Sections: 1 & 3–5 & 8–24 **Abundance:** Common **Height:** 7–36 in. **Flowering:** June–September **Flower Color:** Yellow **Habitat-Community:** Open understories and dry meadows from oak woodlands to subalpine coniferous forests **Elevation:** Below 11,500 ft. **Ecoregions:** Southern California Mountains, Sierra Nevada, Cascades, Klamath Mountains

Ascending, tufted perennial with hairy stems. Leaves alternate, hairy to silky, palmately compound with 5–9 spoon-shaped leaflets to 2.4 in. long and shallowly to deeply lobed or toothed margins. Flowers generally many on ascending to erect branches at stem tips, with 15–25 pistils and generally 20 stamens. Sepals to 0.3 in. long, 5. Petals to 0.5 in. long, 5, yellow. Fruits to 0.1 in. long, pale brown, seed-like achenes.

Potentilla wheeleri

Kern cinquefoil

ROSACEAE ROSE FAMILY

PCT Sections: 4 & 9–10 **Abundance:** Occasional **Height:** 3–13 in. **Flowering:** May–September **Flower Color:** Yellow **Habitat-Community:** Sandy flats, streambanks, meadows, rocky talus slopes in wetland-riparian communities and from lower montane coniferous forests to alpine communities **Elevation:** 5700–11,000 ft. **Ecoregions:** Southern California Mountains, Sierra Nevada

Prostrate, tufted perennial with slightly glandular, spreading-hairy stems. Leaves 1–4 in. long, mostly in basal rosettes, palmately compound with 5 wedge-shaped, toothed, densely hairy leaflets 0.2–1 in. long. Flowers generally >5 per plant and clustered at stem and branch tips, with 15–25 pistils and many stamens. Petals 0.1–0.2 in. long, 5, bright yellow. Fruits tiny, hairless achenes. *Potentilla* is Latin for "slightly powerful," referring to its medicinal properties.

Sibbaldia procumbens

creeping sibbaldia

ROSACEAE ROSE FAMILY

PCT Sections: 4 & 10–24 **Abundance:** Locally common **Height:** 1–6 in. **Flowering:** June–August **Flower Color:** Yellow **Habitat-Community:** Moist, rocky soils in subalpine coniferous forests and alpine communities **Elevation:** 6000–12,200 ft. **Ecoregions:** Southern California Mountains, Sierra Nevada, Cascades, Klamath Mountains

Sprawling, matted perennial with woody stems. Leaves basal, sparsely hairy, pinnately compound with 3 wedge-shaped 3-tooth-tipped leaflets to 1 in. long; petiole to 2.8 in. long. Flowers clustered or scattered on ascending branches along stems, with 5–20 pistils and 5 stamens. Sepals to 0.2 in. long, 5, triangular, > petals. Petals to 0.1 in. long, 5, spoon-shaped, yellow. Fruits to 0.1 in. long, brown, seed-like achenes. The genus name honors Robert Sibbald (1614–1722), a British professor of medicine.

Kallstroemia parviflora

warty caltrop

ZYGOPHYLLACEAE CALTROP FAMILY

PCT Sections: 1–2 **Abundance:** Rare **Height:** 12–25 in. **Flowering:** July–October **Flower Color:** Yellow to orange **Habitat-Community:** Sandy flats and slopes in creosote bush & Sonoran mixed woody scrubs and woodlands **Elevation:** Below 6000 ft. **Ecoregions:** Southern California Mountains, Sonoran Basin and Range

Prostrate to ascending summer annual with hairy to hairless stems. Leaves 1.2–2.3 in. long, generally opposite, pinnately compound with usually 8 (4 pairs) oval, green leaflets. Flowers solitary on long pedicels (longer than the subtending leaf), 5-parted, with coarsely hairy sepals and yellow to orange petals 0.3–0.5 in. long. Fruits 0.1–0.3 in. long, knobby (caltrop-like) capsules with style 1–3 times longer than fruit body. Often seen along the PCT in the Warner Valley region of San Diego County. Germinates after warm-season rains from notoriously long-lived seed banks. Caltrops may go decades between germination events!

▼ 5 PETALS / IRREGULAR COROLLAS

Acmispon argophyllus
var. *argophyllus*

silver bird's-foot trefoil

FABACEAE LEGUME FAMILY

PCT Sections: 1–8 **Abundance:** Locally common **Height:** 3–20 in. **Flowering:** April–July **Flower Color:** Yellow **Habitat-Community:** Sheltered, rocky slopes and canyons in foothill chaparrals, oak woodlands, and lower montane coniferous forests **Elevation:** Below 5800 ft. **Ecoregions:** Southern California Mountains, Sierra Nevada

Prostrate or matted, sometimes ascending perennial with silky-haired stems. Leaves pinnate, with 3 ovoid, silver-silky hairy leaflets (appearing palmate or pinnate) 0.2–0.4 in. long. Flowers clustered in heads of 4–8, sessile, irregular (pea-like), consisting of a banner, keel, and wings, with 5 calyx lobes 0.2–0.3 in. Petals 0.3–0.4 in. long, yellow. Fruits small 1-seeded pods. Numerous varieties occur in California; this is the only one found along the PCT.

Acmispon argyraeus

canyon
lotus

FABACEAE LEGUME FAMILY

PCT Sections: 3–4 **Abundance:** Locally common
Height: 2–10 in. **Flowering:** May–August **Flower
Color:** Yellow **Habitat-Community:** Gravelly to
rocky (granitic) substrates in pinyon-juniper
woodlands and montane coniferous forests
Elevation: Below 8100 ft. **Ecoregions:** Southern
California Mountains

Matted (3–15 in. across) prostrate perennial with silver- or gray-hairy herbage. Leaves pinnate, with 3–4 (appearing palmate when 3) spatula-shaped leaflets 0.2–0.5 in. Flowers in heads of 1–3 flowers, irregular (pea-like), consisting of a banner, keel, and wings, with 5 calyx lobes 0.1–0.2 in. Petals 0.3–0.4 in. long, yellow turning orange-red in age. Fruits 0.6–0.8 in. long, linear, cylindric, mostly straight pods. Confined along the PCT to the San Bernardino Mountains (common) and San Jacinto Mountains (uncommon). *Argyraeus* means "silvery" in Greek.

Acmispon glaber var. *brevialatus*

short-winged
deerweed

FABACEAE LEGUME FAMILY

PCT Sections: 1–6 **Abundance:** Common
Height: 1–3 ft. **Flowering:** March–August
Flower Color: Yellow **Habitat-Community:**
Gravelly to rocky slopes in foothill chaparrals,
Sonoran mixed woody scrubs, and woodlands
Elevation: Below 5200 ft. **Ecoregions:** Southern
California Mountains

Tufted, ascending- to erect-branched perennial or subshrub with hairless or finely hairy, bright green stems. Leaves pinnate, with 3–6 well-spaced elliptic leaflets 0.2–0.7 in. long. Flowers 2–7 in hemispheric clusters, sessile along the stem, irregular (pea-like), consisting of a banner, keel, and wings, with 5 hairless calyx lobes. Petals 0.3–0.4 in. long, yellow (aging reddish). Fruits 0.4–0.7 in. long, oblong pods. Occurs along the PCT in the Peninsular and Transverse Ranges.

Acmispon grandiflorus

large-flowered
lotus

FABACEAE LEGUME FAMILY

PCT Sections: 1–8 **Abundance:** Locally common
(especially in burns) **Height:** 8–30 in. **Flowering:**
April–July **Flower Color:** Light yellow to peach
Habitat-Community: Open slopes and ridges in
foothill chaparrals and oak & pinyon-juniper
woodlands **Elevation:** Below 5400 ft. **Ecoregions:**
Southern California Mountains, Sierra Nevada

Ascending to prostrate, showy perennial to subshrub with variously hairy herbage. Leaves pinnate, with 5–9 spatula-shaped leaflets 0.4–1.1 in. long. Flowers 5–9 in hemispheric clusters, irregular (pea-like), consisting of a banner, keel, and wings, with 5 shaggy-haired calyx lobes. Petals 0.4–1 in. long, light yellow to peach, blushing rose. Fruits 1.2–2.5 in. long, linear, cylindric, ascending, reddish pods with up to 20 seeds. Aka chaparral lotus.

Acmispon heermannii

Heermann's lotus

FABACEAE LEGUME FAMILY •

PCT Sections: 1–6 **Abundance:** Locally common **Height:** 4–20 in. **Flowering:** March–October **Flower Color:** Yellow **Habitat-Community:** Washes, open hillsides, and ridges in chaparrals, Sonoran/Mojave mixed woody scrubs, and oak & Joshua tree woodlands **Elevation:** Below 6400 ft. **Ecoregions:** Southern California Mountains

Matted (10–30 in. across) perennial, spreading along the ground with soft white-hairy stems. Leaves pinnate (sometimes palmately compound) with 4–6 ovoid, green to gray-silver, stiff-hairy leaflets 0.2–0.7 in. long. Flowers 3–8 in hemispheric clusters, irregular (pea-like), consisting of a banner, keel, and wings, with 5 shaggy-haired calyx lobes 0.1–0.2 in. long. Petals 0.1–0.3 in. long, yellow with dark (reddish) lobes. Fruits 0.2 in. long, narrowly oblong pods with 1–2 seeds.

Acmispon nevadensis

Sierra lotus

FABACEAE LEGUME FAMILY

PCT Sections: All (except 6–7 & 11–13) **Abundance:** Common **Height:** 2–5 in. **Flowering:** May–August **Flower Color:** Yellow to orange **Habitat-Community:** Open slopes and ridges in oak woodlands and montane coniferous forests **Elevation:** Below 9000 ft. **Ecoregions:** All (except Sonoran/Mojave Basin and Range)

Matted (7–24 in. across) perennial with wavy- and soft-hairy stems. Leaves irregularly pinnately or palmately compound, with 3–5 spatula-shaped to oblong, green to gray, short-hairy leaflets 0.2–0.5 in. long. Flowers 5–12 in hemispheric clusters, irregular (pea-like), consisting of a banner, keel, and wings, with 5 long-hairy calyx lobes 0.1 in. long. Petals 0.3–0.5 in. long, yellow drying orange. Fruits 0.3 in. long, narrowly oblong pods. Hybridizes with *A. argophyllus*. The specific epithet (from the Latin, "from Nevada") is applied to many species from that state.

Acmispon procumbens

silky California broom

FABACEAE LEGUME FAMILY

PCT Sections: 4–9 **Abundance:** Locally common **Height:** 8–30 in. **Flowering:** April–June **Flower Color:** Yellow **Habitat-Community:** Slopes and plateaus in chaparrals, Joshua tree & pinyon-juniper woodlands, and lower montane coniferous forests **Elevation:** Below 7400 ft. **Ecoregions:** Southern California Mountains, Sierra Nevada

Low-growing, much-branched perennial with short, soft-hairy, grayish herbage. Leaves palmate, with 3 spoon- to spatula-shaped, gray-hairy leaflets 0.2–0.5 in. long. Flowers 1–3 in leaf axils, irregular (pea-like), consisting of a banner, keel, and wings, with 5 hairy calyx lobes. Petals 0.2–0.6 in. long, yellow sometimes tinged orange or red. Fruits 0.4–0.7 in. long, oblong, cylindric pods with up to 3 seeds. Two varieties along the PCT: var. *jepsonii* (corolla 0.4–0.6 in. long) is found in the southern Sierra; var. *procumbens* (corolla 0.2–0.4 in. long) is limited to the Transverse Ranges. Plants become stiff subshrubs in Los Angeles County.

Acmispon strigosus

strigose bird's-foot trefoil

FABACEAE LEGUME FAMILY

PCT Sections: 1–9 **Abundance:** Common **Height:** 1–6 in. **Flowering:** March–June **Flower Color:** Yellow **Habitat-Community:** Sandy to gravelly soils in washes and alluvial plains in creosote bush scrubs, foothill chaparrals, and Joshua tree & pinyon-juniper woodlands **Elevation:** Below 7200 ft. **Ecoregions:** Southern California Mountains, Sonoran/Mojave Basin and Range, Sierra Nevada

Matted (3–15 in. across) annual, branched at base, with short-hairy or hairless herbage. Leaves irregularly pinnate, with 4–9 spoon- to spatula-shaped, sometimes thick and fleshy leaflets 0.1–0.4 in. long. Flower in 1–2-flowered clusters, irregular (pea-like), consisting of a banner, keel, and wings, with 5 hairy calyx lobes. Petals 0.2–0.4 in. long, yellow sometimes tinged orange or red in age. Fruits 0.4–1.4 in. long, linear, slightly flattened, curved-tipped pods with up to 10 seeds. A ubiquitous spring annual of the Desert Southwest with numerous variants.

Hosackia oblongifolia

streambank bird's-foot trefoil

FABACEAE LEGUME FAMILY

PCT Sections: All **Abundance:** Locally common **Height:** 4–24 in. **Flowering:** May–September **Flower Color:** Yellow and white **Habitat-Community:** Moist slopes, meadows, and open places along streams in wetland-riparian communities **Elevation:** Below 7900 ft. **Ecoregions:** All (except Sonoran Basin and Range)

Sprawling or ascending perennial often with hairy herbage. Leaves alternate, pinnate, with 3–11 mostly opposite, oval to oblong, generally hairy leaflets to 1 in. long. Flowers 2–6 in head-like clusters, irregular (pea-like). Calyces to 0.3 in. long, 5-lobed. Petals to 0.5 in. long, 5, consisting of a yellow banner, white keel, and white wings. Fruits to 2 in. long, oblong, hairless, few-seeded stalked pods, each resembling a bird's foot. *Trefoil* ("3 leaflets") is a name used for various lotus plants that have 3 obvious upper leaflets.

Lupinus peirsonii

Peirson's lupine

FABACEAE LEGUME FAMILY

PCT Sections: 5 **Abundance:** Rare **Height:** 1–2 ft. **Flowering:** April–June **Flower Color:** Pale yellow **Habitat-Community:** Loose gravel, talus slopes, and washes in Joshua tree & pinyon-juniper woodlands and montane coniferous forests **Elevation:** Below 8200 ft. **Ecoregions:** Southern California Mountains

Erect, branched perennial with silky silver-hairy herbage. Leaves clustered at base of plant, palmate, with 5–8 broadly spoon-shaped, generally thick and fleshy leaflets 1–3 in. long. Flowers whorled along a short spike, irregular (pea-like). Calyces 2-lipped, lower lip lobes the longest. Petals 0.3–0.4 in. long, 5, pale yellow, consisting of a generally hairy-on-back banner, keel (hairy on upper margin), and wings. Fruits 1.2–1.6 in. long, silky-hairy pod with 3–5 seeds. Endemic to the San Gabriel Mountains. Known from fewer than 20 populations, many of which occur along the PCT from Mt. Baden-Powell to Mt. Islip.

Lupinus stiversii

harlequin annual lupine

FABACEAE LEGUME FAMILY

PCT Sections: 4–5 & 16–17 **Abundance:** Occasional **Height:** 4–20 in. **Flowering:** April–July **Flower Color:** Yellow and pink **Habitat-Community:** Dry, open flats and slopes in well-drained, sandy soils in oak woodlands, foothill chaparrals, and lower montane coniferous forests **Elevation:** Below 6900 ft. **Ecoregions:** Southern California Mountains, Sierra Nevada

Annual with sparsely hairy herbage. Leaves alternate, palmate, with generally 7 leaflets to 2 in. long. Flowers in dense whorls, irregular (pea-like). Calyces upper lip to 0.3 in. long, deeply lobed, lower to 0.3 in. long. Petals to 0.7 in. long, 5, consisting of a yellow banner, white keel (hairy on upper and lower margins), and pink wings. Fruits to 0.8 in. long, hairless 5-seeded pods. The only yellow and pink lupine along the PCT.

Thermopsis californica var. *semota*

velvety false-lupine

FABACEAE LEGUME FAMILY

PCT Sections: 1 **Abundance:** Rare **Height:** 15–35 in. **Flowering:** April–June **Flower Color:** Yellow **Habitat-Community:** Meadows and shaded understories in oak woodlands and lower montane coniferous forests **Elevation:** Below 6400 ft. **Ecoregions:** Southern California Mountains

Erect to ascending, irregularly branched perennial with velvety-hairy herbage. Leaves palmate, with 3 ovoid to spoon-shaped, wavy-haired leaflets 1.3–2 in. long. Flowers scattered on terminal spikes, irregular (pea-like), consisting of a banner, keel, and wings. Calyces 5-lobed with fused upper 2. Petals 1–1.5 in. long, yellow. Fruits 1.1–1.5 in. long, straight pods. Endemic to the southern Peninsular Ranges. Best seen in the pine understory atop Mt. Laguna. *Thermopsis* is Greek for "like a lupine," but lupine leaves typically have more than 3 leaflets.

Viola douglasii

Douglas' golden violet

VIOLACEAE VIOLET FAMILY

PCT Sections: 1–5 & 8 & 16–19 **Abundance:** Occasional **Height:** 1–8 in. **Flowering:** February–July **Flower Color:** Yellow **Habitat-Community:** Vernally moist openings, including serpentine soils, in woodlands and lower montane coniferous forests **Elevation:** Below 7600 ft. **Ecoregions:** All (except Sonoran/Mojave Basin and Range)

Sprawling to erect, many-stemmed perennial with hairy or hairless herbage. Leaves to 2 in. long, alternate, fern-like, 2-pinnately compound, ovoid in outline, with 3–5 leaflets divided into 3–5 segments. Flowers irregular, solitary in leaf axils, with 5 stamens and 1 pistil. Sepals to 0.5 in. long, 5, lance-shaped, hair-fringed, mostly alike. Petals 5, yellow, lowest with base forming a minute spur, red-brown to black on back of upper 2, brown-veined lower 3 (hairy lateral 2). Fruits to 0.5 in. long, hairless capsules with small, pale brown seeds attractive to ants. The name honors Scottish botanist David Douglas (1798–1834), who collected over 500 species in California. Leaves and flowers of violets can be eaten raw, cooked, or used for tea.

Viola pinetorum

pine violet

VIOLACEAE VIOLET FAMILY

PCT Sections: 1–5 & 8–17 **Abundance:** Common **Height:** 2–4 in. **Flowering:** May–July **Flower Color:** Yellow **Habitat-Community:** Vernally moist, shaded places and rocky slopes from lower montane coniferous forests to alpine communities **Elevation:** Below 12,200 ft. **Ecoregions:** All (except Sonoran/Mojave Basin and Range)

Sprawling to erect, many-stemmed perennial with generally gray-hairy herbage. Leaves to 3.8 in. long, alternate, linear to oblong or ovoid, with smooth to toothed margins. Flowers irregular, solitary in leaf axils, with 5 stamens and 1 pistil. Sepals to 0.3 in. long, 5, lance-shaped and not hair-fringed. Petals 5, yellow, lowest with base forming a minute spur, red- to purple-brown on back of upper 2, brown-veined lower 3 (hairy lateral 2). Fruits to 0.3 in. long, minutely hairy capsules with small brown seeds attractive to ants. Two subspecies along the PCT: one type prefers shaded woods, such as pine forest understories; the rare subsp. *grisea* prefers rocky, alpine ridges and slopes.

Viola purpurea

mountain violet

VIOLACEAE IOLET FAMILY

PCT Sections: All **Abundance:** Common **Height:** 1–10 in. **Flowering:** March–September **Flower Color:** Yellow **Habitat-Community:** Open or shaded, dry or moist places, including serpentine soils, from scrubs and woodlands to subalpine coniferous forests **Elevation:** Below 11,900 ft. **Ecoregions:** All

Sprawling to erect, 1–many-stemmed perennial with hairy or hairless herbage. Leaves to 2 in. long, alternate, oblong, triangular, or diamond- to lance-shaped, with smooth to toothed margins. Flowers irregular, solitary in leaf axils, with 5 stamens and 1 pistil. Sepals to 0.3 in. long, 5, lance-shaped, hair-fringed or not. Petals 5, yellow, lowest with base forming a minute spur, red- to purple-brown on back of upper 2 (sometimes lateral 2), brown-veined lower 3 (hairy lateral 2). Fruits to 0.5 in. long, minutely hairy capsules with small, brown to gray or mottled brown seeds attractive to ants.

▼ 5 FUSED PETALS / SYMMETRIC COROLLAS

Amsinckia retrosa

rigid fiddleneck

BORAGINACEAE BORAGE FAMILY

PCT Sections: 1–7 **Abundance:** Locally common **Height:** 10–25 in. **Flowering:** February–May **Flower Color:** Yellow to orange **Habitat-Community:** Open areas in foothill chaparrals, oak woodlands, and lower montane coniferous forests **Elevation:** Below 5200 ft. **Ecoregions:** Southern California Mountains, Sierra Nevada

Spreading to erect-branched annual with spreading, gray, rough-hairy herbage. Basal leaves narrowly spoon-shaped to 5 in. long, withering with age; stem leaves alternate, reduced, lance-shaped, 0.2–1 in. long. Flowers in coiled terminal spikes, with 5 equal-in-length calyx lobes. Corollas 5-lobed, yellow to orange, 0.3–0.5 in. long, with tube exserted. Fruits 4 ovoid nutlets. Found along maritime-influenced segments of the PCT in southern California.

Amsinckia tessellata
desert fiddleneck
BORAGINACEAE BORAGE FAMILY

PCT Sections: 1–8 **Abundance:** Common **Height:** 8–24 in. **Flowering:** February–June **Flower Color:** Yellow to orange **Habitat-Community:** Sandy flats and slopes in creosote bush scrubs, chaparrals, and Joshua tree & pinyon-juniper woodlands **Elevation:** Below 7000 ft. **Ecoregions:** Southern California Mountains, Sonoran/Mojave Basin and Range, Sierra Nevada

Bristly, wide-ranging annual with stout, spreading to erect branches and stiff, spreading-haired herbage. Basal leaves to 4 in. long (withering with age); stem leaves alternate, reduced (often remaining broad), spoon-shaped, green, coarsely hairy. Flowers in coiled ("fiddlenecked") terminal spikes, with 4 (sometimes 3 or 5) unequal-in-length calyx lobes. Corollas 5-lobed, yellow to orange, 0.2–0.3 in. long. Fruits 4 broadly ovoid nutlets. Found along the desert-influenced segments of the PCT. A dominant spring annual of the California desert region; its dried plant matter may enhance fire spread during summer months. *Tessellata* (from the Latin, "checkered") refers to the mosaic pattern on the seeds.

Emmenanthe pendulifolia
whispering bells
BORAGINACEAE BORAGE FAMILY

PCT Sections: 1–9 **Abundance:** Common **Height:** 3–30 in. **Flowering:** March–July **Flower Color:** Yellow to orange **Habitat-Community:** Dry slopes and sandy soils in creosote bush scrubs, foothill chaparrals, and Joshua tree & pinyon-juniper woodlands **Elevation:** Below 6600 ft. **Ecoregions:** Southern California Mountains, Sonoran/Mojave Basin and Range, Sierra Nevada

Erect, branched annual with glandular-hairy stems and medicinally scented herbage. Basal leaves 2–5 in. long, crowded, oblong to lance-shaped, toothed to deeply pinnately lobed; cauline leaves clasping, gradually reduced in size up the stem. Flowers often curved downward, 5-parted, with ovoid sepals 0.2–0.4 in. long and bell-shaped yellow corolla 0.3–0.5 in. long. Fruits 0.2–0.4 in. long, glandular capsules. The only species in *Emmenanthe* (from the Greek *emmeno*, "to bide," referring to the flower not falling as it fades). Dry, hanging flowers make a rustling sound in the wind (hence the common name). Especially abundant in burns.

Cucurbita foetidissima
calabazilla
CUCURBITACEAE GOURD FAMILY

PCT Sections: 1–8 **Abundance:** Occasional **Height:** 5–15 in. **Flowering:** June–August **Flower Color:** Yellow **Habitat-Community:** Sandy to gravelly soils in open, disturbed areas in foothill chaparrals, Sonoran mixed woody scrubs, and oak & Joshua tree woodlands **Elevation:** Below 5200 ft. **Ecoregions:** Southern California Mountains, Sonoran Basin and Range, Sierra Nevada

Rank-smelling, sprawling perennial vine with rough-hairy stems from a large fleshy tuber-like root (that may weigh up to 160 pounds!); monoecious. Leaves 6–12 in. long, alternate, triangular or heart-shaped, somewhat folded upward, with slightly toothed margins. Flowers 1 per node, 5-parted, cup-shaped, 4–6 in. long with curved-outward lobes; petals fused, bright yellow to orange-yellow. Fruits 3–4 in. across, fleshy, green-striped gourds, aging tan or yellow (with a hardening rind), with up to 300 seeds. Can be eaten like squash (*Cucurbita* means "gourd"), but the mature drying fruit rapidly becomes bitter.

Cucurbita palmata

coyote melon

CUCURBITACEAE GOURD FAMILY

PCT Sections: 1–4 & 7–8 **Abundance:** Occasional **Height:** 4–12 in. **Flowering:** April–September **Flower Color:** Yellow **Habitat-Community:** Sandy to gravelly soils in open, disturbed areas in creosote bush & Sonoran/Mojave mixed woody scrubs and Joshua tree woodlands **Elevation:** Below 5400 ft. **Ecoregions:** Southern California Mountains, Sonoran/Mojave Basin and Range, Sierra Nevada

Sprawling (on ground or through shrubs), short-lived perennial or annual vine with coarse-haired herbage; monoecious. Leaves 4–6 in. long, alternate, deeply palmately divided into 5 gray-green lobes with white-mottled veins. Flowers 1 per node, 5-parted, cup-shaped, 2.5–3.5 in. long with curved-outward lobes; petals fused, bright yellow to orange. Fruits 3–4 in. across, fleshy, initially green gourds, aging tan or yellow (with a hardening rind), with white seeds 0.4–0.6 in. long. In Native American mythology, Coyote is a legendary "trickster" hero; these tasty-looking melons may appear edible but are in fact extremely bitter, so don't fall for the coyote's trick! Look for this mythical plant along the lower desert segments of the PCT.

Leptosiphon aureus

golden linanthus

POLEMONIACEAE PHLOX FAMILY

PCT Sections: 5–8 **Abundance:** Occasional **Height:** 2–8 in. **Flowering:** March–June **Flower Color:** Yellow to orange **Habitat-Community:** Open, sandy to gravelly flats, slopes, and washes in creosote bush & sagebrush scrubs and Joshua tree & pinyon-juniper woodlands **Elevation:** Below 6200 ft. **Ecoregions:** Southern California Mountains, Mojave Basin and Range, Sierra Nevada

Erect, spindly, thread-like, branched annual with hairless or hairy, sometimes glandular herbage. Leaves opposite, palmately divided into 3–9 linear lobes 0.1–0.3 in. long. Flowers 1–few per cluster, 5-parted, with tubular calyces 0.2 in. long. Corolla tube funnel-shaped yellow (orange-yellow throat), 0.1–0.2 in. long; lobes 0.2–0.3 in. long; stamens exserted. Flowers close at night. Fruits many-seeded capsules. Found along the PCT where it bisects the Mojave Desert ecotone. *Leptosiphon* (from the Greek, "narrow tube") describes the corolla.

Leptosiphon parviflorus

variable linanthus

POLEMONIACEAE PHLOX FAMILY

PCT Sections: 1–9 **Abundance:** Common **Height:** 2–14 in. **Flowering:** March–June **Flower Color:** Yellow, white, purple, or pink **Habitat-Community:** Open, sandy to gravelly soils in foothill chaparrals, sagebrush scrubs, and oak & pinyon-juniper woodlands **Elevation:** Below 4100 ft. **Ecoregions:** Southern California/Northern Baja Coast, Southern California Mountains, Sierra Nevada

Branched annual with thread-like stems and hairy herbage. Leaves opposite, palmately divided into linear lobes 0.1–0.7 in. long with a sharp-pointed tip on the middle lobe. Flowers in dense heads, 5-parted, with hairy, glandular calyces 0.2–0.4 in. long. Corolla tube trumpet-like, maroon, pink, or yellow, thread-like, 0.5–1.9 in. long, with a yellow, purple or orange throat; lobes yellow, white, purple, or pink; stamens exserted. Flowers close at night. Fruits to 0.2 in. long, many-seeded capsules. Few native plants produce such flower color variation; the yellow and white versions are most common along the PCT.

Navarretia breweri

Brewer's navarretia

POLEMONIACEAE PHLOX FAMILY

PCT Sections: 4 & 10 & 15 & 18 **Abundance:** Occasional **Height:** 1–3 in. **Flowering:** May–August **Flower Color:** Yellow **Habitat-Community:** Moist, sandy to gravelly soils on slopes or in valleys, meadows, and streambanks from foothill chaparrals to subalpine coniferous forests and wetland-riparian communities **Elevation:** Below 10,700 ft. **Ecoregions:** Southern California Mountains, Sierra Nevada

Tiny, slender, few-branched annual with red or brown stems and glandular-hairy herbage. Leaves alternate, deeply pinnately divided into needle-like green lobes. Flowers in compact heads, 5-parted; calyces 0.2–0.3 in. long with needle-like lobes. Corolla tube 0.2–0.3 in. long, yellow, trumpet-like; stamens slightly extended beyond tube. Fruits to 0.1 in. long, few-seeded capsules. No other yellow-flowered navarretia is this small. Curious distribution, making an appearance along the CA PCT in four highly separated locations up and down the state. Best observed in meadows and creek crossings in the eastern San Bernardino Mountains.

Physalis crassifolia

thickleaf ground cherry

SOLANACEAE NIGHTSHADE FAMILY

PCT Sections: 1–4 **Abundance:** Locally common **Height:** 6–30 in. **Flowering:** May–August **Flower Color:** Yellow to cream **Habitat-Community:** Dry, rocky to gravelly slopes and washes in creosote bush & Sonoran/Mojave mixed woody scrubs and Joshua tree woodlands **Elevation:** Below 4200 ft. **Ecoregions:** Southern California Mountains, Sonoran Basin and Range

Perennial or subshrub with zigzagged or ridged, densely short-hairy stems. Leaves 0.4–1.2 in. long, generally alternate, petiole = blade length, ovoid, thick and fleshy, hairless. Flowers somewhat nodding, 5-parted, with calyces 0.2–0.3 in. across (becoming papery and elongating in fruit). Corollas 0.6–0.8 in. across, yellow, with widely bell-shaped tube. Fruits tomato-like berries enclosed in the papery calyx. Look for it at the lower Sonoran Desert crossings from San Diego County to the southeastern base of the San Bernardino Mountains. Though it resembles a tomatillo or tomato, the fruit is toxic, especially when unripe! *Physalis* (from the Greek, "bladder," "bubble") refers to the inflated calyx.

▼ 5 FUSED PETALS / IRREGULAR COROLLAS

Castilleja cinerea

ashgray paintbrush

OROBANCHACEAE

BROOMRAPE FAMILY

PCT Sections: 4 **Abundance:** Rare **Height:** 2–6 in. **Flowering:** May–August **Flower Color:** Pale yellow to rusty brown **Habitat-Community:** Gravelly plains (quartzite) and open areas in sagebrush scrubs and montane coniferous forests **Elevation:** 5500–10,200 ft. **Ecoregions:** Southern California Mountains

Decumbent to ascending, ground-hugging perennial from a somewhat woody base with woolly, ash-gray herbage. Leaves 0.4–0.8 in. long, alternate, usually not lobed, linear. Flowers in densely hairy (branched hairs) spike-like clusters 1–3 in. long, irregular, with 3–5-lobed bracts. Calyces 0.6–0.8 in. long, unequally 4-lobed, branched-hairy, green to rusty brown. Corollas 0.6–0.7 in. long, 2-lipped, pale yellow to greenish yellow (aging red-brown), with 2-lobed, beak-like upper lip and reduced, pouched lower lip. Fruits 0.2–0.5 in. long, ovoid capsules. Endemic to the pebble plains of the Big Bear Lake region. Threatened by development, grazing, recreational activity, and climate change. Hemiparasitic on buckwheat and sagebrush for water and nutrients.

Castilleja lacera

cutleaf owl's-clover

OROBANCHACEAE

BROOMRAPE FAMILY

PCT Sections: 10–24 **Abundance:** Occasional **Height:** 4–16 in. **Flowering:** May–July **Flower Color:** Yellow **Habitat-Community:** Vernally wet places and meadows in woodlands, chaparrals, lower montane coniferous forests, and wetland-riparian communities **Elevation:** Below 9200 ft. **Ecoregions:** Sierra Nevada, Cascades, Klamath Mountains

Erect annual with glandular-hairy stems; hemiparasitic. Leaves 0.4–2 in. long, linear to lance-shaped, 0–5-lobed, with smooth margins. Flowers densely clustered at stem tips with green bracts. Calyces to 0.5 in. long, unequally 4-lobed, lobes ≥ tube. Corollas irregular, 0.5–0.9 in. long, 2-lipped, yellow (purple-dotted at base), with beaked upper lip. Fruits 0.3 in. long, many-seeded capsules. Owl's-clovers tend to have lower corolla lips consisting of 3 obvious pouches at the tip.

Castilleja lasiorhyncha

San Bernardino Mountains owl's-clover

OROBANCHACEAE

BROOMRAPE FAMILY

PCT Sections: 4 **Abundance:** Rare **Height:** 4–10 in. **Flowering:** June–July **Flower Color:** Yellow **Habitat-Community:** Gravelly plains (quartzite) and open areas in sagebrush scrubs and montane coniferous forests **Elevation:** Below 8100 ft. **Ecoregions:** Southern California Mountains

Erect annual with white-woolly, glandular-hairy stems; hemiparasitic. Leaves 0.4–1.2 in. long, alternate, lance-linear, 3-lobed. Flowers in leafy spikes 1–6 in. long, irregular, 2-lipped, with 3–5-lobed bracts. Calyces 0.3–0.6 in. long; corollas 0.6–1 in. long with white-hairy, beak-like upper lip and bright yellow, pouched lower lip. Fruits 0.3–0.4 in. long, ovoid capsules. Occurs along the PCT in the San Bernardino Mountains; historic records and recent observations suggest it also resides in the Peninsular Ranges (San Jacinto and Cuyamaca Mountains). Threatened by development, grazing, recreational activity, and climate change.

Castilleja tenuis

hairy owl's-clover

OROBANCHACEAE

BROOMRAPE FAMILY

PCT Sections: 4 & 8–20 **Abundance:** Occasional **Height:** 4–18 in. **Flowering:** May–August **Flower Color:** Yellow or white **Habitat-Community:** Moist flats and meadows from scrubs to upper montane coniferous forests and wetland-riparian communities **Elevation:** Below 9200 ft. **Ecoregions:** Southern California Mountains, Sierra Nevada, Cascades, Klamath Mountains

Erect annual with glandular-hairy stems; hemiparasitic. Leaves 0.4–2 in. long, linear-lance-shaped, 0–5-lobed, with smooth margins. Flowers densely clustered at stem tips with green bracts. Calyces to 0.5 in. long, unequally 4-lobed, lobes ≤ tube. Corollas irregular, 0.5–0.8 in. long, 2-lipped (upper lip beaked), yellow or white. Fruits 0.4 in. long, many-seeded capsules. *Tenuis* is Latin for "thin" or "slight."

Cordylanthus rigidus

stiffbranch bird's beak

OROBANCHACEAE

BROOMRAPE FAMILY

PCT Sections: 1–10 **Abundance:** Locally common **Height:** 10–40 in. **Flowering:** June–September **Flower Color:** Pale yellow to white **Habitat-Community:** Open areas in chaparrals, oak & pinyon-juniper woodlands, sagebrush scrubs, and montane coniferous forests **Elevation:** 8800 ft. **Ecoregions:** Southern California/Northern Baja Coast, Southern California Mountains, Sierra Nevada

Ascending to erect, weedy-looking annual with bristly, yellow-green to red-brown herbage; hemi-parasitic. Leaves 0.4–1.6 in. long, alternate, sessile, palmately 3–7-lobed with thread-like segments. Flowers 5–13 in short, dense spikes with 3-lobed outer bract and calyx-like inner bracts 0.6–0.8 in. long; calyces sheath-like (enclosing the corolla), 0.4–0.8 in. long. Corollas 0.5–0.7 in. long, tubular, 2-lipped, generally pale yellow to white with upper lip forming a hood ("bird's beak") at the tip of an expanded white pouch. Fruits small, ovoid capsules.

Pedicularis semibarbata

pinewoods lousewort

OROBANCHACEAE

BROOMRAPE FAMILY

PCT Sections: 3–5 & 9–22 **Abundance:** Common **Height:** 1–8 in. **Flowering:** May–July **Flower Color:** Yellow **Habitat-Community:** Dry ridgetops and understories from lower montane to subalpine coniferous forests **Elevation:** Below 11,500 ft. **Ecoregions:** Southern California Mountains, Sierra Nevada, Cascades, Klamath Mountains

Low-growing perennial with most of the stem underground. Leaves 1–8 in. long, alternate, fern-like, lance-shaped, divided into 11–25 segments, with toothed to lobed margins. Flowers clustered at stem tips with hairy bracts. Calyces to 0.4 in. long, 5-lobed, lobes < tube. Corollas irregular, 0.6–1 in. long, 2-lipped, club-like, yellow, tinged red or purple-tipped, with hooded upper lip and 3-lobed lower lip. Fruits to 0.4 in. long, many-seeded capsules. *Pedicularis* ("lice") alludes to an old belief that ingestion by stock animals caused outbreaks of those critters. It takes some hunting to find its yellow flowers hidden within the fern-like leaves.

Diplacus brevipes

wide-throat yellow monkeyflower

PHRYMACEAE LOPSEED FAMILY

PCT Sections: 1–5 **Abundance:** Locally common **Height:** 3–30 in. **Flowering:** April–July **Flower Color:** Yellow **Habitat-Community:** Dry, open sites and burns from oak woodlands to lower montane coniferous forests **Elevation:** Below 6500 ft. **Ecoregions:** Southern California/Northern Baja Coast, Southern California Mountains

Erect, 1–few-branched annual with hairy herbage. Leaves 0.3–3.1 in. long, opposite, lance- to spatula-shaped, becoming hairy on upper stem, with smooth margins. Flowers 1 per leaf axil, irregular, 5-lobed. Calyces 0.4–1 in. long, unequally 5-lobed. Corollas 2-lipped (2-lobed above, 3-lobed below), yellow (red spots in throat), 0.7–1.3 in. long. Fruits 0.3–0.6 in. long, ovoid capsules. *Brevipes* is Latin for "with short stalk."

Erythranthe floribunda

many-flowered monkeyflower

PHRYMACEAE LOPSEED FAMILY

PCT Sections: All **Abundance:** Common **Height:** 0.5–4 in. **Flowering:** April–August **Flower Color:** Yellow **Habitat-Community:** Sandy soils, generally near water, from California prairies to subalpine coniferous forests **Elevation:** Below 9000 ft. **Ecoregions:** All

Erect to decumbent or climbing annual with slimy, hairy herbage. Leaves 0.3–1.4 in. long, opposite, lance-shaped to ovoid with blunt to heart-shaped bases. Flowers from nodes scattered along stem. Calyces to 0.3 in. long, < pedicel, unequally 5-lobed, hairy. Corollas irregular, to 0.6 in. long, 2-lipped, yellow, generally with red spots or blotches. Fruits to 0.3 in. long, many-seeded capsules. Occurs throughout North America. Plants sometimes have many flowers (hence the common name and specific epithet, from the Latin, "full of flowers").

Erythranthe guttata

common yellow monkeyflower

PHRYMACEAE LOPSEED FAMILY

PCT Sections: All **Abundance:** Common **Height:** 2–32 in. **Flowering:** April–September **Flower Color:** Yellow **Habitat-Community:** Wet places in wetland-riparian communities **Elevation:** Below 6900 ft. **Ecoregions:** All

Spreading to erect, 1–many-branched perennial with hairy or hairless herbage. Leaves to 5 in. long, opposite, ovoid to round, lobed. Flowers 1–28, irregular, scattered along stem tips. Calyces to 0.8 in. long, < pedicel, unequally 5-lobed, asymmetrically swollen in fruit. Corollas 0.6–1.6 in. long, 2-lipped, yellow, with red spotted lower lip and smaller, plain upper lip. Fruits to 0.4 in. long, many-seeded capsules.

Erythranthe montioides

mountain monkeyflower

PHRYMACEAE LOPSEED FAMILY

PCT Sections: 8–10 **Abundance:** Occasional **Height:** 0.5–6 in. **Flowering:** June–August **Flower Color:** Yellow **Habitat-Community:** Understories and open streambanks, generally in granitic soils, from pinyon-juniper woodlands to subalpine coniferous forests and wetland-riparian communities **Elevation:** Below 9600 ft. **Ecoregions:** Sierra Nevada

Ascending to erect, multi-branched annual with hairy herbage. Leaves to 1 in. long, opposite, linear to lance-shaped, with smooth margins. Flowers few, at stem tips. Calyces to 0.3 in. long, < pedicel, equally 5-lobed, generally reddish, minutely hairy, with small point at the tip. Corollas irregular, 0.4–0.7 in. long, 2-lipped, yellow, with lower lip generally red-spotted. Fruits to 0.2 in. long, many-seeded capsules. *Montioides* means "mountain species."

Erythranthe moschata
musk monkeyflower
PHRYMACEAE LOPSEED FAMILY

PCT Sections: 3–5 & 8–24 **Abundance:** Common **Height:** 0.5–12 in. **Flowering:** May–September **Flower Color:** Yellow **Habitat-Community:** Partially shaded seeps, meadows, and streambanks from sagebrush scrubs to upper montane coniferous forests and wetland-riparian communities **Elevation:** Below 9600 ft. **Ecoregions:** Southern California Mountains, Sierra Nevada, Cascades, Klamath Mountains

Spreading to erect, multi-branched perennial with slimy-hairy, musky-smelling herbage. Leaves to 2 in. long, opposite, oblong to ovoid, with smooth to toothed margins. Flowers few, at stem tips. Calyces to 0.5 in. long, < pedicel, equally 5-lobed, hairless to hairy. Corollas irregular, 0.7–1 in. long, weakly 2-lipped, yellow. Fruits to 0.3 in. long, many-seeded capsules. *Moschata* means "musk-scented" (as the common name states). Popular as a garden plant in 19th-century England for its musky odor, but for reasons unknown, all cultivated plants lost their perfume at the same time.

Erythranthe primuloides
primrose monkeyflower
PHRYMACEAE LOPSEED FAMILY

PCT Sections: 3–4 & 9–24 **Abundance:** Common **Height:** 0.5–5 in. **Flowering:** June–August **Flower Color:** Yellow **Habitat-Community:** Streambanks, seeps, meadows, and cracks/shelves in rock outcrops from lower montane to subalpine coniferous forests and wetland-riparian communities **Elevation:** Below 11,200 ft. **Ecoregions:** Southern California Mountains, Sierra Nevada, Cascades, Klamath Mountains

Mat-forming perennial with generally rosetted, hairless herbage. Leaves to 1.6 in. long, basal, oblong to spoon-shaped, with smooth to toothed margins. Flowers few, on long pedicels. Calyces to 0.4 in. long, < pedicel, equally 5-lobed, hairless. Corollas irregular, 0.3–1 in. long, 2-lipped, yellow with red-spotted lower lip. Fruits to 0.3 in. long, many-seeded capsules.

Erythranthe suksdorfii
Suksdorf's monkeyflower
PHRYMACEAE LOPSEED FAMILY

PCT Sections: 3–5 & 9–18 **Abundance:** Occasional **Height:** 0.5–4 in. **Flowering:** April–August **Flower Color:** Yellow **Habitat-Community:** Open, moist places, generally in clay or sandy soils, from lower montane coniferous forests to alpine communities **Elevation:** Below 13,200 ft. **Ecoregions:** Southern California Mountains, Sierra Nevada

Compact, generally many-branched annual with glandular-hairy herbage. Leaves to 0.9 in. long, opposite, linear to ovoid, with smooth margins. Flowers few, scattered along stem. Calyces to 0.2 in. long, < pedicel, equally 5-lobed, hairless. Corollas irregular, to 0.3 in. long, 2-lipped, yellow, generally with red spots or blotches. Fruits to 0.2 in. long, many-seeded capsules. *Erythranthe* (from the Greek "red flower") refers to some monkeyflowers.

Erythranthe tilingii

Tiling's monkeyflower

PHRYMACEAE LOPSEED FAMILY

PCT Sections: 3–5 & 10–24 **Abundance:** Locally common **Height:** 1–14 in. **Flowering:** June–September **Flower Color:** Yellow **Habitat-Community:** Seeps, streambanks, and meadows in wetland-riparian communities **Elevation:** Below 11,200 ft. **Ecoregions:** Southern California Mountains, Sierra Nevada, Cascades, Klamath Mountains

Ascending to erect, generally branched perennial with glandular-hairy (slimy) or hairless herbage. Leaves to 1.4 in. long, opposite, ovoid to lance-shaped, generally slimy, with toothed margins. Flowers 1–5 per stem, irregular, from upper leaf bases. Calyces to 0.6 in. long, < pedicel, unequally 5-lobed, asymmetrically swollen in fruit. Corollas 1–1.4 in. long, 2-lipped, yellow with brown-spotted lower lip. Fruits to 0.4 in. long, many-seeded capsules.

Mimetanthe pilosa

downy mimetanthe

PHRYMACEAE LOPSEED FAMILY

PCT Sections: All **Abundance:** Occasional **Height:** 2–15 in. **Flowering:** April–August **Flower Color:** Yellow **Habitat-Community:** Sandy to gravelly soils in washes, moist areas, streambanks, and disturbed sites from foothill chaparrals to upper montane coniferous forests **Elevation:** Below 8000 ft. **Ecoregions:** All

Erect, intricately branched annual with densely wavy-haired stems. Leaves 0.4–1.2 in. long, opposite, lance-shaped to oblong, soft-hairy. Flowers 1 per leaf axil, irregular (appearing somewhat symmetrical), 5-lobed; pedicels 0.4–0.6 in. long. Calyces 0.2–0.3 in. long, 5-lobed, hairy, with lobes unequal and as long as the tube. Corollas 0.3 in. long, 2-lipped, 5-lobed (2 above, 3 below), yellow, often with red-purple dots on lower throat. Fruits 0.1 in. long, ovoid capsules. The only species in *Mimetanthe* (from the Greek, "imitator flower"). Aka false monkeyflower.

▼ MANY PETALS/SEPALS

Nuphar polysepala

Rocky Mountain pond-lily

NYMPHAEACEAE WATERLILY FAMILY

PCT Sections: 10–24 **Abundance:** Common **Height:** Generally floating **Flowering:** March–September **Flower Color:** Yellow **Habitat-Community:** Ponds and slow streams in wetland-riparian communities **Elevation:** Below 8200 ft. **Ecoregions:** Sierra Nevada, Cascades, Klamath Mountains

Aquatic perennial with floating leaves, at least early in the season, and showy flowers. Leaves 4–16 in. long, oblong to ovoid, with rounded basal lobes. Flowers 2–4 in. across, solitary at stem tips. Sepals to 2 in. long, 7–12, yellow to green, reddish or not, petal-like, ovoid to widely spoon-shaped, free. Petals small, stamen-like, many, yellow, reddish or not, free. Fruits to 1.4 in. across, berry-like, leathery, many-seeded. The edible seeds have historically been an important food source for Indigenous peoples.

water plantain buttercup

Ranunculus alismifolius

RANUNCULACEAE

BUTTERCUP FAMILY

PCT Sections: 3–4 & 10–24 **Abundance:** Locally common **Height:** 2–28 in. **Flowering:** April–August **Flower Color:** Yellow **Habitat-Community:** Meadows, swamps, lakeshores, and streams in wetland-riparian communities **Elevation:** Below 11,200 ft. **Ecoregions:** Southern California Mountains, Sierra Nevada, Cascades, Klamath Mountains

Ascending to erect, branched-near-base perennial with hairless herbage. Leaves to 5.5 in. long, alternate, lance-shaped, with smooth to toothed margins. Flowers in loose clusters at stem tips, with many pistils and stamens. Sepals to 0.3 in. long, 5, spreading or recurved. Petals to 0.6 in. long, 4–8. Fruits to 0.2 in. long with straight or curved beak.

California buttercup

Ranunculus californicus

RANUNCULACEAE

BUTTERCUP FAMILY

PCT Sections: 1–4 & 7 **Abundance:** Occasional **Height:** 8–25 in. **Flowering:** March–August **Flower Color:** Yellow **Habitat-Community:** Open, sandy to gravelly soils and meadows from California prairies to lower montane coniferous forests **Elevation:** Below 7000 ft. **Ecoregions:** Southern California Mountains, Sierra Nevada

Erect to decumbent, glossy-flowered perennial with hairless to spreading-hairy stems. Leaves to 3 in. across, basal and alternate, broadly ovate, 3-lobed, with toothed margins (basal). Flowers in loose clusters at stem tips, symmetric, with 5 hairless, reflexed sepals, yellow anthers, and many pistils. Petals 0.3–0.7 in. long, 9–17, elliptic to oblong. Fruits 0.1–0.2 in across, disk-like achenes. The shiny yellow flower vaguely resembles a water lily.

Hartweg's buttercup

Ranunculus canus var. *ludovicianus*

RANUNCULACEAE

BUTTERCUP FAMILY

PCT Sections: 4 & 7–8 **Abundance:** Occasional **Height:** 4–26 in. **Flowering:** March–August **Flower Color:** Yellow **Habitat-Community:** Sandy to gravelly soils and meadows from California prairies to lower montane coniferous forests **Elevation:** Below 7400 ft. **Ecoregions:** Southern California Mountains, Sierra Nevada

Erect to decumbent perennial with hairless to spreading-hairy stems. Leaves to 3 in. across, basal and cauline, narrowly ovate to 3-lobed, hairy, with toothed margins (basal). Flowers in loose clusters at stem tips, symmetric, with 5 hairless, reflexed sepals, yellow anthers, and many pistils. Petals 0.2–0.5 in. long, 5–17, elliptic to oblong, shiny yellow. Fruits 0.1–0.2 in across, disk-like achenes. Intergrades with *R. californicus* in the San Bernardino Mountains.

Ranunculus eschscholtzii

Eschscholtz's buttercup

RANUNCULACEAE

BUTTERCUP FAMILY

PCT Sections: 3–4 & 10–24 **Abundance:** Locally common **Height:** 2–10 in. **Flowering:** July–September **Flower Color:** Yellow **Habitat-Community:** Open, rocky soils and meadows in subalpine coniferous forests and alpine communities **Elevation:** Below 14,100 ft.

Ecoregions: Southern California Mountains, Sierra Nevada, Cascades, Klamath Mountains

Decumbent to erect, tufted perennial with hairless herbage. Leaves to 0.9 in. long, mostly basal, round-ish to heart-shaped, and 2-lobed into 3 segments with rounded or acute tips. Flowers 1–3 at stem tips with many pistils and stamens. Sepals to 0.3 in. long, 5, spreading and falling off early. Petals to 0.5 in. long, 5–8. Fruits to 0.2 in. long with straight beak when mature. Aka snowpatch buttercup: plants prefer growing at the moist edge of melting snow patches.

ORANGE

▼ COMPOSITE / RAY AND DISK FLOWERS

Hulsea heterochroma

redray alpinegold

ASTERACEAE SUNFLOWER FAMILY

PCT Sections: 3–9 **Abundance:** Occasional **Height:** 15–50 in. **Flowering:** May–August **Flower Color:** Orange to red **Habitat-Community:** Open sites and recent burns from oak woodlands to lower montane coniferous forests **Elevation:** Below 8200 ft. **Ecoregions:** Southern California Mountains, Sierra Nevada

Annual or perennial with thick, leafy, green stems and densely glandular herbage. Leaves 4–8 in. long, basal and alternate, reduced on upper stem, elliptic, conspicuously glandular. Flowers in heads; invo-lucres funnel-shaped, 0.4–0.7 in. long, with linear to lance-shaped phyllaries. Ray flowers 0.2–0.4 in. long, 30–75 per head, orange to red. Disk flowers many per head, yellow-orange. Fruits 0.2–0.3 in. long, hairy achenes with short pappus scales. A fire-follower, becoming locally common in recent burns.

Hulsea vestita subsp. parryi

Parry's sunflower

ASTERACEAE SUNFLOWER FAMILY

PCT Sections: 4 **Abundance:** Rare **Height:** 5–20 in. **Flowering:** May–August **Flower Color:** Orange to red **Habitat-Community:** Open, gravelly soils or talus slopes in sagebrush scrubs, pinyon-juniper woodlands, and lower montane coniferous forests **Elevation:** Below 8300 ft. **Ecoregions:** Southern California Mountains

Perennial with thick, short stems and woolly, often glandular herbage. Leaves 1–3 in. long, basal and alternate, spoon-shaped, woolly or felt-like hairy, glandular, with scalloped to deeply lobed margins. Flowers in heads; involucres funnel-shaped, 0.4–0.8 in. long, with sparsely woolly, green (red-tipped) phyllaries 0.3–0.5 in. long. Ray flowers 0.2–0.8 in. long, 9–25 per head, orange to red. Disk flowers many per head, orange to red. Fruits 0.2–0.3 in. long, hairy achenes with short pappus scales. Nearly endemic to the San Bernardino Mountains, where it hybridizes with *H. heterochroma*. Disjunct populations also occur in Joshua Tree National Park.

Hymenoxys hoopesii

owlsclaws

ASTERACEAE SUNFLOWER FAMILY

PCT Sections: 9–16 **Abundance:** Locally common **Height:** 1–3 ft. **Flowering:** May–November **Flower Color:** Orange to yellow-orange **Habitat-Community:** Meadows, streambanks, and openings from lower montane to subalpine coniferous forests and wetland-riparian communities **Elevation:** Below 12,000 ft. **Ecoregions:** Sierra Nevada

Erect, branched perennial with hairy or hairless herbage. Leaves to 3.2 in. long, basal (mostly) and alternate, linear to lance-shaped, hairy or hairless, with smooth or toothed margins. Flowers in heads, 1–12 per stem, with phyllaries in 2 graduated series. Ray flowers to 1.8 in. long, 14–26 per head, orange to yellow-orange. Disk flowers to 0.2 in. long, 100–325+ per head, yellow. Fruits to 0.2 in. long, achenes with 5–7 pappus scales.

Packera pauciflora

alpine ragwort

ASTERACEAE SUNFLOWER FAMILY

PCT Sections: 10–18 **Abundance:** Rare **Height:** 8–16 in. **Flowering:** July–August **Flower Color:** Orange-yellow **Habitat-Community:** Meadows and forest understories in subalpine coniferous forests and wetland-riparian communities **Elevation:** 5900–10,900 ft. **Ecoregions:** Sierra Nevada, Cascades

Erect, 1–3-stemmed, mostly hairless perennial. Leaves to 1.6 in. long, basal rosettes and alternate on stem, variously shaped with some dissected to pinnately lobed, petioled (at least the lowest on the stem), generally hairless. Flowers 2–8 heads per cluster, with 13 or 21, hairless, red to green (red-tipped) phyllaries to 0.4 in. long; outer phyllaries few, reduced, green. Ray flowers to 0.3 in. long, (0)8–13 per head, orange-yellow. Disk flowers 60–80+ per head, bell-shaped to tubular, orange to reddish. Fruits to 0.1 in. long, cylindric, hairless achenes with white bristles.

▼ COMPOSITE / RAY FLOWERS ONLY

Agoseris aurantiaca

orange agoseris

ASTERACEAE SUNFLOWER FAMILY

PCT Sections: 10–24 **Abundance:** Locally common **Height:** 4–20 in. **Flowering:** May–September **Flower Color:** Orange **Habitat-Community:** Meadows, streambanks, and among shrubs from lower montane to subalpine coniferous forests and wetland-riparian communities **Elevation:** Below 11,500 ft. **Ecoregions:** Sierra Nevada, Cascades, Klamath Mountains

Generally erect perennial with clumped basal leaves, milky sap, and naked flowering stems. Leaves to 12 in. long, lance-shaped to ovoid, mostly hairless, generally waxy-coated, spear-tipped, with deeply lobed margins. Flowers in solitary heads on leafless stems; involucres 0.6–0.8 in. long (in flower) with 3 equal series of green or purplish phyllaries. Ray flowers 0.2–0.4 in. long, 15–100 per head, orange. Fruits 0.4–0.8 in. long, beaked achenes with 2–4 series of white bristles. *Aurantiaca* is Latin for "orange." The only orange *Agoseris* sp. along the CA PCT.

desert mariposa lily

Calochortus kennedyi

LILIACEAE LILY FAMILY

PCT Sections: 4–7 **Abundance:** Occasional **Height:** 8–20 in. **Flowering:** April–June **Flower Color:** Orange to red **Habitat-Community:** Gravelly or rocky substrates in creosote bush & Mojave mixed woody scrubs and Joshua tree & pinyon-juniper woodlands **Elevation:** Below 6800 ft. **Ecoregions:** Southern California Mountains, Mojave Basin and Range, Sierra Nevada

Attractive perennial with unbranched, sometimes twisted stems. Leaves 4–8 in. long, basal, withering at flowering, linear, channeled, wax-coated. Flowers 1–6 per plant, erect, symmetric, bell-shaped, with 6 stamens. Tepals 0.8–2 in. long, 6-parted (3 sepals, 3 petals), free, ovoid to spatula-shaped, dark hairy patch at base, orange to red. Fruits 1–3 in. long, erect capsules. Found along the PCT at the desert slopes and crossings bordering the Mojave Desert.

Kelley's lily

Lilium kelleyanum

LILIACEAE LILY FAMILY

PCT Sections: 9–11 **Abundance:** Common **Height:** to 7 ft. **Flowering:** July–August **Flower Color:** Orange to yellow **Habitat-Community:** Seeps, meadows, and streambanks in wetland-riparian communities **Elevation:** 7200–10,900 ft. **Ecoregions:** Sierra Nevada

Erect, unbranched perennial with whorled and alternate leaves. Leaves to 7 in. long, 3–8 per whorl, alternate on lower stem, oblong-lance-shaped, with drooping tip. Flowers 1–15 per plant, pendent, symmetric, with 6 stamens and 3-lobed stigma. Tepals to 2.4 in. long, 6-parted (3 sepals, 3 petals) in a widely bell-shaped perianth, sepals and petals alike, orange to yellow, spoon-shaped, recurved from middle. Fruits to 1.2 in. long, erect capsules with many flat seeds. Lily (from the Greek *leirion*, "lily") ultimately has its roots (pun intended) in Egyptian names used for lotus flowers.

leopard lily

Lilium pardalinum

LILIACEAE LILY FAMILY

PCT Sections: 1 & 4 & 15–24 **Abundance:** Common **Height:** to 9 ft. **Flowering:** May–August **Flower Color:** Orange to red **Habitat-Community:** Seeps, meadows, and streambanks in wetland-riparian communities **Elevation:** Below 6600 ft. **Ecoregions:** Southern California Mountains, Sierra Nevada, Cascades, Klamath Mountains

Erect, branched or unbranched perennial, generally growing in colonies. Leaves to 11 in. long, alternate or 1–8 whorls, 9–15 per whorl, oblong, with smooth margins. Flowers 1–28 per plant, generally unscented, pendent, symmetric, with 6 stamens and 3-lobed stigma. Tepals to 4 in. long, 6-parted (3 sepals, 3 petals) in a widely bell-shaped perianth, generally 2-toned, orange to red with lighter base and maroon-spotted, sepals and petals alike, recurved. Fruits to 2.4 in. long, erect capsules with many flat seeds. *Pardalinum* means "leopard."

Lilium parvum

Sierra tiger lily

LILIACEAE LILY FAMILY

PCT Sections: 10–15 **Abundance:** Common **Height:** to 5.5 ft. **Flowering:** June–August **Flower Color:** Orange to red **Habitat-Community:** Seeps, meadows, and streambanks in wetland-riparian communities **Elevation:** Below 9600 ft.

Ecoregions: Sierra Nevada

Erect, unbranched perennial with whorled and alternate leaves. Leaves to 6 in. long, 2–5 whorls and alternate, broad-lance-shaped to linear, with smooth margins. Flowers 1–26 per plant, unscented, nodding to ascending, symmetric. Tepals to 1.7 in. long, 6-parted (3 sepals, 3 petals), bell-shaped perianth, orange to red, maroon-spotted, sepal > petal width, recurved tips, 6 stamens, and 3-lobed stigma. Fruits to 1.1 in. long, erect capsules with many flat seeds.

▼ 4 PETALS

Eschscholzia californica

California poppy

PAPAVERACEAE POPPY FAMILY

PCT Sections: 1–8 **Abundance:** Common **Height:** 6–24 in. **Flowering:** March–August **Flower Color:** Orange or yellow **Habitat-Community:** Open areas from California prairies to lower montane coniferous forests **Elevation:** Below 7500 ft.

Ecoregions: Southern California/Northern Baja Coast, Southern California Mountains, Mojave Basin and Range, Sierra Nevada

Erect to spreading, showy, large-flowered annual (sometimes perennial) with hairless stems. Basal leaves 1–5 in. long, compact, dissected, hairless; stem leaves alternate, reduced. Flowers few on stalks, symmetric, with 2 sepals, many stamens, and base below perianth funnel-shaped and prominently rimmed. Petals 0.8–2.4 in. long, 4, orange or yellow, sometimes red. Fruits 0.1–0.3 in. long, capsules. The state flower of California. It is often included in highway seed mixes, but native populations of this beauty abound, none more spectacular than those along the PCT in Antelope Valley. John Steinbeck attempted to describe their "burning color–not orange, not gold, but if pure gold were liquid and could raise a cream, that golden cream might be like the color of poppies."

Sphaeralcea ambigua

apricot mallow

MALVACEAE MALLOW FAMILY

PCT Sections: 1–8 **Abundance:** Common **Height:** 20–40 in. **Flowering:** February–July **Flower Color:** Red-orange to lavender **Habitat-Community:** Flats and gentle slopes in creosote bush & Sonoran/Mojave mixed woody scrubs, chaparrals, and Joshua tree & pinyon-juniper woodlands **Elevation:** Below 7800 ft. **Ecoregions:** Southern California Mountains, Sonoran/Mojave Basin and Range, Sierra Nevada

Bushy perennial to shrub with yellow-green or rusty-brown stems covered in coarse, star-shaped hairs. Leaves 0.6–2.1 in. across, alternate, rounded-triangular, palmately 3-veined, wrinkled or smooth, fuzzy, hairy, usually with 3-lobed margins. Flowers symmetric, 5-parted, in open spikes, with yellow to purple anthers. Petals 0.5–1.1 in. long, spreading, spatula-shaped, red-orange to lavender; filament tube 0.1–0.3 in. long. Fruits capsules of 9–17 wedge-shaped segments with 2 seeds per segment. The specific epithet is testimony to the taxonomic uncertainty encountered in the genus.

Sphaeralcea emoryi

Emory's globemallow

MALVACEAE MALLOW FAMILY

PCT Sections: 1–7 **Abundance:** Rare **Height:** 2–4 ft. **Flowering:** February–July **Flower Color:** Red-orange to lavender **Habitat-Community:** Dry places on flats and gentle slopes in Sonoran/ Mojave mixed woody scrubs, foothill chaparrals, and Joshua tree & pinyon-juniper woodlands **Elevation:** Below 3500 ft. **Ecoregions:** Southern California Mountains, Sonoran/Mojave Basin and Range, Sierra Nevada

Perennial or subshrub with white to yellow-green stems covered in coarse, star-shaped hairs. Leaves 1–2.3 in. long, alternate, ovoid-triangular with heart-shaped base, palmately 3–5-veined, usually 3-lobed with the central lobe much longer, hairy, gray-green, with wavy margins. Flowers symmetric, 5-parted, in spikes or open clusters, with yellow to purple anthers. Petals 0.4–0.6 in. long, spatula-shaped, red-orange to lavender; filament tube 0.2 in. long. Fruits capsules of 10–16 wedge-shaped segments with 1–2 seeds per segment. Tolerates saline soils and often abundant in burns.

Amsinckia intermedia

common fiddleneck

BORAGINACEAE BORAGE FAMILY

PCT Sections: 1–8 **Abundance:** Common **Height:** 8–28 in. **Flowering:** March–June **Flower Color:** Orange to yellow **Habitat-Community:** Gravelly soils in creosote bush & Sonoran/Mojave mixed woody scrubs, foothill chaparrals, and woodlands **Elevation:** Below 5800 ft. **Ecoregions:** Southern California Mountains, Sonoran/Mojave Basin and Range, Sierra Nevada

Wide-ranging annual of lower elevations with slender stems, sometimes elongating through shrubs, and covered in spreading, bristly hairs. Basal leaves to 8 in. long, narrowly oblanceolate, withering with age; cauline leaves alternate, reduced, 0.2–1 in. long, lanceolate, green, coarsely hairy. Flowers in coiled (especially at tip) spikes 2–15 in. long, 5-parted, with fused-at-base calyx lobes. Corollas 0.3–0.5 in. long, trumpet-shaped, orange to yellow with dark (reddish) spots, with tube extending from calyx. Fruits grayish nutlets. The genus is named after German horticulturalist Wilhelm Amsinck (1752–1831).

Collomia grandiflora

orange mountaintrumpet

POLEMONIACEAE PHLOX FAMILY

PCT Sections: All **Abundance:** Common **Height:** 4–36 in. **Flowering:** April–July **Flower Color:** Orange (salmon), white, or yellow **Habitat-Community:** Open areas from woodlands and chaparrals to subalpine coniferous forests **Elevation:** Below 10,000 ft. **Ecoregions:** All

Erect, 1–few-branched annual with hairy stems. Leaves to 2 in. long, alternate, lance-shaped to linear, with smooth margins. Flowers in compact heads at stem tips. Calyces to 0.4 in. long, 5-lobed, with lobes connected by a thin membrane with a water pitcher–like projection at the tip. Corollas to 1.2 in. long, funnel-shaped, orange, white, or yellow, with 5 flared lobes. Fruits to 0.2 in. long, capsules that explosively open to scatter seeds. A fun wildflower to spot with its dense heads of salmon-colored mini-trumpets.

Aphyllon californicum

California broomrape

OROBANCHACEAE
BROOMRAPE FAMILY

PCT Sections: 1–9 & 15–18 **Abundance:** Occasional **Height:** 4–12 in. **Flowering:** May–July **Flower Color:** Orange, purple, or white **Habitat-Community:** Open areas from foothill chaparrals to upper montane coniferous forests **Elevation:** Below 8200 ft. **Ecoregions:** Southern California Mountains, Sierra Nevada

Wide-ranging parasitic perennial (lacking leaves and chlorophyll), with single or multiple, thick, fleshy, glandular stems in dense clusters. Flowers in dense spikes, irregular, 5-parted; pedicels 0–2 in. long; calyces 0.5–0.8 in. long. Corollas 1–1.5 in. long, orange, purple, or white (purple- or red-tinged), tubular, 2-lipped, upper lip 2-lobed, lower lip 3-lobed; lips 0.4–0.6 in. long. Fruits 2-valved capsules. Six subspecies occur in California, 3 along the PCT; many use *Artemisia tridentata* as their host. The most common, subsp. *feudgei* in southern California, with a stout stem and floral tube, is often golden-yellow.

Diplacus australis

southern monkeyflower

PHRYMACEAE LOPSEED FAMILY

PCT Sections: 1–2 **Abundance:** Locally common **Height:** 10–32 in. **Flowering:** March–June **Flower Color:** Orange to yellow-orange **Habitat-Community:** Dry, rocky slopes among boulders in foothill chaparrals and oak woodlands **Elevation:** Below 3400 ft. **Ecoregions:** Southern California/Northern Baja Coast, Southern California Mountains

Erect, showy, multi-branched perennial or subshrub with glandular, soft-hairy stems. Leaves 0.6–3 in. long, opposite, linear to lance-shaped, hairless, with smooth to slightly saw-toothed margins. Flowers persistent and sessile (or with a very short pedicel), 2–4 per node, irregular, 5-lobed, tubular, with short-hairy calyces 0.7–1.3 in. long with unequal lobes. Corollas 1.1–1.5 in. long, orange to yellow-orange, 2-lipped, upper lip 2-lobed, lower lip 3-lobed. Fruits 0.7–1 in. long, ovoid capsules. *Australis* (from the Latin, "southern") describes its limited distribution in maritime southern California and northern Baja California.

Erythranthe cardinalis

scarlet monkeyflower

PHRYMACEAE LOPSEED FAMILY

PCT Sections: 1–6 & 13–24 **Abundance:** Locally common **Height:** 10–32 in. **Flowering:** May–September **Flower Color:** Orange to red **Habitat-Community:** Moist slopes, meadows, bogs, and streambanks in wetland-riparian communities **Elevation:** Below 7900 ft. **Ecoregions:** All (except Sonoran/Mojave Basin and Range)

Erect or sprawling, many-branched perennial with glandular-hairy herbage. Leaves to 3.2 in. long, opposite, oblong to spoon-shaped, with toothed margins. Flowers generally many, scattered along stem tips. Calyces to 1.2 in. long, < pedicel, equally 5-lobed, hairy. Corollas irregular, to 2 in. long, 2-lipped, orange to red, with recurved lower lip. Fruits to 0.6 in. long, many-seeded capsules. Very easy to notice from the trail, especially when growing in large colonies that attract scores of hummingbirds.

▼ COMPOSITE / RAY FLOWERS ONLY

Pleiacanthus spinosus

thorny skeltonweed

ASTERACEAE SUNFLOWER FAMILY

PCT Sections: 4–5 & 13 **Abundance:** Rare **Height:** 4–20 in. **Flowering:** June–September **Flower Color:** Pink to red-purple **Habitat-Community:** Gravelly to rocky soils in pinyon-juniper woodlands and montane coniferous forests **Elevation:** Below 9400 ft. **Ecoregions:** Southern California Mountains, Sierra Nevada

Tightly branched, gray perennial or subshrub with rigid, thorn-tipped stems and woolly leaf/stem axils. Leaves to 0.5 in. long, alternate, sparse, bract-like, linear. Flowers scattered along stems and branches; involucres 0.3–0.5 in. long with smooth phyllaries in 2 series (the inner being larger). Ray flowers 0.2–0.3 in. long, 3–5 per head, tips slightly toothed, pink to red-purple or lavender to white. Fruits 0.2 in. long, achenes with many tan bristles of 2 lengths. The only species in *Pleiacanthus*. Look for this well-armed plant along the PCT atop the Blue Ridge east of Mt. Baden-Powell in the San Gabriel Mountains, and from Sonora Pass to Echo Lake in the Sierra Nevada.

Stephanomeria exigua

small wirelettuce

ASTERACEAE SUNFLOWER FAMILY

PCT Sections: 1–10 **Abundance:** Occasional **Height:** 4–50 in. **Flowering:** April–November **Flower Color:** Pink to white **Habitat-Community:** Open areas from creosote bush scrubs to upper montane coniferous forests **Elevation:** Below 8200 ft. **Ecoregions:** Southern California Mountains, Sonoran/Mojave Basin and Range, Sierra Nevada

Single-stemmed, wiry annual with branches on upper stem and milky sap. Leaves 1–3 in. long, basal and alternate (clasping stem and reduced), thin, spoon-shaped, hairless or slightly hairy, with smooth to slightly toothed margins. Flowers solitary or in clusters along branches, and reflexed or straight, glandular or glandless phyllaries. Ray flowers 0.2–0.3 in. long, 5–7 per head, tips slightly toothed, pink to white or white with pink veins. Fruits 0.2–0.3 in. long, smooth or bumpy achenes with white to tan bristles. Five subspecies occur in California, 3 along the PCT: subsp. *deanei* (densely glandular involucre) in the southern Peninsular Ranges; subsp. *coronaria* (one head per stem on short peduncles) in the Transverse Ranges and southern Sierra; subsp. *exigua* (hairless involucre, heads in open clusters) along the desert crossings.

Stephanomeria tenuifolia

narrowleaf wirelettuce

ASTERACEAE SUNFLOWER FAMILY

PCT Sections: 8–18 **Abundance:** Locally common **Height:** 8–24 in. **Flowering:** June–August **Flower Color:** Pink to lavender **Habitat-Community:** Rocky slopes and outcrops from sagebrush scrubs and woodlands to subalpine coniferous forests **Elevation:** Below 10,800 ft. **Ecoregions:** Sierra Nevada, Cascades

Erect to ascending perennial with few to many leafy branches, milky sap, and hairless stems. Leaves 2–3 in. long, linear to thread-like, with smooth to toothed margins. Flowers solitary at stem tips, with hairless involucres 0.2–0.6 in. long. Ray flowers much longer than involucre, 4–5 per head, pink to lavender. Fruits 0.1–0.3 in. long, achenes with 5–40 white, plumose bristles. Pappus bristles are plumose throughout.

Stephanomeria virgata

rod wirelettuce

ASTERACEAE SUNFLOWER FAMILY

PCT Sections: 1–9 **Abundance:** Occasional **Height:** 1–6 ft. **Flowering:** June–October **Flower Color:** Pink to white **Habitat-Community:** Open areas in California prairies, foothill chaparrals, and oak woodlands **Elevation:** Below 6200 ft. **Ecoregions:** Southern California Mountains, Sierra Nevada

Wiry annual with a single, wand-like stem. Leaves alternate, basal withering at flowering, scale-like, usually hairless. Flowers solitary or in clusters of sessile heads along branches; involucres 0.2–0.4 in. long with reflexed or appressed outer phyllaries. Ray flowers 0.3–0.5 in. long, 5–9, tips slightly toothed, dark pink to white. Fruits 0.1–0.2 in. long, smooth to bumpy achenes with white-barbed bristles.

▼ COMPOSITE / DISK FLOWERS ONLY

Ageratina occidentalis

western eupatorium

ASTERACEAE SUNFLOWER FAMILY

PCT Sections: 10–24 **Abundance:** Common **Height:** 5–18 in. **Flowering:** June–October **Flower Color:** Pink or red-purple to whitish **Habitat-Community:** Rocky slopes and ridges, including serpentine soils, from lower montane to subalpine coniferous forests **Elevation:** Below 12,100 ft. **Ecoregions:** Sierra Nevada, Cascades, Klamath Mountains

Erect perennial with woody base. Leaves 0.5–2 in. long, alternate, triangular, glandular below, point-tipped, with toothed margins. Flowers many per cluster, 8–12 disk flowers per head, pink or red-purple to whitish, with hairy phyllaries to 0.4 in. long. Fruits to 0.2 in. long, 5-angled achenes with 5–40 scabrous bristles. Eupatorium is derived from Eupator, king of Pontus and the first to use a related species medicinally.

Cirsium occidentale

cobweb thistle

ASTERACEAE SUNFLOWER FAMILY

PCT Sections: All **Abundance:** Occasional **Height:** 2–6 ft. **Flowering:** April–September **Flower Color:** Red or pink to white **Habitat-Community:** Open sites, including serpentine soils, from woodlands and chaparrals to subalpine coniferous forests **Elevation:** Below 10,500 ft. **Ecoregions:** All

Large, erect biennial with single, hairy stems and whitish foliage. Leaves 3–14 in. long, green above, gray-hairy below, with spiny-winged petioles and spine-tipped lobes. Flowers 1–1.4 in. long, 1–few heads per stem in tight clusters. Disk flowers red or pink to white; phyllaries spiny-margined, cobwebby, with tip-spine to 0.4 in. long. Fruits to 0.3 in. long, achenes with many bristles. It's hard to walk by this thistle without seeing bumblebees visiting the flower heads. Ants are repelled by its cobwebby hairs.

▼ 3 OR 6 PETALS/TEPALS

Allium campanulatum

Sierra onion

ALLIACEAE ONION FAMILY

PCT Sections: 1–5 & 8–24 **Abundance:** Common **Height:** 4–12 in. **Flowering:** May–August **Flower Color:** Rose to purple **Habitat-Community:** Dry slopes and flats from woodlands to upper montane coniferous forests **Elevation:** Below 8600 ft. **Ecoregions:** All (except Sonoran/Mojave Basin and Range)

Erect perennial with 1–2 cylindric stems. Leaves as long as stem, 2–3 per plant, flat. Flowers 10–50 in open, head-like cluster at stem tip, bell-shaped, symmetric. Tepals to 0.3 in. long, 6-parted (3 sepals, 3 petals), rose to purple (rarely white) with purple crescent near base, lance-shaped to ovoid, with smooth margins. Fruits to 0.1 in. long, capsules with black seeds nearly 0.1 in. long.

Allium cratericola

Cascade onion

ALLIACEAE ONION FAMILY

PCT Sections: 3 & 6–7 **Abundance:** Rare **Height:** 2–5 in. **Flowering:** May–July **Flower Color:** Pink to rose **Habitat-Community:** Open, gravelly slopes and plains in foothill chaparrals, sagebrush scrubs, and lower montane coniferous forests **Elevation:** Below 6000 ft. **Ecoregions:** Southern California Mountains, Sierra Nevada

Perennial with a flat, hairless stem from an oval bulb 0.6–1 in. across. Leaves 3–15 in. long, 1–2 per stem, basal, broadly flattened and channeled. Flowers 20–30 per head-like cluster at stem tip, symmetric, with pedicels 0.2–0.7 in. long and 6 stamens with yellow anthers. Tepals 0.3–0.6 in. long, 6-parted (3 sepals, 3 petals), free and spreading from base, pink to rose. Fruits 3-crested capsules. Look for this California endemic along the PCT in the southern San Jacinto Mountains and Sierra Nevada of Kern County. *Cratericola* (from the Latin, "dweller of volcanos") refers to its affiliation with volcanic soils, but it also grows in granitic and serpentine soils.

Allium monticola

San Bernardino mountain onion

ALLIACEAE ONION FAMILY

PCT Sections: 4–5 **Abundance:** Rare **Height:** 3–10 in. **Flowering:** May–July **Flower Color:** Pink to rose-purple **Habitat-Community:** Open, rocky slopes and talus in montane coniferous forests **Elevation:** Below 10,000 ft. **Ecoregions:** Southern California Mountains

Waxy-stemmed perennial from a white to pink bulb, often with small bulblets. Leaves 4–10 in. long, 1 per stem, basal, linear, broad-cylindric, wax-coated. Flowers 8–25 per head-like cluster, symmetric, with 6 stamens and pedicels 0.2–0.5 in. long. Tepals 0.5–0.8 in. long, 6-parted (3 sepals, 3 petals), free and spreading from base, pink to rose-purple. Fruits 6-crested capsules. This endemic is best seen along the PCT atop the Blue Ridge in the San Gabriel Mountains. *Monticola* is Latin for "living in the mountains."

Allium shevockii

Spanish needle onion

ALLIACEAE ONION FAMILY

PCT Sections: 9 **Abundance:** Rare **Height:** 4–8 in. **Flowering:** May–July **Flower Color:** Maroon **Habitat-Community:** Metamorphic rock outcrops and rocky soils from woodlands to upper montane coniferous forests **Elevation:** Below 8200 ft. **Ecoregions:** Sierra Nevada

Perennial with cylindric stems and 1 leaf per plant. Leaves 1.5–2.5 times stem length, cylindric. Flowers generally 12–30 in dense, head-like cluster at stem tip, symmetric. Tepals to 0.6 in. long, 6-parted (3 sepals, 3 petals), maroon with white or green at base, spoon-shaped to ovoid, with recurved tips. Fruits 6-crested capsules with black seeds. A spectacular onion that you have to see to believe! Watch for this beauty on the rocky slopes, both sides of the PCT, at Mile 671.6.

Allium validum

swamp onion

ALLIACEAE ONION FAMILY

PCT Sections: 10–24 **Abundance:** Common **Height:** 20–40 in. **Flowering:** June–August **Flower Color:** Rose to white **Habitat-Community:** Wet meadows in wetland-riparian communities **Elevation:** Below 11,200 ft. **Ecoregions:** Sierra Nevada, Cascades, Klamath Mountains

Clustered perennial with angled stems. Leaves as long as stem, 3–6 per plant, flat or keeled. Flowers 15–40 in dense, head-like cluster at stem tip, symmetric. Tepals to 0.4 in. long, 6-parted (3 sepals, 3 petals), rose to white, narrowly lance-shaped, erect. Fruits to 0.3 in. long, capsules with black seeds. Hard to miss this tall, showy plant while hiking through streamside meadows! Indigenous peoples and early settlers relished the leaves and bulbs as a food and seasoning.

Calochortus palmeri

Palmer's mariposa lily

LILIACEAE LILY FAMILY

PCT Sections: 2–8 **Abundance:** Rare **Height:** 12–24 in. **Flowering:** May–July **Flower Color:** Pink, lavender, or white **Habitat-Community:** Gravelly or rocky substrates in California prairies, chaparrals, and lower montane coniferous forests **Elevation:** Below 6800 ft. **Ecoregions:** Southern California Mountains, Sierra Nevada

Lovely, erect perennial from a bulb with branched and straight stems. Leaves 4–8 in. long, basal, withering at flowering, linear. Flowers erect, widely bell-shaped, with 6 pink, lavender, or white tepals and 6 stamens. Sepals 3, oblong, 1–1.3 in. long. Petals 3, widely spatula-shaped, 0.8–1.2 in. long, with yellow, hairy or hairless nectary glands at base. Fruits 1–3 in. long, erect capsules. Two varieties along the PCT: var. *palmeri* (stem bulblets present; nectary glands yellow-hairy), the most common, is centered on the Transverse Ranges; var. *munzii* (bulblets absent; nectary glands usually glabrous) is limited to the Peninsular Ranges. Both are threatened by development, grazing, recreational activities, and roads.

Calochortus splendens

splendid mariposa lily

LILIACEAE LILY FAMILY

PCT Sections: 1–5 **Abundance:** Common **Height:** 8–24 in. **Flowering:** May–July **Flower Color:** Pink, lavender, or purple **Habitat-Community:** Granitic soils on dry slopes in chaparrals and lower montane coniferous forests **Elevation:** Below 8500 ft. **Ecoregions:** Southern California/Northern Baja Coast, Southern California Mountains

Erect perennial from a bulb with branched, straight stems. Basal leaves 4–8 in. long, withering at flowering, linear; stem leaves 2, 2–7 in. long. Flowers erect, bell-shaped, with 6 pink, lavender, or purple tepals and 6 stamens with bright purple pollen. Sepals 3, lance-shaped, strongly recurved, 0.8–1.2 in. long; petals 3, fan-shaped, 1.2–2 in. long, with densely white-hairy nectary glands. Fruits 2–3 in. long, erect, linear capsules.

Calyptridium monandrum

common pussypaws

MONTIACEAE
MINER'S LETTUCE FAMILY

PCT Sections: 1–9 **Abundance:** Common **Height:** 1–5 in. **Flowering:** February–July **Flower Color:** Pink to white **Habitat-Community:** Sandy to gravelly soils in creosote bush scrubs, foothill chaparrals, and woodlands **Elevation:** Below 6500 ft. **Ecoregions:** Southern California Mountains, Sonoran/Mojave Basin and Range, Sierra Nevada

Ubiquitous matted annual with somewhat succulent stems and hairless herbage. Basal leaves 0.4–2.1 in. long, alternate stem leaves 0.3–0.8 in. long, spoon-shaped, with upper surface puffy around the veins. Flowers inconspicuous, symmetric, with 2 fleshy sepals and 3 pink to white petals to 0.1 in. long. Fruits 2-valved capsules with 4–10 shiny black seeds. These hardy little ground-hugging plants are often overlooked, but they continue to persist along the PCT in southern California, even while being regularly stepped on. Their seeds are valued as a food source by the Chumash and other Indigenous peoples.

trailing windmills

Allionia incarnata

trailing windmills

NYCTAGINACEAE

FOUR O'CLOCK FAMILY

PCT Sections: 1–3 **Abundance:** Locally common **Height:** 2–8 in. **Flowering:** March–September **Flower Color:** Pink to red-purple **Habitat-Community:** Dry, rocky to gravelly slopes and flats in scrubs **Elevation:** Below 5500 ft. **Ecoregions:** Southern California Mountains, Sonoran Basin and Range

Sprawling annual or short-lived perennial with decumbent, elongated, few-branched stems and densely glandular-hairy herbage. Leaves 0.8–1.5 in. long, opposite, ovoid, thick, with undulating margins. Flowers in heads that appear to be a single symmetric flower but are actually 3 strongly irregular flowers, each with 4 golden-yellow stamens, enclosed by a sepal-like involucre. Perianth tube funnel-shaped, the limb 0.1–0.6 in. long, 3-lobed, pink to red-purple. Fruits small, hardened achenes. Two varieties along the PCT, primarily in San Diego County but also at other low desert crossings to the north: var. *villosa* has larger flowers (limb >0.3 in. long) with exserted stamens; var. *incarnata* has small flowers (<0.4 in. long) and stamens included within the tube. The latter is most often an annual and can be abundant following summer rains.

spotted coralroot

Corallorhiza maculata

spotted coralroot

ORCHIDACEAE ORCHID FAMILY

PCT Sections: 1–5 & 10–24 **Abundance:** Common **Height:** 6–22 in. **Flowering:** April–August **Flower Color:** Reddish to yellow-brown **Habitat-Community:** Understories, rich in humus, in montane coniferous forests **Elevation:** Below 9200 ft. **Ecoregions:** Southern California Mountains, Sierra Nevada, Cascades, Klamath Mountains

Erect, 1–few-stemmed, hairless perennial, red to yellow-brown to yellow, with no obvious leaves; myco-heterotrophic. Leaves 0 at flowering but with scale-like bracts 0.1 in. long. Flowers along upper stem, irregular, with stamen and style fused into a column. Sepals 3, to 0.4 in. long, petal-like, the lower 2 spreading, reddish to yellow-brown. Petals 3, lateral 2 similar to sepals, the lowest forming a white lip to 0.3 in. long with red to purple spots. Fruits to 0.8 in. long, pendent capsules with many small seeds. The only spotted *Corallorhiza* along the CA PCT.

red triangles

Centrostegia thurberi

POLYGONACEAE BUCKWHEAT FAMILY

PCT Sections: 2 & 4–9 **Abundance:** Locally common **Height:** 1–8 in. **Flowering:** March–July **Flower Color:** Pink, red, or white **Habitat-Community:** Sandy to gravelly soils in creosote bush scrubs, foothill chaparrals, and woodlands **Elevation:** Below 7800 ft. **Ecoregions:** Southern California Mountains, Sonoran/Mojave Basin and Range, Sierra Nevada

Spreading annual from a basal rosette with a single stem at base and stiff, sparsely glandular branches forked at each node. Leaves 0.4–1.3 in. long, spatula-shaped, hairless. Flowering branches cyme-like, reddish; involucres cylindric with 3 basal awns (succulent lobes with teeth), cream to red. Flowers sessile, scattered along branches, 2 per involucre, each with 9 stamens. Tepals to 0.1 in. long, 6-parted (3 sepals, 3 petals), pink to white. Fruits tiny achenes. Rarely does one see the flowers, but the involucre remains intact long after the basal leaves have dried. The only species in *Centrostegia* (from the Greek, "spurred roof," referring to the basal awns of the involucre).

fringed spineflower

Chorizanthe fimbriata

POLYGONACEAE BUCKWHEAT FAMILY

PCT Sections: 1–3 **Abundance:** Locally common **Height:** 4–12 in. **Flowering:** March–July **Flower Color:** Pink to white **Habitat-Community:** Sandy to gravelly soils in creosote bush scrubs, foothill chaparrals, and oak & pinyon-juniper woodlands **Elevation:** Below 5400 ft. **Ecoregions:** Southern California Mountains

Low, spreading, single-stemmed annual from a basal rosette with stiff, glandular-hairy branches forked at each node. Leaves 0.4–0.9 in. long, lance- to spatula-shaped, densely hairy below, with smooth margins. Flowers clustered at reddish branch tips, 1 per involucre, sessile, with 2-awned bracts and 9 stamens; involucres tubular, reddish, 6-ribbed (each rib toothed), 0.2 in. long. Tepals 0.2–0.3 in. long, 6-parted (3 sepals, 3 petals), with pink to white fringed lobes and yellow tube. Fruits achenes to 0.2 in. long. Two varieties along the PCT: var. *frimbriata* (corolla <0.3 in. long) is primarily on the coastal side of the mountains; var. *laciniata* (corolla 0.3–0.4 in. long) resides on the desert slopes of the Peninsular Ranges. Both have the distinctive fringed perianth lobes. *Chorizanthe* (from the Greek, "divided flower") refers to the deeply lobed perianth of most species.

peninsular spineflower

Chorizanthe leptotheca

POLYGONACEAE BUCKWHEAT FAMILY

PCT Sections: 1–3 **Abundance:** Occasional **Height:** 2–12 in. **Flowering:** May–August **Flower Color:** Rose to red **Habitat-Community:** Sandy to gravelly soils in chaparrals and oak woodlands **Elevation:** Below 5100 ft. **Ecoregions:** Southern California/Northern Baja Coast, Southern California Mountains

Spreading, single-stemmed annual, as wide as tall, with stiff, thinly- to soft-fuzzy branches, forked at each node, from a basal rosette. Leaves 0.2–0.8 in. long, spatula-shaped to elliptic, densely hairy below, with smooth margins. Flowers clustered at reddish branch tips, 1 per involucre, sessile, with 2-awned bracts and 9 stamens; involucres 6-ribbed, reddish, 0.1–0.2 in. long. Tepals 0.2 in. long, 6-parted (3 sepals, 3 petals), rose to red. Fruits achenes to 0.2 in. long. Threatened by development and invasive, nonnative species, but it continues to thrive in recent burns in the Peninsular Ranges.

Chorizanthe staticoides

Turkish rugging

POLYGONACEAE BUCKWHEAT FAMILY

PCT Sections: 4–6 **Abundance:** Locally common **Height:** 3–24 in. **Flowering:** April–July **Flower Color:** Rose-red or pink **Habitat-Community:** Sandy to gravelly soils in creosote bush scrubs, foothill chaparrals, and woodlands **Elevation:** Below 5400 ft. **Ecoregions:** Southern California Mountains

Intricately branched annual with a single, brittle, hairy stem from a basal rosette. Leaves 0.2–1.2 in. long, lance- to spatula-shaped, densely hairy below, with smooth margins. Flowers many in flat-topped clusters at tips of naked branches, 1 per involucre, with 9 stamens; involucres tubular, sessile, deep maroon-red, 6-ribbed, toothed, 0.2 in. long. Tepals 0.1–0.2 in. long, 6-parted (3 sepals, 3 petals), light rose-red to pink (sometimes white). Fruits achenes to 0.2 in. long. Especially common along the PCT in the far western Transverse Ranges (Vasquez Rocks to the Liebre Mountains).

Eriogonum parishii

Parish's buckwheat

POLYGONACEAE BUCKWHEAT FAMILY

PCT Sections: 1 & 3–6 & 9–10 **Abundance:** Common **Height:** 4–16 in. **Flowering:** June–October **Flower Color:** Pink **Habitat-Community:** Open, sandy or loose, gravelly soils in sagebrush scrubs, pinyon-juniper woodlands, oak woodlands, and montane coniferous forests **Elevation:** Below 10,000 ft. **Ecoregions:** Southern California Mountains, Sierra Nevada

Spreading, intricately branched annual with downward-arching hairless stems, sometimes forming dense mounds. Leaves 0.8–2.4 in. long, basal, short-petioled, spatula-shaped, sparsely hairy, green. Flowers many, on diffuse branches, with 9 stamens; peduncles thread-like, to 0.1 in. long; involucres 4-toothed, hairless, minute. Tepals tiny, 6-parted (3 sepals, 3 petals), pink (aging white). Fruits hairless achenes. Forms dense colonies in recent burns, especially along the southern segments of the PCT in the San Jacinto and Laguna Mountains.

Pterostegia drymarioides

woodland threadstem

POLYGONACEAE BUCKWHEAT FAMILY

PCT Sections: 1–8 **Abundance:** Common **Height:** 3–30 in. **Flowering:** March–July **Flower Color:** Pink to pale yellow **Habitat-Community:** Sandy to gravelly soils in crevices or shaded places in creosote bush scrubs, oak & Joshua tree woodlands, and foothill chaparrals **Elevation:** Below 5300 ft. **Ecoregions:** Southern California Mountains, Sonoran/Mojave Basin and Range, Sierra Nevada

Sprawling annual with delicate, hairy stems; monoecious. Leaves 0.6–1 in. long, opposite, lobed, wide fan- or spatula-shaped, green or reddish, with sparsely hairy margins. Flowers symmetric on forked branches, sessile; involucres have a 2-winged bract that becomes folded over. Male flowers tiny, 6-parted (tepals), pink to pale yellow. Female flowers tiny, 6-parted (tepals), greenish white. Fruits hairless, triangular achenes. The only species in *Pterostegia* (from the Greek, "wing covering," referring to the winged involucre bract).

Rumex hymenosepalus

wild rhubarb

POLYGONACEAE BUCKWHEAT FAMILY

PCT Sections: 3–8 **Abundance:** Occasional **Height:** 1–3 ft. **Flowering:** February–May **Flower Color:** Red to pale yellow **Habitat-Community:** Open, sandy areas in mesas, valley bottoms, and dunes in creosote bush scrubs, foothill chaparrals, and oak & pinyon-juniper woodlands **Elevation:** Below 6300 ft. **Ecoregions:** Southern California Mountains, Mojave Basin and Range, Sierra Nevada

Erect, leafy, tuberous perennial with stout, fleshy, hairless stems. Leaves 3–15 in. long, basal and alternate, lance-shaped to oblong, with curly margins. Flowers 0.5–0.7 in. long, whorled in spikes at stem and branch tips, bell-shaped, 6-parted (3 sepals, 3 petals), red to pale yellow. Fruits achenes 0.2 in. across. The tubers, which can reach an enormous size, have been used as a source of tannin (for tanning leather). The leaves and stalks are considered edible when cooked, much like true rhubarb (*Rheum*), which is in the same family.

Rumex paucifolius

alpine sheep sorrel

POLYGONACEAE BUCKWHEAT FAMILY

PCT Sections: 10–18 **Abundance:** Locally common **Height:** to 20 in. **Flowering:** May–August **Flower Color:** Red or green **Habitat-Community:** Moist places in wetland-riparian communities **Elevation:** Below 13,200 ft. **Ecoregions:** Sierra Nevada, Cascades

Erect to ascending, densely tufted perennial with slender, hairless stems. Leaves to 4 in. long, basal (mostly) and alternate, wide to narrowly ovoid, hairless, with smooth, flat margins. Flowers clustered in open, branched spikes at stem tips. Tepals to 0.2 in. long, 6-parted (3 sepals, 3 petals), outer inconspicuous, inner enlarging to cover fruit, red or green. Fruits to 0.1 in. long, brown, winged achenes. *Rumex* and sorrel both mean "sour," which describes the foliage's strong taste. Although a great source of vitamin C, plants can cause sickness if overeaten!

▼ 4 PETALS

Boechera californica

California rockcress

BRASSICACEAE MUSTARD FAMILY

PCT Sections: 1–5 **Abundance:** Common **Height:** 15–40 in. **Flowering:** March–June **Flower Color:** Pink to purple **Habitat-Community:** Gravelly alluvium and rocky slopes in foothill chaparrals, oak woodlands, and lower montane coniferous forests **Elevation:** Below 7500 ft. **Ecoregions:** Southern California Mountains

Single-stemmed perennial, often woody at the base and hairy on lower stem. Leaves 0.1–1 in. long, basal and alternate, spoon-shaped to oblong, hairy, with slightly toothed margins; stem leaves lobed at base. Flowers scattered along stems to tip, 4-parted, with hairy sepals and bright pink to purple petals 0.4–0.7 in. long. Fruits 3–5 in. long, linear, pendent, hairless (or with a few hairs) siliques with 1 row of seeds. The most common rockcress in the Peninsular Ranges, impressively large and showy.

Crassula connata

sand pygmyweed

CRASSULACEAE STONECROP FAMILY

PCT Sections: 1–8 **Abundance:** Locally common **Height:** 1–3 in. **Flowering:** February–May **Flower Color:** Red to green **Habitat-Community:** Open, gravelly alluvium and rocky slopes in creosote bush scrubs, foothill chaparrals, and oak woodlands **Elevation:** Below 5100 ft. **Ecoregions:** Southern California Mountains, Sierra Nevada

Erect, seldom-branched, succulent annual with hairless stems. Leaves to 0.1 in. long, opposite, ovoid, with base generally fused to stem. Flowers 2 per leaf axis node, densely crowded along the stem, minute, 4-parted, with sepals > petals; petals initially green, aging red, orange, or reddish brown. Fruits minuscule, ovoid follicles. This often-overlooked little succulent is especially common in the chaparral communities of the Peninsular Ranges. *Crassula* (from the Latin, "thick") refers to the succulent leaves.

Euphorbia micromera

Sonoran sandmat

EUPHORBIACEAE SPURGE FAMILY

PCT Sections: 1–4 **Abundance:** Locally common **Height:** 1–3 in. **Flowering:** April–November **Flower Color:** Red to pink **Habitat-Community:** Dry slopes and flats in creosote bush & Sonoran mixed woody scrubs **Elevation:** Below 3500 ft. **Ecoregions:** Southern California Mountains, Sonoran Basin and Range

Small, hairless annual with stems lying flat on the ground and hairless herbage containing a milky sap; monoecious. Leaves 0.1–0.2 in. long, opposite, ovoid to oblong. Flowers in small clusters at nodes, each containing a cyathium, bell-shaped involucre, 4 red to pink nectary glands (resembling minute petals), 2–5 obscure male flowers, and 1 female flower. Fruits 3-lobed, hairless capsules. Most common after summer rains but may also appear in late spring. Best observed along the PCT in San Diego County from the eastern slopes of Mt. Laguna to the Warner Springs area, and near the Interstate 10 crossing in Riverside County.

Zeltnera exaltata

canchalagua

GENTIANACEAE GENTIAN FAMILY

PCT Sections: 1–6 **Abundance:** Occasional **Height:** 4–24 in. **Flowering:** April–August **Flower Color:** Pink to white **Habitat-Community:** Moist, usually alkaline soils, in springs, seeps, and streambanks in foothill chaparrals, Sonoran/ Mojave mixed woody scrubs, and oak woodlands **Elevation:** Below 6900 ft. **Ecoregions:** Southern California Mountains

Erect, few-branched, small-flowered annual with slender, grass-like stems and hairless herbage. Leaves 0.4–1.3 in. long, opposite, widely spaced along stem, elliptic to linear. Flowers in open displays at stem and branch tips on pedicels 0.4–2.8 in. long, generally 4-parted, with fused-at-base calyces and trumpet-shaped corollas 0.4–0.8 in. long with narrow tube and lance-oblong, pink to white lobes. Fruits 2-valved capsules. The only *Zeltnera* in California with (usually!) 4-petaled flowers (the others have 5).

Calyptridium monospermum

one-seeded pussypaws

MONTIACEAE

MINER'S LETTUCE FAMILY

PCT Sections: 3–5 & 10–24 **Abundance:** Common **Height:** to 20 in. **Flowering:** April–September **Flower Color:** Pink to white **Habitat-Community:** Open, sandy or gravelly soils from lower montane coniferous forests to alpine communities **Elevation:** Below 13,000 ft. **Ecoregions:** Southern California Mountains, Sierra Nevada, Cascades, Klamath Mountains

Spreading to ascending perennial. Leaves 0.3–2.4 in. long, forming a rosette, with a few along stem. Flowers in dense clusters on 1–many flowering stems. Sepals to 0.3 in. long, 2, round. Petals 0.1–0.3 in. long, 4, pink to white, fused at tips. Fruits to 0.2 in. long, capsules with 1–4 seeds. *Calyptridium* ("capped") refers to the fused petal tips, which form a cap over the fruit.

Chamerion angustifolium

fireweed

ONAGRACEAE

EVENING-PRIMROSE FAMILY

PCT Sections: 4–5 & 10–24 **Abundance:** Common **Height:** to 10 ft. **Flowering:** July–September **Flower Color:** Pink to magenta **Habitat-Community:** Open places, especially after fires, from lower montane to subalpine coniferous forests **Elevation:** Below 10,900 ft. **Ecoregions:** Southern California Mountains, Sierra Nevada, Cascades, Klamath Mountains

Erect, unbranched perennial, usually growing in dense colonies. Leaves 0.6–8 in. long, alternate, lance-shaped, short-petioled. Flowers in dense spikes at stem tips. Sepals to 0.4 in. long, 4, same color as petals. Petals 0.7–1 in. long, 4, pink to magenta, free. Fruits to 4 in. long, cylindric, gray-hairy, many-seeded capsules; the seeds, each with an umbrella-like tuft of white hair, are able to fly long distances and are often the first to sprout after a fire. Young, cooked stems have been used as food in eastern Europe.

Clarkia delicata

Campo clarkia

ONAGRACEAE

EVENING-PRIMROSE FAMILY

PCT Sections: 1 **Abundance:** Rare **Height:** 6–26 in. **Flowering:** April–May **Flower Color:** Pink to rose-lavender **Habitat-Community:** Gravelly to clayey soils in foothill chaparrals and oak woodlands **Elevation:** Below 3500 ft. **Ecoregions:** Southern California/Northern Baja Coast, Southern California Mountains

Erect annual with hairy (below) and hairless (above) stems. Leaves 0.7–1.6 in. long, alternate, lance-shaped to ovoid, green. Flowers from nodding buds, in loose spikes at stem tip, with inferior ovaries, 8 orange-red stamens, and 4-lobed stigmas. Sepals 4, fused at tips. Petals 4, spoon-shaped, pink to rose-lavender with a white base, 0.3–0.5 in. long. Fruits straight, elongated capsules. Look for this beauty along the PCT from the Mexican border to the southern base of the Laguna Mountains.

Clarkia heterandra

mountain clarkia

ONAGRACEAE

EVENING-PRIMROSE FAMILY

PCT Sections: 4 & 6–7 **Abundance:** Occasional **Height:** 4–20 in. **Flowering:** April–August **Flower Color:** Pink **Habitat-Community:** Shady sites in canyons and on north-facing slopes in foothill chaparrals, oak woodlands, and lower montane coniferous forests **Elevation:** Below 5500 ft. **Ecoregions:** Southern California Mountains, Sierra Nevada

Erect, few-branched, delicate annual with glandular-hairy stems. Leaves 0.8–3.2 in. long, alternate, lance-shaped to ovoid, green. Flowers from ascending to erect buds, in open spikes, with inferior ovaries, 8 stamens, and 4-lobed stigmas. Sepals 4, fused at tips. Petals 4, emerging from one side, elliptic, pink, 0.2–0.3 in. long. Fruits rounded, nut-like capsules that bulge on the bottom like a freshwater bass; their shape is highly diagnostic, separating this from all other *Clarkia* spp. in California. Endemic to California. *Clarkia* honors William Clark (1770–1838) of Lewis and Clark Expedition fame.

Clarkia rhomboidea

diamond-petaled clarkia

ONAGRACEAE

EVENING-PRIMROSE FAMILY

PCT Sections: All **Abundance:** Locally common **Height:** 8–22 in. **Flowering:** March–September **Flower Color:** Pinkish **Habitat-Community:** Understories from woodlands and chaparrals to upper montane coniferous forests **Elevation:** Below 8200 ft. **Ecoregions:** All

Decumbent to erect annual with minutely hairy and bent-over tips. Leaves 0.4–2.4 in. long, alternate, lance-shaped to ovoid; petiole to 1 in. long. Flowers from nodding buds, in open spikes at stem tips, with inferior ovaries. Sepals to 0.3 in. long, 4, green, eventually free. Petals 0.2–0.5 in. long, 4, pinkish, diamond-shaped, free. Fruits to 1 in. long, cylindric capsules with many seeds.

Clarkia unguiculata

elegant clarkia

ONAGRACEAE

EVENING-PRIMROSE FAMILY

PCT Sections: 5–7 **Abundance:** Occasional **Height:** 8–30 in. **Flowering:** April–September **Flower Color:** Pink to lavender **Habitat-Community:** Shady sites, canyons, and north-facing slopes in foothill chaparral and oak woodlands **Elevation:** Below 4800 ft. **Ecoregions:** Southern California Mountains, Sierra Nevada

Spindly, few-branched annual with waxy, hairless stems. Leaves 0.4–2.3 in. long, alternate, lance-shaped to ovoid, green. Flowers from nodding buds, in loose spikes, with inferior ovaries, 8 stamens, and 4-lobed stigmas. Sepals 4, fused at tips. Petals 4, emerging from one side, pink to salmon or dark red-lavender, 0.4–1 in. long, with a constricted base (claw) and diamond-shaped blade. Fruits elongated capsules. Common in the coastal zones of California but infrequent along the PCT, best found in the western Transverse Ranges. *Unguiculata* (from the Latin, "with a small claw") describes the petal shape.

Clarkia xantiana

gunsight clarkia

ONAGRACEAE

EVENING-PRIMROSE FAMILY

PCT Sections: 5–10 **Abundance:** Occasional **Height:** 10–30 in. **Flowering:** April–June **Flower Color:** Pink, lavender, or white **Habitat-Community:** Dry, rocky slopes and open areas in chaparrals and oak & pinyon-juniper woodlands **Elevation:** Below 6300 ft. **Ecoregions:** Southern California Mountains, Sierra Nevada

Erect, few-branched annual with hairless, wax-coated herbage. Leaves 0.8–2.4 in. long, alternate, linear to lance-shaped. Flowers from reflexed buds, in loose spikes, with inferior ovaries, 8 stamens, purple anthers, and 4-lobed stigmas. Sepals 4, fused at tips. Petals 4, emerging from one side, pink to lavender, or white, 0.3–0.8 in. long, 2-lobed with a small central tooth. Fruits elongated capsules. Endemic to the southern Sierra and western Transverse Ranges. Two subspecies along the PCT: subsp. *xantiana* (petals 0.6–0.8 in. long) and subsp. *parviflora* (petals 0.3–0.6 in. long).

Epilobium brachycarpum

tall annual willowherb

ONAGRACEAE

EVENING-PRIMROSE FAMILY

PCT Sections: All **Abundance:** Common **Height:** 1–5 ft. **Flowering:** May–October **Flower Color:** Rose-pink to white **Habitat-Community:** Moist grasslands, springs, and shaded understories in wetland-riparian communities and from California prairies to alpine communities **Elevation:** Below 10,400 ft. **Ecoregions:** All (except Sonoran/Mojave Basin and Range)

Erect, willowy annual with hairless and peeling stems near base but glandular-hairy above. Leaves 0.4–2.2 in. long, mostly alternate, linear, sometimes with toothed margins. Flowers scattered along stem tips, 0.2–1.2 in. across, with inferior ovaries, 8 stamens, and 4-lobed stigmas. Sepals 4, erect; petals 4, rose-pink to white (often with dark veins), 0.1–0.6 in. long with notched ("fringed") or 2-lobed tips. Fruits 0.7–1.1 in. long, straight, cylindric capsules with hair-tufted seeds. Widespread throughout Canada and the western US. Often grows with *E. ciliatum* along the PCT.

Epilobium canum

California fuchsia

ONAGRACEAE

EVENING-PRIMROSE FAMILY

PCT Sections: All **Abundance:** Locally common **Height:** 7–48 in. **Flowering:** June–December **Flower Color:** Red **Habitat-Community:** Open, dry slopes, rock outcrops, and ridges from woodlands and chaparrals to subalpine coniferous forests **Elevation:** Below 11,200 ft. **Ecoregions:** All

Matted or upright perennial (sometimes woody at base) with hairy and glandular herbage. Leaves 0.3–2.8 in. long, opposite, lance-shaped to ovoid, with smooth to toothed margins. Flowers in clusters at stem tips. Sepals to 0.4 in. long, 4, free. Corollas 1–1.5 in. long, red, with long funnel-shaped tube, 4-lobed, with lobes shallowly notched. Fruits to 1.2 in. long, cylindric to club-shaped, hairy capsules with hair-tufted seeds. Very showy and usually covered with hummingbirds.

Epilobium glaberrimum

glaucous willowherb

ONAGRACEAE

EVENING-PRIMROSE FAMILY

PCT Sections: 3–5 & 11–24 **Abundance:** Common **Height:** 7–34 in. **Flowering:** June–September **Flower Color:** Pink, purplish, or white **Habitat-Community:** Open, moist, rocky or gravelly soils from lower montane to subalpine coniferous forests **Elevation:** Below 9900 ft. **Ecoregions:** Southern California Mountains, Sierra Nevada, Cascades, Klamath Mountains

Erect perennial forming clumps with generally white-waxy-coated herbage and 0–few stem hairs. Leaves 0.4–2.8 in. long, opposite, narrowly lance-shaped to ovoid, with fine-toothed margins. Flowers scattered along stem tips. Sepals to 0.3 in. long, 4, erect. Petals 0.1–0.5 in. long, 4, pink, purplish, or white, and notched. Fruits to 3 in. long, cylindric to club-shaped, generally sparsely hairy capsules with hair-tufted seeds.

Epilobium obcordatum

rockfringe

ONAGRACEAE

EVENING-PRIMROSE FAMILY

PCT Sections: 10–18 **Abundance:** Common **Height:** 2–6 in. **Flowering:** July–September **Flower Color:** Pink to deep rose-purple **Habitat-Community:** Open, dry, rocky or gravelly soils in subalpine coniferous forests and alpine communities **Elevation:** 5500–13,200 ft. **Ecoregions:** Sierra Nevada, Cascades

Matted, clump-forming perennial with generally white- to blue-waxy-coated herbage. Leaves 0.2–0.8 in. long, opposite, widely lance-elliptic to roundish, with roundish tip. Flowers clustered at stem tips. Sepals to 0.6 in. long, 4, erect. Petals to 1 in. long, 4, pink to deep rose-purple, and notched. Fruits to 1.8 in. long, club-shaped, densely glandular capsules with hair-tufted seeds. *Obcordatum* refers to the heart-shaped petals. Always fun to run into a spectacular show at the higher elevations—have your phone/camera at the ready!

Dicentra uniflora

longhorn steer's-head

PAPAVERACEAE POPPY FAMILY

PCT Sections: 10–24 **Abundance:** Occasional **Height:** 2–4 in. **Flowering:** May–July **Flower Color:** Pink to white or lavender **Habitat-Community:** Gravelly or rocky soils in upper montane & subalpine coniferous forests **Elevation:** Below 10,900 ft. **Ecoregions:** Sierra Nevada, Cascades, Klamath Mountains

Clustered perennial with hairless stems and generally white- to blue-waxy-coated foliage. Leaves 1.5–2.8 in. long, 1–3, alternate or basal, 2–3-divided, white- to blue-waxy-coated below, with fern-like leaflets. Flowers irregular, 1 at stem tips, nodding to erect. Sepals 2, generally shed after flowering. Petals 0.5–0.6 in. long, 4, pink to white or lavender, outer free and pouched at base, with recurved tips > half the total length. Fruits to 0.6 in. long, cone-shaped capsules with few seeds.

Oxyria digyna

alpine mountainsorrel

POLYGONACEAE BUCKWHEAT FAMILY

PCT Sections: 3–4 & 10–23 **Abundance:** Locally common **Height:** to 20 in. **Flowering:** July–September **Flower Color:** Red or greenish **Habitat-Community:** Crevices in rock outcrops and rocky soils in subalpine coniferous forests and alpine communities **Elevation:** Below 13,200 ft. **Ecoregions:** Southern California Mountains, Sierra Nevada, Cascades, Klamath Mountains

Erect perennial with generally red, hairless stems. Leaves to 2.6 in. long, basal (mostly) and alternate, round to heart-shaped, hairless, with smooth, wavy margins. Flowers clustered in open spikes on short stems. Tepals to 0.1 in. long, 4-parted, outer spreading, inner erect, red or greenish. Fruits to 0.2 in. long, reddish, winged achenes. *Oxyria* ("bitter") refers to the leaves. Related to European docks, which are known to relieve the sting of nettles. Although a great source of vitamin C, this plant can cause sickness if overeaten!

Primula tetrandra

alpine shootingstar

PRIMULACEAE PRIMROSE FAMILY

PCT Sections: 3–4 & 9–24 **Abundance:** Locally common **Height:** 2–12 in. **Flowering:** June–August **Flower Color:** Red to lavender **Habitat-Community:** Wet meadows and streambanks in wetland-riparian communities **Elevation:** Below 11,200 ft. **Ecoregions:** Southern California Mountains, Sierra Nevada, Cascades, Klamath Mountains

Erect, generally clumped perennial with hairless herbage. Leaves to 8 in. long, basal, linear to narrowly spoon-shaped, with smooth margins. Flowers 1–10, downturned at stem tips, with 4 anthers. Calyces to 0.3 in. long, 4-lobed, the lobes recurved when flowering. Corollas funnel-shaped with 4 red to lavender, recurved lobes 0.7 in. long. Fruits to 0.3 in. long, many-seeded capsules. Plants in the Klamath Mountains with 5 corolla lobes are apparent hybrids of this and *P. jeffreyi*.

Galium bolanderi

Bolander's bedstraw

RUBIACEAE MADDER FAMILY

PCT Sections: 8–9 & 12–24 **Abundance:** Locally common **Height:** 6–15 in. **Flowering:** May–August **Flower Color:** Red **Habitat-Community:** Rocky soils from woodlands and chaparrals to upper montane coniferous forests **Elevation:** Below 8600 ft. **Ecoregions:** Sierra Nevada, Cascades, Klamath Mountains

Climbing or tufted perennial with woody lower stems; dioecious. Leaves to 1 in. long, 4-whorled in 2 unequal pairs, linear to oblong, hairy or hairless, and generally point-tipped. Male flowers clustered along stems; 1 female flower per each branch along stems. Corollas 0.1 in. across, 4-parted, with spreading, red (rarely yellowish) lobes. Fruits to 0.2 in. across, fleshy, reddish to purplish berries. As the common name implies, plants were historically used to stuff mattresses.

Galium parishii

Parish's bedstraw

RUBIACEAE MADDER FAMILY

PCT Sections: 3–5 **Abundance:** Locally common **Height:** 2–16 in. **Flowering:** June–August **Flower Color:** Pale red to pink or yellow **Habitat-Community:** Arid cliffs, canyons, and rocky slopes in pinyon-juniper woodlands and montane coniferous forests **Elevation:** Below 10,500 ft. **Ecoregions:** Southern California Mountains

Stiff-branched, woody-at-base perennial with conspicuously hairy stems. Leaves 0.1–0.4 in. long, 4-whorled, dimorphic (2 larger, 2 smaller), ovoid to round, short-hairy. Flowers are bisexual or unisexual (but male and female flowers on same plant). Corollas <0.1 in. long, 4-parted, spreading, with pale red to pink or yellow lobes. Fruits 0.1 in. across, 2-chambered nutlets with long white straight hairs. The flowers open briefly, so you'll have only a narrow window of time to see them.

Kelloggia galioides

milk kelloggia

RUBIACEAE MADDER FAMILY

PCT Sections: 3–4 & 9–24 **Abundance:** Common **Height:** 4–10 in. **Flowering:** May–August **Flower Color:** Pink or white **Habitat-Community:** Dry openings in montane coniferous forests **Elevation:** Below 10,200 ft. **Ecoregions:** Southern California Mountains, Sierra Nevada, Cascades, Klamath Mountains

Erect perennial with 4-angled, hairless stems. Leaves to 1.5 in. long, opposite, lance-shaped to narrowly ovoid, with smooth margins. Flowers at stem tips on individual pedicels to 4.7 in. long. Calyx 4–5-lobed; corolla 0.2 in. long, pink or white, funnel-shaped with 4(5), lance-shaped lobes. Fruits to 0.2 in. long, nutlets (2) with hooked hairs. The genus honors California botanist Albert Kellogg (1813–1887).

▼ 5 PETALS/SEPALS / SYMMETRIC COROLLAS

Silene laciniata subsp. *californica*

Indian pink

CARYOPHYLLACEAE PINK FAMILY

PCT Sections: 6–8 & 16–20 **Abundance:** Locally common **Height:** 6–24 in. **Flowering:** April–July **Flower Color:** Red **Habitat-Community:** Open places, including serpentine soils, in chaparrals and lower montane coniferous forests **Elevation:** Below 7300 ft. **Ecoregions:** Cascades, Klamath Mountains

Sprawling or clambering (through shrubs) perennial with sparsely hairy stems and woody base. Leaves 0.4–4 in. long, opposite, lance-shaped to ovoid, smaller on upper stem, with smooth margins. Flowers at stem tips and at upper leaf nodes, ascending to erect, symmetric, with 5-lobed calyces to 1 in. long. Petals 5, free, 4–6-lobed, red, with blades to 0.6 in. long and 2 appendages. Fruits ovoid to oblong, hairy or hairless capsules with many red-brown seeds. The glandular stems help catch flies and other insects, preserving the flowers' nectar for butterflies. The only bright red silene along the CA PCT. The lobed flowers look like they were cut with pinking shears (hence the family and common names).

Silene verecunda

San Francisco campion

CARYOPHYLLACEAE PINK FAMILY

PCT Sections: 1–5 & 7–10 & 13–14 **Abundance:** Occasional **Height:** 4–22 in. **Flowering:** April–August **Flower Color:** Pink to white **Habitat-Community:** Open areas from sagebrush scrubs to subalpine coniferous forests **Elevation:** Below 11,300 ft. **Ecoregions:** Southern California Mountains, Sierra Nevada

Erect perennial from a woody base, with many, generally densely glandular stems. Leaves 1–4 in. long, opposite, lance-shaped, reduced in size up the stem. Flowers few at stem tips and at upper leaf nodes, ascending to erect, symmetric, 5-parted. Calyces 0.4–0.7 in. long, 10-veined, densely short-hairy or glandular; pink to white petals, with 2-lobed spreading tips, extending to 0.3 in. beyond calyx. Fruits small, oblong to ovoid capsules. Occurs from the coast to the Sierran crest, usually in small populations.

Dudleya pulverulenta

chalk dudleya

CRASSULACEAE STONECROP FAMILY

PCT Sections: 1–3 **Abundance:** Locally common **Height:** 5–15 in. **Flowering:** May–July **Flower Color:** Red **Habitat-Community:** Rocky slopes, canyon walls, ledges, outcrops, and roadside cuts in foothill chaparrals and oak woodlands **Elevation:** Below 4100 ft. **Ecoregions:** Southern California/Northern Baja Coast, Southern California Mountains

Erect, succulent perennial with leaf rosettes 4–20 in. across, the entire plant covered with white mealy powder or chalky wax. Leaves 3–10 in. long, 40–60 per rosette, ovoid to oblong, thick, waxy, with powdery white coating and pointed tips. Flowers clustered along branched stem tips, 5-parted, symmetric. Petals 0.5–0.8 in. long, fused to middle (otherwise free), red tinged with green or gold. Fruits small follicles. Rapidly colonizes disturbed areas. *Pulverulenta* (from the Latin, "dust") refers to the plant's chalky coating, which is thought to wash off during rain, coating the ground below the plant and thus preventing soil moisture from evaporating.

Rhodiola integrifolia

rosy stonecrop

CRASSULACEAE STONECROP FAMILY

PCT Sections: 10–15 & 22–23 **Abundance:** Occasional **Height:** 1–6 in. **Flowering:** May–August **Flower Color:** Dark red to deep red-purple **Habitat-Community:** Cliffs, ridges, and moist, gravelly slopes in subalpine coniferous forests and alpine communities **Elevation:** 5900–13,200 ft. **Ecoregions:** Sierra Nevada, Klamath Mountains

Erect, succulent perennial with 1–many, white-waxy stems. Leaves 0.2–1.2 in. long, oval to spoon-shaped, flat, with smooth or toothed margins. Flowers in dense, 7–50-flowered clusters at stem tips, symmetric. Calyces to 0.1 in. long, 4–5-lobed, fused near base. Petals 4–5, free, dark red to deep red-purple, to 0.2 in. long. Fruits erect, many-seeded pods. Aka roseroot, referring to the scent emitted when the roots are cut or bruised.

Chimaphila umbellata

prince's pine

ERICACEAE HEATH FAMILY

PCT Sections: 3–4 & 14–24 **Abundance:** Common **Height:** to 12 in. **Flowering:** May–August **Flower Color:** Pink to red **Habitat-Community:** Well-drained sites in open or dense understories from lower montane to subalpine coniferous forests **Elevation:** Below 9600 ft. **Ecoregions:** Southern California Mountains, Sierra Nevada, Cascades, Klamath Mountains

Stout, slightly woody, evergreen perennial; partially mycoheterotrophic. Leaves 1–2.8 in. long, whorled along stem, narrowly spoon-shaped, shiny bright green above, with toothed margins above middle. Flowers 3–15 in small, loose clusters, symmetric, nodding. Sepals to 0.1 in. long, 5, with hairy margins. Petals to 0.3 in. long, 5, free, waxy, faintly fragrant, pink to red. Fruits to 0.3 in. across, many-seeded capsules. *Chimaphila* ("winter-loving") refers to its evergreen nature. Aka pipsissewa ("breaking into small pieces"): plants were used to dissolve kidney stones.

Zeltnera venusta

charming centaury

GENTIANACEAE GENTIAN FAMILY

PCT Sections: 1–6 & 8–10 **Abundance:** Occasional **Height:** 1–20 in. **Flowering:** May–August **Flower Color:** Pink to rose **Habitat-Community:** Dry, open sites in California prairies, foothill chaparrals, and oak woodlands **Elevation:** Below 5800 ft. **Ecoregions:** Southern California Mountains, Sierra Nevada

Erect, showy annual with 4-sided, light green stems. Leaves 0.2–1.6 in. long, opposite, oblong to lance-shaped, hairless. Flowers 0.6–1.2 in. across, clustered at branched stem tips, 5-parted, with fused-at-base calyces. Corollas trumpet-shaped, 0.4–0.8 in. long, with narrow, white-at-throat tube 0.6–0.7 in. long and elliptic, bright pink to rose lobes 0.2–0.6 in. long. Fruits 2-valved capsules. Usually appears in isolated, highly localized populations. The exserted stamens with yellow anthers twist conspicuously after opening.

Geranium californicum

California cranesbill

GERANIACEAE GERANIUM FAMILY

PCT Sections: 3–5 & 8–10 & 13–14 **Abundance:** Occasional **Height:** 7–28 in. **Flowering:** April–August **Flower Color:** Rose to white **Habitat-Community:** Moist slopes, meadows, and streambanks in montane coniferous forests and wetland-riparian communities **Elevation:** Below 9900 ft. **Ecoregions:** Southern California Mountains, Sierra Nevada

Ascending to erect perennial with soft-hairy stems. Leaves 1–3.1 in. wide, alternate, hairy, palmately lobed into 5–7 segments, with lobed margins. Flowers 1–few at stem tips. Sepals to 0.4 in. long, 5, free, point-tipped. Petals to 0.6 in. long, 5, free, rose with purplish veins to white, with hairy upper surface near the base. Fruits beaked and 1-seeded. *Geranium* ("crane") refers to the long, crane-like, beaked fruit. The drying beak sections of the fruit curl upward as they dry, eventually catapulting the seed into greener pastures!

Lythrum californicum

California loosestrife

LYTHRACEAE LOOSESTRIFE FAMILY

PCT Sections: 1–8 **Abundance:** Occasional **Height:** 8–24 in. **Flowering:** April–September **Flower Color:** Pink to purple or white **Habitat-Community:** Moist soils, marshes, streambanks, and ponds in wetland-riparian communities and oak & pinyon-juniper woodlands **Elevation:** Below 6800 ft. **Ecoregions:** Southern California Mountains, Sierra Nevada

Erect, sometimes branching perennial with 4-angled stems and gray-waxy to light green herbage. Leaves 0.4–2.8 in. long, opposite on lower stem, alternate on upper stem, sessile, linear. Flowers in leafy spikes with 1–2 flowers per axil, symmetric, horn-like, with minute calyx lobes and 6 stamens. Petals 0.2–0.3 in. long, 4–6, spreading, pink to purple or white. Fruits ovoid capsules contained within hypanthium. The Lythraceae includes over 600 species, including pomegranates; this is the only member found along the PCT.

Sidalcea glaucescens

waxy checkerbloom

MALVACEAE MALLOW FAMILY

PCT Sections: 9 & 12–24 **Abundance:** Locally common **Height:** 7–28 in. **Flowering:** June–August **Flower Color:** Pink to pink-purple **Habitat-Community:** Dry meadows in granite or serpentine soils, from lower montane to subalpine coniferous forests **Elevation:** Below 9900 ft. **Ecoregions:** Sierra Nevada, Cascades, Klamath Mountains

Decumbent-ascending perennial with branched hairs on lower stem. Leaves to 2.8 in. wide, alternate, white-waxy, deeply lobed at the base, lobed on lower stem, with toothed margins at lobe tips. Flowers to 15, openly scattered along stem tips. Sepals to 0.4 in. long, 5-lobed, branched-hairy. Petals 0.4–0.8 in. long, 5, free, pink to pink-purple. Fruits 6–8 beaked, glandular-hairy segments, each with 1 seed. *Sidalcea* is a combination of *Sida* and *Alcea*, other names for mallows.

Sidalcea sparsifolia

southern checkerbloom

MALVACEAE MALLOW FAMILY

PCT Sections: 1–3 & 6–7 **Abundance:** Occasional **Height:** 8–24 in. **Flowering:** March–June **Flower Color:** Pink **Habitat-Community:** Seasonally moist soils in meadows and shaded understories from oak woodlands to lower montane coniferous forests **Elevation:** Below 7000 ft. **Ecoregions:** Southern California Mountains, Sierra Nevada

Ascending to decumbent perennial with hairy (hairs sometimes star-shaped) or hairless herbage. Leaves mostly basal, 0.8–2.4 in. across, rounded, heart-shaped, shallowly 7-lobed, with up to 5 alternate and reduced per stem. Flowers >10, 5-parted, in open spikes at stem tips, with white stamens. Sepals to 0.4 in. long, hairy (star-shaped). Petals 0.4–1 in. long, spreading, pink. Fruits 6–7 wedge-shaped segments, each with 1 seed. More tolerant of hot, dry environments than most of the many *Sidalcea* spp. in California. Frequently encountered along the PCT in the Laguna Mountains of San Diego County.

Calandrinia menziesii

red maids

MONTIACEAE

MINER'S LETTUCE FAMILY

PCT Sections: 1–8 & 16–18 **Abundance:** Occasional **Height:** 3–16 in. **Flowering:** March–June **Flower Color:** Deep pink to red **Habitat-Community:** Sandy to loamy soils in California prairies, Sonoran/Mojave mixed woody scrubs, foothill chaparrals, and oak woodlands **Elevation:** Below 6800 ft. **Ecoregions:** Southern California Mountains, Mojave Basin and Range, Sierra Nevada

Decumbent to erect, fleshy annual with hairless (infrequently short-hairy) herbage. Leaves 0.4–3.5 in. long, alternate, linear to spoon-shaped, somewhat succulent, hairless. Flowers clustered at stem tips, symmetric, showy, with numerous stamens and 2 overlapping sepals 0.1–0.3 in. long. Petals 0.2–0.6 in. long, generally 5, bright pink to red, white at the base. Fruits 3-valved capsules with 10–20, small seeds. Often found in disturbed areas, such as along the margins of trails or in burns. The genus name honors Swiss scientist Jean-Louis Calandrini (1703–1758).

Aquilegia formosa

crimson columbine

RANUNCULACEAE

BUTTERCUP FAMILY

PCT Sections: 1–6 & 8–24 **Abundance:** Common **Height:** 7–32 in. **Flowering:** April–September **Flower Color:** Red and yellow **Habitat-Community:** Streambanks, seeps, and moist places from woodlands and chaparrals to subalpine coniferous forests and wetland-riparian communities **Elevation:** Below 10,900 ft. **Ecoregions:** All (except Sonoran/Mojave Basin and Range)

Ascending to erect perennial with hairless, white-waxy-coated stems, at least on the lower portion. Leaves shallowly to deeply lobed or 2-pinnately compound, with lobed leaflets to 1.8 in. long. Flowers 1–few along stem, nodding, with 5 pistils and many stamens. Sepals to 1 in. long, 5, petal-like, red. Petals 0 or 5, yellow blade 0–0.3 in. long, red spur to 1 in. long. Fruits, body to 1.1 in. long, beak to 0.5 in. long. *Aquilegia* ("eagle") refers to columbine's claw-like spurs. *Formosa* means "beautiful." A favorite plant for hummingbirds and large bumblebees with tongues that can reach into the spurs for nectar; while so doing, the bees are often dusted with pollen from protruding stamens.

Enemion occidentale

western false rue anemone

RANUNCULACEAE

BUTTERCUP FAMILY

PCT Sections: 6–8 & 16–17 **Abundance:** Occasional **Height:** 3–14 in. **Flowering:** March–June **Flower Color:** Pink or white **Habitat-Community:** Dry, shaded slopes in oak woodlands, chaparrals, and lower montane coniferous forests **Elevation:** Below 5000 ft. **Ecoregions:** Southern California Mountains, Sierra Nevada

Erect, 1–3-stemmed perennial with white- to blue-waxy-coated foliage (mostly below). Leaves to 4.7 in. long, 2-pinnately compound with 2–3-lobed leaflets to 0.8 in. long. Flowers 1–10 along stem and at tips, with 0 petals, 5–8 pistils and many stamens. Sepals to 0.4 in. long, 5, petal-like, pink or white. Fruits to 0.4 in. long with straight or curved beaks. Rue is a European plant with similar blue-green foliage. *Anemone* means "wind."

Pyrola aphylla

leafless wintergreen

ERICACEAE HEATH FAMILY

PCT Sections: 1–4 & 14–24 **Abundance:** Occasional **Height:** to 2 ft. **Flowering:** June–August **Flower Color:** Pink to whitish **Habitat-Community:** Dry, deep humus, including serpentine soils, from woodlands and chaparrals to upper montane coniferous forests **Elevation:** Below 8200 ft. **Ecoregions:** All (except Sonoran/Mojave Basin and Range)

Evergreen subshrub or perennial; mycoheterotrophic. Leaves basal if present, <0.4 in. long, but often absent or hidden under duff at base of stem, making the plant hard to spot in shaded understories. Flowers 7–25, scattered along stem, irregular, nodding. Sepals to 0.1 in. long, 5, free. Petals to 0.3 in. long, 5, free, pink to whitish. Fruits many-seeded, pendent capsules.

Pyrola asarifolia

bog wintergreen

ERICACEAE HEATH FAMILY

PCT Sections: 4 & 9–24 **Abundance:** Common **Height:** to 2 ft. **Flowering:** June–September **Flower Color:** Pink, pink-purple, or deep red **Habitat-Community:** Moist sites, including swamps, bog, and streambanks, in montane coniferous forests and wetland-riparian communities **Elevation:** Below 9200 ft. **Ecoregions:** Southern California Mountains, Sierra Nevada, Cascades, Klamath Mountains

Evergreen subshrub or perennial with numerous basal leaves; partially mycoheterotrophic. Leaves to 5 in. long, round to narrowly ovoid or heart-shaped, with smooth to toothed margins. Flowers scattered along stem, irregular, nodding, with flower bracts > pedicel. Sepals to 0.2 in. long, 5, free, lance-shaped. Petals to 0.4 in. long, 5, free, pink, pink-purple, or deep red. Fruits many-seeded, pendent capsules. Often grows under alders.

Astragalus lentiginosus var. *variabilis*

freckled milkvetch

FABACEAE LEGUME FAMILY

PCT Sections: 7–9 **Abundance:** Locally common **Height:** 5–20 in. **Flowering:** March–June **Flower Color:** Pink to purple **Habitat-Community:** Dry, sandy slopes and plains in creosote bush scrubs and Joshua tree & pinyon-juniper woodlands **Elevation:** Below 5800 ft. **Ecoregions:** Mojave Basin and Range, Sierra Nevada

Erect, robust annual (sometimes perennial) with reddish stems and sparsely to densely wavy-hairy herbage. Leaves 1–5 in. long, alternate, pinnate, with 11–25 elliptic leaflets 0.1–0.7 in. long. Flowers 10–30 in open spikes at branch and stem tips, irregular (pea-like), with 5-lobed, hairy calyces. Petals 5, pink to purple or white, consisting of a banner to 0.5 in. long, keel, and wings. Fruits 0.5–1.3 in. long, 0.3–0.7 in. wide, inflated (bladdery) pods, firm-skinned, sparsely to densely hairy, with purple freckles. Widespread across California's Mojave Desert, intercepting the PCT from Antelope Valley to the Walker Pass region in the southern Sierra. The species is challenging taxonomically, with 19 varieties in California alone!

Astragalus leucolobus

Big Bear Valley woollypod

FABACEAE LEGUME FAMILY

PCT Sections: 4–5 **Abundance:** Rare **Height:** 3–10 in. **Flowering:** May–July **Flower Color:** Pink to purple **Habitat-Community:** Gravelly to rocky slopes and flats, and shaded understories in sagebrush scrubs, pinyon-juniper woodlands, and montane coniferous forests **Elevation:** Below 9500 ft. **Ecoregions:** Southern California Mountains

Clumpy perennial with short, hairy stems. Leaves 1–3 in. long, alternate, pinnate, with 7–19 widely ovoid, often crowded, white tangly-hairy leaflets 0.1–0.8 in. long. Flowers 5–13, ascending, clustered at stem tips in loose heads, irregular (pea-like), with 5-lobed, hairy calyces. Petals 5, pink to purple, consisting of a banner 0.6–0.8 in. long, keel, and wings. Fruits 0.6–1 in. long, 0.2–0.3 in. wide, slightly incurved, densely white-hairy pods. Found along the PCT in the San Bernardino and eastern San Gabriel Mountains. Threatened by urbanization, mining, and recreational activities.

Astragalus purshii

Pursh's milkvetch

FABACEAE LEGUME FAMILY

PCT Sections: All (except 1–3) **Abundance:** Common **Height:** 1–6 in. **Flowering:** April–August **Flower Color:** Pink to purple or white **Habitat-Community:** Gravelly to rocky soils, from Mojave mixed woody scrubs to subalpine coniferous forests **Elevation:** Below 11,500 ft. **Ecoregions:** All

Low, densely branched, matted perennial with woolly, silvery white hairs covering the foliage. Leaves 0.5–3 in. long, alternate, pinnate, with 3–17 round, white-hairy leaflets 0.1–0.8 in. long. Flowers 1–11, interspersed among leaves, irregular (pea-like), with 5-lobed, hairy calyces. Petals 5, pink to purple or white, consisting of a banner 0.4–0.7 in. long, keel, and wings. Fruits 0.3–1.1 in. long, 0.2–0.5 in. wide, ovoid, densely white (sometimes wavy) hairy pods resembling cotton balls. Several varieties occur along the PCT, separated by calyx size, flower color, and fruit shape.

Hosackia crassifolia

big deervetch

FABACEAE LEGUME FAMILY

PCT Sections: All **Abundance:** Common **Height:** 2–5 ft. **Flowering:** May–September **Flower Color:** Reddish-blotched yellow-green **Habitat-Community:** Open or disturbed places from scrubs, woodlands, and chaparrals to upper montane coniferous forests **Elevation:** Below 6900 ft. **Ecoregions:** All (except Sonoran/Mojave Basin and Range)

Robust, sprawling, hardy perennial with hairy or hairless stems. Leaves alternate, pinnate, with 9–15 oval leaflets, pale below, to 1.2 in. long. Flowers 12–20 in head-like clusters, irregular (pea-like), consisting of a banner, keel, and wings. Calyces to 0.3 in. long, 5-lobed. Petals 5, yellow-green with reddish blotch. Fruits to 2.8 in. long, hairless, many-seeded pods. Like most legumes, absorbs precious nitrogen from soil air and so is often used for restoration.

Lathyrus splendens

pride of California

FABACEAE LEGUME FAMILY

PCT Sections: 1 **Abundance:** Rare **Height:** 1–6 ft. **Flowering:** April–June **Flower Color:** Red to crimson **Habitat-Community:** Foothill chaparrals **Elevation:** Below 3400 ft. **Ecoregions:** Southern California/Northern Baja Coast

Large-flowered climbing perennial vine, sprawling through shrubs with coiling tendrils and hairless (sometimes minutely hairy) stems. Leaves alternate, pinnate, with 6–8 linear to ovoid leaflets 0.8–1.6 in. long. Flowers 4–6 in open spikes, irregular (pea-like), consisting of a banner, keel, and wings, with 5-lobed (upper lobes shortest) calyces. Petals 1–1.4 in. long, bright wine-red to crimson. Fruits hairless pods. Limited distribution, endemic to Baja California and southern San Diego County. Look for it along the trail in the Campo and Lake Morena region.

Lathyrus vestitus

Pacific pea

FABACEAE LEGUME FAMILY

PCT Sections: 1–7 **Abundance:** Occasional **Height:** 1–5 ft. **Flowering:** February–July **Flower Color:** Red to purple or pink **Habitat-Community:** Foothill chaparrals and oak woodlands **Elevation:** Below 4000 ft. **Ecoregions:** Southern California/Northern Baja Coast, Southern California Mountains, Sierra Nevada

Climbing perennial vine with hairless herbage, twining through shrubs with coiling tendrils and sharply angled or flanged stems. Leaves alternate, pinnate, with 8–12 linear to elliptic leaflets 0.8–1.8 in. long. Flowers 8–15 in generally dense spikes, irregular (pea-like), with 5-lobed calyces. Petals 0.6–0.8 in. long, red to purple or lavender, or pink, or white, sometimes bicolored. Fruits to 2 in. long, generally hairless pods. Two varieties along the PCT: var. *alefeldii* is limited to the Peninsular Ranges; var. *vestitus* extends into the Tehachapi Mountains. The specific epithet (from the Latin *vestio*, "dressed") alludes to its propensity to drape itself over shrubs.

Lupinus hirsutissimus

stinging lupine

FABACEAE LEGUME FAMILY

PCT Sections: 1–6 **Abundance:** Locally common **Height:** 8–30 in. **Flowering:** March–June **Flower Color:** Pink to magenta **Habitat-Community:** Dry, gravelly to rocky slopes and recent burns in chaparrals and oak woodlands **Elevation:** Below 6200 ft. **Ecoregions:** Southern California/Northern Baja Coast, Southern California Mountains

Erect, bristly-leaved annual with generally stiff-hairy green stems. Leaves basal and alternate, palmate, with 5–8 oval to spoon-shaped, bright green leaflets 0.8–2 in. long, conspicuously covered in pustulate hairs. Flowers spiraled along stems, irregular (pea-like), 2-lipped, consisting of a banner with a yellowish spot, keel (hairy on lower margins), and wings. Calyces 0.2–0.4 in. long with equal lips, the upper deeply lobed. Petals 0.4–0.8 in. long, at first light pink, aging dark magenta. Fruits 1.2–1.6 in. long, stiff-hairy pods. An easily recognized lupine, armed (as the common name implies) with imposing stinging hairs. In nutrient-rich burns, plants may grow to 5 ft. tall!

Lupinus truncatus

blunt-leaved lupine

FABACEAE LEGUME FAMILY

PCT Sections: 1–6 **Abundance:** Locally common **Height:** 8–40 in. **Flowering:** March–May **Flower Color:** Magenta to purple **Habitat-Community:** Openings and recent burns in foothill chaparrals and oak woodlands **Elevation:** Below 3800 ft. **Ecoregions:** Southern California/Northern Baja Coast, Southern California Mountains

Erect annual with finely hairy to hairless stems. Leaves alternate, palmate, with 5–8 linear, blunt-tipped green leaflets 0.8–1.6 in. long. Flowers sparsely spiraled along stems, irregular (pea-like), 2-lipped, consisting of a banner with a yellowish spot, keel (hairy on both margins), and wings. Calyces 0.1–0.2 in. long with equal lips, the upper deeply lobed. Petals 0.3–0.6 in. long, dark magenta to purple. Fruits 1–1.3 in. long, hairy pods. As both the common name and specific epithet imply, the leaflets are characteristically truncate (squared off at the tips). Common in burns, where plants may reach 4 ft. in height!

Trifolium wormskioldii

cow clover

FABACEAE LEGUME FAMILY

PCT Sections: All **Abundance:** Common **Height:** 2–12 in. **Flowering:** May–October **Flower Color:** Pink-purple or magenta **Habitat-Community:** Open, moist areas in wetland-riparian communities, foothill chaparrals, oak woodlands, and montane coniferous forests **Elevation:** Below 10,500 ft. **Ecoregions:** All (except Sonoran/Mojave Basin and Range)

Decumbent to ascending, matted perennial, branched above, with red-tinged stems and hairless herbage. Leaves basal and alternate, palmate, with 3 elliptic, tooth-margined leaflets 0.4–1.2 in. long. Flowers arranged in head-like clusters 0.5–1.2 in. wide, irregular (pea-like), 5-parted, 2-lipped, with wheel-shaped, dissected, sharply toothed involucres. Calyces 0.2–0.5 in. long, with bristly-tipped tapered lobes. Petals 0.5–0.7 in. long, pink-purple or magenta, and white-tipped. Fruits 0.1 in. wide, oblong pods. One of the few plants in California that can grow from coastal beaches to the high Sierra Nevada. Also quite tasty: the herbage and flowers can be eaten raw in salads, and the roots may be boiled and used in dishes.

Delphinium cardinale

scarlet larkspur

RANUNCULACEAE
BUTTERCUP FAMILY

PCT Sections: 1–5 **Abundance:** Occasional **Height:** 1–8 ft. **Flowering:** March–July **Flower Color:** Red **Habitat-Community:** Dry, rocky slopes in unstable talus from oak woodlands to lower montane coniferous forests **Elevation:** Below 6300 ft. **Ecoregions:** Southern California/Northern Baja Coast, Southern California Mountains

Tall, showy larkspur of rocky areas with short-hairy stems. Leaves 1.2–4 in. across, basal (withered by flowering) and alternate, deeply palmately lobed, round in outline with up to 27 lobes, hairless. Flowers in narrowly pyramidal stalks, irregular; pedicels 1–2 in. long. Sepals 0.9–1.5 in. long, 5, petal-like, hairy, red, with the uppermost spurred 0.6–1 in. long. Petals 0.1–0.2 in. long, 4, flattened and somewhat obscured by sepals, red. Fruits erect, 3-parted follicles 0.5–0.8 in. long. Most common along the PCT in the chaparrals of interior San Diego County, becoming uncommon to the north. *Delphinium* (from the Greek *delphinion*, "dolphin") refers to the bud shape. *Cardinale* is Latin for "red." Caution: most larkspurs are extremely toxic to humans and livestock!

Delphinium purpusii

rose-flowered larkspur

RANUNCULACEAE

BUTTERCUP FAMILY

PCT Sections: 8–9 **Abundance:** Rare **Height:** 1–4 ft. **Flowering:** March–May **Flower Color:** Pink **Habitat-Community:** Cliffs and rocky soils in pinyon-juniper woodlands **Elevation:** Below 5900 ft. **Ecoregions:** Sierra Nevada

Ascending to erect perennial, branched above, with generally hairless stems. Leaves to 3.5 in. wide, mostly on lower stem, maple-like with shallow lobes to 1.2 in. wide, generally short-hairy. Flowers 5–14, in crowded spikes along upper stems, irregular, with many stamens and 3 pistils. Sepals to 0.6 in. long, 5, pink, hairy, generally reflexed, with spurs to 0.8 in. long. Petals 4, white upper, pink lower. Fruits to 1.2 in. long, erect. The only native pink larkspur in North America. The specific epithet honors Joseph Purpus (1860–1932), who made the type collection in 1897. Caution: most larkspurs are extremely toxic to humans and livestock!

▼ 5 FUSED PETALS / SYMMETRIC COROLLAS

Apocynum androsaemifolium

bitter dogbane

APOCYNACEAE

DOGBANE FAMILY

PCT Sections: 1–5 & 9–24 **Abundance:** Common **Height:** 6–16 in. **Flowering:** May–October **Flower Color:** Pink or white **Habitat-Community:** Dry, open slopes and rocky places from scrubs, woodlands, and chaparrals to upper montane coniferous forests **Elevation:** Below 8200 ft. **Ecoregions:** All (except Sonoran/Mojave Basin and Range)

Erect, multi-branched perennial with milky sap. Leaves 1.5–2.5 in. long, opposite, widely oval, hairless, round-tipped. Flowers to 0.3 in. long, clustered at stem ends, pink or white with pink stripes, 5-parted, the fused petals forming a funnel with spreading lobes. Fruits 2.8–4.3 in. long pods with hair-tufted seeds. Caution: poisonous! *Apocynum* ("away from," "dog") refers to its historic use as dog poison.

Hackelia mundula

pink stickseed

BORAGINACEAE

BORAGE FAMILY

PCT Sections: 9–22 **Abundance:** Occasional **Height:** 16–32 in. **Flowering:** May–July **Flower Color:** Pink **Habitat-Community:** Dry openings in montane coniferous forests **Elevation:** 5400–9600 ft. **Ecoregions:** Sierra Nevada, Cascades, Klamath Mountains

Erect, many-stemmed perennial with densely hairy stems. Leaves 2.5–9 in. long, alternate, spoon-shaped, clasping on upper stem, hairy. Flowers in branched, coiled clusters at stem tips. Calyces to 0.1 in. long, 5-lobed. Corollas to 0.7 in. across, 5-parted (petals fused), tube-shaped, pink with pink appendages at base of lobes. Fruits to 0.2 in. long, shiny nutlets covered with barb-tipped prickles. The fruits stick to anything they touch. The only pink hackelia along the CA PCT.

Sarcodes sanguinea

snowplant

ERICACEAE HEATH FAMILY

PCT Sections: 3–5 & 9–24 **Abundance:** Locally common **Height:** 6–18 in. **Flowering:** May–July **Flower Color:** Red **Habitat-Community:** Understories in montane coniferous forests **Elevation:** Below 10,200 ft. **Ecoregions:** Southern California Mountains, Sierra Nevada, Cascades, Klamath Mountains

Stout, fleshy, erect, nongreen perennial with glandular-hairy, leafless red stems; mycoheterotrophic. Flowers many, in a dense cluster along the stem. Sepals 5, free. Corollas to 0.7 in. long, 5-lobed, urn-shaped, fused most of the length, red. Fruits many-seeded capsules. Comes up as the surrounding snowpack is melting (hence the common name). The red really stands out against a snowy white background! Generally found with *Pinus jeffreyi*. Poisonous.

Abronia nana var. *covillei*

Coville's dwarf sand verbena

NYCTAGINACEAE

FOUR O'CLOCK FAMILY

PCT Sections: 4 **Abundance:** Rare **Height:** 3–8 in. **Flowering:** May–August **Flower Color:** Pale pink to white **Habitat-Community:** Dry, rocky, open slopes in limestone-rich soils in pinyon-juniper woodlands and lower montane coniferous forests **Elevation:** Below 9000 ft. **Ecoregions:** Southern California Mountains

Densely tufted, low-growing perennial with red flowering stems and sticky-hairy herbage. Leaves 0.2–0.8 in. long, basal, oblong to round, blue-green, waxy coated; petiole 0.1 in. long. Flowers 7–20 per head-like cluster, 5-parted, symmetric, trumpet-shaped; white to pale pink corolla tube 0.5–0.6 in. long; pale pink to white, spreading corolla lobes 0.2–0.3 in. long with irregularly lobed margins; peduncles 0.8–1.5 in. long. Fruits 0.3 in. wide, 5-winged anthocarps. Known along the PCT only from the eastern San Bernardino Mountains. *Abronia* is Greek for "graceful."

Abronia villosa

desert sand verbena

NYCTAGINACEAE

FOUR O'CLOCK FAMILY

PCT Sections: 1–4 & 7 **Abundance:** Locally common **Height:** 6–16 in. **Flowering:** February–July **Flower Color:** Pink **Habitat-Community:** Sandy flats, dunes, and washes in creosote bush scrubs, Joshua tree & pinyon-juniper woodlands, and lower montane coniferous forests **Elevation:** Below 4000 ft. **Ecoregions:** Southern California Mountains, Sonoran/Mojave Basin and Range

Decumbent to ascending, spreading annual, forming loose mats up to 3 ft. across, with red-tinged stems and long-hairy, glandular herbage. Leaves 0.6–2 in. across, opposite, round to elliptic, glandular-hairy; petiole 0.2–2 in. long. Flowers 0.2–0.7 in. across, 15–35 per head-like cluster, 5-parted, symmetric, trumpet-shaped; pink corolla tube 0.4–1.4 in. long; pink to magenta (whitish at base), spreading corolla lobes with irregularly lobed margins; peduncles 1–1.5 in. long. Fruits 0.6 in. wide, 3–5-winged anthocarps. Two varieties along the PCT: var. *villosa* (corolla tube 0.4–0.8 in. long) inhabits sandy soils along most low desert segments; the rare var. *aurita* (corolla tube 0.8–1.4 in. long) can be observed along roadsides and in open wooded flats near the Highway 74 crossing in southern Riverside County. *Villosa* means "hairy." Despite the resemblance, sand verbenas are not related to the true verbenas of the Verbenaceae.

Boerhavia triquetra var. *intermedia*

fivewing
spiderling

NYCTAGINACEAE

FOUR O'CLOCK FAMILY

PCT Sections: 1–2 **Abundance:** Occasional **Height:** 4–20 in. **Flowering:** July–October **Flower Color:** Pale pink to white **Habitat-Community:** Dry, gravelly to sandy slopes and flats in creosote bush & Sonoran mixed woody scrubs **Elevation:** Below 4100 ft. **Ecoregions:** Southern California Mountains, Sonoran Basin and Range

Delicate, ascending to erect annual with sparsely hairy, sticky (glandular) stems. Leaves 0.4–2.4 in. long, opposite, lance-shaped to ovoid, often brown-dotted. Flowers to 0.1 in. long, generally 3–6 per head-like cluster, 5-parted, symmetric, bell-shaped; tube 0.1 in. long; lobes pale pink to white. Fruits 0.1 in. long, club-shaped achenes with 5 ribs and abruptly rounded tips. Germinates only after substantial summer precipitation. Look for it on the eastern slopes of the Laguna Mountains and San Felipe Hills region of San Diego County.

Mirabilis albida

dwarf
four o'clock

NYCTAGINACEAE

FOUR O'CLOCK FAMILY

PCT Sections: 4 **Abundance:** Rare **Height:** 4–20 in. **Flowering:** May–August **Flower Color:** Pink to magenta **Habitat-Community:** Dry, rocky, open slopes in pinyon-juniper woodlands and lower montane coniferous forests **Elevation:** Below 8000 ft. **Ecoregions:** Southern California Mountains

Erect to decumbent, usually few-branched perennial with often-forked stems and sticky-hairy herbage. Leaves 0.8–2.4 in. long, opposite, lance-shaped or wider. Flowers 3 per cup-shaped involucre in stem axils. Sepals 0.4–0.6 in. long, fused into corolla-like perianth, broadly funnel-shaped, 5-lobed, pink to magenta. Fruits 0.1–0.2 in. long, 5-ribbed anthocarps. Ranges throughout North America but bisects the PCT only in the eastern San Bernardino Mountains. It responds to warm-season (summer) precipitation. Like most species in the genus, flowers open in the evening and close in the morning.

Mirabilis laevis

desert
wishbone bush

NYCTAGINACEAE

FOUR O'CLOCK FAMILY

PCT Sections: 1–8 **Abundance:** Common **Height:** 4–20 in. **Flowering:** February–June **Flower Color:** Pink, purple-red, or white **Habitat-Community:** Dry, rocky, open slopes in chaparrals, Sonoran/ Mojave mixed woody scrubs, pinyon-juniper woodlands, and lower montane coniferous forests **Elevation:** Below 8000 ft. **Ecoregions:** Southern California Mountains, Sonoran/Mojave Basin and Range, Sierra Nevada

Erect to decumbent perennial or subshrub, often growing through larger shrubs, with generally forked stems and sticky-hairy herbage. Leaves 0.4–1.8 in. long, opposite, ovoid, fleshy, often glandular. Flowers solitary in a bell-shaped involucre, sepals fused into corolla-like perianth 0.2–0.7 in. long, broadly funnel-shaped, 5-lobed, pink to purple-red, or white. Fruits 0.2 in. long, ovoid, 5-ribbed anthocarps. All 3 varieties occur along the PCT in southern California: var. *crassifolia* (uncommon in the desert) has showy pink to purple-red flowers; var. *villosa* (glandular-hairy leaves) and var. *retrorsa* (leaves with reflexed hairs) generally have pale pink to white flowers.

Mirabilis multiflora

giant
four o'clock

NYCTAGINACEAE

FOUR O'CLOCK FAMILY

PCT Sections: 1–3 & 6–7 **Abundance:** Locally common **Height:** 12–30 in. **Flowering:** April–August **Flower Color:** Magenta to pink **Habitat-Community:** Dry hillsides and washes in Sonoran/Mojave mixed woody scrubs and Joshua tree & pinyon-juniper woodlands **Elevation:** Below 6600 ft. **Ecoregions:** Southern California Mountains, Sonoran/Mojave Basin and Range, Sierra Nevada

Sprawling, sometimes mounded perennial with leafy, often forked stems and glandular-hairy (when young) herbage. Leaves 1.2–4.8 in. long, opposite, round to heart-shaped, somewhat fleshy, often glandular. Flowers in head-like clusters at branch tips, contained within a 6-flowered, bell-shaped involucre. Sepals fused into narrowly funnel-shaped, 5-lobed, magenta to pink corolla-like perianth 1.7–2.4 in. long. Fruits 0.2–0.5 in. long, club-shaped, variously ribbed anthocarps. Best observed along the PCT in the southern Peninsular Ranges and in the western Antelope Valley and adjacent mountains ranges. The showy flowers open in the evening and may close up during the day. *Mirabilis* means "wonderful" in Latin, and this species certainly earns that description.

Collomia tinctoria

yellowdye
mountaintrumpet

POLEMONIACEAE PHLOX FAMILY

PCT Sections: 10–24 **Abundance:** Common **Height:** 1–3 in. **Flowering:** June–September **Flower Color:** Pink **Habitat-Community:** Open, rocky or gravelly soils in montane coniferous forests **Elevation:** Below 9900 ft. **Ecoregions:** Sierra Nevada, Cascades, Klamath Mountains

Erect or spreading, many-branched annual with glandular-hairy stems. Leaves alternate, linear to lance-shaped, glandular, with smooth margins. Flowers 2–3 at stem tips, 5-lobed. Calyces to 0.3 in. long with lobes connected by a thin membrane with a water pitcher–like projection at the tip. Corollas to 0.6 in. long, funnel-shaped, with maroon to violet tube and pink lobes. Fruits 1-seed-per-chamber capsules that explosively open to scatter the seeds. The common name likely refers to the staining plants cause when pressed.

Gilia cana

showy gilia

POLEMONIACEAE PHLOX FAMILY

PCT Sections: 4–9 **Abundance:** Locally common **Height:** 4–16 in. **Flowering:** March–May **Flower Color:** Pale pink to lavender **Habitat-Community:** Open, sandy areas in creosote bush & sagebrush scrubs, Mojave mixed woody scrubs, and Joshua tree & pinyon-juniper woodlands **Elevation:** Below 7800 ft. **Ecoregions:** Southern California Mountains, Mojave Basin and Range, Sierra Nevada

Spreading to erect, large-flowered, rosetted annual, cobwebby-hairy at stem base, glandular above. Leaves 0.8–1.6 in. long, mostly basal, 1–2-pinnately lobed, woolly-hairy; stem leaves much reduced, alternate. Flowers solitary, each with its own ascending to spreading pedicel, 5-lobed, with anthers within tube. Calyces 0.2–0.3 in. long, tubular, glandular, with acute lobes. Corollas 0.4–1.2 in. long, trumpet-shaped, with purple tube 2–6 times longer than throat; throat yellow below, blue or white above; lobes spreading, pink to lavender. Fruits 0.1–0.4 in. long, ovoid to spherical capsules.

Gilia leptantha

fineflowered gilia

POLEMONIACEAE PHLOX FAMILY

PCT Sections: 4–10 **Abundance:** Locally common **Height:** 7–20 in. **Flowering:** April–August **Flower Color:** Pink to lavender **Habitat-Community:** Open, sandy to rocky slopes in Joshua tree & pinyon-juniper woodlands, sagebrush scrubs, and montane coniferous forests **Elevation:** Below 9000 ft. **Ecoregions:** Southern California Mountains, Sierra Nevada

Spreading to ascending, large-flowered annual, cobwebby-hairy at stem base, glandular above. Leaves 1–2 in. long, mostly basal, 1-pinnately lobed, lobes toothed, woolly-hairy; stem leaves much reduced, alternate. Flowers 2–6 in loose clusters, glandular, 5-lobed, with exserted anthers; pedicels unequal, spreading. Calyces 0.1–0.2 in. long, tubular, glandular. Corollas 0.4–1.1 in. long, trumpet-shaped, with yellow or purple (yellow-veined) tube 1–4 times longer than throat; throat yellow or white; lobes pink to lavender, 0.1–0.3 in. long. Fruits 0.1–0.3 in. long, spherical capsules. At least 3 subspecies along the PCT; one of these, subsp. *leptantha*, is known only from the southeastern San Bernardino Mountains, south of Onyx Peak.

Gilia ochroleuca

volcanic gilia

POLEMONIACEAE PHLOX FAMILY

PCT Sections: 1–9 **Abundance:** Common **Height:** 3–14 in. **Flowering:** March–August **Flower Color:** Pink to white, blue, or violet **Habitat-Community:** Open, sandy to rocky slopes in chaparrals, woodlands, sagebrush scrubs, and montane coniferous forests **Elevation:** Below 8400 ft. **Ecoregions:** Southern California Mountains, Sierra Nevada

Spreading to ascending, intricately branched annual with hairless (generally), glandular, or woolly stems. Leaves 1–2 in. long, mostly basal, 1–3-pinnately lobed with linear, cobwebby-hairy lobes; stem leaves much reduced, alternate. Flowers in loose clusters, thread-like, 5-lobed; pedicels glandular. Calyces 0.1 in. long, hairless, with linear lobes. Corollas 0.2–0.6 in. long, funnel-shaped, with purple tube, expanded throat (yellow below, blue above), and pink to white, blue, or violet lobes. Fruits 0.1–0.2 in. long, spherical capsules. Four subspecies along the PCT, from the flats of Antelope Valley to the high summits of the southern California Mountains.

Gilia stellata

star gilia

POLEMONIACEAE PHLOX FAMILY

PCT Sections: 1–4 **Abundance:** Locally common **Height:** 4–16 in. **Flowering:** March–May **Flower Color:** Pink to white **Habitat-Community:** Open, sandy to gravelly flats, slopes, and washes in creosote bush & Sonoran mixed woody scrubs and Joshua tree woodlands **Elevation:** Below 5200 ft. **Ecoregions:** Southern California Mountains, Sonoran Basin and Range

Erect, generally single-stemmed annual with white hairs bent at a sharp angle (lower half of plant) and glandular upper stems. Leaves 1–3 in. long, mostly basal, 1–2-pinnately lobed with toothed, bent-white-haired lobes; stem leaves much reduced, alternate. Flowers grouped in open clusters, 5-lobed; stamens exserted. Pedicels spreading, hairless or gland-dotted. Calyces 0.1–0.2 in. long, hairy, glandular. Corollas 0.2–0.4 in. long, funnel-shaped, with tube mostly within the calyx, yellow throat with purple spots, and pink to white lobes. Fruits 0.2–0.3 in. long, widely ovoid capsules. A true desert species, turning up along the PCT only at the lower desert crossings, such as near Interstate 10 in Riverside County.

Ipomopsis aggregata

scarlet gilia

POLEMONIACEAE PHLOX FAMILY

PCT Sections: 9–24 **Abundance:** Common **Height:** 12–32 in. **Flowering:** June–September **Flower Color:** Red **Habitat-Community:** Open, dry soils from woodlands to subalpine coniferous forests **Elevation:** Below 10,900 ft. **Ecoregions:** Sierra Nevada, Cascades, Klamath Mountains

Erect, 1–few-branched perennial with hairy, sometimes glandular herbage. Leaves to 2 in. long, alternate, pinnately lobed, with spine-tipped lobes to 0.8 in. long. Flowers 1–7 per cluster, scattered along stem. Calyces to 0.4 in. long, 5-lobed, bell-shaped, with lobes connected by a thin membrane. Corollas to 1.4 in. long, elongate-funnel-shaped, red (rarely pink, yellow, or white) with yellow mottling. Fruits several-seeded capsules. An infusion of the plant was historically used to treat or prevent constipation.

Leptosiphon breviculus

Mojave linanthus

POLEMONIACEAE PHLOX FAMILY

PCT Sections: 4–6 **Abundance:** Common **Height:** 4–10 in. **Flowering:** April–August **Flower Color:** Pink to white or bluish **Habitat-Community:** Sandy to gravelly soils in Joshua tree & pinyon-juniper woodlands, sagebrush scrubs, and lower montane coniferous forests **Elevation:** Below 8200 ft. **Ecoregions:** Southern California Mountains

Erect, thread-like annual with few branches and hairy herbage. Leaves 0.1–0.4 in. long, opposite, palmately divided into needle-like lobes. Flowers in small clusters within leaf-like bracts, 5-lobed; stamens within tube. Calyces 0.2–0.3 in. long with membranes as wide as lobes. Corollas trumpet-shaped, with maroon tube 0.6–1.1 in. long, purple throat, and pink to white or bluish lobes 0.2–0.3 in. long. Fruits several-seeded capsules. Populations often have purple and white flowers in equal numbers. The specific epithet (from the Latin *brevi*, "short," *culus*, "a little") refers to its "somewhat short" stature.

Leptosiphon ciliatus

whiskerbrush

POLEMONIACEAE PHLOX FAMILY

PCT Sections: All **Abundance:** Common **Height:** 1–12 in. **Flowering:** March–July **Flower Color:** Pale to deep pink **Habitat-Community:** Open to shaded slopes from chaparrals and scrubs to upper montane coniferous forests **Elevation:** Below 9500 ft. **Ecoregions:** All

Erect, single-stemmed annual, branched above, with conspicuously hairy herbage. Leaves opposite, palmate, with 3–5 linear lobes 0.2–0.5 in. long. Flowers in dense, head-like clusters, 5-lobed; stamens slightly exserted. Calyces 0.3 in. long with lobes connected by translucent membranes. Corollas trumpet-like, maroon, with thread-like tube 0.5–0.6 in. long, yellow throat, and spreading, pale to deep pink lobes 0.1–0.2 in. long. Fruits few-seeded capsules. The specific epithet (from the Latin *ciliatus*, "fringe") refers to the margin hairs of the leaves and calyces.

Leptosiphon nudatus

Tehachapi linanthus

POLEMONIACEAE PHLOX FAMILY

PCT Sections: 7–10 **Abundance:** Locally common **Height:** 2–12 in. **Flowering:** April–August **Flower Color:** Pink to white **Habitat-Community:** Openings in chaparrals, sagebrush scrubs, oak & pinyon-juniper woodlands, and lower montane coniferous forests **Elevation:** Below 7800 ft. **Ecoregions:** Sierra Nevada

Erect annual with thin, hairy stems. Leaves opposite, deeply palmate, with needle-like, hairy, glandular lobes 0.2–0.5 in. long. Flowers in dense clusters, 5-lobed; stamens exserted. Calyces 0.2 in. long with lobes connected by translucent membranes. Corollas trumpet-shaped; tube hairy, thread-like, 0.5–0.6 in. long; throat yellow; lobes pink or white, spreading, 0.1–0.2 in. long. Fruits 1-seeded capsules. Endemic to the Tehachapi Mountains and southern Sierra Nevada. Some populations have exclusively white flowers.

Linanthus californicus

prickly phlox

POLEMONIACEAE PHLOX FAMILY

PCT Sections: 3–6 **Abundance:** Locally common **Height:** 1–3 ft. **Flowering:** February–July **Flower Color:** Pink **Habitat-Community:** Sandy to gravelly washes and hillsides in foothill chaparrals, oak woodlands, and lower montane coniferous forests **Elevation:** Below 4800 ft. **Ecoregions:** Southern California Mountains

Ascending, widely branched perennial or subshrub with prickly herbage. Leaves alternate, palmate, with sharp-pointed, linear lobes 0.1–0.5 in. long. Flowers at stem and branch tips, showy, open during the day, 5-parted. Calyces tubular, with membranes wider than the lobes. Corollas trumpet-shaped, with white throat and pink lobes 0.3–0.7 in. long. Fruits several-seeded capsules. Look for it along the PCT near Acton and Vasquez Rocks, in the western Transverse Ranges. Handling the sharp leaves will remind you of its common name!

Linanthus dianthiflorus

fringed linanthus

POLEMONIACEAE PHLOX FAMILY

PCT Sections: 1–4 **Abundance:** Occasional **Height:** 2–5 in. **Flowering:** February–June **Flower Color:** Pink **Habitat-Community:** Sandy to gravelly benches and slopes in foothill chaparrals, Sonoran mixed woody scrubs, and woodlands **Elevation:** Below 4400 ft. **Ecoregions:** Southern California/Northern Baja Coast, Southern California Mountains, Sonoran Basin and Range

Erect, few-branched annual with slender stems and white-hairy herbage. Leaves 0.2–0.8 in. long, opposite, linear. Flowers in open to dense, few-flowered clusters, 5-parted. Calyces tubular, 0.4–0.6 in. long, with membranes wider than the lobes. Corollas funnel-shaped, with tube 0.2 in. long, yellow throat, and pink (white at base), fringed lobes 0.3–0.6 in. long. Fruits many-seeded, short-oblong capsules. Often the most striking of the "groundcover" spring annuals in southern California chaparral, though much of its habitat has been lost to urban sprawl. Most common along the PCT at the lower elevations of the southern Peninsular Ranges. The specific epithet (from the Latin, "*Dianthus* flowers") references the flowers' resemblance to carnations.

Linanthus orcuttii

Orcutt's linanthus

POLEMONIACEAE PHLOX FAMILY

PCT Sections: 1–2 **Abundance:** Rare **Height:** 2–4 in. **Flowering:** April–June **Flower Color:** Pink **Habitat-Community:** Dry openings in chaparrals, sagebrush scrubs, and lower montane coniferous forests **Elevation:** Below 6400 ft. **Ecoregions:** Southern California Mountains

Ascending, generally branched (near base) annual with short-hairy stems. Leaves 0.2–0.5 in. long, opposite, deeply lobed with hairy, linear segments. Flowers 1 or clustered at stem and branch tips, 5-parted, open during the day. Calyces tubular, hairless, 0.2–0.5 in. long, with membrane as wide as lobes. Corollas funnel-shaped, with white (becoming purple) tube 0.2–0.6 in. long, white or yellow throat, and pink (2 purple marks at base) lobes 0.2–0.3 in. long. Fruits 0.2–0.3 in. long, obovoid capsules with 6–12 seeds. Endemic to the southern Peninsular Ranges of California. Threatened by recreational activities and urbanization. Best seen along the PCT atop the Laguna Mountains, or along the trail through the Bucksnort Mountains north of Warner Springs.

Microsteris gracilis

slender phlox

POLEMONIACEAE PHLOX FAMILY

PCT Sections: All **Abundance:** Common **Height:** to 8 in. **Flowering:** March–August **Flower Color:** Pink to white **Habitat-Community:** Open slopes and forests from woodlands and chaparrals to subalpine coniferous forests **Elevation:** Below 10,900 ft. **Ecoregions:** All

Erect to decumbent, 1-many-branched annual with glandular-hairy upper stems and foliage. Leaves to 1.2 in. long, opposite (lower stem) and alternate (upper stem), lance- to spoon-shaped, with smooth margins. Flowers 1–few on upper stem. Calyces to 0.4 in. long, 5-lobed, with lobes connected by a thin, narrow (≤ lobe width) membrane. Corollas to 0.6 in. long, funnel-shaped, with yellow tube and blunt or notched, pink to white lobes. Fruits to 0.2 in. long, capsules with 1–3 seeds. *Microsteris* (from the Greek "small, to support") likely refers to its diminutive size.

Navarretia hamata

hooked navarretia

POLEMONIACEAE PHLOX FAMILY

PCT Sections: 1 & 4–5 **Abundance:** Occasional **Height:** 3–12 in. **Flowering:** April–June **Flower Color:** Pink to red-purple **Habitat-Community:** Dry, sandy to hardpacked soils in foothill chaparrals and oak woodlands **Elevation:** Below 4200 ft. **Ecoregions:** Southern California/Northern Baja Coast, Southern California Mountains

Single-stemmed spiny annual, branched above, with green turning reddish, glandular-hairy stems. Leaves 0.7–2 in. long, alternate, oblong, deeply pinnately lobed, the lobes spine-tipped. Flowers in dense heads, sessile, 5-lobed, with glandular calyces 0.2–0.3 in. long and blue anthers. Corollas 0.3–0.4 in. long, funnel-shaped, with pink to red-purple (white at base) lobes 0.2–0.3 in. long. Fruits ovoid capsules. Its skunky odor attracts insect pollinators. Its leaf lobes resemble a grappling hook (hence the common name).

Navarretia leptalea

Bridges' gilia

POLEMONIACEAE PHLOX FAMILY

PCT Sections: 10–19 **Abundance:** Locally common **Height:** 1–13 in. **Flowering:** June–August **Flower Color:** Pink **Habitat-Community:** Open, rocky soils in forests and meadows from chaparrals to upper montane coniferous forests **Elevation:** Below 10,200 ft. **Ecoregions:** Sierra Nevada, Cascades

Erect, branched annual growing in colonies with glandular-hairy (sometimes sparsely so) stems. Leaves to 2 in. long, alternate, linear, spreading, glandular-hairy, with smooth margins. Flowers many in pairs along stem tips, glandular-hairy. Calyces to 0.2 in. long, sparsely glandular-hairy, unequally 5-lobed, the fine-pointed lobes connected by a thin membrane. Corollas 0.3–0.8 in. long, elongate-funnel-shaped, with yellow tube, purplish throat, and pink lobes. Fruits to 0.2 in. long, capsules with 6–12 seeds.

Phlox diffusa

spreading phlox

POLEMONIACEAE PHLOX FAMILY

PCT Sections: 4–5 & 8–24 **Abundance:** Locally common **Height:** 2–8 in. **Flowering:** May–August **Flower Color:** Pink to white or bluish **Habitat-Community:** Dry, open places, including serpentine soils, from lower montane coniferous forests to alpine communities **Elevation:** Below 11,900 ft. **Ecoregions:** Southern California Mountains, Sierra Nevada, Cascades, Klamath Mountains

Decumbent, matted perennial with glandless, hairy or hairless herbage. Leaves to 0.6 in. long, opposite, awl-shaped to linear, with smooth margins. Flowers solitary at stem tips on short pedicels. Calyces to 0.4 in. long, 5-lobed, hairy, with lobes = tube. Corollas to 0.8 in. long, funnel-shaped, pink to white or bluish, with round-tipped lobes. Fruits to 0.2 in. long, capsules with few seeds. *Phlox* (from the Greek, "flame") alludes to the intense flower colors of some species. *Diffusa* ("spreading") refers to the matted growth form.

Phlox dolichantha

Big Bear Valley phlox

POLEMONIACEAE PHLOX FAMILY

PCT Sections: 4 **Abundance:** Rare **Height:** 3–12 in. **Flowering:** May–June **Flower Color:** Pink, white, or lavender **Habitat-Community:** Gravelly soils, pebble plains, and shaded understories in sagebrush scrubs, pinyon-juniper woodlands, and upper montane coniferous forests **Elevation:** Below 8600 ft. **Ecoregions:** Southern California Mountains

Spreading to erect, sparsely branched perennial with hairless to glandular-hairy stems. Leaves 0.8–2 in. long, opposite, lance- or sickle-shaped. Flowers at stem tips, 5-parted. Calyces tubular, 0.4–0.5 in. long, with glandular-hairy lobes and membranes. Corollas trumpet-shaped, with slender tube 1.4–2 in. long, and spreading, pink, white, or lavender lobes to 0.5 in. long. Fruits 0.2–0.3 in. long, 1-seeded capsules. The long floral tube is highly diagnostic. Endemic to the montane zone of the San Bernardino Mountains. Threatened by recreational activities, urbanization, fire management, logging, and mining. *Dolichantha* means "long-flowered" in Latin.

Saltugilia splendens

splendid woodland gilia

POLEMONIACEAE PHLOX FAMILY

PCT Sections: 3–6 **Abundance:** Common **Height:** 5–40 in. **Flowering:** May–August **Flower Color:** Pink to red-purple **Habitat-Community:** Open, gravelly or rocky soils in chaparrals, oak woodlands, and montane coniferous forests **Elevation:** Below 8000 ft. **Ecoregions:** Southern California Mountains

Erect, showy annual, branched above, with glandless to glandular (below) herbage. Leaves 1–6 in. long, basal in an erect rosette, 2–3 pinnately lobed, linear, with long-hairy segments, the hairs translucent; stem leaves alternate, reduced. Flowers few at the tips of glandular pedicels, 5-lobed, with hairless calyces 0.1–0.2 in. long. Corollas 0.4–1.4 in. long, with red-purple, minutely glandular tube extending beyond the calyx and pink throat and lobes. Fruits 0.1–0.3 in. long, ovoid capsules with 35–70 seeds.

Primula fragrans

scented shootingstar

PRIMULACEAE PRIMROSE FAMILY

PCT Sections: 10–11 **Abundance:** Occasional **Height:** 6–24 in. **Flowering:** June–July **Flower Color:** Red to lavender **Habitat-Community:** Moist places in wetland-riparian communities **Elevation:** 7800–11,900 ft. **Ecoregions:** Sierra Nevada

Erect, generally clumped perennial with densely glandular-hairy herbage. Leaves to 16 in. long, basal, spoon-shaped, with smooth margins. Flowers 5–10 at stem tips, downturned, with 5 anthers. Calyces to 0.5 in. long, 5-lobed, the lobes recurved when flowering. Corollas funnel-shaped with 5 red to lavender, recurved lobes to 1 in. long. Fruits to 0.6 in. long, many-seeded capsules. *Primula* ("first") refers to the early blooming of many species.

Primula hendersonii

mosquito bill

PRIMULACEAE PRIMROSE FAMILY

PCT Sections: 4 & 16–24 **Abundance:** Locally common **Height:** 4–19 in. **Flowering:** March–July **Flower Color:** Red to white **Habitat-Community:** Dry, shady places in woodlands, chaparrals, and lower montane coniferous forests **Elevation:** Below 6300 ft. **Ecoregions:** Sierra Nevada

Erect perennial with glandular-hairy to hairless herbage. Leaves to 6.3 in. long, basal, elliptic to ovoid or spoon-shaped, with smooth to toothed margins. Flowers 3–17 at stem tips, downturned, with 4–5 anthers. Calyces to 0.3 in. long, 4–5-lobed, the lobes recurved when flowering. Corollas funnel-shaped with 4–5 red to white, recurved lobes, 1 in. long. Fruits to 0.6 in. long, many-seeded capsules.

Primula jeffreyi

Sierra shootingstar

PRIMULACEAE PRIMROSE FAMILY

PCT Sections: 10–24 **Abundance:** Locally common **Height:** 4–24 in. **Flowering:** June–August **Flower Color:** Red to lavender or white **Habitat-Community:** Moist to dry meadows and streambanks from lower montane to subalpine coniferous forests and wetland-riparian communities **Elevation:** Below 9900 ft. **Ecoregions:** Sierra Nevada, Cascades, Klamath Mountains

Erect, generally clumped perennial with glandular-hairy herbage. Leaves to 20 in. long, basal, narrowly to widely spoon-shaped, with smooth or toothed margins. Flowers 3–18 at stem tips, downturned, with generally 4 anthers. Calyces to 0.6 in. long, 4–5-lobed, the lobes recurved when flowering. Corollas funnel-shaped with 4–5 red to lavender or white recurved lobes, 1 in. long. Fruits to 0.5 in. long, many-seeded capsules. The specific epithet honors Scottish plant collector John Jeffrey (1826–1854).

Primula suffrutescens

Sierra primrose

PRIMULACEAE PRIMROSE FAMILY

PCT Sections: 10–17 **Abundance:** Locally common **Height:** 1–6 in. **Flowering:** July–August **Flower Color:** Red with yellow throat **Habitat-Community:** Crevices in rock outcrops in subalpine coniferous forests and alpine communities **Elevation:** 6500–13,800 ft. **Ecoregions:** Sierra Nevada

Creeping, branched perennial or subshrub with woody lower stems. Leaves to 1.4 in. long, basal, spoon-shaped, hairless, with toothed margins. Flowers 2–many at stem tips. Calyces to 0.3 in. long, glandular-hairy, 5-lobed. Corollas to 0.8 in. long, funnel-shaped, with yellow tube and 5 red lobes. Fruits to 0.3 in. long, capsules with brown, winged seeds. *Suffrutescens* is a reference to its woody base. Occurs at a few locations in the Trinity Alps Wilderness but not along the trail. If you spot it along the PCT in the Klamath Mountains, please let the authors know.

Monardella australis

southern monardella

LAMIACEAE MINT FAMILY

PCT Sections: 3–5 **Abundance:** Occasional **Height:** 4–16 in. **Flowering:** June–September **Flower Color:** Pale rose to pink **Habitat-Community:** Rocky, open slopes in montane & subalpine coniferous forests **Elevation:** Below 10,600 ft. **Ecoregions:** Southern California Mountains

Matted to tufted subshrub with sparsely to densely hairy stems. Leaves 0.2–1.2 in. long, opposite, lance-shaped to triangular-ovoid, green to ash-gray, sometimes with toothed or wavy margins. Flowers in compact clusters, 1 cluster per stem, 5-parted, with leaf-like, rose-tinged outer bracts 0.3–1 in. wide. Calyx lobes hairy. Corollas 0.4–0.6 in. long, 2-lipped (upper lip erect, 2-lobed; lower lip recurved, 3-lobed), with pale rose to pink fused petals. Fruits 4 small, ovoid nutlets. Endemic, comprised of 3 rare subspecies that differ in stem length and leaf and corolla size: subsp. *australis*, the most common, is known along the PCT in the San Bernardino and San Jacinto Mountains; subsp. *cinerea* is endemic to the San Gabriel Mountains; subsp. *jokerstii* (endangered; not yet reported on the PCT) is restricted to the eastern San Gabriel Mountains.

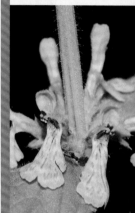

Stachys stebbinsii

Stebbins' hedgenettle

LAMIACEAE MINT FAMILY

PCT Sections: 1–3 **Abundance:** Occasional **Height:** 2–5 ft. **Flowering:** June–September **Flower Color:** Pink to white **Habitat-Community:** Moist to dry, shaded slopes from oak woodlands to lower montane coniferous forests **Elevation:** Below 7600 ft. **Ecoregions:** Southern California/Northern Baja Coast, Southern California Mountains

Erect, resinous, robust perennial with 4-angled, hairy, densely glandular stems. Leaves 4–5 in. long, opposite, oblong, soft-hairy, with truncate to heart-shaped bases and toothed margins; petiole 0.2–0.3 in. long. Flowers 6 per cluster along spikes, 5-parted, with hairy, bell-shaped calyces. Corollas pale pink to white, tube 0.3–0.4 in. long, and lower lip 0.2–0.4 in. long, larger than the upper lip (about the same width). Fruits 4 small nutlets. *Stachys* (from the Greek, "ear of corn") refers to the inflorescence.

Aphyllon fasciculatum

clustered broomrape

OROBANCHACEAE

BROOMRAPE FAMILY

PCT Sections: All **Abundance:** Locally common **Height:** 2–8 in. **Flowering:** March–August **Flower Color:** Pink or yellow **Habitat-Community:** Openings near shrubs from scrubs and woodlands to subalpine coniferous forests **Elevation:** Below 10,900 ft. **Ecoregions:** All

Parasitic perennial (lacking chlorophyll) with various host plants, including sagebrushes and buckwheats. Leaves generally reduced to fleshy scales. Flowers 5–20 in flat-topped clusters at stem tips. Calyces 5-lobed, lobes to 0.3 in. long (< tube). Corollas irregular, 0.6–1.2 in. long, 5-lobed, 2-lipped, funnel-shaped, pink or yellow, glandular-hairy. Fruits many-seeded capsules. *Aphyllon* (from the Greek, "without leaf") refers to the lack of obvious leaves. Broomrapes (the name comes from a related species that is parasitic on Scotch broom) rob their host plants of water and nutrients but rarely kill them.

Parish's broomrape

Aphyllon parishii

OROBANCHACEAE
BROOMRAPE FAMILY

PCT Sections: 1–6 **Abundance:** Occasional **Height:** 6–10 in. **Flowering:** May–July **Flower Color:** Pink to brown-yellow **Habitat-Community:** Openings on sandy to rocky slopes from scrubs to upper montane coniferous forests **Elevation:** Below 9000 ft. **Ecoregions:** Southern California Mountains, Sonoran/Mojave Basin and Range

Parasitic perennial (lacking leaves and chlorophyll) with stout, glandular-hairy, generally solitary stems; attaches to roots of shrubs in the sunflower family. Flowers densely clustered on erect spikes, accompanied by dark-veined bracts, pedicels to 4 in. long, and 5 calyx lobes 0.4–0.8 in. long. Corollas irregular, 5-lobed, broadly tubular, 2-lipped, upper lip 2-lobed, 0.8–1.1 in. long, lower lip 3-lobed, 0.3 in. long, spreading; lobes pale pink to brown-yellow (red-veined). Fruits 2-valved capsules.

wavyleaf paintbrush

Castilleja applegatei

OROBANCHACEAE
BROOMRAPE FAMILY

PCT Sections: All **Abundance:** Common **Height:** 4–32 in. **Flowering:** May–September **Flower Color:** Red or yellow **Habitat-Community:** Open, dry places from scrubs and woodlands to subalpine coniferous forests **Elevation:** Below 11,900 ft. **Ecoregions:** All

Erect, few-stemmed perennial with obviously sticky herbage; hemiparasitic. Leaves 0.8–2.8 in. long, lance-shaped, glandular and hairy, 0–7-lobed, and generally wavy margins. Flowers densely clustered at stem tips with red to yellowish bracts. Calyces to 1 in. long, unequally 4-lobed, lobes ≤ tube. Corollas irregular, to 1.6 in. long, 2-lipped, funnel-shaped, with red margins, beaked upper lip, and dark green lower lip. Fruits many-seeded capsules. Probably the most common *Castilleja* along the CA PCT. Thought to be a snake's best friend: the rocky sites where paintbrushes grow tend to have various reptiles!

desert paintbrush

Castilleja chromosa

OROBANCHACEAE
BROOMRAPE FAMILY

PCT Sections: 4–9 **Abundance:** Occasional **Height:** 10–28 in. **Flowering:** May–September **Flower Color:** Red **Habitat-Community:** Dry, gravelly soils in sagebrush scrubs, Joshua tree & pinyon-juniper woodlands, and lower montane coniferous forests **Elevation:** Below 8600 ft. **Ecoregions:** Southern California Mountains, Sierra Nevada

Densely branched, leafy perennial with short-hairy stems red-purple with age; hemiparasitic. Leaves 1–3 in. long, alternate, simple or lobed with linear to lance-shaped lobes. Flowers in leafy spikes, irregular, with lobed, bright red to yellow-orange bracts 0.8–1.2 in. long. Calyces 0.7–1.1 in. long, unequally 4-lobed. Corollas 0.8–1.5 in. long with yellow-green (red-margined), beak-like upper lip and dark green, reduced lower lip. Fruits 0.4–0.6 in. long, ovoid capsules. Fairly limited to arid zones along the PCT. The colorful bracts attract pollinators that would otherwise ignore the plant's small flowers.

Castilleja exserta
purple owl's-clover
OROBANCHACEAE
BROOMRAPE FAMILY

PCT Sections: 1–9 **Abundance:** Locally common **Height:** 4–16 in. **Flowering:** March–May **Flower Color:** Red-pink to purple **Habitat–Community:** Open plains and valleys in creosote bush scrubs, foothill chaparrals, oak & Joshua tree woodlands, and lower montane coniferous forests **Elevation:** Below 6600 ft. **Ecoregions:** Southern California Mountains, Mojave Basin and Range, Sierra Nevada

Erect, few-branched annual with hairy herbage; hemiparasitic. Leaves 1–2 in. long, alternate, with 5–9 thread-like lobes. Flowers in dense spikes 1–8 in. long; bracts 5–9-lobed, 0.4–1 in. long, with white, yellow or purple-red tips. Calyces 0.4–1 in. long, unequally 4-lobed, colored like bracts. Corollas irregular, 0.6–1 in. long, red-pink to purple, 2-lipped, with beak-like upper lip, pouched lower lip (bright yellow), and white to yellow or rose tips. Fruits 0.4–0.6 in. long, ovoid capsules. The 3 subspecies along the PCT are separated by flower color.

Castilleja foliolosa
woolly paintbrush
OROBANCHACEAE
BROOMRAPE FAMILY

PCT Sections: 1–6 **Abundance:** Locally common **Height:** 12–25 in. **Flowering:** March–June **Flower Color:** Red to orange-red **Habitat–Community:** Open, dry, rocky soils in Sonoran/Mojave mixed woody scrubs, foothill chaparrals, and oak & Joshua tree woodlands **Elevation:** Below 5700 ft. **Ecoregions:** Southern California/Northern Baja Coast, Southern California Mountains

Erect, soft-woolly, multi-branched (from base) perennial with 2-ridged (concealed by woolly hairs) stems appearing gray from a distance; hemiparasitic. Leaves 0.3–1.4 in. long, alternate, simple to lobed below the flowers, and matted in hair. Flowers in leafy spikes 2–6 in. long, with green-purple to vivid orange-red, 3–5-lobed bracts 0.6–0.8 in. long. Calyces 0.4–1 in. long, 2-lipped, tubular, vivid tomato red. Corollas irregular, yellow tinged pink, 2-lipped, with beak-like upper lip 0.7–1 in. long and 3-lobed (bulging between lobes) lower lip. Fruits 0.4–0.6 in. long, ovoid capsules. Responds robustly to fire. A pale yellow form, lacking pigmentation, is frequent along the PCT.

Castilleja lemmonii
Lemmon's paintbrush
OROBANCHACEAE
BROOMRAPE FAMILY

PCT Sections: 10–18 **Abundance:** Locally common **Height:** 4–8 in. **Flowering:** July–August **Flower Color:** Purple-red **Habitat–Community:** Meadows in wetland-riparian communities **Elevation:** 5100–12,200 ft. **Ecoregions:** Sierra Nevada, Cascades

Erect, generally unbranched perennial with glandular-hairy herbage; hemiparasitic. Leaves 0.8–1.6 in. long, linear to lance-shaped, 0–3-lobed, with smooth to wavy margins. Flowers densely clustered at stem tips, with purple-red-tipped bracts. Calyces to 0.7 in. long, unequally 4-lobed (lobes ≥ tube), purple-red. Corollas irregular, to 0.8 in. long, funnel-shaped, 2-lipped, with beaked upper lip and yellow-green lower lip. Fruits to 0.4 in. long, many-seeded capsules. Really stands out and is exciting to find at the higher elevations!

Castilleja linariifolia

Wyoming paintbrush

OROBANCHACEAE

BROOMRAPE FAMILY

PCT Sections: 4–5 & 7–8 **Abundance:** Locally common **Height:** 12–40 in. **Flowering:** June–September **Flower Color:** Red to orange-red **Habitat-Community:** Rocky to alkaline soils in sagebrush scrubs, chaparrals, Joshua tree & pinyon-juniper woodlands, and lower montane coniferous forests **Elevation:** Below 8000 ft. **Ecoregions:** Southern California Mountains, Sierra Nevada

Long-stemmed, few-branched perennial with hairless, yellow-green (aging purple) stems; hemiparasitic. Leaves 0.8–3.1 in. long, alternate, linear, simple to 3-lobed. Flowers in open spikes 2–8 in. long, bright red to yellow, with narrowly 3-lobed bracts 0.7–1.3 in. long. Calyces 0.8–1.5 in. long, tubular, 2-lipped, vivid red. Corollas irregular, 1–1.8 in. long, 2-lipped, with beak-like, yellow-green upper lip and reduced, dark green lower lip. Fruits 0.4–0.6 in. long, ovoid capsules. Highly variable, ranging throughout the intermountain west. Wyoming's state flower.

Castilleja miniata

giant red paintbrush

OROBANCHACEAE

BROOMRAPE FAMILY

PCT Sections: 1 & 3–5 & 9–24 **Abundance:** Common **Height:** 15–32 in. **Flowering:** May–September **Flower Color:** Red **Habitat-Community:** Meadows and streambanks in wetland-riparian communities **Elevation:** Below 11,500 ft. **Ecoregions:** All (except Sonoran/Mojave Basin and Range)

Stout, generally few-branched perennial with green or purplish, slightly sticky stems; hemiparasitic. Leaves 1.2–2.4 in. long, lance-shaped, with smooth margins. Flowers densely clustered at stem tips, with red-tipped bracts. Calyces to 1.2 in. long, unequally 4-lobed (lobes ≥ tube), red. Corollas irregular, 0.8–1.6 in. long, funnel-shaped, yellow-green with red margins, 2-lipped, with beaked upper lip and dark green lower lip. Fruits to 0.5 in. long, many-seeded capsules. The most common paintbrush in wetlands along the CA PCT.

Castilleja minor

lesser paintbrush

OROBANCHACEAE

BROOMRAPE FAMILY

PCT Sections: 1–10 **Abundance:** Occasional **Height:** 1–4 ft. **Flowering:** June–October **Flower Color:** Red **Habitat-Community:** Moist places, wet meadows, and streambanks from oak woodlands to upper montane coniferous forests and wetland-riparian communities **Elevation:** Below 8200 ft. **Ecoregions:** Southern California Mountains, Sierra Nevada

Tall, slender, mostly unbranched annual with green to gray, short-hairy stems; hemiparasitic. Leaves 1.6–3.8 in. long, alternate, well spaced, lance-shaped to linear. Flowers in narrow, open spikes 4–16 in. long, with red-tipped, leaf-like bracts 0.8–2 in. long. Calyces 0.6–1.2 in. long, tubular, 2-lipped. Corollas irregular, 1.1–1.5 in. long, 2-lipped, with beak-like yellow-green upper lip and lower lip yellow, reduced. Fruits 0.4–0.6 in. long, ovoid capsules. Look for it along stream crossings and meadows in the Southern California Mountains, and again in the southern Sierra, especially along the South Fork of the Kern River.

Heckard's paintbrush

Castilleja montigena

OROBANCHACEAE

BROOMRAPE FAMILY

PCT Sections: 4 **Abundance:** Rare **Height:** 10–28 in. **Flowering:** May–August **Flower Color:** Red **Habitat-Community:** Dry, gravelly to rocky soils in openings or understories in sagebrush scrubs, pinyon-juniper woodlands, and montane coniferous forests **Elevation:** 5800–9200 ft. **Ecoregions:** Southern California Mountains

Perennial, branched above, with glandular-hairy gray-green stems; hemiparasitic. Leaves 1–2 in. long, alternate, simple or shallowly lobed, linear to lance-shaped. Flowers in leafy spikes 2–8 in. long, with bright red to orange bracts that have more lobes than leaves do. Calyces 0.6–0.8 in. long, tubular, 2-lipped, unequally 4-lobed. Corollas irregular, 0.8–1.6 in. long, green-yellow, with beak-like upper lip. Fruits 0.4–0.6 in. long, ovoid capsules. Endemic to the eastern San Bernardino Mountains. Often co-occurs with *C. applegatei.*

toothed owl's-clover

Orthocarpus cuspidatus

OROBANCHACEAE

BROOMRAPE FAMILY

PCT Sections: 10–24 **Abundance:** Locally common **Height:** 4–16 in. **Flowering:** June–August **Flower Color:** Purple-pink **Habitat-Community:** Open slopes, including serpentine soils, from sagebrush scrubs to subalpine coniferous forests **Elevation:** Below 10,500 ft. **Ecoregions:** Sierra Nevada, Cascades, Klamath Mountains

Erect, unbranched to many-branched annual with glandular-hairy stems. Leaves 0.4–2 in. long, lance-shaped, 0–3-lobed, with smooth to wavy margins. Flowers densely clustered at stem tips, with purple-pink-tipped, pointed bracts. Calyces to 0.4 in. long, unequally 4-lobed, lobes ≥ tube. Corollas irregular, to 1 in. long, 2-lipped, funnel-shaped, with white pouches and purple-pink, beaked upper lip. Fruits to 0.3 in. long, many-seeded capsules. *Cuspidatus* ("teeth") refers to the pointed bracts. Very showy, especially when growing in large patches.

little elephant's head

Pedicularis attollens

OROBANCHACEAE

BROOMRAPE FAMILY

PCT Sections: 10–22 **Abundance:** Locally common **Height:** 2–24 in. **Flowering:** June–September **Flower Color:** Pink to purple **Habitat-Community:** Wet meadows, streambanks, and bogs in wetland-riparian communities **Elevation:** Below 13,200 ft. **Ecoregions:** Sierra Nevada, Cascades, Klamath Mountains

Erect, unbranched perennial with hairy upper stems. Leaves 1–8 in. long, alternate, linear, divided into 17–41 segments, with toothed margins. Flowers densely clustered at stem tips, with densely hairy bracts. Calyces to 0.3 in. long, unequally 5-lobed, lobes < tube. Corollas irregular, to 0.3 in. long, 2-lipped (the upper trunk-like, the lower 3-lobed), pink to purple. Fruits to 0.4 in. long, many-seeded capsules. When looking closely at the flowers, you really can see 2 drooping ears (the outside lobes of the lower lip) and a trunk (the upper lip). These are fun to see, especially for kids!

Pedicularis densiflora

warrior's plume

OROBANCHACEAE

BROOMRAPE FAMILY

PCT Sections: 2–9 & 16–22 **Abundance:** Locally common **Height:** 2–22 in. **Flowering:** March–June **Flower Color:** Red **Habitat-Community:** Dry places from oak woodlands to lower montane coniferous forests **Elevation:** Below 6900 ft. **Ecoregions:** All (except Sonoran/Mojave Basin and Range)

Erect perennial with brown-hairy stems. Leaves 2–11 in. long, alternate, lance-oblong-shaped, divided into 13–41 segments, with doubly toothed to lobed margins. Flowers densely clustered at stem tips, with brown-hairy bracts. Calyces to 0.3 in. long, unequally 5-lobed, lobes < tube. Corollas irregular, to 0.3 in. long, club-like, 2-lipped (the upper hood-like, the lower 3-lobed), red (rarely yellow to orange). Fruits to 0.5 in. long, many-seeded capsules. The common name relates to the showy flower heads, which resemble a brightly colored headdress. Look for these cute redheads early in the season.

Pedicularis groenlandica

elephant's head lousewort

OROBANCHACEAE

BROOMRAPE FAMILY

PCT Sections: 10–24 **Abundance:** Locally common **Height:** 3–31 in. **Flowering:** May–September **Flower Color:** Pink to red-purple **Habitat-Community:** Wet meadows, streambanks, and bogs in wetland-riparian communities **Elevation:** Below 11,900 ft. **Ecoregions:** Sierra Nevada, Cascades, Klamath Mountains

Erect, single- or multi-stemmed perennial with hairless stems. Leaves 1–10 in. long, alternate, lance-shaped, divided into 25–51 segments, with toothed margins. Flowers densely clustered at stem tips, with hairless bracts. Calyces to 0.3 in. long, mostly equally 5-lobed, lobes < tube. Corollas irregular, 0.3–0.6 in. long, 2-lipped (the upper trunk-like, the lower 3-lobed), pink to red-purple. Fruits to 0.4 in. long, many-seeded capsules. The elephant head–like flowers are pretty cool!

Diplacus bicolor

harlequin monkeyflower

PHRYMACEAE LOPSEED FAMILY

PCT Sections: 8–13 **Abundance:** Locally common **Height:** 0.5–6 in. **Flowering:** May–September **Flower Color:** Magenta or yellow **Habitat-Community:** Granitic, gravelly flats and slopes from lower montane to subalpine coniferous forests **Elevation:** Below 10,800 ft. **Ecoregions:** Sierra Nevada

Erect annual with hairy stems. Leaves 0.2–1 in. long, opposite, linear to oblong, with smooth margins. Flowers 1-few at stem tips. Calyces to 0.3 in. long, > pedicel, equally 5-lobed, dark-ribbed, minutely hairy. Corollas irregular, to 0.6 in. long, 2-lipped, magenta or yellow (hence *bicolor*), lined and blotched with red-brown. Fruits to 0.4 in. long, many-seeded capsules. Yellow-flowering plants are often mixed with magenta individuals, creating a harlequin (varied) color pattern over the landscape.

Diplacus bigelovii

Bigelow's monkeyflower

PHRYMACEAE LOPSEED FAMILY

PCT Sections: 1–9 **Abundance:** Locally common **Height:** 1–10 in. **Flowering:** February–June **Flower Color:** Magenta **Habitat-Community:** Dry gravelly to rocky soils and washes in creosote bush & Sonoran/Mojave mixed woody scrubs and Joshua tree & pinyon-juniper woodlands **Elevation:** Below 6200 ft. **Ecoregions:** Sonoran/Mojave Basin and Range, Sierra Nevada

Erect, few- to many-branched desert annual with hairy, green to reddish herbage. Leaves 0.3–1.4 in. long, opposite, elliptic lower, narrower upper, hairy, with smooth margins. Flowers tubular, with unequally 5-lobed, hairy calyces 0.3–0.6 in. long. Corollas irregular, 0.5–1 in. long, 5-lobed (2 above, 3 below), 2-lipped, magenta, with spreading lobes, yellow throat, and maroon-spotted mouth (top of throat). Fruits 0.3–0.6 in. long, ovoid capsules. Widespread, intercepting the PCT along the low arid segments, such as in San Felipe Valley in San Diego County.

Diplacus constrictus

dense-fruited monkeyflower

PHRYMACEAE LOPSEED FAMILY

PCT Sections: 6–9 **Abundance:** Occasional **Height:** 2–10 in. **Flowering:** May–August **Flower Color:** Pink to red **Habitat-Community:** Gravelly to clayey soils, slopes, and washes in foothill chaparrals, oak woodlands, and lower montane coniferous forests **Elevation:** Below 6300 ft. **Ecoregions:** Southern California Mountains, Sierra Nevada

Erect to spreading, branched annual with coarsely hairy herbage. Leaves 0.2–1.3 in. long, opposite, narrowly elliptic to ovoid, hairy, smooth or slightly toothed at tips. Flowers tubular, with ribbed, inflated, 5-lobed calyces 0.3–0.5 in. long. Corollas irregular, 0.6–1 in. long, 5-lobed (2 above, 3 below), 2-lipped, pink to red, with spreading lobes and white (sometimes yellow) throat streaked with maroon. Fruits 0.4–0.5 in. long, ovoid capsules. Variable, endemic to central California. Intergrades with *D. bicolor*.

Diplacus fremontii

Fremont's monkeyflower

PHRYMACEAE LOPSEED FAMILY

PCT Sections: 1–8 **Abundance:** Common **Height:** 2–8 in. **Flowering:** March–June **Flower Color:** Magenta **Habitat-Community:** Gravelly to sandy soils in creosote bush & Mojave mixed woody scrubs, Joshua tree & pinyon-juniper woodlands, and montane chaparrals **Elevation:** Below 6400 ft. **Ecoregions:** Southern California Mountains, Sonoran/Mojave Basin and Range, Sierra Nevada

Erect, branched annual with hairless to somewhat hairy herbage on upper stems. Leaves 0.2–1.2 in. long, opposite, narrowly elliptic to ovoid, with smooth margins. Flowers 1 per node along the stem, tubular, with 5-lobed, widely ribbed, inflated calyces 0.2–0.6 in. long, reddish with white hairs. Corollas irregular, 5-lobed (2 above, 3 below), lobes equal in size, 2-lipped, magenta; tube and throat 0.4–1 in. long, with yellow and maroon folds on throat floor. Fruits 0.3–0.5 in. long, ovoid capsules. Distributed along the PCT at the lower montane–desert transition of southern California.

Diplacus johnstonii

Johnston's monkeyflower

PHRYMACEAE LOPSEED FAMILY

PCT Sections: 4–6 **Abundance:** Rare **Height:** 2–8 in. **Flowering:** May–August **Flower Color:** Magenta to pink-red **Habitat-Community:** Gravelly to rocky scree on slopes in oak woodlands, montane chaparrals, and montane coniferous forests **Elevation:** Below 9200 ft. **Ecoregions:** Southern California Mountains

Erect, branched annual with fine white-hairy herbage. Leaves 0.3–1.3 in. long, opposite, narrowly to widely spoon-shaped, with smooth margins and narrow tips. Flowers at stem nodes and bunched at stem tips, tubular, with 5-lobed, membranous, reddish calyces 0.2–0.4 in. long. Corollas irregular, 0.3–0.6 in. long, 5-lobed (2 above, 3 below), 2-lipped, magenta to pink-red with maroon-blotched yellow throat; stigma exserted. Fruits 0.3–0.5 in. long, ovoid capsules. This regional endemic intergrades with *D. constrictus* in the far western Transverse Ranges (Liebre Mountains). Best observed along the PCT from Mt. Baden-Powell to the Islip Saddle in the San Gabriel Mountains.

Diplacus mephiticus

skunky monkeyflower

PHRYMACEAE LOPSEED FAMILY

PCT Sections: 9–24 **Abundance:** Locally common **Height:** 0.5–6 in. **Flowering:** May–August **Flower Color:** Magenta, red-purple, or yellow **Habitat-Community:** Open, sandy flats and slopes from sagebrush scrubs to subalpine coniferous forests **Elevation:** Below 11,300 ft. **Ecoregions:** Sierra Nevada, Cascades, Klamath Mountains

Erect annual with glandular-hairy stems. Leaves 0.4–0.8 in. long, opposite, narrowly spoon-shaped to linear, hairy, with smooth margins. Flowers clustered at stem tips. Calyces to 0.4 in. long, > pedicel, equally 5-lobed, hairy. Corollas irregular, to 0.7 in. long and wide, 2-lipped, magenta, red-purple, or yellow, with dark lines and blotches, expanded lobes, and hairy tube. Fruits to 0.5 in. long, many-seeded capsules. Has a strong odor (hence the common name).

Diplacus nanus

dwarf monkeyflower

PHRYMACEAE LOPSEED FAMILY

PCT Sections: 10–24 **Abundance:** Locally common **Height:** 0.5–5 in. **Flowering:** April–August **Flower Color:** Magenta or purplish **Habitat-Community:** Open, sandy flats and slopes from woodlands and chaparrals to subalpine coniferous forests **Elevation:** Below 11,300 ft. **Ecoregions:** Sierra Nevada, Cascades, Klamath Mountains

Tufted or mounded annual with hairy herbage. Leaves 0.1–1.2 in. long, opposite, narrowly spoon-shaped to linear, green above and purplish below, with smooth margins. Flowers clustered at stem tips. Calyces to 0.4 in. long, > pedicel, equally 5-lobed, minutely hairy. Corollas irregular, to 0.8 in. long, 2-lipped, magenta or purplish, with hairless tube and 2 yellow folds on throat floor. Fruits to 0.5 in. long, many-seeded capsules. The specific epithet is Latin for "small."

Erythranthe androsacea
rockjasmine monkeyflower
PHRYMACEAE LOPSEED FAMILY

PCT Sections: 1–8 **Abundance:** Locally common **Height:** 0.5–4 in. **Flowering:** March–June **Flower Color:** Pink to purple **Habitat-Community:** Gravelly to sandy soils on gentle slopes and in washes in Joshua tree & pinyon-juniper woodlands **Elevation:** Below 6200 ft. **Ecoregions:** Southern California Mountains, Sierra Nevada

Tiny, ascending annual with minutely hairy stems. Leaves 0.1–0.6 in. long, opposite, lance-shaped to ovoid, with smooth margins. Flowers tubular, sometimes nodding; pedicels 0.2–1.2 in. long. Calyces 5-lobed, somewhat swollen, hairless, 0.1–0.2 in. long. Corollas irregular, 0.1–0.3 in. long, 5-lobed (2 above, 3 below), 2-lipped, pink to purple; throat maroon-blotched with yellow folds. Fruits 0.1–0.2 in. long, ovoid capsules. Excellent displays can be seen along the PCT in the Scodie Mountains near Walker Pass, but timing is everything, as the flowering window may last just 2 weeks.

Erythranthe breweri
Brewer's monkeyflower
PHRYMACEAE LOPSEED FAMILY

PCT Sections: 3–5 & 9–24 **Abundance:** Common **Height:** 1–8 in. **Flowering:** May–August **Flower Color:** Pink to lavender **Habitat-Community:** Moist slopes and streambanks from lower montane to subalpine coniferous forests and wetland-riparian communities **Elevation:** Below 11,200 ft. **Ecoregions:** Southern California Mountains, Sierra Nevada, Cascades, Klamath Mountains

Erect, 1-few-branched annual with glandular-hairy herbage. Leaves to 1.4 in. long, opposite, linear, with generally smooth margins. Flowers inconspicuous, well spaced at stem tips. Calyces to 0.4 in. long, < pedicel, equally 5-lobed, minutely hairy. Corollas irregular, to 0.4 in. long, 2-lipped, pink to lavender, with yellow-ridged lower lip. Fruits to 0.3 in. long, many-seeded capsules. Often occurs in large colonies.

Erythranthe erubescens
pink monkeyflower
PHRYMACEAE LOPSEED FAMILY

PCT Sections: 10–16 **Abundance:** Occasional **Height:** 0.5–3 ft. **Flowering:** June–September **Flower Color:** Pale pink **Habitat-Community:** Moist slopes, meadows, bogs, and streambanks in wetland-riparian communities **Elevation:** Below 11,500 ft. **Ecoregions:** Sierra Nevada

Erect perennial with hairy herbage, spreading from rhizomes. Leaves to 3.5 in. long, opposite, generally clasping stem, ovoid to lance-shaped, with toothed margins. Flowers generally 2 at stem tips. Calyces to 1 in. long, < pedicel, generally equally 5-lobed, hairy. Corollas irregular, to 2 in. long, 2-lipped, pale pink with dark purple veins and (often) maroon dots, with yellow hairy ridges in tube. Fruits to 0.5 in. long, many-seeded capsules. *Erubescens* means "blushing" or "reddening."

Erythranthe palmeri

Palmer's monkeyflower

PHRYMACEAE LOPSEED FAMILY

PCT Sections: 2–6 **Abundance:** Locally common **Height:** 1–7 in. **Flowering:** April–July **Flower Color:** Pink to purple **Habitat-Community:** Gravelly to sandy soils in wetland-riparian communities, chaparrals, oak woodlands, and lower montane coniferous forests **Elevation:** Below 6800 ft. **Ecoregions:** Southern California Mountains

Ascending, small-flowered annual with minutely hairy stems. Leaves 0.1–0.7 in. long, opposite, linear to lance-shaped, with smooth margins. Flowers bilateral, tubular, nodding, with yellow stamens and 5-lobed, ribbed (small hairs at the tips) calyces 0.2–0.3 in. long; pedicels 0.2–1.4 in. long. Corollas 0.4–0.8 in. long, 5-lobed (2 above, 3 below), pink to purple, with narrow throat, spreading lobes, and yellow folds on throat floor. Fruits 0.1–0.2 in. long, ovoid capsules. Primarily distributed in the Transverse Ranges.

Erythranthe parishii

Parish's monkeyflower

PHRYMACEAE LOPSEED FAMILY

PCT Sections: 2–8 **Abundance:** Occasional **Height:** 3–30 in. **Flowering:** May–August **Flower Color:** Pale pink to white **Habitat-Community:** Sandy soils and moist depressions in wetland-riparian communities, foothill chaparrals, and oak & pinyon-juniper woodlands **Elevation:** Below 6400 ft. **Ecoregions:** Southern California Mountains, Sierra Nevada

Ascending, branched annual with hairy stems. Leaves 0.3–2.8 in. long, opposite, spoon-shaped to ovoid, distinctly palmately veined, light green, with smooth margins. Flowers tubular, with white stamens; pedicels 0.6–0.8 in. long; calyces 5-lobed, hairy, 0.3–0.4 in. Corollas irregular, 0.4–0.9 in. long, 5-lobed (2 above, 3 below), 2-lipped, with narrow throat (dark patches on each lobe) and pale pink to white spreading lobes. Fruits 0.3–0.4 in. long, ovoid capsules. Unusual among monkeyflowers in that it is self-pollinated. Populations are usually quite small, limited to a specific spring or riparian corridor.

Erythranthe purpurea

little purple monkeyflower

PHRYMACEAE LOPSEED FAMILY

PCT Sections: 4 **Abundance:** Rare **Height:** 1–3 in. **Flowering:** May–July **Flower Color:** Rose-pink to purple **Habitat-Community:** Sandy soils in shaded flats, washes, and moist understories in montane coniferous forests **Elevation:** 6200–7500 ft. **Ecoregions:** Southern California Mountains

Erect, diminutive annual with slightly hairy stems. Leaves 0.1–0.7 in. long, basal and opposite, elliptic to ovoid. Flowers usually solitary at stem tips, tubular; pedicels 0.7–2.2 in. long; 5-lobed, hairy-tubed (hairless lobes) calyces 0.1–0.3 in. long. Corollas irregular, 0.3–0.6 in. long, 5-lobed (2 above, 3 below), 2-lipped, with red-purple upper lip, rose-pink lower lip, and yellow throat with dark purple patches. Fruits 0.2–0.3 in. long, ovoid capsules. Limited along the PCT to the Big Bear Lake region, where during years of abundant precipitation it grows in dense populations, casting a rosy glow upon the dry understory of pines. Threatened by development, mining, and recreational activities.

Erythranthe rubella

redstem monkeyflower

PHRYMACEAE LOPSEED FAMILY

PCT Sections: 1–5 **Abundance:** Locally common **Height:** 1–12 in. **Flowering:** April–June **Flower Color:** Purple-magenta or yellow **Habitat-Community:** Sandy to rocky soils in Joshua tree & pinyon-juniper woodlands and lower montane coniferous forests **Elevation:** Below 8000 ft. **Ecoregions:** Southern California Mountains

Erect annual with reddish, slightly glandular-hairy stems. Leaves 0.2–1.3 in. long, opposite, linear to elliptic, becoming sessile up the stem. Flowers generally 1 per leaf node, tubular; pedicels 0.2–0.7 in. long; 5-lobed, glandular-hairy calyces 0.2–0.4 in. long with hair-margined lobes. Corollas irregular, 0.3–0.4 in. long, 5-lobed (2 above, 3 below), 2-lipped, with notched lobes purple-magenta or yellow. Fruits 0.2–0.3 in. long, ovoid capsules. *Erythranthe* is Greek for "red flowers."

Antirrhinum thompsonii

chaparral snapdragon

PLANTAGINACEAE PLANTAIN FAMILY

PCT Sections: 4–6 **Abundance:** Occasional **Height:** 1–5 ft. **Flowering:** April–August **Flower Color:** Pink to pale red **Habitat-Community:** Open or disturbed areas in burns or rocky slopes in California prairies, foothill chaparrals, and oak woodlands **Elevation:** Below 6800 ft. **Ecoregions:** Southern California Mountains

Erect, tall (self-supporting) annual or perennial from a woody base, with glandular-hairy, sticky stems. Leaves 0.3–4.1 in. long, opposite near base, becoming alternate on upper stem, sessile, linear to lance-shaped. Flowers in dense spikes, 1 per axil; calyces unequally 5-lobed, 0.2–0.6 in. long. Corollas irregular, 0.6–0.8 in. long, pink to pale red, 2-lipped, short-tubular, with 2-lobed upper lip and swollen lower lip hiding the pistils and stamens. Fruits 0.3–0.5 in. long, ovoid capsules. Seeds remain viable and dormant in the soil for decades, awaiting abundant rains or disturbance, such as fire. *Antirrhinum* (from the Greek, "nose-like") refers to the flower's bulging lower lip.

Penstemon centranthifolius

scarlet bugler

PLANTAGINACEAE PLANTAIN FAMILY

PCT Sections: 1–7 **Abundance:** Common **Height:** 1–4 ft. **Flowering:** April–July **Flower Color:** Red **Habitat-Community:** Dry, open soils from oak woodlands to lower montane coniferous forests **Elevation:** Below 7400 ft. **Ecoregions:** Southern California Mountains, Sierra Nevada

Striking perennial, waxy coated throughout, with long, upright, hairless stems. Leaves 1.6–4 in. long, generally opposite, thick, lance-shaped to ovoid, clasping the stem, gray-green. Flowers often nodding, in well-spaced whorls along the stem, with 4 stamens and hairless staminode; pedicels spreading; calyces 5-lobed, 0.2–0.3 in. long. Corollas irregular, 0.8–1.2 in. long, red, cylindric, 2-lipped (but appearing symmetric), the upper lip 2-lobed, the lower 3-lobed. Fruits small, spheric capsules. Its narrow, tubular flowers are designed for hummingbird pollination.

Penstemon clevelandii

Cleveland's beardtongue

PLANTAGINACEAE

PLANTAIN FAMILY

PCT Sections: 1–3 **Abundance:** Occasional **Height:** 12–28 in. **Flowering:** March–May **Flower Color:** Pink, magenta, or purple **Habitat-Community:** Dry, rocky slopes in Sonoran mixed woody scrubs, pinyon-juniper woodlands, and montane chaparrals **Elevation:** Below 6400 ft. **Ecoregions:** Southern California Mountains

Ascending, much-branched perennial with hairless herbage. Leaves 0.8–2.3 in. long, opposite, thick, dark green, ovoid, the bases sometimes heart-shaped or fused around stem; margins smooth, sometimes toothed. Flowers in whorls along a spike, 5-lobed, with 4 stamens and hairless to hairy staminode; calyces 0.2–0.3 in. long. Corollas irregular, 0.8–1.2 in. long, cylindric, pink, magenta, or purple, 2-lipped (lower side expanded), the upper lip 2-lobed, the lower 3-lobed, with throat 0.2–0.3 in. wide. Fruits small, spheric capsules. Two varieties along the PCT: var. *connatus* (hairy staminode; toothed and fused leaves), a taxon of conservation concern, occurs on the desert slopes of the San Jacinto Mountains; var. *clevelandii* (hairless to sparsely hairy staminode; largely free and entire leaves), the more common taxon, is from San Diego County.

Penstemon eatonii

firecracker penstemon

PLANTAGINACEAE

PLANTAIN FAMILY

PCT Sections: 4 **Abundance:** Occasional **Height:** 1–3 ft. **Flowering:** March–July **Flower Color:** Red **Habitat-Community:** Dry, gravelly to rocky soils in sagebrush scrubs and Joshua tree & pinyon-juniper woodlands **Elevation:** Below 7200 ft. **Ecoregions:** Southern California Mountains

Erect perennial with short-hairy stems. Leaves 1.3–3.5 in. long, basal and generally opposite, widely lance-shaped to ovoid, clasping but not fused around the stem, bright green. Flowers in separated whorls along a spike, 5-lobed, often drooping, with 4 stamens and hairless to sparsely hairy staminode; pedicels spreading; calyces 0.2–0.3 in. long. Corollas irregular, 1.1–1.5 in. long, red, 2-lipped (but appearing symmetric), narrowly cylindric, the upper lip 2-lobed, the lower 3-lobed. Fruits small, spheric capsules. Common throughout the intermountain west, ranging into California only in the semi-arid highlands of San Bernardino County. Named in honor of Yale professor Daniel Eaton (1834–1895), mentor to botanist Sereno Watson.

Penstemon labrosus

San Gabriel beardtongue

PLANTAGINACEAE

PLANTAIN FAMILY

PCT Sections: 1–6 **Abundance:** Locally common **Height:** 12–28 in. **Flowering:** June–August **Flower Color:** Red **Habitat-Community:** Shaded slopes and understories in sagebrush scrubs, pinyon-juniper woodlands, and montane coniferous forests **Elevation:** Below 9500 ft. **Ecoregions:** Southern California Mountains

Slender, erect perennial with hairless stems. Leaves 1.3–3 in. long, opposite, linear, bright green, with margins rolled inward. Flowers in loose, 1-sided spikes, 5-lobed, with 4 stamens and hairless staminode; pedicels short; calyces 0.2 in. long. Corollas irregular, 1.3–1.6 in. long, red, tubular, glandular, 2-lipped, the upper lip 2-lobed and protruding, the lower 3-lobed, prominent, with lobes angled downward. Fruits small, spheric capsules. *Labrosus* (from the Latin, "large lips") refers to the lower corolla lobes.

Penstemon newberryi

mountain pride

PLANTAGINACEAE

PLANTAIN FAMILY

PCT Sections: 9–22 **Abundance:** Common **Height:** 4–12 in. **Flowering:** June–August **Flower Color:** Rose-red to rose-purple **Habitat-Community:** Talus slopes and rocky places, especially granite outcrops, from lower montane to subalpine coniferous forests **Elevation:** Below 12,200 ft. **Ecoregions:** Sierra Nevada, Cascades, Klamath Mountains

Matted perennial to shrub with hairy or hairless, woody (at base) stems. Leaves to 1.6 in. long, generally basal, ovoid, with toothed margins. Flowers clustered at stem tips, with pale yellow-hairy staminode. Calyces to 0.5 in. long, 5-lobed, glandular. Corollas irregular, 0.8–1.4 in. long, 2-lipped, rose-red to rose-purple, glandular outside, hairy inside. Fruits many-seeded capsules. The only rose-red penstemon along the PCT in the Sierra Nevada. The specific epithet honors John Strong Newberry (1822–1892), who made plant collections in California on the Williamson Railroad Survey (1854–56).

Penstemon rostriflorus

Bridge's beardtongue

PLANTAGINACEAE

PLANTAIN FAMILY

PCT Sections: 1–11 **Abundance:** Common **Height:** 12–28 in. **Flowering:** June–August **Flower Color:** Red to orange-red **Habitat-Community:** Dry slopes and openings in sagebrush scrubs, pinyon-juniper woodlands, and montane coniferous forests **Elevation:** Below 11,000 ft. **Ecoregions:** Southern California Mountains, Sierra Nevada

Semi-woody subshrub or perennial, branched from a clumpy base, with finely hairy stems. Leaves 0.8–2.8 in. long, opposite, linear to lance-shaped, with smooth margins. Flowers in loose, generally 1-sided spikes, 5-lobed, with 4 stamens and hairless staminode; pedicels short, glandular; calyces 0.2–0.3 in. long. Corollas irregular, 1–1.5 in. long, tubular, red to orange-red, 2-lipped, with protruding 2-lobed upper lip and recurved 3-lobed lower lip. Fruits small, spheric capsules. Wide-ranging penstemon of the intermountain west, occupying an impressive 10,000 ft. elevational gradient in California!

Loeseliastrum matthewsii

desert calico

POLEMONIACEAE PHLOX FAMILY

PCT Sections: 2–8 **Abundance:** Locally common **Height:** 1–6 in. **Flowering:** March–July **Flower Color:** Pink, lavender, or white **Habitat-Community:** Dry washes and sandy to gravelly alluvium in creosote bush & sagebrush scrubs and Joshua tree & pinyon-juniper woodlands **Elevation:** Below 5800 ft. **Ecoregions:** Southern California Mountains, Mojave Basin and Range, Sierra Nevada

Striking, low-growing, tightly clustered, prickly annual with reddish, white-hairy stems. Leaves 0.4–1.6 in. long, generally alternate, spoon-shaped, with sharply bristle-tipped lobes. Flowers strongly irregular, 5-lobed, with bristle-tipped calyx lobes. Corollas 0.4–0.9 in. long, pink, lavender, or white, with maroon and white blotches at fused base, 2-lipped, the upper lip 3-lobed, 0.2–0.5 in. long, the lower 2-lobed and slightly shorter. Fruits small capsules. This desert plant is named after surgeon and naturalist Washington Matthews (1843–1905).

Scrophularia californica

California figwort

SCROPHULARIACEAE

FIGWORT FAMILY

PCT Sections: 1–4 & 8–10 & 16–18 **Abundance:** Occasional **Height:** 2–4 ft. **Flowering:** March–July **Flower Color:** Red to maroon to yellow-green **Habitat-Community:** Gravelly to rocky substrates in foothill chaparrals, black bush scrubs, oak woodlands, and lower montane coniferous forests **Elevation:** Below 8300 ft. **Ecoregions:** Southern California Mountains, Mojave Basin and Range, Sierra Nevada

Erect perennial or subshrub with 4-sided stems and glandular-hairy herbage. Leaves 3–7 in. long, opposite, triangular-ovoid, with heart-shaped or blunt base and irregularly toothed margins. Flowers 5-lobed, with petals fused at base and mouth constricted; calyces 0.1–0.2 in. long. Corollas irregular, 0.3–0.5 in. long, 2-lipped, with blood red to maroon upper lip and smaller, pale red or yellow-green, strongly reflexed, 3-lobed lower lip. Fruits 0.2–0.3 in. long, capsules. Aka bee plant.

▼ MANY PETALS/SEPALS

Lewisia disepala

Yosemite lewisia

MONTIACEAE

MINER'S LETTUCE FAMILY

PCT Sections: 8–11 **Abundance:** Rare **Height:** to 1.5 in. **Flowering:** March–June **Flower Color:** Pink **Habitat-Community:** Exposed, decomposed granite gravel or sand flats from woodlands to subalpine coniferous forests **Elevation:** Below 11,500 ft. **Ecoregions:** Sierra Nevada

Fleshy perennial with a single flower per stem, held above the leaves. Leaves 0.2–0.8 in. long, basal, rosetted, linear to club-shaped, with blunt tips. Sepals to 0.5 in. long, 2, with smooth to toothed margins. Petals 0.4–0.7 in. long, 5–9, pink, free. Fruits to 0.4 in. long, capsules with dark, generally shiny seeds. Look for this elusive lewisia when snow is still on the ground.

Lewisia pygmaea

alpine lewisia

MONTIACEAE

MINER'S LETTUCE FAMILY

PCT Sections: 10–20 **Abundance:** Occasional **Height:** 1–2 in. **Flowering:** May–August **Flower Color:** Pink, white, or magenta **Habitat-Community:** Rocky slopes, granitic gravel and sand, wet meadows, and streambanks in subalpine coniferous forests and alpine communities **Elevation:** 5600–13,200 ft. **Ecoregions:** Sierra Nevada, Cascades, Klamath Mountains

Fleshy perennial with many, rosetted leaves. Leaves 0.8–3.5 in. long, basal, thread-like to narrowly lance-shaped, with jagged or toothed margins with pale or no glands. Flowers generally 1 per stem, among leaves. Sepals to 0.2 in. long, 2, with gland-toothed margins. Petals to 0.4 in. long, 5–9, pink, white, or magenta, free. Fruits to 0.2 in. long, capsules with 15–24 dark, generally shiny seeds.

Paeonia brownii

mountain peony

PAEONIACEAE PEONY FAMILY

PCT Sections: 1 & 12–18 **Abundance:** Occasional
Height: 8–20 in. **Flowering:** April–June **Flower
Color:** Red to brownish **Habitat-Community:** Open
scrub or forest in sagebrush scrubs, chaparrals,
and lower coniferous forests **Elevation:** Below
9900 ft. **Ecoregions:** Southern California/Northern
Baja Coast, Sierra Nevada, Cascades

Generally clustered perennial with fleshy, white- to blue-waxy-coated leaves. Leaves 1–2.4 in. long, alternate, 5–8 per stem, 2–3-divided into oblong segments. Flowers 1–few, clustered at stem tips. Sepals 5, free, roundish, greenish to purplish. Petals to 0.5 in. long, 5–10, free, reddish to brownish. Fruits to 1.6 in. long with many large, black seeds. *Paeonia* is derived from Paean, physician to the gods of Greek mythology. The roots have a long list of medical uses, including the treatment of nausea and sore throat. Ironically, they also cause nausea if eaten!

Paeonia californica

California peony

PAEONIACEAE PEONY FAMILY

PCT Sections: 1–2 & 4–5 **Abundance:** Occasional
Height: 10–30 in. **Flowering:** January–May
Flower Color: Red to deep blackish red **Habitat-
Community:** Open areas, burns, and dry ridges in
foothill chaparrals and oak woodlands **Elevation:**
4800 ft. **Ecoregions:** Southern California/Northern
Baja Coast, Southern California Mountains

Bushy perennial with hollow, somewhat droopy stems. Leaves 1–4 in. long, 1–3 in. wide, alternate, 8–12 per stem, dissected (into 3 segments) to compound, pale green, hairless, slightly wax-coated. Flowers cup-shaped, rarely opening completely and often drooping downward, with elliptic petals 0.6–1.1 in. across, many stamens, and 2–5 pistils. Sepals 5, free, leathery, 5–10, red to deep blackish red. Fruits 1.2–1.6 in. long follicles with large seeds. Highly fire tolerant, sprouting from its root crown after burns.

BLUE AND PURPLE

▼ COMPOSITE / RAY AND DISK FLOWERS

Corethrogyne filaginifolia

California aster

ASTERACEAE SUNFLOWER FAMILY

PCT Sections: 1–12 **Abundance:** Locally common
Height: 1–3 ft. **Flowering:** July–November
Flower Color: Violet to purple or white **Habitat-
Community:** Slopes, canyons, and disturbed areas
from oak woodlands to lower montane coniferous
forests **Elevation:** Below 8000 ft. **Ecoregions:**
Southern California Mountains, Sierra Nevada

Robust perennial or subshrub, branched from base; stems ascending, white-woolly, with glands near tips. Leaves 0.4–2.5 in. long, alternate, sessile, linear to spoon-shaped, densely woolly, with lobed or toothed margins. Flowers in 1 or more heads per cluster; involucres 0.3–0.6 in. long; phyllaries 30–90 in 4–9 series with hairy, reflexed tips. Ray flowers 0.5 in. long, 10–40 per head, violet to purple or white. Disk flowers 20–110 per head, corolla 0.2–0.3 in. long, yellow. Fruits achenes to 0.2 in. long with many reddish, barbed bristles. An important moth and butterfly host and food plant.

Dieteria canescens

hoary aster

ASTERACEAE SUNFLOWER FAMILY

PCT Sections: 3–5 & 8–24 **Abundance:** Common **Height:** 1–4 ft. **Flowering:** July–October **Flower Color:** Blue or purple **Habitat-Community:** Dry meadows, openings, and streambanks from scrubs, woodlands, and chaparrals to subalpine coniferous forests **Elevation:** Below 11,200 ft. **Ecoregions:** Southern California Mountains, Sierra Nevada, Cascades, Klamath Mountains

Spreading to erect, branched perennial covered with dense, fine, whitish hairs. Leaves 1–4 in. long, linear to ovoid, fine-hairy, uppermost sometimes clasping stem, with smooth to toothed margins. Flower heads in elongated clusters; involucres 0.2–0.5 in. long, with 3–10 series of unequal phyllaries with spreading to reflexed tips. Ray flowers 0.4–0.8 in. long, (0)7–many per head, blue or purple. Disk flowers 0.2–0.3 in. long, many per head, yellow. Fruits achenes with many unequal bristles.

Erigeron algidus

stalked fleabane

ASTERACEAE SUNFLOWER FAMILY

PCT Sections: 10–14 **Abundance:** Common **Height:** 1–12 in. **Flowering:** July–August **Flower Color:** Lavender to pink, blue, or white **Habitat-Community:** Rocky slopes and meadows in subalpine coniferous forests and alpine communities **Elevation:** 8900–12,200 ft. **Ecoregions:** Sierra Nevada

Tufted perennial with unbranched, hairy, glandular stems. Leaves 1–3 in. long, mostly crowded at the base, reduced along stem, spoon-shaped with long petioles, hairy, with smooth margins. Flowers in solitary heads on a leafy stem; involucres cup-shaped with equal, black-purple, hairy, and sometimes glandular phyllaries 0.2–0.3 in. long. Ray flowers 0.2–0.5 in. long, 30–125 per head, lavender to pink, blue, or white. Disk flowers many per head, funnel-shaped, yellow. Fruits to 0.1 in. long, oblong, hairy achenes with 12–20 bristles.

Erigeron barbellulatus

shining fleabane

ASTERACEAE SUNFLOWER FAMILY

PCT Sections: 11–16 **Abundance:** Occasional **Height:** 2–6 in. **Flowering:** June–July **Flower Color:** Purple to white **Habitat-Community:** Rocky or gravelly slopes from sagebrush scrubs to subalpine coniferous forests **Elevation:** Below 10,900 ft. **Ecoregions:** Sierra Nevada

Ascending perennial with short-hairy, unbranched stems. Leaves 0.8–2 in. long, along the lower portion of the stem, alternate, narrowly spoon-shaped, hairy, with hard, white-shiny bases and smooth margins. Flowers 1 per stem; involucres hemispheric, hairy, 0.2–0.4 in. long. Ray flowers to 0.5 in. long, 15–35 per head, purple to white. Disk flowers many per head, narrowly funnel-shaped, yellow. Fruits to 0.1 in. long, generally 2-ribbed achenes, with 25–40 bristles and a few, short outer bristles. The leaf bases inspired the common name.

Erigeron breweri

Brewer's fleabane

ASTERACEAE SUNFLOWER FAMILY

PCT Sections: 3–5 & 8–14 **Abundance:** Common **Height:** 4–12 in. **Flowering:** May–September **Flower Color:** Purple **Habitat-Community:** Rocky slopes from woodlands to subalpine coniferous forests **Elevation:** Below 10,200 ft. **Ecoregions:** Southern California Mountains, Sierra Nevada

Erect to trailing, branched perennial with short-hairy, generally purple stems. Leaves 0.5–1.5 in. long, numerous on stems, alternate, linear to spoon-shaped, hairy, with smooth margins. Flowers 1–10 per stem; phyllaries hairy, sticky or not, with brown midvein. Ray flowers to 0.3 in. long, 0–45 per head, purple. Disk flowers many per head, narrowly funnel-shaped, yellow. Fruits to 0.1 in. long, generally 2-ribbed achenes with 20–50 bristles and a few, short outer bristles.

Erigeron divergens

spreading fleabane

ASTERACEAE SUNFLOWER FAMILY

PCT Sections: 1–5 & 8–17 **Abundance:** Locally common **Height:** 6–18 in. **Flowering:** April–August **Flower Color:** Purple to white **Habitat-Community:** Meadows, slopes, ridges, and disturbed places in montane coniferous forests **Elevation:** Below 8500 ft. **Ecoregions:** Southern California/Northern Baja Coast, Southern California Mountains, Sierra Nevada

Erect biennial with generally branched, hairy stems. Leaves to 2.5 in. long, spoon-shaped, hairy, not clasping, with smooth margins. Flowers 1–many per stem, with equal, hairy, minutely glandular phyllaries. Ray flowers 0.2–0.4 in. long, (0)75–150 per head, purple to white. Disk flowers many per head, funnel-shaped, yellow. Fruits to 0.1 in. long, oblong, 2–4-ribbed, hairy achenes with 6–12 bristles. One of the few non-perennial native daisies along the CA PCT.

Erigeron foliosus

leafy fleabane

ASTERACEAE SUNFLOWER FAMILY

PCT Sections: 1–11 & 22–24 **Abundance:** Locally common **Height:** 8–40 in. **Flowering:** May–September **Flower Color:** Lavender **Habitat-Community:** Rocky slopes, including serpentine, in woodlands, chaparrals, and lower montane coniferous forests **Elevation:** Below 9500 ft. **Ecoregions:** Southern California/Northern Baja Coast, Southern California Mountains, Sierra Nevada

Ascending to erect, branched perennial with hairy or hairless stems and well-distributed foliage. Leaves 0.5–1.5 in. long, numerous on stems, alternate, thread-like or linear to spoon-shaped, hairy or hairless, with smooth margins. Flowers 1–many per stem, with hairy or hairless, glandular, unequal phyllaries in 3–5 graduated series. Ray flowers to 0.6 in. long, 15–60 per head, lavender. Disk flowers many per head, narrowly funnel-shaped, yellow. Fruits to 0.1 in. long, generally 2-ribbed achenes with 20–34 bristles and a few, short outer bristles.

Erigeron glacialis

wandering daisy

ASTERACEAE SUNFLOWER FAMILY

PCT Sections: 10–24 **Abundance:** Common **Height:** 3–18 in. **Flowering:** July–September **Flower Color:** Lavender to blue or white **Habitat-Community:** Rocky slopes, openings, and meadows from lower coniferous forests to alpine communities **Elevation:** 4200–11,200 ft. **Ecoregions:** Sierra Nevada, Cascades, Klamath Mountains

Ascending, branched perennial with sparsely hairy stems. Leaves to 8 in. long, oblong, hairy, clasping, with generally smooth margins (at least the lower stem leaves). Flowers 1–7 per stem; involucres cup-shaped, 0.2–0.4 in. long, with equal, hairy or hairless, minutely glandular phyllaries. Ray flowers 0.4–0.6 in. long, 45–80 per head, lavender to blue or white. Disk flowers many per head, funnel-shaped, yellow. Fruits to 0.1 in. long, oblong, 2–4-ribbed, hairy achenes with 20–30 bristles.

Erigeron pygmaeus

pygmy fleabane

ASTERACEAE SUNFLOWER FAMILY

PCT Sections: 10–13 **Abundance:** Locally common **Height:** to 2.5 in. **Flowering:** July–August **Flower Color:** Blue or purple **Habitat-Community:** Rocky or sandy slopes and ridges in subalpine coniferous forests and alpine communities **Elevation:** 9500–13,500 ft. **Ecoregions:** Sierra Nevada

Tufted perennial with unbranched, hairy, glandular stems. Leaves 0.2–1.4 in. long, generally basal, linear to narrowly spoon-shaped, hairy, glandular, with smooth margins. Flowers in solitary heads; involucres cup-shaped with equal, purple-black, hairy, and densely glandular phyllaries 0.1–0.3 in. long. Ray flowers 0.1–0.4 in. long, 20–37 per head, blue or purple (rarely white). Disk flowers many per head, funnel-shaped, yellow. Fruits to 0.1 in. long, oblong, hairy achenes with 15–25 bristles.

Eurybia integrifolia

thickstem aster

ASTERACEAE SUNFLOWER FAMILY

PCT Sections: 9–18 & 23–24 **Abundance:** Common **Height:** to 2.5 in. **Flowering:** July–September **Flower Color:** Lavender to purple **Habitat-Community:** Dry meadows and openings from lower montane to subalpine coniferous forests **Elevation:** 5200–10,500 ft. **Ecoregions:** Sierra Nevada, Cascades, Klamath Mountains

Erect, colony-forming perennial with glandular upper stems. Leaves 2–9 in. long, basal and along stem, ovoid, hairy, glandular, short-petioled, with smooth margins. Flowers in elongated clusters; involucres bell-shaped with 3–4 graduated series of densely glandular phyllaries, the inner generally with purple tips. Ray flowers 0.4–0.6 in. long, 8–27 per head, lavender to purple. Disk flowers many per head, tube < throat, yellow (pink- to purple-tinged). Fruits densely short-hairy achenes with pappus bristles. *Eurybia* is Greek for "wide" and "few," for leaves or rays for some species in the genus.

Oreostemma alpigenum
var. andersonii

alpine aster

ASTERACEAE SUNFLOWER FAMILY

PCT Sections: 3 & 9–24 **Abundance:** Locally common **Height:** 2–16 in. **Flowering:** June–September **Flower Color:** Purple to white **Habitat-Community:** Meadows, lakeshores, and streambanks in wetland-riparian communities **Elevation:** Below 11,500 ft. **Ecoregions:** Southern California Mountains, Sierra Nevada, Cascades, Klamath Mountains

Decumbent to erect, colony-forming perennial with hairy upper stems. Leaves 2–9 in. long, mostly basal, grass-like, hairy or hairless, with smooth margins. Flowers in solitary heads; involucres top-shaped with 3–4 equal series of phyllaries. Ray flowers to 0.6 in. long, 10–40 per head, purple to white. Disk flowers to 0.4 in. long, tubular, yellow. Fruits to 0.2 in. long, hairy achenes with pappus bristles. Easy to spot, especially when you come to a meadow with a large, showy colony.

Symphyotrichum ascendens

longleaf aster

ASTERACEAE SUNFLOWER FAMILY

PCT Sections: 3–5 & 9–18 **Abundance:** Occasional **Height:** 8–24 in. **Flowering:** July–September **Flower Color:** Violet **Habitat-Community:** Meadows and disturbed habitats from woodlands to upper montane coniferous forests **Elevation:** Below 8200 ft. **Ecoregions:** Southern California Mountains, Sierra Nevada

Erect, many-branched perennial with leafy stems uniformly hairy just below the flower heads. Leaves 2–6 in. long, spoon-shaped, hairy or hairless, with smooth margins. Flowers in many-headed, elongated clusters; involucres hemispheric with 2–6 graduated or equal series of green-tipped phyllaries, outer phyllaries obtuse. Ray flowers to 0.6 in. long, 15–40 per head, violet. Disk flowers 4–60+ per head, tube < throat, yellow. Fruits hairy achenes with pappus bristles.

Symphyotrichum spathulatum

western mountain aster

ASTERACEAE SUNFLOWER FAMILY

PCT Sections: 3–4 & 9–24 **Abundance:** Locally common **Height:** 8–30 in. **Flowering:** June–September **Flower Color:** Violet **Habitat-Community:** Meadows in wetland-riparian communities **Elevation:** Below 9200 ft. **Ecoregions:** Southern California Mountains, Sierra Nevada, Cascades, Klamath Mountains

Erect, many-branched, leafy-stemmed perennial, with few to no hairs on stems just below the flower heads. Leaves 2–6 in. long, linear to narrowly oval, generally hairless, with smooth margins. Flowers in many-headed, elongated clusters; involucres hemispheric with 2–6 graduated or equal series of green-tipped phyllaries, outer phyllaries obtuse. Ray flowers to 0.5 in. long, 15–40 per head, violet. Disk flowers 4–60+ per head, tube < throat, yellow. Fruits hairy achenes with pappus bristles.

▼ COMPOSITE / DISK FLOWERS ONLY

Cirsium andersonii

rose thistle

ASTERACEAE SUNFLOWER FAMILY

PCT Sections: 10–24 **Abundance:** Occasional **Height:** 6–40 in. **Flowering:** July–October **Flower Color:** Rose-purple **Habitat-Community:** Open sites, including serpentine soils, from woodlands and chaparrals to subalpine coniferous forests **Elevation:** Below 10,300 ft. **Ecoregions:** Sierra Nevada, Cascades, Klamath Mountains

Perennial with hairy or hairless stems and whitish foliage. Leaves 3–14 in. long, green above, gray-hairy below, with spiny-winged petioles and spine-tipped lobes. Disk flowers 1–1.8 in. long, 1–few heads per stem, rose-purple; phyllaries spiny-margined with a purple spine at tip. Fruits to 0.3 in. long, achenes with many bristles. Bumblebees and other flying insects are the main pollinators of this and most thistles; ants are repelled by stem hairs.

▼ 3 OR 6 PETALS/TEPALS

Allium fimbriatum var. *fimbriatum*

fringed onion

ALLIACEAE ONION FAMILY

PCT Sections: 1–8 **Abundance:** Locally common **Height:** 4–10 in. **Flowering:** April–June **Flower Color:** Dark purple to red-purple or white **Habitat-Community:** Dry slopes and flats in chaparrals, oak woodlands, and montane coniferous forests **Elevation:** Below 8400 ft. **Ecoregions:** Southern California Mountains, Sierra Nevada

Perennial with leafless stems arising from a bulb 0.4–0.7 in. across. Leaves 6–15 in. long, basal, 1 per stem, cylindric. Flowers 6–35, in an umbel; pedicels 0.3–0.8 in. long. Tepals 0.3–0.8 in. long, 6-parted (3 sepals, 3 petals), radial, free, recurved, dark purple to red-purple or white. Fruits capsules with ≤6 seeds. *Fimbriatum* ("fringed") refers to the deeply cut or toothed ridges on top of the ovary.

Iris missouriensis

western blue flag

IRIDACEAE IRIS FAMILY

PCT Sections: 1 & 4 & 15–24 **Abundance:** Occasional **Height:** 8–20 in. **Flowering:** May–July **Flower Color:** Blue to lavender to white **Habitat-Community:** Seasonally moist flats and meadows from oak woodlands to subalpine coniferous forests and wetland-riparian communities **Elevation:** Below 10,800 ft. **Ecoregions:** Southern California Mountains, Sierra Nevada, Cascades, Klamath Mountains

Showy, rhizomatous perennial, often growing in clonal colonies, with rarely branched stems. Leaves 6–14 in. long, 0.4 in. wide, 2-ranked in a basal fan, with 1–2 reduced stem leaves. Flowers in flattened clusters of 2–3 with outer bracts (spathes) 1.6–3 in. long. Tepals 1.4–2.9 in. long, 6-parted (3 sepals, 3 petals), blue to lavender to white with purple veins, with recurved outer perianth tips, sepals wider than petals, and irregularly toothed margins; floral tube green, funnel-shaped. Fruits to 2 in. long, 3-chambered capsules. The only iris east of the Sierra Nevada and Cascades, ranging throughout western North America. Thrives in very wet springs, followed by very dry summers.

Sisyrinchium bellum

western blue-eyed grass

IRIDACEAE IRIS FAMILY

PCT Sections: All **Abundance:** Occasional **Height:** 4–20 in. **Flowering:** March–June **Flower Color:** Blue-purple to violet **Habitat-Community:** Moist soils from California prairies to lower montane coniferous forests and wetland-riparian communities **Elevation:** Below 8000 ft. **Ecoregions:** All (except Sonoran/Mojave Basin and Range)

Lovely little tufted perennial with flat, bright green stems and compact rhizomes. Leaves grass-like, basal leaves flattened, stem leaves overlapping. Flowers grouped in open clusters, subtended by 2 bracts with distinctive translucent margins; stamens 3. Tepals 0.4–0.7 in. long, 6-parted (3 sepals, 3 petals), free, blue-purple to violet (occasionally white). Fruits 3-chambered capsules. The most widespread sisyrinchium in California but infrequent along the CA PCT. *Bellum* means "handsome" in Latin.

Sisyrinchium idahoense

Idaho blue-eyed grass

IRIDACEAE IRIS FAMILY

PCT Sections: 2–5 & 8–21 **Abundance:** Common **Height:** 4–18 in. **Flowering:** June–August **Flower Color:** Blue to blue-violet **Habitat-Community:** Meadows in wetland-riparian communities **Elevation:** Below 9400 ft. **Ecoregions:** Southern California Mountains, Sierra Nevada, Cascades, Klamath Mountains

Tufted perennial with slender, winged, leafless, mostly unbranched stems. Leaves to 0.1 in. wide, basal (mostly) and alternate, grass-like, 2-ranked, flat. Flowers at stem tips. Tepals to 0.8 in. long, 6-parted (3 sepals, 3 petals), blue to blue-violet with yellow base, sepals and petals alike. Fruits to 0.3 in. wide, sparsely hairy, 3-chambered capsules with black seeds. Plants need sunlight for the flowers to open.

Fritillaria atropurpurea

spotted missionbells

LILIACEAE LILY FAMILY

PCT Sections: 9–24 **Abundance:** Common **Height:** 4–24 in. **Flowering:** April–July **Flower Color:** Purple-brown **Habitat-Community:** Leaf mold under trees, from lower montane to subalpine coniferous forests **Elevation:** Below 10,500 ft. **Ecoregions:** Sierra Nevada, Cascades, Klamath Mountains

Erect, unbranched perennial. Leaves to 4.7 in. long, 2–3 per node, whorled or alternate, linear to lance-shaped, generally with a pointed tip. Flowers generally 1–4 per plant, nodding, symmetric. Tepals to 1 in. long, 6-parted (3 sepals, 3 petals), purple-brown with yellow or white mottling; perianth bell-shaped, sepals and petals alike, oblong to diamond-shaped, with 6 stamens and 3-branched style. Fruits to 0.7 in. long, capsules with many brown seeds. *Fritillaria* ("dicebox") describes the shape of the fruits.

Fritillaria pinetorum

pinewoods missionbells

LILIACEAE LILY FAMILY

PCT Sections: 4–5 & 8–12 **Abundance:** Rare **Height:** 4–16 in. **Flowering:** May–July **Flower Color:** Purple **Habitat-Community:** Open or shaded granitic soils from lower montane to subalpine coniferous forests **Elevation:** Below 10,500 ft. **Ecoregions:** Southern California Mountains, Sierra Nevada

Erect, unbranched perennial with blue- to white-waxy-coated herbage. Leaves to 6 in. long, 2–3 per node, whorled or alternate, linear, above or level with flowers. Flowers 3–9 per plant, erect to spreading, symmetric. Tepals to 0.8 in. long, 6-parted (3 sepals, 3 petals), purple with green-yellow mottling; perianth bowl-shaped, sepals and petals alike, widely ovoid, with 6 stamens and 3-branched style. Fruits to 0.6 in. long, capsules with many brown seeds. *Pinetorum* refers to its association with pine woods.

Brodiaea elegans

harvest brodiaea

THEMIDACEAE BRODIAEA FAMILY

PCT Sections: 4 & 14–24 **Abundance:** Occasional **Height:** 4–20 in. **Flowering:** April–August **Flower Color:** Violet to blue-purple **Habitat-Community:** Meadows, grassy slopes, and open understories, including serpentine soils, in woodlands and lower montane coniferous forests **Elevation:** Below 8000 ft. **Ecoregions:** Southern California Mountains, Sierra Nevada, Cascades, Klamath Mountains

Erect, unbranched perennial. Leaves to 20 in. long and 0.1 in. wide, basal, grass-like, withering before flowers open. Flowers few, openly clustered at stem tip, erect, symmetric. Tepals to 1.9 in. long, 6-parted (3 sepals, 3 petals), violet to blue-purple with curved-back lobes; perianth funnel-shaped, petals wider than sepals, with 3 erect staminodes, 3 stamens, and 3-lobed stigma. Fruits capsules with ridged, oblong, black seeds. Genus named for James Brodie (1744–1824), Scottish botanist.

Brodiaea terrestris subsp. *kernensis*

Kern brodiaea

THEMIDACEAE BRODIAEA FAMILY

PCT Sections: 1 & 3–5 **Abundance:** Rare **Height:** 1–8 in. **Flowering:** April–June **Flower Color:** Violet to purple-blue **Habitat-Community:** Heavy soils and dry meadows from California prairies to lower montane coniferous forests **Elevation:** Below 6600 ft. **Ecoregions:** Southern California Mountains

Striking perennial with slender, straight, leafless stems from a corm. Leaves 1–7 in. long, usually <5, basal, linear, crescent-shaped in cross section. Flowers few, in open head-like cluster, radial, narrowly bell-shaped, with 3 stamens; pedicels 0.2–0.3 in. long. Tepals 1.1–1.4 in. long, 6-parted (3 sepals, 3 petals), fused at base forming an obvious tube, violet to purple-blue, often white in throat and tube. Fruits erect capsules. Occurs in Kern County, just west of the PCT. Best observed along the PCT in the Laguna and San Jacinto Mountains of the Peninsular Ranges.

Boechera arcuata

arching rockcress

BRASSICACEAE MUSTARD FAMILY

PCT Sections: 1–9 **Abundance:** Occasional **Height:** 12–32 in. **Flowering:** March–June **Flower Color:** Bright purple **Habitat-Community:** Rocky slopes and crevices in boulders from oak woodlands to lower montane coniferous forests **Elevation:** Below 6400 ft. **Ecoregions:** Southern California Mountains, Sierra Nevada

Single-stemmed perennial from a woody base, with hairy lower stem. Leaves 0.1–1 in. long, mostly basal, lobed at base, spoon-shaped to oblong, with slightly toothed margins. Flowers 1-sided along stem to tip, 12–70, erect, 4-parted, with hairy sepals and bright purple petals 0.4–0.7 in. long. Fruits linear, spreading to ascending, sparsely hairy siliques with 1 row of seeds. Find it along the PCT at the Kwaaymii Point lookout area atop the Laguna Mountains in San Diego County.

Boechera howellii

Howell's pioneer rockcress

BRASSICACEAE MUSTARD FAMILY

PCT Sections: 10–20 **Abundance:** Locally common **Height:** 2–8 in. **Flowering:** June–August **Flower Color:** Purplish to white **Habitat-Community:** Rocky outcrops or slopes and gravelly soils from upper montane coniferous forests to alpine communities **Elevation:** 5900–12,500 ft. **Ecoregions:** Sierra Nevada, Cascades, Klamath Mountains

Erect perennial from a woody base, with single hairless stem from a basal rosette. Leaves 0.8–2 in. long, basal and 2–4 alternate, narrowly spoon-shaped, with hairs only along the smooth margins. Flowers 2–5 in elongated displays at stem tips, with hairless sepals and purplish to white petals 0.2–0.3 in. long; pedicels hairless, ascending. Fruits 1–2.5 in. long, to 0.8 in. wide, ascending to erect, hairless siliques with 1 row of seeds.

Boechera inyoensis

Inyo rockcress

BRASSICACEAE MUSTARD FAMILY

PCT Sections: 8–13 **Abundance:** Occasional **Height:** 10–26 in. **Flowering:** April–June **Flower Color:** Lavender to purplish **Habitat-Community:** Rocky slopes and outcrops, including limestone and volcanic, from scrubs and woodlands to subalpine coniferous forests **Elevation:** Below 13,100 ft. **Ecoregions:** Sierra Nevada

Erect, short-lived perennial, with single hairy stem from a basal rosette. Leaves 0.8–1.2 in. long, basal and cauline, spoon-shaped, hairy, with smooth margins. Flowers in elongated displays at stem tips, with hairy sepals and lavender to purplish petals 0.2–0.3 in. long; pedicels spreading-ascending to horizontal, hairy. Fruits 1.5–6.5 in. long, to 0.1 in. wide, spreading-ascending to widely pendent, hairless siliques with generally 2 rows of seeds.

Boechera johnstonii

Johnston's rockcress

BRASSICACEAE MUSTARD FAMILY

PCT Sections: 1 & 3 **Abundance:** Rare **Height:** 4–12 in. **Flowering:** February–March **Flower Color:** Purple **Habitat-Community:** Rocky areas and gravelly soils in lower montane coniferous forests and montane chaparrals **Elevation:** Below 6200 ft. **Ecoregions:** Southern California Mountains

Perennial with a single hairy stem from a woody base. Leaves 0.1–0.3 in. long, mostly basal, narrowly spoon-shaped, hairy. Flowers along stem to tip, 10–18, 4-parted, with hairy sepals and purple petals 0.4–0.7 in. long. Fruits 1–3 in. long, up to 0.2 in. wide, linear, spreading to ascending, hairless siliques with 1 row of seeds. Endemic to the San Jacinto and Laguna Mountains in the Peninsular Ranges, known from only 10 occurrences.

Boechera parishii

Parish's rockcress

BRASSICACEAE MUSTARD FAMILY

PCT Sections: 4 **Abundance:** Rare **Height:** 2–8 in. **Flowering:** April–June **Flower Color:** Lavender to purple **Habitat-Community:** Rocky or gravelly soils, sometimes limestone, from sagebrush scrubs and pinyon-juniper woodlands to upper montane coniferous forests **Elevation:** 6000–8600 ft. **Ecoregions:** Southern California Mountains

Single-stemmed perennial from a semi-woody base, hairy on lower stems. Leaves 0.1–0.2 in. long, mostly basal, linear to narrowly spoon-shaped, hairy. Flowers along stem to tip, 5–20, 4-parted, ascending, with dark purple, hairy sepals and bright lavender to purple petals 0.3–0.6 in. long. Fruits 1 in. long, up to 0.1 in. wide, linear, ascending, hairless siliques with 1 row of seeds. Endemic to the pebble plains region of the San Bernardino Mountains. Threatened by recreational activities, limestone mining, and fire management.

Boechera pulchra

beautiful rockcress

BRASSICACEAE MUSTARD FAMILY

PCT Sections: 1–9 **Abundance:** Occasional **Height:** 12–30 in. **Flowering:** March–June **Flower Color:** Purple to pink **Habitat-Community:** Rocky to gravelly slopes, dry ridges, and canyons from sagebrush scrubs to lower montane coniferous forests **Elevation:** Below 9000 ft. **Ecoregions:** Southern California Mountains, Mojave Basin and Range, Sierra Nevada

Single-stemmed, long-lived perennial from a woody base, hairy on lower stems. Basal leaves 1–2 in. long, linear to narrowly lance-shaped, hairy; stem leaves 10–30, lacking basal lobes. Flowers sometimes 1-sided along stem to tip, 8–25, 4-parted, with hairy sepals and purple to pink petals 0.4–0.7 in. long. Fruits 1.5–3.1 in. long, up to 0.2 in. wide, strongly reflexed, hairy siliques with 2 rows of seeds. Most common along the PCT at mid-elevations in the Transverse Ranges and far southern Sierra. *Pulchra* means "beautiful" in Latin.

Boechera retrofracta

reflexed rockcress

BRASSICACEAE MUSTARD FAMILY

PCT Sections: All (except 1–2 & 6–7) **Abundance:** Occasional **Height:** 10–40 in. **Flowering:** April-August **Flower Color:** Lavender to white **Habitat-Community:** Rock outcrops, sandy flats, and shaded understories in sagebrush scrubs, oak woodlands, and montane coniferous forests **Elevation:** Below 10,500 ft. **Ecoregions:** All (except Sonoran/Mojave Basin and Range)

Short-lived perennial from a semi-woody base, with a single, densely hairy stem per rosette. Basal leaves 0.5–1.8 in. long, spoon-shaped, hairy, sometimes with toothed margins; stem leaves 15–40, with basal lobes. Flowers 15–140 at stem tips, 4-parted, with hairy sepals and lavender to white petals 0.1–0.3 in. long. Fruits 1.5–3.5 in. long, to 0.1 in. wide, hairless to sparsely hairy siliques, strongly reflexed, often appressed (to stem). Widespread, from Quebec to Alaska!

Boechera shockleyi

Shockley's rockcress

BRASSICACEAE MUSTARD FAMILY

PCT Sections: 4 **Abundance:** Rare **Height:** 8–20 in. **Flowering:** April–May **Flower Color:** Lavender **Habitat-Community:** Rocky to gravelly slopes, usually on limestone, in sagebrush scrubs, pinyon-juniper woodlands, and montane coniferous forests **Elevation:** Below 8200 ft. **Ecoregions:** Southern California Mountains

Short-lived perennial with thick, hairy (especially on the lower portion) single stem. Leaves 1–3 in. long, up to 0.5 in. wide, gray-green with dense, fine hairs; basal leaves spoon-shaped, hairy; stem leaves 14–60, lobed at base, angled upward, concealing the stem for most of its length. Flowers along stem to tip, 20–70, 4-parted, with hairy sepals and lavender petals 0.2–0.4 in. long. Fruits 2–5 in. long, to 0.1 in. wide, spreading to ascending, straight to arched, hairless to sparsely hairy siliques with 2 rows of seeds. Occurs along the PCT only in the San Bernardino Mountains on limestone outcrops above Big Bear and Baldwin lakes.

Caulanthus amplexicaulis

clasping-leaved caulanthus

BRASSICACEAE MUSTARD FAMILY

PCT Sections: 4–6 **Abundance:** Occasional **Height:** 16–42 in. **Flowering:** April-August **Flower Color:** Purple to straw-colored **Habitat-Community:** Open, sandy to rocky areas, including granitic scree, in chaparrals, oak woodlands, and montane coniferous forests **Elevation:** Below 9200 ft. **Ecoregions:** Southern California Mountains

Erect annual, hairless and wax-coated throughout. Leaves 1–4 in. long, basal (rosette) and cauline (alternate), widely spoon-shaped to oval, reduced toward stem tip, clasping, olive-green to brown, with smooth or toothed margins. Flowers few at stem tip, 4-parted. Sepals hairless, purple, somewhat bulbous or inflated. Petals pale purple to straw-colored, reflexed, 0.4–0.7 in. long. Fruits 2–6 in. long, to 0.1 in. wide, spreading to ascending, cylindric, straight or curvy siliques. Endemic to the Transverse Ranges. A rare white-sepaled form occurs in Santa Barbara County. *Amplexicaulis* (from the Latin, "clasping the stem") is a fitting description of the leaves.

Caulanthus coulteri

Coulter's jewelflower

BRASSICACEAE MUSTARD FAMILY

PCT Sections: 5–9 **Abundance:** Locally common **Height:** 0.5–5 ft. **Flowering:** March–July **Flower Color:** Purple or white **Habitat-Community:** Dry, open slopes in chaparrals and woodlands **Elevation:** Below 6900 ft. **Ecoregions:** Southern California Mountains, Mojave Basin and Range, Sierra Nevada

Erect annual with simple and forked hairs on the stems and leaves. Leaves 0.4–7 in. long, basal and cauline (clasping the stem), oblong to spoon-shaped, unlobed to pinnately lobed, with smooth to toothed margins. Flowers in elongated clusters at stem tips, with purple (brown or yellow-green at base) sepals to 0.8 in. long and purple or white petals 0.3–1.2 in. long. Fruits 1.4–6 in. long, 0.1–0.2 in. wide, spreading to reflexed, cylindric siliques with 70–96 seeds. Named for botanist John Coulter (1851–1928). This purple jewel of the PCT is impossible to miss, even at your fastest pace. You barely need to slow down to enjoy it.

Caulanthus heterophyllus

San Diego wild cabbage

BRASSICACEAE MUSTARD FAMILY

PCT Sections: 1–4 **Abundance:** Locally common **Height:** 10–40 in. **Flowering:** March–May **Flower Color:** Purple to light yellow **Habitat-Community:** Dry openings or burns in foothill chaparrals and oak woodlands **Elevation:** Below 5800 ft. **Ecoregions:** Southern California Mountains

Erect annual, bristly hairy near base of stem, branching and hairless above. Leaves 1–3 in. long, basal and alternate; rosette leaves narrowly spoon-shaped, with coarsely toothed or pinnately lobed margins; stem leaves narrowly lance-shaped, clasping, reduced, with toothed or smooth margins. Flowers 4-parted, urn-shaped, hairless, with purple or creamy yellow sepals and reflexed, purple to cream petals 0.2–0.6 in. long. Fruits 2–4 in. long, reflexed, 4-angled, straight (rarely curvy) siliques. Native to Baja and southern California, extending from the immediate coast to the mountains. Especially abundant in recent burns.

Caulanthus pilosus

chocolate drops

BRASSICACEAE MUSTARD FAMILY

PCT Sections: 8–10 **Abundance:** Rare **Height:** 1–5 ft. **Flowering:** March–July **Flower Color:** Purple to greenish, white or purplish **Habitat-Community:** Dry, open rocky or sandy slopes in woodlands **Elevation:** Below 9200 ft. **Ecoregions:** Sierra Nevada

Erect to ascending annual with moderately to densely hairy stems, especially below. Leaves 1–10 in. long, pinnately lobed, oblong to narrowly spoon-shaped, with toothed margins. Flowers in elongated clusters at stem tips, with purple to greenish sepals to 0.4 in. long and white or purplish petals 0.3–0.5 in. long. Fruits 0.8–7 in. long, to 0.1 in. wide, ascending to spreading, cylindric siliques with 152–198 seeds. A true treat to find along the trail, but don't eat them!

Phoenicaulis cheiranthoides

daggerpod

BRASSICACEAE MUSTARD FAMILY

PCT Sections: 11–24 **Abundance:** Occasional **Height:** 3–12 in. **Flowering:** April–June **Flower Color:** Purple to pink **Habitat-Community:** Dry rocky or sandy soils from sagebrush scrubs to subalpine coniferous forests **Elevation:** Below 10,900 ft. **Ecoregions:** Sierra Nevada, Cascades, Klamath Mountains

Clumped, single-stemmed (sometimes branched near tip) perennial from a woody base with a basal rosette of whitish leaves. Leaves 0.7–4 in. long, to 1 in. wide, spoon-shaped, hairy, lobed at base, with smooth margins. Flowers in elongated displays on horizontal stems, with hairy sepals and purple to pink petals 0.3–0.6 in. long; pedicels spreading. Fruits 0.7–3.6 in. long, to 0.3 in. wide, flat, hairless, dagger-like siliques with 1 row of 6–18 seeds. The stem, with its remnants of petioles, resembles a palm trunk covered with leaves (hence *Phoenicaulis*, "palm stem").

Streptanthus campestris

southern jewelflower

BRASSICACEAE MUSTARD FAMILY

PCT Sections: 1–6 **Abundance:** Rare **Height:** 2–6 ft. **Flowering:** May–June **Flower Color:** Purple **Habitat-Community:** Open, rocky areas and gravelly slopes from oak woodlands to lower montane coniferous forests **Elevation:** Below 8000 ft. **Ecoregions:** Southern California Mountains

Erect perennial with 1–few branches and hairless, wax-coated stems. Basal leaves 3–7 in. long, spoon-shaped, short-hairy, with smooth to wavy, toothed margins. Cauline leaves 1–4 in. long, reduced up the stem, lance-shaped to ovoid, with bases lobed or clasping the stem. Flowers 4-parted, bell-shaped, with purple calyx and purple petals 0.3–0.6 in. long. Fruits 0.3–0.7 in. long, to 0.1 in. wide, ascending to spreading, straight or curved, flattened, smooth siliques. *Streptanthus* ("twisted flower") refers to the wavy-margined petals.

Streptanthus cordatus

heartleaf jewelflower

BRASSICACEAE MUSTARD FAMILY

PCT Sections: 8–9 & 14–17 **Abundance:** Locally common **Height:** 0.5–3 ft. **Flowering:** April–July **Flower Color:** Purple **Habitat-Community:** Open, rocky soils, including serpentine, in woodlands and lower montane coniferous forests **Elevation:** Below 10,200 ft. **Ecoregions:** Sierra Nevada

Perennial with hairless, 1–few-branched stems covered with a whitish or bluish, waxy coating. Leaves to 3.5 in. long, basal and cauline (lobed or clasping the stem), roundish to spoon-shaped, with smooth to toothed margins. Flowers in elongated, open clusters at stem tips, with purple sepals to 0.5 in. long and purple petals 0.3–0.6 in. long. Fruits 2–4 in. long, to 0.3 in. wide, ascending to spreading siliques with 20–38 seeds. Variety *cordatus* is common along the trail, var. *piutensis* found in the southern Sierra at mile 645–650.

Streptanthus gracilis

alpine jewelflower

BRASSICACEAE MUSTARD FAMILY

PCT Sections: 10 **Abundance:** Rare **Height:** 2–14 in. **Flowering:** July–August **Flower Color:** Rose-purple **Habitat-Community:** Open, rocky soils in upper montane & subalpine coniferous forests **Elevation:** 8500–11,900 ft. **Ecoregions:** Sierra Nevada

Slender annual with hairless, generally branched stems. Leaves 0.2–1.2 in. long, basal and cauline (lobed or clasping the stem), spoon-shaped, with smooth to toothed margins. Flowers in elongated, open clusters at stem tips, with rose-purple sepals to 0.2 in. long and purple petals 0.3–0.4 in. long. Fruits 1–3 in. long, to 0.1 in. wide, cylindric, ascending siliques with 24–52 seeds. The only high-elevation annual jewelflower in the Sierra.

Streptanthus tortuosus

mountain jewelflower

BRASSICACEAE MUSTARD FAMILY

PCT Sections: 10–24 **Abundance:** Common **Height:** 2–48 in. **Flowering:** April–September **Flower Color:** Purple, greenish, or yellow **Habitat-Community:** Rocky, sandy, or serpentine soils, and rock outcrops in chaparrals, woodlands, and lower montane coniferous forests **Elevation:** Below 13,500 ft. **Ecoregions:** Sierra Nevada, Cascades, Klamath Mountains

Biennial or short-lived perennial with hairless, 1-many-branched stems. Leaves 0.2–2.5 in. long, roundish to ovoid or oblong, clasping, with smooth to toothed margins. Flowers in elongated, open to dense clusters at stem tips, with purple (greenish or yellow) sepals to 0.5 in. long, and purple or yellow-white petals 0.2–0.5 in. long. Fruits 1–6 in. long, to 0.1 in. wide, cylindric, spreading to pendent siliques with 26–76 seeds. The most common jewelflower along the PCT.

Gentianopsis holopetala

Sierra fringed gentian

GENTIANACEAE GENTIAN FAMILY

PCT Sections: 10–16 **Abundance:** Locally common **Height:** 1–18 in. **Flowering:** July–September **Flower Color:** Blue **Habitat-Community:** Wet meadows, fens, and bogs in wetland-riparian communities **Elevation:** 5900–13,200 ft. **Ecoregions:** Sierra Nevada

Decumbent to erect annual with 1-few, hairless stems. Leaves to 2.8 in. long, basal and opposite, spoon- or lance-shaped to linear, with smooth margins. Flowers 1 per stem or branch. Calyces to 1.4 in. long, 4-lobed. Corollas to 2.2 in. long, blue, funnel-shaped, with 4 ovoid or oblong, smooth to barely toothed lobes. Fruits many-seeded capsules. Gentian schnapps is a popular European alpine liqueur.

Gentianopsis simplex

one-flower fringed gentian

GENTIANACEAE GENTIAN FAMILY

PCT Sections: 4 & 10–22 **Abundance:** Occasional **Height:** 4–8 in. **Flowering:** July–September **Flower Color:** Blue **Habitat-Community:** Wet meadows in wetland-riparian communities **Elevation:** Below 11,200 ft. **Ecoregions:** Southern California Mountains, Sierra Nevada, Cascades, Klamath Mountains

Erect annual with 1 hairless stem. Leaves to 1 in. long, basal (withering early) and opposite, spoon- or lance-shaped, with smooth margins. Flowers 1 per stem or branch (hence *simplex*). Calyces to 1 in. long, 4-lobed. Corollas to 1.8 in. long, blue, funnel-shaped, 4-lobed, the lobes with toothed, jagged, or fringed margins. Fruits many-seeded capsules. Aka hiker's gentian.

Clarkia purpurea

winecup clarkia

ONAGRACEAE

EVENING-PRIMROSE FAMILY

PCT Sections: 1–7 & 16–24 **Abundance:** Locally common **Height:** 10–40 in. **Flowering:** April–August **Flower Color:** Lavender to purple **Habitat-Community:** Open, sandy to clayey soils in California prairies, foothill chaparrals, and oak woodlands **Elevation:** Below 5000 ft. **Ecoregions:** All

Few-branched, wispy annual with reddish, hairless to short-hairy stems. Leaves 0.7–2.8 in. long, alternate, linear to elliptic, green, with smooth margins. Flowers from erect buds displayed in loose spikes, with inferior ovary, 8 stamens, and 4-lobed stigma. Hypanthium cup-shaped, 0.1 in. long; corolla bowl-shaped. Sepals 4, remaining fused in 2s at tip or free. Petals 4, fan-shaped, 0.7–1.1 in. long, lavender to purple (or dark wine with purple spots). Fruits 0.6–1.1 in. long, elongated, cylindric capsules, straight and erect along the vertical stem. More common along the trail in the southern half of the state.

Veronica americana

American speedwell

PLANTAGINACEAE

PLANTAIN FAMILY

PCT Sections: 4 & 8–24 **Abundance:** Common **Height:** 2–24 in. **Flowering:** May–August **Flower Color:** Bluish **Habitat-Community:** Meadows, springs, streambanks, and lakeshores in wetland-riparian communities **Elevation:** Below 10,900 ft. **Ecoregions:** Southern California Mountains, Sierra Nevada, Cascades, Klamath Mountains

Sprawling to ascending perennial with hairless stems rooting at the lower leaf nodes. Leaves to 2 in. long, opposite, lance-shaped to ovoid, hairless, with toothed margins. Flowers mostly symmetric, in long sprays at stem tips, with 2 stamens. Sepals to 0.1 in. long, 4, free, generally unequal. Corollas 0.2–0.4 in. long, 4-lobed, bluish (dark-lined), lower portion fused into a tube. Fruits to 0.2 in. long, round to heart-shaped capsules. The genus is named for Saint Veronica. The edible leaves make a tasty salad green.

Lomatium shevockii

Owens Peak desertparsley

APIACEAE CARROT FAMILY

PCT Sections: 9 **Abundance:** Rare **Height:** 1–5 in. **Flowering:** April–May **Flower Color:** Purple **Habitat-Community:** Rocky places from woodlands to upper montane coniferous forests **Elevation:** 7200–8200 ft. **Ecoregions:** Sierra Nevada

Stemless perennial with hairless, white-waxy herbage. Leaves 0.6–1.6 in. long, pinnate, with 3–5 ovoid to elliptic, sharp-lobed leaflets. Flowers in compact, hemispheric clusters, symmetric, generally with 0 bracts, 3–6 bractlets, and 5–9 rays to 0.4 in. long. Sepals minute; petals 5, free, purple. Fruits to 0.4 in. long, hairless, with wings narrower than body. Easy to spot, even when not in flower, thanks to its white-waxy foliage. Caution: do not eat any part of a lomatium.

Sanicula bipinnatifida

purple sanicle

APIACEAE CARROT FAMILY

PCT Sections: 1–5 & 16–24 **Abundance:** Common **Height:** 6–24 in. **Flowering:** March–May **Flower Color:** Purple or yellow **Habitat-Community:** Openings in various soils, including serpentine, in woodlands, chaparrals, and lower montane coniferous forests **Elevation:** Below 6100 ft. **Ecoregions:** All (except Sonoran/Mojave Basin and Range)

Erect or spreading perennial with hairless, white-waxy or purplish herbage. Leaves 1.5–7.5 in. long, ovoid to roundish, 1-2-pinnately lobed, the lobes generally narrow with sharp teeth. Flowers in spheric clusters, symmetric, with 6–8 bracts and anthers and pistils obviously exserted. Sepals minute; petals 5, free, purple or yellow. Fruits to 0.3 in. long, ovoid to roundish, covered with stout prickles.

Nemophila menziesii

baby blue eyes

BORAGINACEAE BORAGE FAMILY

PCT Sections: 1–8 **Abundance:** Common **Height:** 6–20 in. **Flowering:** February–May **Flower Color:** Blue to white **Habitat-Community:** Slopes and flats in scrubs, woodlands, and chaparrals **Elevation:** Below 6400 ft. **Ecoregions:** Southern California Mountains, Sierra Nevada

Attractive annual with simple to branched, fleshy, brittle, and sometimes angled or winged stems. Leaves 0.5–2 in. long (lower leaves largest), opposite, oblong to ovoid and pinnately lobed into 5–13 segments. Flowers in leaf axils, 5-parted. Corollas 0.2–1.6 in. across, rotate or bowl-shaped, with petals fused at the base (tube not obvious), either bright blue with a white center or pale blue with black dots and blue veins. Fruits spherical capsules 0.2–0.7 in. across. Two varieties along the PCT: var. *integrifolia* (lower leaves 5-7-lobed) and var. *menziesii* (lower leaves 6-13-lobed). *Nemophila* is Greek for "woodland-loving."

Linum lewisii

prairie flax

LINACEAE FLAX FAMILY

PCT Sections: 1–4 & 10–24 **Abundance:** Common **Height:** 2–32 in. **Flowering:** April–August **Flower Color:** Blue **Habitat-Community:** Dry, open places from woodlands to subalpine coniferous forests **Elevation:** Below 12,000 ft. **Ecoregions:** All (except Sonoran/Mojave Basin and Range)

Erect or spreading perennial with hairless herbage, generally growing in tight clumps. Leaves to 0.8 in. long, alternate, linear to lance-shaped or narrowly spoon-shaped, with smooth margins. Flowers scattered along stem tips. Sepals to 0.3 in. long, 5, free, with translucent margins. Petals to 0.6 in. long, 5, free, blue (rarely white), spoon-shaped. Fruits to 0.3 in. across, spherical, with dark brown to black seeds. The cooked seeds are edible, with a nutty taste, but caution: they contain small amounts of compounds that can produce cyanide and should therefore not be consumed in large portions. *Linum* fibers have been a source for linen for thousands of years. The roots were historically used for eye medicine.

▼ 5 PETALS/SEPALS / IRREGULAR COROLLAS

Astragalus didymocarpus

two-seeded milkvetch

FABACEAE LEGUME FAMILY

PCT Sections: 1–8 **Abundance:** Locally common **Height:** 2–15 in. **Flowering:** February–May **Flower Color:** Purple or white **Habitat-Community:** Sandy to rocky slopes and plains in creosote bush scrubs, foothill chaparrals, and Joshua tree & pinyon-juniper woodlands **Elevation:** Below 5000 ft. **Ecoregions:** Southern California Mountains, Sonoran/Mojave Basin and Range, Sierra Nevada

Slender, inconspicuous, prostrate to erect annual with gray-hairy to minutely hairy herbage. Leaves 2.5–3.2 in. long, odd-1-pinnate, with 9–17 linear to spoon-shaped leaflets 0.1–0.7 in. long. Flowers 5–27 in dense, tightly clustered heads, irregular, pea-like, with 5 black- and white-haired, fused calyx lobes. Corollas purple to white, or white-tinged purple, 0.1–0.2 in. long. Fruits 0.1 in. across, spherical, 2-lobed (and 2-seeded), short-hairy (pea) pods. Two varieties along the CA PCT: var. *dispermus* (stems prostrate; calyx with mostly white hairs) is more common in southern California; var. *didymocarpus* (stems erect; calyx with mostly black hairs) is more common in the southern Sierra Nevada.

Lupinus adsurgens

Drew's silky lupine

FABACEAE LEGUME FAMILY

PCT Sections: 4 & 8–9 & 14–17 **Abundance:** Occasional **Height:** 7–24 in. **Flowering:** May–July **Flower Color:** Violet or lavender to pale yellow **Habitat-Community:** Dry slopes from oak woodlands to upper montane coniferous forests **Elevation:** Below 11,500 ft. **Ecoregions:** Southern California Mountains, Sierra Nevada

Erect perennial with hairy, silver to dull green herbage. Leaves alternate, palmate, with 6–9 leaflets to 2 in. long. Flowers spiraled to whorled along stem, irregular (pea-like), consisting of a banner (hairless on back, with a yellow to white spot), keel (hairless), and wings. Calyces, upper lip to 0.3 in. long, 2-toothed, and lower to 0.3 in. long with 0 or 3 teeth. Petals to 0.5 in. long, 5, violet or lavender to pale yellow. Fruits to 1.6 in. long, silky (pea) pods with 3–6 seeds.

Lupinus albicaulis

sicklekeel lupine

FABACEAE LEGUME FAMILY

PCT Sections: 11–24 **Abundance:** Locally common **Height:** 7–24 in. **Flowering:** May–September **Flower Color:** Purple **Habitat-Community:** Dry slopes in montane coniferous forests **Elevation:** Below 9900 ft. **Ecoregions:** Sierra Nevada, Cascades, Klamath Mountains

Erect perennial with hairy to silky herbage. Leaves alternate, palmate, with 5–10 leaflets 0.8–2.8 in. long. Flowers whorled along stem, irregular (pea-like), consisting of a banner (hairless on back, with an indistinct spot), keel (hairless, with exposed tip), and wings. Calyces, upper lip to 0.5 in. long, 2-toothed, and lower to 0.5 in. long with 0 to 3 teeth. Petals to 0.7 in. long, 5, purple (rarely yellow-white). Fruits to 2 in. long, silky pods with 3–7 seeds.

Lupinus andersonii

Anderson's lupine

FABACEAE LEGUME FAMILY

PCT Sections: All **Abundance:** Common **Height:** 8–30 in. **Flowering:** May–August **Flower Color:** Blue to lavender or yellow **Habitat-Community:** Dry slopes and ridges in sagebrush scrubs, oak & pinyon-juniper woodlands, and montane coniferous forests **Elevation:** Below 9800 ft. **Ecoregions:** All

Decumbent or erect, highly variable perennial or subshrub with hairy green herbage. Leaves palmate, with 6–9 lance-shaped leaflets 0.8–2.4 in. long. Flowers whorled in dense spikes at stem and branch tips, irregular (pea-like), consisting of a banner (hairless on back), keel (hairless), and wings that completely hide the keel. Calyces, upper lip 2-toothed, and lower 2–3-toothed. Petals 0.4–0.6 in. long, 5, blue to lavender or yellow. Fruits 0.8–1.8 in. long, silky pods. The cream-flowered form is common in the southern Sierra and Transverse Ranges.

Lupinus arbustus

longspur lupine

FABACEAE LEGUME FAMILY

PCT Sections: 5, 12–19 **Abundance:** Locally common **Height:** 7–28 in. **Flowering:** May–August **Flower Color:** Blue, purple, pink, white, or yellowish **Habitat-Community:** Open flats and slopes from sagebrush scrubs to upper montane coniferous forests **Elevation:** 4900–9900 ft. **Ecoregions:** Southern California Mountains, Sierra Nevada, Cascades

Erect perennial with green or gray-silky herbage. Leaves basal or alternate, palmate, with 7–13 leaflets 0.8–2.8 in. long. Flowers openly whorled along stem, irregular (pea-like), consisting of a banner (hairy on back, with a white-yellow or no spot), keel (hairy on upper margins), and wings (hairy). Calyces, upper lip to 0.2 in. long, spur to 0.2 in. long, 2-toothed, and lower to 0.2 in. long with 3 teeth. Petals to 0.6 in. long, 5, blue, purple, pink, white, or yellowish. Fruits to 1.2 in. long, silky pods with 3–6 seeds. *Arbustus* is Latin for "growing in woods or forest."

Lupinus argenteus
silvery lupine
FABACEAE LEGUME FAMILY

PCT Sections: 10–20 **Abundance:** Locally common **Height:** to 5 ft. **Flowering:** May–October **Flower Color:** Blue or purple to white **Habitat-Community:** Dry, open flats and slopes from sagebrush scrubs and woodlands to subalpine coniferous forests **Elevation:** Below 11,500 ft. **Ecoregions:** Sierra Nevada, Cascades, Klamath Mountains

Erect perennial with hairless to silvery-hairy herbage. Leaves basal or alternate, palmate, with 5–9 leaflets 0.4–2.4 in. long. Flowers whorled or not, irregular (pea-like), consisting of a banner (hairy on back, with a yellow to white or no spot), keel (hairy on upper margins), and wings. Calyces, upper lip to 0.3 in. long, spur to 0.1 in. long, 0–2-toothed, and lower to 0.3 in. long with 0–3 teeth. Petals to 0.5 in. long, 5, blue or purple to white. Fruits to 1.2 in. long, hairy or silky pods with 2–6 seeds.

Lupinus bicolor
miniature lupine
FABACEAE LEGUME FAMILY

PCT Sections: 1–8 & 16–20 **Abundance:** Common **Height:** 4–16 in. **Flowering:** March–June **Flower Color:** Blue **Habitat-Community:** Open or disturbed flats and slopes in woodlands and lower montane coniferous forests **Elevation:** Below 5300 ft. **Ecoregions:** All (except Southern California Mountains, Sonoran Basin and Range)

Erect annual with hairy herbage. Leaves alternate, palmate, with 5–7 leaflets 0.4–1.6 in. long. Flowers 5-whorled along stem, irregular (pea-like), consisting of a banner (with a white, aging red, spot), white keel (hairy on upper margins near tip), and wings. Calyces, upper lip to 0.2 in. long, deeply lobed, and lower to 0.3 in. long. Petals to 0.4 in. long, 5, blue. Fruits to 1.2 in. long, hairy pods with 5–8 seeds. This is the most common annual lupine along the trail below 5300 ft. elevation!

Lupinus breweri
Brewer's lupine
FABACEAE LEGUME FAMILY

PCT Sections: 4–5 & 9–24 **Abundance:** Common **Height:** to 8 in. **Flowering:** June–August **Flower Color:** Blue to violet **Habitat-Community:** Dry, open flats and slopes from lower montane coniferous forests to alpine communities **Elevation:** Below 13,200 ft. **Ecoregions:** Southern California Mountains, Sierra Nevada, Cascades, Klamath Mountains

Prostrate, tufted or matted perennial with silver-silky herbage and a woody base. Leaves clustered near base, alternate, palmate, with 5–10 leaflets to 0.8 in. long. Flowers in dense clusters, irregular (pea-like), consisting of a banner (hairless or hairy on back, with a yellow or white spot), keel (hairy on upper margins), and wings; bracts deciduous. Calyces, upper lip to 0.3 in. long, 2-toothed, and lower to 0.3 in. long with 0–3 teeth. Petals to 0.5 in. long, 5, blue to violet. Fruits to 0.8 in. long, silky pods with 3–4 seeds. *Lupine* is Latin for "wolf/wolfish," due to the erroneous assumption that they rob the soil of nutrients, based on their harsh environments.

Lupinus concinnus

bajada lupine

FABACEAE LEGUME FAMILY

PCT Sections: 1–9 **Abundance:** Common **Height:** 2–12 in. **Flowering:** March–June **Flower Color:** Purple to pink **Habitat-Community:** Sandy to rocky slopes, alluvial plains, and washes in creosote bush scrubs, foothill chaparrals, and Joshua tree & pinyon-juniper woodlands **Elevation:** Below 5500 ft. **Ecoregions:** Southern California Mountains, Sonoran/Mojave Basin and Range, Sierra Nevada

Low-growing, decumbent or erect annual with hairy stems and gray-green herbage. Leaves palmate, ovoid to linear, with 5–9 white-hairy leaflets 0.4–1.2 in. long. Flowers in dense spiraled clusters often tucked in among the leaves, irregular (pea-like), consisting of a banner, keel (hairless margins), and wings. Calyces 0.1–0.2 in. long, with 2 generally equal lips, the upper deeply lobed. Petals to 0.5 in. long, 5, 2-lipped, purple to pink (sometimes partially white). Fruits 0.4–0.6 in. long, hairy (pea) pods. Highly variable, ranging throughout southern California and the southwestern US. Especially fond of washes. A linear-leaflet form, var. *agardianus*, occurs along the PCT at the lower desert crossings of San Bernardino County.

Lupinus covillei

shaggy lupine

FABACEAE LEGUME FAMILY

PCT Sections: 10–12 **Abundance:** Locally common **Height:** 7–32 in. **Flowering:** July–September **Flower Color:** Pale blue **Habitat-Community:** Open, moist, rocky sites in subalpine coniferous forests **Elevation:** 8200–11,500 ft. **Ecoregions:** Sierra Nevada

Erect perennial with hairy to shaggy-hairy, yellow-green herbage. Leaves alternate, palmate, with 4–9 leaflets to 4.3 in. long. Flowers in whorls or scattered along stem, irregular (pea-like), consisting of a banner (hairless on back, with a yellow spot), keel (sparsely hairy on upper margins), and wings. Calyces, upper lip to 0.3 in. long, 2-toothed, and lower to 0.4 in. long with 0–3 teeth. Petals to 0.6 in. long, 5, pale blue. Fruits to 1.6 in. long, woolly pods with 4–6 seeds.

Lupinus elatus

silky lupine

FABACEAE LEGUME FAMILY

PCT Sections: 4–9 **Abundance:** Rare **Height:** 1–3 ft. **Flowering:** June–August **Flower Color:** Lavender to blue **Habitat-Community:** Dry slopes and mesas from sagebrush scrubs to upper montane coniferous forests **Elevation:** Below 9600 ft. **Ecoregions:** Southern California Mountains, Sierra Nevada

Upright perennial covered with silver-silky to woolly hairs. Leaves basal and alternate, palmate, with 6–8 lance-shaped leaflets 1–3 in. long. Flowers clustered in whorls, irregular (pea-like), consisting of banner (hairless on back), keel (hairless margins), and wings. Calyces 2-lipped, notched upper lip to 0.3 in. long, and 3-toothed lower lip to 0.4 in. long. Petals 0.4–0.6 in. long, 5, 2-lipped, lavender to blue (sometimes partially cream). Fruits 0.8–1.2 in. long, wavy-margined, silky (pea) pods. Hybridizes with *L. andersonii* in the Transverse Ranges. Host plant for the rare San Gabriel Mountains arrowhead blue butterfly.

Lupinus formosus

summer lupine

FABACEAE LEGUME FAMILY

PCT Sections: 1–8 **Abundance:** Locally common **Height:** 1–3 ft. **Flowering:** April–September **Flower Color:** Purple **Habitat-Community:** Heavy soils in valley bottoms and on ridgetops in chaparrals, sagebrush scrubs, and lower montane coniferous forests **Elevation:** Below 6700 ft. **Ecoregions:** Southern California Mountains, Sierra Nevada

Erect perennial with densely hairy to tomentose, gray to silver herbage. Leaves basal and alternate, palmate, with 7–9 spoon-shaped leaflets 1–3 in. long. Flowers clustered in whorls, irregular (pea-like), consisting of a banner (hairless on back), keel (hairless margins), and wings. Calyces 2-lipped, 2-toothed upper lip to 0.5 in. long, and 0- or 3-toothed lower lip to 0.5 in. long. Petals 0.4–0.6 in. long, 5, 2-lipped, purple. Fruits 1.3–1.8 in. long, hairy (pea) pods. Often subject to eradication programs by ranchers (many lupines are poisonous to livestock). Food plant for the endangered mission blue butterfly.

Lupinus gracilentus

green slender lupine

FABACEAE LEGUME FAMILY

PCT Sections: 11–12 **Abundance:** Rare **Height:** 7–32 in. **Flowering:** July–September **Flower Color:** Light blue **Habitat-Community:** Open, moist sites in subalpine coniferous forests **Elevation:** 8200–11,500 ft. **Ecoregions:** Sierra Nevada

Erect perennial with hairy, green herbage. Leaves alternate, palmate, with 5–8 leaflets to 3.1 in. long, <0.2 in. wide. Flowers in 4–8 whorls, irregular (pea-like), consisting of a banner (hairless or hairy on back, with a white to yellowish spot), keel (sparsely hairy on upper margins), and wings. Calyces, upper lip to 0.3 in. long, 2-toothed, and lower to 0.3 in. long with 0 or 2–3 teeth. Petals to 0.7 in. long, 5, blue. Fruits to 1.2 in. long, densely hairy pods with 6–8 seeds. Look for it around Tuolumne Meadows.

Lupinus grayi

Sierra lupine

FABACEAE LEGUME FAMILY

PCT Sections: 8–17 **Abundance:** Common **Height:** 7–14 in. **Flowering:** May–July **Flower Color:** Deep purple to pale blue **Habitat-Community:** Open understories in montane coniferous forests **Elevation:** Below 8200 ft. **Ecoregions:** Sierra Nevada

Prostrate to matted perennial with hairy to woolly herbage. Leaves alternate, palmate, with 5–11 leaflets to 1.4 in. long. Flowers generally in whorls, irregular (pea-like), consisting of a banner (hairless or hairy on back, with a yellow, aging red, spot), keel (densely hairy on upper and generally lower margins), and wings. Calyces, upper lip to 0.4 in. long, deeply 2-toothed, and lower to 0.5 in. long with 0–3 teeth. Petals to 0.7 in. long, 5, deep purple to pale blue. Fruits to 1.4 in. long, hairy pods with 4–6 seeds.

Lupinus hyacinthinus

San Jacinto lupine

FABACEAE LEGUME FAMILY

PCT Sections: 3–5 **Abundance:** Rare **Height:** 1–3 ft. **Flowering:** June–August **Flower Color:** Purple to pale blue **Habitat-Community:** Dry slopes and openings in understories from lower montane to subalpine coniferous forests **Elevation:** Below 10,400 ft. **Ecoregions:** Southern California Mountains

Erect, bushy perennial with hairy herbage and stems becoming green with age. Leaves alternate, palmate, with 7–12 linear to narrowly lance-shaped leaflets 1–3 in. long. Flowers clustered in whorls, irregular (pea-like), consisting of a banner (hairless on back, with a yellow spot), keel (hairless margins), and wings. Calyces 2-lipped, 2-toothed upper lip to 0.4 in. long, and 0- or 3-toothed lower lip to 0.5 in. long. Petals 0.5–0.7 in. long, 5, 2-lipped, purple to pale blue. Fruits 1.3–1.8 in. long, silky hairy (pea) pods with speckled seeds. Best viewed along the PCT in the San Jacinto Mountains.

Lupinus latifolius

broadleaf lupine

FABACEAE LEGUME FAMILY

PCT Sections: All **Abundance:** Common **Height:** 1–8 ft. **Flowering:** April–September **Flower Color:** Blue or purple to white **Habitat-Community:** Open understories and moist sites from woodlands and chaparrals to subalpine coniferous forests **Elevation:** Below 11,500 ft. **Ecoregions:** All (except Sonoran/Mojave Basin and Range)

Erect perennial with green, hairy or hairless herbage. Leaves alternate, palmate, with 5–11 leaflets to 4 in. long. Flowers scattered or in open whorls, irregular (pea-like), consisting of a banner (hairless on back, with a white to yellowish, aging purple, spot), keel (hairy on upper and generally lower margins), and wings. Calyces, upper lip to 0.4 in. long, 0–2-toothed, and lower to 0.3 in. long with 0 teeth or notched. Petals to 0.7 in. long, 5, blue or purple to white. Fruits to 1.8 in. long, hairy pods with 6–10 seeds.

Lupinus lepidus

tidy lupine

FABACEAE LEGUME FAMILY

PCT Sections: 4 & 9–24 **Abundance:** Common **Height:** 2–18 in. **Flowering:** June–August **Flower Color:** Blue, violet, or pink to white **Habitat-Community:** Rocky slopes, open understories, and moist sites from woodlands to alpine communities **Elevation:** Below 13,200 ft. **Ecoregions:** Southern California Mountains, Sierra Nevada, Cascades, Klamath Mountains

Prostrate to erect perennial, sometimes matted, with hairy herbage. Leaves mostly basal, palmate, with 5–8 leaflets to 1.6 in. long. Flowers in dense clusters, irregular (pea-like), consisting of a banner (hairless on back), keel (hairy on upper margins), and wings; bracts persistent. Calyces, upper lip to 0.3 in. long, 0–2-toothed, and lower to 0.3 in. long with 0–3 teeth. Petals to 0.4 in. long, 5, blue, violet, or pink to white. Fruits to 0.8 in. long, hairy pods with 2–4 seeds. Of the varieties found in CA, 6 of the 7 are likely to occur along the PCT.

Lupinus polyphyllus
meadow lupine
FABACEAE LEGUME FAMILY

PCT Sections: 3–5 & 9–24 **Abundance:** Locally common **Height:** 1–3 ft. **Flowering:** May–August **Flower Color:** Violet to white or pink **Habitat-Community:** Meadows, bogs, fens, and streambanks in wetland-riparian communities **Elevation:** Below 9900 ft. **Ecoregions:** Southern California Mountains, Sierra Nevada, Cascades, Klamath Mountains

Erect, stout perennial with hairless or sparsely hairy green herbage. Leaves basal and alternate, palmate, with 5–17 leaflets to 6 in. long and 1.2 in. wide. Flowers in elongated, whorled clusters, irregular (pea-like), consisting of a banner (hairless on back, with a yellow to white spot, sometimes turning red-purple), hairless keel, and wings. Calyces smooth, upper lip to 0.3 in. long, lower to 0.3 in. long. Petals to 0.6 in. long, 5, violet to white or pink. Fruits to 1.6 in. long, hairy pods with 3–9 seeds.

Lupinus sparsiflorus
Coulter's lupine
FABACEAE LEGUME FAMILY

PCT Sections: 1–7 **Abundance:** Common **Height:** 6–20 in. **Flowering:** February–May **Flower Color:** Blue to pink **Habitat-Community:** Sandy to gravelly soils on hillsides and washes in creosote bush scrubs, foothill chaparrals, and Joshua tree & pinyon-juniper woodlands **Elevation:** Below 4500 ft. **Ecoregions:** Southern California Mountains, Sonoran/Mojave Basin and Range

Erect, few-branched annual with both long- and short-hairy herbage. Leaves basal and alternate, palmate, with linear to spoon-shaped leaflets 0.7–1.3 in. long; petiole 1–2 in. long. Flowers in spiraled to whorled clusters, crowded below, irregular (pea-like), consisting of a banner (with yellow spot), keel (hairy margins), and wings. Calyces to 0.3 in. long, 2-lipped, lips generally equal, the upper lip deeply lobed. Petals 0.4–0.5 in. long, 5, 2-lipped, blue to pink. Fruits 0.4–1 in. long, coarsely hairy (pea) pods. The yellow banner spot blushes reddish after pollination. Rarely occurs in large populations. Exceptions are burn areas, where plants become dense and grow to 3 ft. tall.

Trifolium albopurpureum
rancheria clover
FABACEAE LEGUME FAMILY

PCT Sections: 1–7 **Abundance:** Locally common **Height:** 3–12 in. **Flowering:** March–June **Flower Color:** Purple and pink-white **Habitat-Community:** Dry, open areas from California prairies to lower montane coniferous forests **Elevation:** Below 6500 ft. **Ecoregions:** Southern California Mountains

Erect, few-branched annual with red-tinged, stiff-hairy herbage. Leaves alternate, palmate, with 3 teardrop-shaped, toothed leaflets 0.2–1 in. long. Flowers clustered in heads 0.4–0.7 in. across, irregular (pea-like), consisting of a banner, keel, and wings, with prominent peduncles 1–2.8 in. long and 0 or minute involucres. Calyces to 0.3 in. long, 5-lobed, lobes > tube. Petals to 0.3 in. long, 5, purple and pink-white. Fruits 2-seeded pods. Highly ephemeral, germinating only in years of high precipitation. California is a center of diversity for native clovers, many of which are annuals.

Trifolium longipes

summer clover

FABACEAE LEGUME FAMILY

PCT Sections: 4 & 9–24 **Abundance:** Common **Height:** 2–15 in. **Flowering:** March–September **Flower Color:** Purple to white **Habitat-Community:** Meadows, streambanks, and gravelly slopes, including serpentine, from lower montane coniferous forests to alpine communities **Elevation:** Below 9900 ft. **Ecoregions:** Southern California Mountains, Sierra Nevada, Cascades, Klamath Mountains

Lax to erect perennial with hairy herbage. Leaves basal and alternate, palmate, with 3 hairy, linear to spoon-shaped leaflets to 2 in. long. Flowers in heads, irregular (pea-like), consisting of a banner, keel, and wings, with pedicels to 0.1 in. long. Calyces to 0.4 in. long, 5-lobed, lobes > tube. Petals to 0.7 in. long, 5, purple to white. Fruits 1-seeded pods.

Trifolium willdenovii

tomcat clover

FABACEAE LEGUME FAMILY

PCT Sections: 1–8 & 15–19 & 23–24 **Abundance:** Locally common **Height:** 6–16 in. **Flowering:** March–June **Flower Color:** Purple to reddish white **Habitat-Community:** Open places, generally in heavy soils, from oak woodlands to lower montane coniferous forests **Elevation:** Below 7500 ft. **Ecoregions:** Southern California Mountains, Sierra Nevada, Cascades, Klamath Mountains

Robust, erect or prostrate, sparingly branched annual with hairless herbage. Leaves alternate, palmate, with 3 linear, spine-tooth-margined leaflets 0.6–2 in. long. Flowers around 25, clustered in heads 0.7–1.2 in. across, irregular (pea-like), consisting of a banner, keel, and wings, with prominent peduncle 1.6–2.2 in. long and wheel-shaped, dissected, sharply toothed involucre. Calyces to 0.4 in. long, 5-lobed, shiny, lobes < tube. Petals 0.3–0.6 in. long, 5, purple to reddish white. Fruits 1–2-seeded oblong pods. Especially common on recently burned slopes.

Vicia americana

American vetch

FABACEAE LEGUME FAMILY

PCT Sections: 1–7 & 13–24 **Abundance:** Common **Height:** to 39 in. **Flowering:** March–June **Flower Color:** Blue-purple to lavender **Habitat-Community:** Open, moist, disturbed areas in montane coniferous forests **Elevation:** Below 7900 ft. **Ecoregions:** All (except Sonoran/Mojave Basin and Range)

Sprawling or erect perennial with hairy or hairless herbage. Leaves alternate, tendril-tipped, pinnate, with 8–16 oval to oblong or wedge-shaped, smooth- to toothed-margined leaflets to 1.4 in. long. Flowers 3–9 in open spikes, downward-pointing, irregular (pea-like), consisting of a banner, keel, and wings. Calyces to 0.2 in. long, 5-lobed, lower > upper lobes. Petals to 1 in. long, 5, blue-purple to lavender. Fruits to 1.2 in. long, hairy or hairless (pea) pods with ≥2 seeds. The young leaves of *Vicia* are folded (like a V).

Vicia ludoviciana

Louisiana vetch

FABACEAE LEGUME FAMILY

PCT Sections: 1–2 & 4 **Abundance:** Locally common **Height:** 12–40 in. **Flowering:** March–June **Flower Color:** Pale blue **Habitat-Community:** Slopes and canyons in foothill chaparrals, oak woodlands, and wetland-riparian communities **Elevation:** Below 4000 ft. **Ecoregions:** Southern California/Northern Baja Coast, Southern California Mountains

Annual vine with hairy or hairless stems sprawling through shrubs or growing along the ground. Leaves alternate, tendril-tipped, pinnate, with 4–10 oblong to elliptic leaflets 0.4–1.1 in. long. Flowers 1–3 in loose clusters in leaf axils, irregular (pea-like), consisting of a banner, keel, and wings. Calyces to 0.2 in. long, 5-lobed, lower lobes = tube, lower > upper lobes. Petals 0.2–0.3 in. long, 5, pale blue. Fruits 0.7–1 in. long, hairless, flattened (pea) pods. Widespread (*ludoviciana* means "of Louisiana") but along the PCT occurs mostly in San Diego County.

Aconitum columbianum

Columbian monkshood

RANUNCULACEAE BUTTERCUP FAMILY

PCT Sections: 9–24 **Abundance:** Locally common **Height:** 3–7 ft. **Flowering:** July–September **Flower Color:** Blue-purple to white or yellow-green **Habitat-Community:** Meadows, streambanks, and seeps in wetland-riparian communities **Elevation:** Below 11,500 ft. **Ecoregions:** Sierra Nevada, Cascades, Klamath Mountains

Generally erect, 1-few-stemmed, unbranched perennial with hairy upper stems. Leaves to 7 in. long, alternate, deeply 3–5-lobed, maple-like, with toothed margins. Flowers many, in open spikes along upper stems, irregular, with 20–50 stamens. Sepals to 1.2 in. long, 5, blue-purple to white or yellow-green, the topmost forming a hood over the rest of the flower. Petals 2, blue to white, concealed by hood. Fruits to 0.7 in. long, dry follicles. Caution: extremely poisonous and can cause death if eaten!

Delphinium glaucum

mountain larkspur

RANUNCULACEAE BUTTERCUP FAMILY

PCT Sections: 4–5 & 10–16 & 20–24 **Abundance:** Occasional **Height:** 3–10 ft. **Flowering:** July–September **Flower Color:** Purple-blue **Habitat-Community:** Seeps, meadows, and streambanks in wetland-riparian communities **Elevation:** Below 10,500 ft. **Ecoregions:** Southern California Mountains, Sierra Nevada, Klamath Mountains

Ascending, clumped, 2-few-stemmed perennial with white- to blue-waxy-coated, hairless herbage. Leaves to 8 in. wide, mostly basal, deeply many-lobed, maple-like, the lobes with sharp tips. Flowers generally >50, in open spikes along upper stems, irregular, with many stamens and 3 pistils. Sepals to 0.8 in. long, 5, dark purple-blue, hairy on back, forward-pointing to spreading, with stout spurs to 0.8 in. long. Petals 4, purple-tipped. Fruits to 0.8 in. long, erect follicles. Caution: most larkspurs are extremely toxic to humans and livestock!

Delphinium gracilentum

pine forest larkspur

RANUNCULACEAE

BUTTERCUP FAMILY

PCT Sections: 9–18 **Abundance:** Locally common **Height:** 6–20 in. **Flowering:** March–June **Flower Color:** Pale blue to white or pink **Habitat-Community:** Damp, shaded understories from woodlands to subalpine coniferous forests **Elevation:** Below 8900 ft. **Ecoregions:** Sierra Nevada, Cascades

Ascending, 1–few-stemmed perennial with hairless lower stems. Leaves to 8 in. wide, mostly basal, generally deeply 5-lobed, the lobes with rounded tips and the terminal lobe widest above the middle. Flowers 8–20, in open spikes along upper stems, irregular, with many stamens and 3 pistils. Sepals to 0.5 in. long, 5, pale blue to white or pink, hairless, curved backward, with spurs to 0.6 in. long. Petals 4, white upper and blue lower. Fruits to 0.6 in. long, erect, curved follicles. *Gracilentum* means "slender." Caution: most larkspurs are extremely toxic to humans and livestock!

Delphinium hansenii subsp. *kernense*

Kern larkspur

RANUNCULACEAE

BUTTERCUP FAMILY

PCT Sections: 7–9 **Abundance:** Occasional **Height:** 13–43 in. **Flowering:** March–May **Flower Color:** Blue-purple to white **Habitat-Community:** Dry, rocky soils in woodlands, chaparrals, and lower montane coniferous forests **Elevation:** Below 6300 ft. **Ecoregions:** Sierra Nevada

Erect, generally 1-stemmed perennial with hairy herbage. Leaves to 8 in. wide, mostly basal (withered by flowering), deeply 3–18-lobed, white-hairy. Flowers generally >12, in crowded spikes along upper stems, irregular, with many stamens and 3 pistils. Sepals to 0.5 in. long, 5, blue-purple to white, hairy, spreading, with spurs to 0.6 in. long. Petals 4, white upper, blue-purple lower. Fruits to 0.8 in. long, erect follicles. Mostly confined to Kern County, as its names suggest. Caution: most larkspurs are extremely toxic to humans and livestock!

Delphinium nuttallianum

meadow larkspur

RANUNCULACEAE

BUTTERCUP FAMILY

PCT Sections: 9–24 **Abundance:** Common **Height:** 2–20 in. **Flowering:** May–July **Flower Color:** Blue **Habitat-Community:** Openings, meadow edges, and streambanks from sagebrush scrubs to upper montane coniferous forests **Elevation:** Below 10,900 ft. **Ecoregions:** Sierra Nevada, Cascades, Klamath Mountains

Erect, unbranched perennial with hairy or hairless stems. Leaves to 2 in. wide, mostly along lower stem, deeply 7–25-lobed, maple-like, generally hairless, with smooth or toothed margins. Flowers <12, in open spikes along upper stems, irregular, with many stamens and 3 pistils. Sepals to 0.7 in. long, 5, blue, generally curved backward and hairless on back, with spurs to 0.8 in. long. Petals 4, whitish. Fruits to 0.7 in. long, erect, generally curved follicles. The name honors American naturalist Thomas Nuttall (1786–1859), who collected extensively in California in 1835. Caution: most larkspurs are extremely toxic to humans and livestock!

Parish's larkspur

Delphinium parishii

RANUNCULACEAE

BUTTERCUP FAMILY

PCT Sections: 1–9 **Abundance:** Locally common **Height:** 1–2 ft. **Flowering:** March–June **Flower Color:** Blue, purple, or white **Habitat-Community:** Sandy to gravelly soils in scrub and woodlands **Elevation:** Below 7500 ft. **Ecoregions:** Southern California Mountains, Sonoran/Mojave Basin and Range, Sierra Nevada

Short-lived perennial with fleshy stems and hairless to short-hairy herbage. Leaves 1.2–2.3 in. wide, basal (withered by flowering in some plants) and alternate, deeply palmately lobed and round in outline, with up to 12 lobes. Flowers 6–75, in open spikes to stem tip, 0.8–1.2 in. long, irregular. Sepals 5, petal-like, blue, purple, or white, the uppermost spurred; spur 0.3–0.6 in. long. Petals 4 (somewhat obscured by sepals), pale blue, 0.2–0.3 in. long. Fruits 0.3–0.9 in. long, erect, 3-parted follicles. Two subspecies occur along the more arid segments of the trail: subsp. *parishii* (sepals curved backward, sky blue), the more common, gives way in San Diego and Riverside counties to the rarer subsp. *subglobosum* (sepals not reflexed, dark blue). Caution: most larkspurs are extremely toxic to humans and livestock!

Parry's larkspur

Delphinium parryi

RANUNCULACEAE

BUTTERCUP FAMILY

PCT Sections: 1–7 **Abundance:** Common **Height:** 10–30 in. **Flowering:** April–June **Flower Color:** Blue-purple **Habitat-Community:** Sandy to gravelly soils in foothill chaparrals and oak woodlands **Elevation:** Below 5500 ft. **Ecoregions:** Southern California/Northern Baja Coast, Southern California Mountains, Sierra Nevada

Short-lived perennial with fleshy, curly-hairy herbage. Leaves 1.2–2.4 in. wide, basal (withered by flowering in some plants) and alternate, deeply palmately lobed and round in outline, with up to 27 lobes. Flowers 3–60, on ascending pedicels in open spikes to stem tip, 0.8–1.3 in. long, irregular. Sepals 5, petal-like, blue-purple, the uppermost spurred; spur 0.3–0.6 in. long. Petals 4 (somewhat obscured by sepals), white, 0.2–0.3 in. long. Fruits erect, 3-parted follicles 0.4–0.8 in. long. A common fire-follower in southern California; plants in burns can reach 4 ft. tall. Caution: most larkspurs are extremely toxic to humans and livestock! Aka San Bernardino larkspur.

zigzag larkspur

Delphinium patens

RANUNCULACEAE

BUTTERCUP FAMILY

PCT Sections: 1–10 **Abundance:** Locally common **Height:** 12–28 in. **Flowering:** April–June **Flower Color:** Dark blue to purple **Habitat-Community:** Sandy to gravelly soils from California prairies to upper montane coniferous forests and wetland-riparian communities **Elevation:** Below 8800 ft. **Ecoregions:** Southern California Mountains, Sierra Nevada

Perennial with fleshy, glandular-hairy herbage. Leaves to 2 in. wide, basal (withered by flowering in some plants) and alternate (confined to lower stems), palmately lobed, broadly 3-parted. Flowers 0.8–1.4 in. long, irregular, in open spikes to stem tip. Sepals 5, petal-like, dark blue to purple, the lateral reflexed, the uppermost spurred; spur 0.3–0.6 in. long. Petals 4, white, exposed, providing a nice contrast. Fruits 0.5–0.9 in. long, erect, 3-parted follicles. *Patens* (from the Latin, "spreading") refers to the leaves. Caution: most larkspurs are extremely toxic to humans and livestock! Aka spreading larkspur.

Delphinium polycladon

mountain marsh larkspur

RANUNCULACEAE
BUTTERCUP FAMILY

PCT Sections: 10–14 **Abundance:** Locally common **Height:** 6–47 in. **Flowering:** July–September **Flower Color:** Blue **Habitat-Community:** Streambanks and wet, rocky slopes from upper montane coniferous forests to alpine and wetland-riparian communities **Elevation:** 7200–11,900 ft. **Ecoregions:** Sierra Nevada

Ascending to erect, 2-many-stemmed, branched perennial with hairless herbage. Leaves to 3.2 in. wide, mostly along lower stem, hairless, many-lobed, roundish in outline, with smooth or toothed margins. Flowers generally 3–35, in open, 1-sided spikes along upper stems, irregular, with many stamens and 3 pistils. Sepals to 0.7 in. long, 5, blue, hairy or hairless on back, with spurs to 0.9 in. long. Petals 4, pale blue upper. Fruits follicles to 0.8 in. long. *Polycladon* means "many shoots." Caution: most larkspurs are extremely toxic to humans and livestock!

Viola adunca

hookedspur violet

VIOLACEAE VIOLET FAMILY

PCT Sections: 4 & 11–24 **Abundance:** Common **Height:** 1–14 in. **Flowering:** April–September **Flower Color:** Pale to deep violet **Habitat-Community:** Vernally moist, usually shaded places from woodlands to alpine communities **Elevation:** Below 11,800 ft. **Ecoregions:** Southern California Mountains, Sierra Nevada, Cascades, Klamath Mountains

Sprawling to erect, many-stemmed perennial with hairy or hairless herbage. Leaves to 2.6 in. long, alternate, ovoid to triangular, with smooth to lobed margins. Flowers irregular, generally 1 per leaf axil, with 5 stamens and 1 pistil. Sepals to 0.2 in. long, 5, lance-shaped, mostly alike. Petals 5, upper 2 pale to deep violet, lower 3 pale to deep violet with white basal spot, lateral 2 hairy, the lowest with base elongated into a (sometimes hooked) spur to 0.5 in. long. Fruits to 0.4 in. long, capsules with small, dark brown seeds attractive to ants. The common name echoes *adunca* ("hooked"). Where it occurs along the northern California and southern Oregon coast, it is an important larval plant for endangered silverspot butterflies.

▼ 5 FUSED PETALS / SYMMETRIC COROLLAS

Asclepias californica

California milkweed

APOCYNACEAE DOGBANE FAMILY

PCT Sections: 1–9 **Abundance:** Occasional **Height:** 6–24 in. **Flowering:** April–July **Flower Color:** Purple **Habitat-Community:** Openings with sandy to clayey soils in sagebrush scrubs, chaparrals, and woodlands **Elevation:** Below 6500 ft. **Ecoregions:** Southern California Mountains, Sierra Nevada

Sprawling perennial with densely white-hairy stems and milky sap. Leaves 0.8–2.5 in. long, opposite, ovoid, often woolly-hairy. Flowers 5-parted, clustered at the tips of stems. Calyx lobes obscured, 0.2–0.4 in. wide. Petals reflexed, purple, with hoods exceeded by the anther head. Fruits 1–3 in. long, pod-like follicles with seeds bearing a cluster of silky white hairs. *Asclepias* produces some of the most complex flowers in the plant kingdom. The genus is named after the Greek god of healing, Asklepios, a tribute to the innumerable medicinal properties of its plants.

Asclepias cordifolia

purple milkweed

APOCYNACEAE DOGBANE FAMILY

PCT Sections: 8–9 & 13–22 **Abundance:** Occasional **Height:** to 2 ft. **Flowering:** March–July **Flower Color:** Dark red-purple **Habitat-Community:** Dry, rocky places in woodlands, chaparrals, and lower montane coniferous forests **Elevation:** Below 6600 ft. **Ecoregions:** Sierra Nevada, Cascades, Klamath Mountains

Ascending perennial with milky sap and purple stems. Leaves 1.5–2.5 in. long, opposite, heart-shaped, clasping, purple, hairless. Flowers in umbrella-like clusters. Corollas 5-parted; petals fused at base, dark red-purple, with spreading to curved-back lobes. Fruits to 5.5 in. long, erect pods with hair-tufted seeds. Easy to spot: just look for a plant covered from top to bottom in purple!

Asclepias fascicularis

narrowleaf milkweed

APOCYNACEAE DOGBANE FAMILY

PCT Sections: 1–10 & 16–19 **Abundance:** Occasional **Height:** 10–40 in. **Flowering:** May–October **Flower Color:** Pale violet to cream **Habitat-Community:** Open, dry habitats and disturbed areas from California prairies to upper montane coniferous forests **Elevation:** Below 7300 ft. **Ecoregions:** Southern California Mountains, Sierra Nevada, Cascades

Erect perennial with hairless stems and milky white sap. Leaves 3–5 in. long, opposite or whorled in groups of 3–5, linear. Flowers in umbrella-like clusters. Corollas 5-parted; petals reflexed, pale violet to cream, with green-white hoods exceeded by anther head. Fruits 2–5 in. long, erect, smooth, pod-like follicles with seeds bearing a cluster of silky white hairs. Can be weedy in overgrazed areas or along roadsides. An important monarch butterfly host plant.

Asclepias speciosa

showy milkweed

APOCYNACEAE DOGBANE FAMILY

PCT Sections: 9–20 **Abundance:** Locally common **Height:** 1–4 ft. **Flowering:** May–September **Flower Color:** Rose-purple **Habitat-Community:** Various habitats, including fields, trail edges, and streambanks in woodlands, chaparrals, and lower montane coniferous forests **Elevation:** Below 6300 ft. **Ecoregions:** Sierra Nevada, Cascades, Klamath Mountains

Erect perennial with milky sap. Leaves 3–6 in. long, opposite, elliptic to ovoid, clasping, woolly, with smooth margins. Flowers in spheric clusters, with hood-like appendages. Corollas 5-parted; petals fused at base, rose-purple, with reflexed lobes. Fruits to 4 in. long, erect pods with hair-tufted seeds. An important food plant for monarch butterfly caterpillars and a nectar source for adults. The ingested plant alkaloids make the butterflies unpalatable, protecting them from predation.

lamb's horns

Cycladenia humilis

APOCYNACEAE DOGBANE FAMILY

PCT Sections: 4–5 & 16–20 **Abundance:** Occasional **Height:** 2–5 in. **Flowering:** April–August **Flower Color:** Rose-purple **Habitat-Community:** Gravelly or sandy soils, generally in the shade of pines, in montane coniferous forests **Elevation:** Below 9200 ft. **Ecoregions:** Southern California Mountains, Sierra Nevada, Cascades, Klamath Mountains

Erect, fleshy perennial with milky sap and white-waxy herbage. Leaves to 3.5 in. long, opposite, roundish to ovoid, clasping, hairless (less often hairy), with smooth margins. Flowers in clusters of 2–6 per stem. Corollas 0.6–0.8 in. long, 5-parted, funnel-shaped; petals fused, rose-purple, with lobes 0.2–0.4 in. long. Fruits to 2 in. long, pods with hair-tufted seeds. *Cycladenia* is Greek for "ring gland," referring to the nectary.

Jessica's stickseed

Hackelia micrantha

BORAGINACEAE BORAGE FAMILY

PCT Sections: 10–24 **Abundance:** Locally common **Height:** 1–3.5 ft. **Flowering:** May–August **Flower Color:** Blue **Habitat-Community:** Meadows, streambanks, and open slopes from sagebrush scrubs to subalpine coniferous forests **Elevation:** Below 11,500 ft. **Ecoregions:** Sierra Nevada, Cascades, Klamath Mountains

Erect perennial with many sparsely hairy or hairless stems. Leaves 3–6 in. long, alternate, lance-shaped, hairy, with pointed tip. Flowers in branched, coiled clusters at stem tips. Calyces to 0.1 in. long, 5-lobed. Corollas to 0.4 in. across, 5-parted (petals fused), tube-shaped, blue, with white or yellow appendages at base of lobes. Fruits to 0.2 in. long, nutlets covered with barb-tipped prickles. The fruits love to stick to your socks, or anything else they touch (hence the common name).

Sierra stickseed

Hackelia nervosa

BORAGINACEAE BORAGE FAMILY

PCT Sections: 11–18 **Abundance:** Common **Height:** 16–28 in. **Flowering:** May–August **Flower Color:** Blue **Habitat-Community:** Moist, open slopes and forest openings from lower montane to subalpine coniferous forests **Elevation:** 5900–9700 ft. **Ecoregions:** Sierra Nevada, Cascades

Erect, multi-stemmed perennial with hairy lower and hairless upper stems. Leaves 1–5 in. long, alternate, oblong to spoon-shaped, hairy, clasping (on upper stem). Flowers in branched, coiled clusters at stem tips. Calyces to 0.2 in. long, 5-lobed. Corollas to 0.7 in. across, 5-parted (petals fused), tube-shaped, blue, with white appendages at base of lobes. Fruits to 0.2 in. long, nutlets covered with barb-tipped prickles. The fruits practically jump onto your clothing as you walk near, thus earning their common name.

Hackelia velutina

velvet stickseed

BORAGINACEAE BORAGE FAMILY

PCT Sections: 11–15 **Abundance:** Common **Height:** 16–32 in. **Flowering:** June–August **Flower Color:** Blue **Habitat-Community:** Moist, open slopes and openings in montane coniferous forests **Elevation:** Below 9100 ft. **Ecoregions:** Sierra Nevada

Erect perennial with multiple hairy stems. Leaves 2–7 in. long, alternate, narrow-elliptic to spoon-shaped, velvety, clasping (on upper stem). Flowers in branched, coiled clusters at stem tips. Calyces to 0.1 in. long, 5-lobed. Corollas to 0.8 in. across, 5-parted (petals fused), tube-shaped, blue, with white appendages at base of lobes. Fruits to 0.3 in. long, nutlets covered with barb-tipped prickles. Aka Sierra forget-me-not: the story goes that a knight was picking European borage (a cousin of stickseed) for his love when he fell into a swift-moving creek and just managed to yell "Forget me not!" before being swept away.

Mertensia ciliata

tall fringed bluebells

BORAGINACEAE BORAGE FAMILY

PCT Sections: 9–18 **Abundance:** Occasional **Height:** 1–5 ft. **Flowering:** May–August **Flower Color:** Blue **Habitat-Community:** Wet meadows, streambanks, and moist slopes from lower montane to subalpine coniferous forests and wetland-riparian communities **Elevation:** Below 11,100 ft. **Ecoregions:** Sierra Nevada, Cascades

Erect perennial with multiple shiny, green, hairless stems. Leaves 2–7 in. long, alternate, elliptic or lance-shaped, conspicuously veined, clasping (on upper stem). Flowers in hanging 1-sided clusters at stem tips. Calyces to 0.2 in. long, 5-lobed. Corollas 0.4–0.7 in. long, 5-parted, narrow bell-shaped, blue, with fused petals. Fruits wrinkled nutlets. Finding these little bells in wet areas is a special treat. Often grows with *Salix* and *Erythranthe*.

Nama demissa

purplemat

BORAGINACEAE BORAGE FAMILY

PCT Sections: 1–8 **Abundance:** Locally common **Height:** 1–4 in. **Flowering:** March–May **Flower Color:** Purple (bluish) to rose-pink **Habitat-Community:** Dry, sandy soils and washes in creosote bush & saltbush scrubs and Joshua tree & pinyon-juniper woodlands **Elevation:** Below 6300 ft. **Ecoregions:** Southern California Mountains, Sierra Nevada

Prostrate annual, forming mats 2–10 in. across, with distinctly forked branching pattern to its hairy stems. Leaves 0.4–1.3 in. long, alternate, clustered at stem forks, linear to spoon-shaped, with no petioles. Flowers 5-parted, in clusters of leaves. Calyx lobes to 0.3 in. long, narrowly lance-shaped. Corollas 0.3–0.6 in. across, funnel-shaped, with purple (bluish) to rose-pink fused petals. Fruits tiny, several-seeded capsules. Found along the PCT only at the lower desert crossings.

Nama rothrockii

Rothrock's fiddleleaf

BORAGINACEAE BORAGE FAMILY

PCT Sections: 4 & 9–10 **Abundance:** Locally common **Height:** 8–12 in. **Flowering:** July–August **Flower Color:** Purple to pale blue **Habitat-Community:** Dry meadows and gravelly, granitic slopes and flats from pinyon-juniper woodlands to subalpine coniferous forests **Elevation:** 5200–10,000 ft. **Ecoregions:** Southern California Mountains, Sierra Nevada

Erect, 0–few branched, sticky perennial with densely glandular- and bristle-hairy stems. Leaves 0.8–2.5 in. long, alternate, lance-shaped to elliptic, with lobed margins. Flowers in spheric heads at stem tips, with stamens hidden inside tube. Calyx lobes to 0.6 in. long, 5, narrowly lance-shaped. Corollas 0.5–0.7 in. long, to 0.4 in. across, 5-parted, funnel-shaped; petals fused, purple to pale blue. Fruits to 0.3 in. long, capsules with pitted, brownish seeds. The purple pom-pom-like flower heads are easy to spot while hiking or riding.

Phacelia austromontana

southern Sierra phacelia

BORAGINACEAE BORAGE FAMILY

PCT Sections: 4–5 & 8–9 **Abundance:** Occasional **Height:** 2–10 in. **Flowering:** May–July **Flower Color:** Pale blue to lavender **Habitat-Community:** Open, sandy to rocky areas from sagebrush scrubs to upper montane coniferous forests **Elevation:** Below 9400 ft. **Ecoregions:** Southern California Mountains, Sierra Nevada

Inconspicuous, erect to spreading, few-branched annual with sparsely stiff-hairy stems. Leaves 0.4–1.2 in. long, lance-shaped, with smooth or slightly lobed margins. Flowers 5-parted, in 1-sided clusters along curving, glandular stalks. Corollas bell-shaped, 0.1–0.2 in. long, with yellow tube and white to lavender lobes. Fruits 0.2–0.3 in. across, capsules with about 30 seeds. Limited along the PCT to the San Bernardino and San Gabriel Mountains and the southern Sierra, where it overlaps with *P. eisenii* in Section 9. *Austromontana* means "from the southern mountains."

Phacelia campanularia

desert bluebells

BORAGINACEAE BORAGE FAMILY

PCT Sections: 2–5 **Abundance:** Locally common **Height:** 6–28 in. **Flowering:** February–May **Flower Color:** Blue **Habitat-Community:** Open, sandy to rocky areas in scrubs and Joshua tree & pinyon-juniper woodlands **Elevation:** Below 5200 ft. **Ecoregions:** Southern California Mountains, Sonoran/Mojave Basin and Range

Stunning, few-branched annual with green or reddish, glandular-hairy stems. Leaves 1–4 in. wide, ovoid to round, shiny dark green, with toothed margins. Flowers 5-parted, loosely arranged 1-sided along curving stalks, with stamens and style protruding; pedicels thick, reddish, glandular. Corollas 0.5–1.7 in. long, rotate to bell-shaped, bright blue. Fruits 0.3–0.6 in. across, ovoid, glandular-hairy capsules. Limited along the PCT to the lower desert regions east and south of the Palmdale region. Intermediate forms make distinguishing between var. *campanularia* (corolla rotate; uncommon) and var. *vasiformis* (corolla funnel-shaped; more common) challenging. Causes contact dermatitis in some people. In other words, don't touch!

Phacelia cicutaria
caterpillar phacelia
BORAGINACEAE BORAGE FAMILY

PCT Sections: 1–9 **Abundance:** Common **Height:** 7–28 in. **Flowering:** February–June **Flower Color:** Pale lavender to yellow-white **Habitat-Community:** Rocky slopes and shaded understories in California prairies, oak woodlands, and chaparrals **Elevation:** Below 6100 ft. **Ecoregions:** Southern California Mountains, Sierra Nevada

Erect, long-branched annual with grayish, glandular-hairy stems. Leaves 1–6 in. long, ovoid in outline, deeply lobed to compound, with toothed segments. Flowers clustered along coiled, fuzzy-haired flowering stalks, 5-parted. Corollas bell-shaped, pale lavender to yellow-white, 0.3–0.6 in. long. Fruits ovoid capsules 0.1–0.2 in. across. Two varieties along the PCT: var. *cicutaria* (yellow-white flowers with brown spots) is most common in the southern Sierra and Tehachapi Mountains; var. *hispida* (lavender flowers) is frequent in the Southern California Mountains. The flowering stalks resemble a caterpillar (hence the common name).

Phacelia ciliata
Great Valley phacelia
BORAGINACEAE BORAGE FAMILY

PCT Sections: 6–8 **Abundance:** Occasional **Height:** 4–20 in. **Flowering:** February–June **Flower Color:** Blue **Habitat-Community:** Sandy to rocky or clayey slopes and flats from California prairies to lower montane coniferous forests **Elevation:** Below 6000 ft. **Ecoregions:** Southern California Mountains, Sierra Nevada

Erect annual, simple or branched at base, with short-hairy, somewhat glandular stems. Leaves 1–6 in. long, ovoid in outline, deeply lobed to compound, with toothed segments. Flowers 5-parted, scattered 1-sided along curving stalks. Calyces short-hairy with opaque margins. Corollas funnel- or bell-shaped, 0.3–0.5 in. long, with blue tube and blue to violet-blue lobes. Fruits 0.1–0.2 in. across, ovoid, short-hairy capsules. Most often found on clayey soils. Limited along the PCT to the far western Transverse Ranges (Liebre Mountains) and southern Sierra near Highway 58.

Phacelia cryptantha
hiddenflower phacelia
BORAGINACEAE BORAGE FAMILY

PCT Sections: 1–7 **Abundance:** Occasional **Height:** 6–20 in. **Flowering:** March–May **Flower Color:** Pale blue to lavender **Habitat-Community:** Canyons, rocky slopes, and shaded understories in Mojave mixed woody scrubs, woodlands, and montane chaparrals **Elevation:** Below 6000 ft. **Ecoregions:** Southern California Mountains, Sonoran/Mojave Basin and Range

Delicate, few-branched annual with stiff-hairy, glandular stems. Leaves 1–6 in. long, elliptic in outline, deeply lobed to compound, with toothed segments. Flowers 5-parted, dispersed 1-sided along coiled stems, with stamens and 2–3-branched style not exserted; calyces stiff-hairy. Corollas narrowly bell-shaped, pale blue to lavender, 0.1–0.3 in. long. Fruits 0.1–0.2 in. across, spherical, stiff-hairy capsules. *Cryptantha* suggests it has a cryptantha-like appearance.

Phacelia curvipes
Washoe phacelia
BORAGINACEAE BORAGE FAMILY

PCT Sections: 1–9 **Abundance:** Common **Height:** 2–6 in. **Flowering:** April–June **Flower Color:** Blue to violet **Habitat-Community:** Slopes, ridges, and shaded understories in woodlands, chaparrals, and lower montane coniferous forests **Elevation:** Below 8400 ft. **Ecoregions:** Southern California Mountains, Sierra Nevada

Low, spreading, much-branched annual with short-hairy, glandular (toward the tip) stems. Leaves 0.4–1.6 in. long, elliptic to lance-shaped, with smooth margins and prominent veins. Flowers 5-parted, 1-sided on open, glandular stalks; calyx lobes unequal. Corollas rotate to bell-shaped, 0.2–0.3 in. long, with white throat and blue to violet lobes. Fruits small-beaked capsules. Often found along the PCT in association with *Cercocarpus ledifolius*.

Phacelia davidsonii
Davidson's phacelia
BORAGINACEAE BORAGE FAMILY

PCT Sections: 1 & 4–8 **Abundance:** Locally common **Height:** 2–12 in. **Flowering:** April–June **Flower Color:** Blue to violet **Habitat-Community:** Ridges and flats in shaded understories in montane chaparrals and montane coniferous forests **Elevation:** Below 8400 ft. **Ecoregions:** Southern California Mountains, Sierra Nevada

Loosely matted, few-branched annual with both fine and sparsely stiff-hairy stems. Leaves 0.4–2.6 in. long, elliptic to lance-shaped, lobed bases to compound, with smooth tip. Flowers in 1-sided clusters, 5-parted. Corollas rotate to bell-shaped, 0.3–0.7 in. long, with white throat and blue to violet lobes. Fruits small, short-hairy capsules. Often found along the PCT in association with *Pinus jeffreyi*. Hybridizes with *Phacelia curvipes* in the San Bernardino and Laguna Mountains, yielding intermediate forms.

Phacelia distans
common phacelia
BORAGINACEAE BORAGE FAMILY

PCT Sections: 1–8 **Abundance:** Common **Height:** 6–32 in. **Flowering:** March–May **Flower Color:** Pale blue **Habitat-Community:** Sandy to rocky soils from scrubs to montane chaparrals **Elevation:** Below 8000 ft. **Ecoregions:** Southern California Mountains, Sonoran/Mojave Basin and Range, Sierra Nevada

Ubiquitous, erect to sprawling (generally through shrubs), few- to many-branched annual with glandular, soft-hairy stems. Leaves 1–4 in. long, 1–2-pinnate, with toothed leaflets. Flowers 5-parted, in coiled 1-sided clusters, with stamens and style exserted or not. Calyx lobes 0.1–0.3 in. long, unequal. Corollas funnel- to bell-shaped, 0.2–0.4 in. long, with pale blue (sometimes dirty white) lobes and dark-lavender-spotted throat. Fruits short-hairy spherical capsules. Widespread, occupying a range of habitats from dry desert scrub to moist slopes of the central coast of California.

Phacelia douglasii

Douglas' phacelia

BORAGINACEAE BORAGE FAMILY

PCT Sections: 4–8 **Abundance:** Locally common **Height:** 2–14 in. **Flowering:** March–May **Flower Color:** Pale blue to purple **Habitat-Community:** Sandy to clayey soils in foothill chaparrals and oak & pinyon-juniper woodlands **Elevation:** Below 5400 ft. **Ecoregions:** Southern California Mountains, Sierra Nevada

Prostrate to erect annual, branched at base, with glandular, short-hairy stems. Leaves 0.4–3 in. long, teardrop-shaped to ovoid, deeply lobed to compound, with rounded segments. Flowers 5-parted, 1-sided along stems, with stamens and style not exserted. Corollas 0.2–0.5 in. long, widely bell-shaped, with pale blue to white throat and pale blue to purple lobes. Fruits 0.2–0.3 in. across, ovoid capsules. Especially abundant in recent burns.

Phacelia exilis

Transverse Range phacelia

BORAGINACEAE BORAGE FAMILY

PCT Sections: 4–5 & 8–9 **Abundance:** Rare **Height:** 2–10 in. **Flowering:** May–August **Flower Color:** Lavender **Habitat-Community:** Sandy to rocky slopes, flats, and shaded understories in oak & pinyon-juniper woodlands and montane coniferous forests **Elevation:** Below 8800 ft. **Ecoregions:** Southern California Mountains, Sierra Nevada

Erect or decumbent annual, branched at base, with minutely glandular, short-hairy stems. Leaves 0.4–1.2 in. long, lance-shaped, with smooth margins. Flowers 5-parted, in loose 1-sided clusters on hairy stems, with white filaments and stamens within or only slightly exserted; calyx lobes unequal. Corollas 0.2–0.3 in. long, 0.3 in. across, bell-shaped; lobes lavender, each with 4 distinctive, linear, translucent patches. Fruits spherical, short-hairy capsules. This California endemic occurs along the PCT in the Big Bear Lake region of the San Bernardino Mountains and in the southern Sierra from the Piute Mountains to Kennedy Meadows.

Phacelia fremontii

Fremont's phacelia

BORAGINACEAE BORAGE FAMILY

PCT Sections: 4–9 **Abundance:** Common **Height:** 2–12 in. **Flowering:** March–June **Flower Color:** Blue to pink **Habitat-Community:** Sandy to gravelly slopes and flats in creosote bush scrubs, woodlands, and lower montane coniferous forests **Elevation:** Below 8500 ft. **Ecoregions:** Southern California Mountains, Sierra Nevada

Low-growing, decumbent to erect annual, branched at base, with short-hairy, minutely glandular (near flowers) stems. Leaves 0.6–2.1 in. long, oblong to teardrop-shaped in outline, deeply pinnately lobed (sometimes compound), with rounded segments. Flowers 5-parted, in 1-sided clusters on curved stems that exceed the leaves; stamens not exserted; calyces glandular. Corollas funnel- to bell-shaped, 0.3–0.8 in. long, with yellow tube and throat and blue to pink lobes. Fruits 0.1–0.3 in. across, ovoid, short-hairy capsules. Highly representative of the Mojave Desert, extending into the arid montane zones of the Transverse Ranges and southern Sierra.

Phacelia minor

California bluebell

BORAGINACEAE BORAGE FAMILY

PCT Sections: 1–6 **Abundance:** Locally common **Height:** 8–40 in. **Flowering:** March–June **Flower Color:** Purple **Habitat-Community:** Gravelly to rocky slopes in Sonoran/Mojave mixed woody scrubs, oak woodlands, and foothill chaparrals **Elevation:** Below 5800 ft. **Ecoregions:** Southern California Mountains

Erect, few-branched annual with glandular-hairy stems. Leaves 0.5–2 in. wide, alternate, round to ovoid, with irregularly toothed margins; petiole longer than the blade. Flowers 5-parted, openly arranged 1-sided on curved stems that exceed the leaves, with bright white anthers and purple (sometimes white) stamens exserted. Corollas 0.4–1.6 in. long, bell-shaped, slightly constricted between tube and throat. Fruits 0.3–0.6 in. across, ovoid capsules with 30–60 seeds. Hybridizes with *P. parryi*. Secretes oil droplets that can cause an unpleasant skin rash, so look but don't touch!

Phacelia nashiana

Charlotte's phacelia

BORAGINACEAE BORAGE FAMILY

PCT Sections: 8–9 **Abundance:** Rare **Height:** 4–16 in. **Flowering:** March–June **Flower Color:** Bright blue **Habitat-Community:** Sandy to rocky slopes in creosote bush scrubs, Mojave mixed woody scrubs, and Joshua tree & pinyon-juniper woodlands **Elevation:** Below 6300 ft. **Ecoregions:** Sierra Nevada

Eye-catching, few-branched annual with black-gland-tipped hairs. Leaves 0.7–2.5 in. wide, alternate, mostly at base of plant, round to ovoid, with prominent veins and shallowly lobed margins; petiole about as long as blade. Flowers 5-parted, openly arranged 1-sided on curved stems that exceed the leaves, with white anthers and stamens somewhat exserted. Corollas 0.4–0.8 in. long, rotate to widely bell-shaped, with bright blue lobes and tube with 5 white spots. Fruits 0.3–0.6 in. across, ovoid capsules with 40–90 seeds. Endemic to the granitic slopes of the southern Sierra–Tehachapi Mountains desert ecotone. Look for it along the PCT in the Scodie Mountains, especially near Walker Pass.

Phacelia parryi

Parry's phacelia

BORAGINACEAE BORAGE FAMILY

PCT Sections: 1 & 5–6 **Abundance:** Locally common **Height:** 4–40 in. **Flowering:** March–May **Flower Color:** Violet to purple **Habitat-Community:** Open, sandy to gravelly soils in foothill chaparrals and oak woodlands **Elevation:** Below 6700 ft. **Ecoregions:** Southern California/Northern Baja Coast, Southern California Mountains

Erect, few-branched annual with stiff-hairy, glandular stems. Leaves 0.4–2.3 in. wide, alternate, oblong to ovoid, with irregularly toothed margins; petiole longer than the blade. Flowers 5-parted, velvety, openly arranged 1-sided on curved stems, with white anthers and stamens exserted. Corollas 0.4–0.8 in. long, 0.5–1 in. across, rotate to widely bell-shaped, with violet to deep purple lobes, white-spotted at base, and a white tube. Fruits 0.3–0.4 in. across, beaked capsules with 40–90 seeds. Most common in burns and along the PCT in southern San Diego County; may turn up in the western Transverse Ranges. Hybridizes with *P. minor*.

Phacelia tanacetifolia

lacy phacelia

BORAGINACEAE BORAGE FAMILY

PCT Sections: 4–9 **Abundance:** Locally common **Height:** 8–45 in. **Flowering:** March–May **Flower Color:** Pale blue to violet **Habitat-Community:** Open, sandy to gravelly slopes in creosote bush & Mojave mixed woody scrubs and woodlands **Elevation:** Below 7400 ft. **Ecoregions:** Southern California Mountains, Sierra Nevada

Erect to spreading (sometimes gaining support through shrubs), few-branched annual with stiff-hairy, glandular herbage. Leaves 1–8 in. long, alternate, generally compound, oblong to ovoid in outline, with intricately lobed and toothed leaflets (hence the common name). Flowers 5-parted, clustered on a several-branched coiled stem, with distinctively long stamens; calyx lobes linear, long-hairy. Corollas widely bell-shaped, pale blue to violet, 0.2–0.4 in. long. Fruits 0.1–0.2 in. across, capsules with 1–2 seeds. Native to the southwestern US and northern Mexico but planted worldwide as a cover crop and to attract pollinators. *Tanacetifolia* means "with leaves resembling *Tanacetum*," a genus in the Asteraceae.

Gentiana calycosa

Rainier pleated gentian

GENTIANACEAE GENTIAN FAMILY

PCT Sections: 9–24 **Abundance:** Locally common **Height:** 2–18 in. **Flowering:** July–September **Flower Color:** Deep blue **Habitat-Community:** Meadows, streambanks, and moist slopes from lower montane to subalpine coniferous forests and wetland-riparian communities **Elevation:** Below 12,800 ft. **Ecoregions:** Sierra Nevada, Cascades, Klamath Mountains

Decumbent perennial with 2–many hairless stems. Leaves to 2 in. long, opposite, ovoid to round, with minutely toothed margins. Flowers 1–few at stem tips. Calyces to 0.8 in. long, with 5 ovoid lobes. Corollas to 2 in. long, deep blue (rarely violet), narrowly bell-shaped, with 5 ovoid to round lobes to 0.5 in. long. Between each corolla lobe are 2–3 triangular appendages with thread-like tips. Fruits many-seeded capsules.

Gentiana newberryi

alpine gentian

GENTIANACEAE GENTIAN FAMILY

PCT Sections: 10–24 **Abundance:** Occasional **Height:** 2–5 in. **Flowering:** July–September **Flower Color:** Blue to white **Habitat-Community:** Meadows, streambanks, and moist slopes in subalpine coniferous forests and alpine and wetland-riparian communities **Elevation:** Below 13,200 ft. **Ecoregions:** Sierra Nevada, Cascades, Klamath Mountains

Decumbent perennial with 1–many hairless stems. Leaves to 2 in. long, opposite, spoon-shaped to linear, with smooth margins. Flowers 1–5 at stem tips. Calyces to 1.2 in. long, with 5 ovoid to linear lobes. Corollas to 2.2 in. long, blue to white (brown-purple on outside below lobes), narrowly bell-shaped, with 5 spoon-shaped to linear lobes to 0.7 in. long. Between each corolla lobe are 2 jagged, triangular appendages with thread-like tips. Fruits many-seeded capsules. Two varieties along the CA PCT: var. *newberryi* (corollas medium to deep blue) and var. *tiogana* (white to pale blue, with brown-purple streaks below lobes).

Gentianella amarella

autumn dwarf gentian

GENTIANACEAE GENTIAN FAMILY

PCT Sections: 4 & 9–21 **Abundance:** Occasional **Height:** 2–32 in. **Flowering:** July–September **Flower Color:** Blue to pink-violet or white **Habitat-Community:** Wet meadows, fens, and bogs in wetland-riparian communities **Elevation:** Below 11,500 ft. **Ecoregions:** Southern California Mountains, Sierra Nevada, Cascades, Klamath Mountains

Erect annual with 1 hairless stem. Leaves to 1.8 in. long, basal (withering early) and opposite, spoon-shaped to oblong, with smooth margins. Flowers generally many from the base of stem leaves. Calyces to 0.7 in. long, with 5 lobes 1–6 times longer than tube. Corollas to 0.8 in. long, blue to pink-violet or white, narrowly funnel-shaped, with 5 ovoid to triangular lobes to 0.2 in. long, with thread-like appendages at base of each. Fruits many-seeded capsules. The plant contains bitter alkaloids (hence *amarella*, "bitter").

Allophyllum divaricatum

purple false gilia

POLEMONIACEAE PHLOX FAMILY

PCT Sections: 3–6 & 15–19 **Abundance:** Occasional **Height:** 4–24 in. **Flowering:** April–June **Flower Color:** Purple or pink to red-purple **Habitat-Community:** Open, sandy areas in foothill chaparrals, oak woodlands, and lower montane coniferous forests **Elevation:** Below 5800 ft. **Ecoregions:** Southern California Mountains, Sierra Nevada, Cascades

Erect to ascending, branching annual with skunk-like odor and glandular-hairy stems. Leaves 0.4–1.6 in. long, alternate, pinnately 3–13-lobed, the lobes lance-shaped and reduced up stem, becoming palmately 3-lobed. Flowers 5-parted, in loose clusters, 2–8 per cluster, pedicelled. Calyx lobes 0.1 in. long, linear, membranous, glandular. Corollas fused into red-purple tube 0.3–1 in. long with spreading, purple or pink lobes. Fruits spherical capsules. All 4 *Allophyllum* spp. occur along the CA PCT–so it's also the Allophyllum Trail!

Allophyllum gilioides
subsp. *violaceum*

violet false gilia

POLEMONIACEAE PHLOX FAMILY

PCT Sections: 1–18 **Abundance:** Locally common **Height:** 4–8 in. **Flowering:** April–July **Flower Color:** Violet or purple to blue **Habitat-Community:** Open, sandy soils from sagebrush scrubs to upper montane coniferous forests **Elevation:** Below 10,400 ft. **Ecoregions:** Southern California Mountains, Sierra Nevada, Cascades

Erect to ascending, many-branched annual with glandular, short-hairy stems. Leaves 0.4–1 in. long, alternate, pinnately 3–7-lobed, the lobes linear and the central lobe largest. Flowers 5-parted, in loose clusters of 1–3, pedicelled. Calyx lobes 0.1 in. long, linear, membranous, glandular. Corolla tube dark purple, 0.2–0.3 in. long, with spreading, violet to blue lobes 0.1 in. long. Fruits spherical capsules. *Violaceum* (from the Latin, "violet-colored") describes the corolla lobes.

Allophyllum glutinosum

sticky false gilia

POLEMONIACEAE PHLOX FAMILY

PCT Sections: 1–5 **Abundance:** Locally common **Height:** 4–28 in. **Flowering:** April–June **Flower Color:** Pale blue to violet **Habitat-Community:** Areas of full sun in foothill chaparrals and oak woodlands **Elevation:** Below 5200 ft. **Ecoregions:** Southern California Mountains

Straggly (often climbing through or over neighboring plants), aromatic, small-flowered annual with densely glandular-hairy (sticky) stems. Leaves 0.4–1 in. long, alternate, the lower leaves pinnately 5–11-lobed, the upper palmately lobed. Flowers 5-parted, in open clusters of 2–8 on glandular stems. Calyx lobes 0.2 in. long, glandular. Corollas pale blue to violet, weakly bilateral (upon close inspection), with 2-lobed upper lip, 3-lobed lower lip, and short tube 0.1–0.2 in. long; stamens exserted. Fruits spheric capsules. *Glutinosum* means "sticky" in Latin.

Eriastrum densifolium

giant woollystar

POLEMONIACEAE PHLOX FAMILY

PCT Sections: 1–9 **Abundance:** Locally common **Height:** 8–24 in. **Flowering:** June–September **Flower Color:** Blue to purple **Habitat-Community:** Open slopes and burns in chaparrals, woodlands, and lower montane coniferous forests **Elevation:** Below 9200 ft. **Ecoregions:** Southern California Mountains, Mojave Basin and Range, Sierra Nevada

Intricately branched perennial from a woody base with hairy to woolly stems. Leaves 0.4–2 in. long, alternate, and pinnately lobed with 3–15 linear, hairless to woolly lobes. Flowers 5-parted, in head-like clusters of 10–20 at the tips of branches. Calyx lobes unequal and funnel-shaped, with long tube. Corollas 0.6–1.4 in. long, blue to purple, with lobes 0.2–0.6 in. long (sometimes appearing bilateral); stamens unequally positioned, exserted. Fruits few-seeded capsules. The only perennial eriastrum in the US. Three of the 5 subspecies in California occur along the PCT; subsp. *austromontanum*, found in Sections 1–9, is the most common.

Eriastrum diffusum

miniature woollystar

POLEMONIACEAE PHLOX FAMILY

PCT Sections: 1–5 & 8 **Abundance:** Occasional **Height:** 1–8 in. **Flowering:** March–June **Flower Color:** Pale blue to white **Habitat-Community:** Open, sandy soils in creosote bush & Sonoran/ Mojave mixed woody scrubs and Joshua tree & pinyon-juniper woodlands **Elevation:** Below 6300 ft. **Ecoregions:** Southern California Mountains, Sonoran/Mojave Basin and Range, Sierra Nevada

Erect, much-branched annual with hairy to nearly hairless, dark red-brown stems. Leaves 0.4–2 in. long, alternate, 1–3-lobed at base, thread-like, hairless to woolly. Flowers 5-parted, in woolly clusters amid leafy bracts; stamens exserted. Calyx lobes unequal; corollas funnel-shaped, 0.2–0.4 in. long, with white, yellow, or pale blue tube and pale blue or white lobes. Fruits minute capsules. Found along the PCT primarily in the desert regions. Despite the specific epithet, it is frequently short-statured and tightly branching, not open or diffuse.

Eriastrum sapphirinum

sapphire woollystar

POLEMONIACEAE PHLOX FAMILY

PCT Sections: 1–8 **Abundance:** Locally common **Height:** 2–16 in. **Flowering:** May–August **Flower Color:** Bright blue to lavender **Habitat-Community:** Open areas in oak & pinyon-juniper woodlands, montane chaparrals, and lower montane coniferous forests **Elevation:** Below 8800 ft. **Ecoregions:** Southern California Mountains, Sierra Nevada

Erect to ascending annual with glandular, woolly stems. Leaves 0.2–2.2 in. long, alternate, smooth-margined to 2-lobed, thread-like, hairless to woolly. Flowers in woolly clusters of 1–4, 5-parted, tubular, radial (to slightly bilateral); stamens (yellow to white anthers) exserted. Calyx lobes glandular. Corollas funnel-shaped, 0.5–0.7 in. long, with white or yellow tube, yellow throat, and bright blue to lavender lobes 0.2–0.3 in. long. Fruits minute capsules. Look for it in isolated but dense populations along the PCT, favoring compacted soils on the edges of scrub vegetation.

Eriastrum signatum

maroon-spotted woollystar

POLEMONIACEAE PHLOX FAMILY

PCT Sections: 4–8 **Abundance:** Occasional **Height:** 2–14 in. **Flowering:** May–August **Flower Color:** Pale blue **Habitat-Community:** Open areas in sagebrush scrubs and oak & pinyon-juniper woodlands **Elevation:** Below 7800 ft. **Ecoregions:** Southern California Mountains, Sierra Nevada

Erect, wiry, slender annual with woolly stems. Leaves 0.2–1.3 in. long, alternate, smooth-margined to 2-lobed, thread-like, cobwebby-hairy. Flowers in woolly clusters of 1–4, 5-parted, tubular, radial; stamens exserted. Corollas 0.3–0.5 in. long, trumpet-shaped, with yellow to white tube, maroon-spotted throat, and pale blue lobes 0.1–0.2 in. long. Fruits minute capsules. This very challenging genus remains ripe (pun intended) for additional taxonomic study.

Eriastrum wilcoxii

Wilcox's woollystar

POLEMONIACEAE PHLOX FAMILY

PCT Sections: 9–11 **Abundance:** Locally common **Height:** 3–12 in. **Flowering:** June–August **Flower Color:** Blue **Habitat-Community:** Open, sandy soils from sagebrush scrubs and pinyon-juniper woodlands to upper montane coniferous forests **Elevation:** Below 9600 ft. **Ecoregions:** Sierra Nevada

Erect, generally robust annual with woolly to almost hairless herbage. Leaves to 1.2 in. long, alternate, and thread-like or 1-7-lobed near base. Flowers 2–3 at stem tips. Calyces unequally 5-lobed, woolly, with lobes connected by a thin membrane. Corollas to 0.6 in. long, funnel-shaped, with blue lobes and yellow or white tube and throat with stamens of unequal length protruding. Fruits capsules with up to 9 seeds. *Eriastrum* means "woolly star" in Greek.

Gilia angelensis

chaparral gilia

POLEMONIACEAE PHLOX FAMILY

PCT Sections: 1–6 **Abundance:** Common **Height:** 5–20 in. **Flowering:** February–June **Flower Color:** Pale lavender to blue or white **Habitat-Community:** Open, sandy to rocky soils in foothill chaparrals, oak woodlands, and lower montane coniferous forests **Elevation:** Below 6200 ft. **Ecoregions:** Southern California/Northern Baja Coast, Southern California Mountains

Erect annual, branching from base, with short, translucent hairs. Leaves mostly basal in erect clusters, 1–3-pinnately lobed, the lobes linear, hairless to short-hairy; stem leaves alternate, reduced. Flowers in open clusters of 1–10, 5-parted, tubular, radial; calyces 0.1–0.2 in. long with blue membranes between lobes. Corollas 0.5–0.7 in. long, funnel-shaped, with white tube included in the calyx and anthers completely within tube; throat yellow and cup-shaped; lobes pale lavender to blue or white, 0.1–0.2 in. long. Fruits minute capsules. Very common in the chaparral of southern California. *Angelensis* means "of Los Angeles County."

Gilia brecciarum

Nevada gilia

POLEMONIACEAE PHLOX FAMILY

PCT Sections: 2–9 **Abundance:** Common **Height:** 4–15 in. **Flowering:** March–June **Flower Color:** Purple **Habitat-Community:** Open, sandy areas in creosote bush & sagebrush scrubs and Joshua tree & pinyon-juniper woodlands **Elevation:** Below 7800 ft. **Ecoregions:** Southern California Mountains, Sonoran/Mojave Basin and Range, Sierra Nevada

Spreading to erect, rosetted annual with skunk-like odor and woolly tufts at stem base and leaf axils. Leaves 1–2 in. long, mostly basal, pinnately lobed; stem leaves alternate, reduced, variously clasping. Flowers in small clusters, 5-parted, tubular, radial, sticky, with minute, black, stalked pedicel glands; stamens exserted. Calyces 0.1–0.2 in. long, thick, densely glandular. Corollas funnel-shaped, 0.3–0.8 in. long, with purple (below) and white (above) tube and white or yellow purple-veined throat. Corolla lobes 0.1–0.3 in. long, purple. Fruits broadly ovoid capsules. Two subspecies along the PCT: subsp. *brecciarum* (shorter corolla; more yellow on the throat) and subsp. *neglecta* (mostly confined to the southern Sierra).

Gilia capitata

bluehead gilia

POLEMONIACEAE PHLOX FAMILY

PCT Sections: 1–9 & 13–24 **Abundance:** Common **Height:** 4–36 in. **Flowering:** March–August **Flower Color:** Blue, purplish, or white **Habitat-Community:** Open, rocky or sandy soils from scrubs, woodlands, and chaparrals to subalpine coniferous forests **Elevation:** Below 9900 ft. **Ecoregions:** All

Erect, branched annual with glandular and hairy to glandless and hairless herbage. Leaves alternate, 1–3-pinnately lobed, the lobes with toothed to smooth margins. Flowers in dense head-like clusters of 25–100 at stem tips. Calyces to 0.2 in. long, 5-lobed, with lobes connected by a thin membrane. Corollas to 0.5 in. long, funnel-shaped, blue, purplish, or white, with linear to oblong lobes. Fruits capsules with ≤25 seeds. Of the varieties found in CA, 4 of the 8 subspecies are likely to occur along the PCT.

Gilia diegensis

coastal gilia

POLEMONIACEAE PHLOX FAMILY

PCT Sections: 1–6 **Abundance:** Common **Height:** 4–16 in. **Flowering:** March–June **Flower Color:** Lavender to white **Habitat-Community:** Open, sandy areas in foothill chaparrals, oak woodlands, and lower montane coniferous forests **Elevation:** Below 6800 ft. **Ecoregions:** Southern California/Northern Baja Coast, Southern California Mountains

Erect annual with basal rosettes and waxy-coated (below), glandular (above) stems. Basal leaves 1–3 in. long, toothed or pinnately lobed; stem leaves alternate, reduced, wide at base or clasping. Flowers generally in loose clusters at stem tips, 5-parted, tubular, radial; stamens (blue pollen) slightly exserted. Calyces 0.1–0.2 in. long, glandular, with white-margined lobes. Corollas 0.3–0.5 in. long, funnel-shaped, with purple (white above) tube, purple to yellow throat, and lavender to white lobes 0.1–0.5 in. long; white flowers are typically as common as lavender. Fruits minute capsules.

Gilia latiflora

broad-flowered gilia

POLEMONIACEAE PHLOX FAMILY

PCT Sections: 4–9 **Abundance:** Locally common **Height:** 4–13 in. **Flowering:** March–June **Flower Color:** Lavender to white **Habitat-Community:** Open, sandy or gravelly areas in creosote bush & Mojave mixed woody scrubs and Joshua tree & pinyon-juniper woodlands **Elevation:** Below 7500 ft. **Ecoregions:** Southern California Mountains, Mojave Basin and Range, Sierra Nevada

Showy, fragrant annual with basal rosette and hairy or hairless lower stems. Basal leaves toothed or lobed, 1–3 in. long; stem leaves alternate, highly reduced, with wide, clasping bases. Flowers clustered on spreading-ascending branches, 5-parted, tubular, radial; stamens exserted. Calyces 0.1–0.3 in. long, glandular, with white-margined lobes. Corollas 0.5–1.4 in. long, trumpet-shaped, with purple tube, white upper throat and lobe bases, and lavender lobe tips. Fruits 0.2–0.4 in. long, capsules.

Gilia sinuata

rosy gilia

POLEMONIACEAE PHLOX FAMILY

PCT Sections: 1–8 **Abundance:** Locally common **Height:** 5–14 in. **Flowering:** March–June **Flower Color:** Lavender to pink or white **Habitat-Community:** Coarse soils in creosote bush & Mojave mixed woody scrubs, Joshua tree & pinyon-juniper woodlands, and lower montane coniferous forests **Elevation:** Below 8500 ft. **Ecoregions:** Southern California Mountains, Mojave Basin and Range, Sierra Nevada

Erect, single-stemmed annual with basal rosette and hairless stems, wax-coated in lower half, glandular above. Basal leaves 1–2 in. long, toothed or pinnately lobed, cobwebby-hairy or hairless; stem leaves alternate, reduced, with wide, clasping bases. Flowers in open clusters at stem tips, 5-parted, tubular, radial; stamens (white pollen) not exserted. Calyces 0.1–0.2 in. long, dark glandular. Corollas 0.3–0.5 in. long, trumpet-shaped, with white-veined purple tube extending above calyx, yellow throat, and lavender to pink or white lobes 0.1 in. long. Fruits capsules with 9–27 seeds.

Linanthus parryae

sandblossoms

POLEMONIACEAE PHLOX FAMILY

PCT Sections: 4–9 **Abundance:** Locally common **Height:** 1–4 in. **Flowering:** March–May **Flower Color:** Blue-purple or white **Habitat-Community:** Sandy flats and gentle slopes in creosote bush scrubs and Joshua tree & pinyon-juniper woodlands **Elevation:** Below 6300 ft. **Ecoregions:** Southern California Mountains, Mojave Basin and Range, Sierra Nevada

Large-flowered annual with very short, inconspicuous, glandular-hairy stems. Leaves crowded below flowers, deeply lobed, the lobes linear, hairy, 0.2–0.6 in. long. Flowers in clusters at ground level, 5-parted, tubular, radial, with yellow anthers. Calyces 0.2–0.3 in. long with obscure tubes. Corollas funnel-shaped, with blue-purple or white (dark purple spots at base) lobes 0.3–0.5 in. long; populations often contain both blue and white flowers. Fruits obovoid capsules. Exclusively pollinated by melyrid beetles. The large flowers and highly reduced stems give the appearance of stemless flowers sitting directly on the ground!

Polemonium californicum

California Jacob's ladder

POLEMONIACEAE PHLOX FAMILY

PCT Sections: 11–24 **Abundance:** Occasional **Height:** 4–10 in. **Flowering:** June–August **Flower Color:** Bluish or purple **Habitat-Community:** Dry, open to shaded areas in upper montane & subalpine coniferous forests **Elevation:** 5200–10,200 ft. **Ecoregions:** Sierra Nevada, Cascades, Klamath Mountains

Sprawling to erect, clumped perennial with soft, gland-tipped hairs. Leaves to 2 in. wide, basal (mostly) and alternate, pinnate, with 9–25 oblong to lance-shaped leaflets, the terminal leaflet generally fused with adjacent pair. Flowers 5–25 in open heads at stem tips above the leaves. Calyces to 0.3 in. long, bell-shaped, 5-lobed, lobes > tube. Corollas to 0.6 in. wide, bell-shaped, with bluish or yellow throat and bluish or purple lobes. Fruits to 0.2 in. long, capsules with 6–10 brown seeds. *Polemonium* is thought to refer to an unrelated Greek plant.

Polemonium eximium

showy skypilot

POLEMONIACEAE PHLOX FAMILY

PCT Sections: 10–12 **Abundance:** Occasional **Height:** 4–16 in. **Flowering:** June–August **Flower Color:** Blue to purple **Habitat-Community:** Rocky slopes and outcrops in alpine communities **Elevation:** 9800–13,800 ft. **Ecoregions:** Sierra Nevada

Erect, clumped perennial with glandular-hairy to hairy stems. Leaves to 5 in. long, 0.4 in. wide, basal and alternate along stem, glandular-hairy, pinnate, with 20–35, 3–5-lobed leaflets. Flowers many, in dense heads at stem tips, with a strong urine smell that attracts pollinators. Calyces to 0.3 in. long, bell-shaped, 5-lobed, lobes < tube. Corollas to 0.6 in. wide, funnel-shaped, blue to purple. Fruits to 0.2 in. long, capsules with ≤6 brown seeds. A skypilot is a person who leads others to heaven; as many skypilots grow on peak summits, they mark a perfect place to start the journey!

Polemonium occidentale

western skypilot

POLEMONIACEAE PHLOX FAMILY

PCT Sections: 10–24 **Abundance:** Occasional **Height:** 15–40 in. **Flowering:** June–September **Flower Color:** Purple to bluish **Habitat-Community:** Meadows and streambanks in wetland-riparian communities **Elevation:** Below 10,900 ft. **Ecoregions:** Sierra Nevada, Cascades, Klamath Mountains

Erect, single-stemmed perennial with glandular-hairy upper stems. Leaves to 16 in. long, to 3.5 in. wide, alternate, pinnate, with 15–23 lance-shaped leaflets, the terminal leaflet fused (or not) to adjacent pair. Flowers 10–35 in open or dense heads at stem tips. Calyces to 0.3 in. long, bell-shaped, glandular-hairy, 5-lobed, lobes > tube. Corollas to 0.7 in. wide at lobes, bell-shaped, purple to bluish. Fruits to 0.2 in. long, capsules with ≤10 dark seeds.

Saltugilia caruifolia

caraway-leaved woodland gilia

POLEMONIACEAE PHLOX FAMILY

PCT Sections: 1–2 **Abundance:** Occasional **Height:** 0.5–3 ft. **Flowering:** May–August **Flower Color:** Lavender to blue **Habitat-Community:** Open, gravelly or rocky soils from oak woodlands to lower montane coniferous forests **Elevation:** Below 7300 ft. **Ecoregions:** Southern California Mountains

Erect, slender, branching (above) annual with hairless to glandular lower stems. Leaves 1–6 in. long, 2–3-pinnately lobed in erect basal rosette, the linear segments covered in long-hairy, translucent hairs; stem leaves alternate, reduced. Flowers on spreading branches at stem tips, 5-parted, tubular, radial, with hairless calyces 0.1–0.2 in. long. Corollas 0.3–0.6 in. long, with purple tube extending beyond calyx, white (or purple) throat, and lavender to blue lobes (with purple marks at base). Fruits ovoid capsules. Of conservation concern in California. Look for it along the PCT in the Laguna Mountains or hills above Warner Springs in San Diego County.

Solanum parishii

Parish's nightshade

SOLANACEAE NIGHTSHADE FAMILY

PCT Sections: 1–2 & 18–24 **Abundance:** Locally common **Height:** 16–32 in. **Flowering:** April–July **Flower Color:** Purple to blue **Habitat-Community:** Open, gravelly or rocky soils in foothill chaparrals, oak woodlands, and lower montane coniferous forests **Elevation:** Below 6200 ft. **Ecoregions:** Southern California Mountains, Sierra Nevada, Cascades, Klamath Mountains

Many-branched perennial or subshrub with angled or ribbed and generally hairless stems. Leaves 1–3 in. long, short-petioled or sessile, lance-shaped to elliptic. Flowers 5-parted, in small, open clusters, with fused and elongated yellow anthers supported by green filaments; pedicels 0.5–0.7 in. long. Calyces 0.1–0.2 in. long, bell-shaped, hairless. Corollas rotate, blue to purple, 0.7–0.9 in. long. Fruits spherical, capsule-like berries. Several nightshades (e.g., tomato, potato, eggplant) are edible, but most (including this) contain toxic alkaloids and are poisonous! *Solanum* (from the Latin, "quieting") alludes to the narcotic properties of some species.

Solanum xanti

chaparral nightshade

SOLANACEAE NIGHTSHADE FAMILY

PCT Sections: 1–10 **Abundance:** Locally common **Height:** 18–34 in. **Flowering:** February–June **Flower Color:** Blue to lavender **Habitat-Community:** Gravelly or rocky soils in chaparrals, oak & pinyon-juniper woodlands, and montane coniferous forests **Elevation:** Below 8300 ft. **Ecoregions:** Southern California Mountains, Sierra Nevada

Many-branched perennial or subshrub with angled or ribbed stems and white-hairy, sometimes glandular herbage. Leaves 1–3 in. long, short-petioled or sessile, lance-shaped to ovoid, sometimes with lobed and wavy margins. Flowers 5-parted, clustered at stem tips, with fused and elongated, yellow anthers supported by green filaments. Calyces 0.1–0.2 in. long, bell-shaped, short-hairy. Corollas rotate, blue to lavender, 0.7–1.3 in. long. Fruits spherical, capsule-like berries 0.5–0.6 in. across. The most widespread nightshade along the trail. All its parts are toxic to humans and wildlife, especially the unripe fruit! The species is named after János Xántus (1825–1894), a Hungarian zoologist who collected in California and Baja.

▼ 5 FUSED PETALS / IRREGULAR COROLLAS

Agastache urticifolia

horse mint

LAMIACEAE MINT FAMILY

PCT Sections: 4 & 10–24 **Abundance:** Locally common **Height:** 3–6 ft. **Flowering:** May–August **Flower Color:** Rose-purple to pink **Habitat-Community:** Moist places from oak woodlands to subalpine coniferous forests **Elevation:** Below 9900 ft. **Ecoregions:** Southern California Mountains, Sierra Nevada, Cascades, Klamath Mountains

Erect, aromatic perennial with sparsely hairy stems. Leaves to 3 in. long, opposite, lance-shaped to triangular, with toothed margins. Flowers in densely clustered spikes. Calyces to 0.5 in. long, 5-lobed, 2-lipped. Corollas to 0.6 in. long, irregular, rose-purple to pink, 5-lobed, 2-lipped. Fruits 4 nutlets. *Agastache* is Greek for "many spikes." The seeds are reportedly edible.

Mentha canadensis

wild mint

LAMIACEAE MINT FAMILY

PCT Sections: 1 & 3–6 & 9–10 & 13–17 & 23–24
Abundance: Occasional **Height:** 6–24 in.
Flowering: July–October **Flower Color:** Pale blue,
violet, or white **Habitat-Community:** Moist soils,
meadows, streambanks, and lake margins from
foothill chaparrals to lower montane coniferous
forests and wetland-riparian communities
Elevation: Below 8000 ft. **Ecoregions:** All (except
Sonoran/Mojave Basin and Range)

Peppermint-scented, few-branched, rhizomatous perennial with generally 4-angled, short-hairy stems. Leaves 0.7–2 in. long, opposite, linear to lance-shaped, slightly reduced up the stem, short-hairy, with scalloped to short-toothed margins. Flowers in compact clusters in the axils of leaves. Calyces 4–5-lobed, radial, 0.1 in. long. Corollas 0.2–0.3 in. long, slightly irregular, 2-lipped, 4-parted, fused in lower half into a tube, with erect (not spreading), pale blue, violet, or white lobes. Fruits 4 small nutlets. California's only native *Mentha* sp. Rich in menthol compared to other mints and cultivated for numerous medicinal and commercial applications. Look for it along the PCT at the margins of perennial wetlands.

Monardella linoides

narrow-leaved monardella

LAMIACEAE MINT FAMILY

PCT Sections: 1–5 & 7–10 **Abundance:** Occasional
Height: 6–24 in. **Flowering:** June–October **Flower
Color:** Purple to pale blue or white **Habitat-
Community:** Open, rocky sites in montane
chaparrals and subalpine coniferous forests
Elevation: Below 8500 ft. **Ecoregions:** Southern
California Mountains, Sierra Nevada

Erect, gray-green perennial or subshrub, few-branched from base, with 4-angled, densely short-hairy stems. Leaves 0.4–1.4 in. long, opposite, linear to narrowly lance-shaped, gray-green, silver-hairy; petiole winged. Flower 5-parted, in clusters 0.3–1.2 in wide with papery, hairy, white- or straw-colored outer bracts. Calyces 5-lobed, stiff-hairy, the lobes spine-tipped. Corollas 2-lipped (the upper lip erect, 2-lobed, the lower 3-lobed, recurved), purple to pale blue or white, 0.4–0.6 in. long, with lobes fused into a tube. Fruits 4 small, ovoid nutlets. Highly variable, with 6 varieties in California.

Monardella odoratissima

mountain monardella

LAMIACEAE MINT FAMILY

PCT Sections: 4 & 8–24 **Abundance:** Common
Height: 4–18 in. **Flowering:** June–August **Flower
Color:** Lavender, purple, or pink to white **Habitat-
Community:** Rocky openings from sagebrush
scrubs to subalpine coniferous forests **Elevation:**
Below 11,500 ft. **Ecoregions:** Southern California
Mountains, Sierra Nevada, Cascades, Klamath
Mountains

Erect, strongly aromatic perennial with generally hairy, green to grayish stems. Leaves to 2 in. long, opposite, oblong to ovoid, with smooth margins. Flowers slightly irregular, in dense, head-like clusters. Calyces to 0.4 in. long, 5-lobed, 2-lipped. Corollas to 0.8 in. long, lavender, purple, or pink to white, 5-lobed, slightly 2-lipped. Fruits 4 nutlets. *Monardella* means "small *Monarda.*" The sweet smell is very obvious as you hike through patches of this delightful plant.

Prunella vulgaris var. *lanceolata*

lanceleaf selfheal

LAMIACEAE MINT FAMILY

PCT Sections: 3–5 & 10–24 **Abundance:** Common **Height:** 4–16 in. **Flowering:** May–September **Flower Color:** Blue-violet **Habitat-Community:** Moist, generally disturbed soils from woodlands and chaparrals to upper montane coniferous forests **Elevation:** Below 8200 ft. **Ecoregions:** Southern California Mountains, Sierra Nevada, Cascades, Klamath Mountains

Erect to prostrate, clumped or single-stemmed perennial with short-hairy to hairless stems. Leaves to 2.8 in. long, opposite, ovoid to lance-shaped, with smooth margins. Flowers bisexual or female only, in dense, head-like clusters above 2 leaf-like bracts. Calyces to 0.4 in. long, 5-toothed/lobed, 2-lipped. Corollas irregular, to 0.6 in. long, blue-violet (rarely pink or white), 5-lobed, 2-lipped. Fruits 4 nutlets. This medicinal plant has been used to fight or treat inflammation, cancer, diabetes complications, and herpes. Tea is commonly made from the leaves, which can also be added to salads. The nonnative selfheal (var. *vulgaris*), found in moist, generally disturbed habitats, has wider leaves and stems prostrate to sometimes erect.

Salvia carduacea

thistle sage

LAMIACEAE MINT FAMILY

PCT Sections: 1–8 **Abundance:** Occasional **Height:** 0.5–3 ft. **Flowering:** March–May **Flower Color:** Lavender to pale blue **Habitat-Community:** Sandy to gravelly soils in scrubs, foothill chaparrals, and Joshua tree woodlands **Elevation:** Below 4600 ft. **Ecoregions:** Southern California Mountains, Sonoran/Mojave Basin and Range, Sierra Nevada

Pungent (odor reminiscent of lemongrass), prickly annual with a single white-woolly stem. Leaves 1–4 in. long, mostly basal, 1-pinnately dissected, spoon-shaped, white-cobwebby, with wavy, spine-toothed margins. Flowers whorled around the flowering stem in clusters 0.6–1.2 in. across, 5-parted, with spiny bracts 1–2 in. long and bright orange anthers. Calyces 5-lobed, the lobes spine-tipped. Corollas erect, 2-lipped (with fringed and jagged margins), lavender to pale blue, 0.6–1.1 in. long, with lobes fused into a tube, the upper lip 2-lobed, the lower 3-lobed and twice as long as the upper. Fruits 4 small nutlets. Occurs along the CA PCT at the lower mountain passes and desert crossings, often in isolated populations. Fittingly, *carduacea* means "thistle-like" in Latin.

Salvia columbariae

chia sage

LAMIACEAE MINT FAMILY

PCT Sections: 1–9 **Abundance:** Locally common **Height:** 4–20 in. **Flowering:** March–June **Flower Color:** Blue **Habitat-Community:** Dry, generally disturbed soils from woodlands and chaparrals to lower montane coniferous forests **Elevation:** Below 8200 ft. **Ecoregions:** Southern California/ Northern Baja Coast, Southern California Mountains, Sierra Nevada

Erect to ascending annual with short-hairy stems. Leaves to 4 in. long, mostly basal, oblong-ovoid, 1–2-pinnately lobed, with minutely bristly margins. Flowers in dense, rounded clusters scattered along stem with awn-tipped bracts. Calyces to 0.4 in. long, 4–5-awned/lobed, 2-lipped. Corollas irregular, to 0.5 in. long, blue, 5-lobed, 2-lipped. Fruits 4 tan to gray nutlets. The nutritive seeds, ready for collection 1–2 months after flowering, have historically been ground into a flour for mush or cakes. A drink can be made from 1 teaspoon of seeds, flavored with sugar or lemon. Chia sprouts, available in many stores, are a popular addition to salads.

Scutellaria siphocampyloides

grayleaf skullcap

LAMIACEAE MINT FAMILY

PCT Sections: 3–9 & 17–22 **Abundance:** Occasional **Height:** 8–22 in. **Flowering:** May–July **Flower Color:** Violet to blue **Habitat-Community:** Sandy to gravelly soils in seeps and dry streambeds from oak woodlands to upper montane coniferous forests **Elevation:** Below 8200 ft. **Ecoregions:** Southern California Mountains, Sierra Nevada, Cascades, Klamath Mountains

Erect rhizomatous perennial, covered with short, gland-tipped hairs. Basal leaves 1–2 in. long, short-petioled, lance-shaped; stem leaves opposite, reduced, ovoid, green to gray-green, with smooth margins. Flowers 2-lipped, scattered along stems in leaf axils. Calyces with distinctive dish-like ridge on the upper lip. Corollas violet to blue, 1–1.5 in. long, with hood-like upper lip and longer, white-spotted lower lip, the fused lobes forming tube. Fruits 4 small nutlets. The genus name (from the Latin *scutella*, "small dish") refers to the shape of the calyx ridge.

Scutellaria tuberosa

Danny's skullcap

LAMIACEAE MINT FAMILY

PCT Sections: 1 & 4–5 & 17–19 **Abundance:** Occasional **Height:** 8–22 in. **Flowering:** March–July **Flower Color:** Violet to blue **Habitat-Community:** Dry sites in foothill chaparrals and oak woodlands **Elevation:** Below 5000 ft. **Ecoregions:** Southern California/Northern Baja Coast, Southern California Mountains, Sierra Nevada, Cascades

Single- to many-branched perennial from tuberous rhizomes with 4-angled, green (aging purplish), glandular-hairy stems. Leaves 0.2–0.6 in. long, opposite, ovoid, densely hairy below, with scalloped margins. Flowers paired at leaf nodes, short-hairy throughout, 2-lipped. Calyces with distinctive dish-like ridge on the upper lip. Corollas violet to blue, 0.3–0.4 in. long, with hood-like upper lip and longer, slightly 3-lobed, white-spotted lower lip, the fused lobes forming tube. Fruits 4 small nutlets. Distributed on the coastal side of California mountains, intercepting the PCT only in a few maritime-influenced areas. Especially common in recent burns.

Trichostema oblongum

oblong
bluecurls

LAMIACEAE MINT FAMILY

PCT Sections: 10–24 **Abundance:** Locally common **Height:** to 20 in. **Flowering:** June–September **Flower Color:** Blue to lavender **Habitat-Community:** Dry streambanks and meadows from lower montane to subalpine coniferous forests **Elevation:** Below 9900 ft. **Ecoregions:** Sierra Nevada, Cascades, Klamath Mountains

Strongly aromatic annual with hairy and glandular stems. Leaves to 1.6 in. long, opposite, widely oblong, with smooth margins. Flowers in clusters at the base of leaves, with 4 stamens that extend far beyond the lobes. Calyx 5-lobed, the lobes >2 times longer than tube and widest at the base. Corollas irregular, to 0.3 in. long, blue to lavender, 5-lobed, the lower lobe forming an orchid-like lip. Fruits 4 hairy nutlets. It is pretty amazing to watch as pollinators land on the flowers and get pollen-tagged on their rump by the stamens.

Aphyllon cooperi

Cooper's
broomrape

OROBANCHACEAE
BROOMRAPE FAMILY

PCT Sections: 1–4 **Abundance:** Occasional **Height:** 2–15 in. **Flowering:** January–May **Flower Color:** Purple **Habitat-Community:** Sandy, alluvial flats and washes in creosote bush scrubs and Sonoran/Mojave mixed woody scrubs **Elevation:** Below 4800 ft. **Ecoregions:** Southern California Mountains, Sonoran/Mojave Basin and Range

Stout, white-hairy parasitic perennial (lacking leaves and chlorophyll); attaches to roots of *Ambrosia*, *Encelia*, or *Artemisia*. Flowers densely clustered on an erect spike about 2 in. wide, with pedicels to 2 in. long and 5 calyx lobes 0.3–0.5 in. long. Corollas purple with white streaks, 2-lipped, glandular-hairy, broadly tubular, 0.7–1.3 in. long, with 2-lobed upper lip and 3-lobed lower lip; lips 0.2–0.4 in. long. Fruits 2-valved capsules. Widespread in southwestern US deserts, intercepting the PCT only at the lower desert crossings of southern California, such as in San Felipe Valley in eastern San Diego County.

Aphyllon purpureum

one-flowered
broomrape

OROBANCHACEAE
BROOMRAPE FAMILY

PCT Sections: 4 & 8–24 **Abundance:** Locally common **Height:** to 4 in. **Flowering:** March–July **Flower Color:** Pale purple to yellow **Habitat-Community:** Moist or dry places in montane coniferous forests **Elevation:** Below 10,200 ft. **Ecoregions:** Southern California Mountains, Sierra Nevada, Cascades, Klamath Mountains

Parasitic perennial (lacking leaves and chlorophyll); specializes on various perennials, such as stonecrops, sunflowers, and saxifrages. Flowers 1 per stem, 2-lipped, held horizontal to ground. Calyces 5-lobed, the lobes to 0.3 in. long and > tube. Corollas 0.5–1.4 in. long, 5-lobed, funnel-shaped, pink or yellow, glandular-hairy. Fruits many-seeded capsules. Often hidden in the foliage of its host species.

Kopsiopsis strobilacea

California ground-cone

OROBANCHACEAE

BROOMRAPE FAMILY

PCT Sections: 3–5 & 8 & 18–24 **Abundance:** Occasional **Height:** 2–12 in. **Flowering:** April–June **Flower Color:** Purple to red-brown **Habitat-Community:** Open, dry places from woodlands to subalpine coniferous forests **Elevation:** Below 9900 ft. **Ecoregions:** Southern California Mountains, Sierra Nevada, Cascades, Klamath Mountains

Cone-shaped parasitic perennial (lacking leaves and chlorophyll); specializes on *Arctostaphylos* or *Arbutus menziesii*. Flowers in dense spikes with many overlapping bracts. Calyces 0–4-lobed, the lobes abruptly tapered, to 0.3 in. long. Corollas irregular, to 0.5 in. long, 2-lipped, 4-lobed, purple to red-brown (rarely yellow), with spreading lower lip. Fruits many-seeded capsules. Easy to overlook: they really do look like small pine cones lying on the ground.

Antirrhinum nuttallianum

Nuttall's snapdragon

PLANTAGINACEAE

PLANTAIN FAMILY

PCT Sections: 1–3 **Abundance:** Occasional **Height:** 1–6 ft. **Flowering:** May–July **Flower Color:** Lavender to purple-blue **Habitat-Community:** Open, rocky (especially burned) areas in California prairies, foothill chaparrals, and oak woodlands **Elevation:** Below 4200 ft. **Ecoregions:** Southern California/Northern Baja Coast, Southern California Mountains

Erect to sprawling annual or biennial with densely hairy herbage. Leaves 1–2.4 in. long, opposite, ovoid, point-tipped. Flowers 1 per leaf axil. Calyces 5-lobed, all lobes about equal. Corollas irregular, 0.3-0.5 in. long, lavender to purple-blue with white patches and purple veins, short-tubular, 2-lipped, the upper lip 2-lobed, the lower swollen (closing throat). Fruits ovoid capsules 0.1–0.3 in. long. Two forms: a vine-like stem that clings to other plants for support and a more traditional, vertically erect form.

Collinsia bartsiifolia

white collinsia

PLANTAGINACEAE

PLANTAIN FAMILY

PCT Sections: 4–8 **Abundance:** Occasional **Height:** 2–8 in. **Flowering:** April–June **Flower Color:** Pale lavender, pink, or white **Habitat-Community:** Open, sandy (especially burned) areas in foothill chaparrals and oak woodlands **Elevation:** Below 4400 ft. **Ecoregions:** Southern California Mountains, Mojave Basin and Range, Sierra Nevada

Erect, few-branched annual with finely hairy and glandular herbage. Leaves 0.4–1.6 in. long, opposite, thick, oblong, with rolled-under margins. Flowers in dense whorls scattered along stem, 5-lobed, with 4 stamens. Calyces fused at base, with blunt-tipped lobes. Corollas 0.4–0.6 in. long, short-tubular, 2-lipped, with reflexed white upper lip and 3-lobed, spreading, pale lavender to pink lower lip. Fruits small capsules. A California endemic, with several varieties along the PCT: var. *davidsonii*, with lavender lower petals, is the most common.

Collinsia callosa
desert collinsia
PLANTAGINACEAE

PLANTAIN FAMILY

PCT Sections: 4–9 **Abundance:** Locally common **Height:** 2–10 in. **Flowering:** April–June **Flower Color:** Blue **Habitat-Community:** Open, gravelly soils in sagebrush scrubs, chaparrals, pinyon-juniper woodlands, and lower montane coniferous forests **Elevation:** Below 7200 ft. **Ecoregions:** Southern California Mountains, Sierra Nevada

Erect, stout, fleshy little annual with hairless to finely glandular herbage. Leaves 0.3–1.2 in. long, opposite, clasping stem, oblong to ovoid, with thick, rolled-under margins. Flowers openly scattered along stem in leaf axils, 5-lobed, with 4 stamens. Calyces 0.1–0.2 in. wide, fused at base, urn-shaped, generally blunt-tipped, reddish. Corollas 0.2–0.4 in. long, short-tubular, 2-lipped (2-lobed upper, 3-lobed lower), with blue lobe tips, white bases, and purple spots in throat. Fruits small capsules. Fairly common in years of high precipitation but never in large populations. Best seen in the pinyon-juniper belt along the PCT in the more arid ranges bordering the Mojave Desert.

Collinsia childii
Child's collinsia
PLANTAGINACEAE

PLANTAIN FAMILY

PCT Sections: 1–7 **Abundance:** Locally common **Height:** 4–15 in. **Flowering:** April–July **Flower Color:** Lavender to white **Habitat-Community:** Shaded slopes from California prairies to lower montane coniferous forests **Elevation:** Below 6800 ft. **Ecoregions:** Southern California Mountains, Sierra Nevada

Erect, delicate annual with hairless to finely glandular, green herbage. Leaves 0.4–1.2 in. long, opposite, flat, spoon-shaped, with slightly toothed margins. Flowers openly scattered along stem in leaf axils, 5-lobed, with 4 stamens. Calyces 0.1–0.2 in. wide, fused at base, urn-shaped, glandular, blunt-tipped. Corollas 0.2–0.4 in. long, lavender to white, short-tubular, 2-lipped (2-lobed upper, 3-lobed lower), with forward-spreading lobes. Fruits small capsules. The folded lower lip of all collinsia flowers forms a narrow pocket that houses the stamens. The weight of a visiting insect depresses the lower lip, exposing the reproductive parts, thus facilitating pollination.

Collinsia concolor
Chinese houses
PLANTAGINACEAE

PLANTAIN FAMILY

PCT Sections: 1–3 **Abundance:** Common **Height:** 6–16 in. **Flowering:** April–July **Flower Color:** Purple to blue-purple **Habitat-Community:** Open slopes and ridges in California prairies, foothill chaparrals, and oak woodlands **Elevation:** Below 6200 ft. **Ecoregions:** Southern California Mountains

Upright annual with hairless to shaggy-hairy (becoming reddish) stems. Leaves 0.5–1.7 in. long, opposite, thin, spoon-shaped, hairless to sparsely hairy, with slightly toothed margins. Flowers clustered in dense whorls, well spaced along stem, 5-lobed. Calyces long-hairy with widely acute lobes. Corollas 0.5–0.7 in. long, short-tubular, 2-lipped, the upper lip 2-lobed, pale purple with purple dots, the lower 3-lobed, blue to blue-purple with notched lateral lobes. Fruits small capsules. Quite abundant along the PCT in the Peninsular Ranges. Early western botanists likened the whorled flowers to the stacked roofs of a pagoda (hence the common name).

Collinsia heterophylla
purple Chinese houses
PLANTAGINACEAE

PLANTAIN FAMILY

PCT Sections: 1–6 **Abundance:** Common **Height:** 4–20 in. **Flowering:** May–August **Flower Color:** Purple to lavender **Habitat-Community:** Shaded sites in foothill chaparrals, oak woodlands, and lower montane coniferous forests **Elevation:** Below 5700 ft. **Ecoregions:** Southern California Mountains

Erect annual with finely hairy to downy stems. Leaves 0.5–1.7 in. long, opposite, thin, spoon-shaped, mostly hairless, with slightly toothed margins. Flowers in dense whorls, well spaced along stem, 5-lobed, with 4 stamens. Calyces hairless to shaggy-hairy, with generally acute lobes. Corollas 0.4–0.8 in. long, short-tubular, 2-lipped, the upper lip 2-lobed, white to pale lavender with wine-colored spots, the lower 3-lobed, deep purple to lavender. Fruits small capsules.

Collinsia parryi
Parry's collinsia
PLANTAGINACEAE

PLANTAIN FAMILY

PCT Sections: 4–6 **Abundance:** Occasional **Height:** 4–16 in. **Flowering:** April–June **Flower Color:** Blue to lavender or white **Habitat-Community:** Dry, open places in foothill chaparrals, sagebrush scrubs, and oak woodlands **Elevation:** Below 5100 ft. **Ecoregions:** Southern California Mountains

Erect to ascending annual with finely hairy herbage. Leaves 0.3–1.1 in. long, opposite, thin, lance-shaped, clasping (on upper stem), with scalloped margins. Flowers in loose whorls of 1–3 on short pedicels, 5-lobed, with 4 stamens. Calyces 1–2 in. long, fused at base, with hairy-margined, blunt tips. Corollas 0.2–0.4 in. long, tubular, 2-lipped, the upper lip 2-lobed, blue to lavender with white, purple-spotted throat, the lower 3-lobed, the lobes minutely hairy along edges. Fruits small capsules. Best observed along the PCT in the lower transition zones between the San Bernardino and San Gabriel Mountains, where it may grow alongside 4 other *Collinsia* spp.!

Collinsia parviflora
small-flowered blue-eyed Mary
PLANTAGINACEAE

PLANTAIN FAMILY

PCT Sections: All **Abundance:** Common **Height:** 2–16 in. **Flowering:** March–July **Flower Color:** Blue **Habitat-Community:** Moist, shaded understories, everywhere but deserts **Elevation:** Below 11,000 ft. **Ecoregions:** All (except Sonoran/Mojave Basin and Range)

Erect, inconspicuous yet ubiquitous annual with reddish to sometimes dark brown stems. Leaves 0.5–1 in. long, opposite, lance-shaped, with prominent central vein and rolled-under margins. Flowers in loose whorls of 1–3 on short pedicels, 5-lobed, with 4 stamens. Calyces 0.1–0.2 in. long, fused at base, with acute lobes. Corollas 0.2–0.3 in. long, tubular, 2-lipped (upper 2-lobed, white; lower 3-lobed, blue), the lips barely angled from the tube. Fruits small capsules. Widespread, ranging from the Yukon Territories to southern California. *Parviflora* is Latin for "small-flowered." Who is Mary? Despite considerable investigation, she remains a mystery.

Collinsia torreyi

Torrey's blue-eyed Mary

PLANTAGINACEAE

PLANTAIN FAMILY

PCT Sections: 4–24 **Abundance:** Common **Height:** 2–10 in. **Flowering:** May–August **Flower Color:** Blue and white or pale lavender **Habitat-Community:** Sandy, generally granitic soils from lower montane to subalpine coniferous forests **Elevation:** Below 13,200 ft. **Ecoregions:** Southern California Mountains, Sierra Nevada, Cascades, Klamath Mountains

Erect, branched annual with glandular-hairy stems. Leaves 0.6–1.6 in. long, opposite, linear to oblong or ovoid, with smooth margins. Flowers 1–few at stem tips. Calyces to 0.2 in. long, 5-lobed, with blunt tips. Corollas irregular, 0.2–0.4 in. long, 2-lipped, with pea-like, blue lower lip and white or pale lavender upper lip. Fruits to 0.1 in. long, 2-seeded capsules with strongly curved pedicels. The specific epithet honors botanist John Torrey (1796–1873), who made plant collections in California in 1865.

Nuttallanthus texanus

blue toadflax

PLANTAGINACEAE

PLANTAIN FAMILY

PCT Sections: 1–4 **Abundance:** Occasional **Height:** 4–24 in. **Flowering:** March–May **Flower Color:** Violet to blue **Habitat-Community:** Sandy to gravelly hillsides and dry plains in foothill chaparrals and oak woodlands **Elevation:** Below 5200 ft. **Ecoregions:** Southern California/Northern Baja Coast, Southern California Mountains

Slender, erect (flowering stems) or decumbent (non-flowering stems) annual or biennial, branched at base, with hairless herbage. Leaves 0.2–1.1 in. long, alternate, narrowly linear. Flowers scattered along stem, 5-lobed, with 4 stamens, becoming dense in fruit. Calyces 0.1 in. long, fused at base, with acute-tipped lobes. Corollas 0.4–1.1 in. long, violet to blue, 2-lipped (2-lobed upper, 3-lobed lower), unequally bilateral, tubular, the tube spurred at base; spur 0.2–0.5 in. long. Fruits small, spherical capsules. *Nuttallanthus* has just 4 species, and this is the only one in California. An important nectar source for honeybees in coastal southern California.

Penstemon azureus

blue penstemon

PLANTAGINACEAE

PLANTAIN FAMILY

PCT Sections: 10–24 **Abundance:** Common **Height:** 7–28 in. **Flowering:** May–August **Flower Color:** Blue **Habitat-Community:** Moist, open woodland or forest from sagebrush scrubs to lower montane coniferous forests **Elevation:** Below 8200 ft. **Ecoregions:** Sierra Nevada, Cascades, Klamath Mountains

Ascending perennial with woody, hairless stems. Leaves to 3.5 in. long, opposite, clasping, lance-shaped to linear, blue-waxy-coated, with smooth margins. Flowers openly scattered along stem tips. Calyces to 0.3 in. long, 5-lobed, hairless. Corollas irregular, 0.8–1.4 in. long, 2-lipped, blue, hairless outside, hairy inside, with hairless staminode. Fruits many-seeded capsules.

Penstemon caesius

San Bernardino beardtongue

PLANTAGINACEAE

PLANTAIN FAMILY

PCT Sections: 4–5 & 9–10 **Abundance:** Locally common **Height:** 8–32 in. **Flowering:** June–August **Flower Color:** Purple to blue **Habitat-Community:** Shaded, rocky to gravelly slopes in montane coniferous forests **Elevation:** 5700–10,800 ft. **Ecoregions:** Southern California Mountains, Sierra Nevada

Sprawling perennial or subshrub with woody lower branches and mostly hairless stems. Leaves 0.6–1.7 in. long, crowded at base of plant, generally opposite, petioled, widely ovoid to round, with smooth margins. Flowers clustered at stem tips in leaf axils, 5-lobed, with 4 stamens and hairy staminode. Calyces 0.2–0.3 in. long, fused at base, with lance-shaped to ovoid lobes. Corollas irregular, 0.7–1.1 in. long, purple to blue, 2-lipped (2-lobed upper, 3-lobed lower), cylindric, glandular outside. Fruits small, spherical capsules. Pollinated by mason bees, which use mud or other "masonry" products to construct their nests. These nests can be found on rocks in close proximity to the plants. *Caesius* (from the Latin, "bluish gray") describes the overall hue of plants in mid-summer flower.

Penstemon californicus

California beardtongue

PLANTAGINACEAE

PLANTAIN FAMILY

PCT Sections: 3 **Abundance:** Rare **Height:** 6–15 in. **Flowering:** May–June **Flower Color:** Purple to blue **Habitat-Community:** Sandy to rocky slopes in chaparrals, pinyon-juniper woodlands, and lower montane coniferous forests **Elevation:** Below 7500 ft. **Ecoregions:** Southern California Mountains

Spreading or ascending, low-growing perennial with appressed-hairy herbage. Leaves 0.3–0.7 in. long, generally opposite, petioled, linear to narrowly spoon-shaped, gray-green, with smooth margins. Flowers clustered at stem tips in leaf axils, 5-lobed, with 4 stamens and hairy staminode. Calyces 0.2–0.3 in. long, hairy, fused at base, with ovate lobes. Corollas irregular, 0.6–0.8 in. long, purple to blue, 2-lipped (2-lobed upper, 3-lobed lower), cylindric; throat white, with dark stripes into the tube. Fruits small, spherical capsules. Known from less than 20 occurrences in California, most in the southern San Jacinto Mountains. Threatened by development, grazing, recreational activities, and vegetation/fuels management.

Penstemon davidsonii

Davidson's penstemon

PLANTAGINACEAE

PLANTAIN FAMILY

PCT Sections: 10–24 **Abundance:** Locally common **Height:** 7–28 in. **Flowering:** June–September **Flower Color:** Blue-purple **Habitat-Community:** Rock outcrops and open slopes in subalpine coniferous forests and alpine communities **Elevation:** 6500–12,300 ft. **Ecoregions:** Sierra Nevada, Cascades, Klamath Mountains

Matted perennial to shrub with creeping, woody, hairy stems. Leaves to 1.2 in. long, mostly basal, clasping on stem, oblong to ovoid, hairless, with mostly smooth margins. Flowers densely clustered at stem tips, with pale yellow-hairy staminode. Calyces to 0.5 in. long, 5-lobed, glandular-hairy. Corollas irregular, 0.8–1.4 in. long, 2-lipped, blue-purple, hairy inside. Fruits many-seeded capsules.

Penstemon grinnellii

Grinnell's beardtongue

PLANTAGINACEAE

PLANTAIN FAMILY

PCT Sections: 3–9 **Abundance:** Common **Height:** 18–32 in. **Flowering:** May–August **Flower Color:** Blue-violet to white **Habitat-Community:** Gravelly, granitic soils on slopes and ridges in chaparrals, pinyon-juniper woodlands, and montane coniferous forests **Elevation:** Below 9000 ft. **Ecoregions:** Southern California Mountains, Sierra Nevada

Squat, many-branched, bushy perennial with hairless, white-waxy-coated herbage. Leaves 2–3.5 in. long, generally opposite, lance-shaped, folded, arching, yellowish green, with toothed margins. Flowers several at each node on ascending pedicels, 5-lobed, with 4 stamens and densely golden-hairy staminode. Calyces 0.2–0.3 in. long, fused at base, with ovoid lobes. Corollas irregular, 1–1.5 in. long, blue-violet to white, 2-lipped (2-lobed upper, 3-lobed lower), broadly tubular; tube 0.4–0.7 in. wide; throat hairy, with dark stripes into the tube. Fruits small, spherical capsules. This classic bee-pollinated plant has one of the most inflated floral tubes of any penstemon in California. Flowers are white to lavender in the southern ranges, trending blue-violet into the San Gabriel Mountains and southern Sierra Nevada. *Grinnellii* honors California zoologist and field biologist Joseph Grinnell (1877–1939).

Penstemon heterodoxus

Sierra penstemon

PLANTAGINACEAE

PLANTAIN FAMILY

PCT Sections: 9–24 **Abundance:** Common **Height:** 2–26 in. **Flowering:** May–September **Flower Color:** Purplish **Habitat-Community:** Meadows and rocky slopes from lower montane coniferous forests to alpine communities **Elevation:** Below 12,800 ft. **Ecoregions:** Sierra Nevada, Cascades, Klamath Mountains

Matted perennial with hairless herbage. Leaves to 5.5 in. long, opposite, narrowly lance-shaped to ovoid, with smooth margins. Flowers in 1–2 whorls at stem tips. Calyces to 0.3 in. long, 5-lobed, glandular. Corollas irregular, 0.4–0.6 in. long, 2-lipped, purplish, glandular outside, yellow-brown-hairy inside, with yellow-hairy staminode. Fruits many-seeded capsules.

Penstemon heterophyllus

bunchleaf beardtongue

PLANTAGINACEAE

PLANTAIN FAMILY

PCT Sections: 5–7 **Abundance:** Locally common **Height:** 1–4 ft. **Flowering:** May–July **Flower Color:** Blue to violet **Habitat-Community:** Sandy to gravelly openings and burns in foothill chaparrals and oak woodlands **Elevation:** Below 5500 ft. **Ecoregions:** Southern California Mountains, Sierra Nevada

Multi-stemmed perennial with woody (at base) stems and hairless or short-hairy herbage. Leaves 1–4 in. long, generally opposite, linear to narrowly spoon-shaped. Flowers in spikes on leafy stalks with clusters at each node, ascending, 5-lobed, with 4 stamens and hairless staminode with spatula-like tip; pedicels hairless or short-hairy. Calyces 0.2–0.3 in. long, fused at base, with lance-shaped to ovoid lobes. Corollas irregular, 1–1.6 in. long, electric blue to violet, 2-lipped (2-lobed upper, 3-lobed lower), cylindric; tube 0.6–0.9 in. wide. Fruits small, spherical capsules. Two varieties along the PCT, overlapping in distribution in the western Transverse Ranges: var. *australis* is short-hairy throughout; var. *heterophyllus* is hairless.

Penstemon laetus

mountain blue penstemon

PLANTAGINACEAE

PLANTAIN FAMILY

PCT Sections: 5–8 & 12–24 **Abundance:** Common **Height:** 6–30 in. **Flowering:** May–July **Flower Color:** Blue **Habitat-Community:** Open understories from sagebrush scrubs to upper montane coniferous forests **Elevation:** Below 12,800 ft. **Ecoregions:** Southern California Mountains, Sierra Nevada, Cascades, Klamath Mountains

Multi-stemmed perennial with hairy, woody (at base) stems. Leaves to 4 in. long, opposite, linear to lance-shaped, with smooth margins. Flowers openly scattered along stem tips. Calyces to 0.6 in. long, 5-lobed, glandular. Corollas irregular, 0.8–1.4 in. long, 2-lipped, blue, glandular outside, hairless inside, with hairless staminode. Fruits many-seeded capsules.

Penstemon parvulus

shortstalk penstemon

PLANTAGINACEAE

PLANTAIN FAMILY

PCT Sections: 10–14 & 20–24 **Abundance:** Locally common **Height:** 6–12 in. **Flowering:** June–August **Flower Color:** Blue **Habitat-Community:** Rocky openings in lower montane to subalpine coniferous forests **Elevation:** Below 10,200 ft. **Ecoregions:** Sierra Nevada, Klamath Mountains

Loosely matted perennial with hairless, blue- to white-waxy-coated herbage. Leaves to 1.8 in. long, opposite, lance-shaped to ovoid, with toothed margins. Flowers openly scattered along stem tips. Calyces to 0.2 in. long, 5-lobed, hairless. Corollas irregular, 0.5–0.8 in. long, 2-lipped, blue, glandless outside, hairless inside, with hairless staminode. Fruits many-seeded capsules. *Parvulus* ("small") describes the flowers.

Penstemon procerus

small-flowered penstemon

PLANTAGINACEAE

PLANTAIN FAMILY

PCT Sections: 10–24 **Abundance:** Locally common **Height:** 2–16 in. **Flowering:** July–August **Flower Color:** Blue-purple **Habitat-Community:** Meadows and barrens from lower montane coniferous forests to alpine communities **Elevation:** Below 11,900 ft. **Ecoregions:** Sierra Nevada, Cascades, Klamath Mountains

Matted perennial with generally hairless herbage. Leaves to 0.8 in. long, opposite, lance- to spoon-shaped, with smooth margins. Flowers densely whorled at stem tips. Calyces to 0.2 in. long, 5-lobed, hairless. Corollas irregular, 0.2–0.4 in. long, 2-lipped, blue-purple, glandless outside, white- to yellow-hairy inside, with orange-yellow-hairy or hairless staminode. Fruits many-seeded capsules. *Procerus* ("high") refers to its place in alpine communities.

Rydberg's meadow penstemon

Penstemon rydbergii var. oreocharis

PLANTAGINACEAE

PLANTAIN FAMILY

PCT Sections: 10–19 **Abundance:** Locally common **Height:** 7–24 in. **Flowering:** May–August **Flower Color:** Blue to purple **Habitat-Community:** Moist meadows and streambanks in wetland-riparian communities **Elevation:** Below 11,900 ft. **Ecoregions:** Sierra Nevada, Cascades, Klamath Mountains

Few-branched perennial with hairless stem base. Leaves to 2.8 in. long, opposite, lance-shaped, with smooth margins. Flowers 1–few whorls at stem tips. Calyces to 0.2 in. long, 5-lobed, hairless. Corollas irregular, 0.3–0.6 in. long, 2-lipped, blue to purple, glandless outside, white- to yellow-hairy inside, with densely golden-yellow-hairy staminode. Fruits many-seeded capsules.

royal penstemon

Penstemon speciosus

PLANTAGINACEAE

PLANTAIN FAMILY

PCT Sections: 4–5 & 8–19 **Abundance:** Common **Height:** 2–24 in. **Flowering:** May–August **Flower Color:** Blue **Habitat-Community:** Dry, rocky places from sagebrush scrubs to subalpine coniferous forests **Elevation:** Below 12,500 ft. **Ecoregions:** Southern California Mountains, Sierra Nevada, Cascades, Klamath Mountains

Spreading perennial with stout, minutely hairy stems. Leaves to 3.5 in. long, opposite, lance-shaped, clasping, sometimes folded lengthwise, with smooth margins. Flowers generally 1-sided along stem tips. Calyces to 0.5 in. long, 5-lobed, generally glandless. Corollas irregular, 1–1.5 in. long, 2-lipped, blue, glandless or glandular outside, hairless (and generally white) inside, with staminode hairless or hairy at tip. Fruits many-seeded capsules.

showy penstemon

Penstemon spectabilis

PLANTAGINACEAE

PLANTAIN FAMILY

PCT Sections: 1–5 **Abundance:** Locally common **Height:** 25–45 in. **Flowering:** April–June **Flower Color:** Blue to purple **Habitat-Community:** Sandy to gravelly areas on slopes and ridges, including burns, in foothill chaparrals, oak woodlands, and lower montane coniferous forests **Elevation:** Below 5700 ft. **Ecoregions:** Southern California Mountains

Striking erect perennial with hairless herbage. Leaves 1.4–4 in. long, opposite (pairs fused at base), lance-shaped to widely ovoid, with toothed margins. Flowers in elongated clusters on branches, several per node, 5-lobed, with 4 stamens and hairless staminode; pedicels generally ascending. Calyces 0.2–0.3 in. long, fused at base, with ovoid to roundish lobes. Corollas irregular, 1.1–1.6 in. long, blue to purple, 2-lipped (2-lobed upper, 3-lobed lower), cylindric; throat 0.3–0.6 in. wide. Fruits small, spherical capsules. As with many penstemons, the 4 stamens are on the roof of the throat and the staminode is on the throat floor. *Spectabilis* is Latin for "showy."

Eriastrum eremicum

desert woollystar

POLEMONIACEAE PHLOX FAMILY

PCT Sections: 1–4 & 8 **Abundance:** Locally common **Height:** 2–12 in. **Flowering:** April–October **Flower Color:** Blue **Habitat-Community:** Open, sandy soils in creosote bush scrubs and Joshua tree & pinyon-juniper woodlands **Elevation:** Below 5700 ft. **Ecoregions:** Southern California Mountains, Sonoran/Mojave Basin and Range, Sierra Nevada

Annual with branching upper stems and woolly herbage. Leaves 0.3–2.2 in. long, alternate, pinnately 2–7-lobed, the thread-like lobes hairless to cobwebby. Flowers 5-parted, in head-like clusters at branch and stem tips, with unequal long-exserted stamens and unequal calyx lobes. Corollas irregular, funnel-shaped, 0.5–0.7 in. long, with yellow or blue tube, dark-purple-striped throat, and light to dark blue lobes 0.2–0.3 in. long. Fruits minute capsules. The flowers vary from being clearly bilateral (the upper 2 lobes closer together than the lower 3) to nearly radial in some plants.

Verbena lasiostachys

western vervain

VERBENACEAE VERVAIN FAMILY

PCT Sections: 2–7 & 19–24 **Abundance:** Occasional **Height:** 15–32 in. **Flowering:** April–September **Flower Color:** Blue to purple **Habitat-Community:** Moist to dry soils in open areas or shaded understories from foothill chaparrals to upper montane coniferous forests and wetland-riparian communities **Elevation:** Below 7800 ft. **Ecoregions:** Southern California Mountains, Sierra Nevada, Klamath Mountains

Erect or decumbent perennial with hairy, 4-sided stems. Leaves 2–4 in. long, opposite, ovoid, soft- to coarse-hairy, with coarsely toothed margins. Flowers on elongated spikes, each with hundreds of flowers (but only several flowers open at a time), 5-parted, slightly 2-lipped, with 4 stamens. Calyces 0.1 in. long, hairy. Corollas blue to purple, trumpet-shaped, 0.1–0.2 in. long, the lower lobes slightly longer than upper. Fruits 4 nutlets. Most occurrences along the PCT are in moist shaded springs and riparian areas. The specific epithet is apt: *lasiostachys* is Latin for "with spikes of woolly flowers."

GREEN AND BROWN

▼ COMPOSITE / DISK FLOWERS ONLY

Brickellia grandiflora

large-flowered brickellbush

ASTERACEAE SUNFLOWER FAMILY

PCT Sections: 5 & 10–24 **Abundance:** Occasional **Height:** 1–3 ft. **Flowering:** July–October **Flower Color:** Pale yellow-green **Habitat-Community:** Dry, rocky slopes or shaded understories in montane coniferous forests **Elevation:** Below 9900 ft. **Ecoregions:** Southern California Mountains, Sierra Nevada, Cascades, Klamath Mountains

Branched perennial with minutely hairy foliage. Leaves 0.6–4.7 in. long, mostly opposite, mostly triangular, hairy, with toothed margins. Flower heads in clusters at stem tips, nodding, 20–40 disk flowers per head, pale yellow-green, with 5–7 rows of hairy phyllaries to 0.5 in. long. Fruits to 0.2 in. long, 10-ribbed achenes with 20–30 bristles. Easy to spot, as it's fairly large.

▼ 3, 4, OR 6 PETALS/TEPALS

Amaranthus blitoides

mat amaranth

AMARANTHACEAE

AMARANTH FAMILY

PCT Sections: 1–6 **Abundance:** Occasional **Height:** 3–8 in. **Flowering:** July–November **Flower Color:** Green to pink or red **Habitat-Community:** Seasonally moist, sandy soils, disturbed areas, and shorelines in wetland-riparian communities and scrubs **Elevation:** Below 8000 ft. **Ecoregions:** Southern California Mountains, Mojave Basin and Range

Prostrate annual, forming mats up to 30 in. across, with hairless, fleshy, green (aging purplish) stems; monoecious. Leaves 1–3 in. long, alternate, petioled, spatula- to spoon-shaped, conspicuously veined, shiny green. Male and female flowers 0.1 in. across, with 4–5 perianth parts, clustered along leafy axils of branches. Fruits small, bladder-like utricles with 1 black seed. Seeds were used as a food source by Indigenous peoples in North America, particularly the Zuni.

Frasera speciosa

monument plant

GENTIANACEAE GENTIAN FAMILY

PCT Sections: 10–14 & 23 **Abundance:** Occasional **Height:** 2–6.5 ft. **Flowering:** July–August **Flower Color:** Yellow-green **Habitat-Community:** Meadows and open woodlands from lower montane to subalpine coniferous forests and wetland-riparian communities **Elevation:** Below 9900 ft. **Ecoregions:** Sierra Nevada, Klamath Mountains

Stout, erect perennial with 1 hairy or hairless stem. Leaves to 20 in. long, basal and whorled, spoon- to lance-shaped or oblong, with smooth margins. Flowers in elongated clusters. Calyces to 1 in. long, with 4 lance-shaped lobes. Corollas to 0.8 in. long, yellow-green with purple dots and streaks, 4-lobed, each oblong lobe with 2 oblong nectary pits (green blotches) on the inner surface. Fruits many-seeded capsules. Plants die after flowering. Aka deers-tongue.

Epipactis gigantea

stream orchid

ORCHIDACEAE ORCHID FAMILY

PCT Sections: 1–6 & 8 & 14–20 **Abundance:** Occasional **Height:** 11–28 in. **Flowering:** March–October **Flower Color:** Green to red or yellow **Habitat-Community:** Seeps, wet meadows, and streambanks in wetland-riparian communities **Elevation:** Below 8600 ft. **Ecoregions:** Southern California Mountains, Sierra Nevada, Cascades, Klamath Mountains

Erect, stout perennial with hairy, leafy stems. Leaves to 6 in. long, alternate, clasping, reduced upward, lance-shaped to oblong. Flowers 3–15, generally along one side, irregular, with stamen and style fused into a column. Sepals to 0.7 in. long, 3, petal-like, green to red, purple-veined. Petals to 0.6 in. long, 3, the lowest forming a green to yellow, red- to purple-marked lip, the laterals purple to red. Fruits to 1.1 n. long, capsules with many small seeds. Can be hard to find, mixed in with dense streamside vegetation. The lower lip looks like a tongue sticking out!

Listera convallarioides

broadlipped twayblade

ORCHIDACEAE ORCHID FAMILY

PCT Sections: 3–4 & 13–24 **Abundance:** Locally common **Height:** 4–14 in. **Flowering:** May–August **Flower Color:** Green **Habitat-Community:** Moist, shaded understories in montane coniferous forests **Elevation:** Below 9600 ft. **Ecoregions:** Southern California Mountains, Sierra Nevada, Cascades, Klamath Mountains

Erect, slender, unbranched perennial with glandular-hairy stems above the leaves. Leaves to 2.8 in. long, 2, opposite, broadly ovoid, clasping at midstem. Flowers 3–15, openly scattered along stem above leaves, small, irregular, with stamen and style fused into a column. Sepals to 0.2 in. long, 3, green, petal-like. Petals to 0.2 in. long, 3, green, the lowest forming a spoon-shaped lip to 0.5 in. long with notched tip. Fruits to 0.3 in. long, glandular-hairy capsules with many small seeds. Martin Lister (1638–1711) was an English naturalist. The common name calls your attention to the *tway* ("two") stem leaves.

Platanthera sparsiflora

sparse-flowered bog orchid

ORCHIDACEAE ORCHID FAMILY

PCT Sections: 3–5 & 10–24 **Abundance:** Occasional **Height:** 9–22 in. **Flowering:** May–September **Flower Color:** Green **Habitat-Community:** Wet meadows, seeps, and streambanks in wetland-riparian communities **Elevation:** Below 11,200 ft. **Ecoregions:** Southern California Mountains, Sierra Nevada, Cascades, Klamath Mountains

Erect, unbranched perennial with leafy stems. Leaves to 6 in. long and 1.2 in. wide, alternate, sparsely spaced, spoon-shaped. Flowers densely to openly scattered along stem to tip, small, irregular, with stamen and style fused into a column and generally curved, linear spur to 0.4 in. long. Sepals to 0.4 in. long, 3, green, petal-like, the upper forming a hood with lateral petals. Petals to 0.2 in. long, 3, green, the lowest forming a linear to lance-linear lip to 0.4 in. long. Fruits ascending to erect capsules with many small seeds.

Rumex salicifolius

willow dock

POLYGONACEAE

BUCKWHEAT FAMILY

PCT Sections: All **Abundance:** Occasional **Height:** 10–24 in. **Flowering:** May–August **Flower Color:** Green to pink or red **Habitat-Community:** Moist soils, streambanks, meadows, canyons, and rocky slopes in wetland-riparian communities and from California prairies to alpine communities **Elevation:** Below 11,500 ft. **Ecoregions:** All (except Sonoran/Mojave Basin and Range)

Ascending to erect, leafy perennial with fleshy, hairless stems becoming reddish with age. Leaves 2–5 in. long, alternate, lance-shaped to broadly linear, with wavy to flat margins. Flowers clustered along a terminal spike and on branches in whorls of 7–20, symmetric. Tepals 0.1 in. long, 6-parted (3 sepals, 3 petals), widely triangular, green becoming pink or red, each lobe with a prominent warty tubercle. Fruits 0.1 in. across, dark red-brown achenes. Well known for its medicinal uses, including the treatment of chronic migraine, back pain, and arthritis. *Salicifolius* (from the Latin, "willow-leaved") suggests the leaves resemble the true willows of *Salix*.

Thalictrum fendleri

Fendler's meadow rue

RANUNCULACEAE

BUTTERCUP FAMILY

PCT Sections: All **Abundance:** Common **Height:** 2–5 ft. **Flowering:** April–August **Flower Color:** Green to cream **Habitat-Community:** Moist, shaded understories in oak woodlands, montane chaparrals, and montane coniferous forests **Elevation:** Below 10,300 ft. **Ecoregions:** All (except Sonoran/Mojave Basin and Range)

Erect to arching perennial with hairless to glandular-hairy (sometimes purplish) stems; monoecious. Leaves mostly cauline, short-petioled, 2–4-pinnately lobed. Flowers pendent, petal-less, with 4 ovoid to lance-shaped, green to cream sepals 0.1–0.2 in. long, 15–28 stamens with thread-like purple anthers (male flowers), and many pistils (female flowers). Fruits 0.1–0.3 in. long, 7–20 per flower, disk-like achenes. Two varieties along the CA PCT: var. *polycarpum* has hairless leaves; var. *fendleri* has subtly glandular-hairy leaves.

Lomatium dasycarpum

woollyfruit lomatium

APIACEAE CARROT FAMILY

PCT Sections: 1–3 & 6 **Abundance:** Occasional **Height:** 5–25 in. **Flowering:** March–June **Flower Color:** Pale green to white or purple **Habitat-Community:** Clayey, cobbly soils and gravelly to rocky slopes and ridges in chaparrals and lower montane coniferous forests **Elevation:** Below 6200 ft. **Ecoregions:** Southern California Mountains

Spreading to erect perennial with stems emerging from base of plant. Leaves 1–5 in. long, short-hairy, divided into many small linear segments, deep green. Flowers in compound, hemispheric clusters, symmetric, with linear to narrowly ovoid bractlets, 10–21 rays to 3.4 in. long, and elongated, yellowish stamens. Petals 5, free, pale green to white or purple, distinctively white-hairy. Fruits 0.3–0.9 in. long, flattened, disk-like, oblong to ovoid, short-hairy, with wings wider than body. Best observed along the PCT from Campo to the rim of the Laguna Mountains in San Diego County. Caution: do not eat any part of a lomatium.

Osmorhiza brachypoda

California sweet cicely

APIACEAE CARROT FAMILY

PCT Sections: 1–2 & 4–7 **Abundance:** Occasional **Height:** 5–25 in. **Flowering:** March–June **Flower Color:** Pale green to cream **Habitat-Community:** Moist ravines, canyons, and wooded slopes from oak woodlands to lower montane coniferous forests **Elevation:** Below 6500 ft. **Ecoregions:** Southern California Mountains, Sierra Nevada

Spreading to erect, aromatic perennial with finely hairy herbage. Leaves 4–8 in. long, short-hairy, triangular, divided into 3-lobed segments. Flowers in compound, hemispheric clusters, symmetric, with linear to lance-shaped bractlets and 2–5 rays to 4.7 in. long. Petals tiny, 5, free, pale green to cream. Fruits 0.5–0.8 in. long, linear, cylindric, oblong, with bristly ribs. Indigenous peoples used the roots in a tonic to treat coughs and stomachaches. But be careful: there are many dangerously toxic lookalikes in the carrot family.

Chenopodium californicum

California goosefoot

CHENOPODIACEAE

GOOSEFOOT FAMILY

PCT Sections: 1–8 **Abundance:** Occasional **Height:** 8–35 in. **Flowering:** March–September **Flower Color:** Pale green **Habitat-Community:** Open areas, often in clayey soils, in foothill chaparrals and oak & pinyon-juniper woodlands **Elevation:** Below 6300 ft. **Ecoregions:** Southern California Mountains, Sierra Nevada

Erect to lateral perennial from a stout, fleshy base, sometimes forming a loose mat. Leaves 2–4 in. long, generally alternate, short-petioled, broadly triangular, deep green, with deeply toothed and wavy margins. Flowers in dense terminal spikes, petal-less, with 5 pale green, hairless sepals fused about half their length. Fruits utricles enclosed by and falling with the dried calyx. The only perennial *Chenopodium* in California. Indigenous peoples utilize the seeds in flour and as a source of soap, and the leaves and shoots as a cooked vegetable. The common and family names refer to the 3-lobed ("goosefoot") leaves of many species.

Pectiantia breweri

Brewer's mitrewort

SAXIFRAGACEAE

SAXIFRAGE FAMILY

PCT Sections: 10–17 **Abundance:** Locally common **Height:** 4–12 in. **Flowering:** May–September **Flower Color:** Yellow-green **Habitat-Community:** Moist, shaded slopes in upper montane & subalpine coniferous forests **Elevation:** 6000–11,500 ft. **Ecoregions:** Sierra Nevada

Tufted perennial with minutely glandular, leafless flowering stems. Leaves to 3.2 in. wide, basal, round, shallowly 7–11-lobed, with round-toothed margins. Flowers generally 1-sided along stems. Calyx lobes 5, green, and curved-back. Petals 5, yellow-green, 5–9-pinnately lobed, 1 pistil, and 5 alternate (attached between petals) stamens. Fruits to 0.2 in. across, bishop's cap-like (mitre) capsules with many shiny, red-brown to black seeds. _Pectiantia_ ("comb") refers to the comb-like petals.

▼ 5 FUSED PETALS / IRREGULAR COROLLAS

Castilleja nana

dwarf alpine paintbrush

OROBANCHACEAE

BROOMRAPE FAMILY

PCT Sections: 10–16 **Abundance:** Common **Height:** 2–10 in. **Flowering:** June–August **Flower Color:** Yellow-green **Habitat-Community:** Dry, open barrens in subalpine coniferous forests and alpine communities **Elevation:** 7800–13,800 ft. **Ecoregions:** Sierra Nevada

Perennial with many hairy, green or purplish stems; hemiparasitic. Leaves 0.4–1.4 in. long, narrowly lance-shaped, 0–5-lobed, with smooth margin. Flowers densely clustered at stem tips with yellow-green-tipped or purplish (green-margined) bracts and calyx lobes. Calyces to 0.8 in. long, unequally 4-lobed, lobes = tube. Corollas irregular, 0.6–0.8 in. long, 2-lipped (the upper beaked), funnel-shaped, yellow-green with purplish blotches. Fruits to 0.5 in. long, many-seeded capsules. Its color makes this high-elevation paintbrush easy to spot along the trail!

Castilleja pilosa

parrothead paintbrush

OROBANCHACEAE

BROOMRAPE FAMILY

PCT Sections: 4 & 9–18 **Abundance:** Locally common **Height:** 3–14 in. **Flowering:** June–August **Flower Color:** Yellow-green **Habitat-Community:** Dry, open barrens from sagebrush scrubs to upper montane coniferous forests **Elevation:** 7800–11,200 ft. **Ecoregions:** Sierra Nevada, Cascades

Decumbent perennial with many stiff-hairy stems; hemiparasitic. Leaves 0.4–2 in. long, narrowly lance-shaped, 0–3-lobed, with smooth margin. Flowers densely clustered at stem tips with green-tipped or purplish (white- or yellow-margined) bracts and calyx lobes. Calyces to 0.8 in. long, unequally 4-lobed, lobes = tube. Corollas irregular, 0.5–0.9 in. long, 2-lipped (the upper beaked), funnel-shaped, yellow-green. Fruits to 0.5 in. long, many-seeded capsules.

Castilleja plagiotoma

Mojave paintbrush

OROBANCHACEAE

BROOMRAPE FAMILY

PCT Sections: 4–8 **Abundance:** Rare **Height:** 12–26 in. **Flowering:** April–June **Flower Color:** Pale green to yellow **Habitat-Community:** Gravelly to sandy soils in Mojave mixed woody & sagebrush scrubs and Joshua tree & pinyon-juniper woodlands **Elevation:** Below 7600 ft. **Ecoregions:** Southern California Mountains, Mojave Basin and Range, Sierra Nevada

Erect perennial often found growing through (and tapping into) low woody shrubs, with gray-green (aging reddish) herbage covered in branched hairs; hemiparasitic. Leaves 0.8–2 in. long, alternate, linear, 3–5-lobed. Flowers in narrow spikes, with pale yellow, white-woolly calyces 0.5–0.7 in. long. Corollas irregular, 0.5–0.8 in. long, yellow, with beak-like upper lip and reduced, pale green lower lip. Fruits 0.3–0.4 in. long, ovoid capsules. Endemic, restricted to the transition zones between the western Mojave Desert and the Transverse and Sierra Nevada ranges. An important host plant for checkerspot butterflies.

▼ NO OBVIOUS PETALS/SEPALS

Datisca glomerata

Durango root

DATISCACEAE DATISCA FAMILY

PCT Sections: 1–10 & 19–20 **Abundance:** Locally common **Height:** 2–6 ft. **Flowering:** May–July **Flower Color:** Green **Habitat-Community:** Sandy to cobbly soils in dry streambeds or washes in wetland-riparian communities from deserts to montane zones **Elevation:** Below 6800 ft. **Ecoregions:** Southern California Mountains, Mojave Basin and Range, Sierra Nevada, Klamath Mountains

Robust, multi-stemmed perennial with leafy ascending shoots covered with glandular, short, club-shaped hairs; androdioecious. Leaves 1.3–9.6 in. long, alternate or whorled, deeply pinnately lobed, the largest divided into 3 leaflets, the terminal leaflet longest, with toothed margins. Flowers clustered at leaf nodes along the stem. Male flowers petal-less, with 4–6 green, unequal sepals 0.1–0.8 in. long and yellow anthers. Bisexual flowers petal-less, with 3–4 green, equal sepals 0.2–1.1 in. long and 3 yellowish, thread-like, 2-branched styles. Fruits 0.3–0.4 in. long, urn-shaped capsules. Superficially resembles *Cannabis*. All parts of this plant are toxic!

Typha domingensis

narrowleaf cattail

TYPHACEAE CATTAIL FAMILY

PCT Sections: 1–6 **Abundance:** Occasional **Height:** 5–14 ft. **Flowering:** March–August **Flower Color:** Orange-brown or yellow **Habitat-Community:** Marshes, meadows, lakeshores, and streambanks in wetland-riparian communities **Elevation:** Below 5500 ft. **Ecoregions:** Southern California/Northern Baja Coast, Southern California Mountains

Erect, aquatic or semi-aquatic, unbranched, stout perennial; monoecious. Leaves to 4 ft. long, to 0.6 in. wide, mostly basal, flat, upright, pale green; stem leaves alternate (when present). Flowers tightly packed into orange-brown or yellow columnar spikes, 1000+ in 2 spikes per stem, male above female and separated by a gap of 1–5 in., with 0 sepals and petals. Wind-dispersed seeds develop from female flowers. The rhizomes are edible, and Indigenous peoples commonly used the stems and leaves for basketry and other building material. *Typha* (from the Greek, "to smoke") aptly describes the disintegrating heads, which mature and fill the air with cottony white-brown fluff!

Typha latifolia

broadleaf cattail

TYPHACEAE CATTAIL FAMILY

PCT Sections: 1–7 & 14–20 & 23–24 **Abundance:** Common **Height:** 5–10 ft. **Flowering:** June–July **Flower Color:** Green to black- or red-brown **Habitat-Community:** Marshes, meadows, lakeshores, and streambanks in wetland-riparian communities **Elevation:** Below 7600 ft. **Ecoregions:** All

Erect, stout, unbranched perennial, growing in dense (sometimes impenetrable) colonies; monoecious. Leaves to 1.2 in. wide, alternate, narrow, flat, pale green, upright. Flowers 1000+, in 2 green to black- or red-brown flower spikes per stem, male above female (no gap between), with 0 sepals and petals, 2–7 stamens, and 1 pistil. Fruits yellow-brown, thin-walled, wind-dispersed, developing from female flowers. The pollen can be mixed with flour, salt, baking powder, vegetable oil, and milk to make cattail biscuits.

Urtica dioica subsp. *holosericea*

hoary stinging nettle

URTICACEAE NETTLE FAMILY

PCT Sections: All **Abundance:** Locally common **Height:** 2–9 ft. **Flowering:** June–September **Flower Color:** Green **Habitat-Community:** Moist soils, streams, meadows, seeps, and marshes in wetland-riparian communities from foothill chaparrals to subalpine coniferous forests **Elevation:** Below 10,500 ft. **Ecoregions:** All

Tall and infamous perennial with few-branched stems covered in stinging hairs; generally monoecious. Leaves 2–8 in. long, opposite, lance-shaped to ovoid, densely hairy, with toothed margins. Flowers in leafy spikes, clustered at nodes. Male flowers petal-less, with 4 green, free (unfused) sepals 0.1 in. long. Female flowers petal-less, with 4 green, generally free, equal sepals. Fruits ovoid achenes. Its long history of medicinal, food, and textile uses notwithstanding, this plant is better known for its stinging hairs, which, upon contact, inject histamine and other chemicals, producing a stinging sensation that can fester for hours. *Urtica* is Latin for "to burn," so take care when walking through shaded, wet areas!

FERNS, HORSETAILS, AND GRASSES

FERNS AND HORSETAILS

Athyrium distentifolium
var. *americanum*

American alpine lady fern

ATHYRIACEAE LADY FERN FAMILY

PCT Sections: 10–23 **Abundance:** Locally common **Height:** to 3 ft. **Habitat-Community:** Rocky slopes and streambanks from upper montane coniferous forests to alpine and wetland-riparian communities **Elevation:** 5500–12,200 ft. **Ecoregions:** Sierra Nevada, Cascades, Klamath Mountains

Tuft-forming fern. Leaves to 3 ft. long, fleshy, fragile, diamond-shaped, 2–3-pinnately lobed, hairy or hairless, with free veins. Sori roundish, along veins near leaflet margins, with no indusia. Lady fern leaves are easily distinguished from other ferns by their diamond shape—"a girl's best friend"!

Athyrium filix-femina
var. *cyclosorum*

common lady fern

ATHYRIACEAE LADY FERN FAMILY

PCT Sections: 3–4 & 10–24 **Abundance:** Locally common **Height:** to 6 ft. **Habitat-Community:** Moist slopes and streambanks from woodlands to subalpine coniferous forests and wetland-riparian communities **Elevation:** Below 10,500 ft. **Ecoregions:** Southern California Mountains, Sierra Nevada, Cascades, Klamath Mountains

Large, showy fern. Leaves to 6 ft. long, diamond-shaped, 1–2-pinnate, with toothed leaflets, hairy midribs, and free veins. Sori oblong to J-shaped, along veins away from leaflet margins, with no indusia. Leaf and root infusions have historically been used to cure everything from gallstones to hiccups.

Woodwardia fimbriata

giant chainfern

BLECHNACEAE DEER FERN FAMILY

PCT Sections: 1–5 & 16–24 **Abundance:** Locally common **Height:** to 10 ft. **Habitat-Community:** Moist slopes and streambanks in woodlands, foothill chaparrals, lower montane coniferous forests, and wetland-riparian communities **Elevation:** Below 9000 ft. **Ecoregions:** Southern California/Northern Baja Coast, Southern California Mountains, Sierra Nevada

Large, showy, evergreen fern. Leaves to 10 ft. long, 1–2-pinnate, with hairless but generally glandular surfaces, lobed to smooth leaflet margins, and free or net-like veins. Sori oblong to linear, parallel to nearest midrib, with taco-like indusia. Lives up to its common name: it has chain-like sori and is the largest fern along the PCT. An important source of basketry fibers for Indigenous peoples.

Cystopteris fragilis

fragile fern

CYSTOPTERIDACEAE

FRAGILE FERN FAMILY

PCT Sections: All **Abundance:** Common **Height:** to 12 in. **Habitat-Community:** Rock crevices, meadows, and streambanks from woodlands to alpine communities **Elevation:** Below 12,800 ft. **Ecoregions:** All

Small fern with pale to red-brown leaf bases. Leaves to 12 in. long, ovoid to lance-shaped, 2–4-pinnate, hairless, with lobed to smooth leaflet margins and free veins. Sori round, scattered along veins, with delicate indusia that are often obscure when mature. One of the most common ferns of shaded rock crevices, especially at high elevations. *Cystopteris* (from the Greek, "bladder fern") refers to the hood-like indusia.

Pteridium aquilinum var. *pubescens*

bracken fern

DENNSTAEDTIACEAE

BRACKEN FAMILY

PCT Sections: All **Abundance:** Common **Height:** to 5 ft. **Habitat-Community:** Open, partially shaded or disturbed slopes from scrubs, woodlands, and chaparrals to subalpine coniferous forests **Elevation:** Below 10,000 ft. **Ecoregions:** All

Large fern, generally forming extensive colonies and with persistent dead leaves. Leaves to 5 ft. long, widely triangular, 3-pinnate, hairy below, with smooth leaflet margins and mostly free veins. Sori in continuous strips, generally along leaflet margins, with obscure or absent indusia. Look for it in various habitats, especially along the trail's edge. Despite the historic consumption of various parts of young bracken ferns, please avoid eating: it has been linked to stomach cancer and poisonings!

Dryopteris arguta

wood fern

DRYOPTERIDACEAE

WOOD FERN FAMILY

PCT Sections: 1–7 **Abundance:** Locally common **Height:** to 40 in. **Habitat-Community:** Dry, open or partially shaded slopes from scrubs to lower montane coniferous forests **Elevation:** Below 8200 ft. **Ecoregions:** Southern California/Northern Baja Coast, Southern California Mountains

Large fern with 1–2-divided leaves. Leaves to 3 ft. long, lance-shaped, with lobed to toothed leaflets, minutely glandular midribs, and free veins. Sori round, along veins, with roundish, centrally attached indusia. Unlike the diamond-shaped leaves of *Athyrium* spp., wood fern's leaves tend to be widest near the base.

Polystichum imbricans

narrowleaf swordfern

DRYOPTERIDACEAE

WOOD FERN FAMILY

PCT Sections: 1–7 & 14–24 **Abundance:** Locally common **Height:** to 20 in. **Habitat-Community:** Granitic or metamorphic rock outcrops and rocky slopes from scrubs to upper montane coniferous forests **Elevation:** Below 8200 ft. **Ecoregions:** All (except Sonoran/Mojave Basin and Range)

Mid-sized fern with a thumb-like lobe at the base of each leaflet. Leaves to 20 in. long, lance-shaped, pinnate, with smooth to toothed leaflets generally turned perpendicular to the stem (Venetian blind–like) and free veins. Sori round, along leaflet margins, with roundish, smooth or toothed, centrally attached hairless indusia.

Polystichum munitum

western swordfern

DRYOPTERIDACEAE

WOOD FERN FAMILY

PCT Sections: 3–5 & 16–17 & 19–20 & 23–24 **Abundance:** Locally common **Height:** to 4 ft. **Habitat-Community:** Shaded slopes from oak woodlands to lower montane coniferous forests **Elevation:** Below 5200 ft. **Ecoregions:** Southern California Mountains, Sierra Nevada, Klamath Mountains

Large fern with a thumb-like lobe at the base of each leaflet. Leaves to 4 ft. long, ovate, pinnate, with toothed leaflets and free veins. Sori round, along leaflet margins, with roundish, hairy margins and centrally attached indusia. This is the common fern of the forest moon of Endor, the home of Ewoks in *Star Wars: Return of the Jedi.*

Polystichum scopulinum

mountain hollyfern

DRYOPTERIDACEAE

WOOD FERN FAMILY

PCT Sections: 3–5 & 12–24 **Abundance:** Occasional **Height:** to 20 in. **Habitat-Community:** Shaded or sunny rock crevices and boulder bases from lower montane to subalpine coniferous forests **Elevation:** Below 10,500 ft. **Ecoregions:** Southern California Mountains, Sierra Nevada, Cascades, Klamath Mountains

Small to mid-sized fern with a thumb-like lobe at the base of each leaflet. Leaves to 20 in. long, elliptic to lance-shaped, 1- to partly 2-pinnate, with toothed leaflets and bristle-tipped leaflet teeth. Sori round, along leaflet margins, with roundish, hairless, centrally attached indusia. Occasionally found even in the state's desert ranges.

Equisetum arvense

field horsetail

EQUISETACEAE

HORSETAIL FAMILY

PCT Sections: 1–5 & 9–24 **Abundance:** Common **Height:** to 2 ft. **Habitat-Community:** Shaded, moist slopes, streambanks, meadows from woodlands and chaparrals to subalpine coniferous forests, and wetland-riparian communities **Elevation:** Below 10,000 ft. **Ecoregions:** All (except Sonoran/Mojave Basin and Range)

Perennial, with both sterile and fertile stems. Sterile stem to 2 ft. long, with wiry, whorled leaf-like branches. Fertile stem to 1 ft., red-tan to white, with terminal, spore-producing cone. Found throughout the world, and the first vascular plant to appear on the decimated slopes of Mt. St. Helens after it erupted in 1980. Young fertile shoots were historically eaten like asparagus. *Equisetum* (with 15 species globally) is the last of a group of sporophytic, vascular plants dating back to the Paleozoic Era.

Equisetum hyemale

common scouring rush

EQUISETACEAE HORSETAIL FAMILY

PCT Sections: 1–6 & 9–19 & 23–24 **Abundance:** Locally common **Height:** to 7 ft. **Habitat-Community:** Shaded, moist slopes, streambanks, meadows from woodlands and chaparrals to upper montane coniferous forests, and wetland-riparian communities **Elevation:** Below 8200 ft. **Ecoregions:** All (except Sonoran/Mojave Basin and Range)

Perennial with fertile stems only (no branches) and stem sheaths with 2 separate black bands. Leaves minute, produced in whorls at each node. Fertile stem to 7 ft. long, green, with terminal, spore-producing, pointy-tipped cone. Historically used in Europe to scour items made of wood or pewter (hence the common name).

Equisetum laevigatum

smooth scouring rush

EQUISETACEAE HORSETAIL FAMILY

PCT Sections: All **Abundance:** Locally common **Height:** to 7 ft. **Habitat-Community:** Shaded, moist slopes, streambanks, meadows from woodlands and chaparrals to upper montane coniferous forests, and wetland-riparian communities **Elevation:** Below 9200 ft. **Ecoregions:** All (except Sonoran/Mojave Basin and Range)

Perennial with fertile stems only (no branches) and stem sheaths with 1 black band. Leaves minute, produced in whorls at each node. Fertile stem to 7 ft. long, green, with terminal, spore-producing, round-tipped cone. Horsetails and scouring rushes are used therapeutically to treat various ailments. Their cell walls contain silica crystals, making them nature's sandpaper.

Polypodium hesperium

western polypody

POLYPODIACEAE POLYPODY FAMILY

PCT Sections: 3–4 & 11–16 & 22–23 **Abundance:** Rare **Height:** to 10 in. **Habitat-Community:** Crevices in rock outcrops and talus slopes in montane coniferous forests **Elevation:** Below 9800 ft. **Ecoregions:** Southern California Mountains, Sierra Nevada, Klamath Mountains

Small fern that remains evergreen, even if summer conditions are extremely dry. Leaves to 10 in. long, lance-shaped to ovoid, thick, pinnate, with toothed leaflets, hairless midrib on upper leaf blade surface, and free veins. Sori round to ovoid, along both sides of midvein, with no indusia. Always grows in rocky habitats, never on trees.

Adiantum aleuticum

five-finger fern

PTERIDACEAE BRAKE FAMILY

PCT Sections: 3–5 & 10 & 13–24 **Abundance:** Locally common **Height:** to 3 ft. **Habitat-Community:** Shaded, moist rock crevices and streambanks, including serpentine soils, from foothill chaparrals to subalpine coniferous forests, and wetland-riparian communities **Elevation:** Below 11,200 ft. **Ecoregions:** Southern California Mountains, Sierra Nevada, Cascades, Klamath Mountains

Delicate, generally colony-forming fern. Leaves to 30 in. long, palmate, with pinnate branches and lobed, fan-shaped leaflets. Sori oblong, along and covered by inrolled leaflet margins, with no indusia. Aka maidenhair fern, for its fine, hair-like, glossy black stems.

Adiantum capillus-veneris

southern maidenhair

PTERIDACEAE BRAKE FAMILY

PCT Sections: 1–6 **Abundance:** Occasional **Height:** to 3 ft. **Habitat-Community:** Cool, moist canyons, rock crevices, seeps in limestone, and hanging gardens in chaparrals, woodlands, lower montane coniferous forests, and wetland-riparian communities **Elevation:** Below 6500 ft. **Ecoregions:** Southern California Mountains

Attractive wiry fern with a nearly global native distribution. Its 2–3-pinnate leaves arise in clusters from creeping rhizomes, with very delicate, light green leaflets that are broad but not fan-shaped like those of *A. aleuticum.* The frond stem is shiny black. Sporangia are borne on the leaf veins; sori lack the yellowish exudate of other maidenhairs. Found in Snow Creek Canyon on the north side of Mt. San Jacinto and other cool, shaded, isolated places along the PCT. Widely cultivated as a garden fern or houseplant.

Aspidotis densa

Indian's dream

PTERIDACEAE BRAKE FAMILY

PCT Sections: 10–24 **Abundance:** Common **Height:** to 1 ft. **Habitat-Community:** Slopes and crevices in rock outcrops, including serpentine soils, from woodlands to subalpine coniferous forests **Elevation:** Below 11,200 ft. **Ecoregions:** Sierra Nevada, Cascades, Klamath Mountains

Densely clustered fern with red-brown stems. Sterile and fertile leaves generally alike, to 1 ft. long, 2–3-pinnate, light to dark brown, thick, with linear to lance-shaped, smooth-margined leaflets. Sporangia clustered or continuous along leaflet and covered by inrolled leaflet margins, with no indusia. The origin of the common name is a mystery and the subject of lots of speculation.

Cryptogramma acrostichoides

American parsley fern

PTERIDACEAE BRAKE FAMILY

PCT Sections: 10–24 **Abundance:** Locally common **Height:** to 1 ft. **Habitat-Community:** Rocky slopes and crevices in rock outcrops from lower montane coniferous forests to alpine communities **Elevation:** Below 12,500 ft. **Ecoregions:** Sierra Nevada, Cascades, Klamath Mountains

Clump-forming, generally evergreen fern with very different sterile and fertile leaves. Sterile leaves to 8 in. long, lance-shaped, 2–3-pinnate, leathery, dark green, with scattered hairs above and scallop-margined leaflets. Fertile leaves to 12 in. long, 2–3-pinnate, leathery, green, with linear leaflets. Sporangia along veins near leaflet margins, generally covered by edge, with no indusia. Important food source for pikas!

Cryptogramma cascadensis

Cascade parsley fern

PTERIDACEAE BRAKE FAMILY

PCT Sections: 10–24 **Abundance:** Rare **Height:** to 10 in. **Habitat-Community:** Moist, rocky slopes and crevices in granitic or volcanic rock outcrops from lower montane coniferous forests to alpine communities **Elevation:** Below 12,000 ft. **Ecoregions:** Sierra Nevada, Cascades, Klamath Mountains

Clump-forming deciduous fern with very different sterile and fertile leaves. Sterile leaves to 8 in. long, lance-shaped, 2–3-pinnate, thin, hairless, dark green, with scallop-margined leaflets. Fertile leaves to 10 in. long, 2–3-pinnate, thin, green, with linear leaflets. Sporangia along veins near leaflet margins, generally covered by edge, with no indusia. Important food source for pikas!

Myriopteris covillei

Coville's lip fern

PTERIDACEAE BRAKE FAMILY

PCT Sections: 1–9 & 16–17 **Abundance:** Occasional **Height:** to 15 in. **Habitat-Community:** Among rocks (typically granitic) in chaparrals, pinyon-juniper woodlands, and lower montane coniferous forests **Elevation:** Below 7500 ft. **Ecoregions:** Southern California Mountains, Sonoran Basin and Range, Sierra Nevada

Perhaps the most common lip fern in California. Leaves 5–10 in. long and up to 4-pinnate, with rounded segments that are cobbled in appearance. Undersides have long scales (compared to other lip ferns) that exceed the leaflet margins. Sporangia are tucked under the scales. The leaflet margins are lip-like (hence the common name). Lip ferns thrive in dry habitats and are most diverse in Mexico.

Pellaea breweri

Brewer's cliffbrake

PTERIDACEAE BRAKE FAMILY

PCT Sections: 4 & 9–24 **Abundance:** Common **Height:** to 10 in. **Habitat-Community:** Shaded, generally granitic rock outcrops from lower montane to subalpine coniferous forests **Elevation:** Below 12,200 ft. **Ecoregions:** Southern California Mountains, Sierra Nevada, Cascades, Klamath Mountains

Tufted fern with red-brown, thread-like rhizome scales and glossy brown stipes. Leaves to 10 in. long, pinnate, linear-elliptic, pale green; leaflets large, lobed, with inrolled margins. Sporangia along and covered by inrolled leaflet margins, with no indusia. The leaflets' thumb-like lobes help one remember this as "Brewer's hitchhiking plant." It is often found on cliffs, and *brake* is an old English term for ferns (hence the common name).

Pellaea bridgesii

Bridges' cliffbrake

PTERIDACEAE BRAKE FAMILY

PCT Sections: 10–16 **Abundance:** Common **Height:** to 14 in. **Habitat-Community:** Crevices in rock outcrops from lower montane to subalpine coniferous forests **Elevation:** Below 11,200 ft. **Ecoregions:** Southern California Mountains, Sierra Nevada, Cascades, Klamath Mountains

Tufted fern with pale to medium brown, linear rhizome scales and glossy brown stipes. Leaves to 14 in. long, pinnate, linear-elliptic, blue-green; leaflets unlobed, round, with inrolled margins. Sporangia along and covered by inrolled leaflet margins, with no indusia. Compare with *P. breweri*: no leaflet hitchhiker thumbs on this one!

Pellaea mucronata

birdfoot cliffbrake

PTERIDACEAE BRAKE FAMILY

PCT Sections: 1–19 **Abundance:** Common **Height:** to 2 ft. **Habitat-Community:** Rocky or dry slopes from woodlands and chaparrals to upper montane coniferous forests **Elevation:** Below 9800 ft. **Ecoregions:** Southern California/Northern Baja Coast, Southern California Mountains, Sierra Nevada, Cascades

Medium-sized fern with linear, brown (darker midvein) rhizome scales and glossy, purple-brown stipes. Leaves to 2 ft. long, 1–3-pinnate, triangular to linear-elliptic, blue-gray or green to purple; leaflets unlobed, linear to elliptic, sharp-pointed, with inrolled margins. Sporangia along and covered partially by inrolled leaflet margins, with no indusia.

Pentagramma rebmanii

Rebman's silverback fern

PTERIDACEAE BRAKE FAMILY

PCT Sections: 1–2 **Abundance:** Rare **Height:** 5–10 in. **Habitat-Community:** Seasonally moist, shaded, rocky slopes in chaparrals and woodlands **Elevation:** Below 4500 ft. **Ecoregions:** Southern California/Northern Baja Coast, Southern California Mountains

Small fern, only recently described by science. Leaves generally 2–3-pinnate, triangular or 5-sided. Sporangia along veins, throughout the leaf undersides. Restricted to San Diego County and northern Baja California, and limited along the PCT to areas south of Warner Springs. Named after Jon Rebman, curator of botany at the San Diego Natural History Museum.

Pentagramma triangularis

goldback fern

PTERIDACEAE BRAKE FAMILY

PCT Sections: 1–6 & 16–20 & 23–24 **Abundance:** Common **Height:** to 16 in. **Habitat-Community:** Shaded, rocky or dry slopes from scrubs to lower montane coniferous forests **Elevation:** Below 7500 ft. **Ecoregions:** All (except Sonoran/Mojave Basin and Range)

Small- to medium-sized fern with lance-shaped to linear, dark-midveined rhizome scales and brown to black stipes. Leaves to 16 in. long, 2–3-pinnate, triangular, golden to white wax-coated below; leaflets pinnately lobed, without inrolled margins. Sporangia cover leaflet surface in lines along branching veins, with no indusia. An easy fern to identify: just look for the namesake coloring on the back of the leaves.

Calliscirpus criniger
Criniger's cottongrass
CYPERACEAE SEDGE FAMILY

PCT Sections: 10–24 **Abundance:** Locally common **Height:** 7–40 in. **Flowering:** June–August **Habitat-Community:** Wet meadows, streambanks, and seeps, including serpentine soils, in wetland-riparian communities **Elevation:** Below 7400 ft. **Ecoregions:** Sierra Nevada, Cascades, Klamath Mountains

Tufted perennial with 3-angled, sparsely hairy stems and cottony flower heads. Leaves to 18 in. long, 0.3 in. wide, basal and alternate, 3-ranked, linear, sparsely hairy. Flowers in spikelets to 0.6 in. long, arranged in 1 head-like cluster at stem tip, with generally 6 barbed bristles, 1 pistil, and 3 stamens. Fruits to 0.1 in. long, 3-sided, seed-like achenes. Cottongrass species have been used for making wicks, diapers, stuffing pillows, and dressing wounds. Aka bog cotton.

Carex breweri
Brewer's sedge
CYPERACEAE SEDGE FAMILY

PCT Sections: 10–18 **Abundance:** Locally common **Height:** 4–10 in. **Fruiting:** July–September **Habitat-Community:** Open, gravelly or sandy soils in subalpine coniferous forests and alpine communities **Elevation:** 6500–12,800 ft. **Ecoregions:** Sierra Nevada, Cascades

Creeping perennial in scattered clumps with roundish (at least above) stems and hairless foliage. Leaves narrow, quill-like, < flowering stems. Flowers in terminal, widely cone-shaped spikelet to 0.4 in. wide, lower portion female and upper male, with 1 pistil (3 stigmas) and 3 stamens. Perigynia to 0.3 in. long, to 0.2 in. wide, 10–40 per spikelet, hairless, ovoid to oblong, flat, gold-brown. *Carex* is the most common plant genus along the CA PCT, with nearly 100 sedges possible! The perigynia of all sedges are edible, with a pleasant, nutty taste.

Carex capitata
capitate sedge
CYPERACEAE SEDGE FAMILY

PCT Sections: 10–18 **Abundance:** Locally common **Height:** 4–14 in. **Fruiting:** July–September **Habitat-Community:** Wet meadows and moist slopes from upper montane coniferous forests to alpine and wetland-riparian communities **Elevation:** Below 12,800 ft. **Ecoregions:** Sierra Nevada, Cascades

Loosely clumped perennial with roundish (at least above) stems and hairless foliage. Leaves narrow, quill-like, < flowering stems. Flowers in terminal, ovoid to cone-shaped spikelet to 0.3 in. wide, lower portion female and upper male, with 1 pistil (2 stigmas) and 3 stamens. Perigynia to 0.2 in. long, to 0.1 in. wide, 6–25 per spikelet, hairless, ovoid, flat around fruit, pale green, with fine-veined upper surface. Sedges are important plants for many reasons, including forage, erosion control, and critter habitat!

Carex congdonii

Congdon's sedge

CYPERACEAE SEDGE FAMILY

PCT Sections: 10–12 **Abundance:** Rare **Height:** 1–3 ft. **Fruiting:** July–September **Habitat-Community:** Rocky soils and talus in subalpine coniferous forests and alpine communities **Elevation:** 8500–12,800 ft. **Ecoregions:** Sierra Nevada

Clumped perennial with tall stems and generally hairy herbage. Leaves to 0.3 in. wide, grass-like, flat or channeled, with hairy, red-dotted sheaths. Flowers in 4–6 linear to oblong spikelets to 2 in. long, male (rarely females at base) terminal spikelet, female lateral spikelets, with 1 pistil (3 stigmas) and 3 stamens. Perigynia to 0.2 in. long, to 0.1 in. wide, minutely hairy, lance to spoon-shaped, 2-ribbed, tapered to short-beaked. Look for this clumped sedge at the base of rock outcrops or boulders.

Carex filifolia

threadleaf sedge

CYPERACEAE SEDGE FAMILY

PCT Sections: 4 & 10–18 **Abundance:** Common **Height:** 2–10 in. **Fruiting:** May–August **Habitat-Community:** Open, dry meadows or flats and slopes from lower montane coniferous forests to alpine communities **Elevation:** Below 12,200 ft. **Ecoregions:** Southern California Mountains, Sierra Nevada, Cascades

Tufted or ring-forming perennial, generally growing in colonies, with wiry stems and hairless herbage. Leaves narrow, quill-like, < or > flowering stems. Flowers in terminal, oblong-lance-shaped spikelet to 0.7 in. long, 0.3 in. wide, lower portion female and upper male, with 1 pistil (3 stigmas) and 3 stamens. Perigynia to 0.1 in. long, to 0.1 in. wide, hairy (at least above), roundish, faintly 2-ribbed, pale green.

Carex senta

rough sedge

CYPERACEAE SEDGE FAMILY

PCT Sections: 1–10 **Abundance:** Occasional **Height:** 20–40 in. **Fruiting:** April–August **Habitat-Community:** Wet meadows and streambanks in wetland-riparian communities, oak woodlands, and montane coniferous forests **Elevation:** Below 9500 ft. **Ecoregions:** Southern California Mountains, Sierra Nevada

Tall perennial, growing in large clumps, with sharp-angled stems and stiff-hairy herbage. Leaves 0.1–0.3 in. wide, < flowering stems. Flowers in 2–4 cylindric spikelets to 0.3 in. long, lower portion female and upper male, with 1 pistil (3 stigmas) and 3 stamens. Perigynia 0.1–0.2 in. long, to 0.1 in. wide, 25–100 per spikelet, ascending, hairless, pale brown with red-brown spots, ovoid, dull, leathery. Most frequent along the PCT at meadow and stream crossings in the San Bernardino Mountains.

Carex subnigricans

nearlyblack sedge

CYPERACEAE SEDGE FAMILY

PCT Sections: 10–14 **Abundance:** Locally common **Height:** 1–8 in. **Fruiting:** July–September **Habitat-Community:** Wet or rocky meadows and slopes from upper montane coniferous forests to alpine communities **Elevation:** 8500–12,500 ft. **Ecoregions:** Sierra Nevada

Creeping perennial, generally growing in colonies, with roundish (at least above) stems and hairless herbage. Leaves narrow, quill-like, < flowering stems. Flowers in terminal, lance-shaped to oblong-lance-shaped spikelet to 0.3 in. wide, lower portion female and upper male, with 1 pistil (3 stigmas) and 3 stamens. Perigynia to 0.2 in. long, to 0.1 in. wide, 10–40 per spikelet, hairless, lance-shaped to ovoid, flat, veinless, gold-brown.

Dulichium arundinaceum

threeway sedge

CYPERACEAE SEDGE FAMILY

PCT Sections: 10–24 **Abundance:** Occasional **Height:** 11–40 in. **Flowering:** June–October **Habitat-Community:** Wet meadows, streambanks, lake and pond margins, and bogs in wetland-riparian communities **Elevation:** Below 7900 ft. **Ecoregions:** Sierra Nevada, Cascades, Klamath Mountains

Perennial with round, hairless, hollow stems, often growing out of water. Leaves to 6 in. long, 0.3 in. wide, grass-like, alternate, 3-ranked, linear, hairless. Flowers in axillary, flat spikelets to 1.2 in. long, 0.1 in. wide, with 6–9 barbed bristles, 1 pistil (2 stigmas), and 3 stamens. Fruits to 0.2 in. long, flat, yellow, seed-like achenes. *Dulichium* means "a kind of sedge." *Arundinaceum* means "reed-like." Very similar to a grass, but look for the bristly flowers.

Schoenoplectus acutus var. *occidentalis*

common tule

CYPERACEAE SEDGE FAMILY

PCT Sections: 1–2 & 4–8 & 14–24 **Abundance:** Occasional **Height:** 3–15 ft. **Flowering:** June–September **Habitat-Community:** Wet meadows, streambanks, lake and pond margins, and bogs in wetland-riparian communities **Elevation:** Below 8000 ft. **Ecoregions:** All

Thick-stalked perennial with round, hollow stems, often growing out of water. Leaves 1–5 in. long, basal, linear (grass-like), with 1–2 blades. Flowers in clusters of 5–100 spikelets at stem tips, with subtending bract 1–4 in. long, 6 brown perianth bristles (equal in length to the fruit), and 3 stamens. Fruits 0.1 in. long, shiny brown, 2–3-sided achenes. Tules once lined the shores of Tulare Lake (hence the name) in the San Joaquin Valley. This giant sedge is of great ecological significance to wildlife and is utilized by Indigenous peoples for making baskets, clothing, and even boats.

Juncus drummondii

Drummond's rush

JUNCACEAE RUSH FAMILY

PCT Sections: 10–24 **Abundance:** Common
Height: 2–16 in. **Flowering:** July–September
Habitat-Community: Moist, rocky or gravelly
soils in wetland-riparian and alpine communities
Elevation: 6500–11,500 ft. **Ecoregions:** Sierra
Nevada, Cascades, Klamath Mountains

Densely tufted perennial with round, hairless, pithy stems and basal foliage. Sheaths to 2.8 in. long with minute blades. Flowers solitary along stem toward tips, with 1 pistil (3 stigmas) and 6 stamens. Tepals to 0.3 in. long, 6, green with brown margins, the sepals > petals. Fruits capsules with many small seeds. *Juncus* ("to bind") refers to an early use of the stems. Unlike most sedges, rushes tend to have round stems and tepals (instead of spikelets of bracts lacking petals and sepals).

Juncus parryi

Parry's rush

JUNCACEAE RUSH FAMILY

PCT Sections: 4 & 10–24 **Abundance:** Common
Height: 2–12 in. **Flowering:** June–October
Habitat-Community: Open, dry, rocky or gravelly
soils from lower montane coniferous forests
to alpine communities **Elevation:** 6500–12,500
ft. **Ecoregions:** Southern California Mountains,
Sierra Nevada, Cascades, Klamath Mountains

Densely tufted perennial with round, hairless, pithy stems and basal foliage. Leaves to 3.2 in. long, similar to stem. Flowers 1–3 along stem toward tips, with 1 pistil (3 stigmas) and 6 stamens. Tepals to 0.3 in. long, 6, pale brown, the sepals > petals. Fruits capsules with many small seeds. The most common rush along the CA PCT in dry habitats.

Bouteloua barbata

sixweeks grama

POACEAE GRASS FAMILY

PCT Sections: 1–3 **Abundance:** Locally common
Height: 3–20 in. **Flowering:** May–November
Habitat-Community: Dry, rocky to sandy slopes
and flats in creosote bush & Sonoran mixed
woody scrubs and pinyon-juniper woodlands
Elevation: Below 5800 ft. **Ecoregions:** Southern
California Mountains, Sonoran Basin and Range

Tufted summer annual, spreading along ground or erect, with green, hairless stems. Leaves 1–2 in. long, basal or alternate. Flowers in spikelets of bracts (glumes, lemmas, and paleas). Spikes 0.3–1 in. long, comb-like, each with 7–40 awned spikelets 0.1–0.2 in. long. Fruits 1-seeded grains. Sixweeks grama gets its common name by having a famously short lifespan, germinating and setting seed in about as many weeks (or less). Rapid growth and reproduction is one of the many attributes of opportunistic summer annuals. Following a summer rain event of at least 0.5 inches, this one can briefly form a groundcover on normally dry desert landscapes.

Bouteloua gracilis

blue grama

POACEAE GRASS FAMILY

PCT Sections: 4 **Abundance:** Locally common **Height:** 5–25 in. **Flowering:** May–October **Habitat-Community:** Dry, rocky to sandy slopes and flats in pinyon-juniper woodlands and lower montane coniferous forests **Elevation:** Below 8500 ft. **Ecoregions:** Southern California Mountains

Erect, long-lived perennial forming dense clumps with hairless, blue-green stems. Leaves 1–3 in. long, mainly basal, the alternate leaves angled away from stem. Flowers in spikelets of bracts (glumes, lemmas, and paleas). Spikes 0.4–2 in. long, comb-like (resembling eyebrows), with 20–90 awned spikelets 0.2 in. long on few-branched inflorescences. Fruits 1-seeded grains. Occurs along the PCT only in the San Bernardino Mountains.

Danthonia unispicata

one-spike oat grass

POACEAE GRASS FAMILY

PCT Sections: 1–4 & 10–24 **Abundance:** Common **Height:** 4–12 in. **Flowering:** May–August **Habitat-Community:** Dry meadows and rocky soils, including serpentine, from scrubs and woodlands to upper montane coniferous forests **Elevation:** Below 10,500 ft. **Ecoregions:** Southern California Mountains, Sierra Nevada, Cascades, Klamath Mountains

Tufted, erect perennial with hairy herbage. Leaves to 3.2 in. long, basal and 2-ranked, hairy, flat to inrolled, ascending. Flowers in 1 (2–3) spikelet of 3–6 florets on erect stalks at stem tips, with 1 pistil (2 stigmas) and 3 stamens. Spikelets to 1 in. long (excluding awns); awns to 0.4 in. long, generally bent near base; 2 glumes to 1 in. long; lemmas to 0.4 in. long, hairy on margins, contained within glumes. Fruits 1-seeded grains. *Danthonia* honors French agrostologist Etienne Danthoine (1739–1794). Unlike sedges and rushes, grasses tend to have a round, hollow stem, 2-ranked leaves, and flowers lacking sepals and petals.

Elymus elymoides

squirreltail grass

POACEAE GRASS FAMILY

PCT Sections: All **Abundance:** Common **Height:** 4–26 in. **Flowering:** July–August **Habitat-Community:** Dry, open sites, including serpentine soils, from woodlands and chaparrals to alpine communities **Elevation:** Below 13,800 ft. **Ecoregions:** All

Tufted, erect to spreading perennial with generally white- to blue-waxy-coated herbage. Leaves to 8 in. long, to 0.2 in. wide, basal and 2-ranked, hairy or hairless, flat to inrolled, stiffly ascending to spreading. Flowers in 2–3 spikelets per node on erect stalks to stem tips, 2–4 florets per spikelet, with 1 pistil (2 stigmas) and 3 stamens. Spikelets to 0.6 in. long (excluding awns); spreading awns to 5 in. long; 2 glumes (awn-like) to 5 in. long; lemmas to 0.5 in. long, not hidden by glumes. Fruits 1-seeded grains. *Elymus* ("covered") refers to the grain being tightly wrapped by the lemma and palea. The large, bottlebrush-like spikelets break apart and potentially get blown long distances.

Elymus glaucus

blue wildrye

POACEAE GRASS FAMILY

PCT Sections: All **Abundance:** Common
Height: 1–5 ft. **Flowering:** June–August
Habitat-Community: Dry, open sites, including serpentine soils, from woodlands and chaparrals to subalpine coniferous forests **Elevation:** Below 9600 ft. **Ecoregions:** All

Tufted, erect to decumbent perennial with green or white- to blue-waxy-coated herbage. Leaves to 0.6 in. wide, basal and 2-ranked, hairy or hairless, flat, loosely ascending. Flowers generally 2 spikelets per node on erect stalks along stem tips, 2–4 florets per spikelet, with 1 pistil (2 stigmas) and 3 stamens. Spikelets to 0.8 in. long (excluding awns); straight awns to 1.2 in. long; 2 glumes to 0.8 in. long with short awns; lemmas to 0.5 in. long, mostly hidden by glumes. Fruits 1-seeded grains. Commonly used in restoration projects, as it does well in disturbed habitats.

Elymus triticoides

beardless ryegrass

POACEAE GRASS FAMILY

PCT Sections: All **Abundance:** Locally common
Height: 16–50 in. **Flowering:** June–August
Habitat-Community: Dry to moist areas in meadows, seeps, springs, and streambanks in wetland-riparian communities **Elevation:** Below 8000 ft. **Ecoregions:** All

Tuft-forming perennial with stiff, slender, blue-green stems. Basal leaves 4–15 in. long, 0.1–0.2 in. wide, nubby-hairy above; stem leaves alternate, angled away from stem. Flowers in spikes 2–12 in. long, with 2 spikelets per node. Spikelets with 3–7 florets, awl-like glumes 0.2–0.6 in. long, and awn-tipped lemma 0.2–0.5 in. long. Fruits 1-seeded grains. Occurs throughout western North America. The specific epithet means "like *Triticum*," the genus of wheat, which it superficially resembles.

Festuca californica

California fescue

POACEAE GRASS FAMILY

PCT Sections: 4–5 & 19–24 **Abundance:** Locally common **Height:** 1–4 ft. **Flowering:** May–June
Habitat-Community: Streambanks and dry, open sites, including serpentine soils, in woodlands, chaparrals, and lower montane coniferous forests **Elevation:** Below 5900 ft. **Ecoregions:** Southern California Mountains, Klamath Mountains

Densely tufted, stout, erect perennial with hairy herbage. Leaves to 40 in. long, to 0.2 in. wide, basal and 2-ranked, hairy, flat or inrolled, firm. Flowers in few spikelets at branch tips, 4–6 florets per spikelet, with 1 pistil (2 stigmas) and 3 stamens. Spikelets to 0.7 in. long (excluding awns); straight awns to 0.1 in. long; 2 glumes to 0.3 in. long, lacking awns; lemmas to 0.5 in. long, mostly hidden by glumes. Fruits 1-seeded grains. One of the most attractive grasses along the trail with its tall stems and drooping branches.

Melica frutescens

woody melicgrass

POACEAE GRASS FAMILY

PCT Sections: 1–4 **Abundance:** Occasional
Height: 16–60 in. **Flowering:** March–May
Habitat-Community: Dry, rocky slopes in foothill chaparrals and creosote & black bush scrubs
Elevation: Below 4800 ft. **Ecoregions:** Southern California Mountains, Sonoran Basin and Range

Clumped perennial, often branched from the lower nodes. Leaves 4–8 in. long, 0.1–0.2 in. wide, basal and alternate, 3–5 per stem, short-hairy. Flowers in spikelets of bracts (glumes, lemmas, and paleas). Spikelets 0.4–0.7 in. long, in narrow spikes, overlapping, each spikelet with 3–5 florets, glumes 0.3–0.5 in. long with translucent margins, and hairless lemmas 0.3–0.4 in. long. Fruits 1-seeded grains. Look for it at the lower desert slopes along the eastern flanks of the Peninsular Ranges. *Melica* (from the Latin, "honey") refers to the sweet smell of the foliage.

Melica imperfecta

smallflower melicgrass

POACEAE GRASS FAMILY

PCT Sections: 1–10 **Abundance:** Common
Height: 12–40 in. **Flowering:** March–June
Habitat-Community: Dry, rocky slopes in foothill chaparrals, creosote bush & Sonoran/ Mojave mixed woody scrubs, and Joshua tree & pinyon-juniper woodlands **Elevation:** Below 5500 ft. **Ecoregions:** Southern California Mountains, Sierra Nevada

Densely clumped perennial bunchgrass, branching from the lower nodes. Leaves 4–8 in. long, to 0.3 in. wide, basal and cauline, with hairless to hairy sheaths and hairy blades. Flowers in green to dark purple spikelets of bracts (glumes, lemmas, and paleas), with 1–2 green to purplish florets per spikelet. Spikelets 0.1–0.3 in. long, on spreading branches, with glumes 0.1–0.2 in. long and hairless lemmas 0.1–0.3 in. long. Fruits 1-seeded grains. Look for it in rocky terrain at low to mid-elevations of southern California, from the coast to the deserts. The glumes of *Melica* spp. (aka oniongrass) have a thin, onion-skin texture.

Melica stricta

rock melicgrass

POACEAE GRASS FAMILY

PCT Sections: 4–6 & 8–24 **Abundance:** Common
Height: 0.5–3 ft. **Flowering:** June–August
Habitat-Community: Dry, open, rocky soils from sagebrush scrubs and woodlands to subalpine coniferous forests **Elevation:** Below 11,000 ft.
Ecoregions: Southern California Mountains, Sierra Nevada, Cascades, Klamath Mountains

Densely tufted, erect perennial with purple stems near base. Leaves to 0.2 in. wide, basal (mostly) and 2-ranked, flat, hairy. Flowers in single spikelets along stems to tip, erect to ascending, lacking awns, 2–4 florets per spikelet, with 1 pistil (2 stigmas) and 3 stamens. Spikelets to 0.9 in. long, mostly spreading, with 2 glumes to 0.7 in. long and lemmas to 0.4 in. long. Fruits 1-seeded grains.

Muhlenbergia rigens
deergrass
POACEAE GRASS FAMILY

PCT Sections: 1–6 & 8–9 **Abundance:** Locally common **Height:** 1–5 ft. **Flowering:** June–September **Habitat-Community:** Damp or dry, sandy to gravelly soils, especially stream channels, in woodlands, chaparrals, lower montane coniferous forests, and wetland-riparian communities **Elevation:** Below 7100 ft. **Ecoregions:** Southern California/Northern Baja Coast, Southern California Mountains, Sierra Nevada

Densely tufted, erect perennial with slender, cattail-like flowering stalks. Leaves to 10 in. long, to 0.3 in. wide, mostly basal, inrolled, hairy. Flowers in tightly clustered spikelets along stems to tip, lacking awns, 1 floret per spikelet, with 1 pistil (2 stigmas) and 3 stamens. Spikelets to 0.2 in. long, 2 glumes to 0.1 in. long, lemmas to 0.2 in. long. Fruits 1-seeded grains. An important source of fine, white thread for baskets. Deer are known to browse young shoots.

Phleum alpinum
mountain Timothy
POACEAE GRASS FAMILY

PCT Sections: 3–4 & 9–24 **Abundance:** Locally common **Height:** 6–24 in. **Flowering:** July–August **Habitat-Community:** Wet meadows, streambanks, and slopes with late snowmelt, from upper montane coniferous forests to alpine and wetland-riparian communities **Elevation:** Below 12,200 ft. **Ecoregions:** Southern California Mountains, Sierra Nevada, Cascades, Klamath Mountains

Loosely tufted, decumbent perennial with single flowering head. Leaves to 4.7 in. long, to 0.3 in. wide, basal and 2-ranked, inrolled, hairy. Flowers in tightly clustered, flattened spikelets forming a single ovoid head (to 1 in. long) at stem tip, 1 floret per spikelet, with 1 pistil (2 stigmas) and 3 stamens. Spikelets to 0.2 in. long, 2 glumes to 0.2 in. long, lemmas to 0.1 in. long, awns to 0.1 in. long. Fruits 1-seeded grains. *Phleum* means "reedy grass." An important forage grass for wildlife. Aka alpine Timothy.

Poa fendleriana var. longiligula
longtongue muttongrass
POACEAE GRASS FAMILY

PCT Sections: 3–4 & 8–18 **Abundance:** Locally common **Height:** 6–25 in. **Flowering:** April–July **Habitat-Community:** Dry openings in sagebrush scrubs, pinyon-juniper woodlands, and montane coniferous forests **Elevation:** 6200–9800 ft. **Ecoregions:** Southern California Mountains, Sierra Nevada

Erect, stout, dense-tufted perennial; dioecious. Leaves 3–7 in. long, 0.1 in. wide, with persistent sheaths and blades reduced up the stems. Flowers in spikelets of bracts (glumes, lemmas, and paleas), 2–7 florets per spikelet. Spikelets 0.2–0.3 in. long, green to tan, in narrow to open displays; glumes 1-3-veined, 0.1–0.2 in. long; lemmas 0.2 in. long, with cobwebby bases. Fruits 1-seeded grains. Male plants may be rare; asexual reproduction is more common in California.

Poa secunda

one-sided bluegrass

POACEAE GRASS FAMILY

PCT Sections: All **Abundance:** Common
Height: 0.5–4 ft. **Flowering:** March–August
Habitat-Community: Dry slopes to meadows
from sagebrush scrubs to alpine communities
Elevation: Below 12,800 ft. **Ecoregions:** All

Densely tufted, erect to decumbent perennial. Leaves to 0.1 in. wide, basal and 2-ranked, flat to inrolled, sometimes white- to blue-waxy-coated. Flowers in spikelets, generally on one side of stem to tip, lacking awns, 2–7 florets per spikelet, with 1 pistil (2 stigmas) and 3 stamens. Spikelets to 0.4 in. long, lemmas to 0.3 in. long; 2 glumes. Fruits 1-seeded grains. An important food source for the remaining wildlife of California's Central Valley.

Stipa comata

needle-and-thread grass

POACEAE GRASS FAMILY

PCT Sections: 3–4 & 8–10 **Abundance:** Occasional
Height: 1–4 ft. **Flowering:** May–July **Habitat-Community:** Dry openings in sagebrush scrubs,
pinyon-juniper woodlands, and montane
coniferous forests **Elevation:** Below 9200 ft.
Ecoregions: Southern California Mountains,
Sierra Nevada

Airy, erect, unbranched perennial bunchgrass with hairless to hairy stems. Leaves 4–12 in. long, 0.1 in. wide, basal and alternate, with inrolled margins. Flowers in spikelets of bracts (glumes, lemmas, and paleas). Spikelets green to tan, in spreading or nodding displays, 1-flowered, glumes 0.7–1.4 in. long, floret 0.3–0.6 in. long, and white-hairy lemmas with wavy or twice-bent awns 3–8 in. long, the longest in the genus. Fruits 1-seeded grains. This magnificent cool-desert species sneaks onto the PCT where Great Basin Desert influences are present, such as in the eastern Sierra Nevada and San Bernardino Mountains.

Stipa hymenoides

sand ricegrass

POACEAE GRASS FAMILY

PCT Sections: 1–10 & 12–14 **Abundance:** Locally
common **Height:** 12–26 in. **Flowering:** April–July
Habitat-Community: Dry, sandy hillsides, flats,
and dunes from creosote bush scrubs to upper
montane coniferous forests **Elevation:** Below
10,800 ft. **Ecoregions:** All (except Cascades,
Klamath Mountains)

Clumped, erect perennial bunchgrass with hairless to fine-hairy stems. Leaves 8–20 in. long, <0.1 in. wide, basal and alternate, with inrolled margins. Flowers in spikelets of bracts (glumes, lemmas, and paleas). Spikelets green to tan, in open displays, 1-flowered, glumes 0.2–0.7 in. long, floret 0.1–0.2 in. long, and hairy lemma with unbent awn 0.1–0.3 in. long. Fruits ovoid, 1-seeded grains. Ranges throughout western North America. A staple food source (seeds) for wildlife and, historically, Indigenous peoples. It is the state grass of both Nevada and Utah.

Stipa parishii

Parish's needlegrass

POACEAE GRASS FAMILY

PCT Sections: 1–5 **Abundance:** Locally common **Height:** 10–30 in. **Flowering:** April–August **Habitat-Community:** Open, dry soils in pinyon-juniper woodlands, sagebrush scrubs, and lower montane coniferous forests **Elevation:** Below 9300 ft. **Ecoregions:** Southern California Mountains

Erect, tufted, unbranched perennial bunchgrass with usually hairless stems. Leaves 4–12 in. long, 0.1–0.2 in. wide, basal and alternate, with flat or inrolled margins. Flowers in spikelets of bracts (glumes, lemmas, and paleas). Spikelets green to tan, in narrow displays, 1-flowered, glumes 0.3–0.6 in. long, floret 0.2–0.3 in. long, and hairy lemma with once-bent awn 0.6–1.4 in. long. Fruits ovoid, 1-seeded grains. Often found in small colonies along the PCT from the San Gabriel Mountains to southern Peninsular Ranges. The inflorescence becomes red-brown with age.

Stipa speciosa

desert needlegrass

POACEAE GRASS FAMILY

PCT Sections: 1–10 **Abundance:** Common **Height:** 12–24 in. **Flowering:** April–July **Habitat-Community:** Dry, rocky soils, canyons, and washes in scrubs and Joshua tree & pinyon-juniper woodlands **Elevation:** Below 7800 ft. **Ecoregions:** Southern California Mountains, Sierra Nevada

Erect, clumped perennial bunchgrass with branched, reddish brown stem bases. Leaves 4–12 in. long, <0.1 in. wide, basal and alternate, with flat or inrolled margins. Flowers in spikelets of bracts (glumes, lemmas, and paleas). Spikelets green to tan, densely clustered along stems, 1-flowered, glumes 0.6–1 in. long, floret 0.3–0.4 in. long, and hairy lemma with once-bent, densely hairy (feather-like) awn 1.5–1.8 in. long. Fruits ovoid, 1-seeded grains.

NONNATIVE PLANTS ALONG
THE PACIFIC CREST TRAIL ———————————

Introduction of nonnative species into the California ecosystem has occurred since the earliest European settlements. Some introductions were intentional, with plants imported as ornamentals or for horticulture; others were accidental, with plants arriving via the myriad activities of a burgeoning human population. More than 1550 nonnative plant species—those whose natural range does not include California—are now established in the state.

Some nonnative species persist locally, or are transitory waifs that colonize disturbed areas. Others are invasive, spreading into natural areas, and these can pose serious problems to an ecosystem by displacing natives, changing community structure, or otherwise altering ecosystem processes in an undesirable way.

Fortunately, the majority of the Pacific Crest Trail in California traverses protected ecosystems, such as wilderness areas and floristic regions where nonnative plants are less prevalent relative to other parts of the state. In general, the lowest concentrations of nonnative species along the PCT are found at higher elevations, such as the subalpine and alpine zones of the Sierra Nevada, or in desert-influenced segments. But even in those areas, nonnatives are present. Disturbed areas, grasslands, and moist habitats, including wetlands, tend to have higher concentrations of nonnative species.

While the focus of this guidebook is on the appreciation of native plants along the PCT, hikers will no doubt encounter nonnative species, some rather ubiquitous, and some even quite showy. In many cases, nonnatives may resemble common natives, causing the observer to ponder a species' nativity. As an aid in the identification of natives versus nonnative species, we include the following photos of a select group of nonnative species commonly found along the PCT.

CLOCKWISE | bull thistle (*Cirsium vulgare*) / red-stemmed filaree (*Erodium cicutarium*) / dyers wood (*Isatis tinctoria*)

OPPOSITE CLOCKWISE | prickly lettuce (*Lactuca serriola*) / common mullein (*Verbascum thapsus*) / yellow star-thistle (*Centaurea solstitialis*)

CLOCKWISE | perennial sweet pea (*Lathyrus latifolius*) / common sheep sorrel (*Rumex acetosella*) / dandelion (*Taraxacum offi cinale*)

OPPOSITE, TOP TO BOTTOM | Russian thistle (*Salsola tragus*) / crimson fountain grass (*Pennisetum setaceum*)

PHOTO CREDITS

GLOSSARY

achene. Dry, 1-seeded fruit

acute. Forming a sharp, <90° angle

alluvium. Soil deposited by flowing water

alternate. Arrangement of leaves occurring singly at a node

androdioecious. Having male (staminate) and perfect (both sexes) flowers on different plants

annual. Plants that complete their life cycle in one year; also applied to ephemerals

anther. Sac at the tip of the stamen containing pollen grains

anther head. Fused anther, forming a head in *Asclepias* spp.

anthocarp. Modified achene

appendage. Structure that is generally smaller than the main part to which it is attached

appressed. Lying close and flat against or nearly so

areole. Area with flowers and/or spines on a cactus

awn. Narrow bristle coming from the tip or back of a structure

axil. Upper angle between a leaf and stem

axillary. Originating from the axils of leaves

banner. In the Fabaceae, uppermost petal of a bilateral flower

berry. Simple fleshy fruit containing one or more seeds

biennial. Plants persisting for 2 years (seed to maturity and death)

bilateral. Having similar halves, such as a flower that has a single axis where it can be divided or folded into mirror-image halves. A type of irregular flower

bisexual flower. Perfect flowers containing both male (stamens) and female (pistil) reproductive structures

blade. Broad portion of a leaf

bloom. An open flower or whitish covering of a surface, usually of a waxy nature

bog. Spongy wetlands, lacking flowing water and generally dominated by mosses and decaying matter

bract. Modified, generally reduced, leaf-like structure at base of flower petioles

bractlet. Bract located in the upper (closer to the flowers) portion of the inflorescence

bristle. Stiff, strong hair

bud. Plant structure that develops into a leaf, shoot, or flower

bud scale. Small, leaf-like structure enclosing the buds of some plants

bulb. Underground bud, such as an onion

bulbous. Growing from a bulb or having a fat, round shape

burl. Obvious growth on a tree trunk

bur. Structure with hooked or barbed bristles/appendages

calyx. Collective term for sepals. Generally green, but may be colored like petals

capsule. Dry fruit that opens in various ways to allow for seed dispersal

carbonate. Rock, such as limestone, containing calcium

carpel. Simple pistil or a section of a compound pistil (female structure of flowering plants)

catkin. Dry, scaly spike of flowers that is generally unisexual

cauline. On or along the stem

clasping. Partly or wholly surrounding a surface

claw. Generally narrowed base of a sepal or petal

composite. Head with many flowers, such as sunflowers

compound. Having 2 or more similar parts. Compound leaves are divided into 2 or more leaflets

cone. A scaly reproductive structure producing spores (as in horsetails), pollen, or seeds (as in conifers and *Ephedra*)

conifer. Woody plants, mostly trees but also shrubs

corm. Bulb-like root structure

corolla. The collective term for petals. Located above the calyx

cyathium. Inflorescence of *Euphorbia* spp. consisting of a cup-like involucre (which itself resembles a flower), single pistil, and male flowers, each with 1 stamen

deciduous. Leaves that fall at the end of the growing season, or organs that fall off at maturity

decumbent. Growing along the ground with the tip pointing up

dioecious. Having male (staminate) and female (pistillate) reproductive structures on different plants. Individual plants are either completely staminate or pistillate

discoid. In the Asteraceae, having only disk flowers

disk flower. In the Asteraceae, the generally symmetric, non-rayed, bisexual flowers

dissected. Divided or lobed structure, but not compound

drupe. Berry-like fruit with a stony endocarp surrounding a usually single seed, as in a cherry or peach

ecotone. Zone of transition between plant communities

elliptic. Generally pertaining to leaves that have a flattened (side to side) circle shape. Not as narrow as oblong, and oval would have rounder sides

endemic. Restricted to a particular region or area

entire. Smooth edge, lacking lobes or teeth

ephemeral. Plants that bloom over a short period of time. Under the right climatic conditions, they can bloom more than once a year. They can also go many years without germinating and blooming at all

evergreen. Plants that stay green throughout the year

exserted. Projecting beyond a particular structure, such as stamens from a corolla

fascicle. Bundle or cluster

fen. Mossy wetland, similar to a bog, but with flowing instead of standing water

filament. Portion of the stamen supporting the anther

flower. Reproductive structure of the angiosperms, generally accompanied by a perianth

floret. Individual grass (Poaceae) or sunflower (Asteraceae) flower

follicle. Dry fruit from a simple pistil, opening along only one side

free. Not fused

free vein. Branched without connecting to adjacent veins

fruit. Ripened ovary, or group of ovaries, containing seeds. May contain other structures fused to the ripened ovary

glabrous. Smooth, without hairs or similar structures

gland. Secreting surface, structure, appendage, or protuberance. Generally glossy and/or aromatic

glandular. Covered with glands

glaucous. Covered with a generally whitish, sometimes waxy coating

glochid. Barbed hair or bristle found on some cacti

glume. The lowest bract/scale of a grass spikelet. Most grasses have 2 glumes per spikelet

head. Group of flowers attached to a common structure, or a dense grouping of flowers forming a spheric or hemispheric structure

hemiparasitic. Produces some of its own nourishment

hood. Hollow, cover-shaped perianth structure as found on *Asclepias* spp.

horn. Curved, pointed, hollow protuberance from the perianth as found on *Asclepias* spp.

hybrid. A plant that is a genetic cross between 2 species

hypanthium. The fused portion of a perianth around the ovary

included. Not extending beyond a particular structure

indusia. Plural of indusium

indusium. Flap of tissue covering a sorus of a fern

inferior ovary. Ovary fused to the floral tube and generally appearing below the perianth

inflorescence. The collection of flowers (or a single flower) on the floral axis

involucre. Collection of bracts or phyllaries (especially Asteraceae and Polygonaceae flowers) beneath a flower, flower head, or flower cluster

irregular. Asymmetric or bilateral

keel. A dorsal ridge like that of a boat. In the Fabaceae, the bottom 2 petals united, located between the wings in the bilateral flower of most plants

lance-shaped. Longer than wide with broader end toward the base and narrower tip, like a sword

lateral. Appearing or attached on the side

leaf axil. Angle formed from the upper side of a leaf and its point of attachment to the stem

legume. Fruit (pod) of the Fabaceae, containing 1 to many seeds

lemma. Lower bract of a grass floret

lenticel. Generally raised, lens-shaped pores or glands on stem surface

limb. Expanded distal portion of a corolla having fused petals

linear. Long and narrow with parallel margins

lobe. Generally rounded segment of an organ

midrib (midvein). Central supporting or conducting structure of an organ such as a leaf or petal

monoecious. Having separate male and female flowers on the same plant

mycoheterotrophic. Generally, a nongreen plant that gets all or part of its carbon, water, and nutrient supply through a symbiotic association with mycorrhizal fungi

node. The portion of the stem where the leaves and/or branches arise

nut. Hard, 1-seeded fruit

nutlet. A small nut

oblong. Widest at middle with essentially straight, relatively long, parallel sides

obtuse. Blunt or rounded

opposite. Plant organs or parts occurring in pairs and sharing a node or a common point of attachment

oval. Broadly elliptic

ovary. Swollen basal portion of a pistil/carpel containing seeds

ovoid. Egg-shaped

palea. Innermost scale subtending the flower parts of a grass

palmate. Lobes or divisions originating from a common point, like fingers of a hand

pappus. Bristly or scaly calyx of most flowers in the Asteraceae

pedicel. Stalk immediately below a single flower in a flower cluster, or the stalk below a grass spikelet

pedicellate. Having a pedicel

peduncle. Branch supporting flowers

pendent. Drooping or hanging down

perennial. Plant persisting from year to year

perfect flower. Flower with functioning pistils and stamens

perianth. Collective of the calyx and corolla, or used with respect to flowers where calyx and corolla are not clearly differentiated

perigynia. In *Carex*, flattened or triangular seed-like structures encasing fruit

petal. A leaf-like, colored (usually) structure, collectively forming the corolla

petiole. Stalk connected to a leaf blade or a common axis of a compound leaf having leaflets attached on each side

phyllaries. Bract that collectively forms the involucre of sunflowers (Asteraceae)

pinnate. Compound leaf with leaflets arranged on each side of a shared petiole

pistil. Female portion of a flower normally consisting of a stigma, style, and ovary.

pistillate. Flowers with only pistils (female)

platyclades. Flattened stems that look and function like leaves

population. A group of sexually reproducing and interbreeding individuals that share the same gene pool

prickle. A sharp outgrowth of the bark or epidermis

prostrate. Growing along the ground

purgative. Having the effect of a laxative

radiant. In the Asteraceae, similar to a discoid head with expanded, often bilateral, peripheral disk flower corollas

radiate. In the Asteraceae, a head with both ray and disk flowers

ray. Secondary axis in a compound inflorescence; in the Asteraceae, the flatted tongue- or strap-like flowers of some spp.

ray flower. In the Asteraceae, the marginal flower with a ray, as opposed to the disk flower lacking rays

recurved. Curved outward or downward

reflexed. Bent or turned downward

regular. Symmetric flower

rhizomatous. Having an underground stem rooting at the nodes and becoming new stems at the tip

rosette. Group of leaves forming a circle, generally at the base of a stem

rotate. Disk-shaped; referring to widely spreading corolla lobes

samara. Winged achene

scabrous. Surface that is rough to the touch

scalloped. Series of small curves along edges

seed. Ripened ovule, containing an embryo (will develop into plant)

sepal. Division of the calyx, usually green and leaf-like

sessile. Without a stalk

shrub. Woody perennial, generally <15 ft.

silicle. In the Brassicaceae, dry fruit capsule that is as broad or broader than long

silique. In the Brassicaceae, dry fruit capsule that is longer than broad

simple leaf. Individual leaf as opposed to compound

sori. Plural of sorus

sorus. Cluster of sporangia (spore-containing structures)

species. Group of closely related individuals classified as the same taxon

specific epithet. Second portion of a binomial scientific name

spike. Simple inflorescence formed by flowers attached to a single flowering axis

spikelet. Cluster of flowers in grasses and sedges

spine. Pointed appendage

sporangia. Plural of sporangium

sporangium. Spore-producing sac or case

spreading. Extending to horizontal; or growing prostrate

stamen. Pollen-producing organ of the flower consisting of a filament and an anther

staminate. Flowers with only stamens (male)

staminode. Sterile stamen

stem. Aboveground portion of a plant that bears the leaves, buds, and reproductive organs

stigma. Portion, generally at the tip, of the style modified to receive pollen and thus initiating fertilization

stipe. A stalk

stipule. Appendage (sometimes leaf-like) attached at the base of a petiole or leaf

stolon. Aboveground prostrate stem or runner capable of rooting

strigose. Covered with sharp, appressed hairs

style. Portion of the pistil between the stigma and ovary

subshrub. Small shrub; or perennial with some woody stems

subtended. Supporting from underneath; normally a bract under a flower

superior ovary. Ovary not fused to the floral tube and attached above the other floral parts

symmetric flower. Regular flower with equal halves no matter how it's sliced

tassel. Cluster of staminate (male) flowers in some plants

taxon. Taxonomic category referring to a species, subspecies, or variety

tendril. Coiling structure providing support for climbing plants

tepal. Perianth segment functioning as a sepal or petal

terminal. At the tip of a structure or stem

ternate. In threes, e.g., having 3 leaflets

thorn. A branch modified into a sharp, woody projection

throat. Expanded portion of corolla (composed of united petals) between the tube and limb

trailing. Sprawling over the ground or other vegetation close to the ground

tree. Perennial, woody plant with an obvious trunk generally >15 ft.

tuber. Underground stem that stores starch, with nodes and buds

tubercle. Small rounded projection

tufted. Densely grouped

twig. Portion of a woody stem or branch produced during the latest growing season

utricle. Small, thin-walled, 1-seeded fruit

vein. Conducting tissue in a leaf or other expanded organ

whorl. Arrangement of flowers or leaves in a circle around the stem

wing. Membranous or thin extension of tissue bordering or surrounding an organ. The lateral petals of a bilateral flower in the Fabaceae

woolly. Large, soft, entangled hairs

FURTHER READING

André, James M., and Fred M. Roberts, Jr. 2022. *The Vascular Plants of San Bernardino County, California–Desert Region*. San Luis Rey, CA: F. M. Roberts Publications.

Baldwin, Bruce G., et al., eds. 2012. *The Jepson Manual: Vascular Plants of California*. 2nd ed. Berkeley: University of California Press.

Charters, Michael, L. 2021. *California Plant Names*. calflora.net/botanicalnames.

Chester, Tom. 2020. *Plants of Southern California*. tchester.org/plants/lists/guides.html.

Croissant, Ann, and Gerald Croissant. 2007. *Wildflowers of the San Gabriel Mountains*. Photography by Shirley Debraal. Chicago: Midpoint Trade Books.

DeCamp, Ken, Julie K. Nelson, and Julie Knorr. 2017. *Wildflowers of the Trinity Alps*. Kneeland, CA: Backcountry Press.

Hickman, James C., ed. 2003. *The Jepson Manual: Higher Plants of California*. Berkeley: University of California Press.

Ingram, Stephen. 2008. *Cacti, Agaves, and Yuccas of California and Nevada*. Los Olivos, CA: Cachuma Press.

Kane, Jeffrey. 2019. The Past, Present, and Future of California Wildfires (Essay). *Humboldt: The Magazine of Humboldt State University* (Fall).

Kauffmann, Michael E. 2013. *Conifers of the Pacific Slope*. Kneeland, CA: Backcountry Press.

MacKay, Pam, and Tim Thomas. 2017. *Southern California Mountains Wildflowers*. Guilford, CT: Falcon Guides.

Mathews, Daniel. 2017. *Natural History of the Pacific Northwest Mountains*. Portland, OR: Timber Press.

Mistretta, Orlando. 2020. *Field Guide to the Flora of the San Gabriel Mountains*. Rancho Santa Ana Botanic Garden Occasional Publications no. 18. Claremont, CA.

Moore, Michael. 1993. *Medicinal Plants of the Pacific West*. Santa Fe, NM: Red Crane Books.

Rebman, Jon P., and Michael G. Simpson. 2014. *Checklist of the Vascular Plants of San Diego County*. 5th ed. San Diego: San Diego Natural History Museum.

Ritter, Matt. 2018. *California Plants*. San Luis Obispo, CA: Pacific Street Publishing.

Roberts, Fred M., Jr., et al. 2004. *The Vascular Plants of Western Riverside County, California*. San Luis Rey, CA: F. M. Roberts Publishing.

Sawyer, J. O., T. Keeler-Wolf, and J. M. Evens. 2009. *A Manual of California Vegetation*. 2nd ed. Sacramento: California Native Plant Society.

Swinney, Dick, and Andrew C. Sanders. 2008. *Plants of the San Gabriel Mountains*. glendoranaturalhistory.com/PSGM.html.

Turner, Mark, and Phyllis Gustafson. 2006. *Wildflowers of the Pacific Northwest*. Portland, OR: Timber Press.

Turner, Mark, and Ellen Kuhlmann. 2014. *Trees and Shrubs of the Pacific Northwest*. Portland, OR: Timber Press.

York, Dana A. 1997. A Fire Ecology Study of a Sierra Nevada Foothill Basaltic Mesa Grassland. *Madroño* 44(4):374–383.

––. 2018. *An Illustrated Flora of Sequoia and Kings Canyon National Parks*. Sacramento: California Native Plant Society.

ACKNOWLEDGMENTS

During our three years of exploring, photographing, and writing, we required the help of many individuals. Above all, we recognize our families for embracing camping and hiking trips to the PCT, as well as for being understanding of our absences from home during the field season.

The online plant checklists for segments of the PCT in southern California by Tom Chester and others were an invaluable resource in planning our trips. Matt Berger's georeferenced photos of rare plants along the trail was an immense help; he also contributed some of his awesome photos to this book. Michael Kauffmann deserves recognition for contributing several outstanding conifer photos. Dana thanks Carol Ralph for sharing orchid locations with him and for her indefatigable work as the long-standing president of the North Coast Chapter of the California Native Plant Society (CNPS). And Jim is eternally grateful for the trail companionship provided by Tasha La Doux, the intrepid Senna and Elias André, and PCT aficionados and close friends Ron and Ursula Kelley.

This book would not have been possible without the vision of Mark Larabee (PCT Association's Advocacy Director and 2007 Pulitzer Prize winner) and Stacee Lawrence (Timber Press), both of whom saw the value in connecting plants with people on one of the most popular trails in the world. Stacee also hung in there with us during the trying times brought about by COVID-19, empathizing with our situation and graciously extending our fieldwork to another full flowering season. Although we gave it our best try, it still proved impossible for us to capture a photo of every plant presented. That's where our contributing photographers come into play: we owe you all a great debt of gratitude.

And finally, thanks to the Indigenous peoples who have explored and used plants in California for thousands of years. Many of our descriptions include plant uses that have been handed down from generation to generation of these first "botanists." No words can adequately describe our appreciation of the value of this accumulated plant knowledge.

INDEX